NETHERLANDS

Turnhout

NTWERP

LIMBURG

Maaseik

Hasselt

Leuven

RABANT

Tongeren

WEST
GERMANY

Waremme

Liège

Verviers

LIEGE

Huy

Namur

NAMUR

Dinant

hilippeville

Marche-en-Famenne

Bastogne

LUXEMBOURG

Neufchâteau

GRAND
DUCHY
OF
LUXEMBOURG

Arlon

Luxembourg

Virton

Modern Belgium

Modern Belgium

*Edited by Marina Boudart, Michel Boudart,
and René Bryssinck*

The Society for the Promotion of Science and Scholarship
Palo Alto, California 1990

The Society for the Promotion of
Science and Scholarship, Inc.
Palo Alto, California
© 1990 by Marina Boudart, Michel Boudart, and René Bryssinck
Printed in the United States of America

The Society for the Promotion of Science and Scholarship is a
nonprofit corporation established for the purposes of scholarly
publishing; it has special interests in British and European
studies.

Library of Congress Cataloging-in-Publication Data
Modern Belgium / edited by Marina Boudart, Michel Boudart, and René Bryssinck.
p. cm.
Includes bibliographical references and index.
ISBN 0-930664-10-8 (alk. paper)
1. Belgium. I. Boudart, Marina. II. Boudart, Michel. III. Bryssinck, René, 1922–
DH418.M6 1990
949.304—dc20   90-61813
                                                                      CIP

H.R.H. Prince Philippe of Belgium

Belgium is a young country with a promising future.

It has acquired a rich experience as a meeting place of Germanic and Latin cultures.

It was therefore quite natural for Belgium to become a driving force of European integration.

Belgium's peaceful quest for unity in diversity makes it a complex but fascinating country.

of Belgium.

Preface

THE IDEA OF *Modern Belgium* was proposed to us by J. Murray Luck, whose nonprofit Society for the Promotion of Science and Scholarship had already published *Modern Switzerland* and *Modern Austria*. The purpose of these volumes on less well known small countries is to give reliable information to the general public as well as to people in contact with consulates, embassies, and foreign trade or banking organizations. These books are written by a number of scholars and specialists, and they present objectively all contemporary aspects of a country.

To start work on *Modern Belgium,* a Board of Directors was first assembled to raise and manage the funds required for the enterprise. Next, an Editorial Committee was assembled, for the purpose of selecting contributors to the book; ultimately, 61 authors were enlisted by eight coordinators of the Editorial Committee. Many essays had to be translated from French or Dutch, and to obtain a text with a certain coherence and style, editing was carried out in both Belgium and California. In this delicate task the hard work of the coordinators has been critical: we thank them for their efforts, just as we thank the authors for bearing with editorial changes, whether minor or more extensive in scope.

While the book was being written, Belgium changed both substantially and rapidly. As a result, the country enters the 1990's as a new federally oriented nation, looking at the European and global economies with realistic confidence in its future.

The symbol of this confidence remains the King of the Belgians and the Royal Family. Without the kind and steady encouragement of H.R.H. Prince Albert, *Modern Belgium* might never have been completed.

We want to acknowledge the very special assistance of a number of other people who contributed to the book in many different ways: in particular, Monsignor Luc Gillon, Professor Emeritus of the Université Catholique de Louvain; Ambassadors Herman Dehennin and Jean-Paul van Bellinghen; Charles-Ferdinand Nothomb, then Minister of Foreign Affairs; Jacques de Groote and Daniel Pyle, of the International Monetary Fund; Dean Ann Fletcher of Stanford University; Mary Godenne McCrea Curnen, M.D., and Professor L. Dupré, of Yale University; Dr. Peter Duignan and Mrs. Agnes Peterson, of the Hoover Institution; Emile L. Boulpaep, N.D., of the Belgian American Educational Foundation.

Michel and Marina Boudart
René Bryssinck
Stanford and Brussels, May 1990

Contents

PART VI: EDUCATION
Gaston Deurinck, Coordinator

PART VII: SCIENCE
André L. Jaumotte, Coordinator

PART VIII: CULTURE
Herman Liebaers and Philippe Roberts-Jones, Coordinators

xiv   *Contents*

Abbreviations and Acronyms

AA   Atlantic Alliance
ABVV/FGTB   Socialist Trade Union Movement
ACLV/CGLSB   Liberal Trade Union Movement
ACV/CSC   Confederation of Christian Trade Unions
AERA   American Education Research Association
AIPELF   International Association of French-language Experimental
   Pedagogy
BBC   British Broadcast Corporation
BC-NET   Business Cooperation Network
Benelux   Economic union between Belgium, the Netherlands, and
   Luxembourg
BF   Belgian franc
BIS   Bank for International Settlements
BLEU   Belgo-Luxembourg Economic Union
BSP   Belgian Socialist Party
CAB   Current account balance
CAD/CAM   Computer-aided design and manufacturing
CBM   Scientific and Technical Center of Brewing, Malting, and
   Related Industries
CCE   Central Economic Council
CCR   Road Research Center
CEN/SCK   Nuclear Energy Research Center
CERN   European Center for Nuclear Research
CESS   Certificate of upper secondary education
CGSLB   General Central Office of Liberal Trade Unions of Belgium
CHD   Coronary heart disease
CNEE   National Committee for Economic Expansion
CNPS/NRWB   National Council for Science Policy

CNRS   French Center for Scientific Research
CODEST   Committee for European Development of Science and
   Technology
COMECOM   Communist Economic Community
COREPER   Committee of Permanent Representatives assisting
   European Council of Ministers
CORI   Covering, Paint, and Ink Research Institute
COST   Cooperative Organization for Science and Technology
CPAS   Public Centers for Social Assistance
CRIC   National Center of Scientific and Technical Research of the
   Cement Industry
CRIF/WTMC   Technical Research Center for the Metalworking
   Industry
CRISP   Center for Industrial, Social, and Political Research
CRM   Metallurgical Research Center
CRSTID   Diamond Industry Scientific and Technical Research Center
CSC/ACV   Confederation of Christian Trade Unions
CSCM   Superior Council for the Middle Classes
CST   Special Temporary Executive
CSTC   Building Industry Scientific and Technical Center
CTIB   Wood Industry Technical Center
CVP   Christian Socialist Party (Dutch-speaking)
DM   Deutsche Mark
EARLO   European Association for Research on Learning and
   Instruction
EC   European Community
ECS   European Communications Satellite
ECSC   European Coal and Steel Community
ECU   European Currency Unit
EEC   European Economic Community
EIV   Economist Intelligence Unit
EMBO   European Molecular Biology Organization
EMF   European Monetary Fund
EMS   European Monetary System
EPU   European Payments Union
ERP   European Recovery Program
ESA   European Space Agency
ESF   European Science Foundation
ESO   European Southern Observatory
ETUC   European Trade Unions Confederation
EURATOM   European Atomic Community

EUTELSAT   European Telecommunication Satellite Organization
FAGEM   State Faculty of Agronomic Sciences at Gembloux
FAIB   Federation of International Associations in Belgium
FAO   Food and Agriculture Organization
FAPOM   Mons Polytechnic Faculty
FAST   Forecast and Assessment of Science and Technology Program
FDF   Democratic Front of French-speaking Inhabitants of Brussels
FEB/VBO   Federation of Belgian Enterprises
FGTB   General Labor Federation of Belgium
FNRS/NFWO   National Foundation for Belgian Scientific Research
FOPES   Open Faculty for Political, Economic, and Social Sciences
FPM   Mons Polytechnic Faculty
FRFC   Fund for Fundamental Cooperative Research
FRG   Federal Republic of Germany
FRSM   Fund for Scientific Medical Research
FUCAM   Catholic University of Mons
FUL   Luxembourg University Foundation at Arlon
FUNDP   University Faculties of Our Lady of Peace at Namur
FUSEL   St. Louis University at Brussels
GAB   General agreements to borrow
GATT   General Agreement on Tariffs and Trade
GNP   Gross national product
GP   General practitioner
IAS   Space Aeronomy Institute at Brussels
IBS   Belgian Welding Institute
ICSDR   International Cooperation for School Development Research
IEA   International Association for Evaluation of School Development
IEA   International Energy Agency
IISN   International Institute for Nuclear Sciences
IMEC   Interuniversity Microelectronics Center
IMF   International Monetary Fund
INEAC   Congolese Institute for Agriculture Research
INR/NIR   National Broadcasting Institute
IPC   International Institute of Cellular and Molecular Pathology
IPEM   Institute for Psycho-acoustic and Electronic Music
IRE   Institute for Radio Elements
IRM   Royal Meteorological Institute at Brussels
IRSAC   Congolese Institute for Scientific Research
IRSIA/IWONL   Institute for Encouragement of Scientific Research in
    Industry and Agriculture
ISNB   Institute of Natural Sciences of Belgium at Brussels

K&G/ONE   Child and Family/ONE
KFA   Atomic Research Facilities (Germany)
KUL   Catholic University of Leuven
LEA   Local Education Authority
LUC   Limburg University Center at Diepenbeek
MARESCS   Maritime Rescue and Communication Satellite
METEOSAT   Geostationary weather satellite
MPH   Ministry of Public Health
MST   Medical school team
NATO   North Atlantic Treaty Organization
NBB   National Bank of Belgium
NCMV   National Christian Association for the Middle Classes
NRF   *Nouvelle Revue Française*
NSDAP   German National Socialist Workers Party
OECD   Organization of Economic Cooperation and Development
OEEC   Organization of European Economic Cooperation
ONSS   National Office of Social Security
OPEC   Organization of Petroleum Exporting Countries
ORB   Royal Observatory of Belgium at Brussels
OSR   Office of the Special Representative
PAIT   Interuniversity poles of attraction
PES   Preparatory educational school
PGS   Plant genetic systems
PLP   Party for Freedom and Progress (Liberal; French-speaking)
POS   Point of sale (terminals)
PRL   Liberal Reform Party (ex PLP)
PS   Socialist Party (French-speaking)
PSC   Christian Social Party (French-speaking)
PVV   Party for Freedom and Progress (Liberal; Dutch-speaking)
RAF   British Royal Air Force
RDA   Regional Development Agency
REREF   European Network for Research in Education and Training
REX   Right-wing party active before and during World War II
RNB/BNR   Belgian National Radio (in London)
RPS   Renewed primary school
RTB/BRT   Belgian Radio and Television
RTL   Luxembourg Radio and Television
RUCA   Antwerp State University Center
RUG   State University of Ghent
RW   Walloon Movement
SDR   Special drawing rights

SHAPE Supreme Headquarters of Allied Forces in Europe
SME Small and medium-size enterprises
SMR Standard mortality ratio
SNR Fastbreeder nuclear reactor (Kalmar, Germany)
SP Socialist Party (Dutch-speaking)
SPPS Scientific Policy Planning Services
SWIFT Society for Worldwide Interbank Financial
  Telecommunications
TCT Third Work Circuit
UCL Catholic University of Louvain
UEB Brussels Union of Businesses
UEL State University at Liège
UEM State University of Mons
UFSAL St. Aloysius University at Brussels
UFSIA Antwerp St. Ignatius University
UIA Antwerp University Institution
ULB Free University of Brussels (French-speaking)
ULG State University of Liège
UNICE Union of European Community Industries
UNO United Nations Organization
UNSC United Nations Security Council
UWE Walloon Union of Businesses
VEV Flemish Economic Union
VNV Flemish Nationalist Party
VUB Free University of Brussels (Dutch-speaking)
VVB Flemish People's Movement
WEU Western European Union
WHO World Health Organization
WMO World Meteorologic Organization

Contributors

Marina D'Haese Boudart was born in Breda (Netherlands). She obtained a degree of Bachelor of Arts and studied law at the Catholic University of Louvain. She has been a resident of the United States since 1948 and studied painting and the history of art at Princeton and at Stanford. She has served as a board member and a volunteer worker for numerous community and educational organizations. She has been president of the University of California at Berkeley Newcomers Group (1962–63), Crystal Springs School Parents Association (1966–67), the Stanford Faculty Women's Club (1972–73), and the Matadero Investment Club (1986–88). In 1987, His Majesty Baudouin I made her a Knight of the Order of the Crown of Belgium.

Michel Boudart earned a diploma in chemical engineering from the Catholic University of Louvain and a Ph.D. in chemistry from Princeton. He was a C.R.B. Honorary Graduate Fellow, 1947–49, and a C.R.B. Special Fellow, 1949–51. He is currently the Keck Professor of Engineering at Stanford University. He is a member of the National Academy of Sciences and of the National Academy of Engineering of the U.S.A., as well as an associate member of the Académie Royale des Sciences, des Lettres et des Beaux-Arts of Belgium. He is a Commandeur of the Order of the Crown of Belgium. He was awarded doctorates honoris causa by the Universities of Liège, Ghent, Notre Dame, and Nancy.

René Bryssinck, born 1922. Engineering degree in Electricity and Aeronautics, University of Ghent; Engineering degree in Electronics, University of Brussels. He became General Manager of Sait Electronics, and he was later appointed President and Managing Director of that company. In 1975 he entered the Management Committee and became Chairman of the Belgian National Institute for R&D in Industry and Agriculture. Since 1978, he has been Chairman of the Research Board of the Belgian Manufacturers Association. In 1984 he became a member of the Steering Committee of the Industrial R&D Advisory Committee of the European Commission. He is also the Executive Secretary of the Belgian Academy Council of Applied Sciences.

Part I

Jacques Groothaert, born 1926. Chairman of Générale de Banque and member of the Belgian foreign service from 1945 to 1980. He was educated at the Universities of Brussels and Ghent. In the diplomatic service he served successively in Prague, Moscow, Mexico, Paris, Kinshasa, San Francisco, and London and was Ambassador to Mexico (1967–72) and to Beijing (simultaneously accredited to Hanoi; 1972–75), before becoming Director-General of External Economic Relations at the Ministry of Foreign Affairs (1967–80). He joined the Société Générale de Belgique in 1980 and is a chairman or director of a number of companies: EBES, SABCA, Transurb Consult, General Trading Co., and Fabrimétal. He is presently also High Commissioner for Europalia Japan 1989 and Chairman of the Belgian-Chinese Economic and Commercial Council and the Belgium–Hong Kong Society.

Jean Stengers, Professor of Contemporary History, University of Brussels. Member of the Royal Academy of Belgium. He has written extensively on the history of modern Belgium (one of his books is devoted to the events of 1940: *Léopold III et le gouvernement*), on the history of Zaïre, and on international relations. He is the editor of the *Revue Belge de Philologie et d'Histoire*.

Robert André, born 1925. Doctor of geographical sciences. Member of the Royal Academy of Belgium. Professor at the Free University of Brussels and head of the Center for Demography. Lecturer at the University of Mons. Alderman of the City of Mons.

Rudolf Reszohazy, born 1929. Doctor of Philosophy, Ph.D. in History, Catholic University of Louvain. Presently Professor at the Faculty of Economic, Social, and Political Sciences of the same university, in charge of research in the field of modern history and social change.

Reginald De Schrijver, born 1932. Studied in Namur and Leuven. He received his Ph.D. (History) at the Catholic University of Leuven (1962), where he became professor in 1965. He teaches the history of the Low Countries, history of historiography, and cultural history of Europe. Visiting Fellow at London, Yale, California (Berkeley), and Kent universities. His main publications are on the early modern period and the modern political and intellectual history of Belgium and Western Europe.

Herman Balthazar, born 1938. Pr.dr. History (University of Ghent). Governor of the Province of East Flanders since July 1, 1985. Part-time Professor at the University of Ghent (contemporary history) and Free University of Brussels (mass media research). Former Chairman of Belgian Broadcasting and Television Network (Dutch Program), 1980–85.

Part II

André de Staercke, born 1913. Honorary Ambassador of Belgium. Doctor of Law (Louvain-Paris). First Secretary of the Prime Minister of Belgium and Secretary of the Cabinet, 1943–45. Secretary to the Prince-Regent of Belgium, 1945–50. Belgian Deputy at the Council of Deputies of NATO, 1950–52. Belgian Permanent Representative at the NATO Council, 1952–76. Dean of the NATO Council, 1954–76.

Hendrik Fayat, Doctor of Law, Brussels University, 1933. Barrister at the Court of Appeals, Brussels, 1935–73. Professor at the Faculty of Law, Brussels University, 1948–78. Emeritus Professor, 1978. Member of the Belgian House of Representatives, 1946–71. Member of the Belgian Government, 1957–58, 1961–66, 1968–73. Member of the Consultative Assembly of the Council of Europe, 1949–50, and of the Common Assembly of the European Coal and Steel Committee, 1954–57.

Alfred Cahen, born 1929. Belgian diplomat. He entered government service as a probationer in the Foreign Service at the Ministry of Foreign Affairs, 1956. Chef de Cabinet to the Minister of Foreign Affairs, 1977–79. Ambassador–Political Director, Ministry of Foreign Affairs, Foreign Trade and Development Cooperation, 1979–85. Secretary General of the Western European Union, 1985. Lecturer at the Free University of Brussels, 1980.

Pierre Cremer (Major General, Ret.). Taught military history and tactics. Was Professor of Strategy and Defense Policies at the Belgian National War College, which he commanded until 1983. Visiting Professor, Universities of Louvain and Liège.

Etienne Davignon (Viscount), born 1932. Doctor of Law, University of Louvain. He joined the Ministry of Foreign Affairs in 1959 and was Chef de Cabinet for P.-H. Spaak and P. Harmel when they were Ministers of Foreign Affairs. He became General Manager of Foreign Policy in 1969 and Chairman of the Management Committee of the International Agency for Energy of the United Nations in Vienna. He was also a member of the Commission of the European Community and later Vice-President for Industry, Energy, and Research. He left the European Commission in 1985 to become a director of Société Générale de Belgique. He is a board member of several international companies.

Hugo Paemen, born 1934. Studied philosophy and literature, social and political sciences. Belgian diplomat, served in Paris, 1965–68; Brussels (Spokesman, Ministry of Foreign Affairs), 1969–74; Washington, D.C. (Economic Minister), 1974–77; Brussels (EC Commission, Chef de Cabinet for Vice-President Davignon), 1977–85, Spokesman, 1985–87. Since 1987, Deputy Director-General for External Relations, EC Commission.

Paul Noterdaeme, born 1929. Doctor of Law and Baccalaureate in Philosophy. He joined the Diplomatic Service in 1956. He served as Deputy Chef de Cabinet and then Chef de Cabinet to the Foreign Minister, 1968–74; Permanent Representative to the U.N. Office in Geneva, 1974–79; Permanent Representative to the EEC, 1979–87. At present he is Permanent Representative of Belgium to the U.N. in New York.

Edmonde Dever (Ms.), born in Brussels. Bachelor of Arts in history and Doctor of Law, Brussels University. Entered the Belgian Foreign Service in 1946. Between stays at the Ministry in Brussels (among other European and NATO desks), she was posted twice in London, was Consul General in Angola, 1959–61, and was Permanent Representative to the U.N., 1966–69. Successively Ambassador to Sweden and Austria (also representative to the U.N. organization in Vienna). Her last post was Ambassador and Belgium's Permanent Representative to the U.N., 1981–87.

Pierre Harmel, born 1911. Doctor of Law, Bachelor of Social Sciences, and licensed Notary Public. Professor at the Law Faculty, University of Liège, 1945–81. Member of Parliament, 1946–71, and Senator, 1973–77. As minister he was successively responsible for Education, Justice, and Scientific Policy, but is best known as Minister of Foreign Affairs, 1966–73. During this period he was the author of the famous Harmel Report on the Atlantic Alliance. He was appointed Minister of State. He is a corresponding member of the Royal Academy of Belgium.

Jean Godeaux, born 1922. Doctor of Law, graduated in Economics from the Catholic University of Louvain, 1944–46. Member of the Bar of Namur, 1944–47. National Bank of Belgium, 1947–49. IMF, Alternate Executive Director, then Executive Director, 1950–54. Manager, then Partner, then President, of Banque Lambert, 1955–74. President, Banking Commission, 1974 to present. President, Bank for International Settlements, 1985–87. Member of the Board of Settlements, Catholic University of Louvain, 1974–present.

Jean-Paul van Bellinghen. Ambassador of Belgium to the Court of St. James, after representing his country in Kinshasa. He has been associated with Belgian policies toward Zaïre, both on the spot and in Brussels, Washington, D.C., and New York. He has been his government's spokesman on foreign affairs and a personal adviser to three foreign ministers.

Part III

André Molitor, born 1911. Doctor of Law, Catholic University of Louvain. Has managed different public administrations. Principal Private Secretary to the King of the Belgians, 1961–77. Professor of Political and Administrative Sciences, Catholic University of Louvain. Author of many books and studies. Until recently chaired the King Baudouin Foundation.

Robert Senelle, born 1918. Doctor of Law, Free University of Brussels. Appointed Judge at the Louvain Court and Prosecutor at the Council of State. First Secretary to the Prime Minister, 1954–58. Appointed Professor of Constitutional and Administrative Law, Ghent University. Elected Dean of the Faculty of Law, Ghent University, 1978. A few years later became a barrister at the Bar in Brussels.

Xavier Mabille, born 1933. Co–General Manager of the Center for Sociopolitical Research and Information. Spent several years as visiting professor at the Catholic University of Louvain, Faculty of Economic, Political, and Social Sciences. Now Professor at St. Louis University Faculties, Brussels. Scientific adviser to Encyclopedia Universalis, Paris.

Part IV

Luc Wauters, born 1926. Doctor of Commercial and Financial Sciences, Catholic University of Leuven. Master of Science, Columbia University, New York. Chairman of the Almanij-Kredietbank group and Janssen Pharmaceutica. Emeritus Professor, University of Antwerp. Member of the State Financial Council of Belgium. Vice-President of the Flemish Economic Association. Director of the Belgian American Foundation and Belgian University-Industry Foundation.

Jan Huyghebaert, born 1945. Doctor of Law, Catholic University of Leuven. President of Kredietbank. Former adviser to the Prime Minister and Alderman for Port and Industry of the City of Antwerp. Director of several industrial companies such as Bell Telephone and Antwerp Gas Co. Vice-President of the Queen Elisabeth Music Festival.

Paul Kestens, born 1939. Bachelor of Economic Sciences, University of

Brussels. Professor at the same university and visiting professor at the Notre-Dame Faculties of Namur. Became Director of the DULBEA Institute in 1980. Was also Vice-President and then President of the Department of Economic Sciences, Brussels University. He has contributed to several publications on economics.

Jan Hinnekens, born 1927. Doctor of Law, Catholic University of Leuven. Legal adviser, Belgian Boerenbond; appointed Chairman of same in 1981. Vice-President of the National Agriculture Board. On international level, member of the Executive Committee of IFAP and the Committee of Agricultural Organizations of the European Community (COPA).

Raymond Pulinckx, born 1924. Licentiate in Economics and Financial Sciences. Postgraduate work at Columbia University. Managing Director and Chief Executive Officer, Belgian Employers' Federation. Regent of the National Bank of Belgium. Chairman of PABELTEC (Paper) and SKF Belgium (Bearings). Honorary Chef de Cabinet for the Minister of Economic Affairs.

Rik Donckels, born 1941. Licentiate in Mathematics, Doctor of Economics, Catholic University of Leuven. At present, Professor at UFSAL in Brussels and KUL Leuven. Founder of the Small Business Research Institute. Special adviser for Small Business to the Belgian and Flemish governments and private institutions.

Alain Siaens, born 1941. Master of Philosophy and Ph.D. in Economics, Catholic University of Louvain. CRB Fellow, Harvard University. Since 1973, Executive Vice-President of Banque Degroof. Director of the Financial Studies Center. Lecturer at Louvain University and in charge of research in the financial and monetary field.

Herman Daems, currently Visiting Professor at Harvard Business School. Former Professor of Applied Economics, Catholic University of Leuven. Director of the European Institute for Advanced Studies in Management. Has special research interest in large European firms and their response to competitive challenges. Adviser to several companies.

Theo Peeters, born 1937. Ph.D. in Economics, Catholic University of Leuven. M.A. degree, University of California (Berkeley). Since 1971, Professor of Economics at Leuven. Chairman of the Flemish Science and Policy Council. Director of Banque Bruxelles-Lambert and Rorento Fund.

Paul Hatry, born 1929. Lecturer at Brussels University since 1958 in international economics, European integration and energy problems, and Dean of ULB Business School established by E. Solvay, 1970–73. From 1961 to 1988, Managing Director, and since 1988, Honorary Chairman of the Belgian Oil Industry Association. Between 1980 and 1985, member of the Belgian Cabinet as Minister of Finance and later of the Brussels Region. Senator since 1981.

Roland Beauvois, born 1920. Economist at the National Bank of Belgium, 1945–65, General Manager, 1965–87. Professor of Monetary Theory at the Faculty of Social, Political, and Economic Sciences, Free University of Brussels. Member of the State Financial Council.

Part V

Roger Dillemans, born 1932. Professor at the Law Faculty, Catholic University of Leuven, 1964; Dean of the Law Faculty, 1978–81; Rector of the university since 1985. Visiting Professor at Kings College since 1970. President of the Institute of Social Law. Founder and first Director of the European Institute of Social Security. Royal Commissioner for the reformulation and reform of the Belgian social security system, 1980–85.

Roger Blanpain, born 1932. Doctor of Law, Catholic University of Leuven. Professor of Labor Law, Law School, at the same university. President of the International Industrial Relations Association (IIRA). Editor in Chief of the International Encyclopedia for Labor Law and Industrial Relations. Senator.

Jacques Delcourt, born 1928. Doctor in Political and Social Sciences and Graduate in Economics, Catholic University of Louvain. Appointed in 1965 to the Department of Sociology of the same university, where he teaches sociology of work and organizations and the sociology of education. His main research field concerns the relations between education, work, the economy, and society. Has lectured at the University of Geneva and the University of Social Sciences of Toulouse.

Herman Deleeck, born 1928. Doctor of Law (1952) and Doctor of Economics (1966), Catholic University of Louvain. Professor at the University of Antwerp and Professor Extraordinarius at Louvain (social policy and social economics) and the University of Leyden. Director of the Center for Social Policy, University of Antwerp. Member of Parliament (1977–81 and 1984–87). President of the Interdepartmental Commission on Poverty.

Dries Simoens, born 1950. Currently Professor of Social Law at Catholic University of Leuven. In 1978 he attained his Ph.D. at the same university. In addition to his teaching experience, he was an attorney at the Bar of Bruges. During 1982 he also served as Press Attaché to the State Secretary of Pensions.

Albert Martens, born 1940, M.D., Ph.D. Appointed Lecturer at the Faculty of Social Sciences, Catholic University of Leuven. Professor of Sociology of Industrial Relations. Chairman of the High Commission for Migrants of the Ministry of Family and Welfare (Flemish Government), 1982–84. Chairman of the work group "Scientific Research on Foreign Minorities in Flanders" of the National Fund for Scientific Research.

Albert Bastenier, born 1940. Sociology graduate. Appointed to the Sociology Department of the Catholic University of Louvain. Chief editor of *Social Compass* (international review on the sociology of religion) and comanager of the Study Group on Migrations and Interethnic Relations (GREM). Member of the Steering Committee of *Revue Nouvelle*. Author of several books in the field of migration sociology.

Raphel Lagasse, born 1949. M.D., Ph.D. Lecturer at the School of Public Health, Faculty of Medicine, Free University of Brussels. Vice-President of the School of Public Health, Codirector of the Center of Health Sociology, Institute of Sociology, of the same university. Temporary adviser to WHO and UNFPA. Member of the Consultative Council for Prevention and Health of the French-speaking Community of Belgium.

Jacqueline Bande-Knops (Mrs.), born 1932. Professor of Medicine at the Faculty of Medicine, Catholic University of Leuven. Secretary General of the Nationaal Werk voor Kinderwelzijn (child welfare). Chairman of the European Union of School and University Health Medicine.

Herman Nys, born 1951. Graduated from Catholic University of Leuven with an M.D. in Law, 1974, Ph.D. in Law, 1980. Associate Professor in Medical Law, Law School and Medical School at Leuven, 1985. Author of books and articles concerning health care law and health care organization. Member of governmental advisory boards in the field of hospital planning, AIDS, medical ethics.

Part VI

Gaston Deurinck, born 1923. Obtained his Civil Engineering Degree at the Catholic University of Louvain. From the beginning of his career has been interested in systematic management of human resources in industry, universities, and public institutions. In 1956 he established the University-Industry Foundation and contributed to the modernization of the universities and the introduction of new technologies in higher and adult education.

Pierre Vanbergen, born 1919. Had a varied career as a secondary school teacher and inspector, then lecturer at the Antwerp State University Center. Adviser, 1954–58, and Chef de Cabinet, 1961–65, at the Ministry of Education; Director General for the Organization of Studies, 1964–78, and Secretary General, 1978–85, in the same ministry. Took an active part in the work of the OECD, the Council of Europe, and the EEC. Author of several books and numerous articles in Belgian and foreign periodicals.

Roland Vandenberghe, born 1939. Full Professor at the Catholic University of Leuven. Chair of the Center for Educational Policy and Innovation. His main research interest is change and innovation in educational settings. He has published several articles and books on innovation in education and school improvement.

Laurent Grimmonprez (Canon), born 1924. Ordained Catholic priest in 1950. M.D. in philosophy and literature, Catholic University of Louvain, 1954. Teacher and principal of a secondary school (Institut St. Boniface, Brussels), 1954–62. President of the Seminary for Philosophy and Theology at Malines, 1962–64. Secretary General of the Federation of the Belgian Catholic Secondary Schools, 1964–79. Assistant General Manager of the National Secretariat of Catholic Education of Belgium since 1979.

Roger Van Geen, born 1935. Ph.D. Head of the Department of Applied Physics and Honorary Vice-Chancellor of the Free University of Brussels. Chairman of the Belgian National Council for Science Policy. His scientific work covers the field of modern optics and its industrial and medical applications.

Gilbert de Landsheere. Professor Emeritus, State University of Liège, where he headed the Department of Empirical Educational Research, 1960–86. Author of seventeen books on education and of some 200 articles. He serves as a consultant to the main governmental and international organizations dealing with education.

Part VII

André L. Jaumotte (Baron), born 1920. Is active both as a scholar, a researcher, and a manager. As a scholar, he was Professor of Rotating Machines at the Free University of Brussels (Faculty of Engineering). As a researcher, he published many contributions on thermodynamics and fluidics of machines. As a manager, he was Rector and Chairman of the Board of the Free University of Brussels and Chairman of the Academic Hospital. He is chairman of several important industrial companies.

Roger Van Geen, see Part VI.

Paul Levaux, born 1937. Doctor in Chemical Sciences, Free University of Brussels. Presently Secretary General of the National Fund for Scientific Research and associated funds. Chairman of the CERN Council in Geneva, 1976 and 1977. Chairman of the Program Committee of the European Cyclotron Radiation Facility, 1980. During the past ten years was several times in charge of the Evaluation Group of the European Education and Training Program on Science and Technology.

Jean Van Keymeulen, born 1929. Ph.D. in Chemistry, University of Ghent, 1958. General Manager of IRSIA since 1970. Vice-President of the World Association of Industrial and Technological Research Organizations and member of the Federation of European Industrial Cooperative Research Organizations.

Roger Van Overstraeten, born 1937. Engineer degrees El. and Mech., Catholic University of Leuven, 1960. Ph.D., Stanford University, 1963. Professor at Leuven since 1965. President of Interuniversity Microelectronics Center. Author or coauthor of more than 100 scientific papers in the field of electronic devices and microelectronics. Fellow IEEE. Honorary doctoral degree INP Grenoble, 1987.

Alain Stenmans, born 1923. Doctor of Law. Member of the Royal Academy of Overseas Sciences of Belgium. Secretary General of the Services of the Prime Minister for Scientific Policy. President of the Belgian Interministry Commission for Scientific Policy, of the Belgian delegations to the Committee for Scientific and Technical Policy of OECD and the EEC Committee for Scientific and Technological Research, 1972–88.

Part VIII

Herman Liebaers, born 1919. Librarian of the Royal Library, 1956–73. Grand Marshal of the Court, 1974–81. Royal Commissioner for the Restructuring of the National Research Institutes, 1982–84. Professor of Library Science at the Brussels University, 1970–84. Member of the Royal Academy of Belgium. Author of books and articles on Flemish literature, library science, and culture in general.

Philippe Roberts-Jones (Baron), born 1924. Doctor of Philosophy. Curator in Chief of the Royal Museums of Fine Arts of Belgium. Professor of History of Arts at the Free University of Brussels. Permanent Secretary of the Royal Academy of Sciences, Literature, and Fine Arts of Belgium. Member of the Institut de France.

Georges Sion, born 1913. Doctor of Law, writer and playwright, Professor Emeritus at the Royal Academy of Music of Brussels (history of the theater). Critic and lecturer, Permanent Secretary of the Royal Academy of French Language and Literature of Belgium. Belgian Member of the Goncourt Academy.

Jean Weisgerber, born 1924. Senior Professor of Dutch and Comparative Literature at the Free Universities of Brussels (ULB and VUB) since 1952. Fellow of the Royal Academy (Dutch Language and Literature). Secretary General, 1967–73, and Vice-President, 1973–76, of the International Comparative Literature Association. Author of books on Flemish literature (Stijn Streuvels, Hugo Claus, the contemporary novel, etc.).

Francine-Claire Legrand (Ms.), born 1916. Doctor of History of Arts, University of Paris. Entered the Royal Museums of Fine Arts of Belgium in 1950, successively librarian, Assistant Curator, Curator, and Head of the Department of Modern Arts. Author of many books and articles, mainly related to the history of painting and painters.

Jacques De Decker, born 1945. Chief editor for cultural matters of the newspaper *Le Soir*. Professor of Theater History at the Royal Conservatory of Brussels. Playwright, novelist, translator, art critic.

Bernard Huys, born 1934. Doctor of Law and Bachelor of Art in History and Archeology, speciality: musicology (both at the Ghent University). Professor of art history and history of music at the Hoger St. Lukasinstituut, Brussels, since 1964 and Head of the Music Department of the Royal Library Albert I since 1970. Since 1980, member of the Royal Academy of Belgium. Member of several musicological societies, both domestic and foreign. Vice-President of the International Association of Music Libraries. Author of various catalogues, bibliographies, and articles in musicology.

Robert Wangermée, born 1920. Doctor of Philosophy and Doctor of History, Free University of Brussels. General Manager and then Managing Director of the Belgian Broadcasting and Television Network (French Program), 1960–84. Professor of Musicology, Free University of Brussels. In 1988 he was appointed Chairman of the High Council for Radio and Television of the French Community of Belgium. Author of many books and articles on musicology, broadcasting, and television.

Léo Moulin, born 1906. Doctor of Literature, University of Bologna. Doctor of Philosophy, Free University of Brussels. Bachelor of Political Science. Professor Emeritus of the Notre-Dame Faculties of Namur. Chairman of the Association of Writers on Gastronomy and Wines. Author of well-known books such as *Tabled Europe* and *Tabled Belgium*.

PART I

The Land and the People

Jacques Groothaert, Coordinator

Introduction

Jacques Groothaert

BELGIUM IS CENTRALLY located at the heart of the European Community, is densely populated, enjoys a high standard of living, counts as one of the ten most important economic powers in the industrialized world, and is a member of NATO. Yet the name Belgium does not always bring a clear picture or concept to mind. Oddly enough its identity seems to be a well-kept secret, except when great battles are fought on its soil (Bastogne, the Battle of the Bulge), or when minor conflicts arise within its boundaries about language issues (whose portent no foreigner is able to grasp). Indeed, its capital city, Brussels, headquarters for NATO and the European Economic Community, is better known and mentioned much more often than the country itself. The publication of this volume, *Modern Belgium*, is therefore timely and useful. Its contributors have assembled a wealth of data, facts, and reflections that should help to introduce some complexities of Belgian reality.

Belgian history is in a sense European history. With its rich heritage and cultural mix, Belgium has been called the archetypal European country. However, the problem of Belgian nationhood may often seem a puzzle to foreigners. National identity is sometimes defined in negative terms, and rightly so, as a clear feeling of difference from neighboring countries. Belgian textbooks tell the story of events that took place on the territories that became present-day Belgium, rather than the history of a people. Indeed, the evolving European Community resembles Belgium in being based on the assertion of a common identity uniting peoples of different languages.

It has been said that to understand Belgian politics one has to "think double." Tensions and problems between Dutch and French speakers, Flemings and Walloons, have dominated national life since independence. Continual adjustments have created a delicate balance that minor incidents can upset, but these have never—contrary to nationality problems elsewhere in Europe—led to violence or bloodshed. This balance is a rather remarkable achievement. It has been made possible through a long evolution of customs, laws, and agreements. Belgians have always understood that such a process allows for loopholes and exceptions, leaving room for interpretation and often uneasy compromises.

Belgians have learned to live with contradictory and sometimes chaotic results: they have developed reflexes that see to it that organized chaos still differs from total anarchy. Belgians indeed have always placed material well-being and a decent standard of living before conflicts of doctrine. They value tolerance, respect for civil rights, and the due process of law. They care little for the class struggle or for ideological disputes. According to John K. Galbraith, Karl Marx once said that the greatest threat to the revolution was the "belgianization" of capitalism.

So far, the chronic and often baffling instability of Belgian political life has not seemed fundamentally detrimental to a convergence of particular interests. This is contrary to appearances and born of a long coexistence in an area with no natural frontiers or clear-cut boundaries. Mastering "belgitude" requires patience, as well as tactical skill and an ability to generate acceptable compromises and a consensus for peaceful, if not always harmonious, coexistence.

The challenge for modern Belgium is not to rely too much on its past achievements. It is still endowed with a central location, an excellent communications network, skilled labor, few social conflicts, and a strongly competitive export capacity. It is in a position to become, in an age of high technology, an efficient multilingual nation providing services and holding a strategic position in an integrated European market.

The following pages describe Belgium: its tangled history, the resilience of its people, the way in which it tries to tackle the delicate problems of devolution and federalism, and—if it manages to solve them—the positive role it is able and willing to play in the community of free nations.

The first essay, on vocabulary, alerts the reader to the country's complexity; its dual-language system at first strikes the observer as a liability, but it also points toward the rich and diversified cultural background of Belgium's inhabitants. The next three chapters describe first the land itself and then its population. Strategically positioned, the country is both a meeting point and a buffer for the European powers. The three basic ethnic groups, Dutch, French, and German, have been augmented by workers from neighboring countries as well as from, among others, Turkey, Algeria, and Morocco. The composition of the population changes continually with the demand for labor, a situation not unlike that of the United States in the last century.

The next chapter explores religious convictions. Belgium is basically a Roman Catholic country. But its residents practice many different religions. A salient feature is the mutual influence of politics and convictions in Belgium.

The next two chapters provide some knowledge of Belgium's long and complicated past. The first covers the history of Belgium up to World War I, a major turning point in European history. The second historical chapter, on Belgium since World War I, is devoted not to the linguistic squabbles of the past few years but to the recent evolution toward federalism. The final chapter in this part analyzes Belgian national sentiment and explains Belgium's identity problem.

The Vocabulary

Jean Stengers

THE COMPLEXITIES OF BELGIUM are reflected in the various pitfalls of vocabulary applying to the country. Belgium (*la Belgique, België*) emerged as the name of the area corresponding roughly to the present-day country at the end of the 18th century. It became the official name of the land at independence, in 1830. Before that, in the 17th and 18th centuries, one spoke generally of the Spanish or, later on, the Austrian Netherlands (*les Pays-Bas espagnols, autrichiens, de Spaanse, Oostenrijkse Nederlanden*), also called later by historians the Southern Netherlands (*les Pays-Bas méridionaux, de zuidelijke Nederlanden*). The territory was approximately the same as that of modern Belgium, except that the Principality of Liège (*Principauté de Liège, Prinsbisdom Luik*) was still a distinct ecclesiastical state.

The inhabitants of the country are Belgians (*les Belges, de Belgen*). The Latin name *Belgae* was used in antiquity, but the Belgians of Roman times occupied a territory much larger than present-day Belgium. Only at the end of the 18th century was the word applied to the people of the Southern Netherlands.

Since 1831, Belgium has been the Kingdom of Belgium (*Royaume de Belgique, Koninkrijk België*). Its sovereign, according to the constitution, is the king of the Belgians (*Roi des Belges, Koning der Belgen*).

There are presently in Belgium three regions. They were constitutionally defined only in 1970, but two have existed as such since the time of independence: the Flemish region (*région flamande, vlaamse gewest*), commonly called Flanders (*la Flandre, Vlaanderen*), and the Walloon region (*région wallonne, waalse gewest*), commonly called Wallonia (*la Wallonie, Wallonië*). The third is more recent: the Brussels region (*région bruxelloise, brusselse gewest*), which comprises the city of Brussels (*ville de Bruxelles, stad Brussel*) and its eighteen suburbs.

The term "Flanders" came to designate the northern part of the country, with its Dutch-speaking population (see below) only after 1830. Before that, the word had two meanings. First, Flanders is the name of an ancient province, the County of Flanders (*Comté de Flandre, Graafschap Vlaanderen*). Second, Flanders refers to the whole of the Southern Netherlands, including sometimes the Principality of Liège. For example, "Flemish artists" can mean artists born in Wallonia as well as in the northern part of the country. The term Flanders is still frequently used in that way, especially in foreign publications, but the Walloons strongly object to that use.

The basic distinction between the two regions is that of the language used by the population. The inhabitants of Flanders are Dutch speakers (*Néerlandophones, Nederlandstaligen*). They speak various Germanic dialects. However, Dutch (*le néerlandais, het nederlands*) is the educated language, and as the official one, it is replacing the dialects more and more, even in daily life. There are, however, some minor regional differences between the Dutch language of Holland and the Dutch language of Flanders. Hence, the latter is commonly called "Flemish" (*le flamand, het vlaams*) or "the Flemish language" (*la langue flamande, de vlaamse taal*). This is also why literary works produced in Flanders are referred to as "Flemish literature" (*littérature flamande, vlaamse literatuur*). This gives rise to the strange geographic difference between the extent of "Flemish art" (see above) and that of "Flemish literature," a difference that may understandably baffle foreigners.

The inhabitants of Wallonia speak Romance dialects bearing the common name "Walloon" (*le wallon, het waals*). But these dialects are disappearing more quickly than their Flemish counterparts. The language of the region is French (*le français, het frans*), with a few differences in vocabulary (for 70 and 90, for example, the Belgians say *septante* and *nonante*, whereas the French say *soixante-dix* and *quatre-vingt-dix*). Accents, naturally, are often somewhat different, but France has a great variety of accents too. Literature written in French in Belgium, unlike literature written in Dutch, has no specific name. It is known either as "French literature of Belgium" (*lettres françaises de Belgique*) or as "Belgian literature in French" (*lettres belges de langue française*).

In eastern Wallonia there is a small group of German-speaking Belgians (*germanophones, duitstaligen*, in German *Deutschsprachigen*). The Brussels region is linguistically mixed. It includes both Dutch-speaking and French-speaking people. The exact proportion of the two groups remains a bone of contention in Belgian public life.

The Dutch-speaking people, whether they live in Flanders or in Brussels, are officially termed "Dutch speakers" (*Néerlandophones, Nederlands-taligen*), but colloquially they are known as "Flemings" (*Flamands, Vlamingen*). French speakers, whether they live in Wallonia or in Brussels, are usually called "Francophones" (*Francophones, Franstaligen*). The word "Walloons" (*Wallons, Walen*) applies to all the Francophones of Wallonia and to those of the Francophones of Brussels who feel they still have roots in the Walloon part of the country. Those whose links are only with the Brussels region itself are called "Brussels francophones" (*Francophones bruxellois, Franstalige brusselaars*). We thus have this complex situation; a Dutch-speaking Belgian is always a "Fleming," whereas a French-speaking one may be either a Walloon or a Brussels francophone.

The difficulty is made worse by the official names for the three linguistic communities of Belgium. The three communities are distinct from the three regions, and each has distinctive institutions. The Dutch-speaking community, which includes all the Flemings, is called the "Flemish community" (*Communauté flamande, Vlaamse gemeenschap*). The small German-speaking community is called the "germanophone community" (*Communauté germanophone, Duitstalige gemeenschap*, in German *Deutschsprachige Gemeinschaft*). So far, so good. The francophone community is called the "French community of Belgium" (*Communauté française de Belgique, Franse gemeenschap van Belgie*); this is the source of many misunderstandings outside Belgium, since some believe that the term refers to French nationals living in Belgium.

The Brussels Francophones and Belgian Germanophones are often disregarded, and the common formula is "Flemings and Walloons" (*Flamands et Wallons, Vlamingen en Wallen*). This distinction is supported by the fact that, apart from Belgian national feeling, the two important collective loyalties are those of the Flemings and of the Walloons. Practically all Flemings speak of themselves as the Flemish people (*le peuple flamand, het vlaamse volk*), or more affectionately as "our people" (*notre peuple, ons volk*). A growing number of Walloons term themselves the Walloon people (*le peuple wallon, het Waalse volk*).

Belgium and the Netherlands (*les Pays-Bas, Nederland*), also commonly called Holland (*la Hollande, Holland*), were politically united in the 16th century. This is why they still bear a common name: the Low Countries. This is purely a geographical term, with no official character. There is no equivalent in French for "Low Countries" (the literal translation, *les Pays-Bas*, applies only to Holland). The Dutch name is *de Nederlanden* (as opposed to *Nederland*, the official name of Holland).

Some foreigners believe that Belgium, the Netherlands, and the Grand

Duchy of Luxembourg are united in a kind of state, or political entity, called "Benelux." This is a total misconception. Benelux is the name of an economic union between the three countries dating from 1944. Apart from that, there is no political link between Belgium, the Netherlands, and Luxembourg.

Geography

Robert André

BELGIUM IS A DIVERSE cultural melting pot situated at the meeting point of the Germanic and Latin worlds, at the crossroads of the seafaring life of the North Sea. One of the busiest marine waterways in the world, it is the continental confluence of central Europe and its vast plains and mountain ranges. It covers an area of 30,000 square kilometers and has almost 10 million inhabitants.

Physical Aspects

Merging with the coal field for many miles, the furrow traced by the Sambre and Meuse rivers cuts across the country from west to east, marking the boundary between the two main regions of Belgium.

Each region has its own unique physical appearance. To the south are the Ardennes Mountains, stretching up into the skyline; to the north the land is near sea level. The Ardennes begin on the edges of Belgium and France, then range across the Meuse stretch of Belgium, and broaden out in the east to reach the Hautes-Fagnes, the highest part. There at the Grand Duchy of Luxembourg the range continues into Germany with the Eifel massif. It is an anticlinal area, containing the most ancient rocks to be found in the country. The altitude gives the region a sense of continuity. These Belgian "peaks" are barely distinguishable from the rest of the landscape, and the relief is not more pronounced than in the northern plains.

Belgium generally enjoys a moderate, maritime climate; however, the Ardennes plateau tends to have certain continental climate characteristics. Winter in the Ardennes, with their altitude and the distance from the sea, is severe, with frosty weather and heavy snow. Summer is rather cool with monthly averages of 15°C to 16°C. The Ardennes have the highest rainfall level in Belgium, between 900 millimeters to 1400 milli-meters per year, spread out over 180 to 200 days. Fall is the main rainy season, followed by summer.

The lower plateaus form the transition land between the Ardennes and the flat Flemish region and are covered by Quaternary alluvium. In the center of the country, in Brabant, the alluvium covers a layer of sand, resulting in quite considerable erosion of the alluvial surface as seen, for example, at Waterloo. This region is filled with deep valleys. To the west, in Hainaut, clay replaces the sandy subsoil, and again rivers cut into the plateau. Higher and more imposing in the south, the pla-teau contains along the Haine the genesis of a vast west-east depression, the most southerly plain of Belgium, where the altitude falls below 20 meters. The dividing line between the waterways of the Meuse and the Scheldt is a few kilometers to the north of the Sambre-Meuse trail. The waterways of the lower alluvial plateaus, such as the Lys, Scheldt, Dendre, Senne, Dyle, Big and Small Gette, form a parallel network stretching from south-southwest to north-northeast.

At about an altitude of 50 meters, the Flemish plain comes up against a scree some dozens of meters high, which forms the northern rim of the lower plateaus. The rim has been torn apart by erosion, resulting in isolated hills (Kemmelberg and Mont de l'Enclus).

The Campine plateau is in the extreme east. It is not of the same ori-gin as the lower alluvial plateaus, but is rather a fragment of an ancient alluvial cone of the Meuse, the boundaries of which were marked by the abrupt screes formed by the northeast slope of the Démer Valley and the west slope of the Meuse's Limburg Valley.

The north of Belgium is part of the immense plain stretching across northern Europe. It arrives in Flanders at its southwestern extremity. This vast stretch of land, with an altitude of under 50 meters, looks deceptively simple. It is in fact the product of erosion caused by water-ways and of land thrown up by the sea and by rivers. Erosion has been concentrated chiefly on the interfluvial area within the water network traced by the Scheldt. The flattened slopes of valleys and the low crests linking them up, on top of wide-ranging alluvial deposits, form an undu-lating surface with an altitude between 20 and 50 meters. On the edge of the North Sea, the marine-origin plain extends at an altitude below 5 meters, consisting of recent marine clays a few meters thick. This area was formed by the filling in of a lagoon formed during the advance of the sea, which reached as far as Diksmuide and Brugge in the fourth century. Geographically speaking, the area was marshland, and in the 12th century, people living on this patch of land, without the protection of a seawall or dike, gave it the name "polders." The region is separated from the beaches by a string of dunes, broken through in the west by the mouth of the Ijzer and in the east by the Zwin, the ancient estuary of Bruges. Unlike the maritime plain, where perfect topographical continuity is to be found, the polders are composed of distinct sections. The main one, between Eeklo, Ghent, Lokeren, and Rupelmond, is focused around an old mouth of the Scheldt. This aggradation zone is detached from strips of plain formed by the alluvial deposits of the Lys, Scheldt, Dendre, Senne, and Dyle.

The plains and the lower plateaus come under the blast of southwest winds, namely the rain-bringing depressions born along the polar front. The moderate and maritime climate is therefore characterized by abundant rainfall, ranging between 700 and 900 millimeters per annum, spread over the entire year, with a maximum in fall and a smaller peak in summer during the most continental part of the season. Average temperatures are low in summer (between 16°C and 18°C in July), and relatively high in winter (2°C to 4°C in January). There are very few days when it actually freezes, ranging from a low of 45 to 50 days in the maritime plain to a maximum of 80 days in the Campine plateau. There are under 25 days of snow per annum, and less than 10 days of snowfall along the coast.

The Human Factor

The regional linguistic framework is a useful one for studying the human geography of the country and identifying the spheres of influences of urban centers, which have been made more powerful by the merger of boroughs.

The Walloon Region

The industrial centers of the Haine-Sambre-Meuse. From Borinage in the west to Liège in the east, the industrial basin of Haine-Sambre-Meuse is superimposed on the coal axis, which was responsible for its birth in the 19th century. It is divided into the eastern Liège area, consisting of the Meuse Valley, and the western region, situated in the Sambre and Haine valleys. The working of coal, which dates back to the 12th century, was industrialized at the beginning of the 19th century, as demonstrated by the monumental bulk of the coal plant at Grand-Hornu in the Borinage. Operations intensified in the course of the 19th century, resulting in a concentration of the coal industry. Decline came in the 20th century, furthered by the depression in the 1930's.

In the 19th century, urban centers in the Haine-Sambre-Meuse area developed in areas where coal mining was flourishing and where mines had traditionally been situated. Village life was destroyed, and the roads linking villages became streets of miners' houses, forming spiders' webs around a number of different nuclei. In some areas, such as the Borinage, green spaces remain between them, whereas in others housing and industry cover all available land, as to the north of the Sambre in Charleroi.

Although these built-up areas closely resemble one another in development and economy, urban structure differs radically from one to another. Liège, for example, is a city, chiefly because it was already the regional capital in the Middle Ages. It amassed all the functions of a metropolis: episcopal, because it was for many years the seat of an ecclesiastical principality; administrative, because it is the provincial capital; judicial, military, commercial, and also intellectual because it possesses a university. The city of Liège has slightly more than 200,000 inhabitants, but if the outlying areas are included, the number rises to 500,000. As a regional center, it is the focal point for around 1.3 million people.

Charleroi is another example of a large urban center. It has 350,000 inhabitants. This population concentration is the consequence of the 19th-century industrial revolution that coalesced around Charleroi because of its role as an urban core based upon a fortress built in 1666 and named after Charles II of Spain. It is therefore a town with a more recent history and a more modest role than Liège. Nevertheless, its modern economic power turned it into a metropolis, with influence over a large part of the Entre-Sambre-et-Meuse area, where 750,000 people live.

The Mons-Borinage center is an amalgamation of two fundamentally different geographical features. The Borinage conurbation on the southern slope of the Haine depression was an industrial sprawl without a town. Mons, on the other hand, built on a hill on the plain, is an old city and the historical capital of the Hainaut Province. The influence of Mons as a provincial seat, a judicial and commercial center, and an educational forum with a number of university establishments prevented the birth of an urban core within the Borinage. Mons, with 90,000 inhabitants and a certain power of attraction for tourists, is the center of a region with 300,000 inhabitants. Between Charleroi and Mons, the central urban area has developed: For want of an ancient urban city, La Louvière has increased in importance, exercising its influence over 150,000 people. Finally, between the Hainaut and the Liège industrial centers, Namur, which forms the core of the rail network at the meeting of the Sambre and the Meuse, is a medieval capital, provincial seat, episcopal seat, and university center; it recently became the regional capital of Wallonia. It is the center of an area extending from the Basse-Sambre to the upper part of the Meuse and the western part of the Ardennes to the Semois, an area with 400,000 inhabitants.

The steel industry is at present the most important industry in the Haine-Sambre-Meuse region. At the beginning of the 19th century, the industry moved from the Ardennes and the northern lands around them to set up next to the coal industry along the Meuse in Liège. John Cockerill set up a business in Seraing in 1817. The first coke blast furnace was fired in 1824 close to the Sambre, and the first coke blast furnace in the Charleroi area entered into service in 1827.

The steel industry is now in crisis. The Walloon coal field supplies only a small quantity of the coking coal necessary, and no iron ore exists in the area. Moreover, the Walloon industrial base is stretched out over more than 100 kilometers and does not form a coherent regional unit. It is more a juxtapositioning of relatively small-scale urban areas that have not succeeded in uniting, in sharply diversifying their activities, or in integrating into much broader production chains. The consequence has been rapid sociopolitical rigidity, preventing the development of wider industrial scope. Consequently, at the end of the 19th century, light industry began to move away from the Haine-Sambre-Meuse axis, and one heavy sector, nonferrous metals, decided to follow suit. Financiers attempted in the interwar period to remedy the shortcomings of this structure and to concentrate Belgian steelworks. However, it was not until the end of World War II that mergers began to take place on a large scale, with the steel concerns of Liège and Charleroi uniting under the impetus of state aid to form Cockerill-Sambre. Today the Belgian steel industry is situated along the banks of the Meuse in the Liège region and on the banks of the Sambre in the Charleroi region. Outside of these two areas, the steel industry is present only in the central region, with the Boël factory in La Louvière.

The nonferrous metals sector is also established in the Liège area. It nurtured the world zinc industry thanks to the inventive genius of J. J. Dony, who succeeded in extracting the metal from the ore, working a local deposit long since exhausted. Metalworking industries sprang up along the Walloon industrial axis. One of the national leaders in this field is the F. N., or National Arms Factory, situated near Liège. The Caterpillar factory in the Charleroi Gosselies industrial estate, next to the aeronautics industry (SABENA and SONACA), is a modern example worthy of emulation.

Transportation is a vital component of a metallurgical industry that buys its energy and raw materials from abroad and manufactures semi-finished goods. This factor stimulated the creation of a wide-ranging canal network and a very dense rail service.

The glass industry was the third main driving force behind the development of Walloon industry in the 19th century. Concentrated in the region around Charleroi, where glass has been manufactured since the 15th century, and in the Namur Basse-Sambre, which also specialized in glassworks, it initially made use of local coal and sand. The glass industry is still essentially concentrated in the Charleroi area and in the Basse-Sambre, but there are also factories in the Hainaut basin and in Seraing close to Liège, where the famous crystal factory Val-Saint-Lambert is still in business despite major difficulties.

Cement works have also made an important contribution to Walloon industry and are clustered chiefly in the region of Mons around the chalk fields and at Visé near Liège around limestone deposits. Chemistry is one of the Walloon region's chief assets, symbolized at the regional level by the name "Solvay." The Solvay firm was founded in 1863 to exploit the soda-manufacturing process invented by Ernest Solvay. The first factory was located in what is now Charleroi and was so successful that by World War I, Solvay had built up a vast international industrial empire with establishments in many countries. Another famous name in Wallonia is Carbochimique at Tertre near Mons, created between the two wars to supply Borinage coking coal. Food-processing plants and breweries are another common feature. Electricity is yet another strong industry. In 1886, a modest firm was born in Charleroi, which in 1904 became ACEC, or Ateliers de Construction Electrique de Charleroi (Charleroi Electrical Works Concern). It became one of Wallonia's most important industrial firms. Many traditional power stations exist along the Haine-Sambre-Meuse, and there is a nuclear power plant at Tihange near Huy.

The motorway network that has grown up over the past two decades is a new factor in regional development, as demonstrated by the growth of industrial estates close to the motorway that cuts across Wallonia from west to east, forming a link between Paris and Germany via Aachen. The existence of the highway network and its location between Paris and Brussels played a part in the choice of Mons as the site for the General Headquarters of SHAPE.

The Ardennes and surrounding areas. The Ardennes and the surrounding areas south of the Sambre-Meuse dividing line are a vast rural region. The landscape is dominated by forest and green open spaces. Forests consist essentially of conifers, with spruce the most frequent species. Deciduous forests also exist, with the native beech much in evidence. In

Haute-Ardennes, for example, on the Bastogne plateau, forest covers between a quarter and a third of the surface area, grasslands account for half, and crops for cattle feed (fodder, spelt, barley, oats, and rye) occupy the remainder. On hillsides, both in the north and the south, the forest takes over, covering two-thirds to three-quarters of available area. The Ardennes region has the lowest population density in Belgium. The area is dotted with traditional houses built in local sandstone, with agricultural outbuildings, grouped into villages clustered around small towns.

The Ardennes plateau is too sparsely populated to support an urban center. Consequently, this vast region is controlled by towns along the Sambre-Meuse, namely Liège, Namur, and Charleroi, and by two regional towns, Arlon on the southern edge and Verviers on the northern edge. Arlon, originally a Roman town, is the capital of Luxembourg Province and the center of the entire Belgian Lorraine. Formerly the base of the now-declining wool industry, Verviers is near Liège and linked to it by the Vesdre valley. Its sphere of influence extends over the eastern part of the Herve area and the northeastern Ardennes, namely the Hautes-Fagnes, and consequently over the entire German-speaking region. This dominance by a French-speaking town of the German-speaking region is explained by the lack of a major German-speaking urban center. The German-language region is split in two by the vast Hertogenwald forest and is locally focused around Eupen in the north and Sankt-Vith in the south, both small towns. Consequently, Aachen, a nearby city in West Germany, is exercising increasing influence over the region; there is even German immigration from the residential suburbs of Aachen.

Industrial activities in the Ardennes region are therefore centered around small towns, such as the paper industry near Virton, the plastics industry in Arlon, the Donnay tennis racket factory in Couvein, the mineral waters at Spa, or, outside an urban context, the Coo hydroelectricity station on the Amblève. It is thus not surprising that the main activity in the region is tourism, chiefly by Belgians, as seen in the concentration of holiday homes in the valleys of the Meuse near Dinant, the Ourthe, and the Semois. However, foreign tourists also come to the Ardennes, attracted by the memory of the Battle of Bastogne, one of the key points in World War II.

Lower plateaus of northern Wallonia. The lower alluvial plateaus, Hesbaye, southern Brabant, and northern Hainaut, have the richest farming and pasture land in Belgium. Crops include wheat, sugarbeets, and oats. The area is a model of high-yield intensive farming. The traditional Walloon farm, built around a closed-in courtyard, can still be seen. Rural life is focused around large villages in Hesbaye, whereas in the Hainaut it is much more scattered around a central core. In Brabant and particularly in Hainaut, the primary substratum is worked in a large number of quarries, producing porphyry in Quenast and Lessines and limestone in the form of cut stones in Soignies and as a raw material for the cement works south of Tournai. The Hesbaye area is dominated by Liège and Brabant and northeast Hainaut by Brussels. The region also falls under the influence of Tournai, an old Roman city and very ancient episcopal seat, in western Hainaut. The Brussels industrial area stretches along the Brussels-Charleroi Canal, and the capital's suburbs extend southward into the Waterloo and Wavre regions, explaining the economic and demographic dynamism of Walloon Brabant. Ottignies, in Walloon Brabant, is the site of a new university, Louvain-la-Neuve, and a big steel factory, Les Forges de Clabecq.

The Flemish Region

Antwerp and Kempen. Antwerp, situated on the Scheldt, began its ascendancy in the 15th century, with the onset of decline in Bruges. During this period, it became the most important trade center in Europe. It is a port on the edge of an estuary on the right bank of the river. Its Achilles heel is access to the sea, along the Western Scheldt. The channel is 85 kilometers long and dotted with narrow passageways. Constant dredging is required to keep it open. In addition, the entrance to the sea is in the Netherlands. Antwerp therefore set out to create another easily navigable waterway linking it to the Rhine. Success was a long time coming, but a broad junction canal running across the Netherlands was inaugurated in 1975.

Since Belgium gained its independence, the port's development has been dominated by its geographical position. Its evolution can be summed up as from transshipment traffic to industrialization and from the right to the left bank. For many years, Antwerp was chiefly a transshipment point, like other ports in northwest Europe. Antwerp therefore invested a great deal in dominating traffic from or to its hinterlands, particularly the industrial centers, practicing a doubled-edged policy of advantageous rates and simple transportation. Early on, the railway became a prime factor in relations between Antwerp and its hinterlands, particularly the German Rhine region. Rail links with the latter were completed in 1843, and an important network with port stations grew up in the 19th century. The same policy was applied to navigable waterways. The Albert Canal linked the port with the Liège area and is a modern illustration of this double-edged policy. Recent enlargement has made it possible to carry tonnages of up to 9,000 tons by using the pushing technique. The same policy is currently being applied in the development of a very dense motorway network, spilling out in all directions.

Just after World War II, Antwerp carved itself out a niche as a very dynamic center, attracting many firms including Bell Telephone, Gevaert (photographic goods), shipyards and a nonferrous metallurgy plant at Hoboken, refining industries, General Motors (the Ford factory specialized in tractor manufacturing after 1964), food-processing industries (margarine and chocolate), and the tobacco industry. However, the most spectacular feature of modern Antwerp is its recent industrial development. A systematic policy of industrialization was adopted in 1961, forming part of the 1956–65 plan for port modernization. The objective was to optimize the benefits to be drawn from modernization. In ten years the port area grew from 5000 hectares to over 10,000. The centerpiece of this operation was the construction of a dock-lined canal, 16.75 meters deep, 430 meters wide and 10 kilometers long, extending operations on the right bank up to the Dutch border, or 20 kilometers further north than the previous docks. The canal is linked to the Scheldt by the impressive Zandvliet lock, the biggest in the world at the time of its inauguration in 1967. The northern end links up with the Rhine Canal. Since the right bank of the Scheldt was saturated within Belgium, development has spread to the left bank, which is linked to the town by two motorway tunnels, and by new docks around Doel in Oost-Vlaanderen, where a nuclear power plant is situated. A number of factors have contributed to this development, including massive imports of crude oil, partly delivered by the Rotterdam pipeline, rapid development of the chemical and petrochemical industries, increased use of imported raw materials, and an influx of foreign investment, notably American, German, and French. Industries in the heart of the new port include refining and petrochemicals, which are relatively less labor intensive than other industries such as automobile assembly but cover a larger area. A number of major firms have set up business in the harbor area. In the oil-refining sector this includes Esso, Chevron, SIBP (Société Industrielle Belge des Pétroles, or Belgian Oil Industrial Company), and Albatros; in the petrochemicals sector Monsanto, BASF (Badische Anilin und Sodafabrik), Bayer, and British Petroleum; and finally in the chemicals sector, Solvay, Petrochim, Degussa, and Rhone-Poulenc.

Antwerp is therefore an international port, the provincial capital, the seat of a diocese, a university town, a judicial and financial center, and also a focal point for the diamond industry. It now has 500,000 inhabitants and is therefore the most highly populated borough in the country.

If the suburbs are included, there are 650,000 inhabitants, making Antwerp the second biggest city in Belgium. Moreover, Antwerp is the hub of the entire surrounding district, stretching beyond the Scheldt into Oost-Vlaanderen, with a population of 1 million. Its metropolitan functions extend its influence to four medium-sized towns, namely Mechelen and Turnhout within Antwerp Province, Sint-Niklaas in Oost-Vlaanderen, and Hasselt in Limburg, reaching a total of 2 million people.

Kempen (Campine), the northern and central areas of the Antwerp and Limburg provinces, was only two-thirds cultivated at the end of the 19th century. It has since become a grassland region supporting livestock. Conifer woods consisting mainly of pines cover between 15 percent and 30 percent of borough areas, making the region the most heavily wooded one in Flanders. The rural landscape consists of small villages, with lines of houses and open fields, and of more recent hamlets. Kempen underwent industrial development at the end of the 19th century, when mineral supplies in the Liège region ran out and zinc and lead factories migrated toward Antwerp, setting up along the canals in north Kempen. In the 20th century, the same path was taken in the copper, nickel, cobalt, tin, uranium, and antimony industries, when ore began to be imported from overseas, particularly from Zaïre. The nonferrous metallurgical industry settled in Lommel and Overpelt in the Limburg Province and in Balen and Olen in the Antwerp Province. The discovery at the beginning of the 20th century of a local coalfield deep underground was another factor in industrial development. The coal face was reached in 1901 but only began to be worked in 1917. This coalfield, which is rich in bituminous coal and partly worked, stretched to the north of the Scheldt, but it is no longer a viable enterprise. Consequently, the government has introduced a rationalization plan with staggered closure of pits.

Local resources also were behind the creation of a glassworks in Mol, using fine local sand. Mol has thus become the main Flemish center of the glass industry. The recent dynamism of Kempen must, however, first and foremost be attributed to the development of Antwerp. Kempen has become an important region for chemical industries manufacturing explosives, pharmaceuticals, photographic goods, and petrochemicals, concentrated mainly in the province of Antwerp, with an offshoot in the Geel-Mol area, which moreover houses the Nuclear Energy Study Center. The industrial success of Kempen is attributed to its very young demographic structure with a labor force reservoir, easy access to land at relatively low cost, and the fact that the area is served by several motorways and by the Albert Canal. The combination of these factors has attracted food-processing concerns, electrical firms (Philips, Bell, ATEA), and the car industry (Ford in Genk). The small town of Turnhout is the focal point for the eastern part of the Antwerp Province, whereas the influence of Hasselt, the provincial center, covers all of Limburg Province (population 700,000). It extends over the Hesbaye area, the location of the old Roman town of Tongeren, where the soil is much richer and tilling the soil prevails over pasture. Orchards are numerous in this area. Mechelen, the archepiscopal seat of Belgium, dominates an area inhabited by 250,000 people from west to east between Antwerp and Brussels. Its geographical location between two large cities explains the importance of market gardening and horticulture, which made a key contribution to its industrial growth. Mechelen, the surrounding region, and the southern suburbs of Antwerp, traditionally devoted to furniture manufacture, have attracted much investment, including foreign investment, in the metalworking and chemicals sectors.

Vlaanderen. The Vlaanderen region, which forms part of the provinces of Oost-Vlaanderen and West-Vlaanderen, is a traditional center of both intensive agriculture and craft industry with an industrial bias. Intensive, high-yield farming has been a feature of this region for a long time. As a matter of fact, in the Middle Ages improvement of the relatively poor soil and the practice of rearing livestock in sheds resulted in the disappearance of fallow land at the same time as the catch-crops technique was developed. The countryside became dotted with small traditional farms with open courtyards, separated by a wealth of hedges and screens of trees, clustered around central boroughs. This type of landscape is typical of inland Vlaanderen, where pastureland mingles with livestock breeding and food crops. Industrial crops, such as flax, sugarbeets, chicory, and tobacco, are important in the west from the Lys Valley to the Ijzer. Specialized crops, such as flowers in the Ghent region, are also found. The overall picture contrasts sharply with the woods and polders of the maritime plain, reclaimed from the sea and bisected by dunes and drainage canals. The maritime region was developed at a much later date and is characterized by much bigger, isolated farms, still with open courtyards but much more imposing. Again, farming is widely varied. Pasture land is a constant feature, whereas industrial crops are more usual in the western part.

The traditional industry in Vlaanderen was textiles. It still plays an important role despite the crisis that has shaken the two regional centers, Ghent and Kortrijk. However, the dominance of textiles has been challenged by up-and-coming industries. Ghent, the largest town in Vlaanderen, provides an example of this recent economic development. Ghent is a major textiles center, situated at the confluence of the Scheldt and the Lys, and is also a port because of the maritime canal connecting the Scheldt to Terneuzen in the Netherlands. Built at the beginning of the 19th century, the canal was initially able to carry boats of up to 10,000 tons. In 1959, a new lock was inaugurated, permitting a rise in capacity to 60,000 tons. An industrial estate has grown up on the banks of the canal, initially on the west bank and then on the east bank as it was enlarged. The estate houses chemical concerns, refineries, coking plants, cement works, electrical power stations, electrical equipment assemblers, paper mills, and automobile assembly plants. The Belgian steel concern Sidmar is an example of the movement of a heavy industry toward the coast, prompted by the fact that ore and 70 percent of the coal used are imported. Sidmar has fully integrated with the local economy, using electricity and fuel oil manufactured in the region and employing local workers. Ghent was a medieval capital and is now a provincial center, the seat of a diocese, and a judicial and university town. It is at the heart of a built-up area with 350,000 inhabitants and forms a focal point for the rail and motorway network. It is the hub of an area with 800,000 inhabitants covering all of Oost-Vlaanderen Province except for the eastern part. The region of Sint-Niklaas, a town of almost 70,000 inhabitants, comes under the metropolitan influence of Antwerp. Its industrial expansion has been tied to growth in the port of Antwerp, particularly since the extension of the latter to the left bank of the Scheldt. The main industrial activities in the Sint-Niklaas region are textiles, food processing, and metalworking. The Aalst region, home to 300,000 people and falling under the metropolitan influence of Brussels, is also dominated by the textile and food-processing industries.

The province of West-Vlaanderen, bordering on the sea, is dominated by the towns of Bruges, Kortrijk, and Ostend. The Belgian coast is more or less a continuous string of bathing beaches, the most famous of which is Knokke-Zoute. It is the country's main tourist region, with holiday homes representing between one-third and one-half of all houses. Ostend, a famous beach and spa at the center of the Belgian coastline, dominates the entire northwest of the province, which has a total of 200,000 inhabitants. A fishing port, Ostend is first and foremost a travel center, because of sea links with Dover and Folkestone in the United Kingdom. The railway line from Brussels connecting with England through Ghent and Bruges leads to Ostend, as does the highway from Brussels to the coast.

Bruges, for its part, was a crossroads of Europe in the Middle Ages and is now famous with tourists throughout the world as the "Venice of the North." Industrially speaking, Bruges was left behind, clinging to its canals due to the silting of the Zwin and the disappearance of its port. Bruges is now a partner in the industrial renewal of Vlaanderen, as seen in the development of Zeebrugge, the sea outlet of the Bruges maritime canal. Zeebrugge was initially a fishing town but has now become an industrial port. Recent construction opened its harbor to ships of 125,000 tons and equipped it with a spectacular terminal for offloading imported natural gas. The sphere of influence of Bruges extends throughout the northeast of the province (over 250,000 people). Industrial activity centers around coking plants, glassworks, and metalworking. Kortrijk dominates the southern part of West-Vlaanderen Province, home to 450,000 people. Situated on the Lys, Kortrijk, which is a focal point of the motorway network, is an important textile center and also houses wood and metalworking industries. Ieper (Ypres) is another interesting small town, with many poignant reminders of the great battles of World War I.

Flemish Brabant. The entire Flemish Brabant region comes under the metropolitan influence of Brussels. However, the eastern part is dominated by Leuven, whereas the rest is directly influenced by Brussels. Market gardens are the main agricultural activity in this region, the most unique product being the "witloof," or Belgian endive, which is obtained from the roots of chicory. The market gardens are ideally situated, just to the northeast of Brussels. Leuven, a university town, extends its influence over 350,000 people. The food and agro-food industries provide the main source of activity in this area, such as flour milling and the Artois brewery. Philips, the electronics manufacturer, is the other main employer. The town of Tienen in the southeast of this region is the main center of the Belgian sugar industry. Western Flemish Brabant includes a large slice of the Brussels suburbs and the industrial areas of Vilvoorde in the north and of Halle in the south, which form part of the main industrial axis of the Senne valley. The chemical industry, automobile assembly, metalwork, manufacture of electrical materials, and electrical power plants are other major activities.

Brussels. Nothing special about the site of Brussels explains why it became a major city. It is situated in the Senne valley, on a rather modest river, and spreads out onto the western slope. Its position at the contact point between the plain and the lower plateaus, on the edges of the German and Latin worlds, is much more important. By the 15th century, Brussels had become the capital of the Duchy of Brabant; later it became the capital of the southern Netherlands. The political factor determined the importance of the town. The decision in 1830 to make Brussels the capital of Belgium only recognized a fait accompli four centuries old.

The central position of Brussels between plain and plateau and between the two linguistic groups was at the root of its success. Demographic evolution reflects its development. In 1831 at the time of independence, there were only 103,000 inhabitants within the current boundaries of Brussels. The 1981 census revealed that the borough of Brussels had 140,000 inhabitants and the city of Brussels 997,000. The city is continuing to expand beyond the boundaries of the city, to the point where Greater Brussels now counts 1.25 million inhabitants, or 1.4 million if the suburbs are included. Brussels is moreover a center of attraction for all of Brabant Province, the southeastern part of Oost-Vlaanderen Province, the northern and western parts of Hainaut Province, all of Namur Province, and the western part of Luxembourg Province, almost 4 million people in all. Brussels is Belgium's main city and yet paradoxically the only one to have escaped the process of borough amalgamation. This has hindered the development of the urban whole by preventing rational planning and use of space. Brussels has yet to be equipped with the necessary administrative services.

Brussels and its suburbs are the main center of industrial activity in the country. It should be emphasized, however, that the existence of a large city has attracted industry, rather than the opposite. Brussels is the home of such specifically urban industries as dressmaking, fashion, gold- and silversmithing, leatherworking, printing, building, brewing, chocolate making, and paper making. The chemical industry is represented in force as are the metalworking industries, in the form of automobile assembly and the manufacture of scientific instruments, electrical materials, and machine tools. Brussels is the headquarters of many banks and insurance companies, large industrial and commercial companies, and a capital market in the form of the Brussels stock exchange, the most active in Belgium. The key commercial role played by Brussels is clearly seen in the number of organized markets and trade fairs. Finally, Brussels is the capital of the country, the official residence of the king, the seat of government and administration, a judicial, university, and intellectual center, and the capital of Brabant Province. As such, it plays a leading role in the political and administrative life of Belgium. It is also the capital of Europe, home to the headquarters of the European Community and NATO, further proof of its current dynamism.

At 130 kilometers from the sea, Brussels is the key focal point for all transport services. It is a port without a hinterland thanks to the Willebroek maritime canal (capacity 6,000 tons), and it is linked to Walloon industry by the Charleroi canal (capacity 1,350 tons). However, activity in Brussels revolves chiefly around the rail, roadway, and airplane networks. Brussels is the convergence point for the road and rail network and enjoys the services of an international airport in the suburb of Zaventem. Considerable construction has resulted in the connection of the two old North and South railway stations to a central station. The motorway network is now complete and links Brussels to all the country's important towns, to Germany through Liège, to Rotterdam through Antwerp, to the coast and to Great Britain via Ghent and Brugge, to Luxembourg via Namur and Arlon, and finally to Paris via Mons. Geographically speaking, Brussels is therefore the central core of the country and its dynamic unifying force provides the firmest guarantee for the prosperity of modern Belgium.

Brussels

Jacques Groothaert

OVER THE YEARS the name "Brussels" has become more famous abroad than Belgium. As the de facto capital of the European Community and the headquarters of NATO, it has become the place where decision makers and observers must come together in order to participate in the integration of the European Community.

In recent years, the visible or perceived image of Brussels has altered substantially owing to its internationalization. Modern industries as well as the various institutions available to foreign residents of Brussels are bearing fruit—a trend that is expected to become stronger in the years to come. Of the foreign subsidiaries in Brussels, there are more than 800 from the United States, over 400 from Germany and Holland, and over 150 from Great Britain, as well as others from France and Japan. Brussels has been confirmed in its dual role as the capital of the European Community and as a city of industry, trade, and services.

There are 12,846 international associations in the world, a figure that is symptomatic of 20th-century culture. Of these, 1,286 have set up headquarters in Belgium, 80 percent of them in Brussels. A further breakdown shows that 841 international organizations have their offices in Brussels, and another 117 have set up secondary or regional headquarters in the city. The main starting point for this process was the decision in 1958 to locate the three European Communities (ECSC, EEC, and Euratom) in the Belgian capital; these were merged on April 8, 1965, into a single entity. In this way Brussels consolidated its international dimension, which was further reinforced in 1967 when NATO headquarters was transferred from Paris to Brussels.

Altogether, 56 intergovernmental organizations have their principal headquarters in Belgium, and another 10 have set up secondary headquarters. The majority of them are located in Brussels. Of these, the

EC institutions and NATO are obviously the most important, both as regards the number of people they employ and their infrastructure.

Four European Community institutions are located in Brussels: (1) the Commission (17 members), which oversees correct implementation of the treaties and proposes and applies the various Community policies; (2) the Council of Ministers, which has its general secretariat in Brussels and makes decisions on the basis of proposals drafted by the Commission (the Council is assisted by the Committee of Permanent Representatives, COREPER); (3) the secretariat of the European Parliament, which meets in Strasbourg and in Luxembourg; and (4) the Economic and Social Committee, with a membership of 156, which is consulted on economic and social matters and represents various trade unions, employers, and consumers associations.

Brussels is the venue also of NATO's most vital arm, the North Atlantic Council. The Supreme Command of allied forces in Europe, SHAPE, is only 50 kilometers from Brussels, at Casteau, near Mons. Both the EEC and NATO together employ in the Brussels area well over 10,000 people, of sixteen nationalities.

International nongovernmental organizations include a substantial number of socio-professional bodies. They have grown up in the shadow of the European Communities, patterning themselves on purely national bodies formed to negotiate with national authorities. It is hardly surprising therefore that 252 of these should have elected to settle in Brussels, including the most important and also the most active professional organizations.

Employers, trade unions, and Commission and Council experts hold frequent meetings. In Brussels there is harmonious coexistence between the European Trade Union Confederation (ETUC), which includes 30 organizations from fifteen different countries, and the Union of European Community Industries (UNICE).

It was decided at a very early stage, in 1949, to set up a Federation of International Associations established in Belgium (FAIB). This was to encourage and facilitate the establishment in Belgium of the headquarters of international organizations, particularly nongovernmental bodies. Governmental associations enjoy better administrative and logistic support. The FAIB operates alongside the Union of International Associations (which also has its headquarters in Brussels), an institute engaged in research, information, services, and publications aimed at international nongovernmental organizations.

A house of the international associations, a long-standing dream of Belgian internationalists, opened recently. At the same time an International Club was set up. In this way, in Brussels, international organizations have at their disposal an unusually wide range of administrative, logistic, legal, and human resources.

Major commercial and cultural exhibitions, fairs, shows, and congresses play an important part in the international life of a city such as Brussels. They provide a gateway to world markets, an overview of new technologies, and an opportunity to exchange information and experience.

In ten years, the number of international meetings recorded officially by the Union of International Associations has gone up by 26 percent, the number of those held in Brussels by 47 percent. As a result, the Belgian capital has won third place in the list of congress sites. In practice, this means that in 1985 no fewer than 255 international congresses were held in the city, bringing together 292,250 people.

As a financial center, classified according to foreign bank holdings, Brussels ranks ninth. The growing importance of international activities in Brussels was a decisive factor in the decision of many big foreign banks to set up offices in the Belgian capital. Of the 83 Belgian and foreign banks operating in Belgium, 64 are located in Brussels. Of these 83 banks, 59 are branches or subsidiaries of foreign banks (from sixteen different countries). Brussels is obviously well placed to become an important center of financial and communication services for the European Community.

Population

Robert André

AMONG THE MANY UPHEAVALS confronting the modern world, those affecting the number, movement, and structure of population have been the most remarkable. The Industrial Revolution was accompanied by vast demographic growth, resulting in heavy population concentrations in Western Europe, including Belgium. Growth was triggered in the 19th century, by a drop in mortality and a sustained birthrate. In a second phase, a drop in both mortality and the birthrate resulted in an aging population. In the 20th century, the birthrate fell faster than mortality, leading to increasing numbers of old people and declining numbers of young people. The demography of Belgium thus evolved from both a high birth and a high death rate at the end of the 18th century to the current situation of low birth and death rates, with almost zero growth and an aging population. This complex evolution can be termed a "demographical transition."

Birthrate in the 20th Century

The Belgian birthrate (number of babies per couple) began to slide at the beginning of the 20th century before tumbling during World War I. After a postwar baby boom, the birthrate again began to fall, reaching another low during World War II (see Table 1) The number of children per woman fell from 2.11 in 1939, a rate that only just sustains population renewal, to 1.67 in 1941. After the traditional postwar baby boom, the birthrate remained around 17 percent until 1964, rising from 2.48 children per woman in 1947 to 2.71 in 1964, a rate that results in a slight population growth. After 1965, the rate fell, to below 12 percent in 1983. The reproduction rate followed a similar path, with the number of children per woman falling to 2, a potential zero growth rate. Similar trends were seen after 1965 in the majority of developed countries; most of them are now below the population renewal level. For all of Western and Northern Europe, the number of children per woman fell from 2.85 in 1964 to 1.53 in 1984.

In Belgium, there were 144,979 births in 1947, 119,273 in 1975, and 117,102 in 1986. Between 1950 and 1964, both the birthrate and the reproduction rate (number of female babies per 1,000 women) rose despite a relatively unfavorable age structure, whereas between 1964 and 1975 the birthrate and the reproduction rate tumbled despite the growing number of women of childbearing age. After 1975, the drop in the number of children evened off, resulting in a rise in the number of births since the age structure remained favorable. The increase in the number of women between 20 and 29 was an important factor in the growth observed between 1975 and 1981. The age structure has remained favorable since 1981 and will continue to be so until 1990. Nevertheless, the number of births has tapered off to below the 1975 minimum, reflecting another considerable drop in the reproduction rate.

The sharp drop in the reproduction rate reflects both a desire among couples for fewer children and the greater effectiveness of modern contraceptive methods. The relatively high reproduction rate at the beginning of the 1960's was due to a rather large proportion of unwanted or untimely pregnancies. A couple can now exercise greater control over the number and timing of children. The new methods not only are more efficient but do not directly interfere with the sexual act. Once the principle of contraception is accepted, as it has been by the majority of Belgian couples, the decision to stop contraception is a deliberate choice for conception. Although the number of people who want no children has not increased, many people are undecided about or delaying pregnancy and may never have a second or third child.

The drop in the reproduction rate has coincided with the development of a new form of family life, characterized by individualism. This has had the effect of producing fewer, as well as more unstable, marriages. With individualism women must find paid employment for their personal development and as a guarantee of an income in case of divorce. The trend toward uniform behavior and ambitions seems to indicate that this new concept of family life is durable. It corresponds to a second contraceptive revolution, in which abortion is acceptable should contraception fail.

The generations born since World War II have benefited from greater access to education and life in a wealthy society, yet they now confront a serious crisis that raises some disturbing questions about their future. Since young people now have simple and efficient birth control methods at their disposal, today's marriages will not be overly fertile.

TABLE I.1
Demographic Evolution of Belgium

	1831	1846	1880	1900	1930	1947	1981	1986
Population								
Total	3,785,814	4,337,196	5,520,009	6,693,548	8,092,004	8,512,195	9,848,647	9,858,895
Growth index	100.0	114.6	145.8	176.8	213.7	224.8	260.1	260.4
Natural movement (average annual rate)	1831–35	1846–50	1876–80	1896–1900	1926–30	1946–50	1981–83	1985–86
Birthrate	33.0	28.5	31.9	28.9	18.5	17.0	12.2	11.7
Mortality[a]	26.1	25.2	21.7	18.1	13.6	12.5	11.5	11.3
Natural growth	6.9	3.3	10.2	10.8	4.9	4.5	0.7	0.4
Births		1845–48	1879–82	1899–1902	1939	1947	1978–81	1984
Number of children per woman		4.04	4.67	3.94	2.11	2.48	1.70	1.53
Life expectancy at birth		1847–56	1881–90	1891–1900	1928–32	1946–49	1979–82	
Men		37.5	43.6	45.0	55.7	61.4	70.2	
Women		39.0	46.6	48.1	59.4	66.8	77.0	
Distribution by age groups (all ages = 100%)		1846	1880	1900	1930	1947	1981	
60 plus		8.9%	9.8%	9.5%	11.8%	15.6%	18.5%	
20 to 50		49.8	47.5	49.2	57.2	56.2	53.4	
0 to 19		41.3	42.7	41.3	31.0	28.2	28.1	
Aging index[b]		21.6	22.9	22.9	38.1	55.4	66.0	

[a] Taking stillbirths into account from 1928 on.

[b] $\dfrac{\% \ 60+}{\% \ 0\text{–}19} \times 100$

The Falling Mortality Rate

Since the beginning of the 20th century, mortality has continued to fall, and Belgium has experienced only one death rate peak—at the end of World War I due to the Spanish influenza epidemic. Life expectancy at birth rose sharply to reach almost 56 years of age for men and 60 for women in the 1930's. Infant mortality fell considerably, from 154.1 per 1,000 live births in 1901–5 to 83.1 in 1936–39.

After World War II, the gross death rate remained stable at around 12 percent. Despite progress, it remained at a high level, due to aging at the peak, until the mid-1970's.

Demographic evolution since World War II has been marked, as was to be expected, by considerable contraction of the death rate attributable to infectious diseases following the discovery of antibiotics, the general use of vaccines, and improvement in the standard of living. Cardiovascular disease and cancers have gradually increased as causes of death. Since the war, deaths due to circulatory diseases have fallen, reflecting progress in cardiology and improved specialized hospital infrastructure, along with changes in diet and lifestyle. However, the unexpected increase in the male death rate in recent years is all the more striking.

Collapse of Population Growth in the 20th Century

In the 20th century, population growth in Belgium has dropped from over 10 percent to near zero at present. The decline was very noticeable at the beginning of the century and in the interwar period; it was interrupted between 1945 and 1964 before plunging to near zero. The demographic transition should therefore be completed, with population at a stationary level. Closer analysis, however, shows that the net reproduction rate, with allowances for the effects of mortality, decreased from 1,054 in 1970–71 to 730 in 1984. The population has not been renewing itself since 1972, and this trend is increasing. The current situation therefore merely gives the impression of being stationary. In actual fact, Belgium has reached a point of potential decline and is on the brink of a population decrease.

Immigration in the 20th Century

One of the first consequences of shrinking population growth was to give immigrants a more important role in the demographic dynamics of Belgium. Since the end of the 19th century, the foreign population has grown sharply. The 1961 census showed that the number of foreigners living in Belgium had doubled since 1900; by 1970 it had tripled and by 1981 it had quadrupled (see Table 2). In 1900, there were 3 foreigners per 100 inhabitants, compared with 4 in 1930 and 1947, 5 in 1961, 7 in 1970, and 9 today. In the decade between the census of 1920 and that of 1930, the foreign population took a demographic leap, with an annual growth rate of 78.7 percent and a rise of 169,553 people. In the nine years between the census of 1961 and that of 1970, the number of foreigners increased even more, with an influx of 242,796 and an annual average growth rate of 48.8 percent. Between 1970 and 1981, this trend continued, despite the economic crisis. In a period lasting ten years and two months, the foreign population increased by 182,295 people, at an annual average rate of 23.5 percent. The rise has been slowing since the last census, and a slight drop was seen in 1983. Net immigration has been transformed into net emigration of the foreign population, which dropped from 891,244 on January 1, 1983, to 890,873 on January 1, 1984.

The growth in the foreign population since World War II occurred in a number of waves of immigration and emigration. National origin varied over time, becoming increasingly distant, as did the regional destinations of immigrants within Belgium. The growth in 1946–61 in the number of immigrants did not necessarily result in a positive immigration balance each year; three net immigration phases and three net emigration phases can be noted. The variations were quite sharp, since in many cases an influx of immigrants reflected a local need for foreign labor, a need that ended as soon as economic crisis loomed. The first phase began in 1946 and ended in 1948 and was the result of a recruitment campaign for miners. A protocol signed with Italy allowed the recruitment of 76,000 Italians, almost 63,000 of whom were sent to Wallonia. In addition, two-thirds of a group of some 21,000 Eastern Europeans were also sent to Wallonia. After a second phase during which the coal mines hired more than 41,000 workers, a third phase began with the recruitment of 31,000 foreigners in 1955–57. During this period recruitment was extended to Spain and Greece, after Italians were discouraged by a spate of mining accidents.

In 1947, for the first time, nationals of neighboring countries made up fewer than half the foreigners in Belgium. This decline, which could already be detected at the beginning of the century, accelerated considerably between 1947 and 1961, cutting the proportion of neighboring nationals to one-third of total foreigners (Table 2). The number of Poles in Belgium, who had arrived during the interwar immigration wave from

TABLE 1.2
The Foreign Population of Belgium by Nationality in the Last Four Censuses

Nationality	Dec. 31, 1947 Absolute number	% total of foreigners	Dec. 31, 1961 Absolute number	% total of foreigners	Dec. 31, 1970 Absolute number	% total of foreigners	March 1, 1981 Absolute number	% total of foreigners
Italy	84,134	22.9%	200,086	44.1%	249,490	35.8%	279,700	31.8%
France	66,416	18.1	61,438	13.5	86,658	12.4	103,512	11.8
Netherlands	63,700	17.3	50,175	11.1	61,261	8.8	66,233	7.5
Poland	58,542	15.9	32,009	7.1	18,370	2.6	7,642	0.9
Germany	14,067	3.8	14,951	3.3	22,956	3.3	26,756	3.1
Great Britain	10,328	2.8	9,979	2.2	15,340	2.2	23,080	2.6
Luxembourg	9,446	2.6	6,850	1.5	7,018	1.0	6,013	0.7
Spain	3,245	0.9	15,787	3.5	67,534	9.7	58,255	6.6
Greece	1,270	0.4	9,797	2.2	22,354	3.2	21,230	2.4
Morocco	—	—	461	0.1	39,294	5.6	105,133	12.0
Turkey	590	0.2	320	0.1	20,312	2.9	63,587	7.2
United States	1,993	0.5	3,458	0.8	12,676	1.8	11,536	1.3
Algeria	—	—	202	0.0	6,621	1.0	10,796	1.2
Portugal	466	0.1	933	0.2	7,177	1.0	10,482	1.2
Other countries	53,422[a]	14.5	47,040	10.3	59,221	8.5	84,622	9.7
Total	367,619	100.0%	453,486	100.0%	696,282	100.0%	878,577	100.0%
Index 1900: 206,061 = 100.0	178.4		220.1		337.9		426.4	

[a] Including Algerians and Moroccans.

Central Europe, fell by 45 percent. Italians, who in 1947 already constituted the biggest group of foreigners in Belgium, made even more spectacular progress between 1947 and 1961, when numbers rose by 115,952. This incredible leap was higher than the overall growth in the remainder of other groups of foreigners (85,867). In 1947, more than half of foreigners lived in Wallonia. By 1961, this figure had risen to almost two-thirds, or 300,000.

The period between the censuses of 1961 and 1970 began with an immigration phase that ended in 1966. Between 1961 and 1966, 125,000 immigration work permits were issued. The coal mines were again seeking workers, as were the metallurgy and construction industries. The addition of the latter two led to concentrations of immigrants in different regions, namely Ghent, Antwerp, and particularly Brussels. During the 1966–70 recession, the net immigration balance fell from +113,864 in 1966 to +20,833 in 1968–70. The 1970 census revealed that the proportion of foreigners originating in neighboring countries had fallen yet again, as had the number of Poles. The overall percentage represented by the four southern European countries remained constant; within this group, the number of Italians fell, but the numbers of Spaniards, Greeks, and Portuguese rose. The most striking feature during this period was the arrival of Moslems, mainly Moroccans and Turks. On December 31, 1970, more than half of the foreign population resided in Wallonia, a little under a quarter in Flanders, and another quarter in Brussels, which saw a 2.5 percent increase in its foreign population between 1961 and 1970.

Between the censuses of 1970 and 1981, there was a period of immigration between 1971 and 1975. After 1976, economic crisis caused a contraction in the immigration balance, resulting even in negative rates in 1978 and 1980. During this intercensus period, existing trends continued. The relative proportion represented by nationals of neighboring countries fell, despite a rise in overall numbers. The number of French citizens in Belgium rose above the 100,000 mark; the number of Moroccans tripled to 105,000, ahead of the French and in second place behind the Italians. The number of Italians grew to 280,000, or one-third of foreigners; the number of Turks grew threefold, whereas the number of Poles dropped by more than 50 percent. New trends include a drop in the number of Spaniards (from third place to sixth place), as well as a fall in the number of Greeks. The March 1, 1981, census showed that just under half of all foreigners were living in Wallonia and a little more than a quarter in each of the two other regions. Foreigners represent 4 percent of the population of Flanders, about 12 percent that of Wallonia and almost 25 percent that of Brussels.

Aging Phenomena in the 20th Century

Since the end of the 19th century, the age structure in Belgium has followed a similar path to that of other European countries. The population is aging at both ends (see Table 3). The number of old people has almost doubled in the space of a century (9.8 percent of people were age 60 or more on December 31, 1880, compared with 18.5 percent on March 1, 1981), whereas the proportion of young people has tumbled by one-third (42.7 percent under 20 in 1880 versus 28.1 percent in 1981). The double-ended aging of the population and the slowdown in population growth are the two features characterizing the demographic revolution that accompanied the Industrial Revolution.

It may appear that the aging at the peak (older people living longer) results from longer life expectancy and a greater proportion of new-borns reaching old age. But the existence of a greater proportion of old people in a generation does not necessarily imply a greater proportion of old people in the population, since generational sizes vary. Moreover, life expectancy at birth ignores variations by age, which are not shown in the average. The preservation of the life of a baby under one year in fact corresponds to the gain of a birth and demonstrates the medical progress made in the 20th century; all else being equal, this should result in a younger society. In contrast, the drop in the reproduction rate causes a

TABLE I.3
Age Distribution in the Main Linguistic Regions
According to the Last Three Censuses

Distribution by age groups	Brussels–Capital			Wallonia[a]			Flanders			Belgium		
	1961	1970	1981	1961	1970	1981	1961	1970	1981	1961	1970	1981
All ages = 100.0												
60 plus	21.9	22.1	22.3	19.7	20.4	19.1	16.1	17.5	17.5	17.9	19.0	18.6
20 to 59	54.5	52.4	53.6	51.3	49.4	52.7	51.3	49.8	53.7	51.6	49.9	53.4
0 to 19	23.6	25.5	24.1	29.0	30.2	28.2	32.6	32.7	28.8	30.5	31.1	28.0
Index of aging[b]	92.9	87.0	92.5	67.8	67.5	67.9	49.2	53.5	60.9	59.0	61.0	66.0

[a] Including the German-speaking region.

[b] $\dfrac{\%\ 60+}{\%\ 0\text{--}19} \times 100$

drop in the proportion of young people and an increase in that of adults and old people. The contraction in the birthrate therefore appears to be the dominant factor in the double-edged aging of the population in Belgium. Medical progress in the field of heart disease and cancer treatment will result in considerable reductions in mortality, among older people.

Regional Demographic Split in the 20th Century

According to the administrative subdivisions set up in 1963, the proportion of Belgians who are Walloons has been falling considerably, dropping from 34.7 percent on December 31, 1947, to 31.8 percent on January 1, 1986. Since a similar trend occurred within Brussels, which represented 12.2 percent of the population in 1947 and only 9.9 percent in 1986, the relative importance of Flanders is continually growing. It increased from 53.5 percent in 1947 to 57.6 percent in 1986. The German-language region grew slightly, from 0.6 percent in 1947 to 0.7 percent in 1986. Between 1947 and 1986, the population of Flanders rose to 5,676,184 inhabitants, and that of the German-speaking region grew to 66,445. Brussels (population of 976,536 in 1986) lost almost 100,000 inhabitants between 1970 and 1986. Wallonia also experienced a drop between 1981 and 1986, when it counted 3,139,720 inhabitants.

The reason for this is the faster drop in the birthrate in Wallonia than in Flanders, which has accentuated the trend toward twofold aging of the population. Brussels, which has a French-speaking majority, has exhibited the same trends as Wallonia. A difference still existed between the reproduction rate in Flanders and that in the two other regions in 1961–62. The average number of children per woman was 2.9 in Flanders, 2.6 in Wallonia, and 2.2 in Brussels. However, this difference gradually evened out to 1.6 in the three regions by 1982. The birthrate has evolved in a similar manner. Differences were very sharp in 1964, but had dropped to 12.1 percent in Flanders, 11.7 percent in Wallonia, and 11.6 percent in Brussels by 1983. The regional demographic split therefore no longer exists as far as the birthrate is concerned.

However, although less pronounced comparatively, the natural rate of increase in Flanders is still higher than in the other two regions. In 1964, it stood at 8.2 percent, compared with 2.3 percent in Wallonia and 1.1 percent in Brussels. In 1983, the contrast was still present, with Flanders showing a rate of 1.4 percent compared with negative rates of −1.2 percent in Wallonia and −1.6 percent in Brussels. Since trends in regional birthrates have been similar, the difference lies in a lower death rate in Flanders. The continuation of higher rates in Wallonia and Brussels is due to the more marked aging of these two regions. In 1979–82, male life expectancy at birth was 68.6 years in Wallonia, 70.2 in Brussels, and 71.1 in Flanders, and female life expectancy was 76.2 in Wallonia, 77.3 in Brussels, and 77.4 in Flanders.

Another very clear difference is the proportion of foreigners in each of the linguistic regions. The 1981 census showed that foreigners numbered only 4.1 percent of the population in Flanders (Dutch nationals represented almost one-quarter of this). Foreign nationals therefore influence the demography of Flanders only to a very slight extent. In Wallonia, foreigners make up 12.7 percent of the population. Italians account for more than half of this group, with the French the only other large group. Wallonia is therefore the region where the majority of immigrants from the first waves of immigration are concentrated, and they have had considerable impact on regional demography. On the other hand, Brussels has been the focal point for more recent immigrants, among whom the Moroccans are numerically superior, outstripping the Italians, Spaniards, and French. At the time of the 1981 census, out of 100 people in Brussels under 20 years, 36 were foreigners, compared with 18 per 100 in Flanders and 6 out of 100 in Flanders. The same census discovered that out of 100 adults living in Brussels aged between 20 and 39, 32 were foreigners, compared with 13 in Wallonia and 5 in Flanders. Foreigners have thus clearly had quite considerable impact on the demography of Brussels.

Demographic Policy and Outlook

This analysis leads inevitably to the conclusion that four points must be considered in defining demographic policy. First, the influx of immigrants has led in the Brussels region to an extreme concentration of foreigners and to the appearance of national groups of Moslem origin. Second, the numerical inferiority of Walloons is tied to the greater number of foreigners in Wallonia and the fact that the majority in Brussels is French-speaking. Third, the generations are not being renewed throughout the country, which is already apparent in Brussels and Wallonia. Finally, there is the twofold aging of the population, seen throughout Belgium but again more acute in Brussels and Wallonia. As a consequence, it is not surprising that those Belgians who stress the need for a demographic policy have been, and remain, Walloon.

The problem of low birthrate in the Walloon region and its consequences were already a cause for concern in certain circles before World War II. The world-renowned demographer Alfred Sauvy wrote in May

1953: "A country without youth is doomed to become a country of old people chewing over old ideas in old houses." In 1962, the Walloon Economic Council called on the services of Sauvy. The Sauvy Report was original because it considered the demographic problem from the point of view of ethnic culture, on the grounds that "when there is a duality, each of the two parties must be in a position to properly conduct its own life. . . . There can be no doubt that a biologically threatened ethnic culture must make every effort to correct the situation." The objective was therefore to stop the aging of the population, both at the peak and at the base. Sauvy recommended a policy to encourage people to have children by increasing the grants-in-aid for second and third children and creating indirect aid measures. He demonstrated, however, that such a policy, even in a regional framework, would have insufficient results in the medium term. The second point in his report was therefore to recommend sizable immigration.

The Delpérée Report, also published in 1962, was the government's answer to the Sauvy Report. It proposed two policies, one concerning the population in general and the other the family. The first was designed to influence the number and structure of the population, the second to guarantee the standard of living of families. There are vast differences between the two reports; the Delpérée Report dealt with the entire country and was inspired by social and family concerns, whereas the Sauvy Report was intended much more clearly to boost births and was of ethnic inspiration. The Delpérée Report, on the other hand, recognized that the labor shortage in Wallonia would inevitably discourage investment; it therefore proposed that measures be taken to facilitate recruitment of foreign workers and that the scale of immigration be determined by the number of jobs available. It therefore chose to adopt a policy of economic recovery, which was concentrated in Wallonia because industry in this region was experiencing shortfalls in unskilled labor. This differed from Sauvy's view that an immigration policy was an indispensable prop for struggling Walloon demography. The government did not adopt Sauvy's suggestion of a policy to encourage people to have children.

The demographic situation has since gone downhill not only in Wallonia and Brussels but also in Flanders. Recent forecasts issued by the National Statistical Institute predict a drop in mortality, a rise in the reproduction rate, and a continuation of a negative foreign migration balance. These forecasts show a general trend toward a contraction of the total population between 1980 and 2010, observable in Brussels and Wallonia by the end of this century and in Flanders in the early 21st century (see Table 4). The number of Belgian nationals will drop throughout the

TABLE 1.4

Demographic Forecasts by Linguistic Regions According to the National Institute of Statistics

Year	Brussels-Capital			Wallonia[a]			Flanders			Belgium		
	Belgians	Foreigners	Total	Belgians	Foreigners	Total	Belgians	Foreigners	Total	Belgians	Foreigners	Total
1980	762.235	237,134	999,369	2,815,216	407,810	3,223,026	5,397,441	231,964	5,629,405	8,974,892	876,908	9,851,800
1990	639,027	271,066	910,093	2,736,466	417,476	3,153,942	5,421,468	247,994	5,669,462	8,796,961	936,536	9,733,497
2000	565,295	288,670	853,965	2,670,524	422,753	3,093,277	5,409,117	258,863	5,667,980	8,644,936	970,286	9,615,222
2010	509,127	291,708	800,835	2,576,428	412,397	2,988,825	5,320,322	256,764	5,577,086	8,405,877	960,869	9,366,746

[a] Including the German-speaking region.

country after 1990, and the foreign population will continue to increase everywhere until the end of the century before dropping off in Wallonia and Flanders. The institute predicts this apparent paradox will result from the natural positive growth of the foreign population, counterbalanced by the negative net migration. Between 1980 and 2000, the total population of Belgium will, according to the institute, decrease by 2.4 percent, that of Wallonia will decrease by 4.0 percent, and that of Brussels by 14.5 percent, whereas the population of Flanders will increase by 0.7 percent.

The aging of the population is undoubtedly a formidable threat. Clearly, the financial cost of supporting retired people will continue to grow, and the pressure on health care services will become dangerous. In a period of economic recovery, the delicate problem of the retirement age will have to be tackled, for without an influx of immigrants the policy of lowering the retirement age will have to be reconsidered, while keeping in mind the need for social well-being. Paradoxically, this objective could perhaps be better attained by extending the working life, subject to a number of conditions. An incremental retirement system should be considered, to give everyone the opportunity to make the transition from working to nonworking life without a major break. It will be impossible to shut one-quarter and perhaps one-third of the population out of working life. What if, however, Alfred Sauvy was right? He declared that "the ethnic nature of a population is not immune to a change in its age composition . . . for the aging of a population is not beneficial for it. Naturally, an older person has more experience, but the key question is that of vitality." The connection between aging and senescence has not been proven; if it exists, it could undoubtedly be attenuated by medical progress. Nevertheless, it does constitute an additional risk.

These reflections on the evolution of the reproduction rate and structures show that immigration appears to be inevitable to counterbalance the population drop and to reverse the aging of the population. However, this will be possible in the 21st century only if the reproduction rate increases. The current economic crisis has in fact transformed immigration into emigration, and the governments of industrial Europe, including that of Belgium, are encouraging immigrants to return home and are erecting barriers to a new influx of foreigners. With an aging and diminishing population, fresh immigration appears inevitable but in light of the current situation and of Belgium's failure to adopt a policy on immigration, such a solution would appear utopian. The fundamental contradiction between demography and economics is a dilemma preventing governments from doing anything more than integrate the already established foreign population.

Religion, Secularism, and Politics

Rudolf Rezsohazy
(with Jacques de Groote and Daniel Pyle)

Religion in Belgium to 1830

THE STATUS AND CONDITION OF religion and ideology in present-day Belgium cannot be understood without reference to history. The gradual withering of the Roman state and the gradual withdrawal of the Roman armies from northern Europe were roughly contemporary with the arrival of the first missionaries of the Roman church, who succeeded in establishing the general dominance of that church throughout Europe. In the 16th century, the Reformation began as a movement to purge the church of the accumulated excesses of its long dominance, but Rome's resistance to reform soon forced the reformers' energy into new channels, where it gave rise to competing religious systems.

The effects of the Reformation on European societies were anything but uniform and affected each region and population differently. As elsewhere, this drama had profound effects in the regions now occupied by Belgium and the Netherlands, which at that time belonged to the Spanish crown. In the southern parts of this Spanish Catholic territory, Luther's disciples were the harbingers of the Reformation, followed after 1540 by the followers of Calvin, who made rapid inroads in both the Flemish and Walloon provinces. The main center of Calvinism was Antwerp, even then a prosperous and cosmopolitan seaport. In 1566, the Calvinists revolted against the proscription of their public worship, and the Duke of Alva, Philip II's envoy to the Low Countries, launched a campaign to put down the rebellion. In the north, organized resistance to Spanish orthodoxy coalesced under the leadership of William, Prince of Orange. The outcome of this skirmishing was the partition of the Spanish possessions. Many educated and skilled Calvinists from Antwerp fled to Amsterdam, laying the ground for the Netherlands' Golden Century. In the end, the northern part gained its independence and was reborn as the Netherlands, where Calvinism enjoyed undisputed sway, whereas the southern fiefs (called "conscriptions") resolved their differences with Philip and remained Catholic.

From the end of the Calvinist rebellion in the 16th century until the spread of Freemasonry and secular philosophy in the early 18th century, Catholicism continued to enjoy a virtual monopoly in the formation of the accepted worldview in the area occupied by modern Belgium, and until late in the 18th century it was more powerful there than all other influences combined. In 16th- and 17th-century Europe, religious hegemony was the rule: freedom of conscience developed only later, after two centuries of religious warfare following the Reformation. Indeed, in the early 17th century, church and state collaborated in the southern Lowlands to establish a Catholic Reformation. Sometimes called the Counter-Reformation to emphasize its role as a bulwark against the menace of Protestantism, the Catholic Reformation—by successfully pitting pageantry, processions, and pilgrimages, "the rich Roman life," against the severe Calvinism of the Netherlands—consolidated its powerful influence over the society of the south.

These events and circumstances formed or foreshadowed certain characteristics of Belgian society and social organization that have persisted to the present. For one thing, even today, only about 1.0 percent of Belgium's population of nearly 10 million are Protestant. Precise figures are difficult to obtain because of differing definitions of membership among the various Protestant denominations, though since 1978 most Belgian Protestants have become affiliated with the ecumenical Eglise Protestante Unie de Belgique. And perhaps because of this religious uniformity, collaboration between state and church has been accepted as natural in Belgium, even providing, in 1958, a welcome compromise to end the long and bitter controversy over whether state or church should be responsible for the education of the young.

During the long period of Catholic dominance, religion was the basis of the common system of values. Religious observances and rituals marked the main life stages from cradle to coffin, religious rules governed behavior, and religious principles informed consciences. Religion interpreted daily and historical events, organized social pressure, lent themes to art and philosophy, imbued life with significance, and made it sacred.

This unanimity could not endure forever, though. Freemasonry appeared between 1720 and 1730 and organized itself as it spread. The spirit of the Enlightenment shed its light from nearby France. In 1794, soon after the French Revolution had overturned the Old Regime in France, the Belgian territories were incorporated into the new French republic and subsequently into the French empire. In Belgium, as in France, the ideas of philosophers began to supplant the teachings of the church as a source of values. Secularization, de-Christianization, and even anticlericalism appeared.

As these and other trends made inroads, Catholicism began to feel beleaguered. Viewing each event and trend through the lens of its significance for Catholicism, the orthodox saw only two camps: the Catholic and the temporal. But in fact the "temporal camp" contained a whole range of camps, associations, and individuals, only a minority of whom were hostile or disdainful toward the church and its influence.

Between the extremes represented by dogmatic orthodox Catholics and hardcore liberal Freemasons was a large grey area inhabited by the less doctrinaire. These persons, whether Catholics, liberals, or, later on, socialists, did not base their political allegiances mainly or at all on attitudes of respect or hostility toward the church. Religion is only one of the three threads of dissension and tension in Belgian state history: the religious opposition of Catholicism and secularism, the linguistic opposition of the Dutch-speaking Flemish and the French-speaking Walloons, and the socioeconomic opposition of liberals and socialists.

In 1815, at the Vienna Congress following Napoleon's defeat, the great European powers assigned both the Belgian and Dutch peoples to the Dutch kingdom. Although this arrangement was economically profitable, the French-speaking part of the Belgian bourgeoisie accumulated many grievances. They were underrepresented in state bodies, complained of insufficient liberty, and were galled by the restrictions and controls they felt the central government run by Dutch Protestants was attempting to impose on Belgian Catholicism. The growing pressure of these discontents eventually led, in 1830, to an uprising that ended in independence for Belgium.

Independence and Constitution

Belgian independence was the fruit of a successful alliance between activists of two very different stripes: liberals inspired by 18th-century rationalism who felt cramped by Calvinist orthodoxy, and traditional Catholics sensitized and made more receptive to ideas of freedom by their resentment of Protestant oppression. Each group made characteristic and essential contributions to a constitution that was the most advanced of its day in Europe, the liberals insisting on freedom of thought and of the press, and the Catholics on freedom of worship, education, and association.

Thus, although it was no longer the sole source of values and convictions, Belgian Catholicism found itself accepting and promulgating the rules of democracy at a time when the papacy was still strongly inclined toward absolutism. The strict separation of church and state adopted by the framers of the U.S. Constitution, among others, in reaction to religious strife in Europe and in the New World, did not seem necessary or desirable to the Belgians, who were accustomed to seeing these two estates pursue common goals for the common good. Since it was the Catholics who had insisted on freedom of worship, what need was there to protect that freedom against the Catholics?

The initial coalition of liberals and Catholics did not do away with fierce divisions based on religious or philosophical conviction or on one's mother tongue; on the contrary, it soon was swallowed by them. In the new constitutional democracy, the existing religious, socioeconomic, and linguistic divisions led to development of the "pillarization" or "vertical pluralism" that was one of Belgium's distinctive and essential political features at least until the 1960's and is still quite visible today. Relying on the constitutionally guaranteed freedom of association, the Catholics, the socialists, and to a lesser degree the liberals organized themselves into so-called "pillars," each with a political party at the top and whole networks of social organizations below.

In the period just following independence, electoral contests were organized largely on the basis of personal associations. The liberals were the first to create a political party in the modern sense (1846) and gained control of the parliament. The Catholics then began to create an effective political machine, the Parti Catholique, which gave them an absolute majority from 1884 to 1914 and assured their participation in every government between then and World War II. In 1945, the word "Catholique" was replaced by "Social Chrétien"; later this Parti Social Chrétien split into two autonomous parties with the departure of the Flemish-speaking members, who formed the Christelijke Volkspartij alongside the Parti Social Chrétien. Together these two parties now make up the strongest political bloc in Belgium.

The Church and Its Rivals

The Catholic "pillar," with its extensive and close institutional network operating under the supervision of the bishops, was often compared with a citadel. The word accurately reflects the strategy adopted by Catholic leaders confronting a society that was becoming less and less "Christian." Their strategy was to surround the faithful with a protective environment to shield them from the "de-Christianizing" influences of this changing world. One of the main characteristics of Belgian Catholicism, as of Belgians in general, is the tendency to respond to problems through organized solutions. This inclination toward organization also explains the efficiency of Belgian Catholicism in the international sphere, its position in the Roman Catholic church, and the success of its missionary work.

As one among several pillars of society, competing with the organizing activities of the other pillars seeking to better the lot of their adherents, the Belgian church applied itself assiduously during the 19th century to constructing a tight network of social institutions. Down to the present day this network surrounds Belgian Catholics in nearly every aspect of their lives.

The following account may seem to credit Belgian Catholicism with a disproportionate share in the creation of many institutions. The brief history of religious and civil wars given above may help the reader understand why during the 19th century and until the end of World War II no other single institution or party could rival the church's ubiquity and influence. Once the church began, none outdid it in seeking organized solutions to the social problems it undertook to address on behalf of the country's almost wholly Catholic population. But since the church's social activities were paralleled by other groupings based on regional, linguistic, political, or occupational affinities, the development of the citadel as sketched in the following paragraphs can serve as a kind of paradigm of pillarization in general.

The oldest element in the church-created social network was probably the hospitals and clinics that enabled the church to express the concerns it has always felt for the sick, disabled, and handicapped. Dependent in the beginning on the monastic orders and the charity of the faithful, these institutions were later incorporated into, and financed by, the social security system, which is based in Belgium largely on associations.

Schools were another essential element in the Catholic social system, for education, like healing, is a traditional task of the church. Whereas in most other countries education was left largely to the state, in Belgium the church preceded the state in developing and maintaining a nationwide system of schools at the primary, secondary, and higher levels. Today, Belgium has two educational systems, which have become nearly equal since the 1958 School Pact: the public school system administered by the national government, the provinces, and the municipal communes; and the "free" or Catholic school network. "Equality" here refers to their financial treatment by the treasury, which is responsible for supporting both.

Also supported by the state is the Catholic University of Louvain, founded in 1425, which is the largest and oldest Catholic university in the world. It now consists of two autonomous institutions, one in Leuven teaching in Dutch and the other in Louvain-la-Neuve teaching in French. Besides these two complete institutions with a combined student population of 40,000, there are major universities in other cities all over the country.

A wide range of social problems were addressed by church-sponsored "friendly societies," which first appeared in the 18th century with patron saints and which proliferated throughout the 19th century among both workers and farmers. These mutual-benefit societies, financed by members' premiums, insure their members against illness, accident, and disability by indemnifying lost income. The Catholic friendly societies amalgamated in 1906 into the Alliance nationale des Mutualités Chrétiennes, which today has the largest number of affiliates of any similar umbrella group.

The trade union movement in Belgium did not originate with the church, but with trade associations pure and simple. In the beginning the church had no answers to the huge problems created by industrialization, and Catholic concern for workers' interests grew very slowly. It was not until the 1860's, when the First International penetrated the workers' movement and lent it a socialist, anticlerical, or even antireligious color, that the church became specifically involved with workers' issues and problems and, launching its own trade unions, began to make up for lost time. Today, the affiliated membership of the Confédération des Syndicats Chrétiens (Algemeen Christelijk Vakverbond) is slightly larger than that of the socialist Fédération Générale du Travail de Belgique (Algemeen Belgisch Vakverbond).

Other social service agencies, educational associations, and cooperative economic alliances sponsored by the church were brought together under the aegis of the Flemish Algemeen Christelijke Werknemersverbond and the Walloon Mouvement Ouvrier Chrétien, which not only guide and coordinate activities, but also safeguard and further the political interests of their adherents. In rural areas, agricultural leagues were formed under the general auspices of the Boerenbond (1890) and the Alliance Agricole Belge, which serve the general needs of farmers for marketing, cooperative purchasing, savings and credit, insurance, and political representation.

The various agencies of the Action Catholique first appeared during the interwar years. This movement appealed to various social groups (workers, farmers, businessmen, professionals, intellectuals, women, and young persons) to support apostolic activities directed at the deepening of faith through such groups as the Jeunesse Ouvrière Chrétienne, Jeunesse Agricole Chrétienne, Jeunesse Etudiante Chrétienne, Fédération des Scouts Catholiques, and others.

In the world of Belgian journalism, the church has also been preeminent since the 19th century. In Flanders, Wallonia, and Brussels, Catholic daily and weekly newspapers and monthly magazines are more numerous and have a larger readership than the liberal and socialist press combined, but without any loss of individuality: *La libre Belgique, De Standaard, Vers l'Avenir, La Cité, Het Volk*—each has its own style, personality, and audience.

The Church from 1950 to the Present

However, the "citadel" approach also turned out, especially after World War II, to have two major drawbacks: the "clerical temptation," the tendency of church officials to become preoccupied with winning and wielding political power; and a marked and crippling insulation of the denizens of the citadel from trends and people outside the Christian milieu. Since the late 1950's, great changes have taken place.

The first is the phenomenon of declericalization. The bishops and the clergy no longer intervene in political life, and the faithful have become completely independent in choosing their political commitments. The Liberal party welcomes Catholics, many of whom see their religion as no obstacle to voting for ecologists (the Greens) or for the candidates of a linguistic party, or as a factor in choosing schools for their children or in forming other affiliations, although most still prefer institutions with a Catholic spirit.

But even as the members of Christian organizations assign less and less importance to the external symbols of Catholicism, the high quality of the services these organizations offer attracts many who are not practicing Catholics and even "seculars" with no religious affiliation. So although the level of religious observance is diminishing, the numbers of pupils in Catholic schools and membership in Christian trade unions continue to grow. The Catholic institutional network has thus ceased to be a monolith and has been transformed into a diversified sociological web with a common inspiration offering its services to the whole society.

As a result of the greater autonomy of people and organizations, and the debates preceding and following Vatican II, Belgian Catholicism seems less unified now than it did a quarter of a century ago. The new ideas introduced by the tremendous cultural ferment of the 1960's, such as the "sexual revolution," women's liberation, political protest, and liturgical reform, gave rise to a multiplicity of moral, theological, and political positions, especially among intellectuals. (These ideas are discussed more fully at the conclusion of this chapter.) Among the Catholics, as among the secular segments of the population, the bitter divisions engendered by these upheavals have faded and given way to coexistence, which, though sometimes ambiguous, is favored by the strong Belgian inclination toward compromise and by the tolerance of the bishops. It is fair to say that the center of gravity of Belgian society has shifted from Catholicism to sociocultural Christianity.

How can we characterize the state of Catholicism in Belgium today? Of the whole population, 77 percent say they believe in God, 12 percent are atheists, and 11 percent are agnostics. Fifty-two percent believe in the existence of the soul, and around 40 percent in life after death. Forty to 45 percent believe that Jesus Christ is the son of God; 56 percent either pray or meditate, and 69 percent claim to be "religious."

This last figure may seem high in the light of those preceding it, but it is supported by the population's recourse to the major sacraments: 82 percent of newborns are baptized; 83 percent of funerals are religious; and 76 percent of all weddings are performed in church, though in connection with the last statistic it should not be forgotten that the frequency of cohabitations has increased.

All these indexes may reflect only a peripheral attachment to religion. The numbers of those with a stronger involvement in religious life may be judged by attendance at Sunday mass: in the early 1980's, 27 percent of Belgians over 18 attended church during the weekends compared with 45 percent in 1964. The distribution of the faithful is irregular: they represent 32 percent in Flanders, 23 percent in Wallonia, and only 4 percent in Brussels.

No account of religion in Belgium would be complete without mention of the Moslem and Jewish communities. Of the approximately 900,000 foreigners residing in Belgium, around 20 percent are Moslems, mostly from North Africa (especially Morocco) and Turkey. Of the others, about 40 percent are from Italy and Spain, and 20 percent are from France and the Netherlands. The Belgian state accords to Islam the same status as to the Catholic, Protestant, and Jewish faiths.

The 35,000 Jewish Belgians are concentrated in Brussels and Antwerp. Their congregations cover the spectrum from Orthodox (in Antwerp, there is a strong Hasidic revival) through Conservative to Reformed. Although their numbers have always been too small to give them much direct influence on Belgian culture, the Jews, like the Protestants, have provided, and continue to provide, Belgium with prominent leaders.

History of Secularism in Belgium

"Secularism" is the church's term for the huge cultural movement that developed in the Western world from the 16th and 17th centuries onward and which, looking outside the church for answers, gave birth to science and technology through its efforts to examine the mysteries of the universe by the light of reason and still looks to these for improvement of the human lot through discovery and invention. Secularism proclaims freedom and equal opportunity as human rights and aspires to earthly happiness. As this vast movement gained momentum, a number of key ideas appeared and gained strength and currency: human beings are mortal; their will is free, and they are entitled to define their own rules; they were not created, but evolved; humanity and society can be perfected; human beings can overcome their contradictions and conflicts to perfect themselves and human society by modifying life on earth appropriately.

In the 19th and 20th centuries, many currents of ideas have borne these themes forward: positivism, evolutionism, scientism, Marxism, Freudianism, Existentialism. In the end, god and humanity have become separated. Human beings feel less need for god to enable them to explain the universe, to live in it, to find happiness in it. Society becomes more secular, and religion less and less the source of its rhythms, customs, celebrations, and daily practices.

Although this great movement follows a basic trend, it cannot be said that secularism, in Belgium or anywhere else, has a common basic doctrine. From the beginning, it has been a great flow of many smaller streams that have divided, flowed together, influenced one another, disregarded one another, and passed each other through successive stages of development. Today it includes atheists, deists, agnostics, persons indifferent to religion, Marxists, "humanists" of various persuasions, and more. Most favor the principle of "free inquiry," which asserts that scientific and philosophical research should recognize no *a priori* limitations.

Since in the case of Belgium we begin with the religious unanimity of the 16th and 17th centuries, with the church's influence dominant and uncontested, it seems most convenient to examine the successive and successful challenges to that unanimity and influence by which the present diversity and pluralism of Belgian society arose and, without taking sides, to group these challenges under the very broad term "secularism."

As mentioned earlier, the first breach in Belgium's religious unanimity was made by Freemasonry. Arriving between 1720 and 1730, Freemasonry began to spread a little later on and continued to gain influence and adherents into the 19th century. At first bearing the spirit of the Enlightenment, it later took on the coloration of contemporary political changes: Bonapartist during the French occupation, Orangist during the Dutch kingdom (1815–30).

The Grand Lodge of Belgium was founded in 1833 under the auspices of Léopold I, the first Belgian king. In 1834, Theodore Verhaegen founded the Université Libre de Bruxelles, which took an opposite course from the Université Catholique de Louvain by adopting the principle of free inquiry. The Free University became the intellectual guide of freethinkers, easily adopted the views of Voltaire, had links with Freemasonry, and was liberal in its politics. It spawned philosophical societies, philanthropic associations, and leagues with specific objectives, all based on a rationalist humanism.

Although Freemason lodges professed deism, they opposed clerical influences, and it was not surprising that the Belgian episcopate condemned them in 1837. Belgian Freemasonry continued to develop, abandoned metaphysical references, and dropped allusions to the Great Architect of the Universe and to the immortality of the soul.

As might be guessed from the foregoing, there was a certain affinity, verging on alliance, between Freemasonry and establishment politics, and the Belgian Liberal party of today owes its name more to its philosophical than to its socioeconomic antecedents, which tend toward conservatism. The Masonic-liberal milieu flourished more strongly in Brussels and Wallonia, where French influence was strongest, than in Flanders, where the church maintained a firmer grip.

When socialism appeared around 1860, it ran a similar course. It was more successful in Wallonia, which was home to heavy industries such as coal, steel, and glassmaking, than in Flanders, though the latter was always pre-eminent in textiles and had important industrial centers like Ghent.

Belgian socialism drew its doctrine from both Proudhon and Marx and was thus at the start quite materialist in its leanings. Socialists not only opposed the liberals, but were often antireligious as well. Its intellectual adherents and workers' leaders joined secular circles. The latter then experienced a class rift. From the middle-class ranks, wedded to classical liberalism, appeared progressive personalities open to new ideas who joined the vanguard of the struggle for universal suffrage, toward which Belgian society took a long first step hedged with some restrictions in

1894 and a second step to "one man—one vote" in 1919, completing the process by finally allowing women to vote in 1948. Some of the suffragists joined socialism, which was also producing, little by little, working-class leaders.

Belgian socialists characteristically began by organizing a large number of associations of all types—trade unions, cooperatives, friendly societies, educational institutions, people's centers, a political party—in a word, a pillar, as a way of involving socialism in the social system in order to transform it. Thus the revolutionary socialist movement, when transplanted to Belgian soil, very quickly became reformist.

The Secular Spectrum

In the end, in addition to the Catholic network (the "citadel") there grew up a close web of social institutions (or pillars) organized by the socialists, and a much less complete set organized by the liberals. Moreover, in the politically unaffiliated "common space," there also arose a whole series of associations and movements of every description, some of a general character (e.g., Cercles de la Libre Pensée, Amis de la Morale Laïque, Centre d'Action Laïque, Centrale Vrijzinnige Raad, Unie Vrijzinnige Verenigingen) and others promoting specific objectives (such as family planning, liberalization of abortion, women's movements, human rights). About the only principles they had in common were those of free inquiry and opposition to clerical domination.

This diversified universe united itself around the central issue of education. As early as 1864, a Ligue de l'Enseignement was formed to promote and defend public schools while the Catholics were working on the development of their institutions, and the conflict continued through the rest of the 19th century and the first half of the 20th. The struggle culminated in the outbreak of a so-called "school war" in the mid-1950's, which had to be quelled by the Socialist-Liberal coalition government with the 1958 School Pact mentioned earlier, still in force today.

One wing of the secular spectrum is eager to offer the same services as the Catholic church. Thus, it has organized a secular Youth Feast, parallel to the Holy Communion, solemnized civil weddings, and established a ceremony for civil funerals. It trains and sends "lay counsellors" to hospitals, to the army, and to prisons; ensures the teaching of secular morality in public schools (where pupils may choose this course or the religious one); and broadcasts programs on radio and television. Other seculars, especially intellectuals, mistrust the institutionalization of secularity, which to them is only a substitute for the church. They believe the individual should maintain an independent conscience, practice autonomy, and remain free of commitments to any enrolling or official ideology.

It might be interesting to attempt to define criteria revealing the population's adherence to the secular sphere, like those cited above for Christian faith and practice. These might include attendance at a public school; election there of the course on secular morality; matriculation at the Université Libre de Bruxelles or the Vrije Universiteit Brussel; membership in a Socialist organization (but not a Liberal one, since during the 1960's the Liberal party formed a coalition with the Parti Social Chrétien); civil marriage without religious ceremony; refusal to baptize one's children; refusal of first communion and confirmation; membership in a Freemason lodge; or affiliation with secular associations or organizations. However, since no one has ever gathered statistical data on these matters, and since the significance of such criteria cannot be precisely defined, there is no possibility of determining the numerical strength of the secular sphere.

The social ferments of the 1960's, whose effects on Belgian Catholics were touched on earlier, did not spare the secular world, which is supposed by its nature to be more open to new ideas and new influences. Certainly many of the ideas that emerged then were congenial to individualists and freethinkers to begin with.

First was the protest against any authority whose legitimacy was suspect. Morals based solely on authoritarian arguments were no longer acceptable, and personal experience became the final basis of ethical choices. The individual became autonomous with respect to any institution wishing to impose its standards and behaviors, becoming in effect the keeper of his or her own conscience. Under these conditions, freedom emerged as a major value. Fierce, absolute, unbridled freedom conflicts with commitments, belonging, and lasting faithfulness, and it generates mistrust, but since society changes so quickly, one must have free scope if one is always to be able to recover independence.

Women's liberation and the rediscovery of the body combined to form a new concept of sexuality, in which sexual energy is no longer a drive to be controlled, but becomes a source of pleasure and happiness. Sexual taboos, demystified, were no longer seen as absolute imperatives but as socially created restrictions on the natural right to sexual success, which is part of a complete life. This applied as well to the other forms of sexuality, which are simply the expression of diverse tastes and must be tolerated too.

Rousseau's ideas came once more into vogue. Humanity is good in itself but corrupted by social institutions and repressive practices. Liberation becomes the order of the day: the establishment of schools without constraints or competition, where learning takes place according to each individual's interests and rhythms; the recognition that delinquency is a social, not an individual ill, and that prisons must therefore be used as a tool of rehabilitation rather than as a means of revenge and expiation; the emptying of psychiatric asylums; the questioning of the need for armies and the advocacy of conscientious objection; pacifism while recognizing Third World wars of liberation as righteous; antiracism; worker management to overcome workplace alienation; the championing of the purity of nature against pollution by safeguarding the environment and defending the food chain against chemical contamination.

From an institutional and political standpoint, the ferment of the late 1960's and early 1970's has left few traces. The ecology and pacifist movements are probably its most obvious heirs. And although the faithful were more vigorous in their resistance to many of the ideas of that turbulent time, and more vociferous in their rejection of them, many of the themes these debates planted in people's minds and consciences have continued to develop and have deeply influenced the culture and practices of modern societies, secular and religious segments alike, in ways we are not as yet fully aware of.

Belgium Until World War I

Reginald De Schrijver

Romanized Belgium and Germanic Settlements

IN ITS BROADEST SENSE, history in Belgium starts with the earliest human habitation on Belgian soil some 400,000 years ago. The transition from the original primitive way of life to agriculture took place in the late fifth and the fourth millennia B.C. Agriculture remained the base of the economy until the 19th-century Industrial Revolution. The expansion of the Celts, who originated in central Europe, led to their settlements over present-day Belgium after the 7th century B.C. On the eve of the Roman invasion, all tribes in Belgium seem to have been Celtic or at least celticized. Among these were the Nervians, the Eburons, the Menapians, and others. Julius Caesar called all the tribes living in northern Gaul between the Seine and the Rhine "Belgae," and their country occasionally was indicated as "Belgium"; moreover, he added that "of all the peoples of Gaul the toughest are the Belgae." In spite of that they were subjugated by the Romans between 60 and 50 B.C., and around 15 B.C., their country became the Roman provincia Belgica. This province later was divided into several provinces, and each of them was subdivided into *civitates,* which more or less coincided with the territory of the various Belgian tribes. More profound romanization dates from Emperor Claudius on; it equally affected some Germanic tribes such as the Tungri, who were allowed to settle within the borders of Belgica after the extermination of the Eburons. The administrative language in Roman Belgium was, of course, Latin, and this language gradually supplanted the Celtic tongues among the Belgae. In late Roman times some towns flourished in Belgica; among them were Turnacum (Tournai) and Atuatuca Tungrorum (Tongeren). In these towns appeared the first Christian communities.

From the middle of the 3rd century A.D. on, Frankish infiltrations or raids took place from Germania, anticipating the massive crossing of Germanic tribes on New Year's Eve 406. As a consequence of these events, Roman authority and civilization collapsed during the 5th century in the Belgian provinces and elsewhere in Gaul. The Frankish and other Germanic (Saxon and Frisian) settlements radically changed the ethnic and linguistic physiognomy of Roman Belgium. The northern part of present-day Belgium became an overwhelmingly germanized and Germanic- (Frankish) speaking area, whereas in the southern part people continued to be Roman and spoke derivatives of Latin. The linguistic border across Belgium today, from east to west, is the result of a complicated process in the early Middle Ages. Roman and Germanic settlements constitute the distant base of the present-day Flemish-Walloon or Dutch- and French-speaking ethnic·division in Belgium.

The Frankish Monarchy

For a while the center of gravity of the Franks lay in Roman Belgium; King Childeric I (d. ca. 481), whose grave, with its many fine artistic works, was discovered in 1652, even considered himself as a *foederatus* of the Romans. This cannot be said of his son and successor Clovis I (d. 511), who defeated the last Roman commander-in-chief in Gaul and extended his authority over nearly all of Gaul. Clovis's baptism in 506 marks the beginning of the Christianization of the Franks and the re-Christianization of other populations in Belgium during the 6th–8th centuries. This was done mainly by monks from middle and southern Gaul or from England and Ireland. Dioceses were organized, mainly along Roman administrative borders, and basically they were maintained within these limits until the reorganization in 1559 by the Spanish king Philip II. In those times, mainly in the 7th century (the Age of the Saints), nearly 25 abbeys were founded on Belgian soil; most of them continued to exist through the end of the 18th century (French Revolution). Along with its specific religious functions, the Catholic church exercised intellectual and economic functions as well.

Under the Merovingian dynasty, the Belgian territory constituted a border area. This changed under the new Carolingian dynasty, from the middle of the 8th century on, when an enlargement to the north and the east took place. The center of this enlarged Frankish monarchy was between the Meuse and the middle Rhine, covering an important part of eastern Belgium. The Carolingian empire was more Germanic than the Merovingian kingdom. On the other hand Charlemagne re-established in 800 the old Roman empire, and he and his successors patronized a renaissance of arts and letters (the Carolingian Renaissance). As in previous times, monasteries upheld culture and transmitted ancient Roman and Christian culture and literature. The library of Saint Amand on the Scheldt preserved vernacular literature as well, among which was the oldest Romance text, *Séquence de Sainte Eulalie* (ca. 880).

Charlemagne's Frankish "Roman" empire was inherited by his son Louis; after the latter's death, it was divided into three parts by the Treaty of Verdun (843): Francia occidentalis, Francia media, and Francia orientalis. Some decades later, the northern part of the central empire was conquered by eastern Francia or Germany; it coincided largely with old Lotharingia. Most of present-day Belgium falls within Lotharingia, whereas a smaller part, between the Scheldt and the North Sea, was French territory. Judicially and politically this situation—the Scheldt constituting the border between France and Germany in the north—was maintained until the early 16th century. During the 9th century the Scheldt valley was a main target for Norse invasions. These Norsemen, along with the gradual disintegration of central political power, promoted feudalism.

Medieval Principalities

Administratively the Frankish territory was divided into *pagi*, or counties. In the troubled second half of the 9th century, the *comes* (count) of a small territory near the North Sea called Flanders (*pagus flandrensis*, first known mention in the early 8th century) extended his authority, at the expense of the French king, over several *pagi* between the Scheldt and the North Sea. His successors continued to do so southward to the Somme and eastward, beyond the Scheldt, into the German empire. All these possessions constituted in the Middle Ages the powerful county of Flanders. This county continued to exist under this name and as a separate territory until the French annexation of 1794–95. However, its borders changed, mainly in the south. This Flanders coincides only partially with present-day Flanders; the latter constitutes the Dutch-speaking north of Belgium, the former only the actual Belgian provinces of West and East Flanders or the eastern part of present-day Flanders, along with French Flanders (in the north of France) and Zealand-Flanders in the Netherlands.

Whereas the collapse of the central power in France from the 9th century on enabled the rise of powerful regional rulers such as the counts of Flanders, the East Francian, or German, kings and emperors at first maintained a better grip on local vassals, even in distant areas such as Lotharingia. In this territory, no principalities comparable to the Flemish county can be found in the 9th or 10th century. At the end of the 10th century, however, the prince-bishopric of Liège was to emerge within the imperial church. In the 11th century, some Lotharingian aristocratic families started to set up real principalities with their own dynasties. This process of usurpation of imperial power was facilitated by the emperor's defeat in the struggle of the Investitures. The principalities, which came to bear names such as Hainaut, Brabant, Namur, and Luxembourg, did not develop before the end of the 11th century and were no longer threatened after imperial power was eliminated in the 12th century. These principalities constitute the origin of the historical provinces of Belgium, which lasted to the end of the 18th century; that past remains influential in the historic consciousness of modern Belgium. Most of the present-day Belgian provinces bear the names of the medieval principalities, but much more remains than just the names.

There are political as well as cultural differences between Flanders and the Lotharingian principalities. Until the struggle of the Investitures in the 12th century, the Lotharingian principalities had strong cultural connections with the German empire. Liège, whose capital of the same name was called the Athens of the North, took part in the Ottonian Renaissance (10th and 11th centuries), and the immense church of Saint Gertrude in Nivelles in Brabant is comparable to the Dome of Mainz. In the Scheldt valley, French influence in intellectual life was stronger, in architecture and in language, not least at the court of the counts of Flanders.

The principalities were involved in the late medieval interdynastic conflicts, the best known of which is the one between the French and the English kings. Juridically the counts of Flanders were vassals of the French kings, and their county was part of the French monarchy. Economically, however, the Flemings were highly dependent on wool imports from England. Mainly from King Philip Augustus (d. 1223) on, the French kings aimed at enlarging their crownlands. They directed their efforts mainly against Flanders, a county important for both political and economic reasons. Philip Augustus is quoted as having said: "France will absorb Flanders or will be destroyed by her." Flanders turned to England and joined with the Holy Roman emperor and the duke of Brabant to form an anti-French coalition; their combined armies, however, were defeated at the Battle of Bouvines (July 27, 1214). The immediate consequence of this was increased influence by the French king in Flemish affairs in the 13th century; eventually it resulted in Flanders's annexation to the crownlands. But the Flemish towns did not accept this. The murder of royal garrison soldiers and francophile patricians in Bruges on

May 17, 1302, induced King Philip IV (the Fair) to send an expedition. On July 11, 1302, near Kortrijk (Courtrai) a battle took place between the royal French army, which consisted of aristocrats, and a Flemish army basically composed of craftsmen and peasants, but under the direction of princes and knights of various neighboring principalities. As a result of the Flemish victory, the annexation of the county of Flanders to the crownlands was undone. (It is noteworthy that the county of Flanders is the only part of medieval France that does not belong to present-day France.) Another consequence of the Battle of Kortrijk was the establishment of democratic government in Flemish towns at the expense of the ruling patricians. Modern Flanders celebrates July 11 as its national holiday.

Relations between Flanders and its French suzerain came to a head in the opening phase of the Anglo-French Hundred Years' War (1337–1453). Because of wool imports from England, Flanders, under the direction not of the Flemish francophile count, who had fled to the French court, but of a patrician of Ghent, Jacques van Artevelde, shifted from neutrality to an active alliance with England. After the murder of Artevelde in 1345, mainly because of local rivalries in Ghent, Flanders returned to neutrality.

In contrast to Flanders, the equally powerful duchy of Brabant enjoyed a peaceful 13th century, which enabled it to annex, on the road to the Rhine, the small duchy of Limburg. In the 14th century, the financial needs of the duke led to the granting of a share in the government to the three estates: clergy, nobility, and towns. The Charter of Kortenberg (1312) and the Blijde Inkomst or Joyeuse Entrée (1356) have much in common with Magna Carta and were the basis for the development of representative government in the Low Countries. In Flanders the estates originated at the end of the 13th century; at first the aristocracy took part in them, but later representation was restricted to the clergy and some towns.

In the prince-bishopric of Liège also, 13th-century struggles between popular classes and the aristocracy resulted, in the early 14th century, in the so-called Sens du Pays, a kind of popular representation, and in a co-government with nobility, clergy, and the prince-bishop (Paix de Fexhe, 1316). By that time Liège was already alienated, politically and culturally, from the German empire, though juridically it remained part of the Holy Roman (German) Empire. In the second half of the 14th century, Liège was enlarged with the county of Loon, a territory nearly coinciding with present-day Belgian Limburg. Herewith the principality reached borders that basically were maintained until the end of the 18th century.

The Communes of Medieval Belgium

Belgian medieval history and society are not only deeply marked by the rise and the development of principalities, they are no less strongly dominated, from the late 11th century on, by the "communal revolution." The difference between the medieval towns and the surrounding rural areas was primarily economic, although cultural differences were also important. Before the establishment of the duchy of Brabant or the prince-bishopric of Liège, the county of Flanders became a land of towns: Bruges, Ghent, Ypres, and, in French-speaking Flanders, Lille, Saint-Omer, and Douai; the oldest charter in Flanders is that of Geraardsbergen (1068). In Brabant the most famous towns were Louvain (Leuven), Brussels, Antwerp, 's-Hertogenbosch and—as an autonomous small principality in the middle of that duchy—Mechlin (Mechelen). In Brabant and Flanders the textile industry was the main economic activity. Nowhere more than in Flanders, towns were the offspring of commerce. The textile industry started in the French-speaking south of that country, and later expanded to Ghent and Ypres. Bruges was in the late Middle Ages a great commercial center, first of an active international trade controlled by the Flemings and later, in the 14th and 15th centuries, of a passive trade. By the end of the 13th century, Ghent was the biggest producer of cloth in western Europe, and in the next century it counted 60,000 inhabitants.

In the prince-bishopric of Liège, the most important towns were Liège and Huy, where the textile industry also flourished, and Dinant, which was famous for its copper and metal industries. Of all Belgian towns, Huy has the oldest charter (1066). The principalities of Hainaut, Namur, and Luxembourg largely remained agricultural regions, but in Brabant and Flanders by the end of the Middle Ages one-third of the population is said to have lived in towns, which means to a large extent that the economy depended on industry and commerce.

In Belgium most of the towns—and most of the villages as well—came into existence after the second half of the 11th century. These 11th-century trading colonies, or *portus*, lacked legal sanction. For their transformation into towns with "burghers" and institutions, the intervention of the sovereign power was necessary. The city law—*keure* or *charte*—granted by the princes or extorted by the towns contained political, social, and financial privileges. The communal revolution led to real political and juridical autonomy and for the inhabitants of the towns to personal freedom. In Belgium, however, no more than elsewhere in the Low Countries, city-states did not come into existence. Personal liberty did not exclude clear social differences. At a very early stage a minority of wealthy patricians arose and exercised municipal power for a long time. Most important was that "the air of the city makes one free," and communalism undermined feudalism. After the 13th century, most of the peasants in the Belgian principalities were free, whereas in Germany, not to mention eastern Europe, servitude still existed at the end of the Middle Ages or in some places beyond. Communalism thus equals a process of personal and collective freedom and is the basis of a deep love of liberty and of democracy. The internal political life of the principalities—at least in Flanders, Brabant, and Liège—was to a large extent dominated by the communes.

The Burgundian Netherlands

The development of largely autonomous and often rival principalities (Flanders, Hainaut, Brabant and Limburg, Mechlin, Namur, Luxembourg, Liège) changed profoundly during a process that started about 1400 and lasted for nearly a century and a half. With the exception of the prince-bishopric of Liège, the above-mentioned principalities were all grouped within a dynastic and political union that received the name Low Countries (Pays-Bas, Nederlanden). Never before had these countries been grouped along that politico-geographic concept, and, as a matter of fact, there was no intrinsic reason for the union.

The starting point was the marriage in 1369 of Margaret, daughter of the Flemish count, with Philip the Bold, son of the king of France and himself Duke of Burgundy. Margaret was heir not only of Flanders, but of Artois, Franche-Comté, Nevers, and other territories in France and the German empire. The actual government of Philip and Margaret started in 1384. Subsequently the reign of Philip the Bold's grandson, Philip the Good (d. 1465), was most important. To the inherited principalities (Flanders, Artois, the two Burgundys, etc.), the new ruler added, by inheritance, purchase, or—to a lesser degree—military action, successively the counties of Namur, Hainaut, Zeeland, and the duchies of Brabant-Limburg and Luxembourg. All together these territories constituted ten Pays d'en bas (Low Countries) along with some Pays d'en haut (High Countries: Burgundy, Franche-Comté). Moreover, Philip the Bold held a protectorate over three prince-bishoprics: Cambrai, Liège, and Utrecht. The Burgundian state was not a unified or centralized state but rather a personal union; in spite of later centralizing measures that character of loose union was maintained throughout the Old Regime. And yet the Burgundian union fits within the postfeudal tendencies toward territorial unification and more absolutist rule, though, on the other hand, no one can deny Philip the Good's exceptional fortune and real statesmanship.

Since there was no intrinsic reason to group the principalities over which Philip the Bold reigned, one should not be surprised to hear of his son Charles's dream to restore Lotharingia. Charles the Bold tried to realize this in an alliance with the English king against the French king and at the expense of the powerless German emperor. So the ambitious duke occupied Liège, purchased Upper Alsace, and conquered Guelders, but these three territories shook off Burgundian rule upon hearing of Charles's death before Nancy (1477).

The Burgundian 15th century is not only the era of a political union of large parts of the present-day Benelux countries, but also an age of great artistic and cultural achievements that constitutes a peak of Western civilization. Elsewhere in this book are the names of famous sculptors, painters, musicians, and architects orginating from various principalities of the Burgundian union or even attracted from abroad to work in the Low Countries by the splendor of Burgundian civilization. The products of their talents constituted a series of luxury industries concentrated in the towns. The late medieval depression was likewise lessened in the countryside where people improved agriculture techniques, produced more new specialized products such as butter, cheese, meat, and beer, and initiated rural industries, using cheaper Spanish wool to produce cheaper cloth or producing flax for the linen industry.

Finally, we should not omit the founding in 1425 of the first university in Belgium and the Low Countries at Leuven (Louvain) as well as the work of such famous historians of the late 14th and the 15th centuries as Jean Froissart, from Hainaut, and Georges Chastellain and Philippe de Commynes, from Flanders. Their names rank among the more glorious ones of French literature in the late Middle Ages.

The Hapsburg Seventeen Provinces

The Burgundian heritage went to Charles the Bold's daughter Mary who, however, died prematurely in 1482. As a consequence of this, the Burgundian Netherlands were governed first for a decade by her husband, Archduke Maximilian of Austria, then after his succession as German emperor (1493) by their son Philip I the Handsome (d. 1506), and then by the latter's younger sister. With that, Belgium became part of the Hapsburg dominions, which soon comprised the central European territories of the Hapsburgs, the Low Countries, and Spain and its Italian and overseas colonies. The first and only ruler over all these territories was Philip the Handsome's son Charles, born in Ghent in 1500, the second of the name in Spain and Emperor Charles V in the Empire. Needless to say, Belgium became involved in the Hapsburg European and world policy.

The new Hapsburg rulers continued the political work of their Burgundian predecessors. Warfare with France led to the conquest of Tournai (1521), a French island in the former Burgundian Netherlands. In the peace treaties of Madrid and Cambrai (1526, 1529), Francis I renounced French sovereignty not only over Tournai but over the counties of Flanders and Artois as well. So the 9th-century border between France and Germany shifted from the Scheldt to a more southern line. The Hapsburg Low Countries were furthermore enlarged, within the borders of the German Empire, by the acquisition of Friesland, Utrecht and Overijssel, Groningen, and Guelders and by a protectorate over Cambrai. These extensions date from the years 1524–43. The enlarged Low Countries along with the Franche-Comté were grouped in the Burgundian Circle, one out of 10 *Kreise* of the German empire; the Burgundian Circle, however, enjoyed an almost independent status. Moreover, constitutionally, the Low Countries were declared an indivisible whole (1549). Besides Pays-Bas or Nederlanden, they were also called after Flanders, one of the powerful principalities, or the Seventeen Provinces. The usual Latin name was Belgium.

When Emperor Charles V abdicated, his brother succeeded him in the Austrian-Hapsburg dominions, and his son Philip II inherited the Spanish part along with the Low Countries. For a century and a half, Belgian history remained closely connected with Spanish history. Note, however, that the large principality of Liège, about one-fifth of present-day Belgium, politically never belonged to the Netherlands or Belgium in early modern times.

Like the Burgundian Netherlands, the Hapsburg Seventeen Provinces, with the duchy of Brabant as the center of gravity, experienced another golden age of artistic and intellectual life. A splendid series of names fills fields such as architecture, painting, music, printing, sciences, and letters. One can trace their activity not only in the Low Countries but all over greater western Europe as well. Closely connected with political strength and cultural life was economic prosperity. The economic expansion of Belgium in the sixteenth century until about 1570 brought the late medieval economy to a brilliant close. The Low Countries constituted a dominant pole of growth in the world economy. Antwerp, heir of Bruges, served as the international market where Portuguese, Germans, and the English did business and where the Flemings (inhabitants of the Low Countries) offered their luxury products (tapestries, furniture, clocks, musical instruments, paintings, fashion, embroideries, and weapons) as well as linen and other textile products.

The economy, however, was disturbed, first by Hapsburg tax pressure and fiscal policy, which led to revolts in Ghent and Antwerp and a clash between the Hapsburgs' world imperialism and provincial particularism; and second, by foreign competition, mostly German and English. The latter occurred mainly in the 1560's. The 16th century offers, of course, still another fascinating side of history, that of religious renewal and agitation. Luther's early writings were known in Belgium from about 1518–19. Leuven's Faculty of·Theology condemned Lutheranism in 1519, one year before its condemnation by Pope Leo X. Also, in 1520, Emperor Charles V issued his first decree calling for book burning, and in 1522 the state inquisition was installed in the Netherlands. More Protestant groups sent preachers to these countries, but Calvinism became the most influential, not least in the southern Low Countries or Belgium. Its greatest success came after Philip's departure for Spain in 1559.

To Protestant religious unrest, one should add the discontent provoked by the creation of fourteen new dioceses in the Low Countries (1559) and the aversion of the nobility to growing absolutism (the Prince of Orange and others versus Cardinal Granvelle). In 1566 an iconoclast movement, starting in the Flemish town of Steenvoorde and spreading over various parts of the Low Countries (Tournai, Valenciennes, Flanders, Brabant, Holland) had primarily religious motives, but the largely violent action of the iconoclasts was equally a release of political, economic, and social tensions and dissatisfaction.

In order to chastise the rebellious and "heretic" subjects, Philip II sent, in 1567, the Duke of Alva to Flanders. About 1,000 people were executed; among them were two members of the Council of State in Brussels: Count Egmont and Count Horne. William, Prince of Orange, fled from the country. His first military action took place in 1568 in Groningen and marked the opening of the Eighty Years' War against the Spanish king. Alva's repression caused an emigration of about 20,000 people, and many more followed later on. In the provinces under Spanish control, the Catholic faith was re-established as the only legal religion, and an already weakened economy received fatal blows. Revolts broke out over Alva's tax reforms, and Philip II recalled him in 1573. After the sudden death of his successor in 1576, most of the Low Countries sided with William the Silent.

The real Spanish *reconquista* began in 1578 with the new governor

Alexander Farnese, a great warrior and shrewd diplomat. By diplomacy or warfare, he reconquered almost all of the Low Countries south of the Big Rivers in the present-day Netherlands. Ultimately the "war of independence," the Spanish *reconquista,* succeeded only partially. The Seventeen Provinces were divided into two parts of a similar size: the rebel-controlled and eventually independent Calvinist republic of the United Provinces in the north (Holland), and the Spanish Catholic Netherlands in the south (Belgium). The demarcation line between the two camps at the end of the war (1648, Peace of Westphalia) coincides with the present-day Belgian-Dutch border. With a short interruption (1815–30), the northern and the southern Netherlands have had a separate history ever since. In the Low Countries, from the end of the 16th century on, the point of gravity, economically, politically, and culturally, shifted from Flanders and Brabant to Holland; emigration from Belgium contributed greatly to Holland's golden 17th century.

The Southern Netherlands and the Principality of Liège in the 17th and 18th Centuries

Since he did not succeed militarily, in 1598 Philip II of Spain transferred sovereignty over the Seventeen Provinces, actually only over the southern provinces, to his daughter Isabella (d. 1633); she married Archduke Albert of Austria, who had acted as a governor-general in the Spanish Netherlands since 1595. These two concluded the Twelve Years' Truce (1609–21), which they were not able to renew. At the death of the childless Archduke Albert (1621), Spain re-established sovereignty over the southern Netherlands and resumed its war with the rebels. The outbreak of a new Spanish-French war in 1635 increased the French threat to the southern Netherlands. The Eighty Years' War ended in 1648: Spain recognized the independence of the northern provinces, which, moreover, severed all ties with the German empire. The southern provinces continued to be Spanish but remained a loose member of the German empire as well. During that first half of the 17th century, there was an economic recovery in the southern Netherlands following the dramatic decline during the last third of the 16th century; but that recovery was not comparable to the golden age before 1560. In the second half of the 17th century and in the early years of the 18th century, the economy declined again, primarily because of military events and international competition.

The Spanish-French war, which started in 1635, ended in 1659 with the loss of Artois for Spain (Peace of the Pyrenees). Shortly afterwards

Louis XIV started his long personal reign (1661–1715), which amounted to an uninterrupted struggle for hegemony in Europe and to a series of wars against the Hapsburgs and the sea powers (the Dutch Republic and Great Britain). In all these wars the Spanish Netherlands were Europe's main battlefield and Louis's main objective. Spain lost further territories in the Burgundian Circle to France: the Franche-Comté and parts of Flanders and Hainaut (e.g., Lille and Valenciennes). The last of these wars was the War of the Spanish Succession (1701–13), when initially the southern Netherlands came under the control of the Bourbon successor of the last Spanish Hapsburg. As a consequence of the Peace of Utrecht (1713), the territory of the onetime Spanish Netherlands returned to the Hapsburgs and became Austrian, and the Dutch Republic was allowed to install in these Austrian Netherlands an anti-French barrier, which remained for 65 years. The borders with France as agreed in the Peace of Utrecht coincide almost exactly with the present-day Franco-Belgian border.

The southern Netherlands were not only Spanish but also Catholic. Catholicism in Belgium is closely connected with the Spanish *reconquista* and the Counter-Reformation. This Catholic reform movement did not really start until the reign of Albert and Isabella and took the whole 17th century to be realized. As was the case elsewhere, many exemplary bishops and abbots, the organization of seminaries, the activities of new religious orders (among them the Jesuits), and church participation in scholarship and science constitute basic aspects of the Catholic reform. Catholicism continued to be the established state religion, and there was no room for Protestants in Belgium until Joseph II's Act of Tolerance (1781). Belgian Catholicism and the religious situation in Belgium have been for three centuries determined by the 17th-century Counter-Reformation. Closely connected with this movement is Baroque art, which was so important in Belgium in fields such as architecture (Baroque churches), painting (Rubens!), and sculpture. In the 18th century, although painting does not offer names comparable to the old masters, Rococo and Classicist secular architecture deserve particular attention. In the intellectual sphere, on the other hand, the Austrian Netherlands made almost no contributions to the Enlightenment; the main influences came from France and Austria.

The Austrian sovereignty over the southern Netherlands, which started after the Peace of Utrecht and the Barrier Treaty (1713, 1715), constitutes a break with conservative Spain and a link to a more progressive Austria. During the 80 years of Austrian-Hapsburg sovereignty, Belgium suffered from only one foreign occupation (France, 1744–48).

Empress Maria Theresa's reign exists in Belgium's historical consciousness as a particularly happy era. Peace went hand in hand with economic renewal following the old industrial and commercial traditions.

Maria Theresa was a moderate enlightened monarch; her son, Joseph II, who was sovereign over the Austrian Netherlands from 1780 until 1790, was an even more outspoken enlightened despot. During an incognito visit to the country, he found its institutions outdated. His reform policy, which can be considered a general rehearsal of the French Revolution, led among other things to the abolishment of "obsolete" privileges and institutions. Since this was not appreciated by large segments of the population, resistance resulted in the Brabant Revolution (1789–90); the name of this revolution derives from the important part played by the province of Brabant in the struggle against reform. With the exception of Luxembourg, all the provinces of the Austrian Netherlands denied Joseph II's sovereignty and proclaimed their independence. This indicates how strongly, even in 1789, the union of the provinces still rested on a common sovereign and how, without him, each province or principality remained a separate small fatherland. But there was a more general consciousness as well. Inspired by the United States' Articles of Confederation, the former Austrian Netherlands (without Luxembourg) formed a Confederation of the United Belgian States and set up a "congress." Since the revolutionaries were divided, the conservatives eliminated the progressives, whose leaders fled to France. Within one year, Austrian authority and the Old Regime were restored.

In the neighboring prince-bishopric of Liège, revolution also broke out in 1789. Unlike the Brabant one, it was a progressive movement; it was directly influenced by the French Revolution and installed a democratic regime. But here, too, one year later the Old Regime was reinstated and the progressives had to flee to France. From this country came a new and lasting revolution.

Annexation by France and Union with the Netherlands, 1794–1830

The decapitation of Louis XVI and his Austrian wife, Marie-Antoinette, provoked the first Coalition War of Austria and Prussia against France (1791–97). During this war France occupied and annexed the Austrian Netherlands and Liège. Unlike the situation under Hapsburg sovereignty, under French rule the provinces of the southern Netherlands and Liège lost their autonomy and identity. France wanted the Belges and Liègeois to become Frenchmen and aimed at assimilation.

Society was, indeed, profoundly changed: the institutions of the Old Regime were abolished, church property was expropriated, French became the only official language, and the former autonomous provinces were replaced by nine departments, administrative divisions of a unitary state that almost coincide with the present-day nine Belgian provinces. These departments sent representatives to Paris, provided recruits for the never-ending French wars, and took advantage of the nascent Industrial Revolution and of all France as a market for Belgian products. Discontent was general, and conscription and religious persecution became the immediate causes of an anti-French uprising during the last months of 1798; this so-called Peasants War, confined almost entirely to the Flemish-speaking areas, was crushed in early December and was followed by new persecutions. Relief came after Napoleon Bonaparte's coup; a concordance between state and church was signed in 1801.

Napoleon's administration and dictatorship, however, ended in the catastrophes of Leipzig and Waterloo (1813, 1815), and France was reduced to its borders of 1791. However, 20 years of revolutionary reforms and frenchification left a lasting impression. Moreover, for the first time, the southern Netherlands and Liège had had a common history. That new whole was more and more called Belgique, a name that as a matter of fact originally was just an adjective. The large majority of the inhabitants of the *départments belgiques* had not wanted to be French. Although differences were noted between Belge flamand and Belge wallon, nobody at that time thought of a Flemish or a Walloon people; one just referred to two language groups. Much more important were the survival of the old provinces and of the old provincial consciousness and the new Belgian consciousness, which, however, was equally a continuation of general national sentiments already existing in the southern Netherlands in the 17th and 18th centuries. But the Congress of Vienna, drawing a new political map of Europe, decided, without consulting the population or without taking notice of the wishes of the inhabitants, to form out of the former Republic of the United Netherlands (Holland) and the former Austrian Netherlands and Liège (Belgium) an anti-French barrier: the United Kingdom of the Netherlands. This new kingdom was a constitutional monarchy and a unitary state. In this respect, too, there was no return to the Old Regime or to the boundaries of the old principalities.

The Belgians in the southern half of the kingdom never stopped causing troubles for the king, and large groups contested the amalgamation from the outset. Many Belgian Catholics did not accept the Constitution of 1814–15 due to its recognition of religious freedom. New difficulties with the Catholic church arose because of the king's education policy: elementary and secondary schools came largely under state control. In 1817 King William I founded three state universities: Ghent, Liège, and Leuven. The old university of Leuven had been suppressed by the French in 1797. The royal concern with education and the king's attention to industry and trade deserve appreciation. Mainly among industrialists but among anticlerical liberals as well, the king had strong supporters, the so-called Orangists. William I was less successful with his language policy, which aimed at the recognition of Dutch as the only official language in the Flemish provinces. The French-speaking bourgeoisie in these areas did not accept this unilingualism; moreover, many people, speaking only their particular Flemish dialects, considered Holland's the language of Protestantism and not really their own tongue. In addition, the population in the Walloon provinces felt threatened by the overwhelming Dutch-speaking majority in the kingdom.

The Belgian Revolution and Belgium's Independence

In the late 1820's, a new generation of Catholics (Liberal-Catholics) and liberals, in a common hostility to William and the Dutch, formed the so-called Union des oppositions (1828) aiming at a parliamentary regime and at the introduction of freedom of the press, association, religion, education, and language. King William gave in to the demands for liberty in education and language (1829–30), but refused to grant freedom of the press or to introduce a parliamentary regime. The Belgian bourgeois discontent coincided in 1830 with a bad harvest and the negative consequences of industrialization. In late August 1830 a proletarian upheaval broke out in Brussels, Liège, and Verviers; it was suppressed by the bourgeoisie, who used these events as a pretext to ask the king for an administrative separation between Holland and Belgium; but the king postponed his answer. Since Brussels remained a center of unrest and radical agitation, William I ordered an attack on the capital. There was heavy fighting by the lower classes during September 23–27 (the September Days); the royal army withdrew, and the whole south (including all of Limburg and all of Luxembourg) joined the revolution. A provisional government proclaimed Belgium's independence and called for the election of a congress on November 10, 1830. This congress confirmed independence, provided the country with a constitution, and chose a king. The Belgian constitution of 1831 was influenced by the French constitution of 1791, the Dutch one of 1814–15, and the French charter of 1830. Belgium became a parliamentary monarchy with ministerial responsibility and royal inviolability, and it was conceived as a unitary state composed of nine provinces; the constitution recognized the modern liberties of religion, education, association, meeting, press, and language. Actually, French became the only official language at the state level. The separation of church and state was another modern attribute. Freedom of education allowed the Catholic church to expand its school system.

An international conference at London recognized Belgium's independence (December 20, 1830), imposed a guaranteed and eternal neutrality (compare the southern Netherlands as a barrier in the late 17th and 18th centuries), agreed upon the provisional control by Belgium of all of Limburg and all of Luxembourg, and asked Belgium to accept Leopold of Saxe-Coburg-Gotha as its first king. Leopold I took the oath to the constitution on July 21, 1831 (Belgium's National Celebration Day). Not until 1838 did King William accept the loss of Belgium; in 1839 he agreed on the final peace treaty. According to this, Belgium had to cede to the Dutch king half of Limburg (present-day Dutch Limburg) and half of Luxembourg (the present-day Grand Duchy). This reduced Grand Duchy remained in a union with the king and the Netherlands until 1890; since then the Grand Duchy has been independent. Belgium (as well as Luxembourg since 1867) stuck to its imposed neutrality. The main threats to its independence came first from France (the Revolution of 1848; Napoleon III) and later from a unified Germany and pan-Germanism. In early August 1914, the army of the German (Second) Reich, one of the guarantors of a neutral Belgium, invaded the country.

Belgium's 19th century history followed the same broad lines as its European neighbors: industrialization (Belgium was the first on the Continent), bourgeois rule, the rise of a working class, social legislation, and expanding democracy. After a period of political Unionism in the 1830's and 1840's, the bourgeoisie, who alone had the right to vote for 60 years, split up into two parties that dominated Belgium's internal political life: the Liberal party (founded in 1846), which was increasingly anticlerical, and the Catholic party. The philosophical division became clearer after 1834, when two new universities were founded: the anticlerical Free University of Brussels and the Catholic University of Leuven (succeeding King William's state university in Leuven); the philosophical clash peaked when a radical liberal government (1878–84) dedicated itself to the realization of a lay state (the School War). In 1884 the Catholic party regained power, reversed the situation, and remained in power until World War I.

The Catholic governments in this period were confronted with proletarian upheavals (1886) and socialist extra-parliamentary opposition. In 1885 the Belgian Workers party was founded; however, under the ruling electoral system it remained without representation in parliament. Under socialist pressure, the first social legislation was introduced and a constitutional reform (1872–93) granted general male suffrage with multiple votes. In 1894 the Socialist party entered the Belgian parliament, and became the third so-called traditional and national party in modern Belgian society. The Catholic party got a Christian-democratic wing and Catholic trade unions were organized, especially in the Flemish provinces (where industrialization came later). Mechanization, industrial modernization, anticlericalism and socialism were earlier and more important in the Walloon industrial areas (heavy industry in Liège and Hainaut) than in the Flemish-speaking provinces where Ghent (textiles) was the only modern industrial center. A dynamic Wallonia had "poor Flanders" (potato famine in 1847 and succeeding years, intellectual decline, etc.) as its northern neighbor. In 1846 half of the Belgian population still earned its living in the agrarian sector; in the second half of the 19th century this situation changed radically along with major growth of the population. Between independence and the outbreak of World War I, Belgium's population nearly doubled.

Belgium was involved in 19th-century "imperialism" and colonialism, with King Leopold II becoming in 1885 the absolute sovereign of the Independent Congo State. The Congo was taken over by Belgium in 1908 and remained a colony until independence in 1960.

Belgian Consciousness and the Origins of Belgium's Biculturalism and Binationalism

Essentially the Belgian revolution was a national revolution confirming Belgium's separateness. The differences between the Flemish and the Walloon provinces during the Belgian revolution had little or nothing to do with Flemish or Walloon consciousness or with the existing Flemish and Walloon peoples' reacting in their own way. The battles of September 1830 took place mainly in Brussels and in the industrialized Walloon areas (not least in Liège, the former capital of the principality of Liège). Once the troops of William I withdrew from the Flemish-speaking provinces, these areas, where anti-Dutch feelings were even stronger, enthusiastically joined the revolution.

Unlike the United Kingdom of the Netherlands of 1815–30, the new Belgian state was not—or at least was far less—an artificial state. The southern Netherlands constituted a clear prefiguration of modern Belgium. Interpreting Belgium's early modern history as a succession of foreign dominations, the national historiography identified the country and its history with the principalities of the later Middle Ages. The 19th-century Belgians strongly believed in their nationality. Internationally, Belgium was recognized as a stable state, not least because of its economic strength. And yet 19th-century Belgium was the basis of present-day biculturalism and the binational state.

It was not surprising that after the Belgian, or anti-Dutch, revolution of 1830, and with a French-speaking upper class, French would be the official language of state even in unitary Belgium. The masses spoke mostly Flemish or Walloon dialects and had neither political rights nor socioeconomic power. However, Flemish remained the vehicle for elementary education and local administration, with the exception of the more important towns. During the decades following the imposition of the French language, a gradually increasing number of intellectuals in the Flemish provinces protested against the neglect of their Dutch (Flemish) mother tongue. Thus the Flemish movement was born. Primarily it was a struggle for official recognition of the Dutch language in Belgium; basically it remained an emancipation movement of Dutch-speaking Belgians. Belgian authorities accepted that Flemish movement as a literary movement and as a component of Belgian culture and identity, but rejected for several decades its political demands as unfounded or dangerous to Belgian unity.

But the Flemish movement was a political movement as well. In the years 1873–83 linguistic legislation introduced bilingualism in the Flemish areas; the French unilingualism of the Walloon provinces was not disputed. In fact, the system of regional bilingualism in the Flemish areas, which gradually took Flanders (with the new geographic content) as their common name, did not prevent the French-speaking upper class from continuing to use French. On the national level and for all major functions, the French language (which quantitatively never had a majority position in independent Belgium) maintained its exclusive position. With the Flemings constituting a majority in unitary Belgium, and Flemish speakers in Flanders representing more than 95 percent of the population, in the long run political democracy and general manhood suffrage around the turn of the century were to undermine bilingualism in Flanders. By 1900 the Flemish-speaking Belgians had to a large extent already acquired a consciousness of being or at least becoming a people. Never before in history had a Flemish people or a Flemish nation existed. So the Flemish movement gave birth to the present-day Flemish people, just as 19th-century independent Belgium gave birth to that movement.

In the 19th century, a Walloon movement also came into existence, but its context was quite different. For some decades the Walloon movement was a literary movement without, for obvious reasons, linguistic grievances against the Belgian state; it was interested in preserving and enriching Walloon linguistic patrimony and not in replacing French with Walloon. From the 1870's on, a political Walloon movement emerged because of the first linguistic laws, which in the eyes of Walloons foreshadowed obligatory and generalized bilingualism. If the Flemish movement originated as a revolt against official francophone Belgium, the Walloon movement originated as a reaction against legal concessions to the Flemish population. The Flemish movement was much less directed against the Walloon population or Wallonia as such. As long as the Walloons and other francophones could identify sufficiently with a Belgian unitary state (their state) and with prosperous industrial Belgium, Walloon consciousness remained weak. In the 1930's and even more after World War II, this changed profoundly.

Conclusion

Belgium's past offers a particularization and a mirror-image of European history and civilization. Belgium has, however, very distinct features and traits as well; without an appreciation of its history, modern Belgium does not seem understandable. In very different epochs indeed, Belgium came into existence as a name, as a country, and as an independent state, with very unnatural borders. History explains that Belgium's biculturalism is a recent phenomenon whereas the base of that ethnic diversity lies in Roman times. It also explains why Belgium ranks among the Roman Catholic countries. One sometimes reads that the nine Belgian provinces were created after the French annexation, about two centuries ago, but in fact these provinces and their names originated in medieval principalities. Nearly all Belgian towns were founded between the 10th and the 14th centuries; these towns not only constitute an ancient tradition of commerce and industry but have been centers of great culture and promoters of democratic ideals as well. Twenty centuries of history have left indelible traces among the Belgian people and in monuments throughout their country.

Belgium Since World War I

Herman Balthazar

World War I

Dialogue between the German kaiser and King Albert:
The kaiser: So you see—you've lost everything.
The king of the Belgians: Not my soul!

WORLD WAR I is still the most important turning point in European history, in all its aspects. The same is true for Belgium, which was recognized by the Great Powers as a neutral country in 1839, only to be dragged against its will into the worldwide conflict on August 4, 1914, because it would not accede to Germany's request to allow an attack on France through its territory.

Neither public opinion nor the army was adequately prepared for the sudden violence of the war, which had many civilian victims. On October 15, after German troops had occupied most of Belgium's territory, the bulk of the Belgian army took up positions in the extreme northwest of the country, behind the Ijzer river between Nieuwpoort and Ypres, where a cruel battle was fought with the help of the British and French troops and the German advance was halted. For four years, the Belgian front held, as part of a trench line from the North Sea to the Vosges.

The war had far-reaching consequences both at home and abroad. The measures taken by the Germans created a gulf between them and the native population in the 90 percent of the country they occupied. Apart from the occupying forces' discourtesy and their escalating claims on the population, there was economic disruption and the dismantling of a resolutely export-minded industrial nation. As agricultural production fell and food prices climbed, people lost their purchasing power, and more and more of them lost their jobs. In 1916, the hated compulsory service and deportation of workers were introduced. Hunger and poverty reigned. A National Assistance and Nutrition Committee

(NHVC) was formed as early as August 1914, with the impetus and the leadership coming from a number of prominent industrialists and bankers. This committee was assisted by a number of eminent Americans, notably Herbert Hoover, who founded the Commission for the Relief of Belgium (CRB). The psychological and material importance provided by the CRB was immeasurable. At home, the NHVC grew into a powerful shadow government and prepared the country for the postwar period. This reduced the impact of the Germans' *Belgienpolitik*, by which they sought to draw Belgium into their sphere of influence. But their somewhat vague *Flamenpolitik*, a policy aimed at satisfying a number of demands and desires of the Flemish population, was a time bomb. A small group of Flemish politicians collaborated with this German policy. This was one of the crucial factors in the postwar language conflict.

Nonetheless, the feeling of unity in Belgium had never been so strong, embodied as it was by the charismatic King Albert, leading the Belgian army on the Ijzer front. A book by King Albert, which came out in December 1914 and was distributed on a massive scale, gives a true picture of an almost mythological battle, propaganda being yet another characteristic of war. Thus suffering, struggling Belgium won increasing support in both the Allied and the neutral camp, especially in the United States, and was recognized as an independent nation after the Armistice, although not as the greater Belgium some nationalists had dreamed of achieving through annexation.

The Interwar Period, 1919–1940

The best way to evaluate Belgian domestic and foreign policy in the interwar years is to follow trends in western Europe as a whole. Until 1921, postwar reconstruction problems and fears of a social revolution claimed most attention. Monetary stability and the problems of economic recovery went hand in hand until 1926, when the great period of growth began, only to be transformed abruptly into depression in 1930. Things did not change until 1935, and then only in the direction of increasing tension in both international relations and the functioning of parliamentary democracy.

The Belgian economy emerged from the war greatly damaged. First, in addition to the destruction, for four years no investments in capital equipment were made, while elsewhere the processes of industrial innovation and relocation had accelerated. This was especially serious because Belgium was a leading exporter of manufactures, primarily in the traditional industries of the first industrial revolution. In addition, Belgians had made major investments abroad before 1914, mainly in central and eastern Europe, and these investments had become worthless as a result of the Russian Revolution. The total loss is estimated at 10 billion gold francs, or approximately one-fifth of national assets. A return to the prewar situation by a reduction in the quantity of money, which had increased fourfold, and in the national debt, which had risen sharply, was but a forlorn hope. Like the French, the Belgians were too confident in the miracle cure to be provided by German reparations.

Although a revival was not long in coming, financial and monetary problems continued to hamper recovery efforts until 1926. Nonetheless, the results achieved by 1929 were impressive: a 35 percent growth in GNP over 1920, an 80 percent increase in industrial production, and a 70 percent increase in foreign trade. During the same period, real wages rose by 35 percent, and people were making good money.

Overall, Wallonia continued to be by far the most important region in terms of industrial output, despite signs of recession. The Walloon coal mines, for instance, were in slow decline, whereas the production of the new mines in the Flemish area of Limburg was growing fast. The increased influence of the Congolese economy was also noteworthy. In 1920, 45 percent of its exports by value were still natural products. By 1939, this figure had fallen to just 7 percent, and the export value of mining products (copper, tin, diamonds) continued to grow. This gave rise to new industrial processes, for the most part in Flanders.

In this process of industrial change, the role of larger units arising out of mergers and of the banks became more important. Brussels was the center of this expansion. It was there that the heart of united Belgium beat, despite its many internal divisions and problems.

Postwar Belgium found itself in a whole new political landscape. Both the government-in-exile in Le Havre and leading circles in the occupied homeland had begun as early as 1916 to understand that the *Union sacrée* would no longer work without considerable social and political concessions. This meant that the Belgian Working Men's party had to be involved in political administration, and that universal suffrage, the freedom to organize trade unions, and new social legislation had to be considered. Another potential battleground was the language conflict. In general, the vast majority of Flemings supported king and country in 1914. Only a radical minority of *Flamingant* activists wanted independence for Flanders, with the help of the German occupying forces if necessary. But starting in 1916 a broader current of dissatisfaction and impatience could be detected among the Flemish, particularly at the front. Both the king and the government were too late and too repressive in reacting to this current. In analyzing the postwar situation, we must bear these social and Flemish problems in mind.

The first elections under universal manhood suffrage were held in 1919 (women did not obtain the vote until 1949). Three parties dominated the political stage: the older Catholic and Liberal movements, and the younger Socialist Working Men's party. Until 1936, these three parties garnered some 90 percent of votes, although none of them could do better than 40 percent nationally. Given the proportional representation system, coalition governments were a necessity. In Flanders the Catholic party generally won an absolute majority, and in Wallonia the Socialists were dominant. Only in Brussels did the relative strength of Catholics, Liberals, and Socialists vary. The Catholic party won 48 percent of the seats in Flanders as opposed to 38 percent in Wallonia and 14 percent in Brussels.

From November 1918 until 1940, Belgium was governed by eighteen different administrations. This number is in itself an indication of the political instability. During the difficult years of national reconstruction up to 1921, most administrations were governments of national unity (Catholics-Liberals-Socialists). The same formula was tried in the difficult years after 1935. For the most part, however, Belgium was ruled by Catholic-Liberal coalitions. This meant that socioeconomic problems and interests played a leading role in determining the composition of the coalitions. From 1830 until 1914, Catholics and Liberals had been on opposite sides, and the opposition between clerical and anticlerical forces had been the most important dividing line in the country. Although this was still the case after 1918, the phenomenon had less effect on the composition of coalitions, in which the royal house played a silent, but far from negligible, part.

A new aspect in the political picture was the role of Flemish radicalism. A Flemish Front party gained representation in the Lower House, with 5.2 percent of the votes, and the strength of the Flemish nationalist movement grew with every election, gaining 15 percent of the vote in 1939. It evolved from a pluralistic democratic front in the 1920's to a predominantly Christian and authoritarian movement in the 1930's. Its main electoral role was as a rival for the Catholic party, which also had a strong Flemish contingent in the Lower House.

Until 1926, the Socialist party was strong, well-structured, and aggressive. As well as winning new social rights, it had an integrating function. Until 1932, strikes were few and far between, social unrest unheard of.

After 1926, the language problem had a growing effect on political debate. The postponement, in some cases the outright refusal, of concrete demands, such as the conversion to the Dutch language of the University of Ghent (which did not take place until 1930), elicited powerful reactions. Flemish activism was so harshly condemned that many came to see it shrouded in a halo of martyrdom. The cohesion of the unitary Belgian state ebbed. This was the period during which the foundations of current political problems, *mutatis mutandis*, were laid. The only element missing from the interwar era is the Walloon movement, which, from its marginal beginnings, grew into the more popular and virulent *Wallingantisme* after 1960.

However, a reasonably satisfactory equilibrium continued to reign in politics and in other spheres of authority until 1932, when the drastic consequences of the economic crisis and deflationary policy began to take their toll. Unemployment shot up. Disquieting forms of social unrest, over which the organized labor movements had no control, began to occur, particularly in the older industrial districts of Wallonia. From 1934 on, the mixed banking system of Belgium encountered increasing difficulties in the granting of credits and direct involvement in firms.

These difficult years of crisis reached a peak in the 1936 elections, when the three largest parties, particularly the Catholics, suffered heavy losses to the Flemish Nationalist party (VNV) and to new, right-wing authoritarian parties (Rex, primarily in Brussels and Wallonia). The government came in for increasingly heavy criticism: everything was the fault of a weak parliament and of the excessive power of parties, unions, and bankers. Leadership and power became the motto. Many believed that the only solution was to be found in a corporate state; other felt that the king's authority should be reinforced.

The popular and almost legendary King Albert had tragically perished in a climbing accident in the Ardennes in February 1934. The young King Leopold III wished to pursue his father's basic program with vigor. The spirit of the age made him the most stable factor in society. This had considerable influence on a radically changing foreign policy, in which the king played a crucial supporting role. After 1918, Belgium abandoned its traditional neutrality. Looking primarily to France for military support, Belgium committed itself wholeheartedly to the new system of alliances and treaties. The growing atmosphere of crisis and tension in the 1930's brought a return to a policy of strict neutrality.

The king himself presented the guidelines of the new policy on October 14, 1936, and received the full backing of parliament. At the time, the policy was much disputed, especially after the fact. Independence implied distancing Belgium from a rapidly escalating series of events: the growing power of Hitler's Germany, the people's front and the civil war in Spain, rearmament, the colonial expansion of Italy, the persecution of Jews. This foreign policy inevitably had a destructive effect on domestic policy. Only the growing fear of war did away with the contradictions.

When war broke out on September 3, 1939, Belgium declared itself neutral and mobilized all troops to show that this neutrality would be defended dearly. But to no avail. On May 10, 1940, for the second time in a quarter-century, the Germans invaded Belgium.

World War II

The military campaign of May–June 1940 is deservedly known as the Blitzkrieg. Events moved swiftly, and a completely new situation took everyone by surprise. The generation in power, and public opinion as a whole, had little information on which to base perceptions and make decisions: there was the experience of 1914–18, the governmental crisis of the 1930's, and the overwhelming power of a Germany that had confidence in its own victory.

After an eighteen-day campaign, King Leopold III bowed to the inevitable and surrendered. The vast majority of the troops and the people as a whole were certainly relieved and thankful, although it was not clear what would happen next. An almost irreconcilable dispute now arose off-stage as to the king's character and actions. As far as the government was concerned, the function of constitutional head of state took precedence over that of commander-in-chief of the armed forces. This was the first of two areas of conflict concerning the interpretation of the constitution; the second, and more serious, revolved around Belgium's obligations to its allies. For the government, the surrender did not end the war or the country's commitments to France and the United Kingdom, the guarantors of its safety, but the king, as commander-in-chief, wished to remain with his troops and did not regard the new situation as signifying the end of the policy of independence. This implied that Belgium could negotiate its own fate with Germany "with a free hand." This conflict lay at the heart of the royal question, which was to plague the political climate until 1950.

Thus, in the midst of great confusion, a twofold policy, whose adherents were diametrically opposed, came into being. The Germans established a military government in occupied Belgium. Initially, this government was responsible for law and order only and was happy to allow Belgian institutions to function normally, insofar as they did not harm German interests. Besides, Germany did not yet have a blueprint for Belgium's future. The king and his entourage, and representative groups of civil servants, the church, banks, employers, and unions, were willing to accept this offer of normalization, with caution. There were many people who wanted to reorganize Belgian institutions, each seeing matters according to personal interests and preferences. This situation prevailed until the autumn of 1940.

For the government, which, along with tens of thousands of Belgians, had sought refuge in France, the situation became highly perilous. On the one hand, it had to face the painful fact of the breach with the king and public opinion in Belgium; on the other hand, there were the military collapse of France and the formation of Pétain's Vichy government. In its increasing isolation, the government became lost. The ministers disagreed over the path to follow. Originally only a minority pleaded for a government-in-exile in London, where a Belgian National Committee was created as early as June, following the Free French example. In July, matters became clearer, as Gutt and De Vleeschauwer, the ministers of finance and the colonies, went to London. It was of great importance to the Allies to have the economic potential of the Belgian Congo on their side, and this was one reason why the British were anxious to see a recognized and lawful political authority installed in London. After many difficulties and obstacles, a representative nucleus was finally set up in Eaton Square in October 1940. This decision contributed to Belgium's reintegration into the Allied camp as a recognized and respected member.

From the summer and autumn of 1940 on, occupied Belgium faced a choice between a policy of Belgian identity and unconditional collaboration with Germany. We must, however, avoid reasoning too schematically or too simplistically here. The occupying regime gradually became harsher and more merciless, and the totalitarian structure of Nazi Germany was complex. In addition to the military administration itself, the Nazi party and the SS made frequent intrusions into policymaking, seeking genuine supporters and rewarding them with benefits and influence. Thus the German authorities were vying with one another in a way to which many Belgians were initially blind. But after one year of occupation, the vast majority of the public and of those in authority had got the message, and resistance began to flourish everywhere. There were, however, those, in Wallonia as well as in Flanders, who were deeply committed to collaboration. The VNV, for instance, saw a political future for Flanders in a policy of active cooperation. In the confusion and power vacuum of the early months, they were only too eager to accept positions of authority, which they could hold onto only by increasing their commitment to collaboration. This was the second factor contributing to the Belgian language conflict.

World War II was a veritable ordeal by fire for Belgium. For the population as a whole, it meant a prolonged wage freeze, price inflation, rationing of the scanty food supply, a flourishing black market, the high cost of the occupying forces, forced labor first at home and then in Germany, racially and politically motivated deportations, increasing counterterrorist activities by the German police against resistance operations, and bombings.

Second, there was the complex phenomenon of collaboration. Immediately after the Liberation in September 1944, the public vented its rage. Between 1944 and 1949, the War Tribunals dealt with 405,000 cases. The vast majority were dismissed without action being taken, but the 58,000 guilty verdicts (33,000 of them in Flanders) had weighty consequences, particularly as regards their political and ideological aspects. Unjustly, but irresistibly in the spirit of the age, Belgian patriotism overwhelmed temporarily a number of continuing sources of tension. Patriotism was defined in one way only; this prevented a number of continuing sources of tension from being resolved.

From 1942 on, the London government was able to prepare for the postwar period with genuine authority, thanks in part to more frequent contacts with the resistance movements. Here too, however, the ideological character of the war played a part. The left-right polarization of the resistance movement was a decisive factor, particularly the increasing influence of the Communists. The talks between a representative cross-section of employers and the unions were nevertheless very fruitful. It was in these talks that, even before the Liberation, the basic charter was drawn up that was to serve as the government's point of departure for a new and satisfactory collective bargaining system.

In the end, the relationship between government and king was to prove the most intractable problem. On June 7, 1944, King Leopold and his family were whisked off to Germany. On September 19, 1944, the government returned from London. Parliament convened on September 20, and in the king's absence, appointed his brother, Prince Karel, as regent. Those in the know were aware that the king had not budged an inch from his declarations of 1940. Added to that was everything that had happened during four years of war. Belgium and its allies were clearly divided as to whether the king's return was desirable and whether it could contribute to national reconciliation. For five years, this was to be the theme of a passionate debate.

After 1945

The most confusing and incomprehensible aspect of Belgium is the country's political and institutional development. Other contributors to this work will elucidate these structures and deal more completely with economic and demographic evolution. However, this sketch of sociopolitical development since 1945 may supply perspective.

As a participant in the approaching Allied victory, the Belgian government in London rejected neutrality. This decision is still a feature of foreign policy. In London, and in a decisive phase of the postwar period, one man retained responsibility for foreign policy throughout several successive administrations. That man was P. H. Spaak, secretary-general of NATO from 1957 to 1961. Belgium took the initiative in the Benelux Treaty (September 5, 1944) and was one of the first signatories of the UN charter (June 26, 1945). It participated in the Bretton Woods conference (July 1945), took part in the Marshall Plan, joined the Organization for European Economic Cooperation (April 16, 1948), and was the host of, and a partner in, the Brussels Pact (March 17, 1948). Thus Belgium was from the very beginning one of the moving forces behind the foundation in 1949 of the Council of Europe, the European Coal and Steel Community (ECSC), and NATO. This foreign policy was of course determined by the international context, but it also grew out of the need to insert an export-oriented industrial country into an open supranational structure.

All in all, Belgian industry emerged from the war less damaged than it had been in 1918. A highly successful monetary operation, known as Operation Gutt, which involved cutting the money supply to one-third of its previous level, the immediate reopening of the port of Antwerp as soon as hostilities ceased, and above all the great demand for goods from export markets restored the Belgian economy back to its 1938 level as early as 1947. However, this was achieved with the old industrial infrastructure, with no investments in new capital goods and no correction of the considerable regional inequalities. These same shortcomings continued to be noticeable in the succeeding years, with sluggish growth until 1960. In 1958, as the Brussels World Fair displayed the glittering delights of the new consumer society, the Belgian economy was suffering from severe problems and weaknesses. At least 200,000 people were out of work, far too many workers, particularly in Flanders, had to commute, and, most serious of all, the irreversible decline of the old industrial base, especially coal and textiles, had begun.

The initial postwar social setting offered good prospects for a peaceful equilibrium between capital and labor. Underground contacts between employers' and workers' organizations had taken place during the war years. The regained confidence in parliamentary democracy was to be reinforced with a new approach to social peace. This implied a new qualitative leap toward a unified social security system, with equal membership on the new management-worker committees and collective bargaining.

The basic agreement was unveiled at the first National Labor Conference on September 16, 1944, before the first postwar government had even come into being. It was the basis for the act of December 28, 1944, that gave form to the new state social security system. This was the starting point for a succession of acts that created a complex institutional system in which the government, employers, and unions sought to regulate ever-growing areas of socioeconomic life. This practice of regulation and social pacification was a characteristic of the Belgian system. By 1972, the Central Economic Council knew of no less than 156 different socioeconomic bodies where management and workers met.

When the Pierlot administration returned to Brussels in an RAF plane on September 8, 1944, Allied forces had already liberated more than half of Belgium within a week, moving so quickly that resistance groups had made almost no active contribution. This was of great significance, since the resistance movements, although deeply divided, considered themselves to have priority in forming the government of the newly liberated country. The influence of, and support for, the Communist party had grown to significant proportions in the resistance.

On September 27, Pierlot formed the first postwar cabinet of national union, in which he included, in addition to prominent Catholics, Liberals, and Socialists, two Communists and the leader of the left-wing Independence Front. For months, this administration sought stability in difficult and uncertain circumstances. The final elimination of the resistance as a political factor took place after a demonstration in Brussels got out of hand on November 25, 1944.

On December 16, 1944, the Battle of the Bulge got under way in the Ardennes, and for several weeks the situation was perilous. In addition to the internal political and economic difficulties, this provided the Allied Supreme Command with another reason to hope for a more stable administration. The Socialist Achiel Van Acker seemed the best man to reconcile the hopes for change with the necessity of pursuing the war effort because of his powerful and authoritative pragmatism. His government of national union, which also included Communists, took office on February 12, 1945. In the intervening period, the traditional political groupings had started renovating themselves and were on the lookout for programs that would win them a foothold in public opinion.

Tragically enough, the theme that polarized public opinion most effectively was the royal question, which blew up again on May 7, 1945, when it was announced that the U.S. 7th Army had encountered the royal family near Salzburg and taken them under its protection. On June 16, the Van Acker administration tendered its resignation on the grounds that it could not accept responsibility for what would happen if the king were to return immediately. The lines of battle began to take shape. The former Catholic party restructured itself as the Christian Socialist party (CVP/PSC), with the aim of uniting all social groups. A vast majority of its members formed the "king's party," which favored a referendum on the king's return. Their partners in the government wanted to have parliament settle the matter.

The first legislative elections, on February 17, were completely dominated by the royal question. This very polarization contributed to the victory of the old political groupings. The Walloon-Flemish division was every bit as pronounced as before 1940. The Catholics won 42.4 percent of the vote and dominated in Flanders; the Socialists' score was 31.5 percent, and they were stronger in Wallonia.

Apart from a temporary drop in support for the Liberals (8.9 percent), there were two new factors: the disappearance of Flemish nationalism as an autonomous power in politics and the rapid rise of the Communist party. We will return to the Flemish problem later. The Communists came out of the war greatly strengthened, but lost ground very quickly. By 1950, they were already down to less than 5 percent, and their support was to dwindle further into the marginal presence of the 1980's.

In 1950, the royal question was finally solved, after a nonbinding referendum, which was held under extremely difficult conditions. The result was indecisive: 57 percent of the participants voted for Leopold III's return. In Flanders 72 percent were in favor, in Brussels 48 percent, and in Wallonia only 42 percent. Amid serious disturbances, Leopold III came home, but he soon asked parliament to vest his prerogatives in his son Baudouin. This reconciled all political tendencies with the crown.

Nonetheless, the polarization engendered by the royal question continued to make itself felt and almost immediately became linked to the oldest political division in Belgium, that between the clerical and anticlerical camps. This time, the old school problem was the target. The Liberals and Socialists defended the state schools, and the Catholics fought for Catholic education, known as free education. For eight years, the school question remained one of the principal electoral themes: during four years of a CVP administration (1950–54), then, even more severely, during four years of a Liberal-Socialist administration (1954–58). Here too the conflict ended in a compromise, the School Pact, signed by the three main national parties on November 16, 1958.

In the meantime, a new age had dawned, both at home and abroad. Foreign policy is covered in Part II. The new domestic tensions were both socioeconomic and "communitarian," i.e., the Flemish-Walloon conflict.

Belgium too was part of the Golden Sixties. From 1960 to 1973, GNP grew an average of 5 percent per year, and the growth in industrial production was sometimes spectacular. New investments flooded in, as part of a fast-growing internationalization, or multinationalization. This was partly the result of economic conditions, but it also was due to the determined pursuit by successive administrations of a policy first seen in the 1950's. Great efforts were made to set up a new infrastructure of highways, waterways, and port installations. The initiatives taken in a series of economic expansion acts were even more significant. Belgium had developed a consultation economy, in which the role of the administration was subsumed in the social consultation system created at the end of 1944. More than ever before, the social partners, employers and unions, were involved in decision making at the ministerial level, and parliament was assigned a secondary role, as a kind of rubber stamp.

This remarkable expansion was by no means smooth. During the winter of 1960–61, a massive and savage strike broke out, centering in Wallonia. The effects of the overhasty decolonization of the Congo, Rwanda, and Burundi made themselves felt, although the economy was not hit too hard, between 1959 and 1964. The increased control and institutionalization of medical consumption led to a spectacular strike by doctors in 1966. Moreover, starting in 1960, the language and "communitarian" conflict began to occupy the center stage.

Overall, it is undeniable that Flanders had been afforded relatively few opportunities linguistically, culturally, economically, educationally (at the university level), and scientifically. This was the fundamental cause of the birth of the Flemish movement and its growing political impact from 1870 on. We have already explained why this process slowed after 1918, and how it broke loose with even greater force ten years later, to give rise to a series of fundamental language acts in the 1930's. *Mutatis mutandis*, the same process was repeated after 1944. Other areas were given priority in the postwar reconstruction, and many people found it easy to consider the Flemish movement a phenomenon of collaboration with the Nazis. As early as 1954, a new Flemish nationalist party, known as the Volksunie, appeared in parliament. But outside parliament too, in pressure groups and in the Flemish sections of the major parties (initially the CVP in particular), the voice of the Flemish movement gained volume. Paralleling this trend was the increasing economic and demographic pressure from Flanders, in contrast to an opposite tendency in Wallonia, which was aggravated by the structural decline of the old basic industries. From 1960 on, a broad-based movement developed in Flanders to protest changes in the language boundary and the increasing frenchification of the Brussels "oil slick," to press for a redistribution of parliamentary seats, and so on. The same year saw the great social upheavals that gave birth to a more virulent strain of Walloon nationalism in protest against the decline of Wallonia and Flemish predominance. The Belgian unitary state was caught in the cross fire. Attempts to provide regional economic stimuli generated a climate of rivalry, with each region trying to outbid the other. No attempt has as yet been made to take stock of these measures in an objective and noncontroversial fashion. If, for instance, we try to gauge the results of the various support initiatives taken during the 1960's in terms of their effect on job creation, Wallonia, with more funds allocated, achieved less because defensive and rationalization measures absorbed more of the funds than in Flanders.

From October 1962 on, the Lefèvre-Spaak administration (CVP-BSP) decided to attempt to quell the disturbance by means of a constitutional amendment. From that moment on, Belgian political life was subjected to continuous communitarian tension. In 1965, the major national parties split into Flemish and Walloon wings. In 1971, language-based parties like Volksunie (Flanders and Brussels), Front des francophones (Brussels), and Rassemblement wallon (Wallonia) achieved their highest score of 22.3 percent of the vote. Although these language-based parties lost much of their support in the next few years, the search for equilibrium made it much more difficult to achieve a coherent administration and to see what was going on in the day-to-day workings of the institutions. It is nonetheless noteworthy that the three great political families—Catholics, Liberals, and Socialists—retain the allegiance of more than 80 percent of the electorate, just as they did in 1918, and have done ever since, and that they are still the only constant coalition members. After two constitutional amendments in 1970 and 1980, the Belgian state has undoubtedly acquired a new, irreversibly regionalized structure. This structure is explained elsewhere in this book. Meanwhile, the consensus view is that the reform of the state is not yet complete. It is difficult to predict the future evolution of this process, but it will surely be influenced by other than purely communitarian considerations.

Belgian National Sentiment

Jean Stengers

Misconceptions About Belgian Nationalism

IN FOREIGN COUNTRIES, especially in France, Belgium has often been considered an artificial state with no real nationality—that is, with no real national identity or national will. The will behind the origin of Belgium, it has been thought, was that of the Great Powers, which decided in 1830 that to avoid annexation by France, Belgium had to become an independent state.

This view is not hard to explain. In common opinion, a nationality, to be recognized as such, generally needs two characteristics, or at least one of two. Since the 19th century, one has been prepared to see a nationality wherever there is a common language. In the nineteenth century, this criterion was so important that the "principle of nationalities" came to be interpreted mainly as the right of people united by a common language to be politically united and independent. One is also prepared to recognize as a nation a people that have long lived in an independent state with an independent life. When one thinks of the French nation, one is more impressed by its great history than by the bonds created by the French language. Preferably, the two characteristics are present simultaneously. Nobody has any doubts about the British nation or—bordering Belgium —the Dutch nation.

But Belgium does not seem to have either of the characteristics required. It has no common language; in fact, there is no language barrier at all between southern Belgium (Wallonia) and France. Furthermore, the Belgians were never independent before 1830. They just passed from one foreign regime to another—the Spanish regime, the Austrian regime, the French regime, the Dutch regime. That does not denote a nation.

Such is the very general view long prevalent among foreign observers.

One could compile a very long anthology of statements about Belgium that cruelly underline its lack of nationality. This anthology is now being enriched by statements from Belgium itself. Many Belgians, from both Flanders and Wallonia, consider that Belgium was created quite artificially in 1830. They generally add—and this is typical of the Belgian view—that what happened in 1830 was that Flemings and Walloons were compelled by the will of the Great Powers to live together in one state. To the idea of the artificial character of Belgium, which is a very old idea indeed, has now been added the idea that there have long been two "natural" groups, the Flemings and the Walloons, that were artificially herded together.

From a historian's point of view, all these interpretations are total misconceptions. The basic misconception is that Belgium lacked a national life prior to the nineteenth century. It must be admitted with some shame that this misconception has long been encouraged by the very words of the Belgian national anthem. The *Brabançonne*, as it has been sung since 1860 (when a new *Brabançonne*, with the old music but with new words, was introduced) begins with the words:

Après des siècles d'esclavage,
Le Belge sortant du tombeau . . .
[After centuries of slavery,
The Belgian, rising from the grave . . .]

Thus Belgium enjoys the dubious privilege of having a national anthem that is a total distortion of history. It is, I am afraid, a rather unique case.

Nation-building Before 1815

I use the term "total distortion" because the idea of foreign rule (*dominations étrangères*), which is rendered poetically in the *Brabançonne* by "slavery," is a legend. Belgium in the 16th, 17th, and 18th centuries had rulers who lived outside the country (the sovereigns of Spain and later of Austria), but these were in the eyes of the Belgians their *princes naturels*, their legitimate sovereigns, the legitimate heirs of the dukes and counts of the various principalities of the Middle Ages. Apart from some high officials from the outside sent by the sovereign, the whole system of administration, justice, police, and so on had a national character. The idea of foreign oppression was absent from the minds of the inhabitants of the various principalities. What they saw before them and what was essential to them was their principality—their province, as it came to be called—with its own administration, and above the various provinces, the common institutions of what was virtually a state.

It is because there virtually was a state that out of that state a nation appeared. This was the natural process of nation-building under the Old Regime. Wherever there was a state, the people who lived together in that state and had the same political destiny came to consider themselves a "we-group" with common characteristics, a group apart, a nation. The most venerable European nations have no other origin. The French nation grew out of the French state. Before they were annexed to France, the populations who lived outside that state—for instance, those of Artois, Flanders, or Franche-Comté, or of Arras, Lille, or Besançon— were strongly anti-French. The French nation was simply a product of the foreign policy of the kings of France.

What happened in Belgium happened strictly according to this general European pattern of nation-building. After the unification of the Low Countries in the 15th and first half of the 16th centuries under the dukes of Burgundy and under Charles V, the state of the Seventeen Provinces corresponded roughly to what are now Holland, Belgium, and the Grand Duchy of Luxembourg. In that state emerged a national feeling that covered the whole of the Seventeen Provinces. The "patriots" who fought in the religious revolution of the second half of the 16th century celebrated the Netherlands—that is, the Seventeen Provinces—as their cherished homeland. Thus the struggle that developed at the end of the century between the north (which had gained complete independence) and the south (which remained Catholic and under the Spanish king) was felt and described by contemporaries as a "civil war," a war between brethren of the same nation.

This changed in the 17th century, when the two new states, that of the north and that of the south, were strongly established. Two new national feelings grew out of the two new states. The Belgian national feeling, which arose in the south, can best be perceived at the end of the 18th century, at the time of the so-called Brabant Revolution, which was a general revolt against the Austrian emperor Joseph II. The Belgians took to arms against a prince whom they considered a tyrant—not, it must be stressed, against foreign oppression. None of the innumerable pamphlets of the Brabant Revolution is directed against foreign oppression, nor did the revolutionaries sing anything resembling the future *Brabançonne* of the 19th century.

But what appeared in the pamphlets, in the songs, at every corner, one might say, of the revolution, was a solid belief in the strength, virtues, and glory of the Belgian nation, a proud nation, which, by ridding itself of a tyrant, gained national self-government. This psychological aspect sometimes escaped the analysis of historians because they saw the Brabant Revolution as a rather ridiculous effort that collapsed because of the political incompetence of the revolutionaries and their petty divisions.

Even if this was in no way a "glorious revolution," it was most certainly a national revolution. What was said about the Belgians in some pamphlets amounted to a decidedly chauvinistic form of nationalism. "The industrious Belgian nation," one of these pamphlets reads, "has filled the earth with its glory and its might. It always gloriously repelled the attacks of its most formidable neighbors and made them tremble sometimes in their very homes. The Belgians always defended the rights and the glory of their sovereigns." One sees how far we are from the idea of a continuous foreign oppression.

Unfortunately, the talent and the organization of the revolutionaries did not equal their bombast, and the revolution proved a total failure. But without any doubt its inspiration had been a national one.

When they became French citizens—and they were French citizens for two decades (1795–1814)—the Belgians did not forget that they were a special human group, a people with their own characteristics. In 1807, when a local society of poets—a so-called *chambre de rhétorique*—organized a competition for the best piece of poetry on "the Belgians," it met with great success. The competitors, who came from all parts of Belgium, rivaled each other in praise of their countrymen. One of the competitors, a Flemish poet, wrote: "As far as perfection still exists in our world, the Belgians are the people nearest to it, and from century to century they come nearer and nearer. Who can compare with the Belgian under the vault of heaven? He has no equal, except himself." A competition of that kind had the full approval of the authorities. This means that it did not appear in any way to be anti-French. The Belgians had a right to commemorate their past glory and to celebrate their virtues just as the Bretons or the Burgandians were entitled to celebrate Brittany or Burgundy. A striking reminder of this is that the first *Histoire de la Belgique*, in seven volumes, was published in 1805–7. Its author was an official of the French regime, the *sous-préfet* of Saint-Hubert in southern Belgium.

Nation-building, 1815–1830

When the Belgians were united with the Dutch in the Kingdom of the Netherlands, which lasted from 1815 to 1830, they felt more Belgian than ever. Two centuries of separate life had made the Belgians and the Dutch two separate peoples, each considering the other as foreign. They were separated by religion and even, to a large degree, by language, because half of Belgium was French-speaking—as were, in addition, the upper classes in the Flemish part of the country. They were still more separated by a feeling of otherness: the other was different.

Fifteen years of life in common did not lead to any fusion of the populations; on the contrary, it led to a growing opposition between the Belgians and the Dutch. This is a case where the state did not work as a nation-building instrument. It did not work because the Belgians did not consider the state as *their* state but as a Dutch state: the king was a Dutchman, the majority of the high officials were Dutch, the government measures most resented in Belgium were supported by the Dutch deputies in the House of Representatives. The idea of "domination," which had not been present in the Old Regime, now came to the front: the Belgians considered themselves dominated by the Dutch. This is the fundamental and simple explanation of the Belgian Revolution of 1830.

The fusion of the populations, an "amalgam," had been the great purpose and hope of King William I. It failed signally. But what William helped to create was another kind of amalgam he had not foreseen—namely, an amalgam between the Belgians and Liégeois. When we discuss Belgian national feeling at the time of the Brabant Revolution at the end of the 18th century, we use the word "Belgian" as it was used at the time, but the Belgium of that time did not correspond strictly to the Belgium that was to become an independent state in 1830. It did not comprise the territory of the episcopal principality of Liège, which was governed by the prince-bishop of Liège and had a separate political status. This principality covered about one-sixth of what is now the Walloon part of Belgium, as well as the greater part of what is now the Flemish province of Limburg. The inhabitants were not Belgians: they were Liégeois. They had a national feeling of their own.

After the fall of the French empire in 1814, when the future of the liberated territories was discussed, the discussion involved the future destinies of Belgians *and* Liégeois. In 1814 the distinction had still been present. By 1830 it had completely disappeared. The former Liégeois joined the Belgians' opposition against the Dutch. They were in one camp against the other. In 1830 they had simply become Belgians. In this way, which certainly did not correspond to King William's wishes, the Kingdom of the Netherlands was actually nation-building.

1830: National Revolution and Independence

The Belgians rose up in 1830 as a nation. This is clear and obvious to anyone who has studied the documents of the time. When the son of King William I, the Prince of Orange, addressed a manifesto to the

Belgians in 1830 in an effort to be accepted by them as their ruler, he declared that the movement that had developed in Belgium (he euphemistically used the term "movement" rather than revolution) would lead to a new state of things "to which nationality would give its force." Thus the son of the king bowed to the Belgian nationality.

This national revolution was in no way—and this is the primary erroneous interpretation of it—a beginning, the beginning, the birth of a nation. It was the explosion of a national feeling that had old and deep roots. It was, from a national point of view, an outcome.

In some respects, 1830 appears as a repetition—but a successful repetition this time—of the unhappy Brabant Revolution. The Belgians of 1830 bore many resemblances to their forefathers of 1789. For instance, they often appeared as proud and even as vain. They described themselves throughout the revolution with the highest praise: they were (they said) the bravest and most virtuous people possible. This self-esteem was undoubtedly, just as it had been at the time of the Brabant Revolution, a naïve but true mark of nationality. The difference was that this time there was much better organization and much more political competence. The Belgians of 1830 worked out a constitution that was to become a model for liberal Europe: their pride, in that respect, was not wholly unjustified.

Self-praise, let us finally observe, was poured out upon Belgium and the Belgians. It never went to Flemings or Walloons. The terms *Flamands* and *Wallons* existed in 1830, but they did not correspond to any collective sentiments. National feeling reigned supreme and without competitors.

Nationalism in the 19th Century

This remained true for many years to come. Belgium in the 19th century had a very strong and coherent national consciousness. Obviously the strength of national feeling cannot be measured with delicate scales. A delicate measurement would necessitate a distinction among the social classes, the regions, and the like. This is difficult. However, if one sticks to the general dimensions of the phenomenon of nationalism, the signs in Belgium were quite clear.

A first sign was the development of a national mythology, which is almost a necessary accompaniment to national convictions. This was apparent, for instance, in 1860 in the new words of the Belgian national anthem. I have already quoted the beginning of the *Brabançonne* ("After centuries of slavery, the Belgian, rising from the grave"). What follows is:

A reconquis par son courage
Son nom, ses droits et son drapeau.

[Has recovered by his courage,
His name, his rights and his flag.]

These words call forth the idea of a Belgian people who had already asserted their national personality in a distant past (some said as distant as Roman times because Caesar had praised the courage of the Belgians), had later been enslaved, and had finally revived. This mythology led to long dissertations showing how the Belgian national character had remained true to itself since the earliest ages. It was confirmed in some ways by the work of Belgium's greatest historian, Henri Pirenne. Pirenne was too good a historian—actually he was a very great one—to attach any importance to the *Brabançonne* or to dissertations about the permanence of the Belgian national character. Unlike many of his contemporaries, for instance, he never used the phrase *l'âme belge* (the Belgian spirit). But his thesis was that Belgium was created out of a common civilization whose characteristics were already evident in the Middle Ages. Thus he too ascribed very old roots to the nation. It now appears that this scholarly thesis is questionable, to say the least, but it undoubtedly contributed to the national mythology.

A second clear sign of nationalism was the rage with which the Belgians tried to preserve their national integrity. I refer here mainly to the tragedy of 1839. When in 1839 King William of the Netherlands accepted the conditions set forth eight years before by the Great Powers for the independence of Belgium—which he had refused to do until then—Belgium had to evacuate the provinces that today are the Grand Duchy of Luxembourg and Dutch Limburg. Both provinces had taken part in the 1830 revolution and—except for the towns of Luxembourg and Maastricht—had since then been part of Belgium. The inhabitants had not (as one is inclined to say now) "joined" the Belgians; they *were* Belgians. There was no difference of heart between a man of Echternach in the present Grand Duchy and a man of Arlon in the present Belgian province of Luxembourg; there was no difference between a man of Roermond, in the present Dutch Limburg, and a man of Hasselt, in the present Belgian province of Limburg. All these Belgians, just as the people of Alsace-Lorraine would do in 1871, ardently begged to remain in their fatherland. What speaks for the strength of the national feeling is that a large number of Belgians were prepared to go to war to save these compatriots. Reason finally prevailed, and the two provinces were abandoned, but only after a real national tragedy.

It is interesting to note that 80 years later, in 1919, Belgium, as one of the victorious countries in the Great War, saw a chance to recover the two provinces lost in 1839. Many Belgian nationalists sincerely believed that

Belgian feeling was still present among their inhabitants as it had been 80 years before, and that in Echternach, just as in Roermond, people would be happy to rejoin the former fatherland. They were surprised and shocked to discover that the people of the Grand Duchy considered themselves Luxembourgeois and no longer Belgians at all, and that the people of Dutch Limburg were now faithful Dutch patriots. The state, once again, had been a nation-builder.

A third significant sign of Belgian nationalism in the 19th century was the unanimous reaction of the population against any foreign threat. The threat, in the middle of the century, came mainly from France, especially from Napoleon III. The whole Belgian population, without exception, fervently declared that it was Belgian and would resist any foreign encroachment.

What must be stressed here above all is that at least until the end of the 19th century, all political reasoning was in terms of national interests, Belgium being considered as a whole, and that Flanders and Wallonia had very little place in that political reasoning. Let me cite only one example, which is, I think, very striking: the results of the general elections of 1894. These elections were the first following major constitutional changes in 1893. The changes included the introduction of a universal male franchise, as well as a system of plural voting that gave supplementary votes to some categories of citizens. Universal franchise meant that for the first time the Socialists would be in a position to enter Parliament. But if the suffrage had been changed, the system of balloting had not. It remained a majority poll (proportional representation was not introduced until 1899). As a result, in most districts of the country, *all* the seats of the district went to the same party—that is, to the party that won the majority. In Flanders and in the district of Brussels, 100 percent of the seats were captured by the Catholic party, which won an overall majority. The Socialists, on the other hand, captured most of the seats in the industrial districts of Wallonia.

Nowadays such a result would provoke fierce reactions, for it would appear to be a Flemish victory and a Walloon defeat. Nothing of the kind happened in 1894. The political comments of the time focused only on the parties—Catholics, Socialists, Liberals (the last having been squeezed between the other two)—and not on the differences between north and south. Practically no Walloon voice was heard complaining about a "Flemish victory." In other words, all the political reasoning took place along *national* lines. This was a clear proof of the moral cohesion of the country.

Belgian nationalism probably reached an apex in 1914, when the German invasion provoked an outburst of patriotic rage and enthusiasm. The king, Albert I, appeared as the symbol of a proud, united, morally strong nation.

The Birth of Flemish National Sentiment

Unity, however, did not remain absolutely intact during World War I. The Belgian nation witnessed the emergence in its midst, in what was still at that time a very small minority, of a real competitor: a Flemish nation. This marked the emergence of Flemish versus Belgian nationalism. For the first time in Belgian history, language, and not the state, was to be a nation-builder. This development of linguistic nationalism paralleled developments throughout Europe, but it was in some ways quite peculiar.

For one thing, the development in Flanders was unusually slow. The motto *De tael is gansch het volk* (A language is the total identity of a people) was coined in Flanders in 1834. Generally in Europe, once such a motto appeared, linguistic nationalism soon followed. In Flanders, however, it took several decades before the logical consequences of the motto were apparent—before some began to give preference to Flemish identity above everything else. According to the European model, linguistic nationalism should already have developed in Flanders by the middle of the 19th century. Actually there was a long delay. This may be explained by a social factor. Wherever linguistic nationalism developed in Europe, it found its most enthusiastic supporters among the intellectuals and the middle classes. But in Flanders, precisely these classes had become largely French-speaking. Thus most of those who were the usual supporters of the movement elsewhere in Europe did not support it in Flanders and, what is more, insofar as they spoke French, they even opposed it. That caused the delay.

By definition, linguistic nationalism can be expected to develop fundamentally along linguistic lines. Since the differences between Flemish and Dutch are for the most part minor (it is fundamentally the same language), one would logically have expected linguistic nationalism to extend over the Flemish-Dutch linguistic area as a whole. However, this did not happen. The phenomenon developed and was contained inside the frontiers of Belgium: it was Flemish nationalism only. The groups who in the 20th century tried to give to their linguistic nationalism a wider and more logical scope by advocating the political unity of Flanders and Holland did not meet with any popular response. In its propaganda in the 1930's, the Vlaamsch Nationaal Verbond (VNV) used the Greek character delta as a symbol of the unity of the peoples living along the great rivers flowing to the sea. This never aroused any enthusiasm. All the enthusiasm went to the Lion of Flanders.

This is easy to understand too. The struggle for the Flemish cause, for the rights of the Flemish language, occurred within the frontiers of Belgium. It was within these frontiers that the Flemish militants lived and worked and met with success or defeat. Their united efforts gave them a growing group consciousness. Since they encountered strong opposition to their demands, a number of them came to regard the Belgian state as their enemy. Nonetheless, it was that state that molded their group consciousness; they had espoused its frontiers. In this case, where a nation developed within a nation, the state was still a nation-builder.

Logically, once the linguistic and political frontiers had become salient, two parallel linguistic nationalisms should have developed: one Flemish and one Walloon. But nothing of the kind happened. For a long time, only a Flemish national consciousness was present, and it grew stronger and stronger, whereas in the Walloon part of the country, Walloon feeling remained very vague, except in limited circles.

What are the reasons for this unequal development? There are many. The ideology of *De tael is gansch het volk*, which was of German origin, more easily penetrated the Germanic part of Belgium. Linguistic nationalism, on the other hand, is necessarily cultural nationalism; but it was difficult for the Walloons to assert their own culture because they prided and glorified themselves on being heirs and partakers of the great French civilization. Above all, the key word is the one we used above: *struggle*. It was through the Flemish struggle that the Flemish nation was born. There was no parallel Walloon struggle because for a long time Walloons simply supported traditional Belgium and reacted, in the name of Belgium, against Flemish demands. Indeed for a time, the main grievance of the Walloons and the French-speaking Belgians against the leaders of the Flemish movement was that they were grievously betraying Belgium. This criticism in the name of Belgium was not a way to Walloon nationalism.

In the 20th century, Flemish national consciousness has progressively taken precedence over Belgian national feeling. At the time of World War I, a Flemish militant wrote: "We are Flemish first, and after that Belgian. Flemish we are by nature and by decree of God. Belgian we are only by a political pact." Seventy years ago, this was the conviction of only a minority. Except for the reference to the decree of God, today in Flanders it is the conviction of the great majority.

This means that, just as happened in the case of Belgian nationalism, Flemish nationalism has produced its mythology, and that mythology is now an integral part of the national consciousness. To hail Flanders and the Flemish people as "natural" and to consider Belgium as merely a political construction is self-contradictory since Flanders was originally only a by-product of Belgium. It is irrational indeed. But almost everywhere in the world, irrationality is one of the main elements of nationalism.

Contemporary Nationalism

To try and summarize in a few words the present situation is a rather bold, and even risky, attempt. At present in the country three coexisting national symbols, three flags, exist: the Belgian tricolor flag, the Flemish flag with the Lion of Flanders, and the flag with the Walloon cock, which is the flag of the whole French-speaking community. This means that it is the emblem of the French-speaking inhabitants of Brussels, the majority of whom do not consider themselves Walloons.

The impact of these three emblems could be described succinctly as follows. The Belgian flag means most to the francophones of Brussels (who, when they are not Walloons, are rather indifferent to the Walloon cock); it means much to most Walloons, who often see themselves as victims of the predominance of the Flemings in the Belgian state and sometimes profess that a "Belgian-Flemish" state cannot be their true fatherland, but who nevertheless remain in most cases true—if somewhat disillusioned—Belgians at heart. Among the Flemings, the Belgian flag still has a real significance for the older generations, but among the younger generations it no longer arouses, in a majority of cases, any real emotion; it appears as the emblem of a state that offers the Flemings only a convenient political framework for their development. These are naturally only general tendencies, and one could point to young Flemings who are still really devoted, emotionally speaking, to Belgium; but they are not characteristic of their generation.

For the majority, the real national emblem is the Flemish flag: it is the emblem of the Flemish nation, to which they feel they belong, and which they currently call *ons volk*, "our people." Their emotions are related to *ons volk*. The Flemish community has not only its flag, but also its national anthem—the *Vlaamse Leeuw*, the Lion of Flanders—and, like every authentic nation, its intangible frontiers. Hence the determined will to keep tiny bits of territory like the celebrated Voeren (les Fourons in French). One could say that little of what is "Belgian," even if it continues to have a strong impact, is still considered "sacred." But many aspects of the Flemish identity are "sacred."

The flag with the Walloon cock is "sacred" only for a tiny minority, which sometimes makes much noise but does not represent much. There still is no real Walloon nationalism. But the flag is nevertheless a symbol too: the symbol of the solidarity of the French-speaking Belgians, who think it is necessary for them to be united in order to counterbalance the strength of the Flemish community.

Belgium is not at present a country containing two nations. Inside the Belgian nation are two linguistic communities, one of which is a nation.

PART II

International Policy

André de Staercke, Coordinator

Introduction: From Compulsory Neutrality to Multilateral Commitments

André de Staercke

FEW BELGIANS REMEMBER the names of their country's ministers for foreign affairs between 1830 and 1914—from the date of Belgium's independence to World War I—for obvious reasons. As an independent state, Belgium was guaranteed perpetual and compulsory neutrality by those powers interested in its independence. These powers either had accepted this neutrality or had, to varying degrees, resisted it. Therefore the concerns of Belgium's ministers for foreign affairs during this period were restricted to (1) protecting Belgian citizens, (2) promoting Belgians' interests, and (3) safeguarding Belgium's neutrality.

Through the institution of the monarch, Belgium was nonetheless able to play an effective role in international politics. The nation's first king, Leopold I, ascended the throne in 1831. Leopold I was a member of the ruling family of the small German duchy of Saxe-Coburg-Saalfeld, which, following the complexities of inheritance connected with the breakup of Germany, became Saxe-Coburg-Gotha. The eighth child in a large family, Leopold enrolled in the Russian army and served with distinction during the Napoleonic wars. In 1816, he married Charlotte, Princess of Wales and heir to the British throne. She died a year after their marriage, leaving the future king a widower.

Shortly after ascending the throne, the king realized that it was better for the Belgian people to be allowed the greatest possible measure of self-government. With this in mind, he was able to give full scope to his talents and personality, particularly in the area of foreign policy. Europe's monarchical system provided him opportunities to make foreign alliances through the skillful handling of his family's royal marriages.

Leopold himself remarried, this time to Louise-Marie d'Orleans, a daughter of Louis-Philippe, the French king. With the help of the British government, Leopold's nephew Ferdinand of Saxe-Coburg became the second husband of the queen of Portugal, Dona Maria Braganza, daughter of the emperor of Brazil, Dom Pedro. In 1840 another of his nephews, Prince Albert of Saxe-Coburg, married Queen Victoria of Great Britain and became prince-consort. This policy of royal alliances continued into the 1850's with the Austrian marriages of his son, the future Leopold II, to the Archduchess Marie-Henriette, and his daughter to the Archduke Maximilian, future emperor of Mexico and brother of Emperor Franz-Josef. With these alliances and his wisdom and skill, Leopold I established his influence in Europe. "L'Oncle Leopold" became "L'Oracle politique de l'Europe."

Leopold's foreign-alliance policy did not directly involve the Belgian people, but the country benefited greatly from it. At first, the king's plans were carried out by his advisers. Later, Belgians and foreigners were enlisted to develop an effective foreign policy. Thus it became a royal tradition, after 1831, that the king and his appointees guided and defined Belgian's foreign policy. In the 1830's, under the neutral status, the somewhat lethargic Belgian people were content with King Leopold's foreign policy since it was advantageous and profitable and gave them a feeling of importance. This led to problems that alerted Belgians to their destiny in foreign affairs.

Whereas Leopold I's attention centered on Europe, Leopold II's outlook encompassed the world. Leopold II succeeded to the Belgian throne on the death of his father in 1865. As a monarch rooted in the Belgian diplomatic convention, he was a visionary whose genius was well suited to the new age of industrial, economic, and colonial expansion in the 19th century. He was an economic opportunist whose actions galvanized Belgian business to make the country the fifth-largest economic power by the turn of the century.

In an age of European colonization and expansion, capitalistic interests in Europe divided up the African continent according to their economic appetites. The king of the Belgians claimed the region known as the Congo. In 1876 he established the International African Association and, with the help of the English explorer Henry Stanley, set out to explore the Congo basin and abolish the slave trade.

Gradually the king extended Belgian interests in the Congo and was able to organize a political entity, the "Association Internationale du Congo." In 1884 the United States became the first nation to recognize the association as a friendly state. Then in 1885 (partly because of Bismarck's efforts), the Berlin Declaration recognized the existence of the Independent State of the Congo. Leopold II was then invited to assume the role of the Congo's head of state. With some reluctance, understandable because of Belgium's neutral status, the parliament authorized the king to assume the position of sovereign of the new state. Thus Leopold II became head of an area in Africa rich in resources, 80 times larger than Belgium, and under the control of Belgians and foreigners.

Rampant exploitation of the Congo, under Leopold II's leadership, caused repercussions around the world and resentment among the Belgian people. In 1908 Leopold II ceded his authority to the Belgian government. The Independent State of the Congo, under the Belgian government's control, stabilized its economy and became a major African power.

In August 1914, five years after the death of Leopold II in 1909, World War I broke out. Belgium survived the conflict but was broken, a small country, a victim of Germany's perfidy. Leopold II's successor, Albert, "Le Roi chevalier," was the personification of his nation's heroism and martyrdom. Never before had the prestige of the country and the royal house shone so brilliantly.

Allied victory brought a succession of problems for Belgians. The twenty years between the Treaty of Versailles in 1919 and the outbreak of World War II in 1939 were a turning point in world history. For Belgium two basic problems arose, one at home and one in foreign policy. Their fundamental nature made them serious enough to jeopardize the very existence of the nation.

At home the problem of coexistence between the Flemish and French communities was increasingly placing the national identity in question. Abroad, the definition of the nation's future foreign policy was a determining factor in Belgium's destiny. Universal suffrage, promised in 1918 in the aftermath of the Armistice, was to have an important effect on the evolution of these problems, through the influence of a larger and better informed electorate.

The continuation of compulsory neutrality was not acceptable, despite a certain nostalgia for the protection and security that had previously been assured. Furthermore, Belgium, which in 1919 had recognized the League of Nations and in 1920 signed an agreement with France, made it understood that it would not enter into alliances that threatened to drag it into conflicts where no vital Belgian interests were at stake.

After some hesitation the government opted for a policy of guaranteed independence; this allowed it some freedom to practice in fact a policy of neutrality. Its promoters argued that enforced neutrality was not indispensable to a policy of neutrality. This position, although vague, was recognized internationally by the Locarno Treaty of October 1925. England, France, and Germany officially acknowledged Belgium's new policy. In particular, Germany promised to help guarantee Belgium's frontiers. In return, Belgium committed itself to defend its territory against all aggression. Belgium's new status was, quite rightly, considered a great success. With King Albert taking a major role in its implementation and the synergy between the monarch's action and the government's policy, the entire country supported the new policy. Locarno brought hope for a new, lasting peace.

On January 31, 1933, Field Marshal von Hindenburg, the German head of state, called Adolf Hitler to power. Just over a year later, on February 17, 1934, King Albert died suddenly in an accident. It seemed to be the prelude to the events that led to World War II. Hitler's occupation of the left bank of the Rhine on March 17, 1936, not only violated the Treaty of Locarno but also served as a warning for Belgium. France, ignoring her treaty rights, did not react to this move, which placed Strasbourg within the range of the German artillery. The spirit of Locarno faded away.

In view of the *fait accompli* and the lack of any reaction to the successive movements of Hitler's army, Belgium was forced to review its foreign policy. The main concern of Leopold III, who ascended the throne in 1934, was to prevent Belgium from being dragged into a conflict in which it was not primarily concerned. In this he was backed by parliament and the public.

A new definition of the policy of independence, "a foreign policy exclusively and wholly Belgian," called for the strengthening of Belgium's armed forces to enforce its execution. Two famous 1936 speeches, one by Paul-Henri Spaak on July 20, the other by the king on October 14, given before the Council of Ministers, laid down this new policy.

On April 23, 1937, Belgium obtained a unilateral declaration from France and England that freed it from the obligations of the Treaty of Locarno, but maintained the commitments of both the French and British, on the condition that Belgium provide an efficient defense of its territory. A few months later, on October 14, 1937, following substantial negotiations, the Nazi government confirmed its lasting commitment to respect Belgium's borders. Thus the newly defined policy was complete and in effect.

On September 1, 1939, Poland was invaded by the Germans. Belgium, still faithful to its idea of independence, made a renewed declaration of neutrality a few days later on September 3, in the feeble hope of avoiding the maelstrom of war. Unfortunately this policy did not last long. The German offensive of May 10, 1940, swiftly brought Belgium under the Nazi yoke. The policy had been praiseworthy, costly, and yet hopeless.

With hindsight it is, perhaps, astonishing to see how many nations and men, with few exceptions, failed to realize what was at stake in this war. Previous wars, like that of 1914, were waged in the light of common concepts of human dignity, and although smudged by conflict, these concepts were accepted as a principle. With Hitler, war involved a basic rejection of any noble concept of civilization and its replacement by what Pope John-Paul II described as a satanic ideology, utilizing the most barbaric methods.

The fate of Belgium, neutral or not, had been sealed in advance, as had the fate of other nations that fell before the Nazi war machine. It was not until the Allied victory that the world finally realized the horrors of the Nazi philosophy. The capitulation of Belgium on May 28, 1940, was a tragic event for the Belgian people. While King Leopold III remained a prisoner in Brussels, part of the government reassembled in London to join the Allied war effort. In October 1940, the prime minister (Pierlot), the minister for foreign affairs (Spaak), the finance minister (Gutt), and the colonial minister (de Vleeschauwer), were recognized as the official and legal Belgian government.

A month later, Spaak sent a statement to the Belgian diplomatic missions explaining the government's position. The text officially declared executive and legislative powers to be in the hands of the ministers convened in council under the provisions of the constitution. Furthermore it stated that since a state of war existed between Germany and Belgium, the government, representing Belgium and the Congo, without being legally allied with Britain, was closely associated with the latter's policies. Having been recognized by more than 50 nations and having won the support of exiles and the resistance movement, the Belgian government-in-exile assumed a wider range of powers. It benefited from having few restraints, except for the thought that it would have to answer for its actions before a postwar parliament.

The question of Belgian's future foreign policy swiftly became apparent. It was clear that the previous policy of independence and neutrality would not survive in the prevailing postwar situation. The war illustrated the archaic nature of this policy by showing the need for interdependence among nations. Rephrasing the passage "Woe to him who is alone when he falls and has not another to help him up" from Ecclesiastes, Winston Churchill once said to the author, "Woe to the lonely nation, whether small or large, who without even falling will cease to exist."

During those boring days of the war, as Churchill called them, the Belgian government and the Allies had some time to discuss the shape of their postwar world. Their wish, or, one might say, their obsession, was to create a multi-tiered system of international solidarity that would lead to a lasting peace and would stop any attempt at universal domination. In 1941 the Belgians found themselves at the forefront of the debate. Less than a year after the fall of Belgium, new ideas put an end to the traditional path of Belgium's foreign policy. The lessons learned from the defeat were important. Gone was the nostalgia for neutrality and its false advantages. Gone was diplomacy that balanced a policy of limited engagements and one of quasi neutrality.

Now there was talk not only of international cooperation among allies but also military integration. The results were to be found later in programs of reconstruction and organization, such as the Marshall Plan and the Organization of European Economic Cooperation (OEEC), and also in associations of states such as Benelux and collective organizations such as those of Europe, NATO, and the United Nations.

On January 1, 1942, the Belgian government signed the Washington Declaration; though not creating an alliance, it demonstrated adhesion to the principles of the Atlantic Charter (adopted by Roosevelt and Churchill in 1941) and approval of the creation of the United Nations. In short, the government of Free Belgium in London was ready to adopt a foreign policy of multilateral commitments.

In the footsteps of the Allied victory, the Belgian government returned to Brussels on September 8, 1944. Before a reassembled parliament, it swiftly received ratification of its intermediary role on the Allied side. Among other problems it had to face was the question of the absence of Leopold III, who together with his family had been deported by the Germans. On September 20, 1944, parliament bestowed the title of Prince-Regent on the king's brother, Prince Charles, Count of Flanders, who had secretly escaped from the clutches of the enemy. When the king was finally liberated by the Americans the day before the German surrender, the functions of the prince-regent were prolonged because of the controversy surrounding the return of Leopold III. (Leopold was criticized by some for remaining in Belgium after the surrender and for remarrying a "commoner." In 1950 the king abdicated in favor of his son, Baudouin.)

The interregnum, which lasted until July 1950, was one of the most amazing periods in Belgium's history, and was, quite rightly, called the "Belgian miracle." With the stimulus provided by the Marshall Plan, the reconstruction of the nation was swift. To the astonishment of its neighbors, Belgium began a period of prosperity that lasted until the 1970's.

The plans for Belgium's foreign policy drawn up by the government in London were merged with the conclusions of clandestine policy studies made by Belgians under German rule. Parliament approved the plans, and the public unanimously greeted the new policy with enthusiasm. The people saw that the only way to ensure national independence was in the context of a collective system aimed at peace. From 1945 to 1957 the foundation stones of postwar Western solidarity were laid. Thanks to the role of dedicated Belgians such as Paul-Henri Spaak, Belgium played an important role in these first steps, as the following list shows: the United Nations in 1945; Benelux and the Marshall Plan in 1947; the OEEC in 1948; the Treaty of Brussels also in 1948, the first dim ray of hope against the menacing threat of communism, followed shortly afterward by the North Atlantic Treaty; the Council of Europe in 1949; the beginning of the European Coal and Steel Community in 1950; the European Defense Community (disbanded in 1954 in favor of the entry of West Germany into NATO and the creation of the Union of West Europe in 1954); and in 1957 the Treaty of Rome establishing the Common Market. Such were the first steps in the long march toward the multi-tiered structure that was to assure peace, prosperity, and progress for our planet.

This brief account is evidence of extraordinary dynamism. With the establishment of the Common Market, progress toward the ultimate goal had truly begun. What the world and Belgium can hope for may be found in the chapters that follow.

Benelux: An Aspect of Belgium's Dynamic Foreign Policy

Hendrik Fayat

BETWEEN THE TWO world wars, Belgium took part in efforts to minimize for small countries the effect of the rising customs tariffs to which more and more governments were resorting. Neither the International Economic Conference of 1927, nor the debates of 1929 in the League of Nations, nor the Trade Convention of March 24, 1930, achieved any practical results.

By the end of 1930, with Luxembourg, the Netherlands, and four Scandinavian countries, Denmark, Finland, Norway, and Sweden, Belgium signed the Oslo Convention, which called for preliminary negotiations with any country that wanted to raise its tariffs. By the Ouchy Convention (July 18, 1932), the Belgium-Luxembourg Economic Union (formed in 1922) and the Netherlands went considerably further and undertook to cut their tariffs toward each other by 50 percent over a period of five years. But, since their trade partners insisted on retaining the advantages of the most-favored-nation clause, the Ouchy Convention did not work.

During these prewar years, Belgium and the Netherlands were reluctant to go beyond commercial cooperation. In political matters they adhered to strict neutrality, even in the face of an imminent common threat to their territorial integrity, as military incidents clearly showed in January 1940. In May 1940, the three countries were invaded and occupied by Nazi Germany. Their governments found themselves in exile in London. There they realized how small they were separately and how beneficial it would be if they could act jointly. History—and even more geography—were to make the Benelux integration desirable and possible. From 1814 till 1830, the three countries had been united. Their separation in 1830 was, at the time, politically inevitable, but all historians agree that economically this short-lived reunion had been highly profitable.

Geographically these three small countries huddle among three greater neighbors: France, Great Britain, and West Germany. Their territories consist mainly of the estuaries of three rivers: the Rhine, the Maas, and the Scheldt, where two of the major seaports of the world are situated: Rotterdam in the Netherlands and Antwerp in Belgium. Their total population (ca. 25 million) is equal to the combined population of the states of New York and New Jersey, but their total territory is only half the size of these two states put together. Though small in size and population, the Benelux is the fourth-largest trading unit in the world.

From 1943 on, the three governments decided they would work more closely together. Paul-Henri Spaak, the Belgian foreign minister, who was to play such a spectacular role in so many areas of international and European cooperation, was one of the architects and signatories of the Treaty of London of September 5, 1944, establishing the Benelux Customs Union. This customs union did not encounter the obstacles that had beset the implementation of the Ouchy Convention, because the General Agreement on Tariffs and Trade (GATT) exempts a customs union from the generalization rule of the most-favored-nation clause, a formula agreed upon during the first world conference on tariffs in 1947. The Benelux Customs Union became a reality on January 1, 1948, when all tariffs on trade among the three countries were abolished, a common external tariff for third countries came into force, and all quantitative restrictions to trade inside Benelux were removed. On July 20, 1948, the *New York Herald Tribune* devoted a special issue of its European edition to Belgium. To this issue I had the privilege of contributing an article entitled "Belgian Foreign Policy Is Dynamic," which was reprinted the following day in the *New York Herald Tribune*'s home edition. From this article, written nearly 40 years ago, I quote: "The special relationship between the Benelux countries has gained them several diplomatic successes. Belgium and the Netherlands tend to alternate—and in this way they try to achieve a combined, permanent representation—in the leading organs of the United Nations. For instance, the day it was elected to the Security Council, Belgium renounced its seat on the Economic and Social Council in favor of the Netherlands."

At the Havana Conference on Trade and Employment, the Benelux Customs Union was elected to one of the seats reserved for members of prime economic importance on the Executive Committee of the International Trade Organization's Interim Commission. During the London

Conference on Germany, the Benelux countries acted together as one delegation. Along with Britain and France, they were the only countries in Europe to take part in these negotiations.

By successive agreements, an institutional framework has been established consisting of a Committee of Ministers, which usually meets more than once a year, a Consultative Parliamentary Council, a Court of Justice for the interpretation of the Benelux treaties, and a Secretariat. The Court of Justice and the Secretariat are located in Brussels.

The success of Benelux encouraged its leaders, particularly the Belgian government, to take a historic initiative. After the failure to establish a European defense community during the summer of 1954, the progress toward European integration, which had so hopefully started with the OEEC, the Council of Europe, and the European Coal and Steel Community (ECSC), was in danger of grinding to a halt. Through the Benelux proposals for a wider economic union among the six governments of the ECSC, which were accepted at the conference of Messina (June 1955), the road was cleared for the Treaties of Rome of March 25, 1957.

Article 233 of the EEC Treaty and Article 202 of the EURATOM Treaty provide that the Benelux countries are allowed more integration than that reached at any time by the full membership of the European Communities. In their treaty of February 3, 1958, the three Benelux countries agreed to set up an economic union. This aim has not yet been fully reached, but many steps have been taken. Benelux integration is ahead of the integration achieved by the European Communities.

One remarkable example is that since July 1, 1960, there has been no control on the movement of persons between the three countries, and that passport control takes place only at the outer borders of Benelux. Another example is the fact that at the borders between the three countries there is no control on the movement of goods, except for fiscal reasons, and this type of control has been considerably simplified since July 1, 1984, with the introduction of the so-called single document. The practical result is that these intra-Benelux border formalities take only five minutes.

During recent years, further steps have been taken either by the Committee of Ministers or on the occasion of governmental conferences at the prime ministerial level to coordinate the social, economic, monetary, and budgetary policies of the three countries. Apart from these measures toward "internal" integration, the Benelux governments have since 1982 regularly consulted with each other on the advancement of European integration. This was especially the case during the last Belgian chairmanship, when each meeting of the EC Council of Ministers was preceded by a preliminary meeting of the Benelux ministers.

At Milan, in July 1985, it was partly due to the combined efforts and proposals of Belgium, the Netherlands, and Luxembourg that the European Council of Ministers finally agreed to carry on the negotiations that led to the European Act, which was agreed upon when Luxembourg held the chair (February 17, 1986) and signed when the Netherlands held the chair (February 28, 1986). Belgium believes in the necessity of a continuing close cooperation within Benelux to maintain its lead and the example it sets for the unification of Europe.

European and Atlantic Interests

Alfred Cahen

WHEN IN 1945 THE WORLD awoke from the long nightmare of World War II, it found itself in a situation profoundly different from what it had known in 1939 and pregnant with important change to come. New directions in foreign policy were evolving in every country. Belgium was no exception to this rule. Its wartime government-in-exile in London and those in Belgium who were preparing to shoulder their full responsibilities in a liberated country were already thinking about these new directions. At the end of the war, two main aspects of Belgian foreign policy emerged that are still in place today: the commitment to European construction and Atlantic solidarity.

An alliance was something of a novelty in light of Belgium's history of foreign relations. Ever since its independence, Belgium's neutrality was both imposed and guaranteed by the European Great Powers. In 1914 this status was violated by Germany. Belgium's compulsory neutrality was ended by the treaties following World War I. Frightened by the international situation, however, Belgium sought protection by returning voluntarily to neutral status in 1936. Hitler's invasion of the country on May 10, 1940, revealed the ineffectiveness of this policy. Learning from this experience and disillusioned about the benefits of neutrality, at least in its own case, Belgium thereafter sought security in alliance with other nations. Allied first with France, Luxembourg, the Netherlands, and the United Kingdom by the Brussels Treaty in 1948, it was to become a determined and faithful member of the Atlantic Alliance.

As for European construction, the Belgian state found itself quite naturally drawn into it, not only by its relative influence in the world but also by virtue of its geographic and cultural positions, its economic interests, and its undeniable vocation. When it is isolated, a small country has some difficulty in making its voice heard. As a member of a group, it can use that group to reinforce the weight of its options and its attitudes. Belgium occupies within Western Europe a central situation at the crossroads of two of the great European civilizations (the Latin and the Germanic). As a highly industrialized country, with a considerable dependence on external trade, Belgium cannot but benefit from the market to which European cooperation and then integration were to give it easier access. Finally, as one of the most open of nations, it can be proud of an old European tradition.

Not one of the Belgian governments since 1945 has repudiated these two options or indeed felt any contradiction between its European and Atlantic policies. This attitude was most effectively expressed by the king and by Paul-Henri Spaak, a Belgian statesman celebrated both as a European and as an Atlanticist. Addressing U.S. president Gerald Ford on June 26, 1974, King Baudouin said: "From Belgium's point of view, the two choices—European and Atlantic—are complementary. Without the achievement of a genuine European union on the political level, the European states and the European community will be unable to assume the responsibilities imposed on them by their economic success." Spaak, at the end of his memoirs, as a summation of his achievements, wrote: "In this way, my parliamentary life ended with a decision to remain faithful to one of the great courses that I had defended [the Atlantic cause]. . . . I did indeed feel somewhat sad that day, but I consoled myself by recalling the struggles I had taken part in and the results that had been obtained. I had contributed, through the Atlantic Alliance, to ensuring peace in Europe, and I had contributed to the building of a United Europe. I had thus achieved two of my aims."

The Atlantic Alliance—without which there can be no credible defense of the West and therefore of Western Europe—has preserved peace on the Continent and thus made European construction possible. But the alliance increasingly needs a strong Europe: that is, a Europe that has organized itself in all the essential areas, particularly the economic, foreign policy, and security fields. It was against this background that Belgium—a founding member of all organizations for European cooperation and integration—was to play a vital part in several of the key events in the history of European construction.

Even before the end of World War II, the Belgian government-in-exile, together with those of the Netherlands and Luxembourg, signed, on September 5, 1944, in London, a transitional convention for a "customs union"; this was to become Benelux and was to some extent the example subsequently followed by the "Six" and later the "Nine," the "Ten," and finally the "Twelve" with the Common Market.

In the immediate postwar years, Belgian governments, diplomats, and senior officials played an important part in launching the movement for the organization of Europe. Whether in the Brussels Treaty Organization, the Organization of European Economic Cooperation (OEEC), or the Council of Europe, their contribution strongly influenced developments. The names of Paul-Henri Spaak and Paul van Zeeland—both of whom held the posts of prime minister and foreign minister in Belgium—and of Baron Snoy et d'Oppuers, the secretary-general for economic affairs, Hubert Ansiaux, the governor of the National Bank, and Ambassador Roger Ockrent, the permanent representative to the OEEC, are closely linked with that period of European construction and with subsequent phases of that construction.

Whereas the European Coal and Steel Community (ECSC)—the first stage in European economic integration—owed its existence to Jean Monnet, Robert Schuman, and Konrad Adenauer, it was largely on the initiative of Paul-Henri Spaak and his quite exceptional team—Baron Snoy et d'Oppuers, Ambassador Forthomme Rothschild, and Ambassador Albert Huppers—that the other two elements of this integration were to come into being at a particularly critical stage. The European Defense Community and subsequently the European Political Community had just been rejected. Not surprisingly, the future of the European enterprise was in doubt, and fresh impetus was urgently needed. The initiative was taken by Spaak—in close collaboration with his Luxembourgeois and Netherlands colleagues (Prime Minister Bech and Foreign Minister Beyen, respectively). Their contributions were considerable and, on the basis of the Spaak Report, led to the signing by the Six on March 25, 1957, of the Treaties of Rome setting up EURATOM and the European Economic Community. Along with the ECSC, these two new institutions were to provide the economic dimension to the European enterprise.

Between 1955 and 1970, European construction developed haltingly, alternating between considerable successes and serious crises; it failed to extend beyond the field of economic integration to embrace other dimensions. The year 1970 was to be a turning point, and once again Belgium was to give powerful support to its partners. In December 1969, representatives of the Six met in the Hague at a moment when it seemed possible and highly desirable to relaunch European construction. The twelve-year transitional period provided for by the Treaty of Rome was to expire one month later, and the community was set to enter its definitive phase. The United Kingdom, Ireland, Denmark, and Norway were knocking on the door. The internal squabbles and clashes that had punctuated the life of the community for a number of years seemed to become less intense. Among other important decisions, the community instructed its foreign ministers "to study the best way of achieving progress in the matter of political unification." At issue was the problem of creating a genuine European union.

In fact, this task was to fall to a committee composed of the heads of the political departments in the six foreign ministries. The man who was to preside over this committee and be its "catalyst" was a Belgian: Viscount Davignon. The committee's report—the Davignon Report— approved by ministers in October 1970, created "European political cooperation." It paved the way for harmonization of action among the member-countries of the European Communities in the field of foreign relations, thus adding a foreign policy dimension to the economic dimension already available to the Six—now the Twelve.

Again, it was a Belgian, Prime Minister Leo Tindemans, who put forward the fundamental proposal that the governments appoint a "committee of three wise men," chaired by a prime minister, who, in the space of one year, would prepare a plan outlining such a union. This program was adopted, but at the suggestion of British prime minister Harold Wilson, the committee of three was abandoned in favor of having one man only. The man chosen by his peers, the heads of state or of government, was none other than Leo Tindemans.

The Tindemans Report, published in January 1976, remains a key element in the continuing process of building Europe. The report was a complete operational program for establishing a European union. It has had considerable influence, even though it has not been possible to implement all of its proposals.

From Paul-Henri Spaak in the early 1940's to Prime Minister Wilfried Martens and Foreign Minister Leo Tindemans today, practically every Belgian head of government and foreign minister has worked strenuously to further the process of European construction and, ultimately, to bring about the drafting and adoption of the Single Europe Act. It is not surprising, therefore, that the Belgian capital, Brussels, has come to be one of the headquarters—in fact, the main headquarters—of the Europe of the Twelve, since it is host to the EC Council of Ministers, the EC Commission, and, since 1986, the Secretariat of European Political Cooperation; it is also where the vast majority of the community's ministerial meetings and the meetings of its assembly committees are held.

Yet none of this precludes Belgium from playing a dynamic and determined Atlantic role. Belgium has provided the alliance and NATO with one of its greatest secretary-generals, Paul-Henri Spaak; one of the most famous doyens on its Council of Representatives, André de Staercke; its main headquarters in Europe, Evere and Casteau; and a doctrine that has underpinned its activities since 1968, the "Harmel Doctrine."

As NATO's secretary-general from 1957 to 1961, Paul-Henri Spaak steered the organization through a very difficult period, during which the strength of his Atlantic convictions and his extraordinary talents for diplomacy were to work miracles. During his four years in office, he was an ardent advocate of wider consultation among the partners. The smoothness of the discussions within NATO at times of international tension, such as the U-2 incident or the Cuban missile crisis, which happened a year after he left office, testifies that his efforts bore fruit. The fact that he came from a small country undoubtedly had something to do with it. His second aim, which he never abandoned during his term of office, was East-West détente. His visit to Moscow as secretary-general of NATO in 1958 and meetings with Khrushchev confirm this. But he always set his support for dialogue with the East in the context of unbroken Atlantic solidarity and observed the utmost firmness in his relations with his opposite numbers in the Warsaw Pact.

In the 22 years from 1954 to 1976, Ambassador de Staercke was the doyen of the permanent representatives on the North Atlantic Council. His exceptionally long tenure, his extraordinary professional, intellectual, and human qualities, and his vigorous commitment to the Atlantic cause led to his becoming the conscience of that council.

In 1966, after the French decided to withdraw from the integrated military structure, the other member-states had to find a suitable location for the Atlantic institutions and forces, which had been asked to leave France. Benelux was designated by the member-states as the most appropriate alternative. The honor of receiving the main Atlantic bodies stationed in Europe fell to Belgium. On March 31, 1967, SHAPE was installed at Casteau near Mons, and on October 18 of the same year, NATO headquarters was set up just outside Brussels at Evere.

The Atlantic Alliance, which was set up in 1949, has had from time to time to rethink its aims and objectives. This was particularly the case in 1956 and in 1960–61. In 1966, developments again called for such a process of reflection. On the initiative of Pierre Harmel, Belgian foreign minister at the time, this process came about under his guidance, in the form of what immediately became known as the "Harmel exercise." In December 1967, this exercise was set out in the "Report on the Future Tasks of the Alliance," which was adopted by the allies' foreign ministers and continues to be known as the Harmel Report. This report was of special significance. First, it dealt with essential problems and principles of the alliance at a time when the very existence of alliances was being questioned. Second, it vigorously reaffirmed the aims of the Atlantic Alliance. Third, while recognizing that the international situation had changed since 1949, it underlined once more the continuing political and military usefulness of the alliance.

The Harmel Report is still topical. It clearly enunciates that the ultimate political purpose of the alliance is to "achieve a just and lasting peaceful order in Europe accompanied by appropriate security guarantees." Two fundamental tenets, defense and dialogue, were adapted to the new international conditions by the North Atlantic Council at its ministerial meeting in Washington, D.C., in 1984, at the prompting of Tindemans, who was then Belgian foreign minister.

Moreover, Belgian governments have always sought to play a full part in the alliance's major decisions and in their implementation, even when —as now—budgetary or other problems make matters difficult. Thus, Henri Simonet, foreign minister from 1977 to 1981, played a highly important role in the adoption of the dual-track decision of December 1979 on the deployment of Euromissiles; without that decision, it is doubtful whether the Soviet-American arms negotiations would have developed as they have.

Belgium's dual European and Atlantic vocation has been particularly apparent recently in the context of what is known as "the reactivation of Western European Union," in which the Belgian government has played a considerable role. The Western European Union (WEU) was created by a treaty of alliance in March 1948 originally signed by Belgium, France, Luxembourg, the Netherlands, and the United Kingdom; it was extended in 1954 to include Italy and the Federal Republic of Germany with the particular aim of enabling Germany to join the alliance and enter NATO. Living under the shadow of the Atlantic Alliance, this organization found its activities progressively reduced, and it became moribund until 1984. As far as Belgium was concerned, there were two reasons for its reawakening.

On the one hand, there was a need to add a security dimension to the economic aspects (the Communities) and foreign policy (political cooperation) of Europe. Of course, this should have happened among the member-states of the Communities, but it was not possible because of the refusal of three of them: Denmark, Greece, and Ireland. The only solution therefore was to reactivate the WEU. On the other hand, there was a growing urgency to create this European pillar of the Atlantic Alliance, a concept President John F. Kennedy had evoked years before. Indeed the reactivation of the WEU—particularly as far as Belgium is concerned—is taking place within this alliance, which is quite logical since all WEU members are also members of the alliance and all their governments agree that there can be no credible defense of the West—and hence of Western Europe—without the alliance. Recent experience has shown, moreover, that it is indeed high time that this base for a European pillar of the alliance should start to develop.

The end of the 1970's and the beginning of the 1980's were a fairly comfortable period for the alliance in which there was little change in the status quo. There are several reasons to believe that this period is now coming to an end. First, Soviet leaders want to make a substantial change in relations with the West. At present, this change is particularly evident in the field of arms control. Second, technological progress will have a significant impact on Western strategies. Moreover, the balance of power in the world is transforming the exclusively bipolar (East-West relations) situation that existed from 1945 to 1965 into a multipolar situation. Local and regional tensions are coming to assume ever greater importance with repercussions for the economic, political, and security situation of the West. Furthermore, the intensifying debate on both sides of the Atlantic on the changing transatlantic relationship is a key indicator of changes to come.

Thus, within the Alliance the determination of the North Americans on one side and the Europeans on the other is likely to be put to the test. An example is the West European reactions following the Reykjavik summit of October 1986 and the vacillations over the double-zero option regarding the Euromissiles. Atlantic solidarity, which must be preserved even as the transatlantic relationship changes, cannot happen unless the European allies are able to formulate their own security identity. This will bring a better balance to the alliance as far as distribution of responsibilities is concerned—a process now under way. Within the WEU, the seven European countries—which include the four major ones—have recently undertaken a study of what they consider to be their joint security interests as perceived in the context of Atlantic solidarity. A security study completed in 1987 is an important and positive element in the transatlantic debate.

It is essential for the North American allies, in particular the United States, to comprehend that this development in no way represents a distancing from them or from the alliance. Belgium strongly supports the aim of strengthening both the North American–Western European relationship and the alliance. The alliance needs a robust and organized Europe, a view to which Belgium strongly subscribes.

It is fitting to conclude by quoting Henry Kissinger. Though extremely critical, particularly in his memoirs, of certain aspects of Europe's organization and its impact on U.S.-European relations, he nevertheless had this to say in 1984 with reference to "a plan to reshape NATO":

Many in this country seemed to fear that a militarily unified Europe might give less emphasis to transatlantic relations or might botch its defense effort and thus weaken the common security. The opposite is almost certainly the case. In the economic field, integration was bound to lead to transatlantic competition, even to some discrimination. What defines a common market, after all, is that its external barriers are higher than its internal ones. In the field of defense, by contrast, increased European responsibility and unity would promote close cooperation with the United States. A Europe analyzing its security needs in a responsible manner would be bound to find association with the United States essential. Greater unity in defense would also help to overcome the logistical nightmare caused by the attempts of every European nation to stretch already inadequate defense efforts across the whole panoply of weapons.

Such a stand is consistent with Belgium's view and the policy it is pursuing in the dual European and Atlantic contexts, a policy recognized and appreciated beyond its own frontiers. Proof of this may be found in the telegram sent by German chancellor Helmut Schmidt on September 7, 1980, to the king of the Belgians: "On your 50th birthday, I offer Your Majesty my sincere congratulations. Under Your Majesty's unifying guidance over the past thirty years, the Belgian people have cooperated outstandingly and tirelessly in the building of Europe and have made a vital contribution to the alliance."

Military Policy

Pierre Cremer

THE FIRST MAJOR CAMPAIGNS OF World War II eloquently demonstrated that a military policy centered on an independent and isolated defense effort could no longer guarantee the preservation of a small country such as Belgium. An autonomous Belgian defense policy against the modern military potential of more powerful nations was quite untenable because of the country's geography—a lack of geostrategic depth, the small scale and open nature of the Belgian landscape, and a sensitive communications position with major port capacity. This is why Belgium in 1945 enthusiastically joined security and defense systems revolving around multilateral political and military commitments: the Atlantic Alliance, NATO, and the Western European Union (WEU). The WEU has concerned itself chiefly with the coordination of the specifically European security policies of its members. However, with the exception of France, NATO and its military strategy are the dominating commitments for its member-countries.

Belgian defense policy therefore revolves around the idea of a jointly assured deterrent. This takes both direct and indirect forms. It takes the direct form of the placing at the disposal of NATO of a certain number of units from the three branches of the armed forces and of the primary use of reserve units for the defense of Belgian territory and its numerous sensitive points. Indirect Belgian participation in NATO takes the form of partial handing-over of certain infrastructure resources, participation in alert and detection systems, the location of the headquarters of NATO and SHAPE and stores on Belgian soil, and certain communications and transit resources.

The *ground forces*, which in peacetime number 60,900 men and which in wartime would swell to 210,000, have two major responsibilities. The most important one, which is the responsibility of an "Intervention Force" consisting chiefly of an army corps, is participation at very short notice in the joint land defense of the Federal Republic of Germany at the inter-German border and in a sector of around 50 km allocated to it by NATO. Next in importance is the responsibility of the "Home Forces" to ensure, under national command, the defense of sensitive points and national and allied communication lines. The Intervention Force includes two (one reserve) divisions of three brigades each. In addition, it has at its disposal a reconnaissance group, combat-support troops including nuclear-capacity artillery battalions and. others equipped with ground-to-air missiles, combat engineering units, amphibious units, various signaling units, light aviation squadrons, and logistic support troops. The brigades of each division have armored equipment and include, in addition to tank battalions and armored infantry battalions, conventional and nuclear artillery units, engineering units, and logistic troops.

The *air force*, which numbers around 20,300, plays a role in allied air superiority in the areas of air defense, offensive operations including nuclear missions, reconnaissance, and transport. Its combat planes (fighter-bombers) are the most up-to-date models and are organized in two wings with two or more squadrons. At present, two wings of remote-controlled ground-to-air missiles (Nike-Hercules) form part of the defense cordon around the center of Europe. Finally, two important radar and control stations, situated underground, form part of NATO's general system of detection.

The *navy* has only 4,500 men, but despite its smallness it takes part in the important task of protecting the sea passages in the English Channel and the North Sea. This involves notably antisubmarine equipment and the protection of surface convoys, minesweeping operations, and the operational monitoring of coastal waters. It currently has four modern escorts for antisubmarine measures and will soon have 30 minesweepers including 10 ultra-modern ones. It is also equipped with on-board helicopters on two command and logistic support ships.

Finally, there is an interforce *medical service* employing in peacetime 5,800 people, as well as 15,000-strong *state police force*, which is partly under the wing of the Defense Ministry and which, in wartime, can be instructed to carry out operational tasks as well as to maintain public order. In all, therefore, Belgium has a modern military force of 100,000 in peacetime and 250,000 in wartime.

Belgium and the European Community

Etienne Davignon, Hugo Paemen, and Paul Noterdaeme

AFTER 1945, BELGIUM MADE A clean break with its meandering inter-war policy of neutrality and firmly committed itself to a three-tier network of international organizations. Seen as symbols of the interdependence of states and solidarity among nations, these organizations were the United Nations, NATO, and the European Community (EC). This complete about-face was engineered by the sheer will of a generation that had lived through a terrible conflict and wanted to render its repetition impossible.

This evolution was to a large extent inspired and guided by Paul-Henri Spaak, who was minister of foreign affairs for over twenty years between 1936 and 1966 (from 1957 to 1961 he was secretary-general of NATO). The key role he played in the negotiations for the founding of these new multilateral organizations was recognized in his successive appointments as first president of the U.N. General Assembly, the Council of the Organization of European Economic Cooperation (OEEC), the Parliamentary Assemblies of the Council of Europe, and the European Coal and Steel Community.

Belgium had become convinced that absolute sovereignty was an illusory and outdated objective and that national security should be based upon multilateral foundations. Belgian foreign policy–makers therefore invested all their efforts in promoting this viewpoint, with mixed success. The Charter of the newly born United Nations was the first source of disappointment. The five winners of the war were given a veto in the Security Council, the very body whose chief responsibility is to maintain international peace. Spaak, haunted by the pitiful inertia of the League of Nations, warned against the paralysis such a provision would create. However, nothing could destroy the connivance of the "major" nations. The dream was shattered, and all remnants of illusion evaporated when, barely a year after the end of the war, Spaak echoed the concern of all Europeans in declaring to the Soviet Union: "We are afraid."

Belgium then focused its efforts on rebuilding a strong Western Europe, one that would be independent and free to guide its own destiny and security, within the framework of Atlantic solidarity. The rapprochement between Belgium, the Netherlands, and Luxembourg (Benelux), already planned during the war, was the first concrete and symbolic step in this process.

For Paul-Henri Spaak, the future of Belgium was indelibly tied to the construction of a European community, the end objective of which should be a United States of Europe. Unlike other European politicians, Spaak did not perceive a contradiction between this goal and the strengthening of the alliance with the United States. Together Western Europe and North America could guarantee the balance essential for the maintenance of peace. The longevity of this partnership could be ensured by formalizing it in organizational form. On the other hand, European integration would remove the danger of European subordination by the Americans.

In his memoirs, Spaak emphasizes that fear of Stalin and the bold vision of George Marshall pushed Europeans along the path of cooperation. General Marshall had reached the conclusion that the superhuman task of rebuilding the ruined European countries and their tottering economies could not be done in the traditional manner. He therefore suggested accelerating the process. In a famous speech at Harvard University on June 5, 1947, he proposed a recovery plan to all the nations of Europe. The government of the Soviet Union refused point-blank, and its satellites were obliged to follow suit. However, the Western nations decided to organize themselves in response to this offer. The Soviet Union retaliated by creating COMECON. Thus, the two blocs of East and West were born.

The European countries, particularly the small ones such as Belgium, discovered that national interests could be guaranteed by multilateral cooperation embodied in an organization giving them a voice rather than by bilateral diplomacy. Under the broad payment transferability of the European Payments Union in the framework of the OEEC, many quantitative import and export restrictions were gradually abolished. This dismantling of economic barriers among the European nations gave considerable impetus to the harmonization of national policies. The United States shored up European cooperation efforts with a decisive financial contribution to the success of the project. The political significance of economic activity was clearly understood and became a powerful instrument in the new diplomacy.

From this point on, the priorities of Belgian policy were clear. First, Germany had to participate fully in the process of integration and collective security. Concretely speaking, this meant giving a democratic Germany a fresh chance in a new European context. Belgium translated its beliefs into action by giving up the territorial "corrections" granted in the agreement of the Allies. "European integration is the correct manner of resolving the German problem," Paul-Henri Spaak wrote around this time to Anthony Eden, then British prime minister.

Second, the policy of the United Kingdom disappointed those who favored European integration, particularly Belgian leaders. They wanted the United Kingdom to turn its back on insularity and join forces with other Western European countries. A speech made by British prime minister Winston Churchill in Zurich on September 19, 1946, stimulated hopes that were not borne out. In 1951, when there was talk of taking the technical cooperation organized by the OEEC one step further, Churchill stated his support for European integration, but only on the Continent. The United Kingdom was to his mind a separate entity, and its diplomacy was organized along the lines of traditional alliances. What was worse, after initial indifference arising from a profound skepticism, British leaders adopted a hostile position vis-à-vis the preparatory work for the foundation of the European Economic Community and even attempted to discourage German leaders from cooperating. Belgium has not harbored any grudge against the United Kingdom for this error of judgment. Convinced that the EEC could not assume its full political dimension without the United Kingdom, it supported British entry requests both in 1961 and in 1967. Meanwhile, the EEC had demonstrated its viability. Belgium was particularly in favor of enlargement because this coincided with the aims of integration.

A third policy goal was the political union of EEC member-states, covering economic, political, and military matters. In this respect, Belgian thinking in the 1950's was largely in tune with that of Jean Monnet and Robert Schuman, French foreign affairs minister. In 1950, the birth of the European Coal and Steel Community brought together France, Italy, Germany, and the Benelux countries. The objective was to substitute a merger of essential interests for long-standing rivalries through the creation of an economic community and to lay the first foundations of a much wider and much more profound community among long-divided nations.

Emboldened by initial success, all the more remarkable because in the past adversaries had hoarded their most precious economic resources, namely, steel (heavy industry) and coal (primary energy), the six countries were keen to go much further. Proposals were made in 1952 for a European defense community and a European political community. Unfortunately, despite intense diplomatic activity by Spaak, these proposals failed to bear fruit.

Since the political path appeared to be blocked, the advocates of European unification returned to their original method—namely, economic integration leading finally to political integration. This final stage was essential for maintaining the ability to arbitrate inevitable conflicts of interest. Spaak, chairman of the negotiating conference (Spaak Committee), supported by eminent senior officials such as André de Staercke, Forthomme Rothschild, Baron Snoy d'Oppuers, and Van der Meulen, masterminded the birth in 1957 of the European Economic Community and EURATOM. This was no easy matter, for although the younger generation was enthusiastic about this revolutionary concept, more traditional political and economic circles were hesitant.

Even when, in later years, Belgium has had to make do with plans of more limited scope, because of the more pragmatic or opportunistic concepts of the French or British governments, it has tirelessly emphasized that Europe makes sense only if it radically transforms the relationships between its members and its nations. At each fresh stage, a political document was drawn up, such as the Davignon Report in 1970, the Tindemans Report in 1974, and the Declaration on European Identity in 1976.

Relations with the United States have always played a leading role in Belgium's European policy. Belgians have a spontaneous liking for Americans, whom they admire for their economic success. They like to think that they share with Americans belief in certain "middle-class" values, a certain sense of pragmatic efficiency and opportunism that dispenses with pointless regulations. At the governmental level, the warmth of personal relations and mutual trust between politicians have given the dialogue an intimacy that is perhaps surprising considering the balance of forces. In pursuit of its European objectives, Belgium has never for a moment considered that it should subordinate its destiny to American protection, which would inevitably have become condescending and overbearing. Belgian politicians continue to consider that relations with the United States must gradually evolve toward partnership between a strong European community and its ally, the United States of America.

For Spaak, the European community could not become inward oriented if it were to remain faithful to its values. He was one of the forces behind the establishment of institutional links between the community and African nations. In order to convince his more reluctant partners, he even agreed that Belgium would shoulder a disproportionate share of the financial responsibility for the development fund that was subsequently created. This first stage led to one of the most innovative features of community policy; namely, cooperation with 46 African, Caribbean, and Pacific states. Belgium stuck firmly to its European ideals in implementing these priorities. In response to a colleague who questioned him on the best way of protecting Belgian national interests, Spaak replied: "Nothing can safeguard our national interests better than the attainment of our European objective; in any discussion resolutely take the side of the most radical solution."

European integration presented a paradox for most of the 1960's. On the economic front, the community was highly successful, inaugurating a customs union two years earlier than scheduled. In the political arena, however, tension reigned and was aggravated by French resistance, led by General de Gaulle, to the gradual integration specified in the Treaty of Rome. Although it did not abandon its commitment to the supranational nature of community institutions, Belgium strove to avoid a split within the community to safeguard what had already been achieved and to promote short-term progress, which was possible despite the difficult situation. This included notably the establishment of the customs union and the development of a common agricultural policy.

Pierre Harmel took over from Paul-Henri Spaak and was at the head of Belgian foreign policy when, at the end of 1969, the heads of state and government of the community met in the Hague. General de Gaulle had meanwhile left the French political scene. The Hague summit agreed that the community could survive only if further progress was made and that Europe had to revive faith in its own destiny. The creation of an economic and monetary union enlarged to include the United Kingdom, and more coherent cooperation in foreign policy matters formed the foundations for a fresh burst of activity in line with the objectives of the Belgian government. It had as usual spoken for even more binding commitments.

Belgium, which held the presidency of the EEC's Council of Ministers during the first half of 1970, made the most of this fresh impetus. In April, a decision was taken to give the community its own budgetary resources; in June entry negotiations were opened with the United Kingdom, Ireland, Denmark, and Norway; in February the central bank governors entered a system of short-term monetary support; in October the Werner Report called on the Council of Ministers to discuss a plan to gradually align economic policies and create a monetary union with a common currency. Belgium was fully behind this report, written by the then prime minister of Luxembourg. Finally, a committee chaired by the director-general of Belgian policy, Etienne Davignon, wrote a political report approved by the member-states on October 27. After almost fifteen years of splits, the members of the community were finally committing themselves to the purely political objective of aligning viewpoints and actions in the foreign policy field.

In the 1970's this fresh spurt of activity came to grief. The oil crisis caused international monetary stagnation. Solidarity among the EEC member-states was severely shaken by their inability to define a community policy to counter the oil blockade imposed by OPEC. Belgium attempted to stimulate solidarity. Although this initiative failed at the community level, it met with more success on the general Western level.

The member-countries of the Organization for Economic Cooperation and Development concluded a treaty providing for organized solidarity in the event of an oil shortage. As a mark of the role played by Belgian diplomacy, the conference was chaired by Davignon, who became the first president of the International Energy Agency when the treaty was signed. This treaty was a source of great satisfaction for Belgium and was remarkable in at least two respects. First, a place in the agency was set aside for the European Community, to be assumed when it had attained its own energy policy. Second, in order to guarantee the actual implementation of the crisis provision for the sharing of oil resources, it was decided that the United States would not have a veto.

A climate of permanent uncertainty and instability was kept alive by three conditions: unemployment, which had been creeping up unnoticed since World War II, the absence of a coordinated monetary policy in the free world, and the timidity with which the community asserted itself. States hid behind their national interests. The fledgling authority of community institutions began to suffer.

Although doubts flourished within the community, Europe's main partners, except for the Soviet Union, began to consider the European Commission as the main spokesman for Europe. The community was thus gradually able to assert its personality. The community had grown to nine member-states by the time it agreed in 1973 to open multilateral trade negotiations in the framework of the General Agreement on Trade and Tariffs (GATT). Negotiations were opened with 46 African, Caribbean, and Pacific countries with a total of 240 million inhabitants for the extension and strengthening of special links that already existed between the Community of Six and certain African countries (including former Belgian colonies, which became independent in the 1960's). The

Yaoundé Convention was signed on February 28, 1975. It was founded on the equality of signatories and on high-level cooperation in trade, industrial, and financial matters.

Despite a number of declarations of good intent (notably at the Copenhagen summit), the community failed to define a common energy policy, and the second stage of economic and monetary union was not begun in 1974 as initially scheduled. Faced with economic crisis and institutional deadlock just after the enlargement of the community, Belgian prime minister Leo Tindemans was asked by the nine member-states, meeting in Paris in December 1974, to draft a report with a view to transforming the community into a European "union" that would cover all forms of relations between the member-states. At the same time, they agreed to elect the European Parliament on the basis of universal suffrage, a long-standing objective of Belgian European policy. The summit admitted that European construction could be brought about only with direct participation.

The long-standing foundations of Belgium's European policy were reproduced in the Tindemans Report, which was published on December 29, 1974. Tindemans tempered his federalist approach with realistic proposals. The method he recommended was adopted by the founders of the community and reflected the pragmatic nature of Belgians. Specific action in specific fields was to be used as building blocks for the process of European union. European policy is only credible insofar as it provides a tangible response to the challenges of new circumstances. In the long term, Tindemans suggested, a joint policy should be conducted in the economic and social sector, in external relations, and in defense. Foreign policy cannot be defined without considering security. However, the plan was still too ambitious for the governments of the time, which were absorbed in the prevailing economic crisis.

Another ten years went by before some of the proposals contained in the Tindemans Report were formally approved by all the community governments during the preparations in 1985 to amend the Treaty of Rome. The "Single Act," which contains all the decisions taken, formally reintroduces majority voting and draws into the community's sphere of responsibility matters such as monetary policy and research. Finally, it contains the all-important decision to aim for complete implementation of the single market by 1992.

Belgium has not moved from its front-line position of advocating the integration of the Western European nations. Politicians, economic and social operators, and the majority of Belgians, feel consciously or intuitively that Belgium's essential interests, security, economic development, social harmony, the equilibrium of its democratic institutions, and the personal, social, and cultural development of its citizens would best be protected by a more coherent European Community. Without a doubt, the size and relatively short history of Belgium and the absence of highly specific economic interests have smoothed the transition from the traditional concept of national interests to that of European interests. The process of identifying national interests with the objectives of the European Community has taken place most naturally in Belgium among all the members of the European Community. Because of this clear-sightedness and its idealism and belief in European integration, Belgium has constantly adopted positions that have contributed to the peaceful unification of Europe, a phenomenon unprecedented in the history of nations.

Belgium and the United Nations

Edmonde Dever

MANY TIMES WHEN I was head of the Belgian mission to the U.N., I was asked what role a small country such as Belgium can play in the organization. Experience has shown that in international life in general, and at the U.N. in particular, the size of a country is not the only factor determining its influence. More than once, small states, even very small states, have been able to stimulate movement and progress on specific issues through their determination, the action of an outstanding national statesman, the vision of their representatives, or their influence at the level of their regional group.

Belgium was one of the 51 founding states of the U.N. Belgians, although they shared the ideals that inspired the creation of the organization, had from the outset misgivings about some provisions of the proposed charter, recalling the difficulties encountered by the League of Nations. The Belgian delegation tried, not always successfully, to amend some wording in order, for instance, to increase the strength of the organization or to prevent an abuse of the veto right by the five permanent members.

The first session of the General Assembly was presided over by Belgian foreign minister Paul-Henri Spaak, who demonstrated throughout his career how a strong and brilliant personality can enhance the weight of his country on the international scene. From the start, Belgium contributed people and money to the peacekeeping operations, one of the more valuable initiatives of the U.N. The events in the Congo in the 1960's and what was considered unfair treatment by the U.N. temporarily clouded Belgian relations with the organization. Gradually things returned to normal, and in 1971 Belgium gained a term on the Security Council. Disarmament (chemical arms, regional disarmament), humanitarian and social matters (torture, rights of the handicapped), human rights, and legal matters (peaceful use of space, deep-sea problems) are among the fields in which Belgium has been specially active.

Being geographically located at the crossroads of Europe and with an internationally oriented economy, Belgians attach great importance to regional and multilateral arrangements, and they respect the virtue of dialogue. These considerations have always inspired Belgian foreign policy. This applies equally to the U.N., especially following its evolution after the massive entry of the newly independent countries. This entry brought different preoccupations and interests and caused a fundamental modification in the organization. Progress cannot be expected without permanent dialogue among the member-states, which is certainly facilitated by good bilateral contacts and a maximum of trust and goodwill.

Belgium supports every effort to promote dialogue, be it in an East-West or a North-South context. As a small country and because of its history and policy, Belgium cannot be suspected of any special or selfish interests and thus can more easily act as an honest broker. Furthermore, having been compelled through the centuries to cope with aggression and occupation, Belgians have by necessity developed some skills for compromise, mediation, and conciliation. It is also easier for small countries to put out feelers or to launch ideas successfully, as long as those ideas do not drift away from the main trend of their partners.

Belgium is of course conscious of the influence of relations between the superpowers on the state of the world in general and on the work of the U.N. in particular. In fact the state of relations between the two superpowers has prevented a full use of the system laid down by the Charter to maintain peace and security.

In respect of its obligations toward its allies, Belgium always tries to promote East-West détente. The role played by another Belgian minister of foreign affairs, Pierre Harmel, in the definition of the dual policy of defense-détente of NATO is well known, as is the role played by Belgium in the drafting and the conclusion of the Final Act in Helsinki.

Belgium's good relations with the developing countries and its special links with Africa allow it to participate usefully in the North-South dialogue. The appreciation of the Belgian middle-of-the-road position is illustrated by the fact that it is the only member of NATO to be a member of the Council of Namibia and the ad hoc committee on Kampuchea, of which it has held the vice-presidency.

The U.N. has been criticized for lack of progress in the political field. Belgium is realistic in this regard and conscious of the weak performance of the organization in numerous areas. But it is still convinced of the importance of the U.N. as a meeting place for all the countries of the world and as a unique venue for discreet and informal contacts that would be unthinkable anywhere else. Even its worst critics recognize that fact. For small countries, multilateral organizations allow participation in decisions of direct or indirect concern to them. The U.N. can also supply a safety valve and help defuse regional conflicts that threaten to spread.

The efficient work done by the U.N. in fields other than the political is too often overlooked. In matters of social and humanitarian concerns (help to refugees, children, the fight against drugs) and in the specialized agencies, the balance is much more positive. Taking into account the de facto limits of the organization, Belgium in the future will continue to participate actively in the work of the U.N. and join efforts to make it more efficient. Belgium will continue to act within the framework of European political cooperation among the twelve member-states of the European Community. It is little publicized that at the U.N. the twelve member-states increasingly consult on every problem, especially during meetings of the General Assembly, at all levels to analyze and coordinate their views in order to achieve, if possible, common positions. More and more they speak through the voice of the acting president of the twelve, who announces common positions. Increasingly, other states and regional groups are taking the EC's position into account in defining their own position. This action by the twelve EC states is not directed against anybody, but constitutes on the contrary a positive development since they share the ideals of democracy, justice, and peace on which the U.N. was built. Through their special relationship with associated countries in the developing world, they can help to promote constructive solutions.

Belgium, which has always defended European unity and European political cooperation, takes an active part in the work of the twelve states at the U.N. Its good contacts with the other regional groups give it the ability to explain and promote the EC's position. On the other hand, it can inform the twelve EC states of others' stands in order to facilitate an eventual compromise.

In recent years, the U.N. has experienced a financial crisis. This situation has caused numerous voices to denounce the failures of the organization. Belgian policy is to promote better use of the means offered by the Charter to achieve the goals of the organization. After all, the tools are there, but they are not being properly used. The U.N. is not a supranational organization; it cannot do more than its members are ready to do or go further than they are ready to go. To condemn the U.N. is to condemn its members.

On the fortieth anniversary of the signing of the Charter, Belgian foreign minister Leo Tindemans stressed two ways to reinforce the organization: "The Security Council and in particular those of its members which have the veto right should become aware anew of their worldwide responsibilities, taking into account the legitimate aspirations of other nations, members of the organization. Perhaps one ought also to increase and better define the role of the secretary-general, whose good offices throughout the years on many occasions were most useful. The General Assembly and the Security Council should grant to the secretary-general a more extended mission in the field of mediation and diplomatic exploration." It seems to Belgium that in a world increasingly interdependent, it is more essential than ever to dissipate mistrust and misunderstanding among states by worldwide contacts and dialogue. The U.N. offers this opportunity if all member-countries are ready to respect the letter and the spirit of the Charter.

The Reduction of International Tensions

Pierre Harmel

GEOPOLITICS OR GEOGRAPHY INFORMED by lessons of the past is still a key factor in a nation's foreign policy. To understand Belgium's foreign policy, a brief study of a map of Europe is sufficient. Belgium is a small, populous country, with no natural frontiers except for a short coastline bordering the North Sea. The experience of war has taught it, the hard way, that given the position of the country neither neutrality nor self-defense can protect it.

Thus for nearly 50 years Belgium has learned that its security and the needs of a modern economy require its foreign policy to follow four objectives: the establishment of a stronger European union; an integrated defense, bringing Western European and Mediterranean nations together with the United States and Canada; a continuous attempt to control East-West relations; and the creation of a balanced relationship between industrialized nations and Third World countries, thus establishing a new social and economic order.

As Belgians know, these four pillars of the nation's foreign policy are being affected to an ever increasing degree by multilateral agreements. It is thus through these channels that Belgian diplomacy has been most active. However, the chief objective of successive postwar governments in Belgium has been the creation of a unified Europe and an Atlantic Alliance. These efforts in turn have reflected a persistent policy of the government to treat the two issues of collective security and a unified Europe as inseparably joined.

For Belgian diplomacy, the words "collective security" have always implied many converging efforts: a common European and Atlantic defense, constant political action aimed at reconciling and uniting those peoples devoted to democratic liberty in Western Europe, and the setting up of a dialogue between European states whose ideologies differ. As an example of the continuity of this policy, I would like to cite four critical junctures during the last 40 years that make the philosophy of Belgian foreign policy apparent.

The first and most dramatic situation dates to the period between 1946 and 1950. With the war hardly over, danger signs were already apparent. In March 1946, Russian troops invaded Iran and steadily advanced toward Teheran. The United Nations Security Council intervened and ordered the Soviet Union to pull out of Iran before May 9. In August 1946 there was a new offensive by Soviet forces, this time in the Dardanelles, with the USSR claiming the right to ensure with Turkey the defense of the straits. The U.S. fleet took up a position off Istanbul, and the Soviets withdrew. Then came the attempted takeover of Greece by communist forces helped by neighboring nations. On March 11, 1947, the Truman Doctrine granted American aid to democratic nations forced to resist attempted coups by armed minorities helped by foreign pressure. In early 1948 the danger signs lit up again with the coup d'état in Prague and the advent of communist control in Czechoslovakia. President Truman's advisers cabled him from Europe, saying war could break out in 60 days. From June 1948 to May 1949, Berlin was blockaded, and in 1950, the Korean War broke out.

During these volatile years, when the world was brought to the brink of war four times, the first steps were made toward worldwide cooperation. On June 5, 1947, a speech by George Marshall at Harvard University laid the foundations for American aid in the economic recovery of Europe. In Europe itself, France and Great Britain agreed to a mutual defense pact in the Treaty of Dunkirk, which was signed on May 4, 1947. A year later, on March 17, 1948, the Benelux countries joined Britain and France, and committed themselves by the Treaty of Brussels to offer all help and support in their power to any of the five countries, should one of them fall victim to armed aggression. The Treaty of Brussels went further by proclaiming "their commitment to take the necessary steps toward promoting unity and encouraging the progressive integration of Europe by strengthening the economic, social, and cultural links that already contribute to the unity of Europe."

What the Treaty of Brussels emphasized had already been affirmed by Paul-Henri Spaak, then minister of foreign affairs, when the Belgian government was in exile in London during the war. In 1941, he noted that "the European nations have become clearly dependent upon each other for their security." A year later he added, "There can be no political solution without an economic solution. In tomorrow's Europe the problems of security and prosperity will be inseparable."

For U.S. president Truman, the Treaty of Brussels was an important step toward the unification of Europe. Even as the foreign ministers of the five nations involved were exchanging signatures, he telephoned Spaak and, after congratulating the ministers, said, "Now that five European nations are united for their defense, the United States will, in her turn, join this initiative." Indeed, a few months later the North Atlantic Treaty was signed in Washington, thereby uniting the United States, Canada, and ten European nations in a common defense.

Thus, the ideas of a collective defense pact and a European political union were first formulated in Brussels at a time of great danger. However, the ideas were the culmination of a period of history that stretched back to the times when the three neighboring states of Belgium, the Netherlands, and the Grand Duchy of Luxembourg (who have since allied to create Benelux) were sworn enemies.

The second situation that I would like to discuss developed from the events of May 9, 1950. On that day Robert Schuman, the French foreign minister, at the suggestion of Jean Monnet proposed to Dr. Conrad Adenauer, the first chancellor of the Federal Republic of Germany, the reconciliation of the French and German states and the merger of their coal and steel industries in a single economic structure with a strong supranational identity. However, it appeared that more than two nations should be linked in this way. Before meeting Adenauer, Schuman contacted Paul van Zeeland, Spaak's successor as minister of foreign affairs, told him of his plans and asked him to announce his government's decision within a few days. The Belgian government reacted swiftly to encourage further commitments by other nations to Schuman's plans. Indeed, the response to the declaration by van Zeeland was immediate and positive; on June 3, 1950, the six future members of the Coal and Steel Community decided to begin negotiations.

Before going any further, let us look at the background of Franco-German relationships. For two centuries hostilities between the two powers had fueled war. Twice these conflicts became worldwide, carrying death and destruction to the four corners of the globe. It was thus essential and yet daring to propose a reconciliation five years after the cessation of the latest outbreak of hostilities. To do such a thing required courage and a firm commitment to peace. It has often been said, both in the East and the West, that the reduction in tensions and the increase of security in Europe have been assured by a major political achievement: the meeting and mixing of former enemies. What the statesmen of all nations, even those in the communist bloc, did was to help erase the hatred between former enemies and to construct a peaceful future between nations formerly opposed. Looking back, one can see, especially in the light of the role Paul van Zeeland played in the creation of the Coal and Steel Community, that the founding fathers of postwar Europe discovered in Belgium understanding, cohesion, and immediate support.

Paul van Zeeland, a renowned prime minister before the war, was a man who never ceased to serve his country or, during the war, the Allied cause. In 1942, Spaak asked him to examine the economic problems that would have to be faced after the war. Van Zeeland's studies resulted in a memorandum that contained the basic elements of the Marshall Plan, the Common Market, and the GATT. As foreign minister between 1950 and 1954, he was to use his skills to play an important role in three talks that exemplify the idea that the security of a nation calls for a regional understanding in matters of politics, economics, and defense. Thus it was decided to build around the Franco-German reconciliation three concentric European organizations: the supranational organization of the European Coal and Steel Community; a political federation of European nations; and a European defense community acting within the Atlantic Alliance.

The European Coal and Steel Community, which in 1957 became the cornerstone of the Common Market, was established in Luxembourg on April 10, 1952. Its founding treaty had been signed in Paris on April 18, 1951. The creation of a European political community "of federal or confederal structure" was called for on September 10, 1952, by the foreign ministers of the six member-states of the Coal and Steel Community. The General Assembly of the European Coal and Steel Community was placed in charge of formulating a plan, and in March 1953, assembly president Paul-Henri Spaak presented a draft treaty. The chairman of this project was another Belgian, Fernand Dehousse.

On August 11, 1950, some time before the formation of the European Coal and Steel Community, Winston Churchill recommended the creation of a unified European army that would operate within the Atlantic Alliance. This would allow West Germany to contribute to the defense of European liberties. Dean Acheson, U.S. secretary of state, strongly supported the project. The negotiations, which emphasized the federal and supranational characteristics of a European defense community, resulted in the signing of a treaty in Paris on May 27, 1952. André de Staercke represented Belgium. The treaty was ratified by the Belgian parliament in November 1953, but it was rejected without any discussion by the French parliament on August 30, 1954. This was a double blow for the European defense community and for the political community, dependent upon one another as they were.

In order to integrate the West German military forces, the Treaty of Brussels of 1948 was modified in 1954, and on October 23, 1954, the Union of Western Europe was established. However, the momentum continued. Spaak had been reappointed minister of foreign affairs so that, in the words of Ambassador Robert Rothschild, his private secretary, "he could give all he had." This period saw a process more fully described in Alfred Cahen's chapter. The result was the birth of the European Community in Rome, in 1957. Although the other well-known Belgian civil servants such as Baron Snoy et d'Oppuers, Ambassador Albert Huppers, and the legal expert Yves de Vadder played an important part, at this point I want to pay tribute again to the memory of Paul-Henri Spaak, who dedicated his wide-ranging talents, unflagging energy, and exemplary impartiality to peace and the building of Europe.

The third situation that I would like to discuss concerns the French decision in 1966 to pull out of NATO. On May 29, 1966, the government of General de Gaulle issued a timetable outlining the evacuation of NATO headquarters from France before February 1, 1967. Moreover, the Atlantic Council might also soon have to leave its headquarters in the Place Dauphine in Paris. The questions arose: Where would the NATO headquarters now be situated and which country would house the seat of the Atlantic Alliance?

However, another question was even more fundamental—a question raised by the imminent twentieth anniversary of the North Atlantic Treaty. The fifteen member-states were, according to Article 13 of the treaty, obliged to remain within the alliance for twenty years, but in the twenty-first year any member-state could leave the alliance, provided it gave a year's notice. What were the fifteen states going to do? For Belgium the period was one of reflection and decision. Spaak had just left the government, but as his successor, I knew that I could rely on his support. I still remember the meeting in which Manlio Brosio (his predecessor), Spaak (secretary-general of the Atlantic Alliance), Viscount Davignon (the Cabinet principal's private secretary), and myself all tried to find an answer to the questions being raised. The location of the headquarters and the seat of the Atlantic Alliance depended on the preference of the member-states. As for the alliance itself, on the eve of its twentieth anniversary patience was of the essence. In-depth studies were needed to achieve a solution that could be accepted unanimously by all the member-states.

Within a short period of time, Belgium was asked to accept first the

SHAPE headquarters and then the seat of the Atlantic Alliance. The government did not rush the talks with other nations or within its own organization. Consequently, Prime Minister Van den Boeynants was able to give a positive response. SHAPE was quickly installed near Mons, and the headquarters of NATO were placed on the outskirts of Brussels.

To understand the intentions of the fifteen governments concerning their commitment to the treaty, we thought it best at the time to undertake a common study on the future of the alliance. The study began in November 1966, with consultations with Dean Rusk, U.S. secretary of state, and then with our colleagues from the other member-states. The decision to undertake such an exercise was settled by the Atlantic Council in December 1966, and soon the work began. The report took very little time, thanks to the diplomatic finesse of Manlio Brosio, the secretary-general of the alliance, to the intelligence of the doyen of permanent representatives, Belgian ambassador André de Staercke, and to the active cooperation of their colleagues. The conclusion was that the West should remain vigilant, and even without the danger of attack, the defense system should also continue as a collective effort, as laid down in Article 3 of the treaty.

With the lull in East-West tensions, the two superpowers together with Great Britain were able to prepare an agreement on containing nuclear proliferation. This was finally presented on July 1, 1968, to all non-nuclear states. In this treaty, the United States, the Soviet Union, and Great Britain committed themselves to open negotiations leading to the reduction of their nuclear arsenals. Thus the age of bipolarity was at a close, and a move to create a joint effort within the Atlantic Alliance to help encourage détente was begun. This was at a time when bilateral contacts with countries of opposing regimes were intensifying.

Twelve months later, on December 16, 1967, the fifteen member-states presented a report on the future tasks of the alliance. Also known as the "Harmel Report," the document proved to be concise and sound. The alliance proposed to carry out two essential and complementary functions. The first was the maintenance of military strength and political solidarity sufficient to discourage aggression or other forms of political pressure and to defend the territories of member-states in times of aggression. The second function was diplomatic. In the words of the report, "The alliance must be used in a constructive manner, in the interests of détente, and, in doing so, continue its efforts to progress toward sounder relationships which will allow fundamental political problems to be solved."

The Harmel Report implied that the political role of the alliance had to be stressed, but it called for no innovations. On April 16, 1953, President Eisenhower appealed to the Soviet Union for peace. On July 23, 1955, a conference of the four major powers in Geneva called for détente. Until 1965, none of the Atlantic Councils, despite an occasionally unfavorable atmosphere, failed to point out the Western desire for détente.

In this situation Belgium yet again showed its fidelity to "regional understanding" by welcoming the NATO institutions to its soil and by bringing a valuable contribution to NATO studies. Among our closest colleagues, such as Ambassador André de Staercke, Viscount Davignon, and Baron Fr. X. Van der Straeten-Waillet, a certain creative and friendly sense of agreement could be found. The process of fostering regional understanding was also considerably helped by a number of statesmen from allied nations. I would especially like to mention U.S. Secretary of State Dean Rusk, an honorable and farsighted statesman whose contributions were greatly welcomed. His compatriot, Assistant Secretary of State G. Rostow, a warm man of shrewd intelligence, also played an important role. Likewise, French foreign minister Couve de Murville made considerable personal contributions to the project.

For Belgium itself, the document corresponded entirely to its vision. Security is always a complex issue, and its main objectives are both to ensure an efficient collective defense system and to carry out endless negotiations to ensure a good chance of peace. The development of security within Europe by implication called for reinforcing the European union. At this stage no institution existed to formalize the diplomatic union within the European Community, but the director-generals who formulated the policy of the foreign affairs departments of the six original members consulted one another and coordinated their efforts. In Belgium, Viscount Davignon had become the director-general of policy in the Ministry of Foreign Affairs, and he assumed the initiative of trying to establish a centralizing body. The committee that bore his name was officially established by the European summit of 1969 in the Hague. The Davignon Committee's work in fact laid the basis for many of the conclusions drawn by the European security conference that began in 1973 in Helsinki.

The fourth critical period, one that lasted from 1974 to 1983, was particularly full of instability. Tension increased and abated, only to develop once again. Apart from the inevitable political differences between East and West, other elements intervened to upset the balance between nations: the economic depression; the monetary instability following the renunciation of the gold parity of the dollar in 1971; and the energy crisis that followed the sharp rise in oil prices in 1973. For the first time in history, it felt as though the world had lost a center of influence and that Belgium's problems were the world's problems. At the same time, relations were poor. Belgium's allies resented all too late the mistake made by the Soviet Union in placing within range of Western Europe hundreds of medium-range nuclear missiles. Neither did Moscow resist the temptation to expand its power to the south by entering Afghanistan and imposing its authority there.

At the end of 1983, Belgian foreign minister Leo Tindemans, who had in 1975 at the request of Europe's heads of state drawn up a report on the European union, posed a question: Should the Allies continue with the policy they had decided on in 1967? Had not the search for détente been paradoxical, even fanciful? Had the alliance's attitude in dealing with the Eastern bloc not been ambivalent, treating the Soviet bloc nations both as potential military adversaries and as partners?

To reply to these uncertainties and questions, the alliance's Standing Council commissioned a "re-evaluation of East-West relations with a view to establishing a more constructive dialogue." The conclusions were given in a report to the Standing Council and put into words in the Washington Declaration of May 31, 1984. This document left no room for doubt: "The balanced approach laid down in the 1967 Report on the future of the alliance is still valid, that is to say, the upholding of sufficient military strength and political solidarity. And by using this as a base, an effort can be made to establish a more stable relationship between the East and West through dialogue and cooperation." The declaration added that "experience has proved that it is still necessary to carry out the two main tasks of the alliance, as laid down in the 1967 Report, in an integral, coherent and realistic fashion."

Such was the most recent—and characteristic—contribution of Belgian diplomacy to the movement for peace that the great democracies founded. It is not necessary here to outline the complete history of Belgian foreign policy over the last 40 years; other chapters in this book take up that subject. What I have described reveals the trends of political philosophy that characterize those European nations I would call "moderates."

International Monetary Arrangements

Jean Godeaux

THE BELGIAN ECONOMY is small and extremely open. Its degree of openness is, among industrial countries, exceeded only by that of Luxembourg. The degree of openness can be measured by the ratio of imports of goods and services to final expenditures in the economy. This ratio is twice as high in Belgium as it is in France, Germany, and the United Kingdom and four times that of the United States. It is estimated that the import content of private consumption is about 40 percent. For every 100 francs a Belgian consumer spends, 40 are spent on foreign goods or services. The import content of exports is on the order of 50 percent. The import content of industrial investments is probably 60 percent. Thus, the cost of foreign inputs is a crucial element in domestic costs and prices. The level and the stability of the exchange rate are therefore, by necessity, important objectives, or constraints, of monetary policy for Belgium.

This implies that the autonomy of domestic economic, financial, and monetary policies is limited, and it explains why, throughout its history, Belgium has attached paramount importance to free trade, stability of exchange rates, and international monetary cooperation. In other words, Belgium has sought to belong to what contemporary economics calls an optimum currency area. It would be tedious to dwell at length on the distant past. Nevertheless, some elements of history throw some light on the present aims and objectives of Belgian authorities.

This paper was prepared with the assistance of Jan Michielsen, inspector general, Guy Noppen, inspector general, and Frank Moss, attaché, all of the Foreign Department of the National Bank of Belgium.

Before World War II: The Latin Union

When Belgium became independent in 1830, gold and silver coins—Dutch, British, French, and, of course, Belgian coins—were the principal currency. Banknotes were rare and were issued by several banks until the establishment of a central bank, the National Bank of Belgium, in 1850. The question then, as students of monetary history will recall, was that of choosing between the gold standard or the silver standard, or bimetallism. Belgium, following the French model, was basically on the silver standard. The national currency was defined in terms not only of a certain weight of silver but also of a certain weight of gold, with a fixed relation between the value of the two metals. The great problem that confronted authorities in those days was Gresham's Law, which came into play whenever the market value of the metal content of coins—gold or silver—differed from their "official" value.

Belgian minister of finance Frère-Orban, who had created the central bank in 1850, suggested to the French government that an international monetary conference be convened to discuss these problems and to arrive at a common definition of currencies in terms of gold. After several years, these endeavors resulted in the conclusion, in December 1865, of an agreement that created the Latin Union, joining France, Belgium, Italy, and Switzerland. Officially these countries had chosen a bimetallic standard; their currencies were defined both in a silver and in a gold weight in a ratio of 1 to 15.5. But the union was constantly plagued by the fact that the market prices of gold and silver often differed from this official ratio, with the result that when the metal value of a coin exceeded its "legal" value, it was withdrawn from circulation and melted into bars. "Bad" money drove out "good" money. Eventually, silver coinage was limited, and the system came to be known as "limping bimetallism."

Meanwhile England was de facto on a gold standard. Germany switched to the gold standard in 1871; the Scandinavian currency union chose the gold standard in 1872, the United States in 1873, and the Netherlands in 1875. Be that as it may, through many, sometimes arduous, conferences, in which Belgian ministers played an active role, the Latin Union survived until 1927. That year Belgium formally left the union and opted for the gold standard.

The Interwar Period and the Gold Standard

Immediately after World War I, the international debate over monetary problems was dominated by (1) the desire, even the will, of most countries to return to the gold standard, if possible at prewar parities, and the fear of a scarcity of gold or, to put it in the terms used in those days, the fear of a "scramble for gold"; and (2) German reparations. Belgian delegates played an active role in the debates on both questions.

As for German reparations, there was a feeling that Belgium, the innocent victim of aggression in 1914, deserved substantial compensation. This was agreed to by the signatories of the Treaty of Versailles. At the time the popular cry in Belgium was "L'Allemagne paiera" (Germany will pay). This expectation, which proved to be an illusion, led Belgium to postpone, or sometimes to simply ignore, some of the problems of adjustment to postwar conditions. As an illustration of the spirit of the times and of the lessons that were to be drawn from it, it may be of interest to quote from the unofficial minutes of the Bretton Woods conference the words, spoken 26 years later, by Lord Keynes, addressing M. Theunis, a Belgian delegate: "I need add little to the eloquent report of our Reporting Delegate, the Delegate of Belgium M. Theunis. But perhaps I may be excused the mention of a personal memory not irrelevant to this occasion. A quarter of a century ago, at the end of October 1918, a few days before the Armistice, M. Theunis and I travelled together through Belgium, behind the retreating German armies, to form an immediate personal impression of the needs of reconstruction in this country after the war. No such bank as that which we hope to create [i.e., the World Bank] was in prospect. Today after a quarter of a century, M. Theunis and I find ourselves brought close together again and engaged in better preparation for a similar event." These words were uttered, let us remember, by the author of *The Economic Consequences of the Peace*. As Keynes had predicted in this famous book, the expectations of those days were inevitably disappointed, but the search for a technical solution to an insoluble problem (the so-called transfer problem of huge reparations) led to the Dawes Plan and later the Young Plan. Belgian finance minister Emile Francqui played a leading role in those negotiations, which led to the creation of the Bank for International Settlements. The bank has survived the disappearance of its initial mission: to channel the payments of German reparations.

But the main preoccupation of those troubled years was the gold problem. The Genoa Conference of 1922 recommended that the gold exchange standard be established as widely as possible in order to avoid "the scramble for gold." Under this system central banks would hold part of their reserves not only in gold but also in currencies convertible into gold. It was also suggested that gold reserve ratios of central banks be lowered in order to "economize" gold. Belgium played its part in these negotiations and, with some reluctance, adhered to their conclusions. The Belgian A. E. Janssen, later minister of finance, was a prominent member of the gold delegation of the League of Nations.

These efforts were to no avail. The gold exchange standard disintegrated. The gold standard itself suffered a severe blow when Britain abandoned gold parity for the pound sterling in September 1931. The Monetary and Economic Conference, held in London in 1933, reflected a bewildering diversity of views, and it was a striking demonstration of a lack of common ground.

There was indeed "a scramble for gold," and the world economy entered a deflationary spiral. Members of the gold bloc, to which Belgium continued to adhere, were held responsible for strengthening the forces of deflation throughout the world. Belgium gave up its deflationary efforts in March 1935 when it devalued its currency by 28 percent, a move that had become inevitable. It was the beginning of the end for the gold bloc; it ceased to exist when France devalued in September 1936.

Soon afterwards, in September-October 1936, the United States, France, and the United Kingdom concluded the Tripartite Agreement, a belated and halfhearted admission that exchange rates should not be altered by arbitrary unilateral action. Belgium greeted the declaration of principle by the three contracting parties with enthusiasm and adhered to the agreement the next day. The National Bank of Belgium participated in the attempt to restore gold and the stability of exchange rates to a central position in the system. Switzerland and the Netherlands joined soon afterwards. It was a feeble attempt, but the Tripartite Agreement provided an experience that played a role in the wartime contacts that led to Bretton Woods and the International Monetary Fund (IMF).

The Bretton Woods Period

As Margaret Garritsen de Vries, the IMF historian, puts it: "The Bretton Woods conference of July 1–22, 1944, was one of the most successful conferences of the twentieth century and a landmark in world economic history. Four decades later, economists, historians, and others still marvel at the vision, determination, and idealism of those who created the International Monetary Fund." (It would be beyond the scope of this short essay to characterize or even summarize the working of the Bretton Woods system and its extraordinary achievements until a major part of it collapsed in August 1971 when U.S. president Richard Nixon made the dollar "temporarily" inconvertible.)

The Belgian government participated actively in the preparatory work, in the Atlantic City preliminary conference and in the Bretton Woods conference itself, where Belgium assumed one of the four vice-presidencies of the conference. Camille Gutt, former minister of finance of Belgium, "an old and trusted friend" as Lord Keynes would say, became the first managing director of the fund and laid the groundwork for the organization of the IMF.

One of Gutt's merits was that he perceived that the "one-world" approach of the Bretton Woods philosophy was not incompatible with regional European arrangements in which Belgians were to play a remarkable role. Gutt created the Paris office of the fund and dispatched there Robert Triffin, who was soon to become adviser to the U.S. delegation, or more precisely to the Office of the Special Representative (OSR), where under Averell Harriman the U.S. government in an extraordinary and farsighted act of leadership and benevolence used the distribution of Marshall Plan aid to force European governments to lay the basis for unification. In those days the action was not in Washington but in Paris at the Organization of European Economic Cooperation (OEEC). The fund itself had been, so to speak, put in "cold storage" when the so-called ERP decision laid down the rule that European IMF members who were receiving aid under the European Recovery Program (the Marshall Plan) were not expected to use the resources of the fund. The latter was therefore confined to organizational and legal work, work that, though probably frustrating for Gutt, was to lay the intellectual basis for future progress and development.

The OEEC and the EPU

Several Belgians played a decisive role in the new monetary system. Robert Triffin has already been mentioned (he was then a U.S. citizen). Hubert Ansiaux, then director of the National Bank of Belgium, later governor of the bank, was chairman of the Payments Committee of the OEEC, and Jean-Charles Snoy et d'Oppuers was chairman of the Trade Committee and at times presided over the OEEC Council. With their colleagues, through weeks of constant negotiations, they hammered out the system of trade liberalization and multilateral payments. This made it possible to do away with the bilateralism in which, after the war, payments and exchanges had become ensnared.

Far from being contradictory to the "one-world" approach of the IMF, the regional approach proved to be the only way in which substantial progress could be made in eliminating trade restrictions, quotas, and bilateralism. After a first experiment at the Benelux level in 1947 and several provisional agreements in the OEEC, a proposal in December 1949 led to the establishment of the European Payments Union (EPU). The EPU set in motion a process that by the late 1950's led to the widespread return to convertibility of currencies, as defined by the IMF Articles of Agreement.

It is not our purpose to write the history of the Bretton Woods system, its achievements and its shortcomings. Two dates must nevertheless be underlined. In 1962, to supplement the resources of the fund, ten countries including Belgium set up the system of the General Agreements to Borrow (GAB). This was the origin of the G-10, which played an important role in world monetary affairs for many years. The emphasis has now shifted to G-7, G-5, or even G-3 meetings, a regrettable development that deprives the concert of great economic powers the effective contribution of small countries to the negotiating process. Second, in 1969 special drawing rights (SDR), a new reserve asset, were created after more than ten years of arduous negotiations. It was hoped that these would become a central element in international reserves, but this grandiose objective is far from a reality.

The 1970's and the 1980's: In Search of a New Monetary Order

On August 15, 1971, two pillars of the Bretton Woods system collapsed: the system of agreed par values and the convertibility of the dollar into gold. The immediate reaction was twofold: to try to establish new par values, and to search for a new international monetary system.

On December 18, 1971, the Smithsonian Agreement, after months of strenuous negotiations in the Group of Ten, determined a new set of exchange rates and raised the price of gold from $35 to $38 an ounce, a dollar devaluation of 7.9 percent. The Belgian delegation agreed to an "upvaluation" of the Belgian franc of 2.8 percent in terms of gold. But from a systemic point of view, the most important decisions were to restore a par value system and to raise the allowable margin of fluctuation of exchange rates on either side of par values from 0.75 percent to 2.25 percent. These margins permitted a total fluctuation range of 9 percent between two currencies other than the dollar, which was "repegged" to gold. In the EEC, particularly in Belgium, this was considered too much. But more on this later. The Smithsonian Agreement, which was hailed as historic, did not last long. In March 1973 a "system" (if it can thus be described) of generalized floating was accepted, very reluctantly by some as will be seen.

In the meantime, studies and negotiations were in full swing to reform the international monetary system. A Committee of Twenty was created by the Board of Governors of the IMF to elaborate proposals within two years. It concluded its activities on June 13, 1974. By then the first oil crisis had jeopardized the prospects for stability. The committee had to limit itself to an Outline of Reform, which basically accepted an "evolutionary monetary system" to be adapted on the basis of experience.

It was left to the "Interim Committee," created on the recommendations of the Committee of Twenty, to pursue negotiations to amend the IMF Articles of Agreement. In January 1976, this committee, chaired by Belgian minister of finance Willy De Clercq, completed arrangements for an "interim reform" of the international monetary system. This interim reform legalized floating rates, under the "surveillance" of the IMF, and simply retained the possibility that the fund might determine, by an 85 percent majority, that international economic conditions might permit "the introduction of a widespread system of exchange arrangements based on stable but adjustable par values."

The Search for Exchange Stability in Europe

Needless to say, this disintegration of the Bretton Woods system did not satisfy the needs of European countries, particularly of Belgium. The Treaty of Rome had not set an economic and monetary union as an explicit objective. It was felt, at the time of signing of the treaty in 1958, that the international monetary system as it then existed provided an acceptable background. But the treaty specified that exchange rates and the coordination of monetary policies were "matters of common interest."

Even before the collapse of the Bretton Woods system, efforts were being made to achieve in Europe greater stability and closer coordination. In all these endeavors, Belgian authorities played an active role. Only the main stages can be mentioned. In February 1969, the EEC Commission issued a plan that was to be known as the "Plan Barre," after the then vice-president of the commission. The European summit at the Hague in December 1969 decided, on the basis of the Plan Barre, to achieve, step by step, a full economic and monetary union. A study group was created under the chairmanship of Pierre Werner, prime minister of Luxembourg. Within the group, a committee of experts, presided over by Baron Ansiaux, governor of the National Bank of Belgium, was entrusted with the monetary and foreign exchange aspects of the plan. The Werner Report was endorsed by the European Council in March 1971.

However, it proved impossible to achieve even the first steps of the plan, which foresaw in three stages over ten years the achievement of a full economic and monetary union (EMU).

Soon the immediate problem became the necessity to react to the dislocation of the world monetary system. Two days after the "suspension" of U.S. dollar convertibility on August 15, 1971, the Benelux ministers proposed to the EEC Council a plan under which EEC currencies would float "together" vis-à-vis the dollar within narrow margins of fluctuation vis-à-vis each other. An agreement could not be reached. Thereupon the three Benelux countries decided to put the plan into effect among themselves. On August 21, 1971, the Nederlandsche Bank and the National Bank of Belgium concluded the necessary technical agreements. This precursor of the "snake" thus happened to be created in the premises of the National Bank of Belgium. Zoological comparisons were in favor at the time, and this arrangement was sometimes referred to as the Benelux "worm."

From the Snake to the EMS

As mentioned earlier, the wide margins of fluctuation of exchange rates in the Smithsonian Agreement appeared excessive to many European countries. Their response was the Basel Agreement, which set margins of fluctuation between their currencies at the same level as those agreed at the Smithsonian vis-à-vis the dollar. The margins with respect to the dollar were called the "tunnel," within which the narrow band of European currencies would move together as a "snake." When the Smithsonian system disintegrated in March 1973, the tunnel ceased to exist and only the snake was left.

The snake had an agitated existence: some currencies joined, then left, then joined again, then left again, and eventually the snake became a mini-snake in which the Belgian and Luxembourgois currencies were, with a few other "small" currencies, cohabitating with the two strongest EEC currencies: the Deutsche mark and the Dutch guilder. The system had in fact become a Deutsche mark in which the adjustment burden fell solely on the debtor countries.

A larger zone of foreign exchange stability, in which the adjustment process would be more symmetrical (that is, "shared" between surplus and deficit countries), was needed. The Tindemans Report of December 1975 on the European Union had already pointed out that these general provisions would have to be achieved by a consolidation and an enlargement of the snake. However, not until 1978 did a meeting between French president Valéry Giscard d'Estaing and German chancellor Helmut Schmidt open the way for the European Monetary System (EMS), which may succinctly, and not totally accurately, be described as the snake, plus the European Currency Unit (ECU), plus the divergence indicator.

Here again, Belgian representatives played an important role. At the time Jacques van Ypersele de Strihou chaired the Monetary Committee of the EEC, and Cecil de Strycker, governor of the National Bank of Belgium, headed the Committee of Governors. The two played a decisive role in working out the technical implementation of the Giscard-Schmidt blueprint and in finding appropriate compromises between French and German views.

The EMS was greeted with skepticism by many, disappointment by some, and downright hostility by a few. The agreement provided for a two-stage development. The initial stage was to be followed after two years by an "institutional" stage in which a European Monetary Fund would come into existence and the ECU would play a full and complete role as a reserve asset and a means of settlement.

The EMS began in March 1979. By December 1980 the European Council decided that the institutional stage would be indefinitely postponed. Despite this setback, despite many difficulties, despite the need for a number of adjustments of central rates, the EMS, if it has not fulfilled all the hopes of its advocates, has given the lie to many of its critics. With the benefit of hindsight, it may be said that the EMS has attained many of its objectives and that it has created a zone of relative stability of exchange rates in Europe. It suffices to compare the volatility and misalignment of exchange rates between floating currencies to what has happened within the EMS. The EMS has been instrumental in leading to a remarkable convergence of economic conditions and policies between its partners.

Much remains to be done. The years to come may prove more difficult. Progress in Europe does not decrease the need for, and is even in part dependent on, the restoration of an acceptable international monetary order. Despite the difficulties and obstacles, however, some hope is permitted. Almost everyone is now convinced that floating exchange rates have failed to produce the results envisioned by their proponents and that exchange rates are too important to be left solely to market devices. This is at least a promising starting point. Some lessons can be drawn from the experience of the EMS, but the system cannot be simply transposed to the world as a whole.

Belgium, with its small and open economy, believes that progress toward a new monetary order is not only in its interest, but in that of world economic growth, free trade, welfare, and, in the final analysis, peace. The voice of small countries is not very loud; we must hope for strong and farsighted leadership like that of the 1940's.

Belgium and Africa

Jean-Paul van Bellinghen

IN THE EARLY 1960'S, when most of the black African colonies achieved their independence, the term "Belgian Africa" was often better known and understood in many parts of the world than the name of Belgium itself. Belgian Africa meant, in essence, the Belgian Congo, today consisting of the Republic of Zaïre (the second largest country in sub-Saharan Africa both in terms of size, after the Sudan, and in terms of population, after Nigeria) and the present Republics of Rwanda and Burundi (two small countries east of Zaïre, spanning the area from the northern shores of Lake Tanganyika to the hills of Uganda). Together the three countries today represent a little over 10 percent of sub-Saharan Africa's total area and population, Zaïre being the giant with almost 2.5 million square kilometers (80 times the size of Belgium) and a population exceeding 30 million (three times the number of Belgians).

Belgian Africa, which covered almost the whole of Central Africa, was the most inaccessible part of the continent and was described by Joseph Conrad as "the heart of darkness." This part of Africa has been associated with one person, King Leopold II of Belgium, and with one country, Belgium, a very small European power with no previous colonial experience and no influence in the world. This was bound to arouse great curiosity, vigilance, and scrutiny on the part of the Great Powers and world public opinion.

Authors such as Joseph Conrad, Mark Twain, C. S. Forester, John Gunther, and Graham Greene brought this part of Africa into the limelight. Far from remaining the heart of darkness, it became the center stage for every human drama, thus creating some clichés that need to be put in context. "The only dark aspect of the dark continent," wrote Robert Audrey in *African Genesis*, "is our knowledge of it." This essay attempts to put the story of Belgium and Africa in overall perspective.

Stanley's Discovery

Central Africa excited the imagination in the 19th century, for it remained unmapped, unexplored, and totally unknown until in 1872 Henry Morton Stanley, a British-American correspondent writing for the Paris-based *New York Herald,* succeeded in finding Dr. David Livingstone, the lost British missionary, at Ujiji on Lake Tanganyika. In 1874, Stanley undertook a second expedition from Zanzibar. He was accompanied by a party of 400 Africans and six Europeans. He reached Lake Tanganyika again and pushed on to the west and discovered a wide river, the Lualaba, which flowed from south to north and turned out to be the Congo River, whose mighty and often tumultuous rapids, waterfalls, and cataracts, turning gradually to the west, brought an exhausted and decimated party to Boma, 70 miles from the Atlantic Ocean.

In 1877, Stanley returned to London, where he gave a conference before the Royal Geographic Society, received with great applause but no concrete response in terms of action. Stanley, the first explorer ever to have traversed the Congo River basin, was, for his part, looking for a government or, failing a government, an internationally recognized association that would send him back to Africa with financial backing, a mission, and a flag. He therefore accepted an invitation to Brussels from King Leopold II, whose connections with German, British, and French royalty endowed him with a perception of the world very different from that of his own subjects. In 1876, the king had been elected president of the International African Association, which he had helped to organize. The goals of the association were nothing less than the "eradication of slave trade in Central Africa" and the "dawn of civilization" in this part of the world. The association was now considering an exploration party.

The king and Stanley agreed to cooperate, and in February 1879, the association, with the king's financial support, sent Stanley and an exploration party to the mouth of the Congo River. This time, Stanley would trek from west to east. He moved through the dense bush along the cataracts of the lower Congo. His party established no fewer than 30 stations in three years, planting the association's blue flag with a single yellow star and signing treaties with the local chiefs about protection, trade, and land. The king soon transformed the International Association into the Study Committee of Upper Congo, which in turn became the International Congo Association, which sent several more exploring parties, signed 500 treaties, and founded 40 additional stations.

The Congo Free State

The Belgian government and parliament were content to let the king act in his personal capacity, in the hope of inheriting the fruits of his actions without committing the taxpayers' money in risky enterprises. In fact, the governments of Europe, wary of colonial rivalries and conflicts, eventually saw merit in the creation of a vast area in Central Africa run by a respected head of state of a small and neutral European nation, accessible to traders, missionaries, and explorers from all European nations, and permitting duty-free imports of goods.

It was German chancellor Otto von Bismarck who was most convinced by this scheme. He convened a diplomatic conference in Berlin in 1884, which, after two months of negotiations, adopted the Berlin Act establishing the Congo Free State, a state open to all and under the sovereignty of King Leopold II of the Belgians. The Belgian parliament accepted the scheme but refused to become involved. The government would not give the king or the Free State any financial aid, nor would it provide civil servants, postal clerks, medical doctors, or other personnel.

The king was left to recruit administrators throughout Europe. He called on Stanley to be his first administrator general and later on a British subject, Sir Francis de Winton. In 1890 he would have about 400 Europeans at his service, mostly from Belgium, Britain, Germany, and Scandinavia. They were the ones who led the exploring parties, negotiated with local chiefs, mobilized local recruits, pacified warring groups, fought the slave traders, established stations along the rivers, and raised the flag at the frontiers. Leopold had no governmental backing, but he unleashed the energies of two forces acting with different motivations: the churches in Britain, Scandinavia, and Belgium, which were attracted by the possibility of converts, and the entrepreneurs of Europe, who appreciated the nondiscriminatory "open door" status of the Free State, a novelty in those days.

The pioneering days were those when only brave young people dared to confront the unknown: young missionaries with a spiritual objective, young army officers idled by the peace in Europe, young civil servants who felt that much greater accomplishments awaited them in Africa, and, last but not least, adventurers attracted by the motive of total freedom, opportunity, and greater rewards. All would take matters into their own hands and work hard.

They were quite rapidly hardened by the reality of solitude, the heat, and appalling epidemics. Indeed, the exploring groups had been the vehicle for the transmission of epidemics. Malaria was one, as was small-pox, but more devastating was the tsetse fly, which causes the dreaded sleeping sickness. Most of these men and women died young, as wit-nessed by their tombs all along the rivers, but the number of Congolese who died was catastrophic—possibly one-third of a total population of roughly 15 million at the end of the century. (Disasters of the same pro-portions struck indigenous populations in other continents at the time of exploration and conquest. A recent U.S. archeological survey, quoted by the British *Independent*, estimates that "smallpox and other diseases brought by European settlers in North America wiped out 70% of the 14 million Indian population.")

To meet the cost of exploration, pacification, and administration, the king had to rely on his own personal and limited resources and those of his friends and lenders in the European financial world. Taxing his own 400 agents in order to pay them was inconsistent, and taxing the Africans would not yield any revenue. Import duties and trade monopolies had been ruled out by the Berlin Act. The only conceivable source of reve-nue for the Congo Free State proved to be a tax on exports. Hence, the search for the most readily available and valuable export products: ivory and rubber. The intense chase for ivory, so dramatically described in Conrad's *Heart of Darkness*, was obviously stimulated by greedy hunters. Its political justification was its contribution, in the early days, to the budget of the Free State.

The king's personal resources and his bankers' patience were soon exhausted. The king was already negotiating loans from the Belgian gov-ernment to prevent the Free State's financial collapse when John Dun-lop's invention of the pneumatic tire caused a sudden surge of global demand for rubber. The king had resented the government's failure to come to his aid in previous years, and he was therefore quite relieved to learn of the sudden surge in rubber prices. He stopped the loan negotia-tions and hoped to maintain his autonomy on the basis of an expected improvement in the Congo's income.

Rubber was harvested by Africans sent into the forests by local chiefs who had been assigned rubber quotas in return for protection, trade, and money. The principle involved was forced labor, a familiar feature all over Africa in those days, primarily in the field of public works and the production of crops deemed essential for feeding populations. With the sudden improvement in rubber prices, quotas multiplied, and private as well as state agents were given financial incentives for obtaining ever in-creasing quantities. These incentives provoked human drama when offi-cials allowed private companies' armed guards to pressure, beat, or even kill resistant Africans. Murder and maltreatment were always present in the African forest, but this time they took place in the context of the search for funds to sustain a political system that claimed it was ending suffering and bringing justice and development.

British consul Roger Casement sent evidence collected by missionaries to London and wrote letters to his friend Edgar Morel, who indicted the king publicly in his book *Red Rubber*. The Congo Reform Movement soon found an echo on the Continent and in Belgium itself. The king sent an international inquiry team and eventually instituted corrective measures.

Morel, who resided in the British colonial trade center of Liverpool, then a rival of Antwerp, suggested, without any concrete evidence, that the rubber drama had cost 8 million lives, a figure now repeated as "common knowledge." However, the well-documented book by L. H. Gann and Peter Duignan, *The Rulers of Belgian Africa, 1884–1914* (1979), cites a book by Alexandre Delcommune, *L'avenir du Congo belge menacé*, which indicates that there were only 500,000 rubber harvesters in 1905. Since rubber production went on unhindered after 1901, one cannot assume that the group was substantially depleted, let alone that millions were murdered. Morel presumably chose to inflate his figures so as to shock public opinion.

Whatever the numbers of casualties, the techniques used in the rubber harvest had profoundly shaken public opinion in Britain and Belgium. Consequently the Belgian parliament could no longer maintain its hands-off attitude, and the government eventually showed some willingness to assume responsibility in Africa. In 1908, the government finalized an agreement with the king for transfer of sovereignty.

The king died the next year. In 23 years, he had helped to map the country, establish its frontiers, build its stations, occupy the land, appoint an administration, chase the slave traders, stop internal strife, open up the country through a deep sea harbor and a railway connecting with the navigable upper Congo, launch more than 100 river steamers, create a mining industry, harness waterfalls, and introduce modern farming. In short, he had laid the groundwork for the coming 52 years of a Belgian-administrated Congo.

The Belgian Congo

On May 20, 1908, the Belgian parliament approved a bill, the Colonial Charter, ratifying the transfer of sovereignty within the guidelines and constraints imposed by the Berlin Act. Although Belgium had now acquired sovereignty over the Congo, parliament, still concerned with the people's anxieties about foreign involvement, refused to permit the government to transfer public funds to the colony or mobilize military personnel for Africa. The government had no choice but to keep recruiting volunteers for the Congolese army and to finance the Congolese budget exclusively out of Congolese resources, in particular export taxes.

Exports of cotton, palm oil, and coffee now far exceeded rubber exports but the real backbone of the colony's revenue, however, was copper and precious metals from the province of Katanga (now Shaba). Extraction, mining, and refining began on a grand scale. Four long railroads were built connecting the area with ports in South Africa, Tanzania, Angola, and the Congo. The production of copper, starting from scratch at the end of the century, reached 250,000 tons in 1957, or 8 percent of the world's total production, and made the Congo the fourth-largest copper producer in the world. The Union Minière du Haut Katanga became one of the world's largest and most dynamic companies and helped start the nuclear age by delivering to the United States, in 1942, the first batch of fissionable uranium. Total exports, which stood at $12 million (present value) in 1892, shot up to $120 million in 1908, the year of the transfer to Belgium, and to $3.5 billion, 70 percent of the GNP, at the time of independence in 1960.

The taxes on exports remained the main source of income for the colonial government and stood at $1 billion a year in 1957. This income enabled the colonial government to run its daily affairs and to undertake a vast development program. It set its sights on building a network of roads linking navigable waterways and railways. From 1909 till 1960, it built 87,000 miles of good roads. River transport became a huge enterprise, completely controlled by the colonial authorities; rail transport was built by private companies.

Intensive private investments in production (about $10 billion at today's value) from 1885 to 1987 were "a remarkable investment for a small country," wrote Lord Hailey in his *African Survey*. In the field of agriculture, the Belgians introduced coffee, cocoa, tea, and European cattle and built a network of agricultural research stations (INEAC) that had no rival in Africa. They also built a network of scientific research stations (IRSAC) to study the flora and fauna of tropical Africa.

Out of a total population of 13 million in 1957, more than 1.2 million persons were under contract with companies and public bodies and received salaries, medical insurance, and pension rights. According to World Bank figures, the 1960 GNP per capita was $150 (1960 value), then one of the highest in Central Africa. Housing, provided in the cities by the authorities or around industrial sites by companies, was cited as a model by authors such as John Gunther in *Inside Africa*. Medical care was very extensive, with more than 2,600 medical hospitals and centers, with more than 75,000 beds, staffed by more than 2,500 expatriates and 5,000 Congolese professionals.

Education in 1959, on the eve of independence, was wide at the base. Vocational and technical schools were important, but secondary education was limited and university education was just beginning. The Belgian emphasis on primary education resulted mainly from the vast missionary presence.

The Roman Catholic church in Belgium was, in those days, rich in young, dynamic, and devoted men and women, who came from all over Belgium but particularly from the large families of rural Flanders. These Belgians shared the dream of the early Protestant missionaries from Britain, Germany, and Scandinavia who, since 1878, had settled in the Congo basin in order "to bring the gospel" to the newly discovered people. Thousands of priests and nuns made the long sea journey and the murderous river voyage to their inland posts, where they founded their establishments, devoting their life to evangelization and human compassion without salaries and without ever contemplating a return home. The Catholic and the Protestant missionaries are, in this sense, the unsung heroes of the extraordinarily rapid transformation of the Congo.

In 1960 the Belgian missionaries numbered 6,000 men and women. Their working hours spanned the whole day, and their professional lives sometimes exceeded half a century. The Hollywood film *A Nun's Story* pictures their lives with splendid accuracy, and Graham Greene's novel *A Burnt-Out Case* depicts their dilemmas in one of their leprosy centers in Yonda. British Methodist missionaries had been the first to establish missionary schools, but Catholic missionaries from Belgium soon followed suit, and with numbers swelling, they would establish a vast network of schools for which the colonial authorities granted both land and money. By 1958 they had built more than 20,000 schools, manned by almost 7,000 expatriate teachers and 44,000 Congolese, with an enrollment of 1.5 million Congolese children from a total population, then, of 13 million. The greatest tribute to their effectiveness is given in the World Bank's 1981 report entitled "Accelerated Development in Sub-Saharan Africa," which states that just before 1960 the Zaïrean literacy rate was 31 percent, whereas the average for all sub-Saharan Africa was only 16 percent.

The growth of agricultural and technical schools followed the rhythm of industrial and agricultural development, which, rapid though it was, could absorb only a fraction of the masses now pouring out of the primary schools. Over 19,000 students nevertheless attended classes in such schools in 1957, and 44,000 pursued vocational, secondary, and higher education.

University education, as contemplated by almost all colonial powers, meant a few Africans attending universities, mainly in Europe, and was seen in the context of an assimilation of the African elites with European elites. Algeria was then still seen in Paris as an integral part of metropolitan France. Angola and Mozambique were Portuguese overseas provinces. Most of the French colonies were envisioned as future autonomous members of a French community of nations, and most British southern African colonies as future multiracial, autonomous members of the British Commonwealth. The Belgians, however, never seriously contemplated any association between Belgium and the Congo, but had always suggested an eventual—albeit distant—total independence for the Congo. In the 1950's, they confronted the ultimate consequence of their own logic: open up university training, as other colonial powers had, and create an elite that would demand independence and a withdrawal of Belgian rule.

The Roman Catholic church of Belgium, on the other hand, had early on recognized the need for Africanization of its own hierarchy and did not see its role in a Belgian context but in a universal one. It perceived the quickening Third World yearning for independence and in 1952 invited the Roman Catholic University of Leuven (Louvain) to lay the foundation stone of the first Congolese university, Lovanium. The Free University of Brussels followed suit with the founding of a university in 1956 in Lubumbashi, and the Protestant churches started a third university in Kisangani in 1958.

University education therefore started in the Belgian Congo not much later than in Central and Eastern Africa. The Belgians differed, however, from other colonial governments in their reluctance to admit to universities in the metropole a small group of privileged Africans. Their stated policy was one of gradual evolution to higher education, and they resented the idea of a small, privileged group attending universities in Europe only to challenge colonial rule upon their return to Africa. This policy might have been understood, had the groundswell for independence in Africa not suddenly increased and broken loose all over Africa at the end of the 1950's. Having made no plans for an early emancipation, the Belgians found themselves confronted, at independence, with a small number of university graduates. A similar situation prevailed at the time of independence in Rwanda, Burundi, Zambia, and many other Central and Southern African countries, but the Congo's lack of graduates gained notoriety because it was diagnosed by the world media as the main cause for the civil strife that followed so quickly after independence.

In fact, the three universities of Zaïre, which have since merged into the National University of Zaïre (UNAZA), have an enrollment today of more than 20,000 students, which is a figure far above that in some old independent countries of Africa and many a Caribbean country. Belgian cooperation with the three campuses presently still exceeds the total contribution to those campuses of all U.N. member-states, the United Nations, and U.N. agencies combined, and Belgium is the country where presently the majority of Zaïrean, Rwandese, and Burundese students do postgraduate work. Thus, while it is true that the educational pyramid was not finished on the day of independence, with Belgian assistance it has been completed since.

The Belgian Trusteeship over Rwanda and Burundi

Rwanda and Burundi are situated between Lake Tanganyika and Uganda and densely populated by three ethnic groups: the Hutus, the Tutsis, and the Twas. All three groups lived under two monarchies. Both countries belonged to the German colony known as German East Africa, from which German colonial troops attacked the eastern border of the Belgian Congo in October 1914, two months after the outbreak of World War I. The Congolese army successfully held off the German attack and, strengthened by this victory, helped invade German Cameroon, defend Northern Rhodesia, and invade German East Africa. With the 1919 Versailles Peace Treaty, the German colonies were put under the tutelage of the newly established League of Nations, which mandated some European countries to administer the former German colonies on its behalf.

German East Africa was dismembered, and the mandate to administer the kingdoms of Rwanda and Burundi was given to Belgium. In 1945 the United Nations confirmed the system by making the two territories a "trust area" in Belgian hands. This meant that ultimate political responsibility for administering the territories lay with an organization representing the world community of nations, in particular its Trusteeship Council and the Fourth Commission of its General Assembly. In 1947, Brussels appointed former Governor-General of the Congo Pierre Rijckmans as its representative on the Trusteeship Council in New York, submitted yearly progress reports, and accepted both regular visits of U.N. inquiry teams and petitions to the United Nations from Rwandese and Burundese citizens.

Eventual responsibility for the administration of the two areas was clearly in U.N. hands, and yet, surprisingly, socioeconomic development in Rwanda and Burundi could not keep pace with developments in the neighboring Congo, for both areas were overpopulated and had none of the Congo's rich mineral resources. The theory of fast development on the basis of local income was now being challenged.

With U.N. approval, the Belgian administration ruled both kingdoms with the support of both dynasties, which relied very much on the preponderant influence of the Tutsis, a tall and proud people who, in the past, had migrated from the Ethiopian plateaus. Their relative wealth, ethnic cohesion, and tradition gave them a leading role in both countries, where the majority of the people were Hutu farmers.

With the prospect of independence, however, the Tutsis and Hutus of Rwanda followed different paths. The ruling Tutsis, who constituted a very small minority, demanded immediate independence and were largely supported by a majority in the United Nations. The Hutus, fearing a continuation of Tutsi rule after independence, took note of their own identity and numerical majority, and, taking a hint from the Western parliamentary democracies, demanded instead a Western-style parliamentary election before independence. They hoped that a Hutu-dominated parliament would lead to Hutu rule after independence. No compromise was possible between the two groups, and the Hutus revolted and attacked the Tutsis in 1959. The Belgians could do little to avert or stop the bloody encounter. The Hutus eventually won the elections, abolished the kingdom, and created a republic that eventually received recognition in the United Nations.

In Burundi, the ruling Tutsis, who were more numerous than in Rwanda and more intermarried with the Hutus, succeeded in maintaining a balance, but years after independence a bloody confrontation took place there as well. Both governments today have re-established internal peace, with the Hutus exerting the dominant influence in Rwanda and the Tutsis in Burundi.

Rwanda and Burundi were already the most densely populated areas of sub-Saharan Africa when the Belgians moved in. The introduction of modern medicine caused a demographic growth of alarming proportions. The Belgians therefore introduced high-priced export crops such as coffee and tea, which helped improve the overall economic picture substantially, but affected per capita income more modestly. With independence in 1962, the demographic curve kept climbing, but both countries increased their export crops substantially and, contrary to most African countries, managed to maintain and improve income levels. Rwanda attained in 1986 a per capita income of $310, surpassing the $300 per capita income of prosperous Kenya.

Belgium's Confrontation with the United Nations

Belgium was a founding member of both the League of Nations and the United Nations and cooperated closely with both on managing Rwanda and Burundi. The constant surveillance and prodding by U.N. representatives sometimes irritated Belgian officials and media, but, by and large, the world body began to understand both the complexities of the problems as well as the good faith in which the Belgians were acting. When the Hutus revolted against the Tutsis in Rwanda in 1959, the Belgians were spared the role of scapegoat, and when independence came in the summer of 1962, the United Nations understood the need for both countries to keep Belgian military forces for a while so that law and order could be maintained in the early days of fragile statehood. The Belgian military, indeed, stayed with U.N. approval.

The same had not been the case in the Congo two years before. There, law and order broke down only ten days after independence, provoking a Belgian intervention, which, in turn, brought a confrontation between the United Nations and Belgium. Independence was proclaimed on June 30, 1960, as the result of a determined Belgian policy to confront the explosive tide of African nationalism—which had found its first violent expression in Kinshasa in January 1959—with the message that the Congolese would themselves set the date for independence. In eighteen months, they proceeded with provincial and national elections that permitted the appointment of a president, Joseph Kasavubu, and a prime minister, Patrice Lumumba. This short span of time sufficed to form a fragile Congolese political authority that was expected to cooperate with Belgium in order to manage the country and pursue its development.

But ten days after independence Congolese soldiers and noncommissioned officers, seeing their country now led by their own compatriots and failing to understand why they were still under the authority of expatriate officers, refused to obey further orders. Surprisingly and tragically, the prime minister sided with the soldiers and asked the Belgian military to leave, thereby provoking not only the disintegration of his own army but also the breakdown of law and order throughout the country. Brussels immediately sent military units to help the Congolese government stem the tide of spreading anarchy, but when Moise Tshombe, the prime minister of rich Katanga Province, proclaimed his province an independent state, the central government, fearing that he was encouraged by Belgium, called upon the secretary-general of the United Nations, Dag Hammarskjöld of Sweden, to send a U.N. peacekeeping force to help it re-establish order, restore the unity of the country, and expel the Belgian military units and advisers. The Katangese secession had, in fact, not been conceived by the Belgian government, although it had received encouragement from local Belgian residents and companies. Once independence was proclaimed, however, the Belgian army units stationed in Katanga chose to remain neutral. Their presence had become useless, if not potentially hostile to the central government's interests.

The United Nations, in its varied composition of member-countries, saw Kinshasa's invitation as a call for a crusade against a recolonization attempt, a possible suppression of Western capitalist interests, or, more soberly, as an intervention to forestall a major international confrontation in the Congo. With unprecedented speed, the U.N. secretary-general succeeded in raising a U.N. peacekeeping force from several neutral African, Asian, and European countries, flying them to the Congo, re-establishing a semblance of law and order, and facilitating the withdrawal of all Belgian forces.

The U.N. force, however, could not prevent a deep split in the Congolese government, the eventual constitution of a rival and Soviet-supported government in Stanleyville, the murder of Prime Minister Lumumba, and a massacre in the Stanleyville-dominated part of the country. Neither could the secretary-general implement resolutions of the U.N. Security Council, demanding an end to Katangese secession, because his troops' mandate was, in military terms, limited to self-defense. The secretary-general then resorted to shuttle diplomacy, of which he became the tragic victim when, flying to meet Premier Tshombe in N'Dola, Zambia, his plane crashed minutes before landing. With Hammarskjöld's death, the United Nations, already challenged and financially boycotted by France and the USSR, lost its main source of inspiration and guidance.

It will remain Hammarskjöld's merit to have proved the feasibility of a U.N. peacekeeping operation, to have kept the Congo free from a major international confrontation, and to have paved the way for the eventual restoration of peace and unity. These were achieved in 1965 when the political power structure was finally established by the army commander, Colonel Mobutu, today Marshal Mobutu Sese Seko, the president of Zaïre, who had succeeded in creating a new army, subjugating rebellious areas, ending the Katanga secession, and, last but not least, establishing a nationwide political movement reconciling almost all the surviving political forces.

As the U.N. peacekeeping force was withdrawn from the Congo in 1965, so were the major U.N. assistance programs for lack of proper funding by the member-states, and the Congo (soon to be named Zaïre) turned gradually for assistance to individual donor countries and in particular to Belgium. The vast majority of the 100,000 Belgians who had resided in the Congo before independence had left it. A number, however, were ready to return. As the last U.N. soldiers left Kinshasa, the Zaïrean government asked Belgium to send military advisers, some of whom were the very same officers whose expulsions had been demanded in previous U.N. Security Council resolutions. This time there was no cause for alarm: the bond of trust between Kinshasa and Brussels had been restored.

Belgium and Independent Africa

The relationship between former colonial rulers and former colonies has changed from the 1960's in two fundamental ways. Whereas colonial rulers had mainly achieved an economic development by private entrepreneurial initiative and investment without spending public funds, the newly independent countries felt unable to influence the private and mostly expatriate entrepreneurs and often became openly hostile to them. They thereby discouraged new foreign investments precisely at a point in time when they themselves needed new resources to sustain their own political independence and to meet their people's new expectations. The new countries therefore asked all developed countries and in particular their former rulers to give them financial assistance, which had never been a feature of colonial rule. U.N. resolution 2424 (XV) of 1970 gave the donor countries a target to attain in terms of volume of official aid: 0.7 percent of each donor country's GNP. Belgium never reached the goal, but data from the Organization of Economic Cooperation and Development (OECD) show that it did reach 0.6 percent in 1982. With a contribution of 0.56 percent in 1984–85, it is still among the top five of all Western donor countries. With 3,258 scholarships in Belgium for Third World students and trainees and with almost 3,000 experts in the field, it was the best performer in 1984, according to OECD statistics.

The second change in north-south relations was the reorientation of trade and aid from the bilateral colonial relationship to a fully open and universal one. Belgium's reorientation was facilitated by the availability of experts who returned to Belgium after 1960 and by the establishment in Brussels, since 1960, of embassies of almost all the new Third World countries. Understandably, Third World representatives were eager to tap Belgian personnel resources and the financial resources of the Brussels-based EC Commission.

In 1985, Belgium had undertaken aid programs in almost 50 countries. Of this, 7 percent of its aid went to Latin America, 9 percent to Asia, and 70 percent to sub-Saharan Africa. Its present relationship with the Third World, in terms of aid, is mainly oriented to Africa, where it has formal aid agreements with no less than nineteen countries.

In terms of economic influence, Belgians have lost a large part of their predominant position in Zaïre. Indeed, the government of Zaïre, which inherited the Belgian colonial government's 49 percent stake in the mining companies (in fact, the original shares of King Leopold's Congo Free State), now proceeded to acquire the shares of the other shareholders and eventually became the majority shareholder or full owner of all the mining companies. The Union Minière du Haut Katanga sold its participation in the Shaba (formerly Katanga) mines to the Zaïrean national company, Gecamines, which cooperated with its former Belgian partners in mining the ore, refining the metal, and stockpiling and transporting it. The Zaïrean government, on the other hand, pursued in the late 1960's an ambitious program of forcing foreigners to sell their companies to Zaïrean nationals and proceeded, later, to nationalize all major companies from both Zaïrean and foreign owners. Confronted a few years later with important management problems, it offered a number of smaller nationalized companies back to their former owners. They now confront depressed market conditions and a scarcity of investment resources.

Zaïre's economy has recently suffered mainly from stagnant prices for copper, the country's main export. For the last ten years, copper prices have remained at about a third of the price prevailing during the last years of the colonial era. Hence, the general volume of trade has suffered, as Belgian exports to Zaïre have fallen to approximately a third of the pre-independence days.

With Rwanda and Burundi, where the main crop is coffee, the volume of which has multiplied and the price of which has remained rewarding, the volume of reciprocal trade has remained stable. With the other African countries, Belgian trade has prospered in the wake of the reorientation of their economies from the bilateral colonial pattern to a worldwide pattern. An illustration is the Belgian maritime company CMB, which expanded its African lines from three to twenty, and SABENA World Airlines, which expanded its limited colonial network to 23 African countries, the largest network in Africa.

Belgian missionaries remained in independent Africa and faced the years of turmoil with courage and determination. When other Europeans left, they stayed on, and their continuing presence and altruistic motives gained them an ever growing respectability. Their numbers are dwindling and they are advancing in age, but they refuse to retire and more than 2,000 men and women of the church are still present. They can take pride in creating one of Africa's most dynamic churches and in enjoying the confidence and the active participation of the majority of the people of Zaïre, Rwanda, and Burundi, a truly unique achievement in Africa.

The real heroes of African development are the Africans themselves. Throughout their sufferings under the slave trade, the spread of epidemics, and subjugation under European rifles, they kept their dignity, their optimism, and their eternal and frank laughter. Their capacity to absorb and assimilate has been astounding, and with the benefit of hindsight it appears that only their total geographical separation from the rest of the world kept them from mainstream currents. It was colonialism that brought an end to separation, as it has done throughout history. Colonialism, in fact, provoked a yearning for development and, hence, a desire for an ever widening circle of contacts with the entire modern world. The recent history of independent Africa has shown that pace of development, far from being hindered by the maintenance of good relations with the former colonial powers, instead has been enhanced by it as well as by the establishment of a widening circle of international cooperation. A look at the map of Africa is telling in this respect, and the recent history of Rwanda, Burundi, and Zaïre is no exception to this observation.

The history of Belgium and Africa obviously contains errors and failures. King Leopold's refusal to give anyone any account of his policies left him open to writers' and pamphleteers' most extravagant and absurd accusations. Later, in the 1950's, the Belgian government's blindness to the oncoming tidal wave of African nationalism left it ill-prepared for political emancipation. The true significance of Belgium and Africa, however, lies in the fact that never before in colonial history was such rapid development achieved in such a short time by such a small country in such a vast area of the world.

Today, almost thirty years after independence, it is still from Belgium that Zaïre, Rwanda, and Burundi receive the greatest cooperation, and it is in Belgium that they still have their most important anchorage in the developed world. Development is not the brainchild of ideologists and romantic pamphleteers; it is the product of the effective establishment of a permanent contact and cooperation between human beings. This will remain Belgium's pride in Africa.

PART III

The Constitutional System and the Interactions of Political Institutions

André Molitor, Coordinator

The Current Constitutional System

Robert Senelle

IN THE COURSE OF THE last quarter-century, Belgium has undergone a slow but unquestionable metamorphosis from a nation organized along the principles of Napoleonic centralism to a federal state. This transformation is an essential component of Belgian political and constitutional life. It has to be understood in the context of the multicultural nature of Belgium and of its situation at the crossroads of the Roman and Germanic languages.

Linguistic conflict was absent under the Old Regime, before the French Revolution. Indeed, Belgium's current difficulties arose from French policy after the Revolution. By virtue of the law of 9 Vendemiaire AN IV (October 1, 1795), the Austrian Netherlands and the principality of Liège were occupied and annexed by France. The French felt that linguistic unification offered a key to political amalgamation between France and the Belgian provinces, which had been annexed by force and against the will of the Belgian people. Consequently, the French government attempted to systematically root out the Dutch language. French became the official language of government, the army, education, justice, culture, and all national affairs. Energetic steps were taken to ban the use of Dutch. This iniquitous legislation was gradually phased out between 1815 and 1830, when the nineteen provinces of the Netherlands were united under the scepter of King William of the Netherlands, who had brought back together the seventeen provinces of the old Netherlands. Unfortunately, after the 1830 revolution, the Belgian government held that use of French would cement the unity of the new state. A significant insight into the reasoning behind this policy is given in a letter written in 1832 by Minister of Justice Charles Rogier to Jean-Joseph Raiken, an influential Belgian politican. "The rudiments of good government are based on the exclusive use of a single language, and it is clear that the single language of the Belgians must be French. In order to accomplish this, all civil and military posts will be entrusted to Walloons and Luxembourgeois; in this manner, the Flemish, temporarily deprived of the advantages attached to such posts, will be obliged to learn French, and the Germanic element in Belgium will gradually be destroyed."

A Flemish cultural revival in the second half of the 19th century and the economic expansion of most of the Flemish provinces later in that century thwarted this attempt at total gallicization of the Flemish provinces of Belgium. This provided the impetus for the slow but irrepressible urge to write into the constitution and legislation the cultural pluralism of Belgium and the differences of sentiment between the Flemish and the Walloon peoples. The Belgian constitution was fundamentally overhauled on three occasions: 1970, 1980, and 1988. On each occasion, the federalist trend was accentuated. It should be emphasized that the overwhelming majority of Belgians are happy to live together in Belgium, under the guiding hand of a monarchy that has indisputably had a moderating influence politically and is an eminent source of unity for the various different Belgian provinces.

Belgium is bisected by a linguistic border, giving it a cultural split personality: the Dutch-language culture in the north and the French-language culture in the south. The principle of "unilingualism" is applied in each region. In other words, the regional language is the official language and is used in government administration, education, and so on.

After World War I, neutral Mosenet and the districts of Eupen, Malmedy, and Saint-Vith were ceded by Germany to Belgium in the Treaty of Versailles (June 18, 1919). Together they form the German-speaking region of Belgium, which has a population of around 75,000. The city of Brussels is situated in the Dutch-speaking region. However, its inhabitants are a mixture of French- and Dutch-speaking Belgians, and it therefore forms a meeting point for the two major population groups. The city of Brussels is a bilingual region.

The existence of four linguistic regions is recognized by Article 3(a) of the constitution. The geographical boundaries of the linguistic regions were laid down in the laws of August 2, 1963, and December 23, 1970, on the official use of the different languages. The French-speaking region comprises the provinces of Hainaut, Liège (excluding the cantons in the German-speaking region), Luxembourg, Namur, and the Nivelles district in Brabant Province (1.7 million km²). The Dutch-speaking region consists of the provinces of Antwerp, Limburg, West Flanders, East Flanders, and the districts of Hal-Vilvorde and Louvain in Brabant Province (1.4 million km²). The German-speaking region is made up of the boroughs of Amel, Büllingen, Burg-Reuland, Bütgenbach, Eupen, Kelmis, Lontzen, Raeren, and Sankt-Vith (85,377 km²). The bilingual region of the city of Brussels has nineteen boroughs: Anderlecht, Auderghem, Berchem-Sainte-Agathe, Brussels, Etterbeek, Evere, Forest, Ganshoren, Ixelles, Jette, Koekelberg, Molenbeek-Saint-Jean, Saint-Gilles, Saint-Josse-ten-Noode, Schaerbeek, Uccle, Watermael-Boitsfort, Woluwe-Saint-Lambert, and Woluwe-Saint-Pierre (16,178 km²). As of January 1, 1986, the population of the various regions was as follows: Dutch-speaking region, 5,676,194; French-speaking region, 3,206,165; German-speaking region, 66,445; and Brussels, 976,536.

The question often arises as to why Belgium has not transformed the various Belgian provinces into administrative units with a constitutional status more or less similar to that of Swiss cantons. The answer is twofold. First, the linguistic problem has until now largely dominated relations between the French- and Dutch-speaking communities. Second, the Catholic party has a very comfortable majority in the provincial governments of Flanders. Consequently, the Socialist and Liberal parties have preferred not to adopt the Swiss option, which would reinforce the electoral strength of the Social-Christian parties.

Belgium is no longer a unitarian country. It has become a federal state. This chapter attempts to shed some light on its specific nature. It will deal first of all with national institutions. Then it will move on to the regional institutions, which are the base of federal Belgium. Finally, it will deal with the organization of the judiciary and the individual freedoms guaranteed by the constitution.

National Institutions

The 1831 Constituent Assembly was inspired by two essential principles: national sovereignty and separation of powers. Although theoretically the various powers are separate and supreme within their own sphere of competence, there are certain links between them.

The constitution is the overriding authority for all the powers, including the legislative power. It precedes the separate existence of each of these powers. The legislative power is, however, in a privileged position with respect to the constitution.

First, the same bodies hold both constituent and legislative authority. Only the procedures and the majorities required change. Second, the legislature disposes of residual power, whereas the two other wings of authority have only those powers specified by the constitution. Residual power is taken to mean that the legislature has all powers except those formally denied to it by the constitution. Third, the judiciary is not allowed to judge the constitutionality of a national law, but the Court of Arbitration is competent to judge if the national government, the Communities, and the Regions have respected the limits of competence as established by the constitution and the laws and to determine whether the corresponding articles of the constitution have been applied. Fourth, Article 28 of the constitution stipulates that only the legislature has the power to interpret laws, including the basic law. This privileged position of the legislature explains the legal supremacy it has acquired vis-à-vis the two other branches of authority. However, this supremacy has altered over the course of time, and the legislature now seems to be losing ground to the executive branch, particularly to the government.

There has been considerable growth in de facto powers, alongside legal powers. Political parties are the main force in this regard, and they are now considered the holders of political power because they are the electorate's means of political expression. Belgian political parties are permanent citizens' organizations, representative of the various different threads of public opinion. Their objective is to win and exercise political power in order to put into practice a particular program. Political democracy is, in fact, founded on the pluralism of political parties, which gives electors a choice in free and democratically organized elections. Although they are the true holders of political power, the parties are de facto organizations without any precise legal status. They are, however, officially recognized by the regulations governing parliamentary assemblies, which define them as political groupings. They must have a minimum of three members and must meet at least once a week in order to appoint official speakers, agree upon their political strategy, or define their policy aims. Nevertheless, these powers, though extensive, are restricted in a number of areas. The power the political parties hold varies, since some of them, because of their composition, length of existence, and representativeness, are considered to a greater extent national parties with a governmental vocation. They therefore have a weightier say in political affairs, even if they are momentarily in the opposition.

The powers of political parties are restricted in a number of other ways, and they themselves are subject to the activities of a growing number of pressure groups. The most important of these are the "social partners": business and large trade union organizations. These groups significantly influence social and economic matters. Other groups are more specialized: professional organizations such as those of pharmacists or doctors, farmers, women's rights movements, war veterans, the retired, young people, linguistic groups, or religious ones. The role of the press in political life is especially important.

The legal and de facto powers naturally must have an interface, and in Belgium the government plays this role. This is why, apart from a few rare exceptions, governments have increasingly become coalition or "cabinet" governments. Since 1919, there has only been one majority government, between 1950 and 1954, when all ministers belonged to the same party. Moreover, this majority was the result of special circumstances. Apart from two slight exceptions in 1925 and 1946, all other governments since 1919 have been coalition governments. This has inevitably influenced the exercise of power, although the constitution has always been formally respected.

Coalition or cabinet governments are brought about by a preliminary agreement between the ruling parties, given concrete form in a governmental pact, which is then submitted to parliament for approval. In this fashion, as will be explained with reference to Article 65, the king's power to appoint and dismiss ministers has taken on a rather different form. A new institution has appeared on the political stage, the cabinet (Conseil des Ministres). The importance acquired by the cabinet has been sanctioned by the constitution, which, in addition to the recognition of its role in exceptional circumstances in Article 79, confirms the permanence of its existence in Article 86(a). Therefore, the government is no longer formed of individual ministers, but rather of the ministers as a body.

Similarly, when a parliament is dissolved before the end of its term of office, this is generally due not to a vote of no-confidence by the legislature but to the disintegration of the governmental team. Consequently, parliamentary conflicts are no longer between the legislature and the executive but between the majority parties and the opposition, with the government reflecting the views of the former. The executive, and more especially the government, has thus acquired an increasingly important role, for it is in some ways the executive mouthpiece of the political parties making up the majority. The battle between parties is thus for control of the executive, and it is through the executive that the majority parties attempt to implement their policy program.

The government gains more prestige if it is backed by parliament or, in other words, by the majority. Parliament's role has evolved as a result, because parliamentary work is first of all prepared by the government, which must keep a watchful eye on the parliament if it is to successfully pass its policy program. Generally speaking, the bills that stand a good chance of adoption are introduced by the government. It also proposes the budget and is ensured in advance of its approval—at least as far as it enjoys the confidence of the majority, both in parliament and among the electorate. A wider role for the government does not therefore violate the basic precepts of democracy.

If, in 1831, the Constituent Assembly was wary of executive power, it was because the authority of the executive depended to a large extent on the personal influence of the king. When, however, government represents the leading political parties brought to power by the electorate, the constituent body senses that its legitimacy is directly derived from a healthy democracy. In such a case, the opposition parties must limit themselves to checking and criticizing governmental action. As a consequence, the separation of legislative and executive powers has become vague. On the one hand, the parliament is all-powerful through the government formed by its majority, and on the other hand, the government itself, because of its majority, is no longer afraid of being disclaimed by the parliament.

In order to have a clear idea of the relationship between the legislative chambers and the government in Belgium, it must be borne in mind that the activities of the executive power cannot be dissociated from the operation of the legislative power. Aside from its role of constantly watching over the use of public money, the parliament—notably the parliamentary majority—has the key role of providing and then maintaining on behalf of the nation a government in which it has confidence and which can enjoy stability for the implementation of its program. For its part, the government, which in turn relies on the parliament, must ensure that parliamentary activity is in the same general policy direction. The government has thus become the motor driving parliament and directing its work. Governmental stability requires a disciplined majority, which, for important matters, often results in party-line voting. Such discipline can exist only in political parties so tightly organized that frequent changes in the composition of the government can be avoided.

The separation of executive and legislative powers has been replaced by a kind of cooperation, with the decision-making power increasingly falling into the hands of a coalition of varying composition. The leading political forces of the moment and socioeconomic groups attempt to influence this coalition.

It should, however, be emphasized that this form of the exercise of power still falls within the constitutional framework. Due to its flexible nature, the constitution has allowed such an evolution without serious upheaval. Thus, in the eyes of nearly all Belgians, parliamentary democracy represents, despite its imperfections, the best and, in any event, the only admissible form of government. For the vast majority of citizens, the parliament, created by the will of a sovereign people and representing the supreme authority, is the cornerstone of democracy.

The National Executive

The national executive is the branch of government responsible for implementing laws, ensuring state security, and maintaining public order. Article 29 of the constitution invests this power in the king.

Articles 63, 64, and 89 of the constitution stipulate that the king's powers can be exercised only upon countersignature by ministers, who alone are responsible to the legislative chambers. The role of the monarchy in a modern parliamentary system is limited, and the government clearly holds the reins of political initiative and everyday administration. The current concept of the monarchy, to use a time-honored phrase, is that of the "king in his cabinet"; in other words, the king and the members of the government, who, separately, are politically and constitutionally without power. Political action by the king without the consent of the ministers is absolutely excluded. This system of cabinet government, in which the ministerial team reflects the parliamentary majority, necessarily implies that the government is the active element. The very nature of such a system dictates that the government plays a key role in guiding and coordinating the management of state affairs.

Modern constitutional democracy in Belgium cannot simply be considered a monarchical system in which the monarch plays a diminished role. The king, when exercising his prominent attributions, applies the well-known statement of the English juridical adviser Bagehot that the king's main duties are to put his ministers on their guard, to advise them, and to warn them in case of necessity. It is obvious that the king's role becomes particularly important during a governmental crisis, as the constitution requires the king to take steps to see that a new government is formed within the shortest possible time. On the contrary, the psychological role of the king as a figurehead of unity is of central importance. The head of state's lack of any political responsibility within a parliamentary democracy absolves him of any suspicion of bias. Strikingly, all surviving monarchies in Europe are parliamentary monarchies. A dual monarchical-parliamentary system seems to exercise a two-way protective influence.

The King

Belgium is a representative constitutional monarchy. As stressed in the introduction, the king acts as a moderator and is a very important source of unity within multicultural Belgium. A hereditary monarchy has indisputable advantages over a presidential system. The king never owes his appointment to a particular party and is therefore independent of any ideological trends. He is never subject to re-election. If he is called on to intervene personally in the relationship between the various wings of power, notably between the government and the legislature, his impartiality will be much more difficult to question than that of a politician. He is thus in a better position to encourage compromise in the event of crisis. The current head of state is King Baudouin.

The constitutional powers of the king are hereditary in the direct line of descent from King Leopold I, from male to male and by order of primogeniture. Women and their descendants are excluded from the throne. The powers granted to the king by the constitution can be divided into those relating to the exercise of (1) executive power, (2) legislative power, and (3) judicial power. Special attention will be paid in this chapter to powers falling within the first group.

These powers are (1) the execution of laws (the king is invested with the power, within the limits laid down by the constitution and by legislation, to issue compulsory provisions known as decrees or regulations; this is known as the rule-making power); (2) the appointment of civil servants to general administrative and diplomatic posts (the king sees to these appointments and is responsible for the arrangement and organization of the general administration); (3) public order and state security (the king holds this power by virtue of policing regulations and decrees and can summon the state police, armed forces, courts, and tribunals); and (4) national defense and foreign policy (the king confers the various military ranks, commands the armed forces, declares war, and signs peace treaties, alliances, and trade agreements). By virtue of Article 68 of the constitution, trade or other agreements that could encumber the state or individually bind the Belgian people enter into force only after approval by parliament.

In addition to powers connected with the exercise of legislative and judicial powers and the ones mentioned above, the king supervises regional and local administrations (this area of authority was considerably pruned in the revision of the constitution in August 1980); coins money; bestows titles of nobility, without, however, attaching any privileges to these; and awards civil and military honors.

The Government

Ministers meet in principle once a week, traditionally on Friday mornings. The agenda of the cabinet meeting is set by the prime minister. A few days before the meeting, the king is informed of the agenda and provided with copies of papers to be put before the cabinet. This allows the head of state to discuss any problem with the prime minister. The king receives a copy of cabinet decisions within a few days after the meeting.

By virtue of Article 86(b) of the constitution, the cabinet must contain an equal number of French- and Dutch-speaking ministers, excepting the prime minister. This provision was inserted into the constitution on December 24, 1970, in response to three objectives. First, it consecrated in the constitution official recognition of the prime minister; second, it officially recognized the cabinet as a permanent institution rather than one used in exceptional circumstances (Article 79); and finally, it rendered compulsory a linguistic balance in the cabinet, excluding the prime minister, members of the government from the German-speaking part of the country, and state secretaries.

The prerogatives and working principles of the cabinet have been determined by tradition. Shortly after the formation of a new government, the prime minister sends his colleagues a circular in which he indicates the manner in which he intends the cabinet to meet. This circular in principle defines the prerogatives of the cabinet, specifying areas in which its agreement is required, its opinion requested, or verbal information submitted to it. The circular also gives practical instructions regarding internal and external procedures, notably the way in which documents should be presented. Finally, it defines working procedures, such as the frequency of meetings, the advance notification required for the presentation of affairs, and the way in which information about decisions and notifications is to be passed on.

The cabinet is the most important political and administrative body. In its role as a political body, it adopts general policy guidelines and supervises the execution of this policy. In its role as an administrative body, it is responsible for making decisions on important matters involving one or several ministers. Ministers must submit information to the cabinet on current affairs of importance and of potential impact on national public opinion.

The cabinet's sphere of competence has expanded considerably since 1945. Many laws and royal decrees formally require cabinet deliberations for their implementation. The personal responsibility of each minister has naturally grown in direct proportion to this growth in the scope of the cabinet. Generally speaking, the role of the cabinet has expanded to provide satisfactory accountability to the country as a whole. This evolution is also connected with the existence of coalition governments, with each party keeping the others in check within the cabinet. So the cabinet had become one of the most important actors on the Belgian political stage, notably in the day-to-day management of public affairs.

Legislative Power

In Belgium, by virtue of Article 26 of the constitution, legislative power is collectively exercised by the king, the Chamber of Representatives (Chambre des Représentants), and the Senate (Senat). All three have a role to play in the adoption of any legislative act, and all three have the right to initiate legislation. Since 1921, universal suffrage and proportional representation have been the two cornerstones of the Belgian electoral system.

The *Chamber of Representatives* is made up of 212 members elected by universal suffrage. Members are elected for four years, unless the parliament is dissolved. Only the Chamber of Representatives has the right to charge a minister or to bring him before the supreme court (Cour de Cassation) in order to be tried.

The *Senate* consists of several categories of members: (1) directly elected senators; they number exactly half of the number of chamber members (currently 106); (2) senators elected by provincial councils, or provincial senators; their numbers are proportional to the population of each province; there are currently 51 provincial senators; (3) members appointed by directly elected senators and provincial senators; these are known as "co-opted senators"; their number is equal to half of the number of provincial senators (currently 26); and (4) "ex officio" senators: the royal princes or, if the king has no sons, Belgian princes of the branch of the royal family called upon to reign, become "ex officio" senators at the age of 18. All members of parliament are divided into linguistic groups.

The procedure for drawing up laws is as follows. The initiative may come either from the government (a "government bill") or from a member of parliament (a "private member's bill"). After its reading, the bill is sent for committee discussion and report. It is then placed on the agenda of the Chamber or the Senate, depending on where it was introduced. After a public discussion of the bill article by article, the house discussing it votes first on each article and then on the whole text. Once it has been approved by the originating house, it is handed over to the other house, where the same procedure is followed. Once the bill is adopted, it must receive royal assent. On approval, the bill will be promulgated, or, in other words, signed by the king. The final step in the procedure is official publication in the *Moniteur Belge*. It enters into force on the tenth day after publication.

Brief mention should be made here of a procedure inspired by the multicultural nature of Belgium. It is known as the "alarm bell procedure" and can be set off when a piece of legislation might harm relations between the communities. This procedure was set up by Article 38(b) of the constitution and is an important limitation on parliamentary powers.

Because there is a considerable imbalance between the linguistic groups (91 French-speaking members and 121 Dutch-speaking members), it is necessary to guard against clashes between the two or unilateral action on the part of the Dutch-speaking majority. Consequently, under the alarm bell procedure a motion, signed by at least three-quarters of the MPs belonging to a linguistic group, can be introduced after the filing of the report and before the final vote, declaring that the bill would seriously damage relations between the communities. This procedure can apply to all bills apart from budgets and those requiring a special majority. If such a motion is introduced, parliamentary procedure is suspended and the motion is referred to the cabinet, within which, as seen above, there is linguistic equality. The cabinet has 30 days to give its reasoned opinion on the motion and then invites the relevant house to decide either on the basis of this opinion or on the basis of an amended bill. This procedure can be brought into play only once by a particular linguistic group for each bill.

Provincial and Borough Institutions

The guiding principles for provincial and borough legislation are given by Article 108 of the constitution. The members of provincial and borough councils must be elected directly. All matters that are of provincial and borough interest fall under the exclusive sphere of competence of the provincial and borough councils. This notion of interest is not clearly defined legally but is taken to mean everything that the provincial and borough authorities consider as being attributed to them, excluding matters reserved by the constitution or by legislation to another authority. To ensure transparency of a council's affairs for the electors, all meetings, accounts, and budgets must be public. The central government exercises general control through the power to suspend or annul council decisions. Specific control may take the form of opinions, authorizations, expert counsel, and judgments.

The Regional Institutions

The transformation of the Belgian state will take many decades to complete. The foundations for this change were made between 1921 and 1935, when the legal and official language of Belgium was changed from French to both Dutch and French. Belgium was divided into four linguistic regions by the laws of August 2, 1963, and December 23, 1970, both of which pertain to the language used in administration. These regions are the Dutch-speaking Region, the French-speaking Region, the German-speaking Region, and the bilingual Brussels-Capital Region. Consequently, with the exception of the bilingual Brussels-Capital Region, the language of the region also serves as the administrative language.

The state reform of 1970–71 ended the unitary state. Three new territorial divisions were included in the constitution: the linguistic Regions mentioned above (Article 3bis); the Cultural Communities (Article 3ter); and the Regions (Article 107quater). Since the state reform of 1970, a competent legislature can determine and change the boundaries of the linguistic Regions simply by passing a special law by a majority vote in both chambers of the respective linguistic groups. It is a prerequisite for the passing of such laws that a majority of members of each linguistic group have met and that the total count of all yes votes in both linguistic groups amounts to two-third of all votes cast. The territorial powers of the Cultural Communities are determined by the demarcation of the linguistic Regions.

Two branches are distinguished in the Belgian constitution: the Cultural Communities and the Regions. The Cultural Communities are responsible for cultural, educational, and linguistic matters; the Regions for matters of socioeconomical importance. Since the 1970 reform, the Cultural Communities have been able to issue decrees. These decrees have the power of law and are not subordinate to national legislation. The Regions, however, were not given the power to issue decrees.

The French-speaking minority was awarded constitutional equality on the national level. The equal linguistic composition of the State Council is stipulated in the constitution. The legislative chambers are divided into a Flemish and a French group. These linguistic Communities can adjourn a debate on a bill with a three-fourths majority and can refer the bill to the Council of State. The fact that laws dealing with federalization are special laws ensures the French-speaking community that no such initiative can be completed without its consent. This equality introduced a federal principle into a constitution that had not yet been federalized.

With the state reform of 1980, a further step on the road toward federalization was taken. The Cultural Communities were remodeled into Communities. This change of name was necessary, because these legislative bodies henceforth were also in charge of health and social services. Thus the range of cultural affairs was enlarged. In addition, many socioeconomic matters were also sanctioned in the special law of August 8, 1980, to reform the institutions of the Flemish and the Walloon Regions.

These Regions too could henceforth issue decrees with the power of law that are not subordinate to national legislation. In the northern part of the country, the Flemish Council and the Flemish Executive look after communal and regional matters on the basis of this special law. Article 107ter introduced a new body, the Court of Arbitration, into the organization of the country. This court settles all conflicts of competence between the state, the Communities, and the Regions.

Many problems, however, still need to be solved. Article 59ter was reformed in 1983, and the German-speaking Community was granted autonomy. With the exception of language regulations, its powers resemble those of the Flemish and French Community. No definite statute, however, covered the Brussels Region. Dissatisfaction about the inadequate division of responsibilities between the State Council on the one hand and the Regions and Communities on the other hand grew. The few transfers of power that were made, such as giving the Communities authority in matters of education, did not constitute any real transfer of power. Thus there was a growing demand to take a third step toward a federal state.

The progressive transformation of the nation's institutions influences every aspect of public life. Consequently, it was decided to accomplish the reform of 1988 in three steps. The first step encompasses the revision of Articles 17, 59bis, 107ter, 108ter, and 115 of the constitution and the special law of August 8, 1988, pertaining to the powers vested in the Communities and the Regions. The reform of Article 17 of the constitution guarantees the freedom of education. This constitutional guarantee became a philosophical necessity once the Communities were endowed with new powers in matters of education. Revision of Article 59bis allows the transfer of all decision-making in the field of education to the Communities. Only the ages for compulsory school attendance, the minimum conditions to obtain a diploma, and the pension regulations of the teaching staff remain a national prerogative. The Communities are allowed to make their own mutual cooperation agreements as well as decisions concerning international relations. Financial matters are also to be decided by the competent legislature.

The revision of Article 107ter of the constitution puts the Court of Arbitration in charge of settling all conflicts of competence between laws, decrees, and ordinances. The competence of the court has been augmented so that it can arbitrate by a law, a decree, or an ordinance whenever a law or a decree violates the constitutional principle of equality (Articles 6 and 6bis of the constitution) or the constitutional guarantee of freedom of education (Article 17). The competent legislature can also

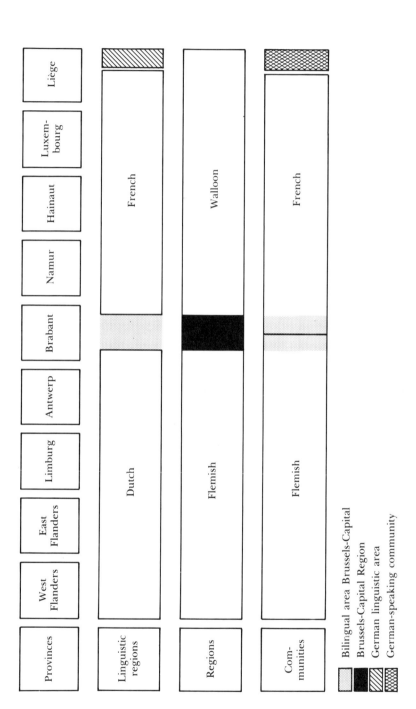

| Provinces | West Flanders | East Flanders | Limburg | Antwerp | Brabant | Namur | Hainaut | Luxem-bourg | Liège |

Linguistic regions: Dutch — French

Regions: Flemish — Walloon

Communities: Flemish — French

▨ Bilingual area Brussels-Capital
■ Brussels-Capital Region
▧ German linguistic area
▨ German-speaking community

Fig. III.1.   The asymmetric structure of Belgium

commission the court to investigate laws, decrees, and ordinances for their constitutionality. The revision of Article 108ter determines the specific modalities to be used to create a coherent structure for the Brussels-Capital Region. The revision of Article 115 reserves the determination of the financial regulations of the Regions to the designated legislature. The special law of August 8, 1988, concerning the reform of institutions implements the transfer of new powers to the Communities and the Regions.

The second step began during the parliamentary session of 1988–89. It implements the following constitutional principles approved during the first stage: the expansion of the Court of Arbitration's competence (special law of January 6, 1989); the specific statute concerning the Brussels-Capital Region (special law of January 12, 1989, concerning institutions in Brussels); and the financing of the Communities and the Regions (special law of January 16, 1989).

The third step will complete the reform of the Belgian state. There is no agreement when this phase should be completed. The following matters must be decided in phase three: abolition of the double mandate (members of the Flemish Council, the French Community Council, and the Walloon Regional Council are not elected directly but are members of the national parliament); reform of the Senate; allocation of heretofore unassigned powers; delegation of exclusively national powers; and the international jurisdiction of the Communities and the Regions.

This study will not further consider the third step. Below I quickly survey the structure of the Belgian state after the second stage and the financing of the Regions and the Communities.

The Structure of the Belgian State Since the Second Phase

The Belgian national territory is structured asymmetrically. The territory is divided into nine provinces, four linguistic Regions, three Communities, and three Regions. These different substructures overlap. Figure III.1 bears witness to the complex structure of the Belgian state at present. The demarcation of the Regions and the Communities is founded on the division of the national territory into linguistic regions. No correspondence, however, is intended between the different subdivisions. The consequences of this are (1) the province of Brabant belongs to three linguistic Regions: the Dutch, the French, and the bilingual Brussels-Capital Region; (2) the province of Liège belongs to two linguistic Regions: the French and the German; (3) the bilingual area of Brussels-Capital constitutes a Region, but not a Community (the Flemish and the French Communities are responsible for institutions that, because of their occupation or their organization, are to be regarded as belonging exclusively to their respective Community); and (4) the German linguistic area constitutes a Community, but not a Region. The regional affairs of the area are overseen by the Walloon Region.

The two different types of territories, Communities and Regions, have consultative bodies (the Council) and executive bodies (the Executive). The Councils of the two types of territories do not have the same powers. The constitution has left the responsibility for the organization of the bodies of the Regions in the hands of the competent legislature. Article 26bis of the constitution ordains that the power to issue decrees can be assigned to the regional bodies. In order to characterize this regional structure, the competent legislature has established a different management for the Flemish and the Walloon Regions on the one hand and the Brussels-Capital Region on the other hand. The constitution awards equal powers to issue decrees to the councils of the Flemish and Walloon Regions. A special structure of powers has been created for the Brussels-Capital Region. The distinct characteristics of this region had to be represented. This urban area, inhabited by members of both Communities, is after all the capital of Belgium and a city of international importance. As a region, Brussels-Capital enjoys the same powers as the Flemish and the Walloon Regions, but its Council may issue only ordinances, not decrees. The ordinances have the power of law.

Ordinances and decrees differ in the following ways. (1) The judicial branch may verify the constitutionality of ordinances (with the exception of those articles of the constitution reserved to the Court of Arbitration) and may check their conformity to the special law of January 12, 1989, concerning regulations in Brussels. Decrees, on the other hand, completely escape the scrutiny of ordinary judges. (2) The Senate can annul ordinances pertaining to spatial planning, city planning, public works, or transportation. This repeal must be passed by the majority of senators from both linguistic groups within 120 days following publication of an ordinance. The national legislature does not have similar powers to annul decrees. (3) If the Council of the Brussels-Capital Region is remiss in making decisions in matters of regional and city planning, public works, and transportation, the Senate may then substitute its own decisions upon approval of both linguistic groups. This right of substitution docs not cxist in regard to decrees.

The Brussels Region also plays a supra-communal role. The regional institutions take over those powers formerly vested in the institutions of the agglomerations, such as the fire department, emergency medical care, garbage collection and disposal, subsidized public transportation, and the coordination of communal activities. The nineteen community administrations within the Brussels-Capital Region remain in existence. The Council's decisions in these matters are called "dispositions," whereas the ones made by the Executive Branch are called "resolutions." None of them has power of law. They are submitted to the verification of ordinary judges.

Because members of the two major linguistic communities live together in the capital, a special structure of powers was established pertaining to the Council's field of competence. A distinction is made depending on whether an institution dispensing personal assistance or health care (including the relevant scientific research) belongs exclusively to a single community (the so-called unicommunal institutions) or not (bicommunal institutions). The Joint College rules over the bicommunal institutions by way of ordinances. The Community Committees rule in matters of education in their respective community by means of dispositions. The Joint College and the Community Committees implement their executive power by means of resolutions.

The territorial asymmetry is increased by organic asymmetry. The northern part of the country has a Flemish Council as its decreeing body and a Flemish Executive Branch as its executive for matters pertaining to the Flemish Community and the Flemish Region. The southern part of the country has a different council with an executive for each Community and Region. The French Community Council and the Walloon Regional Council can transfer executive powers from the Walloon Region to the French Community Council by a two-thirds vote in each Council.

There exist on an organic level a Flemish Council and a Flemish Executive for Flemish communal and regional affairs; a Walloon Regional Council and a Walloon Regional Executive for Walloon regional affairs; a French Community Council and a French Community Executive for matters concerning the French Community; a Council and an Executive of the German-speaking Community for matters concerning the German-speaking Community; and a regional Council and a regional Executive for Brussels-Capital dealing with Brussels.

Only the Council of the German-speaking Community and the Council of Brussels-Capital are directly elected. The other councils are assembled out of members of the national parliament (see Fig. III.2). After reform of Articles 53 and 54 of the constitution pertaining to the Senate, members of the Chamber of Representatives will no longer be represented on the councils. Dutch-speaking members who have been elected from the

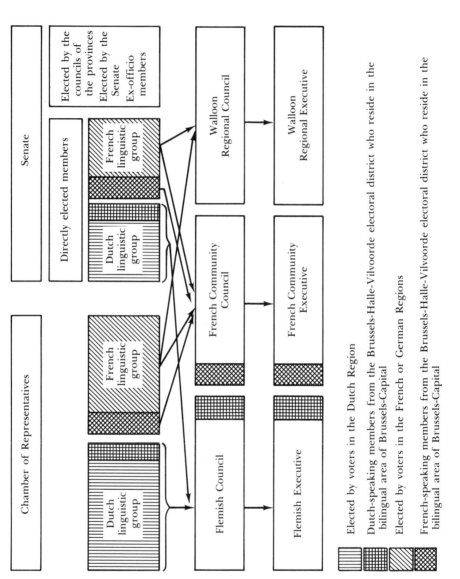

Fig. III.2.   The composition of the councils

electoral district Brussels-Halle-Vilvoorde and who reside in the bilingual area of Brussels-Capital have no right to vote in the Flemish Council in matters concerning that region.

The Flemish Executive has eleven members. At least one member must be elected from the electoral district of Brussels-Halle-Vilvoorde and must reside in the bilingual area of Brussels-Capital. The French Community Executive has four members. At least one member has to be elected in the electoral district of Brussels-Halle-Vilvoorde. The Walloon Regional Executive has seven members. Membership on the Flemish Executive is apportioned during the present legislature according to the numerical strength of the political parties in the respective councils. The French Community Executive and the Walloon Regional Executive during this legislative period, as well as all Executives in future legislatures, are directly elected from and by the respective councils.

The Council of Brussels-Capital has 75 directly elected members. The Council is completely renewed every five years. The candidates must declare which linguistic group they belong to and may not reverse their choice during a later election. The nominees form two groups, a Dutch one and a French one, inside the Council. Each linguistic group can, except during the planning of the budget, call upon the so-called alarm-bell procedure. This nonrepeatable procedure enables three-fourths of a linguistic group to declare that certain regulations in a draft or a proposal for an order could seriously endanger relations between the Flemish and the French Communities. This procedure refers the motion to the Executive of Brussels-Capital. The Executive must propose changes to the Council within 30 days.

The Executive of Brussels-Capital has five members. Aside from the president, it is composed of two members from each linguistic group. The whole of the Executive may be chosen in one election provided the five members obtain a majority of the votes in the Dutch and the French linguistic groups. If not, each linguistic group elects its own two members of the Executive, and the Council elects the president by secret ballot.

The Executive, its president, and its members may be removed from office only by a constructive vote of no confidence by the Council. This implies that the successor(s) of the dismissed member(s) is (are) mentioned in the motion of no confidence. The proposal also needs a clear majority, depending on the body or the person against which it is directed. If it is directed against the Executive as a whole, it has to be adopted by the majority of Council members and the majority of the members of each linguistic group; if against the president, it has to be adopted by the majority of Council members; and if against a mem-

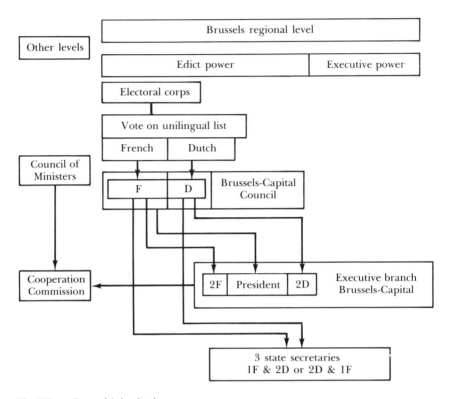

Fig. III.3.   Brussels's institutions

ber, it has to be adopted by the majority of the members of each of the concerned linguistic groups.

Even though the collegial Executive decides by assent, it can divide responsibilities concerning the preparation and the execution of its resolutions among its members. The division of powers into five task groups is applicable only if the Executive cannot reach an agreement about these concerns. The five task groups are economy and energy policy; public works and traffic; employment and local authorities; regional planning, the procuring of living space, the environment, conservation, reallocation of land, and the water supply; and finances, the budget, public offices, and external relations.

The adoption of resolutions by agreement does away with the necessity to vote within the Executive. A member of the Executive who does

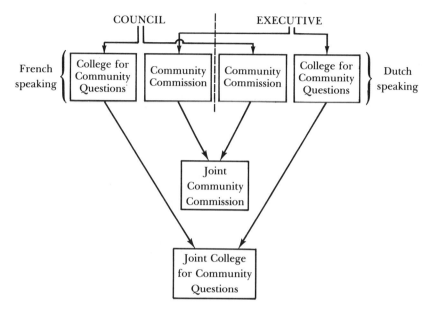

Fig. III.4.   Community-affairs institutions of the Brussels-Capital region

not agree with the decision can either accept that decision or leave the Executive. The president may indicate his decision first. Then a member of the larger linguistic group (in this case the French one) does so. After that a member of the smaller linguistic group (in this case the Dutch one) indicates his preference, followed by a member of the larger linguistic group, who in turn is followed again by a member of the smaller linguistic group.

Because the Executive is also in charge of the responsibilities of the former Executive Board of the Brussels agglomeration, an official allocation of these responsibilities has been made. This allocation is effective only when there is no agreement within the Executive about this allocation of responsibilities. These responsibilities are divided into three groups: fire department and urgent medical care; garbage collection and disposal; and subsidized public transportation and coordination of the Community's activities.

The three regional state secretaries are elected by the Executive following the same procedure as for the Executive's members. They are not part of the Executive but may attend its meetings. Each state secretary becomes an adjunct to a member of the same linguistic group. It is this member who delineates the competence of the state secretary. The state secretaries are responsible to the Council in the same way as the members of the Executive are.

The Commission for Cooperation is, observing the principle of linguistic equality, assembled of an equal number of members from the national Council of Ministers and from the Executives. Its duties are (1) to develop and consolidate the international role and function as capital of the Brussels-Capital Region; (2) to submit to the Executive the necessary measures to reach this objective. If there is no agreement, it is up to the Council of Ministers to ask the competent national legislature to approve the measure by a majority of votes in the two linguistic groups; and (3) to debate with the Executive the suspension of Council ordinances and of the Executive's resolutions, which are decided by the king upon deliberation with the Council of Ministers. This can apply only to matters concerning city planning, development planning, public works, and transportation. The suspension is valid for 60 days and may be prolonged only for one term of the same duration. If the designated legislative chamber does not invalidate the ordinance by a majority vote of both linguistic groups within the deadline, the suspension is lifted permanently.

There are also a Flemish Community Commission, a French Community Commission, and a Joint Community Commission. These Commissions have as their respective bodies: a Flemish, a French, and a Joint Assembly, consisting of the members from the affected linguistic group(s) in the Council; and a Flemish, a French, and a Joint College, consisting of the members of the affected linguistic group(s) of the Executive.

The Powers of the Communities and the Regions

Since the state reform of 1970, the Communities have had jurisdiction over cultural affairs, language, international cultural cooperation, and the school system. In the case of the school system, however, the Communities' powers were restricted to responsibility for art education. The state reform of 1980 enlarged the scope of the Communities' responsibilities to include such personnel-related matters as the social services and the health service. The state reform of 1988 reserves the following matters to the national level: the ages for compulsory school attendance; the minimal conditions for the awarding of diplomas; and pension regulations for the staff. Apart from the almost complete transfer of educational responsibilities, the 1988 reform gave the Communities responsibility for fundamental scientific research; advertising on radio and TV and support of the press; protection of children and young people; and social assistance for prisoners.

The Regions are responsible for environmental and urban planning; the environment; reallocation of land and nature conservation; housing; water supply and water distribution; economic policy; energy policy; subordinate authorities; employment policy; and public works and traffic. The changes in the responsibilities of the Regions took place on two levels. Of all the newly awarded responsibilities, the sector of public works and of traffic as well as the employment programs are of the utmost importance. The other responsibilities have been allocated as homogeneously as possible. There are, however, limits on the powers allocated to the Regions.

The competent legislature of 1988 planned for the transfer of homogeneous packages of responsibilities concerning economic policy. The enumeration of regional responsibility for economic matters in the special law of August 8, 1980, seemed rather fragmentary. The competent legislature of 1988, however, allocated the responsibility for economic policy to the Regions. This includes such previously national sectors as the steel industry, shipbuilding, coal mining, textiles, and glass packaging. The special law of August 8, 1988, however, limits the autonomy of the Regions in economic matters due to the economic and monetary union. This enables the national parliament to establish general regulations pertaining to the responsibilities of the authorities, consumer protection, the organization of industry, and the optimal conditions for economic expansion. Parliament is also responsible for monetary policy; financial policy; conservation; regulation of and control over the savings, credit, and insurance agencies; banking and insurance law; prices and pay policy; the right of competition; trade practices; commercial and company law; residency requirements; industrial law; and social law.

Agreement for Cooperation

The special law of August 8, 1988, provides for a very fragmentary cooperation only. Where the Communities were concerned, there was the matter of the French-speaking authorities already in place on the territory of the Flemish Community before 1980. This situation cannot be changed without the agreement of both Community Councils. The Regions generally were given the right to make agreements for cooperation.

The commitment to such an agreement was made in the following interregional matters: hydrology and commerce on those waterways that cross the borders of a Region; harbors that extend over the territory of more than one Region; and works for common city traffic and local traffic and taxi companies that extend over more than one Region. Agreements are made between the Regions and the state to cover aid, usage, and development of telecommunications and telecontrol networks that cross regional boundaries in matters of commerce and security. Agreements are made between the Communities over the merchant marine training colleges in Ostend and Antwerp and their boarding schools.

Disputes arising because of an obligatory agreement for cooperation are to be mediated by a college of judges established by law. Each party nominates a member of the college. These members co-opt their president. If the nomination of a member or the co-option of the president should fail, the acting president of the Court of Arbitration will make the nomination.

The Special Law of August 8, 1988, further provides for advisory procedures pertaining to all supra-regional matters. The national parliament is committed to discuss the outlines of national energy policy; technical safety measures for traffic; European and international institutions; air traffic; and the preparation of negotiations and the implementation of plans for European institutions insofar as they pertain to agricultural policy or to matters that belong to the specific fields of competence of the Regions.

It is clear that this fragmentary way of proceeding can be only a temporary solution. The Concerting Committee is still the body in which discussions between the national government and the Executives take place. The first and foremost function of this committee, however, is to prevent and clarify conflicts of interest. The development of an advisory body will be one of the most urgent tasks of the third phase.

The Court of Arbitration

The special law of January 6, 1989, regarding the Court of Arbitration has caused a fundamental change in the court's responsibilities. The court passes judgment on appeals for annulment and on prejudicial actions. Appeals for annulment may be introduced because of a violation by law, decree, or ordinance of one of two principles: the distribution of powers between the state, Regions, or Communities as determined by the constitution and the competent legislature; and the principle of equality as defined by Articles 6 and 6bis of the constitution and the principle of freedom of education defined by Article 17. The appeal for annulment may be introduced by (1) the Council of Ministers or the Executive of a Community or a Region; (2) any individual or institution with a vested interest; or (3) the president of the legislative assemblies when two-thirds of the members request it.

An appeal for annulment must be introduced within six months of the contested regulation's publication. This deadline is reduced to 60 days if the contested regulation allows an agreement by assent of the chambers. This period of time may be renewed by the Council of Ministers or the Executive of a Community or a Region.

The party making the appeal may ask the court to delay implementation of the contested regulation for a period of three months, which may not be extended. The appeal is granted only if (1) the contested regulation could cause irreparable and serious damage; or (2) the contested regulation is identical to another regulation adopted by the same legislature that the court had already rejected. An order by the court to deny an appeal has from its publication in the Belgian state gazette absolute power of law. The rejection of an appeal is final and may not be appealed.

Prejudicial questions may arise in cases that might lead to an appeal for annulment. They may also arise in cases of contestation of norms or conflicts between decrees or between decrees and ordinances. This refers to disputes where there has been no overstepping of competence but where, for example, the geographical boundaries of authority may be in doubt. Prejudicial questions must be introduced by the judicial council involved. Except for the Court of Cassation or the State Council, the judicial council in question is not obliged to introduce a prejudicial question if (1) the introduction is inadmissible; (2) the Court of Arbitration has already pronounced on the same subject; (3) no answer to the question is necessary to settle the conflict; or (4) the introduction has no foundation. The Court of Cassation and the State Council are always obliged to introduce a prejudicial question unless it is inadmissible. The ruling on a prejudicial question sets a precedent for other judicial councils ruling on the same problem. The rulings of the court are final and may not be appealed.

The court has twelve members: six Dutch-speaking and six French-speaking. They are appointed for life by the king out of a pool of candidates that is twice as large and that is proposed by the Senate with two-thirds of the votes of the attending members. Each linguistic group elects one of their number president. There is linguistic as well as jurisdictional equality. One-half of the judges in each linguistic group must be former members of the Executive, and the other half must have held one of the following offices for at least five years: (1) councillor, public prosecutor, deputy chief public prosecutor, or deputy public prosecutor for the Court of Cassation; (2) councillor of state, chief disciplinary counsel, deputy chief disciplinary council, or first referendary of the State Council; (3) adviser to the Court of Arbitration; or (4) full professor, associate professor, professor, or associate professor of law at a Belgian university. One of the members in each linguistic group must show proof of sufficient command of the German language. Fourteen advisers assist the Court of Arbitration. They are appointed by means of a competitive examination. After a trial period of three years, they are appointed on a permanent basis by the king.

The Financing of the Communities and Regions

It is explicitly mentioned in the special law on the financing of the Communities and Regions that the system for financing them will be similar to the one used in other federal states. The system is based on two principles: the financial responsibility of the Communities and Regions and reversible solidarity.

This solidarity works only at the level of Regions, not at that of the Communities. It operates through a final and reversible process of contribution to the national solidarity in the same proportion as the one between the real capability of the Regions and the national average. The passage from the present distribution of allocation to the new system of financing will be harmonious thanks to a transition period of ten years in which differences will be progressively eliminated. In the new system, the means at the disposal of the Communities earmarked for education correspond to a percentage of the value-added tax. For the Regions and other Community matters, those means correspond to a percentage of the individual income tax. The starting point is the level of allocations in 1989, and these amounts will be indexed annually during the transition period. Because the index will not grow as fast as receipts from the personal income tax and the sales tax, the part allocated to the Regions will diminish. Only from the eleventh year on will this percentage become a fixed amount.

In the final phase (from the year 2000), the revenues each Region derives from the personal income tax will fluctuate in tandem with the revenue from this source in that Region. Personal income tax receipts reflect the nominal growth of the gross national product. From the transition phase on, the Communities are entitled to a share of the receipts of radio and television fees and the Regions to the product of their own taxes as set out in Table III.1.

TABLE III.1
Sources of Funds for the Communities and Regions

Source	Percentage of tax	Basis of tax	Exemption	Profit
Gambling and betting	yes	yes	yes	yes
Automatic gambling machines	yes	yes	yes	yes
Liquor licenses	yes	yes	yes	yes
Inheritance tax	yes	yes	yes	yes
Property tax	.yes	no	yes	yes
Transfer fees of real estate	in the future	no	in the future	partly
Motor vehicle license fees	no	no	no	in the future

The Judiciary

The judiciary is responsible for ruling on disputes arising from the application of rules of law. The structure of the judiciary is governed by a number of main principles. For example, only the legislature has the power to create courts of law, and no extraordinary commissions or tribunals of any type can be created. Court hearings must be public unless this would imperil public decency. Rulings must be substantiated and given in public. Courts and tribunals can apply local and provincial decrees and regulations only insofar as they do not transgress national legislation. The rulings and judgments of courts and tribunals do not apply generally and relate only to the parties involved in a particular dispute. Courts and tribunals are independent of each other. They are not bound by the decisions of other courts and tribunals or by their own decisions in previous cases. The independence of judges vis-à-vis the Executive is guaranteed by their appointment for life and by their irremovability, as laid down in Article 100 of the constitution.

The following types of courts exist. The *police courts* have jurisdiction over the least serious infringements of criminal law, namely petty offences; they punish through police reports. There is one *justice of the peace tribunal* for each judicial district. These courts deal with lawsuits for sums up to BF50,000 and with disputes in certain areas reserved by law for this type of tribunal regardless of the sum at stake. There is one *court of first instance* for each judicial division. Each such court includes one or several chambers in three sections known as civil court, correctional court (penal), and juvenile court. Each judicial division also has a *labor tribunal*, which has wide authority extending over all disputes relating to labor relations. In addition, each judicial division has a *commercial court*, with wide powers over conflicts between businesses, acts of commerce as defined by law, disputes relating to bills of exchange and promissory notes, conflicts arising from bankruptcies, and so on. Finally, there is one *divisional court* in each judicial division. It consists of the chief magistrate of the court of first instance, the chief magistrate of the labor court, and the chief magistrate of the commercial court. It rules on the competence of the appointed judge if this is called into question.

There are presently five *courts of appeal*, at Ghent, Antwerp, Brussels, Liège, and Mons. They rule on appeals against decisions rendered by courts of first instance and by commercial courts; they also deal with appeals against the election decisions of colleges of mayors and aldermen and by chief division offices. However, the Conseil d'Etat, which is the administrative tribunal of last resort, is responsible for hearing appeals regarding rulings on the validity of borough elections. Finally, the courts of appeal decide on appeals against the decisions of regional and provincial tax directors on matters relating to direct taxes. Each territorial area covered by a court of appeal also has a *labor court*. It hears appeals against the decisions of labor tribunals.

Each province has a *criminal court of first instance* for criminal, political, and press offenses. It is composed of a court and a jury. The jury is made up of 12 jurors drawn at random from the register of voters of Belgian-born or naturalized citizens who enjoy civil and political rights and have reached the age of 30.

The *military tribunals* consist of courts martial and of the military court. They act in cases of offenses against military penal law and offenses under civilian criminal law committed by persons belonging to the armed forces at the time of the offense.

The *Court of Cassation* is the supreme court. There is only one such court, and it meets in Brussels. It has general authority and is the court of last instance for decisions arising from the infringement of a law or substantial procedural or regulatory violation under penalty of nullity. It does not judge the merits of the case. In the event of annulment, the court sends the case to another court competent to rule on its merits. The court to which the case is referred has to take account of the decision of the Court of Cassation only if the latter twice annuls the ruling for the same reasons. The Court of Cassation has specific jurisdiction over conflicts regarding the competence of governmental bodies. Finally, the Court of Cassation is responsible for judging cases concerning government ministers, should the need arise. The Chamber of Representatives has the formidable task of charging a minister and bringing him before the Court of Cassation.

The *Conseil d'Etat* was set up by the law of December 23, 1946. Although this tribunal operates according to the same standards employed by the judiciary, it is uniquely answerable to the Executive. It is therefore the most important administrative tribunal of the Belgian system. The Conseil d'Etat is divided into two sections, one legislative and the other administrative.

The legislative section is responsible for giving a reasoned opinion on all governmental or private member's bills or governmental and private member's proposals for decrees, amendments to these, and proposals put before it by the speaker of the Senate, the Chamber of Representatives, or one of the community or regional councils. These speakers are obliged to ask for the opinion of the legislative section on amendments to parliamentary or governmental bills when at least one-third of the members of the legislative chamber or council in question request an opinion in accordance with the procedures laid down in the regulations; and parliamentary or private member's bills and amendments to the former when the majority of members of a linguistic group in the legislative chamber in question request an opinion in accordance with the procedures laid down in the regulations.

Except for urgent cases with special justification and bills relating to budgets, accounts, borrowing operations, state operations, and armed forces quotas, ministers and members of the community and regional executives, each in areas concerning them, must submit all draft bills, preliminary drafts of decrees, or proposed regulatory decrees to the legislative section of the Conseil d'Etat for a reasoned opinion. The opinion of the legislative section of the Conseil d'Etat is required even when a draft bill or preliminary draft decree is deemed urgent. In such a case, it concentrates on defining whether the preliminary draft or draft bill deals with matters within the scope of the state, community, or region.

Ministers and members of community or regional executives, in their respective areas of competence, can request a reasoned opinion from the legislative section of the Conseil d'Etat on all bills or proposed decrees and on all amendments to private member's or governmental bills or proposed decrees. The prime minister and the presidents of community or regional executives can, in their respective areas of competence, give the section responsibility for drafting preliminary bills, preliminary draft decrees, regulations, or amendments of which they determine the subject matter and purpose. Finally, the legislative section can issue opinions on draft royal decrees rendering collective labor agreements binding.

The scope of the administrative section falls in both the jurisdictional and the nonjurisdictional spheres. The administrative section issues judgments or renders opinions. Its most important task is to issue judgments on proceedings for annulment of laws on the grounds of infringement of substantive procedural elements or prescribed forms and on the grounds of misuse or improper use of power, directed against acts and regulations of the various administrative authorities, or against contentious administrative decisions. The section also rules on disputes over the respective competence of provincial and borough authorities or of public establishments. In cases where there is no competent jurisdiction, the administrative section rules on the basis of fairness, taking account of all the circumstances of public and private interest, on requests for compensation for exceptional moral or material injury caused by an administrative authority. The administrative section, which in some ways acts as a legal adviser, gives opinions to ministers and members of community or regional executives on all nonlitigious administrative questions and cases that fall under the scope of the executive.

Civil Liberties

All civil liberties guaranteed Belgian citizens are also granted to all foreigners on Belgian territory, apart from the exceptions provided for in law. The following rights are guaranteed by the constitution.

Personal freedom is guaranteed by Article 7 of the constitution, which protects citizens against arbitrary detention and barbarous legal penalties and guarantees due process of law. The constitutional principle of *inviolability of domicile* (Article 10) stipulates that the authorities may enter a residence only in cases provided for by the law and in the form prescribed by it.

The general principle of *equality before the law* bans the application of a different system to people in the same general, objective, and impersonal situations. Under this principle, all distinctions of rank have been abolished; tax privileges of whatever nature are banned; extraordinary tribunals are banned; ideological and philosophical minorities are protected; and equal access of Belgians to state posts is guaranteed.

Article 11 (*inviolability of property*) stipulates that no one can be deprived of property other than for reasons of public interest and in a manner provided for by the law and in return for just compensation, paid in advance. *Freedom of political opinion* in all matters is guaranteed by Article 14, except for offenses against this freedom. *Freedom of religious worship* allows for the practice of the religion of one's choice, the celebration of religious ceremonies, and the organization of religious communities. *Educational freedom* is provided for in Article 17, paragraph 1 of the constitution, and consists of the freedom to open a school and to provide teaching in it, along with the freedom for each citizen to choose the education he or she wishes to receive.

Article 18 guarantees *freedom of the press*, bans censorship, and makes it illegal for suretyship to be required of writers, publishers, or printers; the same article acknowledges the principle of complicity by setting up a system of vicarious liability from the author to the publisher, the publisher to the printer, and the printer to the distributor. *Freedom of assembly* is stipulated in Article 19 of the constitution, which states that Belgians have a right to assemble peacefully and without arms and in accordance with the laws that may govern the exercise of this right, without preliminary authorization. This provision does not apply to outdoor assemblies, which are completely subject to police laws. Article 20 guarantees citizens *freedom of association*, thereby implying the freedom to choose to join or not to join an association. The constitution further guarantees *the secrecy of correspondence* and gives citizens the *freedom of petition*, the right to bring to the attention of the public powers any grievance, wish, or claim.

Finally, *freedom of language use* is guaranteed. Use of the languages currently employed in Belgium is optional. Language use can be governed only by the law and only as regards public authorities or judicial affairs. Through application of the 1970 constitutional revision, the councils of each linguistic community have been recognized as competent to decide by decree on the use of language for administrative affairs, education, and relations with the public.

State Reform, 1988–89

One of the most remarkable political phenomena in Europe in the second half of the 20th century has undoubtedly been the awakening of cultural and linguistic awareness among subgroups in culturally diverse states. This has notably been the case in Spain and Belgium. Generally speaking, the unitarian and centralized state has been obliged to adapt constitutionally to these new trends. The history of Belgium since the end of World War II is a typical example of the slow yet unavoidable transformation of a unitarian state into a state with a federal-type structure, culminating in the institutionalization of the cultural diversity of its component parts. The existence of French-, Dutch-, and German-speaking cultures has become a federal reality in modern Belgium. However, it is important to remember that the Belgian provinces are the descendants of the former principalities of the Austrian Netherlands. These principalities, with the exception of Liège, were brought together under the same throne during the 14th and 15th centuries, thanks to the political genius of the dukes of Burgundy. The Belgian provinces have therefore been under the same political umbrella for centuries. The federalization of Belgium is thus a return to an earlier era. The Walloons, Flemish, and German-speaking Belgians can live together in harmony, and thus ensure the common well-being of the state, only in a federal Belgium, as they did for a number of centuries.

Belgium will be a federal monarchy. Without the monarchy, the gradual transformation of the Belgian state would have been impossible. The king is currently the irreplaceable symbol of Belgian unity. King Baudouin, in a rather strange return to the past, has assumed the same task as his Burgundian predecessors; namely, rallying and keeping together the component parts of a multicultural Belgium.

Political Decision-Making

Xavier Mabille

ALTHOUGH WRITTEN LAW describes official mechanisms governing the workings of institutions, it generally does not touch on de facto mechanisms and real decision-making processes. It also says little about the centers of decision-making and the major operators in the decision-making process. This is true of the Belgian constitution, which only incidentally mentions the cabinet and the prime minister.

Whereas the institutions form the backdrop to the exercise of political decision-making, parties and groups are the main collective operators. Whereas political decision-making essentially takes place in the arena of elected assemblies and executive bodies, whose composition chiefly reflects that of the assemblies, election to the assemblies is almost entirely carried out on the basis of lists of candidates put forward by the parties. In other words, the parties are responsible for breathing life into the decision-making forum.

The Real Decision-Makers: Parties and Groups

As in any representative system, parties give tangible form to various vague trends by drawing up electoral programs, setting up an organizational structure from the local to the national level, and putting forward lists of candidates at elections.

In Belgium, this structuring of political trends has a considerable history. It dates to the middle and end of the 19th century, when the three main political families (liberal, Catholic, and socialist) were born. The political parties of today are their direct descendants. This political structuring reflected the various different divisions of Belgian society—philosophical, religious, social, linguistic, and cultural. Society first split over the relative roles to be accorded the Catholic church (and the structures it had put in place and sponsored) and the state authorities, particularly in areas such as education and social assistance. The Catholic party confronted the Liberal and Socialist parties over this issue for a long time. A second area of dispute was fueled by different social and economic interests. The two anticlerical parties were opposed in this area, whereas the Catholic party professed, at least when the workers movement obtained political expression, to transcend this split by representing all classes. The right and left did not split at the same point on these two issues. In the first, opposition was between a clerical right wing and a secular left wing; in the second, it was between a conservative right and a progressive left.

This simplified breakdown of the political scene does not, however, make allowance for the complexity of the Belgian situation or for its evolution. Reality is in fact much more complex and must make allowance for a third consideration. The dispute over the form of the state and its internal balances was largely a reflection of the demands of the Flemish and Walloon movements. They brought about considerable institutional reform and caused a split within the three main parties, each of which formed a Flemish and French-speaking wing. The situation is in fact continually fluctuating. For example, in 1961, the Liberal party rejected its traditional anticlericalism. This change had important consequences for the political system.

The respective weight of the three main political trends has remained relatively stable over time. The Catholic (or Social Christian) wing has generally obtained the greatest number of votes throughout the country; it was outstripped by the Socialists only at the national elections of 1925 and 1936 and at the European elections of 1984. At all other elections since the introduction of universal suffrage for all men over 21 just after World War I (women gained the vote in 1948), Socialists have come in second, followed by the Liberals (except at the national elections of 1946, when the Communists overtook the Liberals).

The gaps between the three main political trends have closed with time, particularly with losses by the Social Christians in 1965 and 1981, losses by the Socialists in 1965, and gains by the Liberals in 1965 and 1981. At the 1985 national elections, the Social Christians obtained 29.3 percent of the vote, the Socialists 28.3 percent, and the Liberals 20.9 percent. However, results vary widely at the regional level. The Social Christians have always led the field in Flanders, and the Socialists in Wallonia.

In addition, all three national parties have split into Flemish and

French-speaking wings. The Social Christians split into the Christelijk Volkspartij (CVP) and the Parti Social-Chrétien (PSC) in 1968, the Liberals into the Partij voor Vrijheid en Vooruitgang (PVV) and the Parti de la liberté et du progrès (PLP) in 1972, and the Socialists into the Parti Socialiste (PS) and the Socialistische Partij (SP) in 1978. The French-speaking and Walloon liberals reunified as the Parti réformateur libéral (PRL) in 1979. All these parties are recognized as capable of governing. It is extremely rare for other parties to participate in coalition governments.

Coalition governments have been the norm since the introduction, just after World War I, of universal manhood suffrage. The extension of suffrage accentuated the effects of a system of proportional representation and prevented any single party from gaining an absolute majority in either of the two houses. The only exception came in 1950–1954, when the Social Christians had an absolute majority. The big parties more or less have a monopoly on governing. In the four decades between 1946 and 1985, the Social Christians participated in the government for 34 years and 6 months, the Socialists for 22 years and 10 months, and the Liberals for 19 years and 5 months. Respectively, they participated in 21, 16, and 10 different governments. Over the same period, the Social Christian party held the post of prime minister for 30 years and 10 months, and the Socialist party held it for 8 years and 10 months.

The Social Christians have always been part of the national government since 1958. Before this date, alliances between the Socialists and Liberals were occasionally strong enough to force the Social Christians onto the opposition benches, notably in the immediate postwar period and during the 1954–1958 government. The dynamics of coalitions join the Social Christians and Liberals in conservative coalitions, the Social Christians and Socialists in coalitions that the Liberals accuse of being extremely left-wing, and the Socialists and Liberals in coalitions defending secularism. After the reform of the Liberal party and its rejection of its traditional anticlericalism and "anti-leftist extremism" in 1961, coalition possibilities were to all intents reduced to two; the Social Christians now occupy a kingpin position in the interplay and can choose between joining forces with the Socialists in a left-wing coalition or with the Liberals in a right-wing government. Even though the parties have split into Flemish and French-speaking sections, the sections have always found themselves in the same political situation as their linguistic opposite numbers; namely, in the government or in the opposition.

Other parties are or have been represented in parliament, and some of them have even had brief tastes of governing. The Communist party, which was a breakaway party formed by left-wing factions from the Socialist party, was represented in parliament from 1925 to 1985. On the eve of, and in the aftermath of, the February 1946 national elections (when its support reached a peak, and it overtook the Liberals as the third party), it participated in a number of coalition governments.

The Volksunie has been represented in parliament since 1954. It is the continuation of a tradition of political expression among the Flemish movement, distinct from the major parties. It reached its electoral peak in 1971, when it was the third biggest party in Flanders. It participated in government from 1977 to 1978 and after this unique taste of government experienced its greatest electoral defeat.

The Democratic Front of French-speaking Inhabitants of Brussels (Front démocratique des Bruxellois francophones; FDF) was formed in 1964 to give political expression to French-speaking opinion in Brussels strongly hostile to the linguistic legislation of 1962 and 1963. The FDF entered parliament immediately after its formation, with the 1965 national elections, and between 1971 and 1981 it was the leading political party in the Brussels region. The FDF participated in government from June 1977 to the beginning of 1980. Racked by serious tensions and weakened by the loss of several leading figures, it suffered electoral defeats in 1981 and 1985.

The Walloon Union (Rassemblement wallon) was set up by the first two federalist Walloon members of parliament, elected in 1965, who did not belong to the major political parties. It was represented in parliament from 1968 to 1985. It was the second largest Walloon party at the 1971 elections and participated in the government from summer 1974 to the beginning of 1977. It was also weakened by dissent and departures, suffered electoral defeats in 1977 and 1981, and has not fought as a party in elections since 1985.

A new political group, with ecological leanings, has been represented in parliament since 1981. The Flemish section (Agalev) and the French-speaking section (Ecolo) both originated in groups concerned with the preservation of the environment and interested in the search for alternatives. Since 1981, Agalev has ranked fifth among the Flemish parties, and Ecolo fourth among the French-speaking parties.

Two other parties have been represented in parliament, although to a very minor extent, since 1978. They are the Democratic Union for the Respect of Labor (Union démocrate pour le respect du travail), which chiefly attacks what it considers to be excessive taxation, and the Flemish Block (Vlaams Blok), an extreme right-wing Flemish nationalist party.

Parties not presently represented in parliament include the Belgian

Labor Party (Parti du Travail de Belgique), which is Maoist-inspired, and the Trotskyist Socialist Workers Party (Parti ouvrier socialiste). Both are on the extreme left of the political spectrum. A number of other groups are extremely right-wing, although some of them would deny this description.

Outside the party framework, but sometimes in close contact with it, exist a large number of groups that reflect the various lines of division running through Belgian society. For example, the division over the question of the relationship between the Catholic church and the state has led to a proliferation of Catholic groups and anticlerical circles. Anticlericalism was for a long time the trademark of the Liberals and the Socialists, before it became a trait of other secular groups.

Catholic groups are characterized by the existence of what can be termed "church structures." The intervention of the Catholic hierarchy in public life, which was frequent in the past, has gradually died away since around 1960, and connections with other Christian organizations have become more supple. The proliferation of groups is explained chiefly by a desire to protect practicing Roman Catholics. This desire originated in the conflicts of the last century, when certain parties and groups favored a high degree of secularization.

The Catholic organizations carry out a wide range of functions and address different groups of public opinion. They range from associations for proselytization to social organizations with varying purposes. Some of these groups have also grafted themselves onto other splits in Belgian society. But the Catholic world has its own individual profile, which often cannot be compared with the Liberal or the Socialist world.

Roman Catholicism is the main religion in Belgium. The law of March 4, 1870, also recognized the Protestant, Anglican, and Jewish churches. However, these churches have a much smaller membership and no political role as such. A more recent law, of July 19, 1974, recognized the Islamic church.

From the outset, anticlericalism left its mark on liberalism and socialism in Belgium. The split over the secular issue persists in Belgian politics, even if the heat has started to go out of the religious dispute. The opposition line is drawn today within certain pluralist political groupings.

In addition to the various parties, a number of associations defend secularism. The world of secularism, traditionally characterized by a large number of societies and groups with varying leanings, now has three coordinating bodies: the French-speaking organization, the Secular Action Center (Centre d'action laïque), formed in March 1969; the

Dutch-speaking Union of Liberal Associations (Unie der Vrijzinnige Verenigingen), formed in spring 1971; and finally, at the national level, the Central Council of Nondenominational Philosophical Communities of Belgium (Conseil central des communautés philosophiques non confessionnelles de Belgique / Centrale Raad der Niet Confessioneele Levensbeschouwelijke Gemeenschappen van België), formed in 1972. The last is known under the shortened name of Central Secular Committee (Conseil central laïque / Centrale Vrijzinnige Raad).

Labor organizations, representing salaried workers and employees in the private sector and civil servants, are one of the main actors in the group system. They are also among the most representative from a numerical point of view. The impetus behind them was the desire to change the working and living conditions of workers and to improve their social position. These reforms could only come about by law and thus required political pressure.

The three main national interprofessional trade union organizations are the Confederation of Christian Trade Unions (Confédération des syndicats chrétiens; CSC), the General Labor Federation of Belgium (Fédération générale du travail de Belgique; FGTB), and the General Central Office of Liberal Trade Unions of Belgium (Centrale générale des syndicats libéraux de Belgique; CGSLB). The structure of the CSC and FGTB is two-tier, consisting of professional central offices and interprofessional regional federations. For a number of years there have been Walloon, Flemish, and Brussels sections. The percentage of union membership is very high in Belgium, currently standing at more than 80 percent of those eligible. Trade union organizations have a wide range of activities, some of which demand mobilization of the militant potential represented by their members and others oriented more toward the provision of services.

Other social organizations have mushroomed among the ranks of salaried workers and employees. These include, for example, mutual benefit insurance organizations for a specific sector of the working population (civil servants, the self-employed). Five such organizations exist at the national level and are "federations of federations" of individual mutual benefit insurance societies: the National Alliance of Christian Mutual Benefit Insurance Companies, the National Union of Socialist Mutual Benefit Insurance Companies, the National League of Liberal Mutual Benefit Insurance Federations of Belgium, the National Union of Professional Mutual Benefit Insurance Federations of Belgium, and the National Union of Neutral Mutual Benefit Insurance Federations.

Trade unions deal at the sectional and national level with professional and interprofessional organizations of company heads. In January 1983, the main business organizations fused into a single national interprofessional organization, the Federation of Belgium Enterprises (Fédération des entreprises de Belgique; FEB).

Three regional interprofessional organizations also exist: the Flemish Economic Union (Vlaams Economisch Verbond; VEV), the Walloon Union of Businesses (Union wallonne des entreprises; UWE), and the Brussels Union of Businesses (Union des entreprises de Bruxelles; UEB), which notably represent employers' interests in economic decentralization bodies, such as regional economic councils and regional development societies. The VEV is much older than the other two, and its history is to a certain extent tied up with that of the Flemish fight for the "flemishing" of business in Flanders.

Representatives of trade union and business organizations are often to be found within consultative bodies. They negotiate with one another, within businesses, within joint committees, and within the National Labor Council. The decisions of joint committees can be rendered binding by royal decree. The end product of these negotiations is collective agreements or, in the framework of social programming, biannual interprofessional agreements.

The major business organizations are composed of representatives of companies of varying sizes. This heterogeneity can give rise to internal tension. Separate groups representing heads of small and medium-sized businesses and the self-employed exist within specific professional and interprofessional organizations. They are concerned chiefly with professions that are still very much trades or with small distribution or service firms. The main interprofessional organizations representing these groups are, in addition to the National Federation of Chambers of Commerce and Industry of Belgium, the National Christian Self-employed and Trades Union (Nationaal Christelijk Middenstandsverbond), which is Social Christian, in Flanders; and the Federation of Trade Unions of the Self-employed (Federation des Unions syndicales de classes moyennes), which is not aligned with a political party, in the French-speaking part of the country. The Walloon Alliance of Associations of Employees, the Self-employed, and Executives and the Intertrade Union of Self-employed in the Brussels Region, which were created more recently, are respectively responsible for the representation of these groups in the decentralized economic bodies of Wallonia and Brussels.

Farmers have their own organizations. The three largest are the Belgian Farmers Union (Belgische Boerenbond; Catholic) in Flanders, the

National Federation of Belgian Professional Agricultural Unions (Fédération nationale des Unions professionnelles agricoles belges; unaligned), and the Belgian Agricultural Alliance (Alliance agricole belge; Catholic) in Wallonia.

The economic and social interest groups mentioned above participate, according to their individual sphere of competence, in advisory committees or councils or in the management of state-approved bodies. Many other organizations, chiefly of a professional nature, exist. They are growing in number, paralleling a trend toward increased regulation of the professions in terms of access and procedures. Organizations of this type occasionally rise to the forefront of the political stage. Medical organizations in particular have been in the spotlight on a number of occasions, particularly since 1964.

This brief overview illustrates that the group system is not rigid; on the contrary, there is constant fluctuation as groups emerge, disappear, or merge. A recent newcomer, for example, concentrates exclusively on representing executives.

One type of group is of especial importance in the Belgian political context; namely, the component parts of what are known as the Flemish movement and the Walloon movement. The Flemish and Walloon movements are very real and important phenomena, but they cannot always be boxed into a formal structure. In both cases, a very diverse range of organizations unites to exercise pressure at given moments and for specific objectives.

The permanent nature of the Flemish movement is guaranteed by the bedrock provided for it by certain large cultural associations, led by the Davidsfond (Catholic), Willemsfond (Liberal), and Vermeylenfond (Socialist). The Flemish movement includes a political pressure group for federalism, the Flemish People's Movement (Vlaamse Volksbeweging; VVB). Coordinating bodies (Consultative Center of the Flemish Associations, Egmont Committee) have overall responsibility for all the component organizations of the Flemish movement and coordinate activities in the fields of cultural autonomy and state organization. Activity groups, such as the Language Action Committee TAK, are more marginal in political terms, but sometimes their activities have considerable impact.

For its part, the Walloon movement is essentially represented by Free Wallonia (Wallonie libre), Walloon Renovation (Rénovation wallonne), and the Walloon People's Movement (Mouvement populaire wallon), which have promoted federalism among the public and in political circles. Since September 1986, a new movement, known as Wallonia—A Region of Europe, has gradually gathered support.

Decision-Making Mechanisms

Coalition governments are, as mentioned earlier, a chief characteristic of political decision-making in Belgium. Coalitions have become almost inevitable since 1919 because of the aggregate effect of universal suffrage and proportional representation. This has influenced the role of the monarchy in two ways. First, the chairing of the cabinet by the king has become increasingly rare. His influence has been felt to a lesser extent through attendance at meetings and to a greater extent through personal contact with ministers. Second, the king has come to play a key role in defusing governmental crises.

Traditionally, after parliamentary general elections, the prime minister offers his resignation to the king. If the resignation is accepted, then the outgoing government becomes a caretaker one. If the prime minister offers to resign during a term of parliament, the king must consider whether to accept the offer, to turn it down, or to withhold a decision while asking the prime minister to attempt to solve the crisis. A decision by the king to refuse to accept the resignation or to delay replying can only temporarily prevent the collapse of the government.

Once the king accepts the resignation of the government, a series of consultations and negotiations takes place, whose nature and form have been laid down by tradition. First, the king consults a number of high-ranking officials. His choice is determined by the importance of their posts. They generally include the speakers of the houses, party leaders, heads of socioeconomic groups, the leaders of parliamentary groups, and so on. The king then appoints either an information agent (*informateur*) or a person responsible for forming the new government (*formateur*).

In the first instance, the information agent also organizes consultations. The choice of persons consulted at this stage is dictated by the information agent's need to assess the negotiating chances of a governmental program and the chances of forming a coalition with a majority in each of the houses. The information agent reports back to the king. Once the king has discharged the informateur, he appoints a formateur. The two may be the same person. The appointment of a formateur is a signal that consultations are over and that negotiations to form a new government are being opened. The choice of a formateur is often a clue to the political color the new coalition will take. In actual fact, "the resignation of a government, the formation of a new ministerial team, and the dissolution of the houses are moments in national politics where the monarchy is especially in the spotlight. . . . This area is perhaps the one where the king acts, if not with the greatest degree of liberty, then in any event with the least constitutional cover or guarantee" (André Molitor, *La Fonction royale en Belgique*, Brussels, 1979, p. 26).

Coalitions express a political accord that may not reflect electoral outcomes. There are coalitions of losing as well as of winning parties. Negotiations between parties concentrate on the contents of the governmental program and on the division of influence within the government. The governmental agreement is a very precise document stipulating the intentions of the new team; it lists concessions granted and advantages obtained for each member of the new coalition. The composition of the government is determined by precise requirements. Apart from an equal number of French- and Dutch-speaking ministers (if need be, excepting the prime minister), allowance must be made for the various different political colors of the government members (including internal trends within the coalition parties) and for the parliamentary assemblies and regions, provinces and subregions, to which they belong. Although the parties are responsible for the negotiations on the division of powers in the various sectors of governmental activity, "the king appoints and dismisses his ministers" (Article 65 of the constitution), and "the king appoints and dismisses state secretaries" (Article 91). He also announces the composition of the new team.

Royal decrees confirm the resignation of outgoing government members, appoint the members of the new government, and stipulate their functions. These are published simultaneously in the *Moniteur belge*. The appointment of the new prime minister is countersigned by his predecessor; all other decrees are countersigned by the new prime minister. Constitutional prescriptions regarding ministerial responsibility are thus respected. Finally, the members of the government swear an oath to the king.

The community and regional executives are formed in a different way. In 1981, the first such executives were composed in proportion to the numerical weight of the political groups in the corresponding councils. After 1985, majority rule came into use. Consequently, the Flemish parties in the national coalition (CVP and PVV), which have a majority of seats on the Flemish Council, together negotiated the formation of the new Flemish Executive. Similarly, the heads of the French-speaking parties in the coalition (PRL and PSC), which scraped together a majority in the French-speaking Community Council and obtained half the seats in the Walloon Regional Council, were appointed as informateurs for the formation of the two corresponding executives. The two parties monopolized the two negotiations.

Coalitions are also negotiated for the formation of permanent deputations in all the provinces where no party holds a majority of seats in the provincial council. The only party ever to have such a majority was the Socialist party in Hainaut Province in 1985. Provincial alliances have their own logic, distinct from that prevailing at the national level and at the community and regional levels. In all cases where there is no majority, coalitions are also the norm at the borough level for the appointment of members of the college of the mayor and aldermen (election of aldermen, proposal of a candidate for mayor).

The Belgian political system has, over the course of time, reinforced the position of the government and weakened the role played by parliament. This is notably due to the fact that the coalition practice obliges the parties in the government to devise an agreement specifying the intentions of the new team. This agreement is a binding contract on the members of the government. The governmental agreement must be very exact in order to establish a balance between the concessions made and the satisfaction obtained by each of the coalition members. Consequently, the freedom of the major parliamentary groups is restricted, for any initiative that might upset the balance behind the coalition is untenable.

Care must therefore be taken not to blindly repeat the classic theory of the parliamentary system regarding the separation and balance of the executive and the legislative powers. The dividing line between a governmental coalition, which rests on a parliamentary majority but acts almost exclusively through governmental initiative, and the opposition, which has abundant recourse to parliamentary initiative, through the submission of private member's bills, and to parliamentary procedure, through questions and heckling, provides the most eloquent demonstration of its true nature. The activities of the opposition are chiefly concentrated on influencing public opinion since its prospects for success within the parliamentary system are limited. Private member's bills are much more numerous than governmental bills. However, the latter are the source of most laws adopted by the parliament. The same situation is seen at the community and regional levels.

In a system like the one in Belgium, the decision-making process cannot be pigeonholed. A decision-making chain does, however, exist and can be summarized as follows: (1) formulation of a demand by a group; (2) the incorporation of this demand into a party program; (3) following elections and negotiations between parties, the inclusion of the proposal based on the demand, in its original form or a modified one, in the governmental agreement, which is the list of the government's intentions; and (4) legislative adoption of a bill and implementation by the relevant ministry of the principle contained in the governmental agreement. The governmental agreement, which is now traditionally published in an appendix to the declaration read to the houses by the prime minister when he presents his government, is therefore an important reference for future political decisions.

In all decisions of assemblies and colleges, majority voting is the rule. Under Article 38 of the constitution, "all resolutions must be taken by an absolute majority of votes, excepting matters established by house regulations regarding elections and nominations. Should the votes be evenly divided, the proposal under discussion is rejected. Neither of the two houses can adopt a resolution unless a majority of its members are present." In the majority of cases, members of political groups supporting the government vote in favor, and opposition members vote against. The occasional abstention is usually intended to justify a particular stance or opinion; for example, abstention often expresses regret that the bill does not go far enough to warrant opposition.

The practice of coalition governments requires a high degree of discipline among the majority parties. It is rare that different majorities, known as "alternative majorities" (*majorités de rechange*), are formed under one and the same government.

Some decisions require special majorities in the Chamber or the Senate, for example, revision of articles in the constitution. Each house can deliberate only if at least two-thirds of its members are present, and no changes can be adopted without at least a two-thirds majority (Article 131 of the constitution). It is worth noting that the third revision of the constitution passed even though the government at the time did not have a two-thirds majority in either of the two houses. Success was due to dissension within the ranks of the opposition.

Decisions of a similar nature can require very different procedures. For example, the minimum age for voting in borough elections is stipulated by law, whereas the constitution (Articles 47 and 53) sets the age for voting in elections to the Chamber of Representatives and the Senate. A law was thus all that was required to lower the voting age to 18 for borough elections, but the same decision for national elections required revision of the relevant articles in the constitution. This step was eventually taken in 1981.

The 1970 Constituent Assembly decided that certain laws, to be adopted, must obtain a majority of votes in each linguistic group in both houses, provided that a majority of members of each group is present and that the sum of votes in favor in the two linguistic groups equals at least two-thirds of total votes cast. The laws in question concern changes in provincial boundaries (Article 1), changes in the boundaries of linguistic regions (Article 3b), and determination of the way in which community bodies exercise their powers and adopt the list defining the scope of their powers (Article 59b). This provision also covers the law granting elected regional bodies competence over matters stipulated in the same law, except those mentioned in Articles 23 and 59(b), within the scope and according to the manner defined in the law (Article 107d). The 1970 constituent assembly also set up the so-called "alarm bell" mechanism (see preceding chapter).

Certain laws are adopted unanimously or with a large majority, for example, social security legislation and ratification of treaties, agreements, and other international acts. But unanimity or consensus on issues of considerable political significance is rare.

Many decisions in a political system such as Belgium's are compromises, either because they are negotiated within coalitions and are thus the result of reciprocal concessions or because their negotiation draws together all potential decision-makers. Compromise and coalition go hand in hand and have prompted general use of consultations and dialogue. Typically, compromises involve agreements either on a large number of disparate points such as governmental agreements between coalition parties, which are "governmental majority contracts," or as large a number as possible of participants, whether from the majority or opposition. Typical examples of the latter are the School Pact or the Cultural Pact, which were major agreements drawing in all the parties, in and out of the government.

In the past few decades, a large number of advisory bodies representing the various economic and social operators have been formed. Their task within their sphere of competence is to issue opinions either on their own initiative or at the request of members of the government. Such organizations exist in a large number of sectors. Many of them date, in their current form, from the postwar period, including the Central Economic Council (founded 1948), which corresponds at the sectoral level to professional councils and at the business level to plant councils; the High Council of the Self-employed and Trades (1949); the National Labor Council (1952); the National Council of Scientific Policy (1959); the Consumers Council (1964); and the Economic Regional Councils (1970), which advise on economic planning and decentralization. These are the main and best-known advisory bodies, they have the most general objectives, and they represent the major economic and social circles. However, advisory committees and councils exist in all fields and at all levels.

The system was originally set up to help the political authorities obtain information on the opinions of the major interest groups outside of the parliamentary framework and to give these groups an opportunity to express their opinions on upcoming legislation. The groups can render unanimous or mixed opinions. In the latter case, an enclosed memorandum explains the position of the minority. Advisory bodies are also occasionally set up on a precise issue and with a limited brief. This is the case for committees made up of so-called sages or senior experts. The National Committee for Ethical Problems is one such example. Finally, informal consultation procedures also exist. Interest groups sometimes play a more active role in political decisions. For example, they may be associated in the adoption and application of specific decisions and policies or in the administration of state-approved management bodies. The genesis for consultation practices is perhaps to be found in major collective negotiations of the type conducted by National Labor Conferences or major agreements such as the draft social solidarity agreement of 1944.

Groups are also associated in the drafting and application of sectoral policies. This is the case, for example, with the Gas and Electricity Control Committee, the Oil Consultation and Control Committee, and a number of others. Each such body was set up individually, and each has its own characteristics. For example, the Steel Policy Consultative Committee (now disbanded) was set up by an agreement concluded on April 18, 1967, between the Belgian state, the Belgian Steel Committee, and trade union organizations. The Oil Consultative and Control Committee was set up by royal decree on April 8, 1974. The composition, competence, and even the efficiency of such organizations varies from one to another. For many years now, these groups have also been involved in the management of state-approved bodies, through representation on boards of directors, for example, of semi-state institutions (particularly widespread in the credit sector) or of social security organizations. The groups most frequently represented in this system are business and trade union organizations, but others are present as well. For example, the General Council of the National Sickness and Disability Insurance Institute includes representatives of insurance firms and the health-care professions, in addition to representatives of business, self-employed people, and workers organizations. The National Council on Economic Expansion includes both members of the government and leaders of the main organizations representing businesses, the self-employed, the professions, farmers, and workers.

Because the consultation "system" grew up gradually and in an empirical manner, it is difficult to draw a full picture. The growth of this parallel system has caused a devolution from a purely parliamentary political system based on elected assemblies using a majority voting system. Paralleling the reforms introduced in political institutions has been a certain regionalization of consultation practices. Moreover, since the international economic crisis hit Belgium, these consultation groups have become increasingly restless. Business organizations have become much more radical, tending to blame the unemployment problem on such factors as increased costs and taxation, an unfavorable investment climate, shortfalls in vocational training, and overgenerous social security benefits, particularly unemployment benefits. Trade unions have found themselves increasingly on the defensive, with priority being given to defense of wages and social security benefit levels.

This distortion of social relations has aggravated difficulties in concluding collective agreements, particularly interprofessional agreements. It has also led to a gradual erosion of consultative bodies and practices. The organization at the head of what once seemed to be a real consultative system, the National Council on Economic Expansion, has not met once since the onset of economic crisis.

The Workings of the System

A small country, a recently formed state, and a society divided by tensions, Belgium is in some ways a political science laboratory. Political decision-making in Belgium is strongly affected by the interplay of past and present tensions. But in practice the system operates so as to defuse tension: "The complex interplay of divisions, which are both the result and source of conflict, also encourages compromise" (X. Mabille, *Histoire politique de la Belgique*, Brussels, 1986, p. 380). This has been true in all fields: educational, social, institutional.

True, the system gives rise to inconveniences. In many cases, it tends to muddy the situation. A compromise *à la belge* is generally so complex that it is difficult to shed light on all its aspects. It is also an expensive system, even though sometimes it is difficult to assess costs. It generates an overabundance of institutions and normative and regulatory provisions. Such a system can also give rise to wariness about politics or even a rejection of politics. On the positive side, however, the system has diminished the risk of violent confrontation, apart from short-lived crises.

The system can sometimes be termed a "partycracy." Responsibility for all upsets is thrown back on the parties and their leaders. The omnipresence of parties is a fact, demonstrated, among other ways, by the high degree of politicization of the administration. However, the parties are not omnipotent. They must cooperate with one another and also with groups that in certain cases wield just as much influence as they do.

The division of the onetime national parties along linguistic lines has meant that any government consists of a coalition of at least four parties. The coalition formed after the November 1981 elections and retained after those of October 1985 is therefore both a coalition of two parties from each of the associated political families (Social Christian and Liberal) and a coalition of two parties from each of the communities (Dutch- and French-speaking). This coalition by its very nature is subject to much internal tension along the various dividing lines, due to the antagonism between the parties of which it is composed, with the Social Christians and the Liberals coming to blows over economic and social issues, and the Dutch- and the French-speaking members splitting over different problems.

The parties must also strike up compromises with the various interest groups and factions. The need for compromise is heightened by the ties between the political parties and some of these groups and by the close relationship between politics and the economy in regard to collective decision-making. Although the interplay of institutions is conditioned to a considerable extent by the activities of parties and pressure groups, it would probably be an exaggeration to say that the rule of law is subordinated to de facto powers. In light of the representative nature of the political parties and of the pressure groups, their activities are undeniably legitimate, within the rules of the game, and identical to those governing the coalition. It is also true, however, that the state is considerably weakened as a result.

The paradox of the Belgian state lies in the fact that it conjures up mutually incompatible images in diametrically opposed circles. The weakness of the state has its roots in the distant past. It has always been considered by Catholics as the specter of secularization, yet the anticlericals have always thought of it as being overly influenced by the Catholic church. The workers movement denigrates it as a bourgeois state, but for the Liberals it poses the threat of state interventionism. The Flemish movement has for a long time considered it as a French-speaking (or at least French-dominated) state, whereas in recent years many French-speaking people have come to fear what they consider the growing influence of the Flemish.

The future evolution of the role and position of the state is a matter of primary importance. The state could become a forum for reducing or even eliminating tension, a forum for redistributing political and administrative functions, or a battleground over the privatization of economic and administrative operations. For a century and a half now, the scope of the public authorities has continually been growing, without, however, the state becoming impervious to private groups and invulnerable to their pressure. Moreover, it has often been at the request of these groups that the state has broadened its activities.

The state administration is currently going through a critical phase. The international economic crisis has forced a rethinking of employment, social security, and social assistance policies, for which businesses and trade unions were unprepared.

Institutional reform is sometimes blamed for the malfunctioning of the system. It has certainly increased the system's complexity, but it cannot be held responsible for that. Institutional reform can be traced back even beyond the French-speaking nature of the young Belgian state to the process of gallicization of the ruling classes at the end of the ancien régime. The Flemish movement, which is as old as the Belgian state itself, has been a factor of key historical importance. (Similar reform is also occurring in other Western European countries.) From 1970 on, the movement for regional and community autonomy has gathered force in Italy, Spain, Great Britain, and even France.

Western European states, particularly Belgium, have had to cope with a twofold shift of decision-making centers. On the one hand, the European Community influences or is active in a number of sectors, some of which are subject, such as in Belgium, to strong interregional tensions. Thus, when the law of December 30, 1970, on economic expansion replaced the laws of July 18, 1959, and July 14, 1966, the demarcation of development zones proved to be a source of conflict between the Belgian state and the European Community, arising from a Flemish-Walloon conflict within Belgium. Similarly, EEC decisions to cut back on steel production and capacity, particularly since the Davignon Plan in 1977, came at a time when political debates on the matter in Belgium were particularly acrimonious.

There is a major difference between on the one hand Belgium and the other countries undergoing regionalization and on the other hand federal states such as West Germany, Switzerland, and Austria. In Belgium, there are two or three national subdivisions, depending on one's point of view, whereas the federal states have many more such divisions. In Belgium, centralization has been challenged not by relatively marginal autonomist movements but by a Flemish movement and a Walloon movement. The first has a longer history, but both have a considerable political impact.

The Belgian case is unique. For more than a century after independence, Brussels was the political and administrative focal point of the state and the hub of private economic power. It was also a focus for Flemish resentment because of its gallicization and for Walloon resentment because of a feeling that it ignored the regional interests of Wallonia. If the rail network built in 1840–50 from the geographical center of the country is compared with the motorway network built in 1960–70, considerable evolution can be seen. The double-edged pressure of the Flemish and Walloon movements has eroded the position of the onetime center. Unlike other examples of federalism or regionalism in Western Europe, Belgium cannot be classed either with the centralization model contested by marginal autonomists or with the polycentric federalist model. The latter is nevertheless a source of inspiration, at least implicitly, for advocates of provincial federalism, but they have not yet succeeded in gaining widespread support or in obtaining decisive decision-making capacity. The existence of only two or three subnational entities creates the risk of scission.

The decision-making autonomy granted to the communities and regions under the reforms of 1970 and 1980 should certainly help defuse the conflict. Although it is too early to predict whether post-unitary Belgium will have more harmonious intercommunity relations, Flanders, the French-speaking Community, the Walloon Region, and the German-speaking Community will now have more leeway to expand their decision-making powers without running into conflict. Sources of dispute nevertheless still exist in the gray areas around the respective decision-making zones, arising from the complex nature of the division of powers and related means and from the status of boroughs along linguistic borders. Moreover, these "community" tensions surface at the central government level, particularly when the distribution of funds and authority is at stake, as seen recently in the educational and industrial sectors (such as coal and steel) and, persistently, in public works and procurement contracts. These problems occasionally hinder the operation of the central government and frequently affect the functioning, which until now has been very bad, of the government/executive consultative committee. There is therefore an element of risk in any political dispute once it takes on what is known in Belgium as a "community dimension." The absence—or in any event lack—of reciprocal exchanges of information between regions and communities constitutes another threat to unity. This area has been deteriorating for the last 20 to 25 years.

"But the political history of Belgium, although it is a history riddled with crises, is also . . . a history of avoiding rupture. In society and in a state, division is not synonymous with a centrifugal tendency and is not a contributory factor to rupture. On the contrary . . . the complex interplay of division gives rise to compromise. Similarly, the asymmetries long since present and now reflected in the institutions are perhaps a barrier to rupture, to the point where it can be asked whether the cornerstone of a certain unity is not to be found precisely in a certain degree of asymmetry" (X. Mabille, *Histoire politique de la Belgique*, p. 388).

The recent evolution of the system has been marked by repeated and extended use of special powers, by a tendency to exercise ministerial functions in a collegial manner, by the strong pre-eminence of the prime minister over his peers, by a growing and sometimes new role for the high law courts, such as the administrative tribunal of last resort (Conseil d'Etat), and for the economic courts. The system has also been tilted, to the detriment of the parliament, toward the government, relying on the courts. The use of special powers allows the government, following the passage by parliament of a law devolving special powers in certain areas and for a precise period of time, to take decisions by means of royal decrees debated in the cabinet. The use of special powers, frequent in recent years, reopens on each occasion a debate of both a legal and a political nature regarding the relationship between the executive and the legislature and perhaps more particularly regarding the relationship between the majority and the opposition. By using special powers, governments can lessen the risk that one of the wings of the coalition might refuse its support during a vote in a public sitting. The advantage of these special powers is therefore twofold. On the one hand, decision-making time is decreased by restricting the formation of normative measures to cabinet deliberations, thus circumventing the process of parliamentary discussion and approval, and on the other hand, the risk of insurrection within majority groups is avoided.

Since 1981, the coalition of Social Christians and Liberals has used special powers on a number of occasions in order to push through its policy of economic and financial recovery. The opposition (notably the Socialists) has criticized the government for its repeated use of practically identical special powers, claiming this indicates that the measures adopted have not had the hoped-for results. With a government undertaking to submit draft royal decrees for the reasoned opinion of the legislative section of the Conseil d'Etat and to consider its remarks, the Conseil was obliged to emerge from the relative obscurity, to which it had been condemned since its creation in 1946, to supervise the normative activity of the executive.

Moreover, certain offices of the Administrative Section of the Conseil d'Etat have had to decide on appeals against the election or the appointment of political officials in boroughs with special linguistic status situated on the edge of the city of Brussels or along the border between the French- and the Dutch-speaking regions. The rulings of the Flemish offices of the Conseil d'Etat calling on French-speaking officials elected in Flanders (even if in a majority in certain borough councils) to prove that they can speak and understand Dutch provoked strong reactions among French-speakers, who accused the Conseil d'Etat of overstepping its role and usurping that of the legislature by imposing a new eligibility condition. This is not a unique case. Other jurisdictional bodies have also acquired increased importance, such as the Court of Arbitration or the economic magistracy, whose role has evolved under the impact of the economic crisis. For the past fifteen years or so, the international economic crisis and the process of institutional reform have placed considerable strain on political decision-making. Their impact has been so durable that they can no longer be considered short-term factors.

A counterweight to the changing shape of political power will be vital in the years to come. The questions are: Where can it be placed, and, How can it operate? The question of organizing the relationship between the government and the public sector on the one hand and the independent authorities and the private sector on the other must also be settled. Finally, Belgium must succeed in striking a balance between communities and regions in a manner that guarantees the smooth operation of the whole.

PART IV

The Economy

Luc Wauters and Jan Huyghebaert,
Coordinators

Introduction

Luc Wauters and Jan Huyghebaert

THE ECONOMY OF A small country like Belgium is strongly affected by the world economy and the economies of its European trading partners. In this part, general trends in the Belgian economy over the past 35 years are examined and attention is paid to general achievements, the relative contributions of the most important economic sectors, and macroeconomic structural changes.

In the primary sector, agriculture, which includes forestry and fisheries, is the main contributor. Mining, mainly coal mining, is becoming an ever decreasing activity. Belgian farmers are mostly stockbreeders and market gardeners engaged in intensive land management.

In the secondary sector, the manufacturing and construction industries are the most important contributors to GNP. The manufacturing industry has undergone considerable restructuring as a result of competition within the EEC and the oil crises of the 1970s. Small and medium-size enterprises employ nearly 50 percent of all workers and can be considered an indispensable component of the Belgian economy.

In the tertiary sector, including commerce and financial and insurance services, considerable changes and progress have been made. Financial services and markets have experienced a continuous high growth rate and employ 12 percent of the work force. The final integration of the European market in 1993 will be another incentive for development and international mergers in banking and insurance. Complementary to the growth of financial and insurance services is the extension of nonfinancial services, such as hotels, health care, knowledge and information distributors, and advisory and administrative services of all kinds. Export and internationalization can be expected in this area.

In a small industrial country with an open economy but without natural resources, it is difficult either to overestimate the importance of foreign trade (65 percent of total Belgian production is exported) or to underestimate the competitiveness in high-tech manufacturing. Both will be affected by the changes to be expected from the full opening of the European market and the increasing use of nuclear energy for the production of electricity.

Last but not least, monetary, fiscal, and budgetary policy illustrate the way wealth is taxed, redistributed, and used by the government for the welfare of the citizens. Since monetary policy is sensitive to external influences, it is coordinated with the other European countries within a fixed exchange rate. Successive governments have labored to reduce the budget deficits and expenditures. These efforts, a favorable international environment, and a coherent economic policy have decreased annual government deficits and contributed considerably to a sounder economy.

General Trends

Paul Kestens

THIS CHAPTER IDENTIFIES the major trends influencing the Belgian economy on the basis of the main macroeconomic data available. The most important source of these data is government accounts. The observation period stretches from 1953 to 1987; no official data on government accounts are available before 1953. The performance of the Belgian economy over this period can be assessed in the light of two parameters. The first is the rate of achievement of general economic policy objectives such as growth, employment, price stability, and balance of payments. The general economic health of the country from 1953 to 1987 can be diagnosed by evaluating these four variables. The second parameter deals with changes in the relative contribution of each sector of activity to the national product. This analysis reveals factors affecting the overall economic performance of Belgium.

Medium-Term Performance of the Belgian Economy

The overall success of the Belgian economy can be illustrated by looking at the achievement rate for general economic policy objectives (see Table IV.1). This section focuses on results obtained during three subperiods: the two decades (1953–73) when the international economic situation was favorable; the period 1973–82, which was characterized by a downturn in general economic growth and strong instability both in the world economic situation and in currency markets; and the period 1982–87, when exchange instability remained strong but the amplitude of economic cycles eased.

The Period 1953–1973

Up to the eve of the first oil crisis in 1973, the different economic and employment objectives had met with varying degrees of success. On

TABLE IV. 1
Achievement of Main Policy Objectives, 1953–1985
(percent per year)

Year	GNP growth (constant prices)	Consumer price growth	Unemployment rate	Current account balance
1953–57	3.3%	1.3%	3.9%	0.9%
1958–62	3.6	1.0	3.2	0.9
1963–67	4.4	3.5	1.6	0.2
1968–72	5.7	4.0	2.5	2.5
1973–77	3.1	9.7	5.0	0.7
1978–82	1.6	6.4	10.0	−2.4
1983–87	1.3	4.2	13.5	2.0

the one hand, the economy had continued to grow, and the balance of payments had improved. On the other hand, results in the areas of full employment and price stability were unimpressive. On the positive side, the economic growth rate accelerated continuously over the two decades in question. The modest average growth rate of 3.3 percent in the mid-1950's rose gradually to 4.5 percent ten years later before leveling off at 5.5 percent in the early 1970's. Belgian economic growth was initially below the levels experienced in the other EEC member-states but gradually attained comparable levels after the creation of the Common Market.

Over the same period, a monetary policy of balancing the books ensured that Belgium's balance of payments was not systematically in disequilibrium. However, just before the first oil crisis, officially satisfactory results concealed an actual imbalance. The appearance of a permanent and large trade surplus in the early 1970's in fact reflected an underevaluation of the Belgian franc. On the darker side, prices became more and more unstable in these two decades, reflecting a worldwide trend. This deterioration took place even though price stability was a priority policy objective, particularly in light of the increasingly open nature of the Belgian economy. Early in this period, foreign trade prices remained relatively stable; they then gradually rose at a rate close to domestic inflation.

Over the same period, the employment balance fluctuated. Up to the mid-1960's, general economic expansion led to a considerable upturn in the labor market. The unemployment rate, which stood at 4.5 percent in the early 1950's, gradually fell to below 1.8 percent in the mid-1960's. A stagnation in the size of the working population during this same period reinforced the effectiveness of government efforts to wipe out structural unemployment. However, restructuring efforts by the government proved insufficient to reabsorb unemployment in regions entering a new structural recession, chiefly in the Walloon industrial basin (coal mining, metallurgy, and steel making). Moreover, after stagnating between 1953 and 1964, the Belgian work force began to grow continuously from 1965 on, when the postwar generation entered the labor market. The percentage of working women sharply increased. Consequently, there was no drop in unemployment in the last phase of economic growth before the first oil crisis; on the contrary, unemployment rates stood at 2.0 percent and 2.5 percent, respectively, during the last two economic peaks (1969–70 and 1973); these rates were significantly higher than the average observed during previous cycles.

The Period 1973–1982

After the first oil crisis, the negative impact of the international environment reversed previously good performances. At first the under-evaluation of the Belgian franc cushioned the impact of the oil crisis on Belgium's balance of payments. The balance of payments remained more or less in equilibrium for the period 1973–77. The first annual deficit as a percentage of GNP was recorded in 1977 (−0.5 percent). Economic recession set in from the second half of 1974 to the second quarter of 1975 as companies used up available inventory. Domestic demand sagged only very slightly. The economic upswing provoked by the process of rebuilding inventory in 1976 improved results to a satisfactory level. This gave rise to the mistaken belief that economic difficulties were only cyclical. However, a clear downturn in growth was registered later, with a near halving of the growth rate in the two five-year periods following the first oil crisis. Moreover, the range and frequency of cyclical ups and downs altered in the last ten years of this period, with falls in absolute terms registered in 1975 and 1981. This contrasted with the previous two decades, when growth fluctuated but never turned negative except for a slight fall in 1958. This break was closely tied to the world economic situation. Indeed, exports, which depend largely on the economic situation in consumer countries, accounted for a considerable part of Belgian GNP.

The inability of the labor market to absorb growth in the working population after the mid-1960's was exacerbated by this slowdown in growth. This evolution in Belgium's labor market foreshadowed a similar trend among its European partners in the early 1980's. The rapidity of the labor market reaction in Belgium arose from the attempt by sectors facing international competition to maintain a sufficiently competitive level to overcome internal inflationary pressures and a general contraction in international demand. Because exports consisted chiefly of raw materials and semifinished products (only very few products had a high value added), export prices could be varied only within limits reflecting price rises in the main competitor countries. Market shares could be preserved only by boosting productivity, to the detriment of full employment. Increased productivity was also essential to compensate for automatic salary raises to keep pace with inflation.

In the period 1978–82, when economic and currency turmoil were rife, results for all four main objectives were negative. In addition, inflation and underemployment became more acute, growth decreased, and a large trade deficit surfaced.

The Period 1982–1987

The second readjustment of oil prices and the rise in the value of the dollar, which took place in the international upheaval at the beginning of the decade, prompted further deterioration in Belgian buying power. This deterioration was much more marked than that experienced after the first oil crisis. It became clear that economic policy should concentrate on limiting the medium-term impact of a weaker Belgian economy and spreading the burden between the main macroeconomic operators —households, companies, and the government. The Belgian franc was devalued in February 1982, and a more restrictive incomes policy was adopted. These economic policy U-turns and a new, more favorable international environment in the period 1985–87 with a lower dollar and a reverse swing of the oil pendulum gave mixed results.

The evolution of the world economy facilitated achievement of external economic objectives. In other words, the competitive position obtained thanks to the February 1982 devaluation and the income policy was more easily preserved. Consequently the current account balance rapidly moved back into equilibrium, and by the end of the period in question a sizable surplus had been generated. Moreover, the rapid rate at which fluctuations in international prices affected domestic prices led to a fall in the inflation rate, which again reached a level comparable with that of Belgium's main competitors.

On the other hand, the international context did not allow any improvement in performance on the two other objectives. At the very most, it allowed compensatory growth for the deflationary effects of income and the government's financial adjustment measures. The annual GNP growth rate stabilized at around 1.5 percent. This rate was not strong enough to allow reabsorption of unemployment, which continued to grow, although at a slightly slower rate. The gradual reduction in the number of young people joining the labor market partly explains this deceleration.

Evolution of Macroeconomic Structures

GNP by Sector

Belgium industrialized early and has undergone a special sectoral evolution. Thus, the share of GNP represented by primary industries has fallen, with the slack being taken up first by the secondary sector and then by the tertiary sector. Table IV.2 compares the sectoral breakdown of GNP at intervals of seventeen and fifteen years. The decline of mining has been particularly marked, as has that of agriculture, forestry, and fisheries. In the first subperiod, added value was partially transferred to the secondary sector, notably in the form of the building and metalworking industries, and to the tertiary sector as a whole. Between 1970 and 1985, primary activities ceded ground exclusively to the services sector. Losses in competitiveness suffered by heavy industry provoked "deindustrialization" toward the end of the period in question, weakening the relative importance of industrial value added. This process was even more accentuated in employment. In 1985, industrial jobs represented only 32 percent of total employment, compared with 42 percent fifteen years earlier and 45 percent in 1960.

The first point to be deduced from Table IV.3 is that the Belgian economy depends increasingly on foreign trade. Over the long term, this

TABLE IV.2

Relative Contribution of Sectoral Added Value to GNP, 1953–1985

(at market prices and in current francs)

Activity sector	1953	1970	1985
Primary sector	11.9	4.6	3.0
Agriculture, forestry, fisheries	7.7	3.7	2.4
Mining	4.2	0.9	0.6
Secondary sector	37.0	40.1	33.9
Manufacturing industries	29.7	31.9	24.2
Construction	5.3	6.9	6.0
Tertiary sector	51.1	55.3	63.1
Commerce	14.9	17.3	20.0
Financial services and insurance	2.1	3.2	5.2

TABLE IV.3
GNP by Activity Sector, 1953–1985
(as percent of GNP)

Activity sector	1953	1963	1974	1980	1982	1985
Private consumption	70.3%	66.8%	59.7%	63.5%	66.2%	65.9%
Public consumption	12.8	13.2	15.0	18.4	18.8	17.8
Gross domestic investment	16.6	20.6	24.4	21.5	17.2	15.3
State investment	1.8	2.9	3.4	3.4	3.2	2.2
Net exports of goods and services						
Total exports	29.4	36.5	57.3	65.5	79.3	84.2
Total imports	29.1	37.1	56.4	69.0	81.5	83.2
Net exports	+0.3	−0.6	+0.9	−3.5	−2.2	+1.0
GNP at market prices (adjusted)	100.0%	100.0%	100.0%	100.0%	100.0%	100.0%

has resulted in growth of the share accounted for both by exports and imports. Their share rose from around one-third in the mid-1950's to one-half before the first oil crisis to over 80 percent by 1985. By the end of the period in question, Belgium could boast the highest amount of exported goods per capita in the entire industrialized world.

Public consumption has been the only sector to make up a relatively even proportion of national product throughout the observation period. The continual rise in the relative share of current public expenditure does not differ notably from trends in other industrialized countries. On the other hand, the amounts taken up by private consumption and investment took a different path over the period in question.

In the first phase, between 1953 and 1974, the more or less steady drop in the relative importance of private consumption corresponded to considerable growth in the investment slice. Consequently, the propensity to invest in the Belgian economy, which was structurally weak at the beginning of the observation period, gradually grew to a level comparable with that of Belgium's Common Market partners by the early 1970's. Some experts feel that this evolution is the main factor behind the accelerated GNP and productivity growth since 1960.

Investment growth is naturally also tied to government policy. Government investment has expanded considerably. Growth at all levels of government has been much stronger than that of the national product. It has varied from time to time, partly because of budgetary restrictions but also because of a deliberate policy of economic balance. In addition to this, investment projects became easier to put into practice under laws of July 1959 and December 1970 designed to stimulate economic development that increased and broadened the advantages offered by the government to private investors.

Throughout this period, the strong growth in the propensity to invest in companies has been encouraged by the rapid development of a range of financing sources. Two specific factors must be mentioned in explanation. First, the volume of household savings increased because of the rise in available income. The proportion of income saved, which stood at only 7 percent of household income in 1950, doubled during the third quarter of the 20th century to reach 14 percent on the eve of the first oil crisis. The development and diversification of systems of savings collection by financial institutions have mobilized household savings to a greater extent. Moreover, diversification by individuals extended the buying power of available income, regardless of the growth in current income, under the joint effect of capital gains on property and the optimization of financial assets. Second, an influx of foreign funds reinforced investment-funding capacity within Belgium. This influx has essentially been due to the creation of the Common Market, which encouraged foreign investors, chiefly American, to export capital to Europe rather than to export real goods. This trend was reinforced by the overvalued dollar.

Since the first oil crisis, however, the evolution in the relative shares of private consumption and investment has been turned on its head. The weakening of the Belgian economy did not initially decrease overall available household income, for private consumer spending grew faster than the national product. However, the favorable situation that had previously encouraged investment rapidly deteriorated. The government's financial situation did not leave any room for growth in public investment and was a barrier to a policy encouraging private investment. Companies had to cope with a drying-up of their main sources of financing. The supply of equity capital was much less dynamic, due to savers' reluctance to invest in risky ventures. Massive recourse to third-party funds gradually became more difficult due to government financing requirements and the austere monetary policy adopted to defend the Belgian franc. Since 1978, nominal interest rates have remained at levels higher than expected inflation and expected investment viability. The composition of Belgium's GNP has therefore gradually moved back to that at the beginning of the 1950's and is characterized by a high proportion of private consumer expenditure and low investment.

Income and government finance policy became much more restrictive after 1982, thus acting as a brake on this structural evolution. There has been a slight drop in both public and private shares in overall consumption. Greater investment in fixed assets by private companies has, however, not compensated for the drop in state investment and housing construction.

Agriculture

Jan Hinnekens

THE CASUAL OBSERVER of Belgium must have the impression that in this densely populated country with its highly developed service and industrial sectors, there is no room for agriculture. This is an understandable error: the country is heavily urbanized, with little space available for agriculture. The figures tell it all. Belgium has a total area of 30,521 sq. km. Some 10 million people live in this confined space, with an average density of 325 per sq. km. The population density is particularly high in the Flemish region. Agricultural land occupies barely half of the kingdom. Woods take up about 20 percent, mostly in the Walloon region. In the past, the loss of agricultural land to urbanization, industrialization, and road building was high (more than 0.5 percent per year), especially in the Flemish region; this has decreased in recent years. There are less than 14 ares (about 0.3 acres) of agricultural land available per Belgian today.

Belgium has a mild, damp climate. On the North Sea coast, the temperature and the number of frost-free days in a year are favorably determined by the warm waters of the Gulf Stream. In the western part of the country, which is low and flat, the average yearly temperature is 10°C. In the extreme southeastern corner, almost 700 meters above sea level, it is just over 6°C. From west to east, the annual rainfall increases from 800 to 1,200 mm.

There are relatively large differences in fertility among the various areas. The Leemstreek (claylands), which run west to east, and the polders, with their heavy soil deposited by the sea, are the most fertile areas. The least fertile soils are to be found in the Kempen and in the Ardennes, the High Ardennes and the Jura, in the southeast. This area is recognized and subsidized by the European Community as a "less-favored region." Among the remaining agricultural areas, which have average fertility, there are also some typical meadowland areas.

The climate, the soil composition, and structural and other factors combine to determine which crops and animals are most suitable for Belgian agriculture. Obviously, the soil is exploited intensively. But capital is also an important means of production, since farmers want to put as much value added as possible into a limited area, and that calls for capital, in the form of buildings, machinery, livestock, and inputs such as feed and fertilizer. It should come as no surprise then that the Belgian farmer is a stockbreeder and a market gardener rather than a grower of cereal grains. This can be seen clearly from data on overall production value: stockbreeding accounts for around 66 percent, market gardening for about 18 percent, and grain production for some 15 percent.

Stockbreeding

Cattle rearing is the main stockbreeding activity. This sector takes up 58 percent of the area devoted to agriculture (grazing and crop land) and accounts for 21 percent of the value of agricultural production in the form of beef products and 17 percent in the form of milk production. Belgian cattle (around 3 million head, less than one-third of them milk cows) for the most part belong to five native breeds, originally raised for both meat and milk production. The most common breed, the Belgian Witblauw, is raised for its meat and is well known beyond Belgian borders. This is why average milk production per capita (just under 4,000 kg) is somewhat low.

Toward the end of the 1960's and in the 1970's, pig farming expanded considerably. Since then, it has made a slightly larger contribution to overall agricultural production value than cattle breeding. Pig farming is highly concentrated in the Flemish region, particularly in small farms in the Zandstreek area. These farms, faced with the impossibility of expansion, have been trying to improve their quality by moving toward a capital-intensive, soil-dependent sector that offers them good prospects in a unified Europe. There are at present 5.5 million pigs in Belgium, most of them Belgian Landrace, a breed internationally known for its quality, thanks to selective breeding. The Piétrain is also a world-renowned breed, unsurpassed for its net meat yield. One-third of pork production is exported.

Finally, there is poultry farming. Laying poultry and table poultry account for 4 percent and 3 percent, respectively, of the total value of agricultural production.

Market Gardening

With only 4 percent of agricultural land, market gardening accounts for 4 to 5 times as big a share of agricultural production. Market gardening is labor intensive, and often capital intensive as well. In Belgium, market gardening means vegetables (about 50 percent of production value). First and foremost is chicory (Belgian endive), a product created some years ago in the Belgian Botanical Gardens in Brussels. Chicory is exported to some forty countries. In addition, various vegetables grown outside are used in the canning industry and the frozen food industry. This industry has grown considerably in recent years and is 80 percent export-oriented. Vegetables grown in hothouses include primarily tomatoes and lettuce.

Next in order of importance are nonedible market gardening products, including decorative plants. The azalea is the most important of these. The cultivation of this plant is based on years of tradition and research, which have made Belgium the world's leading azalea producer. The azaleas can be admired in their glory at the Ghent Flower Show, a magnificent floral spectacle held every five years in the center of the decorative plant industry. Among bulbs and corms, begonias and gloxinias have brought Belgium much international fame. Every year, hundreds of hectares of blooming begonias can be admired in the Ghent area, where carpets of begonias adorn the market squares of towns. Belgium's share of the European begonia and gloxinia industry is 60 percent. Tree growing (particularly conifers and trees for forestry) is also important. The cut-flower industry, both under glass and in the open air, has experienced difficulties in recent years.

Fruit production consists primarily of dwarf apples and pears and the Belgian table grape. This quality grape is the only one to come on the market during winter, but rising energy prices have led to a decline. Of the tens of thousands of greenhouses, covering 450 ha south of Brussels in "glass villages," less than 20 percent are still devoted to the production of this speciality.

Crops

Crops, with about one-fourth of the area devoted to agriculture, produce about one-seventh of the value of agricultural production. They therefore lag behind market gardening and stock breeding. In European and international terms, however, Belgian crop farming holds its own, thanks to high yields per hectare. Cereals production is primarily winter corn and winter barley, because considerable increases in yield can be achieved with these cereals. Sugarbeet is next, with an area less than a third that of cereals production. The sugar yield is at a record level, over 7,000 kg per hectare. Further down the scale, and with an area fluctuating to a greater extent, comes the potato.

Farm Income and Labor

The high yields achieved by Belgian agriculture can be explained partly by high intermediate consumption, that is, by a high consumption of production enhancers. No less than 56 percent of the value of agricultural production goes to purchase inputs, a percentage not exceeded anywhere in the European Community. Of course, the limited area and the strong tendency toward stock breeding, pig farming in particular, have considerable influence here, since both factors mean that stock feed has to come from outside Belgium. Stock feed expenses account for about half of all expenditure for intermediate consumption. Expenses on energy, fertilizers, planting, and sowing lag well behind. Among other deductible items are depreciation of around 6–7 percent of the value of agricultural production and the interest paid on loans (about 1.5 percent) and leases (4.5 percent). Only 34 percent of agricultural land is worked by the owner. Expenditure on wages is low since laborers account for only 3 percent of the working farming population. Finally, 30 percent of the total final value generated by Belgian agriculture is operator's income.

The total agricultural labor force has never been so small. Some 100,000 people are employed in farming and market gardening, and another 60,000 work part-time in agriculture. Altogether, this represents less than 3 percent of the total working population of Belgium, and this percentage is falling. About three-quarters of the agricultural population are owners or tenant farmers, and the farms have a pronounced family character. Wage-earners account for only a small percent of the work force.

Smallness is a characteristic of Belgian farms. The average is about 20 ha for professional farms, and 2.75 ha for the 8,000 or so professional market-gardening farms. Of course, this average size must be put into perspective, in view of the intensive character of farming in Belgium. The Belgian agricultural worker generates the highest average value added in Europe.

With a 2.5 percent share of GNP, agriculture cuts a reasonably successful figure in the Belgian economy as a whole. For years, it achieved better productivity increases than industry, and increases in income matched the general increase in salaries, but through a reduction in the number of employees rather than through an increase in value added. Agricultural production nonetheless continues to grow, and certain products are increasingly finding their way abroad. Among the traditional export products, sugar, pork, milk, butter, and various market-gardening products are the most important. Belgian agriculture accounts for about 6 percent of Belgian exports. Among the products imported, the most important are oilseeds and other raw materials for animal feed. The agricultural balance of payments is traditionally negative, if the products of the food industry, such as oils, fats, and sugar, are ignored.

Manufacturing and Construction Industry

Raymond Pulinckx

BELGIUM WAS THE FIRST country in continental Europe to be drawn into the industrial revolution, following in the footsteps of Great Britain. Belgium was spurred by the existence of a powerful textile cottage industry in Flanders, dating back to the Middle Ages, and of an arms and metalworking sector in Wallonia. In addition, coal reserves around the Sambre and Meuse, exploited on a small scale since the 13th century, provided the energy necessary for industrial development. Industrialization proceeded rapidly in the first decades following Belgian independence. The annual growth rate of industrial production between 1842 and 1872 has been estimated at 5.2 percent. Coal mines, iron and nonferrous metalworks, glass factories, and textile plants formed the backbone of Belgian industrialization. The number of workers employed in factories increased from 406,000 in 1846 to 1,069,000 in 1910. Most firms ground to an almost complete halt during World War I. Then, protectionism in the majority of countries in the interwar period caused difficulties for sectors producing finished goods. Production increasingly switched to raw materials and semifinished products. World War II had a less disastrous impact on the industrial apparatus than World War I. After the war, demand for semifinished products remained very firm as both Europe and the world restructured. After 1960, the gradual creation of the European Economic Community completely overturned the normal rules of competition. The slow but sure removal of customs barriers between the six, and later the nine, member-states opened the way to the free movement of all goods and more particularly to that of finished products.

The geographical situation of Belgium, at the heart of the Community and surrounded by its most densely inhabited and most prosperous regions (100 million inhabitants in a radius of 300 km around Brussels), along with the decision to set up the Community's main institutions in Brussels, attracted a large number of foreign companies to Belgium. Labor force availability in the north of the country oriented the bulk of investment toward this region. Chemical, metalworking, electrical, and automobile industries grew up. Belgium then entered the Golden Sixties, which in this case ran until 1974. During this period, it experienced rapid growth, at an annual rate rising as high as 5 percent, and industrial structures were considerably modified and diversified. Industry then lived through a difficult few years. The excessive salary increases that characterized the last few years of prosperity, combined with economic policy errors after the two oil crises, brought a loss in competitiveness for most Belgian industries. In an economy so dependent on the export market, the consequence was blanket restructuring, sometimes on a massive scale. Many companies were forced to close down or went bankrupt; others were able to survive only through reconversion and abolition of jobs. In the course of eight years, between 1974 and 1982, job losses in industry totaled 381,000, or 25 percent. In 1982, the government adopted a new approach, consisting of a currency devaluation, a wage freeze, and tax incentives for venture capital. Competitiveness and viability were largely restored as a result, followed after 1985 by a recovery in productive investments.

Table IV.4 illustrates just how badly industrial growth was affected after 1974. Between 1960 and 1974, the average annual growth rate of the entire manufacturing and construction industry reached 5.4 percent, causing output to double in the space of fourteen years. The chemical, wood, metalworking, and steel industries significantly outstripped this average with annual growth rates of 8–10 percent. Textiles, nonferrous metals, and, to a lesser extent, construction and foodstuffs generally had below average growth. In the following eleven years, industrial production stagnated, with growth never exceeding on average 0.6 percent per annum. The chemical industry alone escaped stagnation, succeeding in almost maintaining its previous growth rate. The nonferrous metals, metalworking, foodstuffs, and paper sectors held on to a positive growth rate. All other sectors experienced negative rates, particularly textiles and clothing, steel, construction, and nonmetallic (building) materials.

The last two columns in Table IV.4 show the results of the battle for growth, in the form of the respective importance of each sector. The sectors are ranked according to the value added to input costs, which measures the real contribution of the various activity groups to GDP between 1960 and 1985. Three branches climbed a considerable way up the ladder. The chemical industry practically doubled in importance (6.1

TABLE IV.4
Growth and Relative Importance of Different Industrial Sectors, 1960–1985

Branch	Annual growth		Relative importance[a]	
	1960–74	1974–85	1960	1985
Steel	7.9%	−0.6%	8.3%	4.4%
Nonferrous metals	2.7	3.8	2.0	1.8
Metalworking, machine construction, electrical	8.0	1.4	19.8	25.1
Chemical	9.7	7.7	6.1	11.8
Foodstuffs	4.0	1.4	16.7	16.0
Textiles, clothing	2.2	−1.5	12.0	6.2
Wood	10.0	0	3.6	3.2
Paper, printing	5.1	0.8	4.5	4.5
Quarries, nonmetallic (building) materials	5.0	−1.3	6.7	3.9
Construction	3.9	−1.6	17.4	18.4
Miscellaneous	8.2	1.4	2.9	4.7
Total manufacturing and construction industry	5.4	0.6	100	100

[a] Value added to input costs as a percent of total value added by manufacturing and construction industry.

percent to 11.8 percent), and metalworking, machine, and electrical construction gained 5.3 points. The miscellaneous sector also increased its share, probably because of the diamond industry. On the other hand, three branches fell considerably: the steel industry, textiles and clothing, and nonmetallic materials. The concentration of activities has therefore shifted toward branches, such as metalworking and electronics or the chemical industry, that make use of high technology and are therefore better placed to compete with countries with cheap labor.

Main Features of the Various Sectors

The Steel Industry

The steel industry is oriented toward the production of semifinished products and has undergone the most thorough restructuring in recent years. A cornerstone industry in the first industrial revolution, steel concerns grew up in Belgium in the 19th century around the Sambre and Meuse close to the coal fields. Most of the output was exported. In 1910, 1.9 million metric tons were produced. Output doubled between 1910 and 1950 and quadrupled between 1950 and 1974, reaching the record level of 16 million metric tons.

After this date, plummeting demand in Europe and competition from certain Third World countries led to the introduction by the European Community, made responsible for this sector by the European Coal and Steel Community (ECSC) Treaty, of severe production quotas and restructuring measures. Belgian steel production has been brought down to 10 million tons and concentrated in the most profitable concerns, particularly the maritime steel sector in the Ghent region. Oxygen-fed and continuous casting steelworks have become general practice, and production of flat products, notably sheet materials, has outstripped that of long products. However, the future of this sector is still in doubt despite investment and restructuring, because overcapacity remains a problem in Europe.

Nonferrous Metals

The origins of this sector date back to the early 19th century. The oldest zinc processor was founded in 1837. The relative importance of nonferrous metals is explained by the fact that Belgium had close ties with Katanga (present-day Shaba) in Central Africa. Some of the minerals extracted in this region were and still are refined in Belgium.

This sector has invested heavily in technological research. In addition to traditional metals such as zinc, copper, and lead, it also produces some thirty more or less rare metals. The metallurgy is in some cases very complex and demands considerable know-how. Companies have also tended to evolve up the production chain, producing semifinished products and alloys. More than 73 percent of output is exported, making Belgium one of the world's major exporters of nonferrous metals. Some companies also make money by selling their manufacturing procedures abroad.

Metalworking, Machine Construction, and Electrical Works

This sector, which accounts for 317 billion francs in value added and employs 250,000 people, holds a key position in the manufacturing industry. Diversity is the key word for products, manufacturing procedures, markets, and company size. Four large subsectors of more or less equal size can be identified.

1. Metalworking, including in particular the first-stage processing of metals (foundry and especially wire drawing, in which one of the world leaders is a Belgian firm), sheet work, building accessories, and heavy metalworking. Generally speaking, this subsector has experienced diffi-

culties in recent years because of a contraction in demand and competition from substitutes and from countries using cheap labor.

2. Machine construction, mainly capital goods. The well-being of this sector depends on investment throughout the world, particularly in industrialized countries. The sector exports 70 percent of its output. The majority of large firms are subsidiaries of multinational groups. The automation of manufacturing has caused a flurry of change in both production methods and products.

3. Electrical works and electronics. Growth in electricity consumption has slowed, with inevitable effects for the production of electrical capital goods. On the other hand, expansion is still in its heyday in the electronics sector, embracing specialized electronic goods, telecommunication materials, and consumer goods. Markets are evolving rapidly and hold out great promise for the future.

4. Automobile construction. Five major manufacturers have subsidiaries in Belgium building or assembling cars. Annual output has risen to 1 million units, of which more than 90 percent is exported.

Companies in this sector have invested heavily in new plants to automatize and robotize their workshops and assembly lines. Belgian factories have a high reputation for productivity and quality.

The Chemical Industry

The chemical industry is both vast and highly diverse. It encompasses companies working with the basic substances of mineral or organic chemistry products and those companies, which through various mixing and transformation processes, produce fertilizers, fungicides and pesticides, paints, pharmaceuticals, soaps and cosmetics, photography products, and processed plastics. The chemical industry has experienced strong and regular growth for 25 years; it was less affected, relatively speaking, than other sectors by the recession that followed the oil crises. Unlike the situation in other branches, employment has remained stable.

Again, a large proportion of companies are subsidiaries of multinational groups. The remainder are Belgian companies that have a number of foreign subsidiaries. Chemistry is the industrial sector that spends the most on R&D (17 billion francs per annum). It is a strong exporting sector and has the biggest trade balance surplus (167 billion francs in 1986). The Belgian chemical industry traditionally produces caustic soda, chlorinated products, photographic goods, and certain proprietary medicinal products. Finally, it is noteworthy that some companies have already carved themselves a niche in biotechnology, undoubtedly a sector of the future.

Foodstuffs, Beverages

This vast sector accounts for 16 percent of the entire manufacturing industry. A wide range of activities falls under its umbrella, all with the same starting point: agriculture. The end products are destined for human consumption or animal feed. Although the foodstuffs sector is a time-honored human activity, it has nevertheless had to keep up with modern technology. The first step was the transformation of cottage industries into industrial concerns. Subsectors such as baked goods and meat products, which in the· past were totally controlled by individual tradesmen, are increasingly falling into the hands of industry. Supermarket distribution is one factor in this evolution. The self-service system also requires individual packaging in small quantities, increasing the value added by industry.

The food industry has undoubtedly been the sector most affected by the removal of customs barriers within the EEC. Previously, tariffs on foodstuffs were very high. External trade has developed rapidly, and company concentration has been stimulated. The majority of Belgian firms were previously family concerns; some of them have been or will be obliged to integrate into multinational groups. Finally, the EEC's Common Agricultural Policy and directives on consumer protection have also influenced the fate of this industry. Generally speaking, the Belgian foodstuffs industry has coped very well with the pressure for change. Despite relative saturation of demand, the sector has continued to grow and was only marginally affected by the recession that followed the oil crises. The sector's most important activities are sweets, chocolate, oil, cookies, beer, soft drinks, and cattle feed.

Textiles and Clothing

This sector, which produces mainly consumer goods, has a long tradition. A number of fresh challenges have had to be confronted in recent years, from competition from the newly industrialized countries and Eastern European states to intra-European competition, very important technological advances in equipment and fibers, and changes in consumer tastes and in commercial networks. The sector could cope only by investing heavily. But the majority of companies were family concerns and, because of the low profit level in the sector, were unable to scrape up sufficient funds. The government drew up a "textile plan" to separate out the most viable companies from among the existing ones. These companies were then given the financial means to carry out the necessary investments. Restructuring of this sector was very positive.

One of the most noteworthy activities in this sector is the production of carpets, of which Belgium is one of the world's biggest exporters. Other important sectors include furniture and automobile fabrics, along with a range of fabrics for industrial uses. Almost 80 percent of textile output is exported. This sector has a large trade surplus. The same cannot be said for the clothing sector, which is experiencing considerable difficulties in making a market name for itself.

Wood

This sector is not as important as the ones just discussed. It has a turnover of 75 million francs and employs 25,000 people. The main products are furniture and chipboard, but a wide range of other goods are produced. Efforts to create new materials, improve furniture design, and in particular to automate workshops demonstrate the dynamism of the sector and augur well for its future.

Paper and Printing Industry

This branch covers all paper processes: production of pulp, manufacture of paper and cardboard, the processing of these, and finally printing and publishing. Belgium's relatively small forest resources do not entirely cover its paper and pulp requirements. Consequently, it is a net importer of these raw materials. However, Belgium is highly active in the processing of paper and cardboard, a sector that has become increasingly internationalized in recent years because of the rapid technical evolution of manufacturing. Computer technology has become an integral part of the industry and, after considerable investment, has paved the way for substantial progress in productivity. Current consumer trends have ensured that demand remains strong.

For its part, the graphics industry employs 22,000 workers, which is more than the two other subsectors combined (6,600 for pulp and paper; 10,400 for processing). Its services are targeted essentially on the domestic market, although some export breakthroughs have been recorded in recent years. The Belgian publishing industry has led the way in a number of instances such as pocket books and comic strips. Again, manufacturing procedures have become internationally competitive in recent years.

Nonmetallic (Building) Materials and the Construction Industry

These two branches are closely interlinked because they aim at the same market. The building materials sector consists essentially of stone and sand quarries, brickworks, cement works, ceramics concerns, glassworks, and prefabricated parts. The majority of these products have a low specific value and are therefore not viable for transport over a long distance. The market is therefore within Belgium and in neighboring countries.

The glass industry is, however, an exception. Three-quarters of its output is exported. Again, technical change has upset the smooth routine of this sector. Many new products have been launched, often overstepping the narrow limits of the construction industry, for example, safety glass for vehicles, particularly cars, fiberglass for the reinforcement of plastics, packaging glasses, and special high-technology glasses with a multitude of uses. Generous R&D budgets will guarantee the glass industry a healthy future.

Construction has lived through a difficult period in the past decade. Saturation of demand, high interest rates, and low levels of discretionary income among households and building contractors have led to a decline in the number of houses, office buildings, and industrial plants being built. Finally, the government's financial difficulties have led to job losses in civil engineering. Construction companies have only marginally been able to turn to the export market to compensate for the recession on the domestic market. In some cases, they have been able to participate in the construction of large units on foreign soil or have carried out dredging work.

Diamond Industry

This review of the various branches of Belgian industry would not be complete without mention of the diamond industry. Although statistics for the diamond sector are not kept separately from other industries, diamond cutting is nevertheless very important for the Belgian economy.

The industry is situated essentially in Antwerp and the surrounding area. It keeps in close touch with the Antwerp market, which is the biggest diamond market in the world. The level of activity has nevertheless diminished in recent years because of competition from Israel and India. However, the latter two have concerned themselves chiefly with small stones. Antwerp remains the world's most important center for cutting large, high-quality stones. More than 95 percent of the goods produced are exported, particularly to the United States, Japan, and Hong Kong. Customs data, which probably underestimate the scale of the trade, showed exports worth 180 million francs in 1986.

This brief overview has illustrated the fact that Belgian industry has suffered more acutely than the industries of other European countries from the crisis in the secondary sector. However, Belgium has to a large extent carried out the necessary restructuring. The majority of its industrial sectors and companies are now in a strong position to face the challenges of the last decade of the 20th century. Belgian industry is naturally still very dependent on external economic events, in that most of its industrial branches export a very high proportion of their output. In this age, that is the inevitable fate of a small industrialized country. In certain sectors, this dependency has been accentuated by the overwhelming presence of subsidiaries and multinational groups. Consequently, Belgium's future is largely tied to the economic health of the outside world, especially that of the EEC. It will also depend on the extent to which employers, workers, and government are capable of maintaining the competitiveness of Belgian industry.

Small and Medium-Sized Enterprises

Rik Donckels

IN BELGIUM AS WELL AS in most industrialized countries, small and medium-sized enterprises (SME) have attracted a lot of attention in recent years, probably because of the many restrictions facing larger-scale organizations. Underscoring the importance of this problem, the EEC proclaimed 1983 the European Year of SME.

The contribution of SME to economic development is difficult to quantify. Indeed, according to Belgian law, SME are defined according to the number of employees, turnover, or balance sheet. For the sake of simplicity, a definition of SME as firms with under 100 employees is used in what follows. Data for 1986 show the importance of SME to the Belgian economy (Table IV.5). Over 98 percent of private firms are SME, but 71 percent of them employ under four people. The total contribution of SME to employment is 47 percent, an impressive figure. In addition, the contraction of employment in the 1973–86 period was remarkably smaller for SME than for big firms (Table IV.6). Moreover, the share of the smaller enterprises grew from 7.68 percent in 1973 to 10.19 percent in 1986.

General Climate

In connection with the European Year of SME in 1983, the Economist Intelligence Unit (EIU) published an outstanding study on SME entitled *General Climate for Small Business: A Ten Countries Study* (London, 1983). For each of a number of indicators such as taxation and financial markets, a classification from 1 (top) to 10 (bottom) was drawn up. Belgium ranked sixth overall. For specific indicators, Belgium was third in labor market conditions, first in physical infrastructure, last in taxation, third in financial market, and sixth in specific SME-legislation. On the whole, Belgium was neither in the vanguard nor the rearguard.

TABLE IV.5
*Number of Private-sector Firms and Employees in Small and
Medium-sized Enterprises and in Larger Firms, 1986*

Size of firm (number of employees)	Number of firms		Number of employees	
	Total number (ooos)	Percent of total	Total number (ooos)	Percent of total
1–4	115	71%	199	10%
5–9	22	13.5	143	7
10–19	12	7	159	8
20–49	8	5	260	13
50–99	2	1	154	8
Total SME	159	98.5	915	47
100 or more	2.5	1.5	1,035	53
TOTAL	161.5	100.0%	1,950	100.0%

SOURCE: National Social Security Office.
NOTE: Figures may not add to totals shown because of rounding.

TABLE IV.6
*Evolution of Employment by Number of
Employees in Firm, 1973 to 1986*

Size of firm (number of employees)	Percentage change in total number of employees
1–4	+16.25%
5–9	+ 9.69
10–19	+ 0.13
20–49	− 2.24
50–99	−29.24
Total SME	− 3.09
100 or more	−19.28
TOTAL	−12.42

SOURCE: National Social Security Office.

The specific indicators furnish some interesting additional information, however. Belgium got the top ranking for infrastructure. This is certainly not surprising given the great efforts public authorities put into creating industrial parks and special SME parks all over the country. There has even been an effort to renovate old and abandoned premises. As a result, available premises certainly meet SME needs. Where taxation is concerned, it is the other way round. In 1983, Belgium had the most unfavorable taxation system of all states in the EEC. Hence, taxation is clearly the most urgent candidate for reform.

New Ventures

In Belgium and elsewhere the decline of the SME sector has been halted in recent years. Indeed, the number of new ventures has risen to some 60,000 a year, a clear sign of a regained vitality. These new ventures are quite important to the Belgian economy. Nevertheless, a recent study on start-up companies revealed several sobering trends. First, 67 percent of the Belgian start-ups are in the trade sector, and only 0.01 percent of them are firms based on new technology. Second, job creation in new ventures is remarkably low. Third, starters show but a limited interest in innovation. Fourth, only a third of the starters are involved in export activities. Finally, the attrition rate is quite high: about 23 percent of the new ventures fail within 24 months, mostly those in the trade sector.

The study also revealed that a starter takes calculated risks, beginning typically in a familiar and local market after a well-considered decision preceded by a serious preparation, including expert advice. Second, family attitudes toward the starter prove to be an important and stimulating environmental factor—entrepreneurship creates entrepreneurship. Finally, only 7 percent of the starters were unemployed when they decided to start their own business.

Position in the Socioeconomic Network

Sales potential. In general, SME are forced to operate in a local market as a result of their enormous heterogeneity.

Inputs. The EIU study shows that Belgian SME are doing quite well on the labor market. They experience no great difficulties in financing: banks play only a secondary role, and self-financing remains the most important source of funds, as befits the pursuit of independence by Belgian small business people. As to "venture capital," its role in Belgium remains small since only five firms have subscribed to the "over the counter" market launched in January 1985. Nevertheless, a few successful "management buyouts" have been realized recently. Also some family businesses tend to sever family ties to strengthen their financial basis toward growth and expansion.

Other SME. In general, Belgian small business people are individuals who avoid cooperation, but there are exceptions, for example, export deals. The aim of such initiatives is to counsel and to support SME exporting to the same country, for instance, Algeria, Great Britain, or China. Assistance may consist of collective hiring of stands at trade fairs, providing logistic support, or organizing the common use of exhibition grounds.

Big enterprises. It often is alleged that SME and big firms have conflicting interests. This might be true for a number of sectors, but in Belgium, however, this antagonistic attitude is eroded by a search for complementarity. Thus, because of the increasing importance of subcontracting, especially in industry, subcontracting fairs are organized periodically to match supply and demand. A second example is the "business in the community" idea, as big enterprises show an ever growing interest in the economic situation of the region where they operate. This is expressed mainly in the so-called local employment initiatives by which small and big firms exploit in common local possibilities so as to meet local needs. Effectively, this offers SME people expert managerial support. Undoubtedly, this form of cooperation will grow.

Organizations. Many Belgian organizations are directed toward SME, both professional ones, linked with certain professions, and interprofessional ones. The latter often originated on ideological grounds and make no distinction between different professions. Both categories are important pressure groups when it comes to defending the interests of SME. Another of their activities is communication of information, especially on specific matters such as wages, administration, social security, tax law, and the like. Almost all Belgian SME people belong to at least one of these organizations. Many of them belong to groups in both categories.

Training and assistance. Since the end of the 1950's, Belgian public authorities have been making great efforts to extend training possibilities for SME people. This has resulted in the creation of 36 training centers throughout the country. Every year, thousands of small business people take part in these activities. The training offered deals with technical as well as with managerial subjects. One major advantage of the decentralization of these training centers is a relationship based on trust, since they cooperate closely with professional and interprofessional organizations that also organize a number of educational activities. An ideal situation would lie in a basic education complete with customer-tailored assistance. Being aware of this opportunity, the private sector has set up an increasing number of private consulting agencies explicitly directed toward the new generation of SME people, which has come to realize the importance of training. It is clear that a larger use of training and assistance possibilities will induce considerable changes in the future, for example, cooperation with universities or other research centers. At present, there still exists an information and communication gap, but the improvement in this area is noticeable.

SME and public authorities. Different hierarchical levels are involved in

SME-oriented policy: local, provincial, regional, national, and suprana-tional. Since 1985, *local authorities* have started to play a stimulating role in the local economy. This evolution should be attributed to more than just the granting of financial or fiscal advantages. Certainly more impor-tant is the assistance for all sorts of initiatives, such as stands at trade fairs, communication of information to starters and SME, establishment of contacts between small and big enterprises, and so forth.

At the *provincial* level, it is mainly the regional development agencies (RDAs) that play an important role. Seven of these RDAs exist: one in each of the Flemish provinces, one in the Brussels region, and one in Wallonia. Some of these RDAs actively participate in the organization of export deals and provide vital information, for example, by creating databases on firms belonging to their activity area.

At the *regional* level, regional authorities define planning practices for stimulating the economy. This is illustrated by the so-called expansion law, which grants financial (soft loans and capital grants) or fiscal advan-tages when investments are made or personnel recruited. Application of this law varies from region to region. Lately, regional authorities have been playing an important role in launching business centers. In the centers, known as industrial nurseries, new ventures can benefit from office space, secretarial support, and business advice from an experi-enced manager on site. Most of the time these nurseries involve public authorities as well as the private sector and are essential to any policy aimed at promoting entrepreneurship.

At the *national* level, public authorities mainly play a regulating role. First, the "no free entry to the market" principle implies that the poten-tial entrepreneur has to prove his/her technical ability and managerial know-how before receiving the needed certificate. This applies to 41 pro-fessions: 16 in the building industry, 9 in electronic and precision instru-ments, 15 in trade and services, and 1 in the restaurant trade. The num-ber of certificates granted reached 16,808 in 1985. Despite the objections of free marketeers, there is an increasing demand for barriers to guar-antee quality and protect consumers. Second, 102 activities are subject to statutory obligations. Some examples are the production and selling of pharmaceuticals, chemicals, or food products, the selling of specific products (e.g., weapons), and the liberal professions. Besides their regu-latory role, public authorities also engage in promoting entrepreneurship (see below).

Finally, at the *supranational* level within the EEC, a "small business task force" draws up measures aimed at improving the general climate for small businesses, stimulating new ventures, and strengthening the financial infrastructure. Examples of these measures are realization of

the free market, introduction of fiscal stimuli in the member-states, improvement of competition, attention to education and training programs
(CEDEFOP in Berlin), accessibility for SME to the new information technology (via the DIANE network), organization of a "business cooperation
network" (BC-NET) to stimulate the cooperation between small and big
firms, and promotion of the dispersion and transfer of new technologies
to SME (the SPRINT project).

Finally, with respect to the relation between SME and the public
authorities, regional governments subsidize the wages of unemployed
people hired by SME to carry out R&D, energy-savings-related work, and
export projects. Launched at the end of 1983, this project had covered
the wages of 2,226 people employed in 1,224 ventures by January 1987.

Unemployed people who start their own businesses get a loan of
500,000 francs. Introduced in 1984, this initiative resulted in the creation of 3,092 ventures, implying a government investment of 1.45 billion
francs for its first year. By the end of 1985, a rising government investment (1.8 billion francs) matched the creation of 3,697 ventures. Up till
now, this initiative has led to the creation of some 10,000 ventures. It
undoubtedly has had a considerable impact on Belgium's annual number
of start-ups.

According to a scheme called the Plus-One-Plan, an individual trader
gets a grant on hiring a first employee. In 1987, the Plus-Two-Plan granting an allowance to employers who enroll a second employee was invented. Another new initiative in all nine Belgian provinces is that small
business people can call upon a small business adviser specializing in
technological innovation and exports.

In conclusion, SME in Belgium should be considered not an anach-
ronism but an indispensable and successful component of a modern
economy, given the opportunities they enjoy as well as the constraints
they are confronted with. Further progress depends on the attention of
SME leaders to professionalism, integration into the socioeconomic network, and delegation of decision-making power. On the side of public
authorities, there is need for concern. Only a small number of SME are
in foreign trade, and most of those deal only with neighboring countries.
Besides, direct taxes, social security payments, and red tape burdens
are too heavy. Finally, new initiatives are needed to stimulate synergy
and complementarity between small, medium, and large enterprises and
the organization of technology transfer to bridge information and communication gaps and to build up an efficient, user-friendly consulting
infrastructure.

Financial Services and Markets

Alain Siaens

BELGIUM HAS A MATURE ECONOMY. Industrialization and internation-alization have been taking place for over 150 years; it has always been an open economy, dependent on its neighbors and commercial partners, to whom it sells 65 percent of its production; and its frontiers have traditionally been open to foreign corporations and activities. Its smallness does not present only disadvantages.

Market forces and political impulses coexist in a flexible way, through cooperation and "gentlemen's agreements" more than through authoritarian centralism. Regulation is relatively liberal. The traditional free circulation of capital accustomed financial institutions to direct cross-border competition. Even public financial institutions like the Central Bank or the National Industrial Credit Company have made half their equity available to the general public and are quoted on the stock market. Public utility companies are private and are also quoted on the stock market. Belgium is the most Anglo-Saxon of the "Latin countries" and the most Latin of the northern countries.

The figures for 1987 show that about 68 percent of the Belgian work force is employed in the tertiary sector; 46 percent of them are in the private sector and 12 percent in the financial sector, where the growth rate is higher than average. Developing a service economy is a natural option for Belgium. After 1992 there will be a unified common European market with free movement of labor, free competition, and total freedom for capital to circulate throughout the EC. One may expect further concentration and international mergers in banking and insurance.

The International Dimension

Due to its location in the heart of Europe, its position as EC capital, and the favorable fiscal treatment given to financial and corporate income, Belgium has attracted many financial institutions. Brussels is fast becoming a financial center because of the presence of international institutions (EC, NATO, etc.) and multinational firms and also because of an active multilingual population. Office rental prices and the cost of living in general are very competitive.

Foreign-owned banks represent 15 percent of value added in the banking sector. They established themselves in Brussels in order to service their national and multinational clients and to engage in international lending and borrowing, taking advantage of an attractive fiscal system called *quotité forfaitaire d'impôt étranger.* Under this system, any interest income they receive from abroad is considered as having been partially taxed, even if this is not the case. As a result, foreign banks benefit from a kind of tax credit and pay practically no income taxes. Furthermore foreign bank subsidiaries are allowed to ignore capital ratio requirements for their international business.

This explains why, of the 84 banks operating in Belgium, 28 are under foreign law and 33 are under Belgian law but controlled by a foreign majority. In 1987, the foreign banks, of fifteen nationalities, represented 51 percent of the banking sector's total balance sheet; 86.8 percent of their balance sheet was made up of activities in foreign currencies or with the foreign sector. In this group, Japan heads the list with fifteen units, ahead of France and the United States. On the other hand, 23 purely Belgian banks have a presence in 56 countries by way of subsidiaries or through shareholdings in foreign banks.

Altogether, 70 percent of the sector's balance sheet is composed of transactions in Belgian francs with the rest of the world, or in foreign currencies, mainly through heavy involvement in the Eurodollar market, which is an "entrepot" business, engaging in lending and borrowing abroad. The importance of an international financial center may be measured by the external assets of its banking system. According to this criterion, in 1986 Brussels ranks seventh with 3.8 percent of the world market, behind London (22 percent), New York (16.9 percent), Tokyo (8.9 percent), France (6.5 percent), Luxembourg (4.3 percent), and Frankfurt (4 percent). Brussels is a leader in ECU operations, holds 8.5 percent of all Euro-managed deposits, and places 3.5 percent of Euro-bonds.

Two institutions serving the international financial community are worth mentioning. SWIFT (Society for Worldwide Interbank Financial Telecommunications) organizes the standardized and automatic international communication of messages and data among 1,286 banks in 58 countries. Euroclear serves more than a thousand financial institutions in the world, acting as a general custodian and clearing mechanism for Eurobonds; it held more than U.S. $400 billion worth of securities at the end of 1986.

Belgium is attracting the financial and administrative activities of large multinational companies through generous fiscal incentives given to so-called coordination centers that confine themselves to a range of inter-group services. This is an imaginative attempt to establish the country as an attractive environment for financial services. Centralized financing operations can be carried out in a favorable tax climate, taking advantage of Belgium's dense network of double-taxation treaties as well as its respected position as an EC member.

Savings and Financial Wealth

The savings ratio of Belgian households from 1980 to 1986 was on average 17.4 percent as compared with 12.3 percent for all OECD countries. Savings in financial assets constitute a higher proportion than they do abroad. Since 1974 the corporate sector has enjoyed an abnormal financing capacity, with cash flow and new equity exceeding gross capital formation.

The huge excess saving of the private sector has structural counterparts: a huge public debt (122 percent of GNP in 1987) and private capital outflows that over twenty years have structurally offset current surpluses in the balance of payments. A fifth of the public debt is in foreign currencies, the heritage of the difficult years (1975–82) when both private capital movements and the current balance showed deficits.

The Belgian private sector is used to being a net buyer of foreign securities, and foreigners bring in capital for direct investment. Whereas between 1982 and 1987, the value of Belgian shares represented on average 28 percent of liquid assets and 27.5 percent of bonds, they now represent 50 percent and 39 percent, respectively. There was a true revolution in venture capital during the 1980's because of powerful fiscal incentives. The fiscal deductibility of investment in Belgian shares and little or no tax on dividends from various sources stimulated venture capital.

Financial Intermediaries

Three types of institutions hold money in forms ranging from demand deposits to long-term bonds. Banks dominate the domestic market for assets less than one year old, and public institutions, assets of more than one year's maturity. Banks also dominate operations on the international financial markets.

Public institutions were historically created (1) to lend for special purposes or to certain categories of borrowers, such as long-term credit to industry, and (2) to mobilize popular savings, act as banks for local public entities, and manage cash transmissions via the postal checking office. But despecialization began about twenty years ago, and all intermediaries now compete on all markets despite the specific fields each category or each institution tries to develop. The Central Bank (NBB) has macroeconomic responsibilities for monetary policy, and the Banking Commission exercises microeconomic supervision over financial institutions.

The important interbank lending swells transaction totals. In 1986 the international interbank market provided banks located in Belgium with 32 percent of their resources net of uses, most of which involve credit to foreign entities or securities issued by them (part of which are lent in turn to the Belgian public sector). The public sector has huge financing needs; 36.7 percent of the banks' net resources were lent to it in Belgian francs.

Securities held by clients for which banks act as custodian represent approximately the same amounts as deposits and bonds in the balance sheet. Securitization is growing in importance in Belgium as it is in the rest of the world. Commercial banks are moving more and more into investment banking.

The Belgian financial system is technologically advanced. Computerization and telecommunications are fast modifying methods of payments and ways of banking. International experts consider the payment system one of the most efficient in the world: based on the principles of normalization, harmonization, and automation, the interdisciplinary transaction exchange system operates around the clock. The public has become accustomed to automated bank tellers, where funds are electronically transferred. Corporate electronic banking is even more developed.

The Money Markets

By definition, these concern all assets of less than one year's maturity and consist of the four markets discussed below. The amount in billions of Belgian francs at the end of 1986 is indicated in brackets (1 U.S.$ = 39 BF). The first market is the *interbank market*, where financial institutions borrow from each other, deal with call money [9.5] and the interbank markets [592] internationally connected with Euromarkets, and benefit from money in Belgian francs lent again by Luxembourg banks. Second, the market for *treasury bills* [710.1] functions like an auction market organized by the Central Bank, and only financial intermediaries are allowed to subscribe. The third market is the *private credit market*, where the importance of acceptances and trade bills [55.1] is declining and that of overdrafts [165] and straight loans [60] is growing. The Belgian Banking Association suggests a range of interest rates, which each bank remains free to adopt or reject, for advances, trade bills, and acceptances. Finally, deposits by the *nonfinancial sector* amounted in 1986 to U.S. $98.4 billion [3,837.6]. The total increased by 10.4 percent annually between 1977 and 1986, or 6.1 percent in real terms.

About three-quarters of the term deposits of non-bank depositors are held in foreign currencies. The proportion of Belgian francs when bank depositors are included is in fact higher, due to borrowing by Belgian banks of Belgian deposits held in Luxembourg banks.

Only big deposits, above 5 million BF, receive rates closely connected with the interbank market. Demand deposits earn 0.5 percent interest but no charges are levied on checking accounts and payments made in bank money. Interest rates are determined collectively by banks for small term deposits, by "savings" banks for saving accounts, and by public institutions for the so-called *bons de caisse* (savings certificates with a maturity of around five years); each variation has to be approved by the Central Bank.

The Capital Markets

The Primary Market

In international terms, about 3.5 percent of Eurobonds are placed by banks in Belgium. The management, by private undertakings, of new issues of securities and of the official listing of hitherto unlisted securities, is usually carried out by banks and requires the approval of the Banking Commission, a financial control authority equivalent to the Securities and Exchange Commission in the United States. In addition, the Comité de la Cote has the right to refuse the listing of any securities and to suspend or remove any. The listing of foreign securities requires the further authorization of the Ministry of Finance.

The Secondary Market in 1986

In June 1987, 296 Belgian companies and 148 foreign companies were quoted on the stock market. The market for state bonds is relatively large, even by international standards. Foreign investors are becoming increasingly interested in Belgian securities, since, for nonresidents, the stamp duty on transactions has been abolished and there is no withholding tax on interest earned by bonds issued by financial intermediaries and public entities.

Government and other public sector issues are traded on the Marché des Rentes, where the Fonds des Rentes (government broker) stabilizes the market. All private-sector issues are traded on the spot market or, when important, on the account market. Price is determined by brokers calling out offers to buy and to sell. In the case of foreign securities, trading is usually in the form of bearer certificates representing the original registered shares. The dominance of bearer securities make personal security holding largely unknown and limits the number issued to shareholders who vote at general meetings.

Stockbrokers still retain a collective monopoly over share and bond issues worth below 10 million BF, with fixed rates and a standard 40 percent share for banks and other financial intermediaries. About half the trading takes place outside the official stock market in the form of trading organized by banks, which receive the bulk of orders. The stock exchange reforms in Britain, France, and Spain have raised questions about the existing system of restrictive practices and fixed commissions. Negotiations are under way to modernize and promote more extensive competition.

The Stock Market

Belgian shares were traditionally cheaper than foreign shares in terms of price-earning ratios, although now the gap has narrowed. The market is no longer as small as it used to be. Market capitalization has increased threefold since 1982 not only because of a strong rise in prices, but also because of massive new issues and new listings of shares, mainly due to Belgium's advantageous fiscal laws. It now represents about 0.8 percent of world capitalization. Turnover is traditionally lower than elsewhere, although stock market statistics underestimate transactions by ignoring market block trading, which is roughly equivalent to transactions made within the stock market.

Holding Companies

Holding companies are the typical shareholders in Belgium. There were 74 at the end of 1986; the three most important originated from universal banks that existed before 1934, when commercial and deposit banking was legally separated from the financial ownership of industrial and commercial companies. However, Belgian banks have always been authorized to take part in the securities and investment banking business. It is envisaged that the four national or regional public holding companies will be able to increase their equity base through new issues available to private investors.

The Foreign Exchange Market

Belgium ranks tenth in the world in terms of volume of exports, which constitute 71 percent of its GNP. Consequently, transactions in foreign currencies are paramount. From 1973 to 1987, the Belgian franc fluctuated between U.S. $0.036 and $0.014. The figure was $0.026 in August 1987.

The Belgian franc represents 7.7 percent of the value of the ECU, a pool of twelve European currencies; the ECU is the core of the European monetary system and is used by the European central banks to settle their transactions. It is also traded privately in deposits and bonds. According to the ranking of nominal interest rates, the levels of which indicate the relative strength of a currency, the Belgian franc is becoming a strong currency. Despite some weaknesses between 1979 and 1982, the Belgian franc once again enjoys the benefits of a domestic inflation rate lower than the European average.

Since 1944, Belgium has had a dual exchange market: an official market for current transactions, where the franc fluctuates within the range agreed on by the Central Bank and is therefore subject to intervention; and the free market, which covers capital transactions and where the value of the franc fluctuates according to supply and demand. This system, which acted as a safeguard against instability in the balance of payments and in monetary creation due to volatile capital movements, will probably be abandoned in order to simplify transactions in accordance with the present trend toward European monetary and financial unification.

The Luxembourg Partner

Luxembourg, with a population of just over 350,000, forms an economic and monetary union with Belgium and has become something of an "offshore" financial center. For financial holding companies, there are no corporate taxes, and dividends are not taxed. Foreigners do not pay any withholding taxes on interest earned on bonds or deposits. Many international bond issues take place in Luxembourg. The exchange controls are similar to and as liberal as those in Belgium and are administered by the Belgo-Luxembourg Exchange Institution.

Insurance and Pension Funds

Neither of these forms of saving is at present as popular as they are abroad. Belgians hold fewer life insurance policies than their neighbors. At the end of 1986, the holdings of private pension funds set up by corporations did not exceed $5 billion. Household savings in life insurance and group insurance were, respectively, U.S. $46 billion and $34 billion. Net premium income in 1986 was about $5.1 billion, and at the end of that year total assets, equity, and technical reserves amounted to a little over $28 billion.

Nonfinancial Services

Herman Daems

THIS CHAPTER DESCRIBES some of the key structural characteristics and trends in nonfinancial services in the Belgian economy. A good way to gain some understanding of service activities in Belgium is to distinguish three types of nonfinancial services. First, there are services that care for people. Examples are hotels and restaurants, barber and beauty shops, shoe repair shops, laundromats, and health care activities. A second type of service creates knowledge and distributes information. Universities and schools are the most obvious examples of this type of services but also included in this category are research laboratories, architects, and consulting engineers. The third type of service helps managers, investors, and consumers operate with greater efficiency in the market system because the services open market opportunities, permit coordination, and monitor contracts. Wholesalers and retailers, stockbrokers, lawyers, accountants, fiscal advisers, and management consultants provide this third type of service.

Important differences also exist among the suppliers of the services. Private business continues to account for the largest share of nonfinancial services supplied in Belgium. Very often the private business is owned and operated by an independent entrepreneur who employs a small number of people. But increasingly some service businesses are part of large multinational service companies that operate with a global strategy. Examples can be found in advertising, accounting, and management consulting. Many of the market leaders in Belgium are well-known British companies. Finally, some service activities are organized inside large nonservice corporations. For example, as is now common in most advanced economies, many of Belgium's large industrial companies and banks operate their own legal departments and rely on outsiders only for special assignments.

Private business is not the only supplier of nonfinancial services. Some services are provided by government departments or by organizations that deliver the service for the government. This is typically the case in education. Other services such as health care are delivered by nonprofit organizations.

Contribution to the Belgium Economy and International Comparisons

The description above clearly shows that nonfinancial service activities and the suppliers of these services are quite diverse. That helps to explain the lack of detailed statistical data about the sector. Table IV.7 estimates the contribution of the nonfinancial services to the Belgian economy. In 1984, the nonfinancial service sector accounted for an astonishing 64.3 percent of total employment in the Belgian economy. This includes employment in the private and the public service sector but excludes employment in financial services. In 1970 the share of employment stood at 51.6 percent. The contribution to GNP is somewhat lower. In 1970, 50.4 percent of GNP was created in nonfinancial services; in 1984, 57.6 percent. The different evolution of employment and GNP illustrates the well-known fact that labor productivity in the service sector is lower than

TABLE IV.7
*Contribution of Nonfinancial Services to the
Belgian Economy, 1970 and 1984*

	Share of total employment	Share of GNP
1970	51.6%	50.4%
1984	64.3	57.6

TABLE IV.8
*International Comparison of
Share of Nonfinancial Services*

Country	Share of GNP
Belgium	57.6%
France	55.1
Italy	49.7
Netherlands	56.0
Germany	51.5
United Kingdom	41.1

in the rest of the economy. An international comparison can be found in Table IV.8. The table documents that a large part of the Belgian economy depends on services.

The Business of Caring for People

Thousands of mostly small firms offer a variety of personal care services ranging from haircuts, shoe repairs, and key making to lodging and catering. From an international perspective three structural characteristics of this subsector are worth noting.

First, most of the businesses are owned and operated by independent entrepreneurs. Sometimes the entrepreneurs rely on family members for additional labor input. If family labor is not available or not qualified, a small number of employees are hired as the growth of the business requires. However, some firms purposely reduce their growth to avoid having to go to the labor market. In contrast to some other European countries, breweries have only occasionally opened retail outlets. The lodging business is somewhat exceptional. Many of the larger hotels in Belgium are operated by foreign hotel chains. These chains have been able to penetrate that segment of the lodging market catering to businessmen. The tourist segment of the market, however, remains in the hands of small, independent hotel owners and operators.

Second, entry into the nonhealth personal care business is relatively easy. In contrast to some other service activities, the government has not imposed many entry regulations on this area. New restaurants and cafes are opened regularly. This creates new competition for existing ones. The association representing small businesses has called for tighter entry regulations to curb competition, but the government has resisted these pleas because it believes that the job opportunities created by easy entry can help solve the unemployment crisis. However, the failure rate among new start-ups is quite high, and it is doubtful that many permanent jobs can be created in this way. For the consumer competition has been beneficial because Belgian personal care businesses offer a rich choice of services in terms of quality and price.

Third, Belgian entrepreneurs have been rather slow in developing franchise concepts that could be used to create national and international chains of service businesses. But there are exceptions. In shoe repair and key making, a chain was successfully developed with the help of an American entrepreneur. Another chain was created to compete with the well-known American fast-food chains. This last example is interesting because no attempts were made to develop an original Belgian food product; instead the chain decided to offer exactly the same products as the American-owned food chains. The relative success of the Belgian chain illustrates clearly that even in personal care services, consumer tastes are becoming more and more international.

In other countries such as the United States, nonhealth personal care businesses have undergone a major consolidation. Several factors may well have hindered the consolidation process in Belgium. The Belgian government until recently did not allow advertising on radio and TV. This certainly made it much more difficult to commercialize a franchise concept. Foreign experience shows that franchising depends strongly on media advertising. Billboard advertising and newspaper advertising are not effective enough to launch a new franchise chain. It can also be argued that the tax system and the social security system have created disincentives against large organizations. The high value-added taxes also have made it less attractive for consumers to buy services in the marketplace. Finally, the small size of the Belgian economy and its deep cultural split have not provided entrepreneurs with a sufficiently large domestic market to attempt new franchise concepts.

Creation and Diffusion of Knowledge

In comparison with other European countries, Belgium is not a large spender on research and development. However, private business spending on R&D compares reasonably well with other countries. Most private research laboratories are owned and operated by large industrial companies. Many of these companies are foreign multinationals that have been located in Belgium for decades. Strong points in research are pharmaceuticals, telecommunications, nuclear energy, metallurgy, and, more recently, biotechnology and semiconductors. All large Belgian universities have created special interface organizations to facilitate the transfer of knowledge between the university and business.

Several large engineering consulting firms exist in Belgium. Typically such firms belong to industrial groups. As such groups have moved into foreign markets, the engineering consultants have helped them develop and design engineering products for these markets. In the past Africa and Asia have been the prime markets for these engineering firms.

Knowledge is also diffused through management and technological seminars. For many years English management and technological programs have been offered at Belgium's largest universities. As yet, a private management school does not exist. But some companies have created in-house training centers. Some foreign multinational companies have located their European-wide training centers in Belgium.

Services to Facilitate the Operation of the Market System

Businesses that help managers, investors, and consumers operate more efficiently in the market system are the most diverse services of all. They include wholesalers and retailers, lawyers, accountants, advertising agencies, market research companies, and computer services companies. Some of these companies are small. Others like the retail companies are among the largest companies in the country. Their degree of independence also differs. The largest advertising agencies, accounting firms, and consulting services are typically controlled by foreign multinationals.

From an international perspective, the structure of the retail sector is most interesting. Some thirty years ago when car ownership became widespread, the modern large-scale supermarket took off in Belgium. Very quickly the supermarkets, nearly all of them owned by two Belgian companies, took a substantial share of the distribution market. The small independent retailers called on the government to set up a site-review procedure. This effectively stalled the rapid spread over the country of the large supermarket chains. The procedure, however, did not cut the market share of the large retail chains. Lately the supermarket chains have experienced a profit squeeze because of stagnating consumer demand. Some believe that as a consequence the small independent shops may have been able to improve their position slightly. Also, foreign retail companies have come into Belgium with new distribution strategies.

In contrast to the United States, Belgium has few shopping malls, probably because free land is scarce and the traditional downtown areas have provided pleasant shopping environments. Another reason for the absence of shopping malls may be that franchising has been slow in developing. Also, Belgian cities have been much slower than their counterparts in the Netherlands and Germany in adopting car-free shopping streets.

The Future of Nonfinancial Services

As in most other countries, there is a growing interest in the service economy in Belgium. It is generally believed that the service economy can provide growth and new jobs. It is also hoped that services can be exported and thus provide an alternative to the export of manufactured products. Some problems exist, however.

First, rapid growth of employment in some services is hindered by the high minimum wage. Despite recent efforts by the government to create specific employment incentives, many small businesses find the implicit wage costs for hiring nonskilled workers too high.

Second, the high wage costs have stimulated service companies to look for labor-saving technologies. A spectacular example of the substitution of labor for capital-intensive technology is found in gas stations. An increasing number of gas stations—in greater proportion than abroad—are completely automated. The use of information technologies is spreading rapidly in all subsectors of the service economy. It is very likely that this technological revolution will reduce the opportunities for creating jobs and drastically alter the structure of the service economy.

Finally, the consolidation movement, which so far has bypassed some of the service sectors, can be expected to leave a mark in the decades ahead. Consolidation and franchising will also be important when Belgian entrepreneurs look for opportunities to market their services abroad.

Foreign Trade

Theo Peeters

FOREIGN TRADE IS ESSENTIAL to the Belgian economy. With a small, open economy, Belgium is more dependent than other countries on selling abroad. This external dependence due to the small size of the domestic market is further aggravated by the absence of natural resources.

Internationalization and the Openness of the Economy

The internationalization of economic activity has become a dominant structural characteristic in recent decades in virtually all industrialized economies. Belgium is no exception. The extent to which a national economy is internationalized is measured by its degree of openness, defined as the ratio of exported goods and services to the total available resources in the economy, that is, the ratio of the sum of GDP to the import of goods and services.

Pertinent data were collected in a 1978 study by the National Bank of Belgium for five of its leading European trading partners, for comparable small economies, and for the United States and Japan. The first point is that the degree of openness is roughly inversely proportional to the area of a country. Large countries such as the United States and Japan have the most closed economies, whereas the degree of openness is highest in the smallest countries. Among this group, Belgium is well out in front. Since the early 1970's, Belgium has overtaken the Netherlands. This means that Belgium is highly sensitive to external developments, particularly to the evolution of the market in its leading trading partners.

The second point is that the degree of openness in all the countries under consideration, large and small, has increased with time. The only apparent exception to this trend is the United States between 1976 and 1979 and 1982 and 1984. This anomaly is explained by the progressive degradation of the American balance of trade due to the country's relatively poor export performance. If, however, we look at the growing penetration of imports (the ratio of goods and services to total available resources), the data reveal a continuous (and rapid) rise in the degree of openness of the American economy. The causes of this universal phenomenon are undoubtedly multiple. The liberalization of international trade under the GATT agreement, coupled with technological advances in transport and communications, is certainly not unrelated to this development, nor is trade liberalization as part of European integration. In Belgium in particular, considerable foreign investments have further contributed to an accelerating internationalization of the production process and a growing dependence on foreign markets. Economic growth depends on foreign demand for national products to a greater extent in Belgium than elsewhere. The external pressure on the Belgian economy therefore requires constant vigilance if a strong competitive position is to be maintained.

Specialization Patterns and Competitive Advantages

As a country lacking in natural resources (raw materials and sources of energy), Belgium is highly dependent on manufactured products for its exports. Finished and semifinished products account for some 75 percent of Belgian exports. The positive balance of payments traditionally results from these products, which are the basis of Belgian prosperity. That is why it is so important for Belgium to defend its position in the shifting international markets for manufactured products.

It is generally argued that Belgium lags behind in this endeavor, owing to a number of structural handicaps. Recent data from the National Bank put this into a wider perspective. These 1987 data divide processing and conversion industries into three categories according to the degree of technological refinement, based on the extent of R&D that goes into manufacturing. In comparison with that of its competitors, the Belgian production structure appears to be largely oriented toward economic activities with a low to medium degree of technological input. The percentage of high-tech activities is lower than for all the other countries examined. However, a certain upgrading of the production structure can be observed, due to a relative reduction of low-tech work and a corresponding increase of medium-tech activities.

The data show, as expected, that with a few exceptions, an above-average share of production is associated with a pronounced comparative trade advantage. The data also confirm that, on average, Belgium scores best in low-tech activities and lowest in high-tech activities in both production and export. However, available data also indicate far from negligible shifts in production and trade structures since the early 1970's. A number of sectors in which Belgium enjoyed a distinct advantage until that time are in decline. This is particularly true of the ferrous metals industry (primarily steel), which is under pressure because of the stagnation of international demand and the rise of new competitors. Nonetheless, the relative weight of this sector in both production and export is still higher for Belgium than for its competitors. A similar, though less pronounced evolution can be observed in the glass industry and in nonferrous metals. While the shipbuilding industry has more or less succeeded in maintaining its share of production, its export position, already weak, has lost more ground. In the textile, leather, and clothing industries, however, the improvements in manufacturing have not led to a stronger export position.

In contrast to these declining industries, a number of noteworthy improvements can be seen, chiefly in the medium-tech sector. The average increase in competitive advantage is strikingly high in this sector, being most pronounced in the chemical, pharmaceutical, rubber, and plastic industries. The particularly strong trade situation, as compared with its relatively low share of production, of the category of "other manufacturing" is largely attributable to the diamond industry, which accounts for a major share of the export figures because of Antwerp's status as the world center of the diamond trade. As regards production (the processing and conversion of raw diamonds), the share is markedly lower.

All in all, the impression persists that Belgium, as a country with a relatively small domestic market, had to build up competitive advantages. Technologically more refined products and production based on product differentiation are easier to launch in countries where firms can count on a large domestic market. Small countries can find a way out of this unfavorable specialization pattern if they can rely on a small number of multinationals of worldwide importance. This may partly explain why Belgium scores low on high-tech activities compared with other small countries, such as the Netherlands and Sweden. It also makes quite clear why the liberalization of international trade and European economic integration are of vital importance to a small country like Belgium. The market expansion that will come with the integration process will permit Belgian firms to avoid the limitations of a small domestic market and the relatively unfavorable specialization pattern they would otherwise be obliged to adopt.

Decline in Market Shares

In view of the growing external dependence of the Belgian economy and the structural weaknesses outlined above, a further look should be taken at the loss of market shares. Since the mid-1970's, Belgium has faced a loss of export market share. A detailed study of this problem can be found in reports by the National Bank of Belgium in 1980 and 1981. More recent and less extensive material on this question is included in a 1986 OECD report on the Belgian economy. The OECD report attempted to explain the change in Belgium's global market share, based on a constant market share analysis, as a function of three elements: (1) the shift attributable to the geographical destination of Belgium's export package; (2) the shift that may be the consequence of the goods structure of the export package; and (3) the residual value, which, in certain circumstances, may be identified with a possible change in Belgium's overall competitiveness. The data were analyzed for five-year periods. In order to measure the effect of the goods structure, total exports were divided into 22 sectors. In order to measure the effect of the geographical structure, eleven destinations were singled out: the United Kingdom, France, West Germany, Italy, the Netherlands, Switzerland, the United States, the rest of the OECD, the COMECON countries, OPEC, and the rest of the world.

The main findings can be summarized as follows. Between 1966 and 1975, Belgium was able to maintain its share of the world export market for manufactured goods. Belgian exports grew at about the same rate as world trade. Since 1975, however, a clear change has taken place, and Belgium's market share has declined. This can be seen from the slower growth of Belgian exports of manufactured goods during this period as compared with the corresponding figures for the world export trade.

Belgian exports, more than three-quarters of which go to its European partners, continued to benefit hugely from the dynamic growth that characterized Europe through the Golden Sixties and into the early 1970's, up to the time of the first oil crisis. The effects of this strong geographical concentration in the EEC were originally positive but became a distinct handicap after the crisis. Because of the slowing of growth all over Europe, Belgian exports were hit relatively harder than those of competitors, and as a result Belgium's global share of the market declined.

The goods that constitute Belgium's export package did not bring many competitive advantages, although a slightly positive influence can be seen up to the end of the 1970's. Since then, however, this slight advantage for the Belgian production package became a disadvantage. Other surveys, that of the National Bank in particular, however, point to a consistently negative contribution by the concentrated goods package of Belgian exports to the evolution of Belgium's market share. The relatively extensive grouping of sectors used in the OECD report probably conceals an even more unfavorable impact by Belgium's product mix.

The residual component, generally considered a yardstick of a country's competitiveness, appears to be negative. This points to an unfavorable competitive status for Belgium. Yet the economic recovery measures passed by the government since 1982 appear to have brought about an upswing after the pronounced decline observed in the second half of the 1970's.

Basic goods and semifinished products still play a relatively important part in Belgium's export package. Compared with its most direct competitors, Belgium has been losing its share of export markets since the mid-1970's. This evolution is primarily the consequence of heavy concentration in European markets, and this is why the pronounced slowdown in growth that has affected Western Europe more than other parts of the world since the oil crises has been particularly damaging to Belgium's exports. The advanced internationalization and high degree of openness of the Belgian economy aggravated the effects of this negative development. As a result, it is vitally urgent for Belgium to maintain its competitive position against its direct rivals. The decline that occurred during the latter half of the 1970's and into the early 1980's has made a deep impact. However, the recovery policy that has been followed since 1982 may have turned the tide to some extent.

In the meantime, the Belgian export structure is still plagued by an unfavorable product mix. Low-tech products still account for much of the goods package. This explains why Belgium is more exposed than its European partners to the growing pressure from the new industrial countries in Southeast Asia and elsewhere. However, changes over the course of time point to a certain improvement and therefore to a certain upgrading of Belgium's export package. Because of its lack of natural resources, Belgian competitiveness will continue to depend on rigorous internal cost control, until such time as Belgium makes a breakthrough in the high-tech markets.

Energy

Paul Hatry

WHEREAS IN THE 19TH CENTURY, Belgium's economic growth was based on the wealth offered by its coal mines, it became a net importer of energy around the middle of the 20th century, when the old coal mines in the south of the country ran out and new ones in the north became uncompetitive. Domestic energy production now meets only a small fraction of requirements. Although Belgium produces very little primary energy, its economic structure and climate mean that it is a large consumer. For the most part, energy consumed is imported. In the 1960's oil became the main energy source used, meeting almost 60 percent of total energy requirements. However, since the oil crises of 1973–74 and 1979–81, energy consumption has been considerably diversified. Imported coal, natural gas, and nuclear energy are now important sources. At the same time, total consumption has contracted in response to economic recession and energy-saving measures.

Belgium, previously an important energy producer and now a large consumer, has developed a remarkable amount of know-how in energy technologies. In the field of energy use, Belgium has been very innovative. This has been seen, for example, in the transportation and interconnection of electricity and gas, in coke consumption in the steel industry, and in the specific consumption of energy per kWh of electricity produced in thermal power stations. In all these fields, Belgian industrialists have brought advanced technologies into play. Belgium's energy policy is also rather interesting in terms of management and pricing policy, which involves price freedom, consumer protection, industrial competitiveness, and a certain amount of government control.

Management of the energy sector was inspired by the consultation between employers and trade unions that grew up clandestinely during World War II and later became the normal form of labor dialogue in

Belgium. The most immediate consequence of this system is that joint control by employers and workers is substituted for state control. Consultation and control are used to guarantee reasonable prices to users in a sector in which a technical monopoly often exists (e.g., gas and electricity). This has meant that, unlike many other European countries where energy industries have been nationalized or where the state has a large stake, Belgium has managed to preserve private enterprise. This independence has helped the Belgian energy industry to remain competitive.

For gas and electricity, consultations are held on energy prices. This point is discussed in more depth below. Oil prices, using procedures described below, and coal prices are largely determined by the international market.

Coal

Historically, Belgium was one of the first energy producers and laid the foundations of modern industry on its coal reserves. The first instances of coal mining date to the 13th century. From these early beginnings coal mining peaked in the 1950's. Although, in the first half of the 20th century, production began to tail off in the southern fields (Liège and Hainaut), it experienced strong growth in Kempen during the same period. The large Kempen coal reserves were discovered by calculations carried out on analysis of geological layers by Belgian mining engineers.

Since the 1960's the coal industry has been in clear decline. The mines in the south of the country have been shut down and output in Kempen cut by two-thirds. This is explained by the availability since 1960 of imported energy at very competitive prices, in the form first of oil and then of natural gas and imported coal. The mines still being worked in Kempen are kept afloat only by a large state subsidy, paid to avoid brutal closures and the disastrous economic and social consequences they would provoke. The industrial base of the region is not sufficiently diversified to be able to survive without the coal industry. Coal consumption naturally followed the same pattern. In 1950, solid fuel represented 90 percent of domestic energy consumption. It now only represents 20 percent, chiefly accounted for by imported coal.

Oil

Practically every inch of Belgian territory has been the subject of prospecting, and drilling has been carried out on a number of occasions, but no exciting discoveries have been made. The oil industry has therefore concentrated on downstream activities. At the beginning of the 1950's, an important refining, transport, and distribution sector developed. Growth was constant until 1973, when the sector suffered from the oil crises of 1973–74 and 1979–81.

These two crises dealt a blow to the competitiveness of oil products in relation to competing products and caused profound changes in the production and distribution structure of the sector. Although demand for light products, such as automobile fuel and aircraft fuel, has remained stable, and sales of products for use in the petrochemical industry and of oil (motor fuel and fuel in general) have contracted only very slightly, use of heavy products has shrunk in alarming proportions. This evolution has been seen both in the processing industry and in electricity production, reversing a trend of strongest growth for heavy products after 1958. Refineries have been obliged to move with the times. Although the refining sector is still an export hub, it has been forced to cut capacity considerably, closing the two biggest refineries and converting units to the structure of demand, which has changed considerably since 1973.

The refining sector rationalized its operations to a considerable extent in the past decade, cutting plant capacity by 40 percent. At the same time, modern reconversion facilities and the distribution sector were developed. For example, the number of fuel sales points was cut by more than 50 percent in a decade, but at the same time the network was modernized and large-scale sales points are now in a majority. Gas stations now have a large number of pumps selling several different types of fuel and a range of oils. The gas station often sells other goods or services (self-service cafeterias or restaurants, for example) and are frequently open 24 hours, using modern payment techniques.

As for prices, the Ministry for Economic Affairs and the Belgian Petroleum Federation, which represents the sector, negotiate a "program contract." This contract uses a number of parameters reflecting the international evolution of oil markets to define maximum prices for the national supply. The system is very flexible precisely because of its contractual nature. The cut in oil prices over the past few years has been passed on to consumers under the contract system, unlike in other countries where prices are "managed" in a more rigid manner by the government. In current francs, present prices are below those reached immediately after the first oil crisis, reflecting the turnaround that took place in 1985–86.

Petrofina, an oil and petrochemical holding company, has subsidiaries in 25 foreign countries throughout the world, including the United States. It is Belgium's biggest industrial company in terms of turnover and results. It is an integrated company, with a full range of exploration, production, transport, refining, distribution, and petrochemical activities. According to *Fortune Magazine*, it is the 23rd largest petrochemical company in the world and the 13th largest among non–North American companies. Like the majority of large international oil companies, Petrofina conducts its refining, distribution, and storage operations via subsidiaries (in Petrofina's case, located in Belgium). In addition to subsidiaries of multinationals, a large number of small and medium-sized oil companies exist in the area of distribution of oil products.

Gas

Although Belgium was a pioneer in the creation of a distribution network for coal gas in urban areas, it is not a producer of natural gas. Prospecting for gas has been as disappointing as that for oil. On the other hand, the discovery of the Groningen field in the Netherlands fundamentally changed the face of Belgian gas supply. The proximity of the Dutch gas, its simple use, and the rapid construction of a modern transport and distribution network meant that natural gas has gained a considerable share of the Belgian energy market. Since the end of the 1970's, gas has accounted for 20 percent of total energy demand, although this has leveled off slightly in recent years.

In the future, Belgium will undoubtedly conclude new purchase contracts for Dutch and Norwegian North Sea gas, thus compensating for the gradual exhaustion of the Groningen field. A purchasing contract was also signed with the state-owned Algerian company, Sonatrach, but it is rather controversial, for it was negotiated at a time when fears of a primary energy shortage were high. The situation has now changed, and Belgium remains bound to buy more gas from Algeria than it can possibly dispose of and at prices not correctly adjusted to the market situation.

The contract concluded with Sonatrach led to the construction of a liquid methane terminal at Zeebrugge, inaugurated in October 1987. At a cost of around 25 billion BF, it is one of the biggest and most modern installations in the world for the reception, storage, and regasification of liquid gas. By 1992, Zeebrugge will also have become a focal point for the supply of mainland Europe with Norwegian gas, through the construction of the "Zeepipe" pipeline.

The structure of the Belgian gas sector is relatively simple. One company, Distrigaz, more or less has a monopoly over the import and transport of gas for private consumption. It is a partly private, partly public company, although mostly state-run. Gas distribution is carried out by so-called interborough companies. In most cases, these are associations between local authorities (provincial or borough) and private distribution companies that are subsidiaries of electricity concerns. There are also a few purely interborough companies, whose capital is 100 percent state-owned. The system is therefore part public, part private, and operates under the watchful eye of the Control Committee for Gas and Electricity, one of the joint consultation bodies born in 1955. The main role of the committee is to agree on prices.

Electricity

Electricity is the most versatile source of energy since it transforms primary sources into useful forms for mechanical, chemical, thermal, and lighting applications. Thus electrical energy plays an ever increasing role in modern countries developing high technology. As a result, in a country like Belgium, even though the total consumption of energy is decreasing, the consumption of electricity keeps rising.

Because the Belgian landscape is almost flat, hydroelectric power accounts for less than 1 percent of the total electric power. At one important installation, water is pumped up and stored at night using excess electrical energy from the nuclear power reactors and then sent back to hydraulic turbines during the hours of peak demand for electricity. Until the 1960's, electricity was generated mostly from coal from Belgian mines. Later, most of the thermal power plants switched to cheap imported oil and gas.

In Belgium, nuclear power plants now play a dominant role in the production of electricity. This evolution finds its origins in the important role the then Belgian Congo played during World War II in supplying the United States with all the uranium necessary for the discovery and development of nuclear energy. As compensation, Belgium insisted on becoming associated after the war in the peaceful applications of atomic energy. Although the Belgians decided to forgo any military application, they started early to develop nuclear reactors for the production of energy and radioisotopes.

In 1958, a plan was drawn to install on the grounds of the Brussels World Fair the first nuclear reactor built in the United States to be exported abroad. The original plan was abandoned, but the same reactor was installed a few years later at the Nuclear Energy Research Center (CEN/SCK) in Mol in northern Belgium. This important center was created in 1952 and employed 1,500 people at its peak. This reactor became one of the first in the world to produce commercial electricity. Thus well before the oil crisis, the electric power industry in Belgium had opted for nuclear energy. By 1973, two nuclear power reactors, at Doel and Tihange, were in an advanced stage of construction. In the following years, more nuclear units were built, and by 1985, seven power reactors producing 5,410 megawatts accounted for almost 40 percent of electric power in Belgium. In 1988, more than 65 percent of Belgian electric energy was produced by nuclear reactors, making Belgium second only to France in the percentage of electricity coming from atomic energy.

Along with the building of these plants, Belgium was engaged in the development of processes dealing with nuclear fuels. Thus, an experimental plant for the reprocessing of nuclear fuels was built in Dessel. This demonstration plant, called Eurochemic, was built as a joint venture with OECD partners, but France and England later decided to build similar plants on their territory and Eurochemic was shut down. Another important Belgian contribution to nuclear fuel technology was the construction of a plant to fabricate fuel elements with oxides of slightly enriched uranium for light-water reactors. That plant, also built in Dessel with French partners, is called Franco-belge de Fabrication du Combustible (FBFC). A third Belgian contribution to nuclear fuel fabrication was the development of mixed oxides of uranium and plutonium fuels first for breeder reactors such as SNR 300 in Kalkar, then for classical PWR reactors, mainly in France. This venture continues to grow, and the Dessel plant has merged with a French partner to form the Commox corporation. Finally, experiments are under way at CEN/SCK to study the storage of nuclear waste in underground clay deposits.

Traditionally, more than 90 percent of the electric power industry in Belgium has been in the private sector. Since 1950, mergers and restructuring have concentrated the industry among three main corporations —EBES, INTERCOM, and UNERG—with a total annual production of 50 terawatt hours. At the distribution level, local communities have traditionally been involved by way of "intercommunal" companies that are in fact mostly run by the three large corporations just mentioned. The development of the Belgian electricity grid in all aspects of production and distribution is handled by a world-renowned engineering company now called Tractebel, following the merging of Tractionel and Electrobel.

Belgium now possesses a very large reserve (40 percent) of electric power. This has led the government to conclude the installed nuclear power is adequate to the needs of coming years, provided that peak demand can be met by gas turbines or cogeneration plants. As it now stands, no additional nuclear power plant is planned in the near future.

The Belgian grid is connected with those of the Federal Republic of Germany and of the Netherlands. Two more links exist to the Netherlands north of the nuclear plants at Doel and to Germany through Luxembourg to Trier. The Belgian grid is connected to France through plants at Gravelines, Chooz, and Cattenon. These international links are used routinely to exchange electricity and to provide emergency relief so that installed power in the interconnected country can be limited in size. With the new European market in 1993, an important French contribution is foreseeable, since France has an excess of nuclear-generated electric power.

Other Energy Sources

Since 1974, an attempt has been made to reduce dependency on imported energy. The Scientific Policy Planning Services (SPPS), attached to the prime minister's office, has used financial aid to stimulate industrial initiatives in the fields of solar energy, dynamic electricity, wind, and biomass energy and to encourage the rational use of energy. Some SPPS activities have been conducted jointly in the framework of European or American projects. However, as in other industrialized countries, this policy has not resulted in significant progress in alternative energy fields. No new source has been developed that is capable of producing by the year 2000 a sizable proportion of primary energy requirements. However, wind energy has had a certain amount of success, particularly in developing countries.

If rational energy use can be considered an energy source, it has been quite successful in Belgium, both as regards joint state/university research and in the field. Projects have been put into practice with the aid of companies and private energy consumers, on the initiative of the state. However, the rise in energy prices in the 1970's produced a stimulus for such research that has not been reproduced since.

Belgium is a highly industrialized country that has for many decades attached considerable importance to energy problems. It has reflected all the changes on the world market in regard to fluctuations in availability and prices. The evolution of the energy picture in Belgium can be summed up as follows: (1) systematic attempts to reduce energy consumption, resulting in a considerable improvement of energy efficiency, independent of the effects of economic recession and climatic problems (e.g., the length and severity of winters); (2) diversification of energy supplies, particularly through the development of the gas market, fresh interest in imported coal, and above all the rise of nuclear energy; and (3) reduced dependency on energy imports from politically unstable regions. Oil, which was most affected by this problem, is now supplied to a considerable extent by more secure regions. Belgium's example clearly proves that a liberal energy policy in regard to initiative and pricing pays off. Unlike many other countries, where energy is often tightly controlled by the government, economic and technical inventiveness has been used to the full in Belgium to ensure that progress continues in this vital field, despite difficult economic circumstances.

Monetary Policy and Organization

Roland Beauvois

The Currency

THE BELGIAN FRANC was created in 1832, two years after the proclamation of Belgian independence. The new currency unit was organized along the same lines as the French franc. It was worth 5 grams of silver and was also linked to gold. A fixed ratio between the official prices of these two metals was laid down by law. Parity was established at 290 mg of pure gold. Belgium rapidly confronted the inconveniences of bimetallism. In 1865, it was called on to join the Latin Union international agreement formed by France, Italy, Switzerland, and, a little later, Greece. Like these countries, it found itself trapped within a hybrid system after the collapse in the price of silver relative to that of gold. After 1876, 5-franc silver coins were only "tokens" minted by the Treasury, and their face value was much higher than that of the metal they contained. The system was therefore dominated in practice by the value of gold, but gold coins were a rarity and were not used for payments. A gold bullion standard grew up. Gold reserves held by the National Bank of Belgium (NBB) served to guarantee the external convertibility of the Belgian franc, at a fixed rate, close to the parity established with other gold-linked currencies.

The damage caused to the Belgian economy by World War I and postwar reconstruction expenditure sparked off inflation. Between 1914 and 1926, the Belgian franc was a floating currency. There was no mechanism guaranteeing the convertibility, in foreign currencies at a fixed rate, of monetary assets held in Belgian francs. In October 1926, the system of fixed exchange rates came back into force. The Belgian franc was stabilized at a gold parity of 41.8 mg of pure gold, or one-seventh of its official prewar value.

During the crisis of the 1930's, the contraction of international trade had serious consequences for the Belgian economy, which was highly centered on foreign markets. In March 1935, the Belgian government devalued the franc by 28 percent in relation to its gold parity in order to avoid further deflation. In September 1944, the franc was devalued again, this time by 32.7 percent, on the initiative of the government-in-exile in London. The official exchange rate was fixed by agreement, notably in relation to the pound sterling and the U.S. dollar. In December 1945, the Belgian parliament ratified Belgian participation in the Bretton Woods agreements. In becoming a member of the International Monetary Fund, Belgium returned to an international system of fixed exchange rates linked to gold via the U.S. dollar.

The restructuring after World War II was characterized by demand-pulled inflation at the international level. During this period, Belgium's overall foreign position was not at risk. Generally speaking, its production plant had suffered less during the war than that of its neighbors. The balance on current account remained in the black, although naturally there was a deficit vis-à-vis the dollar zone. Under the Marshall Plan, Belgium received aid in dollars on the proviso that it give aid in Belgian francs to its debtor neighbors. This, followed by the European Payments Union, enabled Belgium to use its surpluses with European countries to cover its dollar deficit.

When the pound sterling was devalued in September 1949, the Belgian franc was not spared the general downward trend. It was devalued by 12.345 percent in relation to gold and to the U.S. dollar. Many of the European currencies lowered their parities. The average exchange rate of the franc actually rose.

In 1957, the parliament wanted to put the Belgian franc on a clear legal footing. A law adopted on April 12 confirmed the official gold definition of the franc at 17.77 mg of pure gold. It consecrated the international rules that Belgium was obliged to respect as a member of the International Monetary Fund. The effective collapse of the international fixed exchange rate system in March 1973 meant that the 1957 law no longer corresponded to reality. The ratification in 1978 by Belgium of the second amendment to the statutes of the International Monetary Fund, abolishing any official price for gold, rendered the law null and void. However, Belgium has yet to amend its monetary law to adapt to the existing situation. Parliament in fact lost all its powers to define an official rate for the franc. Its last official move was to ratify, in December 1971, an amendment of the parity agreed on during the so-called Smithsonian Conference. Since then, the government alone has decided to modify the official exchange rate.

TABLE IV.9
Exchange Rates Expressed in Belgian Francs, 1914–1987
(legal parities)

	1914	1930	1939	1950	1987
U.S. dollar	5.18	35.831	29.68	50.21	37.34
Pound sterling	25.22	174.22	131.535	140.0	61.11
French franc[a]	1.0	1.406	0.7443	0.1435	0.0621
Swiss franc	1.0	6.9445	6.685	11.619	25.06

[a] Value expressed in old francs, the equivalent of ¹⁄₁₀₀ of the current French franc.

Belgium was one of the countries to sign the so-called Basel Agreement of April 1972. This agreement entered into force after the dollar was allowed to float. Its objective was to set up a stable exchange rate system between the currencies of the member-states of the European Economic Community. Belgium was among the few countries to respect this agreement until its replacement by the European Monetary System (EMS). The EMS was founded by a resolution adopted by the European Council on December 5, 1978, which entered into force in March 1979. By virtue of this agreement, to which Belgium is a party, the Belgian franc has a rate attached to the ECU. Its rate on the exchange market is controlled by the NBB and can fluctuate within a margin of 2.25 percent either way. The official rate of the Belgian franc can be changed only by mutual agreement. The only major change to the ECU rate of the Belgian franc took place during the February 1982 readjustment. It was then adjusted 8.5 percent downwards in relation to the other currencies. In all, the various adjustments within the EMS since its creation changed the ECU rate of the Belgian franc from 39.46 francs in March 1979 to 42.46 francs since January 1987.

The evolution of the exchange rate of a few European currencies and the U.S. dollar in relation to the Belgian franc is shown in Table IV.9. The Belgian currency depreciated sharply after World War I. It resisted the shock of World War II much better. The Swiss franc is used in Table IV.9 as a control, since Switzerland was not involved in either of the wars.

More recent fluctuations in the franc can be measured by looking at the effective exchange rate, or the average exchange rate for foreign currencies weighted according to the importance of each of them for Belgium's foreign trade. Under a system of floating exchange rates, the effective rate is the best measure of variations in the value of one currency in relation to others. In the case of the Belgian franc, the effective rate rose gradually and evenly between 1970 and 1980. In 1980, the index (base year 1970) stood at 124. This was followed by a period of retreat and depreciation of the franc. In 1984, the index stood at 97. A recovery then took place, partly due to the fall in the dollar, and the index crept up to 109 by 1987.

The Central Bank (NBB)

The National Bank of Belgium was established by the law of May 5, 1850, which granted it the privilege of issuing bank notes. At the outset, the bank was a private company whose shares were held by the general public. However, its governor was appointed by the king. As in many other countries, control of the bank gradually slipped into the hands of the government. In 1948, the capital was doubled, and the shares were subscribed by the government. The bank became an independent establishment charged with public duties and regulated by public law. Half of its shares remain in private hands and are listed on the stock exchange. The state now exercises official and permanent control through a public representative. In addition, frequent contacts between the bank governor and the minister of finance enable the latter to keep up with the bank's policy and, if need be, exercise influence on it. The government also has some say in the appointment of members of the NBB Board of Directors. In addition, three of the ten members of the Regency Council, an advisory body that plays a considerable role in fixing the bank's rates, are appointed by the minister of finance. The remaining regents are nominated either by organizations representing industry, trade, and agriculture, by trade union organizations, or by public sector credit institutions.

Like other central banks, the NBB plays the role of lender of last resort. It can intervene on the supply side of the monetary market and thereby influence short-term rates. It exercises this role in conditions very different from those known in the past. First, notes have lost much of their importance. They now represent only one-third of the total money supply and less than 10 percent of total financial assets held by residents through domestic financial institutions. This reduction in demand for notes has increased the multiplier effect of bank deposits and rendered financial intermediaries less dependent on the central bank. They no longer have to resort to its services so frequently to replenish their funds. Second, intervention by the NBB as a lender of last resort on the monetary market is not implemented through the same instruments as in the past. For a long time, the rediscounting of bills of exchange was the typical way in which the money market procured resources from the bank. Today, banks and other financial intermediaries in Belgium organize their liquid assets through use of the vast portfolio of Treasury certificates (public debts with terms of between one month and one year) that they hold. When they want to procure funds, they request the repayment of certificates from the Treasury. Therefore the state rather than the banks turns to the central bank. This has a twofold effect. First, the central bank cannot conceivably place the Treasury in difficulty by refusing it funds. Second, the bank's assets, other than exchange reserves, consist for the most part of direct or indirect claims on the Belgian state.

In addition to these roles, the National Bank is responsible for the execution of exchange and payments agreements with foreign countries. It also manages the official exchange reserves. This role dates back to the gold convertibility of the Belgian franc and has always been exercised by the NBB. There is no separate organization responsible for managing the exchange market. However, the form taken by this role has again changed considerably. The bank is now obliged to intervene under international agreements. Since the International Monetary Fund suspended exchange stability, the impetus for this duty has come from the EMS. The composition of exchange reserves has changed. Gold no longer acts as an instrument of international settlement, except for the creation of official ECUs within the EMS. Reserves consist of assets in various foreign currencies. The U.S. dollar is by far the most important of these. ECUs are also held, along with claims on international organizations such as the International Monetary Fund (unconditional and special drawing rights). During the several years when the balance of payments (current operations and private capital movements) was heavily in deficit, NBB exchange reserves were used to cover a part of this deficit. However, the main resource fueling the financing of this was foreign currency from loans contracted abroad by the government.

Since the end of World War II regulations have been in force governing payment transactions with foreign countries. They apply to both Belgium and Luxembourg by virtue of the monetary association that exists between the two. Decisions are taken by the Belgo-Luxembourg Exchange Institution, whose board is made up of representatives of the two countries. The NBB is responsible for administration of current affairs. These regulations rapidly became more liberal, with general authorizations replacing the system of special authorizations. Since the beginning of the 1950's, a two-tier exchange market has existed. One is "regulated"; the other "free." Payments for goods transactions and certain service transactions must be carried out on the regulated market. Currency from export earnings must be brought back into the country and sold on this market, which importers use to obtain currency supplies, in fact without restriction, at a rate close to the official rate. Payments with respect to capital operations, with certain exceptions, are carried out on the free market. Payments with respect to funded income can be carried out on either market. In practice, outgoing payments are carried out on the regulated market and incoming ones on the free market. Rates fluctuate on the free market, in principle without restriction.

In creating a two-tier exchange market, the Belgo-Luxembourg Exchange Institution aimed to liberalize financial transactions without posing a threat to official exchange reserves. The free market was supposed to find its own balance through small fluctuations in the exchange rate, as does any floating exchange rate system. However, in periods of strong speculation, for example at the beginning of the 1980's, the gap between the "regulated" and "free" rates widened. The regulations are still in force and are still strictly applied to the exchange positions commercial banks must adopt. However, the abolition of customs checks within the European Economic Community, the development of multinationals, and, generally speaking, the internationalization of the Belgian economy have rendered the control of transactions by the regulated market less effective. Moreover, the two-tier system no longer covers the official exchange reserves of capital outflows, which are in much stronger supply on the free market due to considerable growth in revenue in the form of capital income. In contrast, very large payments abroad of this type of income are carried out on the regulated market. The abolition of capital movements planned in the framework of the European Economic Community will oblige Belgium and Luxembourg to change their legislation. A single market will remain, which will be free and will operate using a fixed rate.

Unlike other central banks, the NBB has no microeconomic control over financial intermediaries. In certain cases, it does have advisory power. Other authorities are responsible for monitoring financial intermediaries in regard to prudential rates. The Banking Commission, which is an independent institution with public duties, was created in 1935. It monitors the commercial banks, including the Government General Savings Bank, private savings banks, and consumer credit organizations. It also monitors public issues of securities in order to protect savings. State credit institutions are under government control. The government is represented within each of them by one or several public representatives appointed by the ministry or ministries responsible for controlling the organization.

The NBB's authority in the marketplace rested for many years on a de facto situation. When bank notes represented an important part of the money stock, commercial banks were obliged to refund a large part of their new credits by calling on the central bank. In granting credit, commercial banks therefore had to take into account the NBB's rediscount rates and, generally speaking, its conditions for the acceptance of bills for rediscounting. The gradual reduction in demand for notes weakened the central bank's de facto powers.

It therefore requested that it be granted powers de jure, calling notably for the creation of a compulsory reserves ratio. This was accomplished by a law of December 1973 that granted the NBB the right to invite financial intermediaries to respect ratios between certain of their assets and certain of their liabilities and to impose limits on certain balance sheet components. These powers were extended to all categories of financial institutions and were very wide. The NBB did not have any statutory power, as stated above, and therefore had to proceed by issuing recommendations and, if need be, by requesting those holding statutory power —notably the Banking Commission—to take steps in line with its recommendations. However, the procedure for the consultation of financial institutions laid down in the law was cumbersome. Moreover, recommendations were in effect only for six months; after that the entire procedure had to be started again from scratch. Finally, the government clearly intended the bank to use these powers only in situations requiring restrictive policy. During the 1970's, the bank made use of these powers. It has not done so since. In an economic situation characterized by slow growth and marked underemployment, a policy restricting demand would have been inappropriate. Inflationary pressures were either imported or due to increases in income. The correction of domestic inflation had to revolve around policies other than those pertaining to credit and currency.

The NBB's main policy instrument, whose objectives and limits are described below, has become interest rates. The bank exercises direct influence on short-term rates; it does not have to attempt to influence them indirectly by operating on the money supply. Acting with Treasury agreement, it is responsible for fixing the rates of one-, two- and three-month Treasury bills. These bills form, as already mentioned, an extremely important investment for banks and other organizations operating on the money market. Consequently, variations in the rates of Treasury bills are echoed in rates for interbank loans, large deposits, and, therefore, short-term credit rates.

Other Financial Institutions

Money is created in the form of demand deposits. Part of these deposits is then transformed into notes, when salaries are paid or when households withdraw the amounts they need for everyday expenses. Deposits represent around 60 percent of the money supply. Private commercial banks manage the largest proportion of these assets. The Postal Checking Office, a state body subordinate to the Postal Board, has lost importance. Demand deposits are the only form of asset it offers, and it grants credit only to the state. Since financial institutions have become less specialized, as explained below, organizations that previously did not offer banking services now offer their clients a demand deposit service. However, they still manage only less than 20 percent of money deposits.

Money demand is falling. The general public is better informed, and management of financial assets has been rationalized. High interest rates have resulted in demand for nonmoney financial assets. The internationalization of financial markets has encouraged foreign currency investments. In recent years, Belgian companies and households have devoted only between 5 and 10 percent of new financial savings on increasing their monetary assets. The transformation rate of money into income is undergoing a structural acceleration.

In comparison with others, Belgians invest large amounts in financial markets. In recent years, around 10 percent of the available income of private individuals has been so invested. If companies are added to this equation, the two sectors together annually accumulate net financial assets (assets less liabilities) of upwards of 10 percent of GNP.

In recent years, 80 percent of savings have been on the domestic market; the remainder has been invested abroad. On the domestic market, around two-thirds of funds pass through the hands of the main financial institutions. These include private banks, private savings banks, mortgage and consumer credit companies, and public sector credit institutions, including the Government General Savings Bank. On June 30, 1987, assets held by Belgian residents with these financial institutions amounted to 6,200 billion francs, or the equivalent of just under 120 percent of GNP for the year. The private banks manage a little under 40 percent of this total, as do public sector credit institutions. Private savings banks manage slightly under 20 percent. The remainder is in the hands of the other categories of financial institutions, which have much less weight.

Investment opportunities are highly diverse. However, this spectrum has not been broadened in recent years by as many innovations as have occurred in other countries. Belgium has not used the "aggregate" control technique for monetary policy, whereby limits are imposed on the growth in the supply of certain clearly defined financial assets. Belgian financial institutions have not therefore been obliged to be as imaginative as their foreign counterparts in inventing new types of financial assets not falling under these restrictions.

The Evolution of Financial Institutions

Two trends have been discernible in the evolution of financial institutions in recent decades: a move away from specialization, and a move toward internationalization. The latter has been particularly true of the banks.

The distinction between establishments specializing in short-term transactions and those who do not has become blurred. Banks have developed investment credits, issue mortgages and bonds, and offer savings accounts. Their capacity to hold share portfolios is still limited by law. Savings banks have become involved in company credit operations and have increased their participation in the payment mechanism. Public sector credit institutions have been set up by the government in stages, each time to overcome a particular shortcoming in the financial market. Each had at the outset relatively precisely defined functions. In the past twenty-five years, they have gradually gone beyond these limits into the spheres of both fund collection and credit operations. Change has continually gathered force, particularly in the large institutions, the Government General Savings Bank, set up in 1865, and the Community Credit Bank, set up in 1860. Both of these institutions have become on the domestic fund market, financial intermediaries similar to the larger private banks as Générale, B.B.L., and Kredietbank. Within the three categories of institutions, the majority do not have the scale to practice the full range of asset and liability operations. Moreover, the majority of commercial banks and private savings banks are geographically restricted to a particular part of the country.

Internationalization has particularly affected the banks. A considerable number of foreign banks or subsidiaries of foreign banks are established in Belgium. At the beginning of 1987, of the 86 banks registered in Belgium, 29 were governed by foreign law. Of the remainder, 23 of the 57 banks coming under Belgian law were affiliated with a foreign bank, and foreign, nonbanking groups were the main shareholder of four others. This penetration of the Belgian banking market is due to the amount of foreign investment in the Belgian economy and to the liberal policy of Belgian authorities toward the introduction of foreign banks. As a result, the balance sheets of banks established in Belgium include a growing proportion of external assets and liabilities. International activity, measured by the balance in Belgian francs and in foreign currency, is more substantial than activity within Belgium. The foreign currency balance exceeds the balance in Belgian francs. This growth in assets abroad and debts with foreign countries results partly from the large number of foreign banks operating on the Belgian market. However, Belgian banks are also highly geared toward international transactions. For the three larger Belgian banks, Générale, B.B.L., and Kredietbank, the balance with foreign countries represents more than 40 percent of the total balance, even though they are highly active on the domestic market and developed as retail bankers.

This growth in external claims and debts is less marked in the other two groups of financial institutions, consisting of around thirty private savings banks all governed by Belgian law and six public sector credit institutions. Even the biggest of these enterprises has only in recent years taken the gamble of developing foreign operations.

Looking at the balance sheet total, one of the private banks is the biggest Belgian financial intermediary. In international terms, however, it is well down the ladder, even in comparison to institutions from countries of a similar size, such as Switzerland and the Netherlands.

Monetary Policy

The Belgian economy is open but dominated because of its size. Belgium's GNP represents only around 1 percent that of all OECD countries combined. From the economic viewpoint, it is one of the most open of comparable countries. Imports account for 40–45 percent of real resources in terms of the national production/import mix. This is a measure of the importance of imports in final expenditure. From the financial viewpoint, the domestic market is integrated to a large extent with foreign and supranational markets.

Consequently, significant changes abroad in the level of activity, prices, rates, or exchange rates affect the Belgian economy. Since the beginning of the 1960's, the main factor in the unit price rise for final expenditure has been rising import prices. The other side of the coin is that economic problems on the Belgian domestic front and resultant anticipations more often than not affect the country's external balance, either as regards current payments or capital movements, or both.

When there is a contradiction between domestic monetary policy objectives and external objectives—and this is often the case—the latter cannot be sacrificed. Belgian monetary policy cannot ignore the external factor, which has become powerful because of the internationalization of the national economy and also because the Belgian public, both companies and households, is increasingly sensitive to price or rate differentials, anticipated or effective changes in exchange rates, and, generally speaking, any fundamental change.

In the late 1970's and early 1980's, when energy prices rose, the Belgian economy went through a bad period. Growth slowed, and unemployment rose. Inflation, after peaking in 1974–75, eased off somewhat but remained high. Similar trends were seen in most industrialized countries, but not with the same force as in Belgium. The relative weakness of the Belgian economy was visible above all in the reversal of the balance of payments on current account. The earlier surplus evaporated, and the deficit broadened from 1977 to reach a maximum in 1981 of more than 4 percent of the GNP. This imbalance was due to deterioration in terms of trade, structural deficiencies in part of the industrial fabric, and by a lax economic policy. The public did not accept the effects of the deterioration in the terms of trade on real available income. On the contrary, a clamor for economic well-being gathered strength. Salary claims and increases in other professional incomes were greatly exaggerated, at least in sectors sheltered from foreign competition, which was disastrous for the profitability of companies subject to this competition. The government developed services to compensate for job losses in industry and increased transfer expenditures to compensate for income losses and to improve social security advantages. Consequently the state deficit expanded, despite higher taxes. In 1981, a recession year, the deficit rose to more than 16 percent of GNP.

In this situation of trailing growth, underemployment, and lack of investment spending, monetary policy could only seek to fight external imbalances by trying to restrict internal demand, just at a time when fiscal policy was attempting to shore it up. Monetary authorities attempted to prevent inflation fueled by a rise in the price of imported inputs. They therefore attempted to shelter the franc from depreciation and maneuvered to ensure that it follow the strong currencies as closely as possible. Interest rate policy was arranged so as to avoid capital outflows, which would have reinforced the impact on the exchange market of the external deficit on current account and would, moreover, have hindered the financing of the government's budgetary deficit. At the same time, the monetary authorities insisted that budgetary and incomes policy be revised.

This "strong franc" policy did not prevent internal inflationary factors from making their existence felt. Price drops, in francs, of imported goods paid in the depreciated currencies were not passed on, whereas rises in foreign prices, notably the second rise in oil prices, were rapidly incorporated into retail prices. This sparked off salary rises, due to cost-of-living adjustments, and rises in other professional incomes, which kept pace with salaries. In sectors competing on foreign markets, many companies were obliged to absorb these increases due to the nature of their product. They were not able to pass on this rise of internal costs in their prices. On the contrary, they were obliged to cut their prices to compete with countries with weaker currencies. The strong franc policy was therefore heavily criticized, particularly since it required high interest rates. This weighed heavily on company costs and on those of the government.

The new government that came to power after the elections of November 1981 adopted a policy designed to restore equilibrium. This policy included the unhooking of the franc. In February 1982, it was depreciated by 8.5 percent within the EMS. In June 1982 and March 1983, it was depreciated by 4.25 percent against the Dutch guilder and by 4.5 percent against the deutsche mark. This devaluation was accompanied by a range of support measures, aimed at temporarily breaking the link between salaries and price rises. Generally speaking, an income and taxation policy was adopted that aimed to restore company profitability. Budgetary policy was changed to reduce the public deficit. The deficit was reduced to a little more than 9 percent of GNP in 1987, partly thanks to new taxes and to the cut in interest rates.

The support measures were not enough to prevent a temporary acceleration in inflation after the devaluations. Inflation then began to fall in Belgium, as in the majority of industrialized countries. This was partly due to moderation in salary increases and partly to the tumbling of oil prices. The trend accelerated when oil prices collapsed and the cost of other industrial raw materials fell. Devaluation of the franc was followed by a recovery in the growth rate. This continued, again as in the majority of industrialized countries, thanks to the effects of recovery in the United States. However, the rate was slower in Belgium than in other countries, for the policy of restricting wage increases and balancing the budget slowed the expansion of domestic demand. This relative deflation facilitated recovery of the balance on current account. The depreciation of the Belgian franc also contributed to this recovery, but its positive effects wore off after 1983. The improved economic situation in industrialized countries had more lasting effects for Belgian exports. Finally, the improvement in the terms of trade was a very significant factor. In 1984, the external current account of the Belgo-Luxembourg Economic Union was balanced again. In 1987, it showed a surplus of around 2 percent of Belgium's GNP.

This return to equilibrium simplified the definition of monetary policy. The major problems that remained were mostly of a structural nature: the level of underemployment, the scale of the government deficit, and the weaknesses of part of the production apparatus, which required expansion investment. Monetary policy could not contribute to solving them; its only contribution would be a cut in capital costs.

The downward trend in interest rates throughout the world, rendered possible by disinflation, made things easier for the Belgian authorities. However, they had to proceed carefully. Since 1981, private capital movements had led to considerable net outflows. These were partly for fiscal reasons, but were chiefly due to the fact that the basic economic picture in Belgium was less favorable than in other countries, particularly in the Federal Republic of Germany. The 1982 depreciations had tarnished the image of the Belgian franc. In periods of tension within the EMS, the Belgian franc was considered by holders of floating capital to be among the weaker currencies and not likely to be revalued. In such periods, Belgian monetary authorities on several occasions had to stop the downward movement of interest rates and make temporary increases. More permanently, holders of assets in Belgian francs had to be offered a premium to attract and hold foreign capital in the short term or to reduce the attraction, for residents, of investments in other currencies. This premium took the form of a positive rate differential. Short-term Belgian rates were systematically kept at a higher level than those for investments in stronger currencies, whose evolution they mirrored. Gradually, the gap narrowed. In 1987, the short-term interest rate differential compared with that for investments in deutsche marks was reduced to around 3 percent. This closing of the differential is an indication that the Belgian economy and consequently the franc are gradually being put back on the right track.

The nature of problems faced by the Belgian economy in the past fifteen years has rendered monetary policy powerless to prevent the appearance of imbalances. Their correction required instruments other than economic policy. During this recovery phase, monetary policy has been adjusted to consolidate the progress made and to prevent it from being overturned by monetary upheaval.

For a long time now, policymakers have been prompted by external factors to watch developments abroad closely. Spontaneously, by the force of circumstances, Belgian monetary policy has been coordinated with that of other countries, particularly with that of countries who have organized their external monetary relations along the lines of the fixed exchange rate system. Belgian monetary policy is intentionally sensitive to external influence. Accelerated integration among the countries of the European Economic Community will go hand in hand with close monetary cooperation. Respecting this requirement will not demand any considerable sacrifice or adjustment on the part of the Belgian authorities.

Government Finance

Roland Beauvois

THE ANALYSIS OF GOVERNMENT finances often centers around central government revenues and expenditures, but it is more appropriate to study a wider concept, namely that of government as a whole, comprising, in addition to the central government, local authorities and social security. Transfers between the first of these three subdivisions and the two others are quite vast and affect the central budget. "Debudgetized" expenditure must also be included, where possible. More often than not, this is capital expenditure that normally falls on the shoulders of the central government. To decrease the official budget, this type of expenditure is often sloughed off on bodies that are legally separate from the state and carry the burden of debt in its place. Interest charges and repayment of the debt of these independent bodies naturally enough have to be covered by the central government.

The data in Table IV.10 refer to total government revenues, expenditures, and deficits. They are expressed with reference to the GNP. During the ten-year period starting at the beginning of the 1970's, real growth amounted to 30 percent. These years were shaken by two oil crises. They ended with an overall weakening of the economic situation and were marked by a serious deterioration in government finances. Fiscal and parafiscal revenues have grown proportionally faster than the GNP. Moreover, their composition has changed. Income from taxes on individuals has expanded particularly strongly. During the 1970's the combination of high inflation and insufficient adjustment of the various tax brackets led to a considerable rise in the real tax burden. Since the value-added tax and stamp duty tend to be proportional and excise duties tend to be regressive, the body of indirect taxation evolved in line with the GNP. Social security contributions were raised on a number of occasions by specific measures.

TABLE IV.10
General Government Revenue and Expenditure
(% of GNP)

	Average 1970–73	Average 1980–82	1986
Revenue			
Direct taxation	12.2%	18.5%	18.5%
Indirect taxation	12.3	12.6	11.8
Social security contributions	11.2	13.4	15.1
Capital taxes	0.4	0.3	0.3
Non-fiscal and non-parafiscal revenue	1.4	2.1	1.6
Total	37.5	46.9	47.3
Expenditure			
Net expenditure on goods and services	13.5	17.7	16.1
Interest payments	3.3	7.8	11.1
Current transfers to individuals	15.1	22.9	22.0
Company subsidies	2.7	3.3	2.8
Current transfers to rest of the world	1.0	1.4	1.4
Total current expenditure	35.6	53.1	53.4
Gross fixed capital formation	4.0	4.0	2.1
Capital transfers	1.6	3.9	2.8
Grand total	41.2	61.0	58.3

Under the heading "net expenditure on goods and services," which represents public consumption, the highest growth area in excess of GNP growth was not general administrative expenditures or expenditures on defense and security. In fact, education took the biggest slice. The average time spent in education per pupil was lengthened and available choices of education were diversified. This caused an increase in the number of teachers per pupil. Competition between state and private schools further increased the cost of education. "Current transfers to individuals" expanded particularly sharply in relation to GNP. Expenditure on pensions has grown mainly because people live longer, benefits have improved, and women who entered the labor market after World War II have reached pension age. Sickness and disability benefits have been influenced by the extension of coverage to broader categories of the population and more extensive recourse to medical consultation and treatment. Unemployment benefits and aid for job creation soared. Underemployment worsened. "Company subsidies" and "capital transfers" were inflated by the considerable aid granted to the transport sector and particularly to sectors in difficulty (coal and steel, notably). The only heading to remain at a constant percentage of GNP was "investment expenditure."

TABLE IV.11
Deficit Funded by the General Government

	% of GNP
Average 1970–73	−3.7%
Average 1976–79	−6.6
Average 1980–82	−14.1
1986	−11.0

A clear upsurge can be seen in "interest payments." There were two reasons for this. The first was the progressive increase in interest rates, due to worldwide inflation and the upheavals in financial markets. The second was the increasing budget deficit leading to the steadily growing indebtedness of the Belgian state. The registering of an overall deficit by the public sector was nothing new (Table IV.11). During the previous decade of considerable prosperity, there was already a deficit, averaging 3.5 percent of GNP. In Belgium, the principle of covering investment expenditure, in the very broad sense of the term, by borrowing was accepted for a very long time. Interest payments were therefore already a relatively large part of Belgian budgets, although the situation worsened considerably during the following difficult decade.

The two years of economic crisis that followed the second rise in oil prices at the end of the 1970's dealt a severe blow to the budget. The government that came to power following the elections at the end of 1981 decided on a series of austerity measures. The economic upturn and a general downward trend in interest rates favored this new policy considerably.

On the income side (see Table IV.10), a number of provisions boosted, occasionally in a very sophisticated manner, income from social security contributions. On the expenditure side, larger expenditure cuts affected investments. The majority of other expenditure categories also felt the pinch, although in a less severe manner, due to various restrictive measures that were relatively moderate on the whole. Only one current expenditure category continued to increase at a faster rate than GNP, namely, interest payments. There were two reasons for this. For each of the years 1983 to 1986, the deficit that had to be funded—namely, new debt—measured as a percentage of GNP, exceeded the GNP growth rate. Public indebtedness therefore grew in relation to GNP. At the same time, the average interest rate paid on the public debt was higher than the GNP growth rate. The combination of these two factors meant that interest payments gradually became heavier. A so-called snowball effect had been triggered. The Belgian government was not in a position to adjust domestic interest rates. First, there was no room to maneuver because Belgian financial markets are highly open to the rest of the world. Second, the interest rate policy had to be defensive to prevent capital outflows, after the 1982 devaluation of the Belgian franc had damaged its reputation. The only efficient manner of stopping the snowball effect was therefore to generate a sufficient budgetary surplus. New austerity measures were taken and began to make themselves felt at the end of 1987. The results are, as yet, insufficient.

Budgetary developments in 1988 and up to the end of the decade were difficult to forecast at the time of writing. Before the early elections at the end of 1987, the government had announced its intention to embark on a fiscal reform that would decrease the tax burden on individuals. If such a reform were not to add to the deficit, these reductions would have to be compensated for either by raising indirect taxation or by reducing certain "fiscal expenditures" (programs agreed to earlier), or by new expenditure cuts. The proposed restrictions and cuts encountered a wave of opposition. On the other hand, public opinion generally admitted that the government's finances had to be straightened out.

This ambiguity does not exist only in Belgium. For historical or contemporary reasons, Belgians find good reasons to oppose government intervention when it interferes with their personal interests. Taxation is often resented as a levy without return and government expenditure as a futile burden. In fact, this is not the case. The major part of total government income is immediately handed back, in money form, to companies and households via transfer flows. In 1986, when government income represented 47.3 percent of GNP, expenditures on interest payments on government debts and current and capital transfers to residents amounted to 38.7 percent, or more than 80 percent of income. The government held on to only 8.6 percent of the national product to cover consumption and public investments—taken together, 18.2 percent of GNP—which both generate income in the national economy. A further 1.4 percent of GNP went to transfers to the rest of the world. In the final analysis, after all the transfers to or from all governments, the available income of "households and individual enterprises" on the one hand and "companies" on the other hand now absorb a larger proportion of GNP than at the beginning of the 1970's, whereas the share of available income in the hands of all governments has diminished.

The surplus on the Belgian current account since 1985 indicates that the government deficit has more than been covered by the financial surplus of "households and individual enterprises" and that of "companies."

The net financing capacity (after investment) is exceptionally high in Belgium, standing at around 10 percent of disposable income, or 8 percent of GNP. The latter sector is still well within its self-financing margins, which have broadened in recent years, fueling investment expenditure and financial markets.

This situation, where the central government deficit does not even absorb surplus national savings and which is expressed as a current account surplus with the rest of the world, is nevertheless precarious. All forecasts currently reject the hypothesis of faster growth in the world and in Belgium. If this pessimism is borne out, the profitability of Belgian companies could be affected by foreign competition, as could domestic savings. Households could choose to maintain their consumption level to the detriment of savings. Should these changes take place, the general government financial deficit, at its current level, would no longer be covered by the surplus from the two other sectors, and then once again the government would have to rely on net borrowing from the rest of the world to cover a current external deficit. This is the specter held up by those who insist on the need to continue with the austerity policy. It is not the only argument in favor of such a choice.

One of the other arguments is psychological. Once international institutions, be they the International Monetary Fund, the European Community, or any other, denounce the dangers of sloppy government finances and disorder, along with the majority of Belgian politicians and the press, people's behavior begins to be influenced by this apocalyptic vision. There is a fear of new taxation, provoking capital outflows. This in turn weighs heavily on the exchange market and can initiate new inflation. This atmosphere becomes one of the factors obliging the government to reduce the public budget deficit. Particularly since the so-called snowball effect has become synonymous with cancer.

In other words, budgetary policy must set itself the objective of reducing public expenditure. It is not a question of increasing the pressure of taxation. Objectively speaking, it is already heavy enough in comparison with international standards. Subjectively speaking, people accept high taxation with increasing reluctance. Tax avoidance and even evasion have become commonplace. Political pressure has led to a range of fiscal expedients. Direct taxation now consists of a complex and opaque body of provisions, the burden of which is often unevenly spread. In addition, declared high income is very heavily taxed. The system is accused of discouraging production. The supply-side theory has gained a great deal of ground. The weight of social security contributions has increased the gap between labor costs to the employer and the net salary pocketed by the employee. The specificities of domestic price formation mechanisms in an economy where employers associations and trade unions are powerful mean that tax increases have an inflationary effect on costs. This severely shackles companies competing on the international market. In any event, governmental legislation is now tending toward a reduction of taxation on individuals.

Significant compression in the general government deficit supposes that expenditure is cut by an amount much higher than the desired one. The reduction in payments made by the government signifies an income loss for those benefiting from them. They in turn cut their expenditures, other incomes are affected, and on it goes. At each stage, direct and indirect taxes and social security contributions are not collected. The reduction in government expenditure therefore leads to a plummeting of public income, particularly since governments levy a larger part of the national product.

It is also true that because the public sector in the broad sense of the term has taken on an important role in the national economy, a cut in expenditures gives rise to numerous difficulties due to the impact on income, employment, and growth. The government's role is threefold: providing public goods and services, redistributing income, and limiting fluctuations in economic activity. The role of the government has gradually expanded and has become an integral part of structures, even if this is not the optimum situation for the latter. Basic change often represents upheaval. Sectoral problems can arise, many employees have to switch to jobs for which they are not trained, and a slide in the distribution of income can give rise to a new category of disadvantaged. Consequently, recovery must be gradual.

The deficit problem has diminished somewhat since 1984 due to improved growth, a drop in interest rates, better terms of external trade, and specific measures. Real income per unit increased as a consequence, compensating for less growth and shoring up private consumption and industrial investment. For a small and open economy like that of Belgium, the international environment is a key element in the success or failure of an austerity policy. In any event, budget policy is not enough to reduce the budget deficit. Economic policy in its entirety must be involved and must be organized in a coherent manner in order to exploit all the advantages that can be drawn from a reduction in government expenditure and to attenuate the spread of deflationary effects on global domestic demand.

PART V

Social Policy

Roger Dillemans, Coordinator

Labor Relations

Roger Blanpain

BELGIUM IS A COUNTRY of small business. Indeed, in 1985, 97.15 percent of the 163,662 enterprises employed under 50 workers. This has important consequences, chief of which is the dual labor system. Taking size into account is a long-established practice in labor legislation and industrial relations. Only enterprises with, on average, at least 100 employees need a labor council. A committee for safety, health, and embellishment of the workplace is needed only if there are 50 or more employees. A firm with fewer than 50 workers has only a union delegation, depending on the existing collective agreements. As a result, there are no labor councils, committees, or union delegations in the majority of enterprises, and for an important number of employees there is no workers' representation at this level. Consequently unions have less influence in smaller enterprises. However, collective agreements covering wages and working conditions, whether at the national interindustry level or at the branch or industry level, can be extended. Thus all employees benefit from the collective agreement, whether it applies to the entire private sector or to a given branch of industry.

In 1982, of the 2,842,981 workers in Belgium, 1,203,370 were blue-collar workers and 1,639,611 white-collar workers; 1,790,911 were males and 1,052,070 females; 1,943,532 worked in the private sector and 899,449 in the public sector (including education). Lately, employment in the private sector has increased, and employment in the public sector has fallen. Unemployment, although decreasing remains high: in June 1987, 470,500 (11.4 percent) workers were unemployed, which is only slightly less than the figure of 481,700 (11.7 percent) for June 1986.

Belgium has benefited greatly from foreign investment. Almost 80 percent of the enterprises employing more than 1,000 employees and 60 percent of those employing between 500 and 999 employees are multinationals.

Social and Cultural Values

The social and cultural values that determine the nature of labor laws and industrial relations in Belgium largely coincide with the legal foundations of economic power in a free-enterprise economy. Economic power in Western society rests mainly on four fundamental options. The first three of these enable individuals or groups of individuals to obtain decision-making power over goods; the fourth gives the same individuals or groups of individuals power over people (employees). The first fundamental option is the *right to own property*; this right enables the owner to dispose of, exploit, and benefit from property and to make a profit from it. The second fundamental option is the *freedom of commerce and industry*, which was introduced in Belgium in 1791 when the medieval guilds and corporations were abolished during the French Revolution. This freedom means that any person has the *freedom of association*; individuals can associate with others in order to engage in industrial or commercial transactions and, to that end, to increase their own capital in order to maximize any profit that may ensue in case of eventual division. The right to own property, freedom of commerce and industry, and freedom of association still constitute the legal basis for the free-enterprise system.

The fourth option is the *freedom of labor*; the worker is free to choose a job and an employer and has the consequent freedom to conclude an individual labor contract. By means of this contract, the employee engages to work in a position of subordination; that is, under the command, authority, and control of the employer. So the employer gains power over workers, and within limits they have to carry out the employer's orders.

Protective labor laws and trade union action, resulting from collective bargaining as well as from the direct intervention of the state in a mixed economy, have had a dramatic impact in Belgium. These basic values are still the pillars of the social system and fundamentally determine the development of the labor relations system. Belgium is a pluralistic society in which individuals and groups are allowed the freedom to promote their own interests. Social conflict is consequently inevitable and indeed is an essential element in decision-making. In the Belgian industrial relations system, employers and employees, enjoying a large degree of autonomy, settle their conflicts by means of industrial warfare. Conflict and strife are seen as essential to the autonomous decision-making process that characterizes the Belgian labor relations system. Free and effective collective bargaining is in fact impossible when the workers do not, for example, have the freedom to stop work collectively and by so doing try to force the employer to accept their point of view. Or, to put it another way, labor relations are, in Belgium, essentially power relations, whereby the decision-making power of the employer is challenged by the collective powers wielded by the workers. In recent years a new factor has changed labor relations dramatically: the average worker is now better educated and has higher expectations.

The Trade Unions

Almost 70 percent of Belgian workers belong to trade unions, giving Belgium the highest degree of unionization in the EEC. The most important trade unions are the Confederation of Christian Trade Unions (ACV/CSC) and the Socialist Trade Union Movement (ABVV/FGTB). Less important is the Liberal Trade Union Movement (ACLV/CGSLB). In the major sectors of industry—construction, metals, chemicals, cement, petroleum, and mining—almost 90 percent of blue-collar workers are organized. Approximately 40 percent of white-collar workers are organized. Staff or supervisory personnel are rarely organized. Belgian trade unions are not organized on a craft or occupational basis; industrial unions prevail. Both the Socialist and Christian unions have separate, cross-sectoral divisions for white-collar workers.

The FGTB is based on principles of democratic socialism corresponding to those of the Belgian Socialist Party. Its goal is a system of social and economic democracy under which the means of production are at the service of the whole community. Different national unions are affiliated with the FGTB. Each union is an independent organization with its own structure, governing body, and statutory rules. To become affiliated, the union must accept the basic principles of the FGTB and promise to carry out all decisions made by the governing body of the FGTB.

Christian workers in Belgium are grouped together in a national organization called the Christian Labor Movement. The aim of this organization is to defend workers' interests in accordance with Christian social doctrine and the principles of democracy. It is composed of specialized national organizations for economic, cultural, and educational action, such as the CSC, mutual insurance companies, cooperatives, youth movements, women's guilds, and other associations. The nationwide CSC directs the activities of all Christian trade unions in Belgium. The CSC has, essentially, the same structure as the FGTB: it is composed of seventeen national unions organized by industry, which are decentralized at the regional and local levels.

Employers' Associations

The principal association of employers is the Federation of Belgian Enterprises (FEB/VBO). The FEB/VBO is composed of 48 sector associations covering some 35,000 affiliated firms. These national associations cover most branches of economic life, with the exception of agriculture, small shops, handicrafts, and the nationalized industries. The Federation of the Middle Class organizes the small firms, and a number of organizations cover agriculture. The employers' associations not only give legal, fiscal, economic, and other advice to their members, but also engage in collective bargaining. The FEB/VBO is active at the national, interindustry level; the industry-wide associations take care of the sectoral levels. Regional organizations like the Flemish Employers' Association, the Walloon Employers' Association, and the Brussels Federation of Employers are becoming more and more important.

Labor Relations

Interaction between organized workers and employers has resulted in different degrees of institutionalization of labor relations at different levels. This working relationship between labor and management results from a long historical process that started at the end of the last century.

At the level of the enterprise or establishment, three different bodies may represent respectively the employers and the employees of the trade unions: the union delegation, the labor council, and the committee for safety and health and embellishment of the place of work. Joint committees function at the branch or industry level, and the National Labor Council, created in 1952, functions at the national interprofessional or interindustrial level.

The Union Delegation

The union delegation represents the unionized employees in the enterprise and has to be established if requested by one or more representative trade unions. The union delegates are employees of the enterprise and are either appointed by the unions or elected by the unionized employees of the enterprise. The union delegation has a demanding and contentious role with regard to wages and working conditions—in the broadest possible sense—in the enterprise. Delegates can present and discuss individual and collective grievances and demands, as well as supervise the application of collective agreements and the maintenance of labor law standards in the enterprise.

The Labor Council

A labor council has to be established in every enterprise employing (on average during the four preceding trimesters) a minimum of 100 employees. The labor council is composed, on one side, of the employer and one or more representatives or their proxies from the enterprise chosen by him. He is free to choose whomever he wants to represent him from among the managerial employees and can have as many representatives as he wants provided that he does not exceed the number of employee representatives. On the other side, the labor council is composed of a number of employee representatives. The number of representatives (with a minimum of 2 and a maximum of 25) varies with the size of the enterprise. The labor council is largely an informative and advisory body; the employer retains the decision-making power.

The Joint Committees

Joint committees have played an important role in Belgian labor relations ever since their introduction into collective bargaining, the settlement of industrial disputes, and the implementation of social legislation and labor standards. The first joint committees were established on a pragmatic basis in the mining and metalworking industries after World War I.

Joint committees are established by royal decree at the request of, or at least after consultation with, the most representative employers' association and trade unions. The joint committees are composed of a chairperson and an equal number of representatives of the employers' associations and the trade unions. The joint committees collaborate in the drafting of collective bargaining agreements between the organizations represented; prevent disputes, or resolve disputes, between employers and workers; and advise the government and the National Labor Council.

One of the most important tasks of the joint committees is, of course, to promote collective agreements between the employers' associations and trade unions represented on the committee. These agreements on wages and working conditions cover, broadly speaking and certainly in the case of an extension by royal decree, every employer and employee in a given branch of industry. The joint committees also play an important role in the prevention and settlement of industrial disputes. To that end, most joint committees have set up a reconciliation committee. In practice the reconciliation committee deals not only with collective disputes (about interests as well as interpretation), but also with individual grievances.

The National Labor Council

The National Labor Council is composed of 24 members equally divided between the employers' associations and the trade unions. The main function of the council is to advise the legislature or the government, either on its own initiative or on request, about general social problems concerning employers and workers. In practice the council has great prestige and is frequently consulted by the government. The law of December 5, 1968, gave the National Labor Council the explicit competence to conclude collective labor agreements. The council has made extensive use of this power. Since 1970 no less than 42 agreements have been concluded.

Collective Bargaining and Industrial Conflict

The Belgian social partners, especially the trade unions, believe in free collective bargaining without any government intervention, particularly with regard to wages. Free collective bargaining has been one of the major characteristics of Belgian labor relations during the past 25 years, with some exceptions. The fact that collective agreements set only minimum conditions makes it possible to conclude collective agreements at different levels and to develop a system of cumulative bargaining: at the national interindustry level, at the sectoral level, at the regional level, and finally at the enterprise level. Belgian employees have a right to strike. Recently the number of strikes has diminished.

Flexibility in Labor Relations

For the Christian Democratic–Conservative government that came to power in 1981, flexibility is one element in its battle to restore the competitiveness of Belgian industry. Flexibility seems to be part of a long-term strategy and can be seen in the Social Recovery Act of 1985, which made changes in provisions concerning the protection of wages, work rules and conditions, closure of enterprises, and the like. An act of March 1987 allows enterprises in general to work for twelve hours a day and, for economic reasons, allows Sunday work, night work for men, and work on holidays provided collective agreements have been concluded to this end.

Although employers have insisted that minimum wages are too high, especially for youth, minimum wages have been neither abolished nor diminished, except in cases of new forms of apprenticeship. A far-reaching wage freeze was enacted during the 1981–86 period, and the cost-of-living clause has been reconsidered.

No two-tier systems of pay have been introduced. Today free bargaining on wages has been reintroduced, and agreements concluded undoubtedly reflect the changed power relationships. Agreements concluded up to March 1987, covering 25 sectors and 1.1 million of the 1.9 million private-sector employees, call for wage increases of between 2.5 and 4.5 percent over a period of two years.

Part-time and temporary workers continue to enjoy equal treatment with full-time or permanent workers. The number of part-time workers has increased considerably. Proposals to remunerate for individual performance and/or performance of the enterprise have not been on the agenda for collective agreements.

A proposal by the government to establish profit-sharing for employees, who would be taxed at only a 25 percent rate, is still pending. To that end a collective agreement would have to be concluded, and the enterprise would have to increase its work force by 1 percent. Employers are not enthusiastic about this proposal.

Overall, flexibility has had, up to now, rather marginal effects. Its greatest impacts were the far-reaching wage freeze (1981–86) and the considerable relaxation in March 1987 of rules regarding working time.

Employment

Jacques Delcourt

BY THE END OF 1973, economic growth had slowed considerably in all European countries, including Belgium. This caused rising unemployment and social integration problems, particularly for young people. A number of theories have been advanced to explain this economic upheaval, including trade union extremism, continual salary growth, and runaway inflation. Spiraling oil and commodity prices following the Israeli-Arab wars and successive oil crises have also been cited as possible causes, along with the suspension of dollar convertibility in 1971. With hindsight, the question can be asked whether these were not merely a series of epiphenomena caused by changes in the international division of labor. This explanation is more fundamental and provides a framework in which the changes since 1973 can be better perceived. Because of these changes, full employment has been replaced by underemployment or unemployment, and both employment status and actual jobs have become more precarious.

The creation of the Common Market in 1958 coincided with a new phase of internationalization of production. Thereafter vast amounts were invested in the internationalization of industrial and trading firms, banks, finance houses, and insurance companies. The trend toward internationalization was set in motion by the communications and transport "revolution," which facilitated the circulation of people, goods, information, finance, and therefore currency. Under the old international division of labor, certain Third World countries, both colonial and independent, exported commodities and raw materials and imported finished goods from the developed world. Trade was already on a world scale, but the same could not be said of production. When the system changed, developing and developed countries alike entered an era of "intercontinental," or world, production. The age of overseas and criss-cross investment on a continental and international scale had begun.

This internationalization of production has had a number of consequences. First, the need for transport and trade facilities between the various points of production has resulted in massive investment in harbor extensions (particularly in deep water), port installations for storage, assembly, and production, motorway links, pipelines, canals, international airports, and intercontinental communications centers. The immense amount of private investment has been matched by expenditure by countries anxious to stake out a good place for their economy on the world development ladder. The internationalization of transport, communications, and trade quickly affected industrial restructuring and redeployment. At the same time, the more wealthy countries continued to follow a policy of high salaries and the extension of the social security umbrella, leading to expansion of the social services sector.

The new countries now entering the industrialization race depend on equipment and technology supplied by more developed countries, which have thus become involved in engineering, design, and implementation of large-scale projects, turnkey factories through company consortiums, or the creation of large assembly plants. In the more developed countries, public and private investment is flooding into ambitious projects. The involvement of the private sector is actively encouraged by the state. Front-line development sectors include chemicals, petrochemicals, electronics, aeronautics, telecommunications, nuclear energy, and the arms industry.

The years leading up to the crisis were marked by land and property speculation. In addition to major public and private civil engineering projects prompted by the growing internationalization of the industrial economy, developed countries have seen strong growth in the service sector. In conjunction with engineering work undertaken to reduce the congestion of large urban centers, great numbers of high-rises, administrative blocks, commercial centers, offices, and car parks have been built. Similar growth has been seen in investment in buildings for community and public service, such as schools and universities, hospitals and homes, sports grounds, and youth and cultural clubs.

By 1974, this period of hyper-expansion, corresponding to the introduction of a global production system and a new international division of labor, became alarming. From this point on, a new phase began. Rationalization investment gained the upper hand over expansion investment. The flurry of technological innovation resulting from microprocessors, revolutionizing the way in which information is registered, processed, stored, and transmitted, added weight to this trend. This is the starting point for the analysis of employment.

Overall Evolution, 1970 to the Present

The figures in Table V.1 give a good indication of the general trend in employment from 1970 onwards. These figures show that the current and future growth of population in Belgium is and will remain very low. Growth has been proportionally higher in the population of working age, but this is expected to slow by 1990, reducing the pressure of new generations entering the labor market. This is due to the low birthrate since 1965. The growth in the working population mirrors the growth in the number of people of working age. Total employment has therefore increased during the crisis period. However, many jobs have become precarious, and in other cases people have agreed to work part-time in order to avoid unemployment. Moreover, the working population also includes people seeking work who are therefore technically speaking unemployed. There has also been a contraction of the male working population and parallel growth in the female segment. This scissor-type evolution appears likely to continue for some time.

Table V.1 reveals growth in the number of people fully unemployed over the period under study, particularly women. This may seem paradoxical in light of the rapid growth in the number of women in the working population, but it signifies that female employment is growing more slowly than the number of women seeking work. Many point to the generous nature of unemployment benefits to explain this expansion of female unemployment. However, the lower educational levels of women vis-à-vis men also play a role. Moreover, just as the crisis began, a number of factors acting in conjunction strengthened women's desire to work, such as growth in the number of one-parent families, the higher cost of living, new family leisure and relaxation requirements, and a general decrease in salary growth.

Breakdown by Main Activity Sectors

Table V.2 shows the changes during the period under study with respect to total employment by the main sectors of economic activity: agriculture, industry, and services. The overall level of employment has remained firm, but the distribution of employment by sector has changed considerably. Employment has contracted in agriculture and industry but grown in the services sector. Moreover, a distinct split between the sexes is apparent. Female employment in the agricultural sector has stagnated, and in industry a sharper fall has been seen in female than in male

TABLE V.1
Evolution of Population and Employment
(000s)

Total Population	1970	1975	1980	1985	1990 (est.)
Total	9,651	9,813	9,863	9,859	9,785.5[a]
Index*	100	101.7	102.2	102.1	101.4
Age 15–65	6,082.5	6,285.3	6,461.0	6,635.8	6,538.1
Index*	100	103.3	106.2	109.1	107.5
Working pop. including armed forces	3,824	3,999	4,156	4,214[b]	4,260[c]
Index*	100	140.6	108.7	110.2	111.4
Percent working	62.9%	63.6%	64.3%	63.5%	65.2%
Fully unemployed	71.3	177.4	321.9	476.6	580.0
Index*	100	248.9	451.7	668.8	813.9
Men					
Total	4,722	4,805	4,821	4,812	4,774.8[a]
Index*	100	101.8	102.1	101.9	101.1
Age 15–65	3,028.6	3,148.6	3,243.5	3,328.2	3,284.1
Index*	100	104.0	107.1	109.9	108.4
Working pop. including armed forces	2,598	2,622	2,605	2,561[b]	2,446[c]
Index*	100	100.9	100.2	98.6	94.1
Percent working	85.8%	83.3%	80.3%	76.9%	74.5%
Fully unemployed	42.4	85.2	120.7	209.2	
Index*	100	200.9	284.4	493.6	
Women					
Total	4,929	5,008	5,042	5,047	5,010.7[a]
Index*	100	101.6	102.3	102.4	101.7
Age 15–65	3,053.9	3,136.7	3,217.5	3,307.6	3,254.0
Index*	100	102.7	105.4	108.3	106.5
Working pop. including armed forces	1,226	1,377	1,551	1,653[b]	1,762[c]
Index*	100	112.3	126.5	134.8	143.7
Percent working	40.1%	43.5%	48.2%	50.0%	54.1%
Unemployed	28.874	92.209	201.176	267.428	
Index*	100	319.3	696.7	926.2	
Female unemployed/ total unemployed	40.5%	52.4%	62.5%	56.1%	

SOURCES: Belgium, National Statistical Institute *Bulletin;* Eurostat; Belgium, Planning Office.
*Excluding those on early retirement, those working a limited number of hours, and those participating in unemployment-reduction programs.
[a] 1991   [b] 1984   [c] 1989

TABLE V.2
Employment by Economic Activity Sector
(000s)

Total	1970	1975	1980	1985
Agriculture	174	136	112	106
Index	100	78.2	64.4	60.9
Percent	4.7%	3.6%	2.9%	2.9%
Industry	1,537	1,458	1,276	1,084[a]
Index	100	94.9	83.0	70.5
Percent	41.6%	38.5%	33.6%	29.8%
Services	1,987	2,189	2,409	2,445[a]
Index	100	110.2	121.2	123.0
Percent	53.7%	57.9%	63.4%	67.3%
Total	3,698	3,783	3,797	3,635
Percent	100.0%	100.0%	100.0%	100.0%
Female employment				
Agriculture	38	30	24	44
Percent of total	21.8%	22.1%	21.4%	21.7%
Industry	308	295	232	202[a]
Percent of total	20.0%	20.2%	18.2%	18.6%
Services	833	946	1,076	1,119[a]
Percent of total	41.9	43.2	44.7	45.8
Total	100.0%	100.0%	100.0%	100.0%

SOURCE: Eurostat.
[a] 1984

employment. On the other hand, female employment has expanded remarkably in the services sector, rising to 64 percent at the end of the period in question.

The changes in Belgium do not differ significantly from those in the other EEC member-states, but they are more pronounced. In 1985, agriculture represented less than 3 percent of Belgian employment compared with an EEC average of 8.6 percent. Belgium is also below average for industrial employment, at 30 percent, compared with 33.8 percent for the twelve EEC member-states. It therefore comes as no surprise that Belgium ranks first in the services sector, which represents 67.1 percent of total employment compared with an EEC average of 57.6 percent.

The following factors have played a role in the "deindustrialization" of employment in Belgium: (1) the internationalization of businesses; (2) the development of offshore (foreign) plants; (3) competition from developing countries as a result of technology transfer; (4) the development of subcontracting, facilitated by the breakdown of goods into more or less standardized components; (5) the reduction of passenger and goods transport costs and of communications costs (increasing remote transmission and monitoring possibilities); (6) the rationalization of production through the introduction of new technologies; (7) the structural decline of a number of sectors, such as coal mining and the steel industry due to market saturation or contraction of demand; and (8) the impact in traditional industrial countries of salary growth, trade union militancy, and the development of new social movements, such as ecology and consumer protection, along with regional and social urban movements.

The growth in the tertiary sector has paralleled deindustrialization. It has affected both public and private services for individuals, companies, organizations, communities, and institutions. High-fliers in this process are research, financial services, legal advice, computer technology, accountancy, advertising, marketing, personnel management, and management services. For want of a better term, such tertiary businesses were initially known as "post-industrial," although no clear dividing line can be drawn between industrial and tertiary activities. Today we speak of the industrialization and "merchandising" of services, or of the development of cultural and leisure industries. In the final analysis, a post-industrial economy is characterized by the pre-eminence of intangible capital over tangible capital, such as buildings and plant. Capital is more and more frequently tied in with the production of goods and services with a high degree of incorporated knowledge, using increasingly sophisticated equipment. Computer resources have become a strategic weapon. Machinery is designed in a cybernetic manner using information that guides and controls. Such machinery can be programmed and reprogrammed and tends to favor the breakdown of mass production. It is versatile and reduces the fragmentation of production tasks. In a post-industrial economy—where a continually growing quantity of know-how and culture is incorporated into production and which is characterized by the key role of information and communications technologies—designers, researchers, scientists, engineers, academics, and graduates form an increasing proportion of company staff and public administration.

Daniel Bell was one of the first to coin the term "post-industrial." He emphasized the importance of cultural infrastructure in such a society. In other words, information and communications infrastructure (cables, fiber optics, satellites and antennas, broadcasting and reception equipment) have become more important than the infrastructure characterizing the industrial society, which is given over to the transportation of goods and persons or the supply of water and energy (gas, electricity, oil). In a society built on the development of know-how and culture and relying on industries operating on the basis of creativity and intelligence, continuous training and adaptation of human resources become a strate-

gic task. This explains the scale of investment in the preservation, reproduction, and development of human capital; this in turn contributes to
the multiplication of jobs in the public sector and the growth in public
expenditure in all cultural and social sectors.

The Public and Private Sectors

Even though total employment and the working population have continued to grow slightly since 1975, salaried employment has tailed off,
as shown in Table V.3. That table also reveals growth in public sector employment. This, however, has not been sufficient to compensate for the
contraction in the private sector, despite the range of measures designed
to promote economic recovery in Belgium. The table also shows the remarkable growth in female employment, which represents the strongest
growth in the public sector. At the end of the period in question, women
represented almost 44 percent of public sector employment, compared
with 33 percent in the private sector.

Private sector employment will probably grow more than public sector employment in the future. This is essential, as public budget deficits
grow, the imbalance of social security accounts worsens, and social security contributions stagnate. This has resulted in a public and social security expenditure freeze and a consequent freeze in public sector recruitment. The impact of this situation has been particularly serious on jobs
for people with higher education and university diplomas, for whom the
public sector offers more than 60 percent of employment opportunities.

Geographical Concentration

These fundamental changes in the Belgian economy have culminated
in growing regional imbalances. In theory, a large number of factors

TABLE V.3
Evolution of Salaried Employment
(000s)

	1970	1974	1984
Private sector	2,287.7	2,399.8	2,026.0
Percent female	29.2%	30.0%	33.0%
Public sector	716.2	799.4	971.5
Percent female	36.4%	37.8%	43.9%
Total	3,003.9	3,199.3	2,997.5
Percent public sector	23.8%	25.0%	32.4%

SOURCE: National Labor Council.

should contribute to the switchover of employment to the tertiary sector, including increased possibilities for product changes to meet demand, their breakdown into a number of more or less standardized component parts, the opportunities offered by information technologies for the remote control and monitoring of different production units, the desire of large companies to reorganize themselves into small or medium-sized businesses (multi-centering), subcontracting, and so on. In theory, all these factors should argue for reduced inequality in regional development opportunities. In practice, however, imbalances have remained and have even been accentuated. Up to the present, regional development and planning activities have not proved capable of counterbalancing forces tending toward concentration of activities and employment. In fact, the internationalization of business and the internationalization of the product system favor port activities and the development of a seafaring economy. A number of factors have contributed to this, including transshipment and storage facilities, the possibilities of obtaining a return cargo or of splitting a cargo and sending it off to a number of destinations, the range of services available in major ports, and access to a large "hinterland." This explains the prosperity of areas in Belgium along the Brussels-Antwerp or Ghent-Terneuzen axes (and perhaps in the future the areas around Zeebrugge and Ghent).

The parallel development of the tertiary sector tends, for its part, to result in economic concentration in large urban centers. This is because of the greater availability there of transportation, production, and business services, research and public facilities, and management and administrative services capable of initiating and designing large-scale projects. This process leads to the expansion of large urban centers, such as, in Belgium, Brussels, Antwerp, Ghent, Liège, and Charleroi. One of the major challenges Belgian society faces is closing this gap between regions. At some point, a concerted effort will have to be made to promote the geographical deconcentration of economic activities and to revitalize declining industrial zones and rural areas.

In the long term, a number of factors favor the decentralization of administrative tasks and the geographical dispersion of activities. This will partially satisfy regionalization aspirations, which have been fueled by world geo-economic evolution. This is essential, for the costs of concentrating activities will continue to grow faster than the resultant external savings.

For a number of years, there has been a rapid extension of functional networks formed by local bank and insurance branches and by the various local branches of central institutions. At the same time, with new technology, it makes more sense to manage information and development locally. The competence and capacity of local and regional management have also encouraged the process. High-performance "peripherals" encourage decentralized access to data banks and expertise.

Information and communications technologies are not the only factors stimulating decentralization. The same is true of various applications of microelectronics, laser technology, genetics, food and pharmaceutical agrichemistry, and low-temperature chemical processes (less than 80°C). Moreover, "soft" energy forms are now becoming feasible for the manufacture of a whole range of products. The use of alternative energies, the miniaturization of production equipment and of the products themselves, along with their simplification and the compression resulting from the use of electronics and new materials, work in favor of regionalization and ruralization of various types of production, as well as a redevelopment of work in the home.

Redevelopment opportunities for the regions are thus to be found in the accelerated diffusion of know-how and technology, in regional capacities for information management, and in increased access possibilities to major collective data banks. Parallel to this, regions have begun searching for a separate identity, a past and a culture that the industrial revolution seemed to have destroyed. Local and voluntary associations have been formed, mobilizing local people and bringing fresh life to the region. Such associations also have new means at their disposal to develop regional identity and culture. Measures for the dilution of business and geographical decentralization are also contributing to this process.

Growth of Unemployment

In addition to this weakening of regional opportunity, the structural changes that have rocked the Belgian economy have resulted in continual growth in unemployment. An increasing number of people seem unable to find a niche in the new economic organization. Table V.1 revealed the rapid growth in unemployment over the period under study, as well as forecasts, which are far from promising. The question of female unemployment is discussed above. The most pressing problem is that of youth unemployment (see Table V.4).

Youth unemployment has continued to grow despite the raising of the school-leaving age to eighteen in 1983. It has expanded despite training courses, government work-creation programs, and the creation of the status "special temporary executive" (CST) and that of "third work circuit" (TCT). It has grown despite measures to cut employers' social

TABLE V.4
Number of Fully Unemployed Persons Under 25

	1970	1975	1985	1990 (est.)
Men	3,134	7,877[a]	54,581	—
Women	7,323	19,110[a]	85,966	—
Total	10,457	26,987	140,547	—
Percent female	70%	70.8%	61.2%	—
Total unemployment	71,261	177,367	476,629	580,000
Percent female	14.7%	15.2%	29.5%	—

[a] 1974

TABLE V.5
Evolution of Youth Unemployment (Under 25) by Educational Level
(monthly averages)

	1971		1976		1985[a]	
	Number	Percent	Number	Percent	Number	Percent
Elementary education	5,142	42.2%	32,851	41.6%	30,123	23.6%
Total lower secondary education	3,241	26.6	21,446	27.1	48,389	37.8
General training	773	6.2	4,069	5.1	6,130	4.8
Technical[b]	1,080	8.9	7,111	9.0	9,621	7.5
Vocational	1,388	11.4	10,266	13.0	32,638	25.5
Total upper secondary	1,522	12.5	15,949	20.2	34,598	27.0
General training	470	3.9	5,455	6.9	7,582	5.9
Technical[b]	723	5.9	6,496	8.2	10,874	8.5
Vocational[b]	329	2.7	3,998	5.1	16,142	12.6
Total higher education	1,727	14.1	7,319	9.2	8,464	6.6
Nonuniversity	1,607	13.2	6,131	7.7	7,670	6.0
University	120	1.0	1,188	1.5	794	0.6
Apprenticeship	440	3.6	1,176	1.5	5,360	4.2
Other studies	127	1.0	284	0.4	929	0.7
TOTAL	12,199	100.0%	79,025	100.0%	127,953	100.0%

SOURCE: National Employment Office.
[a] Year-end 1985.
[b] Including "social advancement" classes (adult education).

security contributions and moderate salary growth and to introduce a longer delay between the time young people become unemployed and the time they are entitled to benefits. But unemployment does not affect all young people evenly. As Table V.5 shows, it tends to hit the least-qualified hardest. The time out of work expands inversely in relation to qualifications. There can therefore be no doubt of the need for more basic and vocational training measures. Adequate and sufficiently specialized training is a prerequisite or at least a help for someone seeking a job.

Youth unemployment is not simply tied in with a lack of training. It is also due to a lack of jobs within developed economies and a considerable contraction in the number of low-qualified jobs due to rationalization investment, the introduction of new technologies and of new forms of work organization, and the decline of certain traditional sectors.

Young workers are the main group to have seen their employment opportunities evaporate in this period, both in urban areas and in what were once industrial basins. The sharpest contractions in the employment of people under age 25 came in the metal-processing and mechanical engineering industries (-50 percent between 1974 and 1984), other manufacturing sectors (-73 percent), construction and civil engineering (-28 percent), and the non-energy minerals and chemical sectors (-23 percent). Between 1974 and 1984, it is estimated that 190,000 jobs were lost in the industrial sectors, or almost one-third (31.5 percent) of employment opportunities.

This decline in employment opportunities is, however, not confined to industry. A similar phenomenon can be seen in the services sector. The use of computer technology and new means of production, communications, and information storage have cut a considerable number of jobs open to low-qualified young people, for example, in the banking, finance, and insurance sectors. Some people claim that this is counterbalanced by growth in various snack and fast-food restaurants. Analysis reveals, however, that such restaurants have eliminated the need for dishwashers, waiters/waitresses, and cooks. All that is required are a few people to assemble and package the food. The extension of the self-service system to various businesses and public sector services has accentuated the impact of this situation.

This explains youth unemployment in towns that are tertiary service centers. In addition to the elimination of opportunities for poorly qualified young people, there is a growing gap between jobs to which they have access and the rest of the qualifications pyramid. The majority of unqualified jobs today offer little hope of promotion to the higher echelons. Although it is possible to learn the job or the rudiments of customer service, it is becoming less and less feasible, on the basis of training in one of these jobs, to build a career or to learn on-the-job qualifications that could lead to promotion. Even though the new economic organization offers opportunities for seasonal, part-time, or weekend work along with a number of other badly paid jobs, young people are not offered any real chance of improving their qualifications or of being promoted.

We must find means to help these young people, who have failed at school or not taken their education far enough, to obtain the necessary professional qualifications to rise above the assistance quagmire. This is especially vital given that the normal rules of social interplay work against them. Companies, for example, operate on the principle of "last in, first out." In addition, employers are wary of poorly qualified young people, who are hastily classed as antisocial or unemployable. Older workers are also wary of their younger counterparts, for in a situation of scarce employment, any steps encouraging the employment of young people could, conversely, threaten that of more experienced workers. The problem of youth unemployment is therefore not only a question of poor training or possible discrimination against young people. It is first and foremost due to a lack of suitable jobs and to economic and technological changes that have aggravated the situation.

Local employment initiatives and encouragement for project promoters whether in the public or private sector offer a glimmer of hope. However, it is not enough to give an unemployed person an opportunity to create his or her own job. If the method is to be fully implemented, a class of socially oriented entrepreneurs must be formed, and project coordination centers must be created. In other words, it is not merely a question of subsidizing investment or employment, or of providing financial stimulus for initiative. Very little has been done systematically on this front to animate and develop a social market economic sector that could use to the maximum the capacities of this underprivileged group of young people. There must be a driving force behind this initiative in order to promote its gestation and to assess projects. This driving force must help form operational links, assess chances and markets, provide means, resources, and expertise, and draw together plant and financial means. In this field, the state, the community, and regional and local organizations must play the role of catalyst. For, in order to develop a viable social market sector, project "nurseries" must be organized, along with structures for gradually moving projects into the real work environment. There must be training for managers and social entrepreneurs. Without this, the parallel economy will flourish.

According to OECD experts, the most developed economies seem to have been emerging from the crisis since 1984. An optimistic note has also been struck by reports published by the Belgian Scientific Policy Planning Services (SPPS). A 1986 report even predicted a shortage of university graduates by the year 2000 because of demographic evolution, particularly the arrival of fewer young people on the employment market, and more especially because of technological evolution requiring highly qualified staff. In addition, replacement requirements appear set to grow. More than forty years have passed since World War II. In this period, a growing number of university graduates have stepped into the shoes of executives who had no university education. This rate of substitution will now probably slow, but replacement demand will soon expand.

Such a hypothesis is perhaps too optimistic. It is difficult to predict the effect of the computer, at least in the public sector. Recent research has underlined that employees in the public sector file, process, and store information using a range of communications systems. Thorough computerization of these services could drastically reduce the number of employees required in public administration. In addition, the slowing of state expenditure, cuts in social security expenditure, and the reluctance of taxpayers and social security contributors to pay more than is absolutely necessary will deal a severe blow to civil service recruitment. In the private sector, on the other hand, the deindustrialization movement seems to have run out of steam, and forms of "reindustrialization" will now take place through the manufacture of products with a high added intellectual and cultural value, the increased use of front-line and new technology, and in particular the proliferation of viable small and medium-sized enterprises (SME).

Fresh growth in SME is due essentially to the gradual transformation of lifestyles and needs, resulting in what Alvin Toffler has termed the "de-massification" of mass production. Thus, despite unemployment and underemployment, the proportion of salaries available for the purchase of new services and goods would seem to be on the rise. This, for example, is seen in people's leisure pursuits and in the high-tech equipment they have in their homes. Cultural activities and tourism are also growing and are reflected in the development of hotels and restaurants. Families are spending more on high-tech equipment and on home decoration. People now have more leisure time, are better educated, feel they have a right to "do their own thing," search for personal well-being, and have an opportunity to develop a taste for luxury and art. Consumption should become more refined and diversified as a result. This has found expression, for example, in the development of craft industries and art, design, and decoration businesses, companies specializing in the production of more or less exclusive articles, body and beauty care concerns, companies manufacturing sports and leisure clothes, furniture firms specializing in the decoration of private houses and institutions, or firms specializing in the production of open-plan offices or background music.

Expanding SME include firms that respond to new and growing requirements for training and culture. Belgian society is becoming highly education-conscious. One group of SME concentrates on the search for the quality of life or for ecological development and fights for the provision of new services to individuals, for the revitalization and improvement of the habitat against various forms of pollution, for water purification and waste recycling in order to stimulate energy savings, and for greater safety at home or at work. SME development has also been prompted by the development of amateur and spectator sports, the explosion of the communications society, and the expanding culture industry. Finally, SME proliferation is a consequence of subcontracting diversification, notably through operational specialization, in areas such as equipment, repair, packaging, handling, or transport and in fields such as cleaning and maintenance. On the whole, expansion in this area will probably absorb qualified, rather than poorly qualified workers, but it will not necessarily absorb the full slack of job seekers.

The Welfare System

Herman Deleeck

IN BELGIUM, WELL-BEING AND POVERTY have to be considered in relation to the welfare system itself and to its effect on the people. The Belgian welfare system is typical of the continental type of Western European welfare system. Welfare systems are features of wealthy societies. In 1985, it amounted in Belgium to $12,420 per capita of the GNP compared with a national income of $10,010 per capita. With the welfare system, the government guarantees basic social rights according to an extensive system of allowances, social goods, and services in such areas as guaranteed income, education, health, housing, and culture. Thus, the amount of social expenditures has become very large (38 percent of the GNP in 1980). The welfare system, therefore, requires a *new type of income distribution.*

The welfare status of a family is determined by income from labor; a large number of social benefits; free or quasi-free social goods and services; and high taxes and social security contributions to finance the above. These four elements must be considered in determining income distribution. The distribution process has therefore become complex politically and socially because the citizens have not always seen the link between what they pay and what they receive.

The welfare system is also a special type of decision-making process in which the government, the social organizations, and private business are involved institutionally. The extensive system of welfare facilities is regulated by the government, but associations of workers, employers, farmers, and shopkeepers are also actively involved. They share responsibility for regulating, managing, and implementing the system by means of a network of councils providing consultation, advice, and administration. The implementation of the welfare system is confined, by law, to social organizations of which the trade unions and welfare societies are the most important. The characteristics of the Belgian welfare system are found to a lesser degree in other continental European countries. The system of welfare funding has, since the end of the nineteenth century, grown out of local initiatives, especially those of labor organizations. From the start, socialist and Christian democratic organizations have been adversaries. Until today, the management and execution of the welfare system have been in the hands of social organizations divided by ideology. Decentralization, pluralism, and liberty of choice are the most essential characteristics of the Belgian system of social administration; they set the tone for the whole political and social life.

Compulsory health insurance is implemented by welfare societies, the Christian and socialist societies being by far the most important ones. Membership in a welfare society is compulsory, but the choice of which one to join is free. The National Institute of Health Insurance is managed by a council of representatives from trade unions, welfare societies, and employers' organizations. Membership in trade unions is voluntary; however, 70 percent of employees are members. There are Christian and socialist unions and a small Liberal one. Unemployment benefits are paid out by the trade unions.

It has been said that the present social security system was founded in 1944. This is not the case. After World War II the existing system of social security was unified and generally made compulsory. During the German occupation (1940–44), representatives of employers and employees agreed clandestinely to a Social Solidarity Union. After the war, both parties wanted to cooperate in rebuilding industry and increasing productivity in order to raise the standard of living and reinforce the social security system. The spirit of this agreement dominated the social security system during the whole period of growth of the welfare system (up to 1975); the main power for social matters was placed in the hands of the social partners, making the trade unions and the welfare societies the most important and powerful actors in the administration of social policies.

An extensive socialization of the national income went, therefore, hand in hand with the maintenance of free enterprise and free choice by the citizens. Thus, the Belgian welfare system is an optimal combination of freedom and solidarity. This is true in theory and in fact. However, a number of problems have arisen, especially since the ending around 1975 of the "golden years."

Economic Growth and Social Expenditure

Belgium's GNP almost tripled in real value between 1950 and 1985; during this time public social expenditure increased from 10 percent

TABLE V.6
Social Expenditure as Percentage of GNP

	1960	1980
Social security	10.5%	25.1%
Education	4.5	8.0
Health care	2.7	5.1
Social housing	(0.5)	(0.7)
Total social expenditure	17.6	38.2
Total public expenditure	30.8	52.5

SOURCE: OECD, *Social Expenditure, 1960–1990.*

TABLE V.7
Social Security as Percentage of GNP in the EEC

	1970	1975	1980	1983
Netherlands	20.8%	28.1%	30.4%	33.9%
Belgium	18.7	24.2	28.1	30.9
Denmark	19.6	25.8	28.7	30.6
West Germany	21.5	29.8	28.5	29.1
Luxembourg	15.9	22.3	25.9	26.5
France	19.2	22.9	25.9	29.0
Italy	17.4	22.6	22.8	27.1
United Kingdom	15.9	19.4	21.4	23.8
Ireland	13.2	19.7	21.0	23.9
Average	19.0	24.7	25.8	28.0

SOURCE: Eurostat, *European Community.*

to 40 percent of the GNP. Table V.6 illustrates the enormous growth of the Belgian welfare system since World War II. The greatest increase in social security expenditure (including assistance) occurred between 1970 and 1975, when it increased 2.5 times.

Within the European Community, Belgium has shown the largest budget and the greatest increase over time in expenditures for social security (see Table V.7). The welfare system developed gradually during the postwar period and was supported by a steadily growing economy. This process peaked at the beginning of the 1970's. From 1975 on, economic growth decreased and unemployment increased. However, social expenditures declined only moderately during the 1980's, thanks to a policy of moderation and recovery.

In general, the growth of social expenditures in Belgium has followed a trend visible in other Western European countries. The influence of employees in the labor force has grown steadily (85 percent in 1984), with a parallel increase in social security benefits (unemployment, disability, retirement). Following an extension in the years of schooling, expenses for education and family allowances increased. The aging of the population and the wastage of manpower due to retirement increased the budget for benefits to the elderly. Higher standards of living, together with great advances in medical technology, increased health insurance benefits dramatically. These factors caused an almost uncontrollable growth in the social system. They are at the root of today's problems with the budget and social security.

The Social Security System

The Belgian social security system is of the so-called Bismarckian type. It is structured around job classification groups and provides social protection to the insured belonging to one of these groups. It comprises three separate systems: social insurance in the private sector organized through the general system for wage-earners; social insurance in the private sector for the self-employed; and a social protection system in the public sector for permanently appointed civil servants.

The Belgian social security system also has its own system of insurance. The right to an allowance depends on contributions made to the system during a certain period of working time. These contributions are based on each employee's wages and on the earnings of the self-employed. The social insurance system thus offers social protection to almost all the population, but, due to its requirements of employment and contribution payments, it is not entirely adequate for providing a minimum income to every citizen at any given time. In order to ensure a minimum income to those few who slip through the social insurance network, the social security system extends protection through a residual system of social assistance benefits (see Table V.8).

There are two main types of social insurance allowances: replacement income and the compensatory benefits. A replacement income makes up

TABLE V.8
Social Security Expenditure as Percentage of GNP

	1960	1985
Health care	1.7%	5.1%
Industrial disability	0.6	2.0
Pensions	3.9	7.2
Unemployment	1.2	4.4
Child allowances	2.3	2.5
TOTAL	10.4	24.5

SOURCE: Belgium, Ministry of Social Affairs.

for labor income lost through sickness, unemployment, or old age. It equals a certain percentage of the lost labor income and thus guarantees maintenance of existing standards of living, within minimum and maximum limits. Compensatory benefits are flat-rate payments compensating for medical care and parenthood expenses. A fixed allowance per child is provided. Medical care expenses are partially reimbursed. In Belgium, medical care is free, and relations between physicians, hospitals, and health insurance providers are regulated by conventions.

For wage-earners, there are seven different schemes in the social security system: pensions, health care allowances, sickness and disability benefits, unemployment benefits, child allowances, compensation for employment-related accidents, and compensation for occupational diseases. Only four schemes exist for the self-employed: pensions, health care allowances, disability benefits, and child allowances. Permanently appointed civil servants who are guaranteed a steady income are covered by statute for old age and disability pensions and for child allowances. Their health care coverage is equivalent to that of wage-earners in general. The social insurance schemes are financed through employer and employee payroll deductions and through payments by self-employed individuals. In addition, they are subsidized by the government.

The Belgian social security system is financed through contributions based on work income (indirect wages). Thus the management of the social security institutions is in the hands of the job category organizations involved (employees and employers), which also participate in decision-making. Depending on the case, social security payments are made by powerful autonomous social organizations such as trade unions (unemployment benefits) and welfare societies (health care and disability benefits). Social assistance benefits, which provide only a safety net, are financed entirely by the government. There are four different areas of social assistance benefits: the unquestionable right of each citizen to a minimum income necessary for survival; the right of the elderly to a guaranteed income, claimable by those who have a pension below the guaranteed income or who have no pension at all; the guaranteed income allowance for the handicapped; and the guaranteed child allowance for mothers of children who cannot claim child allowances within the social security system.

In 1985, about 24 percent of the GNP was spent on social security. The greatest part went to pensions (29.1 percent), then to sickness and disability (28.8 percent), unemployment (18.0 percent), and child allowances (7.5 percent). Employment-related accidents accounted for 3 percent of the expenses, occupational diseases 1.4 percent, and social assistance benefits 2 percent. In 1985, 40 percent of this amount was financed through contributions by employers, 27 percent through contributions by those insured, and 29 percent by government subsidies.

Education

In Belgium, education is provided by the central government, by private organizations (mainly Catholic), and by each of the nine provinces and municipalities. The relationship between the different "school networks" has been a major political issue in Belgian history. The "school war" (1954–58) was brought to an end in 1958 by the School Pact, an agreement among the three main political parties (Christian Democrats, Socialists, and Liberals). It introduced an equitable distribution of state grants for education among all kinds of approved schools. Although 70 percent of students attend Catholic schools, parents are free to choose between state and private schools for their children.

In Belgium, education is compulsory from age six to age eighteen. There are three levels of education: elementary (six years); secondary (six years); and higher education. On completion of elementary school at age twelve, a pupil passes into the secondary education system (see Part VI). The successful completion of secondary education entitles a student to attend higher education courses either at the universities or at non-university schools of higher education. No fees are required for primary and secondary education, and only modest fees are charged for higher education. Allowances are granted by the central government to students in secondary and higher education. In order to qualify, the student must depend on parental or family income below a defined minimum. Allowances are rather low for secondary education students but can be substantial for students in higher education. A quarter of the university students and almost half of those in non-university schools of higher education receive scholarships. At universities, social expenditures such as social services, student accommodations, and health services are subsidized by the state.

The abolition of fees in all schools (up to the university level), both public and private (mainly Catholic), has forced the state to pay for current expenditures, including teachers' wages, in all schools. The state, however, is responsible only for the maintenance of public school buildings. The private schools are, nevertheless, entitled to compensation for building expenses.

The School Pact and the coexistence of two school systems have stimulated the development of secondary and higher education. The Belgian educational system is high in quality but expensive, not to individuals but to the state. The level of schooling is the highest of the European Community. In 1984, 13 percent of eighteen-year-olds attended universities and 40 percent attended non-university schools of higher education. The democratization of the educational system has gone very far; everyone who wants to study can do so without financial barriers. However, because of sociocultural differences in aspirations, there are still large social differences in participation in these educational opportunities. With a welfare system, this situation cannot be changed by decree.

Housing

In Belgium, housing policy is oriented toward private ownership of middle-sized dwellings, especially for moderate- and low-income households. In 1981, some 61 percent of all dwellings were owner-occupied. This is by far the largest proportion of owner-occupied dwellings in the whole of Europe. Because of extensive building, strongly stimulated by the government, there has never been any lack of houses since the end of World War II. The most important support for this policy of "social housing" has been housing construction subsidized by semipublic housing societies and by subsidized private housing construction and acquisition.

Since World War II, half of all new buildings have been directly subsidized. Within the framework of the Belgian welfare system, the social organizations of various ideologies have played an active part in the building and financing of housing through regional housing societies. In the social rent sector, subsidies covered 14 percent of all rented dwellings. The 1948 De Taeye Act introduced three kinds of subsidies for promoting broad social ownership: building premiums for persons building their own home, purchase premiums for private individuals buying a dwelling built by a social housing society, and credit facilities such as low-interest mortgages and fiscal advantages. These three provisions are available only to those under certain ceilings, depending on the type of dwelling and the maximum taxable income. Psychologically, the ownership of a family home is a high priority for the great majority of Belgians.

Poverty and the Paradox of the Welfare System

Even though in 1985 about 24 percent of the GNP was spent on social security, a considerable part of the population still finds itself in a position of financial insecurity. Studies carried out by the Center for Social

TABLE V.9
Number of Financially Insecure Households by Social Categories,
1976–1985

	Percentage of insecure households		Percent of the sample	
	1976	1985	1976	1985
Total population	24%	21%	100%	100%
Unemployed	51	60	3	3
Pensioned	40	35	26	27
Disabled	49	44	2	2
Young heads of families (<age 30)	13	11	11	11
Female heads of families	35	35	13	17
Widows	34	36	13	11
Divorced women	33	36	2	4
Households with two workers	7	4	26	30
Elementary education only	34	38	48	34
Unskilled workers	41	46	14	12

Policy at Antwerp University in 1976, 1982, and 1985 have shown that about 23 percent of households are financially insecure (i.e., their total income was lower than that regarded by the population as being a decent social minimum for various types of households; see Table V.9). The study also found that 7 percent of households were apparently living in a state of poverty. Despite the financial crisis, social insecurity did not increase between 1976 and 1985 because the structure of the socially insecure group changed. There were fewer old people in this group because of improved pension schemes but more working-class people because of unemployment. Analysis of the situation shows that social insecurity is not randomly spread over the entire population but concentrated among the elderly, disabled, long-term unemployed with no other income at their disposal, and, to an increasing degree, separated families. Moreover, these social groups are financially insecure because they remain in a socially helpless situation given their low education and professional training, scanty occupational qualifications, unstable employment, and low social background. Financial insecurity and modern poverty seem linked to the existing social stratification of the population. The paradoxical conclusion of this analysis is that persons who have to live only on social security benefits are in a position of financial insecurity precisely because of low benefits they cannot supplement. In other words, a second income would give a stronger guarantee of financial security than the social security system itself can give!

Poverty is an evolutionary concept; new forms appear while others disappear. The problem of poverty has always concerned—and still does concern—the elderly, a generation with little schooling, a weak position in the labor market, and a less favorable work history. One of the achievements of social policy, the so-called "maturation" of pensions, is that the share going to elderly people defined as poor seems to be decreasing rather than increasing, despite the aging of the population. A few years ago the concept of the "new poverty" was introduced. Various causes for this phenomenon have been suggested: generalized unemployment; destabilization of traditional family structures (i.e., growing number of divorces, of one-parent families, and of single persons), leading to a situation in which proportionally more female than male heads of family belong to the group of poor people. Also, the rise in the number of young families with two wage-earners puts families with one income in a relatively weaker financial position. The new poverty is characteristic more of pure financial deficiencies than of sociocultural factors.

The presence of poverty in the welfare system is an eternal contradiction. How can this be understood? First, it has to be clear that poverty is a relative and gradual phenomenon. For this reason, we prefer to speak about financial social insecurity rather than poverty. One is poor by comparison with the wealth of compatriots. In that sense, Western European poverty is a very serious form of poverty. There are degrees of poverty; the very poor are small in number. Less than 2 percent of the population receives the guaranteed income, the means-tested allowance for those people (working-class people, the elderly, the handicapped) who do not have an income of their own or who have no claim for legal or administrative reasons to social security allowances.

Four elements in the Belgian social security system prevent a serious degree of poverty: unemployment benefits without any time restrictions, universal and generous child allowances, automatic cost-of-living adjustments, and, as a safety net, the guaranteed minimum income. Because of this, the problem of poverty, even during times of crisis, is less acute in Belgium than in some other Western European countries. Why then talk about poverty at all? Because the term *poverty* points at the remaining inequality. Also, the fact that a country with a large budget for social expenditure confronts problems of distribution should stimulate a continuous search to improve the efficiency of the highly developed social security system, using the condition of the lowest class in the population as criterion for an acceptable standard of living.

The Matthew Effect

The efficiency of public social expenditure can be seen from other points of view, such as the unequal consumption by social groups of social goods and services. These are offered to the whole population, universally and quasi free, but because of social and cultural differences in values, knowledge, income, the higher social classes make use of social goods and services more readily than do the lower classes. The length and choice of careers are still socially determined; benefits from home ownership or from allowances from the social housing system to buy a house go preferentially to groups with higher incomes; benefits from the use of specialized medical technology, which can lower mortality, are also socially determined. This phenomenon, which is visible in all Western European countries, has been called the "Matthew Effect" (from Matthew 13.12: "For to him who has, more will be given; but from him who has not, even what he has will be taken away"). Because of a number of political, institutional, and sociocultural factors, many benefits of social policies flow more readily toward the higher social classes than toward the lower ones. A large budget for social expenditure does raise the standard of living for everyone, but the growing socialization of the national income does not automatically lead to a more equal distribution of funds. This is not to condemn the welfare system but rather to reflect critically on its efficiency in promoting equal participation in and equal access to the system. This goal reflects the basic democratic ideal behind the welfare system.

Crisis in the Welfare System: Ends and Means

The large budget for social expenditure weighs heavily on the financial capabilities of the national economy. For many years, Belgian society has lived beyond its means. Since 1981, the government's policy of moderation has tried to solve this problem. The high fiscal and social burden created some resistance among citizens and encouraged the development of the so-called informal labor market. Financing social security by means of wage-related contributions stimulated *labor-saving investments* and consequently was responsible for high unemployment.

The process of decision-making called *democratic corporatism*, in which the social partners (employers and employees organizations) set the tone and the government and parliament play only a subordinate role, reinforced the excessive growth of social expenditure during the years of abundance. The government's policy of moderation has been made possible only by means of special powers authorized by parliament in 1982, 1983, and 1986.

A rather unexpected side-effect of the welfare system has been the excessive growth of regulations and administration. Bureaucratic rules frequently make legal claims difficult and complicated, thus especially disadvantaging persons from the lower social classes. Harmonization and simplification of the social law have been urged from all sides but, as yet, without success. The social efficiency of the system, measured in terms of equality of income, welfare, and opportunities, is smaller than one would expect, taking into consideration the large amounts budgeted.

Finally, a number of new problems are appearing in relation to the aging of the population and to the destabilization of the family. The aging of the population has led to a greater proportion of intergenerational income redistribution, and changes in traditional family units have created problems in the guaranteed income system, with less support for the sick and elderly at home. In 1985, 19.5 percent of the population had reached retirement age (60+ years old). It is expected that this percentage will increase to 21.6 percent in the year 2000 and to 28.4 percent in 2025. The birthrate has decreased continuously since 1965. It was 11.6 percent in 1985, or 1.7 births per woman (2.1 births/woman are necessary to replace the existing population).

Belgium is presently at a turning point. First, a crisis in financial means is forcing moderation. This has occurred in Belgium since 1981 in a careful and pragmatic way. The proposals to greatly reduce benefits in the social sector (e.g., by strongly restricting unemployment benefits and replacing them by the means-tested social assistance) or to privatize the social security institutions have not been implemented. The trade unions have been under pressure, but they have enough political power to prevent radical changes in social policies.

In addition to the crisis in financial means, there is a more fundamental crisis of objectives. The modern welfare system must deal further with deep-rooted sociocultural inequalities, become more selective and goal directed, reformulate the needs that must be attended to, and deal with the new lifestyle, family structure, and the aspirations of the younger generations for a new quality of life. Such a long-term reorientation may already be under way.

In recent years, serious efforts have been made to cope with these objectives, as evidenced by a number of documents, such as the reports of the minister of social affairs on the reform of the social security system (1983); demographic perspectives and their effect on pension schemes and family allowances (1987); health policy, home care, and hospitals

(1987); the report of the Royal Commission on Codification, Harmonization, and Simplification of Social Security (1985); and the first report of the Interdepartmental Commission on Poverty (1987).

The Belgian welfare system performs at a high level of efficiency and appears capable of resisting the economic crisis in an acceptable way. As a minister of social affairs put it, "It's a venerable building that has to be renovated urgently, but it must not be pulled down."

Social Security

Roger Dillemans and Dries Simoens

THE BELGIAN SOCIAL SECURITY system is, at the present time, an institution of great importance. This is already evident from its budget. It amounts to one-fourth of the Belgian national income. Social security has become a permanent feature of Belgian society, along with individual property rights, parliamentary democracy, liability for errors, universal suffrage, and so on. It is a stabilizing factor in the social order. The principles of insurance and solidarity on which social security is based are the basic elements of present-day social thinking.

This immense establishment did not develop overnight. Nor was it the result of a well thought out blueprint, the work of a few farseeing persons. On the contrary, it evolved gradually over a period of more than a century. Much time elapsed between the first laws devised to encourage interest in the aged and the law of August 7, 1974, which guaranteed a minimum income to all Belgians lacking income and not covered (insured) by other branches of social security. This evolution took place in three stages. First, a hesitant start was made by saving banks and mutual insurance funds (*mutualité*), which provided limited insurance coverage for such events as disability, old age, and premature death of the head of the family. Later, in the decades following the turn of the century, the stage of "subsidized freedom" started. Although the state did not take the initiative, it granted ever increasing support (in the form of subsidies) to existing insurance and welfare techniques. Finally, in a third stage, the different branches of social security acquired a compulsory character. This last stage, which represents the modern social security system, became final by the decree-law of December 28, 1944. The decree-law sealed the so-called pact of social solidarity, which developed clandestinely during the last years of the war through semiofficial contacts between a small number of employer and employee representatives.

The main features of this social security decree-law were: all branches are compulsory; one single agency (the National Office for Social Security) collects the contributions of the employers and employees; existing private organizations (trade unions, mutual insurance funds, family allowance funds) are maintained and coordinated through a national office. In this national office employers and employees have equal representation. Social security was extended to the self-employed in the mid-1960's.

Around 1970, just before the outbreak of the economic crisis, social welfare arrangements were finally worked out for persons who are neither employees nor self-employed: the handicapped who have never worked, the elderly without a previous occupation, and orphans. Also included in this group were all Belgians without means of support. Common to all these arrangements was the so-called means test, which requires an investigation into the means of support of the beneficiary. Since World War II and in parallel to all these developments was the global remodeling of social security. This remodeling was aimed at "harmonization." As already indicated, the different systems developed separately. Remodeling and harmonization can be considered the continuing development of social security.

Financing

Financing social security is a central issue in the remodeling debate. Presently 70 percent of benefits are financed by contributions from the groups involved—employers, employees, and the self-employed—calculated on the basis of their wages or income; 30 percent are financed by taxes. The latter stands as a security for the financial integrity of social security. The state also guarantees the payment of benefits when traditional security mechanisms (family, savings, private insurance, individual property) are not capable of providing the same security. Guaranteeing the financial security of citizens is predominantly a task for the state, as is education, medical care, and internal (state police) and external (army) security.

In times like the present with extensive unemployment and an aging population, the size of the contributions from the groups involved, namely the working members of the population, decreases. Increasing contributions as an answer to this problem threatens to expand the burden on wages. This may endanger employment even further and discourage initiatives. All this creates one of the dilemmas with which the present social policy has to cope.

Benefits for Specific Demographic Groups

One series of risks covered by social security can be defined as demographic. The financial consequences of raising children and of old age are met by family allowances and pensions. To a certain degree the authorities can control these risks. For example, the authorities can determine the age at which compulsory education ends and the pensionable age begins, within reasonable limits. Thus, in 1982 the upper limit of compulsory education was increased from age fourteen to eighteen. Similarly, at the other end of the occupational span, the pensionable age has, in certain cases, been lowered. However, the normal pensionable age remains fixed at 65 years for men and 60 years for women (an unequal approach to the sexes, which presently is no longer taken for granted).

For the most part, however, the authorities have no control over these risks that are, after all, linked to life itself and influenced by demographic factors. It is exactly this demographic situation in Belgium that is, as in most surrounding countries, particularly unfavorable. The low birthrate after the baby boom of the 1960's (1.7 births per woman, whereas maintaining the population requires 2.1 births) will be followed by an aging population. For social security, this causes an even more unfavorable distribution of working and retired people and consequently of those who pay contributions and those who qualify for an allowance. The gloomy prospect of a reversed population pyramid will be one of the greatest challenges to social security in the future.

Thus one hears more and more talk of a cost-controlling policy. It should be added that pensions are at a fairly adequate level, at least for employees. They are calculated according to the number of professional working years and according to the wages earned during those years. The pensions approximate 75 percent for a head of family or 60 percent for a single person of the average wages earned during the whole career. Additionally, a retired person is allowed to perform a limited amount of work and still keep a pension. In addition to the retirement pension obtained by the employee on reaching the pensionable age, there is also the survivor's pension obtained by the widow or widower of the employee on the death of the latter.

Pensions for the self-employed are less satisfactory. These began only in 1967 and face the problem of inadequate funds. The amounts awarded are very low, even beneath the minimum needed to guarantee a decent human existence. There is hope for improvement, albeit later, because since 1984 real incomes are taken into account instead of flat-rate amounts.

Efforts are being made to compensate for the aging of the population. One of the objectives of child allowances is to stimulate births, thus achieving the historical objective of adapting the wages of a worker to the composition of the family. The latter goal is in accordance with papal encyclical letters. Child allowances consist of a flat amount monthly, paid to the employee regardless of family income. The child allowance legislation is extremely complicated because the basic amounts differ by birth order. Besides these basic rates, increases are also granted according to the age of the child or for handicaps on the part of the child or the worker, or for orphans, children placed in an institution, or children of retired or unemployed persons. The administrative structure of this branch of the social security system is extraordinarily complicated. Research has shown that the amounts awarded are not sufficient to meet the costs of maintenance and education of a child. It should be noted, however, that not only social but also fiscal legislation provides advantages for raising children. Taxable income is reduced by a certain amount per person. The child allowance branch has long had financial reserves. Questions were raised, however, whether these should be used to encourage employment of the mother (by creating day nurseries) or to reward the mother working at home at educational tasks (the socio-pedagogic allowance). Unfortunately, these reserves have been exhausted because they have been applied to meet financial deficits in the pension branch. This has raised hopes of meeting in part the disadvantageous consequences that low birthrates have imposed on the pension branch by cutting costs in the child allowance branch.

Insurance Coverage for Health Care and Disability

A second category of risks can be defined as health risks. A central position in this area is occupied by health insurance, which pursues two objectives: to protect the health of citizens by reimbursing health care costs, and to provide a replacement income for those unable to work due to sickness or disability. The mutual insurance funds are responsible for both kinds of benefits. These funds are ideologically oriented corporations recognized by the state. They also offer social services to their members, apart from health insurance. All forms of medical care reimbursement are provided, although seldom for the complete amount. To counter overuse of health care and to lighten the financial burden on the health insurance system, part of the costs remains chargeable to the individual. These costs are the so-called threshold fees (*ticket moderateur*).

In principle, social security pays directly to the provider of the care, who receives reimbursement from the fund following an accounting of services rendered. Fees are fixed nationally by agreement between the mutual insurance funds and the associations of doctors. The doctors are free to abide by the agreement, and most of them do. The Belgian health insurance system is unlike a national health service on the English model; the Belgian patient freely chooses his or her doctor for each treatment without having to register with a particular one. For costs of health care other than doctor fees, such as hospital nursing and drug prescriptions, the mutual insurance fund pays directly to the provider of the care (the hospital or the pharmacist). In these cases, the patient need not advance the costs.

For certain categories of the population, the principle of free health care is in force, namely, for widows and widowers, orphans, the handicapped, and retired persons with an income below a certain amount. Among health insurance problems are overconsumption as a consequence of an oversupply of medical care (e.g., too many hospital beds) and enormous costs caused by spectacular technological developments (e.g., clinical biology, scanners) and by the aging of the population (40 percent of the health care costs are for the elderly).

The second largest function of health insurance is to provide a replacement income in cases of sickness or disability. This often causes legal discussions. If the evaluation is carried out within the first six months following the sickness or disability, it is based on the worker's former occupation. If it is carried out after that period, the evaluation is in accordance with the job category to which the person belongs with respect to his vocational training.

The first health insurance benefits mentioned (reimbursement of costs paid for medical care) have been extended to the whole population. Those who do not have the status of employee or self-employed are covered if they live at the expense of an employee or a self-employed person (e.g., a wife or a child). The state considers the protection of health so important that in 1967 it extended health care to "persons not yet insured," a last security net. The second sector (income allowances) is reserved for employees and the self-employed. Again, employees enjoy higher allowances linked to their former wages than do the self-employed, who have to be satisfied with flat-rate benefits.

Besides health insurance, there are two other branches of coverage for disability and life insurance: the Industrial Accidents Scheme, which provides coverage for injuries received during and through the execution of the employment contract or on the way to and from work; and the Occupational Diseases Scheme, which offers insurance against certain occupational diseases. The indemnity procedures are largely the same in both cases. They are more advantageous than health insurance in two respects. After a fatal industrial accident or a fatal occupational disease, the surviving members of the victim's family obtain a benefit. In case of permanent incapacity, the victim obtains compensation amounting to a certain percentage of his or her former wages. The compensation can go up to 100 percent and even up to 150 percent if the victim needs assistance from another person. The industrial accidents branch is run by private insurance companies. Since 1987, the occupational diseases branch has also been partly privately supported.

Furthermore, for handicapped persons who have never worked (such as those born deformed) and who consequently cannot qualify for any of the branches of social security mentioned above, a system of allowances has been developed. In this system handicapped persons are granted amounts corresponding to the minimum for existence (see below); this amount is increased by increments according to the degree to which the capacity to live independently is affected.

Unemployment Insurance

Finally, a third series of risks can be defined as economic. This is the domain of unemployment insurance. It provides approximately 450,000 beneficiaries a means of existence. This branch applies only to employees of the private sector. The self-employed or other groups who are out of work and without income must request the "minimum for existence" benefits (discussed later).

It is difficult to compare the Belgian unemployment scheme with that of other Western European countries. It is often said that it is one of the most generous. First, not only former employees but also young school dropouts are beneficiaries. Second, in principle the unemployment benefits are granted for an unlimited period of time. However, the amount of the allowances, though quite high for unemployed who receive a supplement for family dependence (60 percent of the former wages), decreases very quickly for those who are not in this situation, namely an unemployed person living alone or living with a spouse or with a partner receiving a professional or replacement income (40 percent of the former wages after 24 months and after 30 months possibly a minimal flat rate by day).

Unemployment benefits are reserved for persons who are involuntarily unemployed. Some ten provisions of law uphold this obligation: the unemployed must register with the employment office as a person seeking employment. Moreover, he must not be unemployed through his own fault or initiative. For example, when the unemployed person quits his job without just cause, or when she has been dismissed because of an equitable reason resulting from her attitude. Also, she must be available and willing to accept a suitable job. The last obligation is especially important: a central issue here is the notion of a "suitable job." Very long articles define whether a job is suitable or not and whether it can thus be forced on the individual. Training, work, skill, and physical ability are taken into account. Attention is also paid to the labor conditions such as the distance between the dwelling place and the place of work, the necessary tools, possible family hardships, and the like.

In the last few years the regulations have become somewhat more flexible. A formula has been worked out in which an unemployed person accepts a part-time job but remains registered for employment in a full-time job. Such a person receives an unemployment benefit for the hours or days of unemployment. A formula for voluntary career interruption also exists.

The National Office for Labor Provision plays a role in stimulating employment. It fosters a policy of labor mediation by adding financial benefits to the wage costs of an unemployed individual having great difficulties in getting employed (elderly and disabled) and by offering vocational training so that the unemployed person can learn work skills to fill vacancies.

In 1974 the "minimum for existence" was introduced as a security measure to supplement unemployment regulations, and in fact the whole social security system. This system provides a minimum income for persons who have no or insufficient means of support and who are not eligible to receive this assistance because of other social allowances or because of family members with a legal duty to support them. However, the applicant is required to demonstrate a willingness to be employed unless this is shown to be impossible for reasons of health or compelling social circumstances. Those who can cite social circumstance are, for example, single parents, students no longer maintainable at the expense of their parents, and persons responsible for the care of elderly or ill members of the family.

Since 1982 hundreds of alterations have been introduced in social security legislation, thanks to the full powers given to the government by parliament. The keystone of the policy was the partial disconnection of the cost-of-living index to social benefits. Belgium has a system of automatic cost-of-living adjustments. Furthermore, the accumulations of benefits have been straightened out, regulations have been harmonized, and privileges that were no longer justifiable have been phased out. The threshold fee in health insurance has been increased, and replacement incomes have been brought in line with family circumstances. The full powers given to the government by the parliament contain two restrictions: the purchasing power of those with the lowest incomes cannot be touched, and the basic principles of social security must be safeguarded.

In parallel with these developments, a royal committee for the remodeling of social security has been established. This led to a report submitted in 1985 that applies to all branches of social security. The report proposed to improve existing regulations rather than to seek radical changes: Belgian social security has proved its soundness.

Immigration and Foreign Minorities

Albert Martens, Albert Bastenier, and Felice Dassetto

IN 1944, GUNNAR MYRDAL'S monumental *An American Dilemma: The Negro Problem and Modern Democracy* was published. It has since become renowned both in the United States and in Europe. It begins with the lines: "There is a 'Negro problem' in the United States and most Americans are aware of it, although it assumes varying forms and intensity in different regions of the country and among diverse groups of the American people. Americans have to react to it, politically as citizens and, where there are Negroes present in the community, privately as neighbors."

The "immigrant problem" is now viewed in similar terms in Belgium and in the majority of European countries. Although there have been "immigrants" in Belgium for over fifty years, public opinion began to see coexistence as a "problem to be solved" only a few years ago. Much as Myrdal noted for the United States, Belgians react to the presence of a population group known as immigrants who are perceived as a "problem" both as citizens and as neighbors.

Who Are These "Immigrants" and "Foreign Minorities"?

The main groups under study here are the Italians, Spanish, Greeks, Turks, Moroccans, and Yugoslavs who during World War II or after, during the Golden Sixties (1962–66), came to Belgium to work in the mines, the steel industry, construction, textiles, domestic services, and so on.

Initially, these workers came alone. Later, they settled in Belgium with their spouses and children. The overwhelming majority retain their original nationality, even after two or three generations. This trend has been reinforced by the fact that Belgian nationalization legislation is highly restrictive and until recently did not automatically accord Belgian nationality to children born in Belgium. Only a "Belgian" can hand down Belgian nationality to his or her descendants (*ius sanguinis*). However, people who have been living in Belgium for a number of years can, under certain conditions, request naturalization. This is a long and costly procedure, and its outcome is uncertain. Moreover, few immigrants resort to it. Between 1977 and 1985 around 2,000 foreigners (or 0.2 percent of Belgium's foreign population) requested naturalization each year. From a legal point of view, therefore, an immigrant is (and remains) a foreigner, even if Belgium is (and will remain) the country of residence for the immigrant and his family. This ambiguity between the permanent presence of immigrants, which daily becomes more definite, and political and legal nonrecognition of this situation, forms the heart of the immigration question. Immigrants, originally brought in as an additional work force, currently represent 10 percent of the total population and 25 percent of the population of Brussels.

Economic fluctuations attract new laborers and result in fresh recruitment. Employment is a production factor and is inextricably bound to this cyclical chain. Industrialization initially involved the urban work force and later turned to the rural population to take up the slack. After World War I, industry found itself short of cheap labor. Between 1920 and 1930, Belgian mines recruited 60,000 Poles, 30,000 Italians, and 15,000 Czechs, among others, to carry out difficult or dangerous tasks.

After World War II, despite a high unemployment level and government declarations that Belgium would never again bring in foreign labor, the government ratified an agreement putting 60,000 German prisoners of war to work in the mines. After a year, they were replaced by Italians (77,000), whose mass recruitment reflected the economic situation and the level of coal stocks. Italian workers, who carried out difficult and dangerous work for low wages, accounted for 40–60 percent of the coal production needed for national reconstruction (made possible by the Marshall Plan). By the mid-1950's, Italians were proving more difficult to recruit. The large number of accidents in the mines, especially the Marcinelle catastrophe, which wiped out 200 Italian miners and left a tragic mark on mining history, and the improved organization of Italian workers by the trade unions, forced coal mine employers to look elsewhere for cheap labor. They turned to Spain and Greece in 1956. But gradually the coal mines in the southern part of the country (Wallonia) began to be exhausted, and the need for foreign recruitment dwindled. The mining crisis could therefore have represented the end of foreign labor recruitment. However, this proved not to be the case.

Around 1962, when the economy was in full swing, employers made a concerted effort to avoid a shortage of unskilled workers. Consequently, wages for unskilled jobs rose considerably, followed by across-the-board increases. In order to make good any shortfall, the government stipulated that employers could hire not only Italians, Greeks, and Spaniards, but also Turks, Moroccans, and Yugoslavs, without requesting preliminary authorization from the Ministry of Employment and Labor.

Subsequently workers could enter Belgium with a tourist visa. If they found a job and passed a medical examination, they could regularize their situation on the spot. More than 200,000 foreigners took advantage of this system, known as "tourist immigration." They not only entered the mines, but also took jobs throughout industry, the services sector, and the construction sector. Consequently, pockets of immigrants were no longer concentrated in mining centers (Liège, Charleroi, Campine), but were found in all urban centers (Brussels, Antwerp, Ghent). This labor migration halted only when unemployment began to rise in 1967 and trade unions feared they might lose control over management of the labor market. The halt came in two stages. First, in 1967, there was a return to the legal system. In other words, the Ministry of Employment and Labor again had to authorize recruitment of foreigners. Second, in 1974, it became government policy to turn down any application for foreign recruitment to fill an unskilled job.

Besides considerably slowing foreign recruitment, these actions plunged foreign workers in Belgium for a number of years into hiding, for fear that they might be expelled since they could not regularize their situation, either because of a lack of proof or because of the refusal of certain employers to help them. In 1974, they began to seek a change, and under pressure from the churches, trade unions, and charitable associations, the government was obliged to regularize the position of 7,000 clandestine foreign workers, before declaring a halt to the immigration of unskilled workers. Since this date, only qualified workers, white-collar workers, and company executives have been able to obtain work permits from the Ministry of Employment and Labor. Moreover, these are no longer granted to nationals from southern European countries or from North Africa but only to Swedes, Japanese, or North Americans.

From Labor Immigration to Permanent Presence

With more than 350,000 immigrants at the beginning of the 1950's, 450,000 in 1960, and 900,000 in 1985, more than 10 percent of the permanent residents of Belgium are now of foreign origin. These figures are not simply an indication of the scale of immigration to Belgium in the past four decades. They disguise the fact that immigration represents one of the most important events in Belgian demographic and social history. For many years, the mammoth implications of this new phenomenon were perceived only vaguely. The consensus until the middle of the 1970's was that immigration was only a transitional phenomenon with no impact on the future. It was a simple movement of labor that over the long run concerned mainly the economy and not society as a whole. But when it became clear that the economic crisis had not sparked a return of immigrants to their country of origin, but rather accelerated their putting down of roots, views changed sharply. Gradually and not without a great deal of hesitation, it came to be recognized that there could be no question of sending back immigrants, just as it was not a viable option for the United States in the 19th century to throw the slaves back into the sea. The demographic and social events of the previous years were then correctly perceived as a new episode in the country's economic history.

It is impossible to overemphasize the impact of this discovery on Belgian public opinion. Immigration could not simply be seen as the presence of workers who would gradually fade from the social landscape. On the contrary, it created a new population group, ethnically different in some cases, which had set up home in Belgium, a country that considered itself as a mature and closed society. If this population group was destined to remain in Belgium, it could no longer camp on the outskirts of Belgian society. A period of social redefinition of roles has therefore begun.

Stabilization

Whereas in the past, the immigration question was simply one of work force management, necessitating only administrative measures, the same is no longer true today. Migration policy can no longer be conceived as a component of employment policy. Anthropological and social issues must be examined if Belgium is to cope with the interactions that inevitably accompany the process of stabilizing the settlement of ethnic minorities.

Clearly, integration is not taking place at the same pace for all the different groups or in all areas of Belgium. The chronology of successive migration influxes and environmental factors also play a role in the process. Thus, in the past ten years, some foreigners have found a place in Belgian society, whereas others have only just begun the process of integration. It is not reasonable to expect the same level of integration for North Africans and Turks, who are in the early stages of the process, as for the Italians and Spanish, who are at the end of the road.

Moreover, immigrants naturally prefer certain urban centers, such as Brussels, and social balances have been upset there in a way not seen in other regions. In the final analysis, however, the economic, cultural, and political effects of immigration on a city like Brussels are only a more condensed and more visible version of the social impact mentioned above. Individuals and groups either accept or reject new experiences and experience conflict or adapt to harmonious coexistence. This situation gives rise to the "problems" regularly highlighted by the media when speaking of immigration: the isolation of certain ethnic minorities, disparities in education, inequalities in professional status, intercommunal bickering over access to social resources, presumed or real social deviance or delinquency among certain population groups. These are an expression of the obstacles encountered in the process of social and cultural integration of minority communities. They are imbalances resulting from the upheaval of cultural and social frameworks following a large influx of foreigners.

The Moslem component of immigration (Moroccan and Turkish) has become the focus in recent years of discussions of what is very generally termed the "integration" of immigrants, for a number of reasons. However, the main reason is that the Moslem component, which will have a considerable long-term impact and will shape indigenous society in the years to come, has had an impact not because of its size but rather because of obvious differences in cultural and social values it implants in local society. The fact that these values have been introduced during a period when Moslem countries have been experiencing social upheaval characterized first and foremost by religious fundamentalism has not simplified the integration process. Religious fundamentalism and Islamic radicalism have been cited as possible reasons to explain the integration difficulties of Moslem minorities. This issue contains the seeds of confrontation between Islam and the West, with which many European countries are currently grappling. The question of an ethnic stratification of Belgian society is beginning to loom large.

How Can the Dilemma Be Resolved?

Since the major social phenomenon of recent years has been the gradual integration of immigrant groups, political activists with an eye to the future should tackle its fundamental short- and long-term social implications. To talk of immigrants who do not wish to integrate is only to highlight one aspect of the current situation and postpone the inevitable adaptation in attitudes. If political action is to grapple with these complex but unavoidable issues, it must first identify the ultimate objective. This objective, which neither public opinion nor public representatives seem to perceive, is the successful long-term integration of population groups that live side by side. The gradual transformation of temporary labor migrants into citizens is essential, and there is little point in trying to gloss over this fact or play down the consequences. The process is a long-term one of trial and error to find successful methods of integration. The central starting point is the definition of a path to this objective, without allowing setbacks along the way to result in a premature conclusion that the path chosen is a failure.

Among the necessary measures must be the determination of the social and political status of those foreigners for whom the term "immigrant" is outdated. It is highly unlikely that in the near future simpler naturalization procedures will provide a satisfactory solution to this problem. Consequently, immigration laws must be redefined. As in a number of other Western societies, Belgian legislation appears chronically out of date and badly adapted to the new social factors to which the country committed itself when it resorted to massive, peaceful, and potentially stable immigration of foreign labor. Unless, of course, as some people believe, the perpetuation of legal discrimination is the expression of a desire for domination. This is difficult to reconcile with the democratic values to which Belgians claim to adhere. Regardless of this, Belgium now finds itself in a situation where it must ask whether it is realistic to continue excluding all nationals of foreign origin from political decision-making and whether the precarious legal status granted them is still viable for a population group that has traveled a considerable way down the road to integration. An "enlarged" Belgium faces the need for a new "social contract" among all the various parties present at this point in its history. Belgium can no longer consider itself a finished entity. It is again in the process of formation. However, the absence of a political theory of international migration and the apparent ignorance of the internationalization of many features of everyday life have rendered the legal conceptualization of this process almost "unthinkable."

The current government is moving increasingly toward assimilation, on the grounds that the creation of "non-Belgian citizens" would violate the constitution. However, the slow and relatively unsuccessful nature of assimilation by naturalization raises questions about further evolution under this banner and unfortunately increases the volume of voices raised against democratic coexistence.

Harmonious Coexistence of Communities

Belgium's main claim to fame is the unswerving perseverance of its inhabitants in overcoming community quarrels. The coexistence of linguistic communities (Flemish, Walloon, and German-speaking) and of regional entities (Flanders, Brussels, Wallonia) is both difficult and fragile, particularly since politicians are not above playing on fears of the "other" group. However, national communities are not the only ones to be exploited in this manner. Ethnic (non-Belgian) communities are also exploited in rather unsavory political campaigns. Non-Belgians are frequently and unjustly accused of being responsible for the rising crime rate, of being excessively and dangerously concentrated, of downgrading public order, and of refusing to integrate.

It was thus with astonishment but certainly with approval that foreign residents listened to the speech of King Baudouin on Belgium's national day, July 21, 1987. Immigrants appreciated the exactness of the king's analysis and the pertinence of his suggested solutions much more than did national communities. Some passages of his speech were particularly enlightening.

In the life of men but also in the life of a country, it is easy to spoil one another's existence by fueling mutual worries over the behavior of the other.

Some people are continually worried and pass all their time attempting to protect themselves from the other community. Life is already so short. We cannot spend our time expending our energy merely in defending ourselves. We have much better things to do.

This is the place for the new civic attitude of which I have often spoken to you. It presupposes that we attempt to understand one another and perceive the other person's reasons for worry. Finally, it requires the joint implementation of positive, confidence-building measures.

Tangibly speaking, this means that everyone must demonstrate levelheadedness in this matter. In other words, the media must objectively inform the public of what is going on in the other communities and of their concerns instead of being introspective or blowing out of all proportion local quarrels or wounding or provocative declarations. In other words, we must refuse to exacerbate opposition, for the overwhelming majority of the population wishes to live in understanding and work in peace.

Next, each citizen and in particular representatives of the people must categorically refuse to let themselves be drawn into any form of provocation or arrogance vis-à-vis the other community. We must resist the too easy temptation of escalating antagonism, stirring up passion. To resist is to be truly courageous.

I would like our country to demonstrate within our multifaceted European Community, which is seeking its own unity, that it is possible to see different cultures live side by side, without too many difficulties, within the same political entity.

Such a call will inevitably strike a chord. Let us hope that the response will not be only an attempt to facilitate the coexistence of "national" communities, but also the day-to-day lives of all inhabitants, regardless of nationality. This is the profound wish of all ethnic minorities living in Belgium.

Addendum: Nationality and Place of Residence

The data in the tables are based on W. Dumon and L. Michiels, *OCDE: Système d'observation permanente des migrations. Belgium 1986* (Sociology Department, Catholic University of Leuven, 1987), pp. 13–16. Exact data on the number of foreigners by nationality are available only for census years. However, the National Statistical Institute makes annual estimates. Foreigners originating from the other EEC member-states are in a majority compared with foreigners from non-EEC states. However, follow-

TABLE V.10
Foreign Population According to Nationality

Country of origin	1982 Number	1982 Percent	1983 Number	1983 Percent	1984 Number	1984 Percent
EEC						
West Germany	26,747	3.0%	27,245	3.1%	27,452	3.1%
France	103,729	11.7	103,621	11.6	103,101	11.6
Italy	276,464	31.2	273,002	30.6	270,521	30.4
Netherlands	65,478	7.4	65,304	7.3	65,578	7.4
Luxembourg	5,954	0.7	5,792	0.7	5,771	0.6
United Kingdom	22,634	2.6	22,596	2.5	22,288	2.5
Denmark	1,855	0.2	1,859	0.2	1,887	0.2
Ireland	1,034	0.1	1,065	0.1	1,112	0.1
Greece	21,430	2.4	21,303	2.3	21,055	2.3
TOTAL	525,325	59.3	521,787	58.4	518,765	58.2
Non-EEC						
Portugal	10,473	1.2	10,447	1.2	10,378	1.2
Spain	57,783	6.5	57,004	6.4	55,952	6.2
Yugoslavia	5,940	0.7	5,929	0.7	5,556	0.6
Turkey	66,057	7.5	68,416	7.7	70,033	7.8
Other European countries	18,807	2.1	18,587	2.1	17,413	2.0
Algeria	10,936	1.2	10,864	1.2	10,821	1.2
Morocco	110,200	12.4	115,082	12.9	119,083	13.4
Tunisia	6,945	0.8	6,868	0.8	6,820	0.8
Zaïre	9,240	1.0	9,607	1.1	9,457	1.1
Other African countries	6,382	0.7	6,747	0.7	6,652	0.7
United States	11,094	1.3	10,734	1.2	10,867	1.2
Canada	1,441	0.2	1,416	0.2	1,413	0.2
Other countries	45,106	5.1	47,754	5.4	47,663	5.4
TOTAL	360,404	40.7	369,457	41.6	372,108	41.8
GRAND TOTAL	885,729	100.0%	891,244	100.0%	890,873	100.0%

SOURCE: National Statistical Institute.

TABLE V.11
Total Foreign Population According to Place of Residence

Region	1981[a]	1982[b]	1983[b]	1984[b]
Wallonia				
Number	408,158	407,182	404,645	402,269
Percent of foreigners	46.5%	46.0%	45.4%	41.5%
Percent of population	12.7%	12.7%	12.3%	12.2%
Brussels				
Number	237,875	243,624	248,002	248,217
Percent of foreigners	27.0%	27.5%	27.8%	27.9%
Percent of population	23.9%	24.5%	25.0%	25.3%
Flanders				
Number	232,544	234,914	238,597	240,387
Percent of foreigners	26.5%	26.5%	26.8%	27.0%
Percent of population	4.1%	4.2%	4.2%	4.2%

SOURCE: National Statistical Institute.
[a] On March 1   [b] On January 1

ing a growth period in 1970–80, the number of foreigners from EEC member-states is now falling.

The French, Italians, and Moroccans make up the biggest foreign groups, each exceeding 100,000. The number of French and Italian people has declined since 1981. For the three years shown in Table V.10, the number of Moroccans expanded. This was also true for Turks. The number of Spaniards has been falling steadily.

The largest number of foreigners live in the Walloon region, although this has fallen in the course of the past five years. On the other hand, the number of foreigners residing in the Brussels and Flemish regions has risen (Table V.11). They both have around the same number of foreigners (around 27 percent of the foreign population each). However, an important difference lies in the fact that in the case of Brussels, foreigners represent a much higher proportion of the total population, 25 out of 100 inhabitants compared with 4 in the Flanders region. The high concentration of foreigners in Brussels has been the main catalyst for tensions over the presence of immigrants and is the greatest source of concern for the government. In Flanders and Wallonia, the problem is not as acute. However, certain boroughs in these two regions have a higher concentration of foreigners than boroughs within Brussels.

Health

Raphel Lagasse

AN OVERVIEW OF A COUNTRY'S health is often nothing more than a discussion of the many health problems facing the country. This results in a rather paradoxical situation in which not health but its opposite—disease and death—is described. There are two reasons for this rather negative approach to health descriptions. The first has to do with the ambiguity of the term *health*. For a classic definition we may refer to that of the World Health Organization: "Health is a state of complete physical, mental, and social well-being, and not merely the absence of disease." The problem with this definition is that it is not operational and makes it difficult to measure health or to describe a country's health with any precision. The second reason is that data that describe a population's health are scarce. Furthermore, they consist largely of mortality figures, because these are routinely collected. Some routine data are available on morbidity, from hospital records or from other sources, but a more precise description of morbidity can be produced only by special surveys. Data on health in a positive sense are almost nonexistent. This positive approach to health is still confined to the field of experimental research.

This chapter presents the most recent data available at this time and is based on mortality statistics for 1984, as well as on special surveys on the incidence of disease, medical consumption, and the distribution of some risk factors causing major health problems in Belgium.

Mortality and Life Expectancy

The total number of deaths in 1984 was 111,073 out of a total population of 9.85 million inhabitants on January 1, 1984. This yields a crude mortality rate of 11.3 percent per year. This figure can be compared with 12.4 percent in 1960, 12.3 percent in 1970, and 11.5 percent in 1980.

Among the twelve countries in the European Community, Belgium, in 1980, ranked third after the United Kingdom (11.8 percent) and Germany (11.6 percent). The lowest value that year was for Spain (7.7 percent). However, the crude rates are influenced both by the proportion of males and females in the population under consideration and, most important, by the age distribution. As the Belgian population ages, a higher crude mortality rate is observed than if the Belgian population had maintained the same age distribution as in 1900.

International comparisons or trend analyses are therefore difficult to perform. This difficulty can be avoided by presenting mortality rates by sex and for specific age groups. This has been done in Figure V.1, which shows the evolution of mortality by sex since 1957 in three age groups: 0 to 14, 40 to 54, and 65 to 74. A progressive decrease in the rates can be observed in each category during the past thirty years, with the sole exception of males aged 65 to 74, whose rate increased slightly at the beginning of this period. Another universal phenomenon can be observed in the figure: excess mortality of males, compared to females, regardless of age.

A second way to overcome the difficulty of demographic differences is to standardize data, that is, to calculate the mortality that would be observed if the population under study had the demographic characteristics of a well-defined fictive population, the "standard population." International comparisons of mortality rates are much more valid when done this way. Figure V.2 shows for the year 1982 the ranking of the twelve EC countries according to standardized mortality rates in males and females (the European population is used as the standard population). Belgium ranks fourth by decreasing order for males and fifth for females.

A third way to neutralize the influence of demographic factors in the comparisons is to study life expectancy at birth, the mean number of years of life expectancy calculated from birth. Figure V.3 shows the evolution of this indicator in Belgium since 1900. It is evident that life expectancy at birth has increased sharply, rising from less than 50 years for both sexes to 70.0 for males and 76.8 for females. The magnitude of this striking difference between the sexes is equal to that in neighboring countries.

Life expectancy at birth varies geographically in Belgium. For the period 1979–82, life expectancy at birth varied in males from 65.7 years in the province of Liège to 71.3 in West Vlaanderen, and in females from 75.8 in Liège to 77.6 in Limburg. As a whole, life expectancy at birth is higher in the Flemish provinces than in Wallonia. This geographical distribution is a relatively new phenomenon appearing sometime around

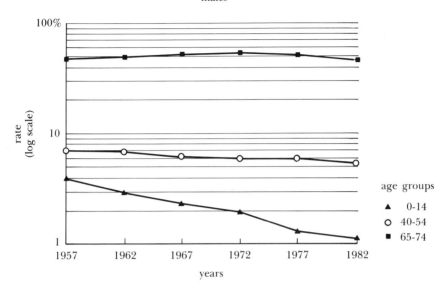

Fig. V.1. Evolution of age-specific mortality rates in Belgium since 1957.

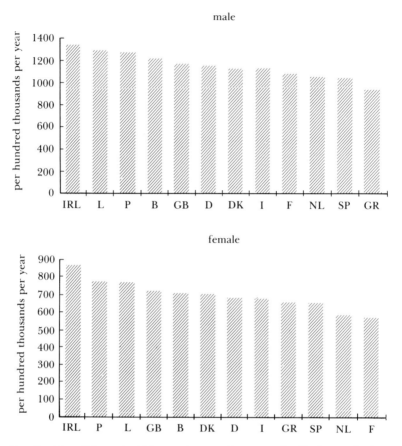

Fig. V.2. Ranking of the twelve EC countries according to standardized mortality by sex. Period around 1982. IRL, Ireland; L, Luxembourg; P, Portugal; GB, Great Britain; D, West Germany; DK, Denmark; I, Italy; F, France; NL, Netherlands; SP, Spain; GR, Greece. Source: WHÓ 1986.

World War II. In the 19th century life expectancy was higher in Wallonia. The difference in the figures for life expectancy between the extreme provinces is sizable for males (5.6 years), but the situation for females is much more homogeneous, with a difference of less than two years. Geographical variations in mortality are, for the most part, due to differences in male mortality.

This can also be observed in the maps presented in Figure V.4. They

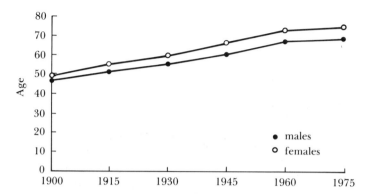

Fig. V.3. Evolution of life expectancy at birth in Belgium since 1900.

are drawn on the basis of the *standard mortality ratios* (SMR) for global mortality in each of the 43 Belgian districts, the mean for Belgium being 100. The districts are ranked by increasing order of the SMR values, and then grouped in sextiles, each sextile corresponding to a specific shading on the maps. Male mortality shows a typical geographical distribution, but no such pattern is present for females. Other types of determinants are probably behind the differences in male and female mortality.

In any case, mortality is unequally distributed in Belgium. However, these inequalities are not only geographically but also socially determined. Unfortunately, for Belgium there are no statistical data on overall mortality by socio-professional categories, but only some indices and partial results from special surveys. The Belgian situation is probably similar to that in the United·Kingdom or France, where general and specific mortality gradients have been demonstrated. For example, life expectancy at birth is much higher for white-collar professional groups than for blue-collar workers, with the unskilled workers group ranking lowest.

What are the causes of death in Belgium? Certainly, they have changed considerably since the beginning of this century, when the impact of contagious and parasitic diseases was still strong. This impact has lessened steadily. By 1954, infectious and parasitic diseases accounted for 3.9 percent of male mortality for all ages; in 1983, the percentage was less than 0.8 percent.

The profile of the causes of death is strongly influenced by sex and age as well as by place of residence. As a whole, in Belgium in 1984, diseases of the circulatory system were by far the leading cause of death, ac-

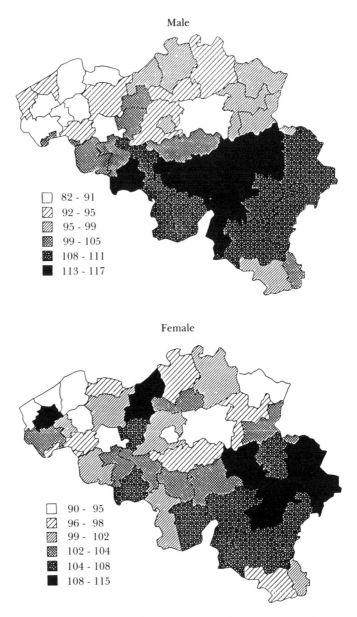

Male

☐	82 - 91
▨	92 - 95
▨	95 - 99
▨	99 - 105
▨	108 - 111
■	113 - 117

Female

☐	90 - 95
▨	96 - 98
▨	99 - 102
▨	102 - 104
▨	104 - 108
■	108 - 115

Fig. V.4. Geographical distribution of overall mortality in Belgium for males (above) and females (below). Presentation in sextiles for standard mortality ratios computed by district (n = 43). Period: 1974–78.

counting for more deaths than all cancers together. These two categories alone account for two-thirds of all deaths. Figure V.5 shows the proportion of deaths in 1979 attributed to seven categories of conditions in both sexes. For diseases of the circulatory system, the proportion is higher in females than in males; the inverse is true for cancers, diseases of the respiratory system, and external causes (accidents, suicides, and homicides). Diseases of the digestive system are found in equal proportion in males and females.

The proportional distribution is very different according to age. Among children less than one year old, two-thirds of all deaths are due to "conditions in the perinatal period" or to congenital anomalies. For the 1–14 age group, even though tumors cause 15 percent of all deaths, the major cause of death is external causes: 47 percent in boys and 30 percent in girls (1984). More specifically, 25 percent of boys' and 12 percent of girls' deaths in this age group are attributable to traffic accidents. In the 15–44 age group those striking figures are still observable: 26 percent and 12 percent, respectively, of male and female deaths are caused by traffic accidents.

Historically, this cause of mortality multiplied threefold between 1954 and 1972; during this time the number of cars increased by a factor of five. The mortality resulting from car accidents peaked in 1972 at 0.30 percent per year. Five years later, this figure had declined to 0.25 percent; in 1983 it stood at 0.21 percent. This striking decrease over a ten-year period most probably resulted from stringent laws combining reductions in legal speed limits, penalties for abuse of alcohol consumption, and compulsory use of safety belts. However, more than 2,000 Belgians are killed each year on the road.

Another major cause of death among young people is suicide. Indeed, even though the highest mortality rates by suicide are observed in those over 75, it is in the 15–25 age group that the proportional weight is at a maximum; this weight is difficult to establish with precision, but it could well lie between 10 percent and 20 percent.

With suicide it is difficult to determine how valid and exhaustive the official data are. Therefore the rising trend of suicide mortality in recent years may be attributable either to a real increase or to better reporting on death certificates. In males, for all ages, the suicide mortality rate remained fairly stable from the end of World War II to 1975–76 (around 0.21 percent). It reached 0.25 percent in 1977, 0.28 percent in 1979, 0.29 percent in 1981, and 0.31 percent in 1983. In females, the same stability was observed (around 0.10 percent) until 1974; the rate then rose to 0.12 percent in 1975, 0.13 percent in 1977, 0.15 percent in 1979, and

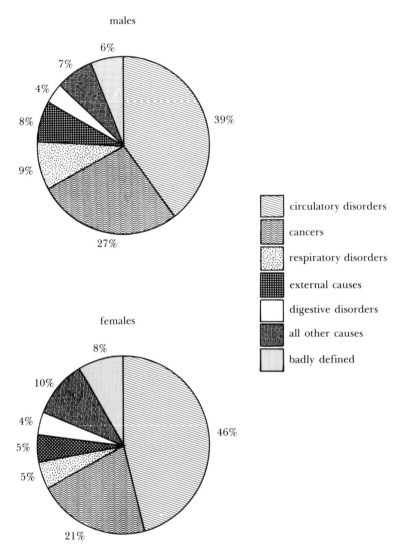

males

6%

7%

4%

8%

9%

39%

27%

circulatory disorders

cancers

respiratory disorders

external causes

digestive disorders

all other causes

badly defined

females

8%

10%

4%

5%

5%

46%

21%

Fig. V.5. Proportional mortality in Belgium in 1984 by sex, all ages, for seven major groups of conditions.

0.16 percent in 1983. It seems difficult to explain this parallel increase as an artifact of reporting, and the coincidence of the phenomenon with the start of the oil crisis cannot be overlooked. The rise in economic difficulties and unemployment could well be a factor.

The geographical distribution of suicide mortality shows low rates in Limburg and Luxembourg provinces and higher ones in Brabant, Hainaut, and Liège provinces. Contrary to common belief, suicide rates are not uniformly higher in cities than in the countryside. Moreover, suicide rates represent only part of a more frequent problem—attempted suicide, which has been estimated to be five to ten times more frequent than suicide itself. This extrapolation brings to 15,000 to 25,000 the number of Belgians attempting suicide each year. A seasonal pattern is observable, with a maximum in March and November and a minimum in July.

Two categories of mortality have evolved in recent years: diseases of the circulatory system and cancers, the first and second leading causes of death. Their evolutions are quite different from each other. Cancer mortality rates have increased during the past 30 years, especially in males, rising from 2.08 percent per year in males and 1.99 percent in females to 3.25 percent and 2.25 percent, respectively. Diseases of the circulatory system in both sexes increased until 1963, maintained that level until 1968, and then decreased, with the exception of a slight increase in females since 1977. This increase has resulted in an inversion of the sex ratio for this condition's crude rates; until 1980 more males than females died of such diseases; now women lead.

Of the diseases of the circulatory system, coronary heart diseases (CHD) have often been studied in Belgium, and prevention programs have been tested and implemented in different locations. Between 1958 and 1968, CHD increased in males roughly 50 percent, but a similar increase was not observed in females. Between 1972 and 1983, a 22 percent decrease was observed in males (from 2.36 percent to 1.84 percent) and a 10 percent decrease in females (from 1.40 percent to 1.26 percent). These figures show both the magnitude of the trends and how males are still hit by an excess mortality compared to females. Females, however, suffer more mortality from cerebrovascular diseases compared to males. The geographical pattern of CHD mortality shows that this condition affects southern Belgium (Wallonia) 30 percent more than the northern provinces (Flanders). Data collected by two CHD registers reveal a correspondingly higher incidence in Charleroi, a Wallonian city, compared to Ghent (a city in Flanders). A possible explanation may be nutritional differences between the two regions.

Another cause of death is lung cancer; this type of cancer is responsible for the steady increase in cancer mortality for males. Between 1954 and 1983 the relative increase in all cancers in males was roughly 56 percent. The rates for respiratory cancers rose from 0.42 percent to 1.30 percent per year, a relative increase of 210 percent. All other cancers together represented a mortality rate of 1.66 percent per year in 1954 and 1.95 percent in 1983, an increase of only 17 percent over 30 years. This striking progression of lung cancer mortality can be linked to tobacco consumption habits in Belgium. Indeed, the relation between cigarette smoking and mortality from lung cancer has been firmly established. In a study conducted on British male doctors, the relative risk was roughly 13 times higher in smokers than in nonsmokers, and 24 times higher in doctors smoking more than 25 cigarettes per day compared to nonsmokers.

The issue of cigarette smoking and lung cancer highlights the new trends in Belgian public health policy, which focuses on identifying high-risk factors (such as smoking and cancer), describing regional disparities for the leading causes of death, understanding the likely causes of impaired health, and implementing special preventive interventions. Behavior patterns appear to be partly responsible for the changing profile of disease and mortality in Belgium. Smoking and nutritional habits are behaviors that require more and more attention from public health researchers and decision-makers.

Health of Neonates and Children

The period around birth and childhood is generally of special interest to those who study community health. Health scientists and clinicians, as well as many lay people, believe that the best foundation for a lifetime of good health is laid at birth. Also, because of their vulnerability, children provide sensitive markers of a community's health problems. In addition, the earlier the prevention of adult diseases begins, the higher its effectiveness.

Approximately 120,000 children are born each year in Belgium, a huge majority (99 percent) in hospitals or maternity centers. This predominance of hospital births did not always exist. In 1954, almost 30 percent of deliveries occurred at home. By 1965, this proportion had fallen below 5 percent. The mean number of prenatal visits in Belgium is 9.4; this figure ranks Belgium ahead of most European countries, including France, Spain, and Switzerland. A survey held in three districts in Wallonia in 1981 showed that 38 percent of pregnant women interviewed had benefited from prenatal physiotherapy, and 22 percent from postnatal physiotherapy. These behaviors were markedly linked to social status.

In recent years, the frequency of teenage pregnancies has decreased slightly. A rate of 19.1 percent per year was observed in 1981 for all women age 15–19. This figure is higher than in many European countries, but below that of the United Kingdom (27.8 percent in 1984) and Spain (27.1 percent in 1979), and far below that of the United States (74 percent in 1982).

For type of delivery, the frequency of caesarean sections in 1983 was 8.1 percent, compared with 7.5 percent two years before. This rising trend is visible in the majority of industrialized countries, but the rate remains below 10 percent, the maximum level recommended by the WHO. This ranks Belgium favorably among European countries.

Of the 118,006 births in 1983, 828 were stillbirths: This corresponds to a mortality rate of 7 percent. Moreover, independent of their survival status, 880 (7.5 percent) were affected by one or more congenital anomalies detectable at birth. A majority of these anomalies concerned the osteo-muscular system (30 percent), the central nervous system (15 percent), and the palate and lip areas (12 percent). Anomalies were the cause of 9 percent of the stillbirths.

In 1983, 5.4 percent of all newborns were of "low birth weight" (less than 2,500 gm), a well-known risk for survival, resulting either from growth retardation in utero or from premature birth. This percentage compares with figures of 7 percent in the United Kingdom and in the United States at the same time and 5 to 6 percent in most West European countries.

Survival of children is generally studied in two very important periods: the first week and the first year. The first period refers to the early neonatal mortality rate, the second to the infant mortality rate. In 1983, 587 children died during the first week (5 percent), and 1,217 during the first year (10.4 percent). If we compare these figures with those for 1960 (17 percent and 31.2 percent, respectively), we see how fast these rates have declined. International comparisons show the excellent position of Belgium among industrialized countries; infant mortality rates vary from 5.5 percent in Japan (1985) to 8.4 percent in the Netherlands (1984), 9.1 percent in France (1983), 12.4 percent in Spain (1980), 14.1 percent in Italy (1981), 14.6 percent in Greece (1983), and 19.3 percent in Portugal (1983). This considerable improvement in child survival in recent years can be attributed both to the development of special health structures, such as the National Funds for Children, and to the more general effects of improvements in socioeconomic conditions. Social factors are still important determinants of the infant mortality differences. It has been demonstrated for the years 1974–75 that the relative risk of death in the first year of life was twice as high in the highest risk category of workers compared to the lowest.

After birth, children are generally seen by pediatricians, either in private practice or in public clinics. In 1980, roughly 85 percent of all children were examined at least once in these clinics. Data collected by a special survey conducted in 1981 in three districts in Wallonia reveal that 98 percent of all children had been examined by a pediatrician during the first week of life. Interviews with the mothers eight months after birth revealed that more than 90 percent of these children never had worrisome health problems and that 86 percent were considered in good or excellent health. In contrast, 8 percent had been hospitalized at least once since birth, and 12 percent had suffered from sleep difficulties. These figures cannot be generalized for the country, but they are a few of the rare indicators available for evaluating morbidity and positive health around birth other than hospital statistics, which refer only to the major problems leading to hospital admissions.

Morbidity

By definition, morbidity refers to "any departure, subjective or objective, from a state of physiological or psychological well-being." Understandably, it is rarely possible to obtain exhaustive and unbiased information on a group in order to determine the frequency of morbid states or events. In every country some infectious diseases are subject to compulsory confidential reporting. In Belgium the list comprises rare quarantined diseases (cholera, yellow fever, plague, and smallpox) and more common diseases (tuberculosis, typhoid fever, viral encephalitis, and viral hepatitis, among others).

Although not required by law, all AIDS cases are in fact registered. Of the 4,542 cases in Europe reported to the WHO up to February 19, 1987, 207 cases were registered in Belgium; 116 of these had died. As opposed to other European countries, most cases (139) involved nonresidents, that is, people who had lived in Belgium for less than five years; among residents, 39 out of the other 68 were homo- or bisexual males.

The problem with legally required compulsory reporting of diseases is the low rate of the cases actually declared; this is particularly true for rather frequent diseases such as tuberculosis, gonorrhea, and hepatitis. For this reason among others, the Ministry of Public Health in 1978 implemented a network of "sentinel general practitioners." Some health problems, such as measles or mumps, are monitored continuously because of their control through vaccination. Other problems are monitored on an annual basis. Fifteen infectious diseases, nine noninfectious diseases, and seven behavior-related problems have been studied in this way, producing a valuable nationwide overview.

Of special interest are the results for domestic accidents and hepatitis. In 1984, 2,656 domestic accidents were registered through the network; extrapolation leads to a figure of 240,000 cases annually for Belgium, and an incidence rate of 24.6 percent of the population. These accidents involve mostly males and mostly the younger age groups—under 5 and then between 5 and 9 years of age. A higher incidence can be observed in females over 60 years. The leading cause of accidents is falling (47 percent). In 11 percent of all domestic accidents hospitalization was required.

For hepatitis, 191 cases were registered during a one-year period in 1982–83. This leads to an extrapolation of roughly 17,500 cases in the country (1.78 percent per year), with a slightly higher incidence in those under 20 years of age. By region, the rates are 1.5 percent in Flanders, 2 percent in Wallonia, and 2.8 percent in Brussels. When comparing these data with the officially declared ones, the ratio is roughly 20 monitored cases to each declared one. This clearly highlights the value of the measuring and monitoring tool instituted by this network of sentinel general practitioners.

Another way to gain insight into morbidity is to look at medical consumption, even though such figures do not correlate perfectly with health-status level or the degree and type of health problems in a community. Medical density and accessibility to health services, for example, also play an important role as determinants of medical consumption. An in-depth study of medical consumption has been conducted over the past ten years in Belgium. The many results of the study show, among other things, that for general practice a mean number of 5.2 consultations or visits per year was observed in 1974 per person covered by the general system of health insurance. Differences are seen between different categories: active people (3.9), handicapped (9.6), retired (8.8), and widows (10.9). Moreover, standardized data reveal regional differences, with a minimum in Brussels and a maximum in Flanders. This study also showed that initially general practice and specialized services both expanded, up to a level at which specialized services developed to the detriment of and in competition with general practice.

In the field of specialized medicine, the relative importance of special technical investigations appeared to correlate highly with the availability of the required equipment in various places. Developments between 1966 and 1977 show an increase of 38 percent in the volume of activity for all specialists together, and a geographical pattern quite different from that of general practice: Brussels is in first position, with roughly a 50 percent higher incidence of use of specialized medicine compared with Wallonia, which has slightly higher figures than Flanders.

In addition to studies of the volume of medical activities, some attempts have been made to discern the main problems treated by the health services. Because of the selection of only the more severe cases in hospitals, the pattern observed in general practice is more likely to reveal common though less severe health problems. A special survey conducted in 1982 in a general practice group showed the relative frequency of cardiovascular diseases (15.3 percent), respiratory diseases (15.1 percent), mental problems (14.6 percent), disorders of the osteo-muscular system (6.8 percent), and infectious or parasitic diseases (5.2 percent) as reasons for seeking medical help. In addition, 12.7 percent of patients came for administrative purposes, prevention, or counseling. This gives a markedly different picture of the relative importance of various health problems from that provided by mortality data analyses.

Health Determinants

In Belgium, as elsewhere in the world, health results from a combination of determinants. Among these factors, the most studied ones lie in the physical environment. In that category, potable water distribution, public hygiene, and improvements in housing conditions were probably the most effective forces at work in the remarkable progress of health conditions in Belgium in this century. More recent progress in this field has come in the reduction of air pollution, bringing the levels in all Belgian towns below the critical levels set by the WHO. This positive result can be credited to a whole set of policies concerning car motors, domestic heating systems, and industrial pollutants.

In the course of this historical evolution, residual health problems appear, more and more, to be related to the social or psychosocial environment and to the many behaviors now considered to increase risk. Tobacco consumption is a well-known risk factor in many diseases, including perinatal problems. In this area, the figures are optimistic: despite the lack of official statistics on this matter, the proportion of smokers among Belgians 18 years or older was estimated at 43 percent in 1976, 40 percent in 1982, and 35 percent in 1985. Males smoke more than females (45 percent versus 27 percent), and no significant difference can be shown among the three regions of the country.

A large interuniversity survey conducted between 1980 and 1984 on nutritional and smoking habits in Belgium shows striking differences in nutritional habits between Flanders and Wallonia, particularly in the consumption of the various fatty acids. For example, in males, polyunsaturated fats represent 8.4 percent of caloric intake in Flanders, but only 6.3 percent in Wallonia. Consequently, the ratios between polyunsaturated and saturated fats in nutritional intake are 0.58 and 0.38, respectively. A higher consumption of margarine in Flanders was shown for a few years, as opposed to butter consumption in Wallonia. Moreover, a statistical correlation was observed in males between the relative importance of unsaturated and saturated fats on the one hand and the serum levels of low density lipoprotein (LDL) cholesterol on the other; this serum level is one of three well-established risk factors for coronary heart disease (the other two are tobacco and hypertension).

For blood pressure, the same survey provided community-based data allowing computation of mean values by age and sex. For example, in males, the systolic blood pressure mean is 13.1 mm Hg in the 25–34 age group and 14.7 mm Hg in the 65–74 age group. For females, the respective values are 11.9 and 15.3 mm Hg. No systematic regional difference was found for mean blood pressure.

The same survey revealed that alcohol represents 5 percent of the caloric intake in men (age 25–74), with a slightly higher proportion in the French-speaking community. The proportion is only 2 percent in females, with a similar regional difference. The most evident consequence of alcohol consumption on mortality is cirrhosis of the liver, and there is a higher mortality due to this condition in those districts with a higher alcohol intake.

Positive Health

Some indicators rely more on health than on disease, especially data on growth, height, weight, and immunization. It would be very interesting to describe a community's health from the standpoint of physical fitness, sports performance, or mental well-being. Unfortunately, data to do so are lacking, and even if it were possible, there are few external references for comparative purposes.

Growth curves for Belgium over time show a significant rising trend: between 1925 and 1960 the mean height increase was roughly 3 cm for 3-year-old boys and 10 cm for 15-year-old boys. The roles of environment and wealth and of protein-intake improvement are easy to understand. Besides this general increase in mean height, historical trends also show a reduction in socio-geographical differences. Around 1960 the mean height of male students (generally a more privileged group) was 1.76 m, and in 1979 for male enrollees in military service, a cross-section of all social categories, it was also 1.76 m.

A secular trend was also observed when comparing adults of different age groups, belonging to different birth cohorts. In males, the mean height was 1.75 m in the 25–34 age group, but only 1.68 m in the 65–74 age group. In females, the respective figures were 1.62 m and 1.56 m. For the same respondents, the mean weight of males age 25–34 was 76 kg compared to 74 kg for the 65–74 age group; the maximum value was 78 kg for those age 35–54: 61 kg for the 25–34 age group compared to 70 kg in the 55–64 age group.

As for immunization coverage, which refers both to a positive health behavior and to a chance for better health, the results are satisfactory. Almost 100 percent of children are immunized against poliomyelitis, diphtheria, and tetanus. For pertussis, coverage rates reach 75 percent. For measles, rubella, and mumps, the rates reach approximately 80 percent in the Flemish Community and 55 percent in the French Community, which decided in 1985, one year later than the Flemish Community, to deliver vaccinations freely throughout the community.

Health Care Policy and Services

Jacqueline Bande-Knops and Herman Nys

IN THIS BRIEF CONTRIBUTION, we discuss health care policy in Belgium and the main services available. In the first part, we look at the main health care policy–related elements, in particular the competent authorities, the financial resources (in which health insurance plays a central role), and some important consultative bodies and authorities. In the second part, the most important preventive and curative health care services are dealt with (health care for the young, occupational medicine, mental health care, hospitals) as well as the most important providers of services (doctors, nurses, pharmacists, paramedics).

Health Care Policy

Like all other government policies in Belgium, health care policy is characterized by a division between the national government and the three regional authorities. An August 8, 1980, act theoretically allocated both curative health care in and out of hospitals and preventive health care, including health education, among the regions. But there are major exceptions, both explicit and implicit. Examples of the latter are furnished by legislation on medication and the act governing the medical profession. Among the explicit exceptions are what are known as the organic provisions in the Hospitals Act, the financing of the operation of hospitals, health and disability insurance, the basic rules for the planning and financing of hospital construction, the installation of large-scale, high-cost medical equipment, the recognition of hospitals insofar as it has any financial effect, and the designation of university hospitals. To sum up, the rule of thumb is that the national government makes the decisions, and the regions are responsible for implementing them.

At the national level, health care policy is to a great extent determined through the mechanisms of health and disability insurance. Such insurance is legally required of almost all inhabitants of Belgium. It is implemented by the mutual insurance funds, which are corporate bodies. They negotiate with health care providers concerning the prices the insured parties are to be charged for services provided. These negotiations are conducted by a committee of doctors and representatives of the mutual insurance funds. In the past, this price fixing was carried out in such a way that health care developed increasingly in the direction of hospital treatment and medical technology (clinical biology, radiology, etc.). Over the past five years, however, a change has taken place, albeit slowly. Another health insurance policymaking body is the technical-medical council, on which the medical faculties are represented along with the mutual insurance funds and organizations of doctors. This body advises on the "nomenclature," the list of medical services reimbursed or paid for directly by the health insurance organizations. Inclusion in or exclusion from this list of certain services helps determine health care policy.

This constant participation of those directly involved is in fact a leading characteristic of government health care policy. This can also be seen in the existence of a great number of official consultative committees and deliberating bodies, in both curative and preventive health care. Efforts are made on these committees to achieve a consensus of all interests involved; the government then enshrines this consensus in its decisions.

Health Care Services

Health Care for the Young

A number of services are closely involved in health care for the young in Belgium. We will mention in particular K&G/ONE and MST.

The National Child Welfare Board was discontinued as a national institution at the end of 1986 and was replaced by two autonomous regional institutions, which are to a great extent building on the former institution's main tasks. They have adapted these to today's family problems, adding a number of specific assignments. The annual allowances the institutions receive from the budgets of the ministries involved are used to a large extent to subsidize institutions and services dealing with maternity care and child hygiene, concentrating on the medico-social support measures of children from birth to 3 years.

K&G/ONE's activities begin before the child is born. In order to supervise the evolution of the pregnancy and with a view to promoting the child's chances for life, a network of prenatal clinics has been built up.

The centers are run by independent committees and recognized by K&G/ONE. A team consisting of a gynecologist and a social nurse provides guidance for expectant mothers and devotes particular attention to high-risk pregnancies.

Children age 0 to 6 can be registered with young children's clinics. A consultant doctor monitors their physical, mental, and motor development, vaccinates them or makes sure they are vaccinated, and advises on their diet. The social nurse attached to the clinic provides medico-social follow-up at home. These consultative centers cover the whole country. In addition, K&G/ONE recognizes and subsidizes a series of institutions and services for day care. It decides on the standards day-care centers (creches and kindergartens) and foster-parent services must meet if they are to be considered for operating subsidies.

Day-care centers must remain open a certain number of hours per day and per year, and they must have sufficient qualified personnel for their capacity. Parents contribute to the cost of day care in proportion to their income. In certain circumstances, children up to 6 years old can be taken care of after school. In addition to the creches and kindergartens, there are also organized foster-parent services. Standards to qualify for a subsidy are also laid down. Registered foster families must meet certain requirements. These services centralize applications and make sure that the children are looked after on a continuous basis. In addition, these services can also organize day care for children aged up to 6 outside school hours and during holidays. Those who wish to foster children for payment outside a foster-parent service can do so if they have municipal authorization. Such parents are known as independent foster parents.

K&G/ONE also recognizes and subsidizes a number of crisis child-care centers. There are day and night child-care centers. Private individuals and public bodies can have children aged up to 3 years taken care of in these centers for a time for social or health reasons in order to remove them from their family environment. The children are monitored by a specialized medico-psycho-social team. K&G/ONE also recognizes a certain number of hostels for mothers. These hostels receive young mothers who are temporarily in need, whether they are expectant mothers or young mothers with a child or children. K&G/ONE also fills the need for short-term day- and night-care centers for children who, because of physical problems or acute family difficulties, would benefit from temporary guidance in a protective environment. Children aged 2 to 14 are eligible for this service.

In addition to its supervisory and subsidizing functions, K&G/ONE also functions in the field of health education and information concerning medico-social child and family problems. In addition to the individual information its employees (social nurses, doctors, and child-care center personnel) provide for families, K&G/ONE develops educational material for the public at large (folders, posters, and films). K&G/ONE also publishes a bimonthly magazine called *Het Kind* (The Child) and maintains a specialized public library where books and magazines are available for consultation. K&G/ONE also has the responsibility to act in connection with prevention and assistance in cases of cruelty to children and neglect.

School Health Services

School health care is compulsory for all children in school (from 3 years until 18 years). School health care aims include (1) primary prevention (health education of schoolchildren and vaccination programs); and (2) secondary prevention (early detection and follow-up of physical and mental disorders). Seven school health examinations are compulsory; supplementary examinations may be performed by the school health team (physician and/or nurse) whenever there is an obvious reason. The school health examinations take place in more than 300 specially designed "health centers." The majority of school doctors and nurses are specially trained for their work. Many physicians involved in school health care have obtained a postgraduate degree in youth health care. Some of the health centers are also equipped for mother-and-child health care examinations as well as for occupational medicine and other activities in the field of preventive medicine for the general population.

School health care services, being exclusively preventive, do not offer any treatment. Whenever a child has to be referred for further diagnosis and/or treatment, the school health team always collaborates with the parents, the general practitioner, and/or the dentist. A letter is sent to the parents after the examination, and on referral the general practitioner is requested to return the completed form to the school doctor. The regular school health examinations are only part of a broader range of preventive measures applied during school life. The school health team also visits the school regularly, takes part in health education programs for youngsters, and works in close conjunction with teachers, educational specialists, psychologists, and social workers.

Occupational Medicine

By a royal decree of 1965 every employer, in the private or public sector, must subscribe to an occupational medicine service or set up a service for employees. More than 500 such services exist. The occupational medicine service is paid for by the employer, and the task is laid down in accordance with the general regulations on the protection of labor.

The some 700 physicians working in the field of occupational medicine engage, among other things, in the detection of health hazards for the employees, in tracing and eliminating as far as possible factors that can threaten health in the work environment, and in giving advice to employers and employees in the field of design and layout of workshops, in the selection and the use of means of production, and in connection with everything that can contribute to humanization of labor.

Occupational medicine services are staffed by specially trained physicians and nurses. Their position is a very special one: they have an important preventive role to play through periodic medical examinations, as well as through free consultation hours for the employees. The organization of first aid, vaccination programs, health education, and early detection of occupational diseases is also part of this program.

Mental Health Care

Mental health care consists essentially of two structures: psychiatric hospitals and psychiatric departments of general hospitals; and outpatient services for mental health care. (For the first, see the section on hospitals below). The mental health care services are of recent origin (most of them started after 1975), and they have both a curative and a preventive mission. They consist of multidisciplinary teams (psychiatrists, psychologists, and social workers). The delimitations of the territory of these services and of other outpatient services is far from clear, and there is talk of a competitive approach to these services. Relationships with the psychiatric hospitals are also generally tense.

Hospitals

There is no doubt that the hospital sector is the most extensive health care service in Belgium. Until a few years ago, almost all the government's efforts in the field of health care went toward the hospitals. It is now generally accepted that this has led to a surplus of hospital beds, and today policy is aimed at cutting back this surplus. One of the ways this is being done is by closure of a number of hospitals with under 150 beds. In addition, there is an attempt to encourage hospitals to get rid of some of their beds voluntarily, by granting closure premiums. Larger-scale hospitals are being encouraged to merge. All these measures are still too recent to have yielded any results. Besides the surplus of beds and the existence of many smaller hospitals, another characteristic of Belgian hospitals is the great number of university hospital beds.

In addition, policy is also aimed at converting existing beds to other specialties. Special hospital services (geriatric wards) are being set up to cope with the aging population. For older people who can no longer look after themselves but who do not require hospital care, rest homes and nursing homes are being set up. Because of the shortage of government funds to pay for these new initiatives, a policy of cutbacks in existing services (especially mother-and-child care) in favor of new services is being implemented. Nursing care in two-person rooms or public wards is fully paid for by the state and the mutual insurance funds. In other cases, a supplement may be required.

Doctors

The most important category of providers of health care services is that of doctors. They have a legal monopoly over the exercise of the medical profession. In order to practice medicine, one must have the required diploma and be registered with the Medical Order. This is an organization created by the government, and its main task is to supervise the observance of the rules of ethical conduct by doctors. In addition, doctors are subject to the authority of civil and criminal law, but the number of liability trials against doctors in Belgium is limited. There is certainly no talk of a "malpractice boom," as is the case in the United States.

Within the medical profession, there is increasing talk of specialization and of differentiation into subspecialties. This phenomenon is expressed through the mutual insurance funds, since certain services are not reimbursed unless performed by a doctor specializing in a particular field. One recent development in this field is the recognition of the GP as a practitioner of first-line health care.

In general, doctors' services are reimbursed by the mutual insurance funds at 75 percent of a price determined by negotiations between doctors organizations and the mutual funds. For a number of years now, these negotiations have taken place annually and been preceded by serious disputes between the two sides. The negotiations increasingly deal with matters that strictly speaking are unrelated to the mutual insurance funds, such as the legal status of hospital staff doctors or the introduction of what is termed a *numerus clausus* (limitation of the number of medical students). In Belgium, admission to medical faculties is still open to anyone with a secondary school diploma. Most doctors in Belgium prefer individual practice. Group practices or health centers are relatively rare.

Nurses

Nurses are the most numerous group in Belgian health care. They are found mostly in hospitals, but their numbers are also on the increase in home health care. The demand for nurses is growing, in spite of the economy measures in the hospital sector, and there has recently been talk of a shortage of nurses. Some attribute this shortage to the less attractive legal status of nurses. Owing to the doctors' legal monopoly over the practice of the medical profession, the circumstances under which nurses can perform certain medical treatments, such as intravenous injections, are uncertain. For years a solution has been sought to this problem, but without success.

One characteristic of Belgian hospital nursing is what is termed "integrative nursing," in which a single nurse is responsible for all the nursing care for a given patient. In this way, the patient does not face many different nurses, each of whom deals with only one aspect of nursing care.

Other Professional Groups

Obviously a considerable number of other professional groups besides doctors and nurses are active in health care. The most important of these are pharmacists, dentists, and a number of paramedical professions, such as physiotherapists, speech therapists, and the like.

PART VI

Education

Gaston Deurinck, Coordinator

The Educational System

Pierre Vanbergen

Organization and Control of Education

IN THE LATE 18TH AND EARLY 19TH centuries, a major issue in Belgium was secularization of education, especially during the period when Belgium was annexed to France (1794–1815) and merged with Holland (1815–30). The fundamental law of the kingdom of the Netherlands stipulated that education was the responsibility of the Dutch government and that it should be secular. The opposition movement that culminated in revolution and the proclamation of Belgium's independence in 1830 consisted of an alliance between the liberal and Catholic opposition. Article 17 of the constitution guaranteed freedom of education and prohibited any measures hindering such freedom. In addition, it stipulated that education at the expense of the government would be organized in accordance with the law. However, the struggle over control of education continued.

Primary education was legally organized in 1842. The law stipulated that borough schools should be set up and run according to two principles: official (public) schools should dispense only supplementary education and the foundations of education should be based on Catholicism. The liberal movement organized itself into a party in 1847. Its political platform called for the organization of public education at all levels by civil authorities, a position that rejected religious interference in public education.

The control of education has continued to be a politically sensitive issue that has occasionally given rise to vigorous strife. A political compromise was reached in 1958 with the School Pact, which covers the entire educational system except universities. The School Pact, as signed by the political parties and followed by a 1959 law, reaffirmed the constitutional provision of freedom to choose between religious and secular education and the government's obligation to support these options. School fees were abolished at every level of education, and government subsidies were guaranteed for all schools, including private schools, that observed the laws regarding the organization of studies and the use of languages in education.

The School Pact gives "organizing powers" responsibility for the administration of Belgian schools. The following classifications of institutions reflect the concept of organizing powers and their relationship to the state.

1. *Official (public) versus free (private) education.* The official organizing powers are state, provincial, or municipal public authorities. Free education is organized by an individual or a corporate or religious body. The National Secretariat for Catholic Education organizes an extensive network of schools.

2. *State versus subsidized education.* State education is directly controlled and financed by the national government. Subsidized education includes official provincial and municipal education as well as free (private) education.

3. *Neutral versus religious education.* A school is considered neutral when it respects all philosophical or religious views held by the parents and when at least three-fourths of the teaching staff hold a certificate from an official, neutral school. Depending upon demand, neutral schools must offer a choice of religious education classes (Catholic, Protestant, Jewish, Moslem) or nonreligious moral education classes for two hours per week. A school is religious (denominational) when at least three-fourths of the teaching staff hold a certificate or diploma from a religious institution.

To qualify for recognition and state subsidies, official and free schools must conform to the legal guidelines for structure, curricula, and programs by adopting a structure existing in state education or approved by the Ministries of Education, following a syllabus that meets legal provisions or is approved by the Ministries of Education, meeting criteria for class size and organization of classes, and allowing monitoring and inspection by the state on subjects taught, level of study, application of linguistic laws, and the like (teaching methods are excluded from this inspection). The organizing authorities must hold consultations before introducing reforms in general policy, duration of study, admissions criteria, or requirements for completion of programs. In the 1980's, the system introduced by the School Pact has experienced problems caused by the government's introduction of provisions without obtaining consensus within the watchdog committee for implementation of the agreement. Control of education continues to be a subject of controversy.

No external examinations are conducted in the Belgian educational system at any level. All certificates and diplomas issued by schools have the same validity, regardless of organizing power, if the school conforms to government regulations and accepts state inspection and control. Certificates and diplomas are granted by teachers in primary schools, by class councils in secondary schools, and by boards of examiners in higher education. This flexible system, which revolves around verification of teaching level and confidence in the judgment of school authorities, results in general monitoring and facilitates preventive intervention. When the teaching level of a school, division, or particular subject appears to be sliding, the government issues a warning. Failure to correct problems can result in loss of certification of a school's certificates and diplomas.

Consultative bodies have been formed, either in a structural manner (e.g., standing councils or senior higher education councils, interuniversity councils, the Senior Council for Psychological, Medical, and Social Guidance, etc.) or in a thematic manner (e.g., Committee for the Renewal of Basic Education, Committee for the Improvement of Equal Opportunity for Boys and Girls in Education, planning committees, etc.). Generally French and Dutch branches of each body exist; they are organized on the basis of equal representation (religious/nonreligious) or in accordance with the division of schools into state, official, and subsidized education.

The policy of liberally creating new schools and departments as provided for in the School Pact and the 1959 law was not tenable for budgetary reasons. The national education budget tripled from 10 billion BF (less than 2 percent of GNP) to 110 billion BF (5.58 percent of GNP) in 1971. When recession in 1960 caused the government to make budgetary cuts, education was spared. But following another recession in 1966, legislation was enacted to suspend the creation of any school or department for one year. This law was renewed, and negotiations for a revision of the School Pact resulted in a protocol in 1973 that introduced educational rationalization and planning. These protocols, which have been developed for all levels of education, have raised the minimum standards for school operation or subsidization. The standards for the creation of new schools are much higher, and existing schools have been reorganized and consolidated regionally within the network of administrative authority.

General Structure of Belgian Education

Belgian education operates at the following levels: preschool (ages 2.5 to 6), primary (ages 6 to 12), secondary (ages 12 to 18), and higher. Since the enactment of legislation in 1983, full-time education is compulsory until the age of 16 and part-time education is compulsory until the age of 18. Higher education includes universities as well as university-level and non-university-level education in six subject areas: agriculture, art, economics, paramedical, social, teacher training, and technical. Special education is organized for handicapped children and adolescents (ages 3 to 21) at the preschool, primary, and secondary level and is divided into eight types of handicap defined by law.

A system of social advancement and continuing education programs offers partial or complete training at the secondary or higher education levels for students who have completed compulsory education. Programs are offered on a reduced schedule, in the evening or on weekends. Legislation has facilitated the release of employees to attend courses. This system plays a significant role in Belgian education, with approximately 200,000 students registered each year. Correspondence courses prepare students for examinations organized by state boards for lower and higher secondary education certificates and diplomas and state recruitment competitions and examinations. This category also includes instruction for Belgian children residing abroad, in-service training for teachers, and the like.

Language and Education

In Belgium, the right to education in one's native tongue is a fundamental freedom and a basic human right. Language laws passed in 1932 and in the 1960's gave the regional language total hegemony: Dutch is the language of instruction in all schools in Flanders, French in all schools in Wallonia, and German in some areas of eastern Belgium. In Brussels and a few communities with linguistically mixed populations, either French or Dutch is the language of instruction in each school, and only those students with the appropriate native or usual language may attend. Although the teaching of languages is a major component of Belgian curricula, there are no bilingual schools. All subjects other than languages must be taught in the language of the school's linguistic region or, in the Brussels area, of the particular school.

Education is the responsibility of the three communities (Flemish, French, and German) except in matters relating to educational disputes, compulsory schooling, teaching structures, diplomas and certificates, subsidies, salaries, and standards, which must be observed by all schools. Oversight of education was segmented into two ministries of education in 1969 and into two community councils in 1971. (A German-speaking community council was established in 1981.) Two education ministers are appointed by the government, one for French and German education and another for Dutch education. The two ministers must agree or jointly propose to the king or to parliament measures that concern all schools, regardless of the teaching language. Each can individually implement measures not requiring reciprocal application in the other community. Thus, since 1970 legislative power in the field of education has been split between the parliament and the community councils. Moreover, since 1981 each community has had its own executive body.

Much power over education still remains at the national level (parliament and government). Power disputes are inevitable, since the scope of legislation and its practical implementation may be interpreted variously. Consequently, advocates of full community control over education are still pursuing their cause. The linguistic controversy also cuts across religious versus secular lines; traditional, private education receives more political support in the Dutch-speaking part of the country, whereas public education is stronger in the French-speaking community. Community control over education could therefore cause major imbalances in each of the two large communities, a prospect that helps explain the government's reluctance to agree to complete community control of education.

Development of Education

The school attendance rate has grown steadily over the past forty years. In 1956–57, 54.33 percent of children between the ages of 15 and 16 were enrolled; the figure is now 100 percent, following the new compulsory education law of 1984. For the 18–19 age group, 23.8 percent were enrolled in 1956–57, compared with 45 percent in 1976–77 and over 50 percent in the late 1980's.

Non-university higher education establishments had a total enrollment of 13,410 in 1954–55, 49,650 in 1969–70, and 115,730 in 1984–85. A similar pattern has occurred in university education, where student enrollments have grown from 23,280 in 1954–55 to 69,630 in 1969–70 and 102,350 in 1984–85. These figures should be considered in light of the birthrate, which rose steadily between 1945 and 1965 but has fallen since 1970.

The democratization of education has been encouraged by free primary and secondary education. Moreover, a system of study grants gives secondary students and higher education students access to financial aid under certain conditions.

Teacher Training

Preschool and primary school teachers and lower secondary teachers study in teacher-training colleges following completion of secondary school. The two-year program has recently expanded to three years. Lower secondary teachers receive specialized training in two subjects in addition to their pedagogical courses. Upper secondary teachers and lecturers in non-university higher education establishments must obtain a university diploma and a teacher-training credential, which requires coursework completed during the last two years of university studies.

Regardless of level, teacher training has a number of shortcomings. On the eve of the 21st century, Belgian teachers are still not termed "professionals." Belgium is by no means the only country in this situation. But tradition, lack of information on the part of decision-makers, short-term economic factors, and institutional inertia have meant that the Belgian teaching profession has not succeeded in moving with the times and becoming fully university trained. This does not mean, however, that the teaching is mediocre, for the teaching profession continues to attract excellent students. But in recent years, recruitment has become more difficult. The danger will probably become apparent only in future years, particularly given the social and scientific changes generated by new technologies. Belgium is capable of meeting the challenge, and proposals for a complete overhaul of teacher training are being developed.

Preschool and Primary Education

Roland Vandenberghe

DURING THE PAST DECADE, serious attention has been given to the future development of Belgian primary education. Like the educational system as a whole, primary education confronts the challenge of identifying and developing the full potential of students at the very moment when the fundamental mechanisms governing the organization of behavior and thought are being established. At a policy level, as well as within schools, the aims, curricula, and structure of primary education are being explored.

The development of preschool and primary education in Belgium was influenced by the Swiss Johann Pestalozzi, the German Friedrich Fröbel, the Italian Maria Montessori, and the Belgian Ovid Decroly (1871–1932). Primary education was originally influenced by Johann Herbart, Georg Kerschensteiner, and John Dewey. Its content and methods are eclectic in nature.

Preschool Education

Though not officially part of the educational system, nurseries and toddler centers are an important component of early childhood care. Daycare centers can be divided into two categories: nurseries for children from birth to 18 months, and toddler centers for children aged 18 to 36 months. Daycare centers usually receive children both of whose parents work and children from families with social or financial problems. Parents pay a fixed daily rate based on their annual income. In 1986, there were 2,422 children in nurseries and 16,044 in toddler centers.

Preschool education for children aged 2.5 to 5 years is free of charge. In most preschools, children are grouped according to age. Especially in schools with small enrollments, however, a family or vertical organizational system is used. Classes are generally coeducational. Preschools are frequently associated with primary schools, both administratively and physically, although a number are independent. Compulsory education does not begin until age 6, but attendance at preschools is very high: an estimated 30 percent for 2.5- to 3-year-olds, 90 percent for 3- to 4-year-olds, and 99 percent for 5-year-olds.

Primary Education

In 1914, legislation was enacted to provide compulsory schooling for all children from the age of 5 to 14 years. Belgium was one of the last countries in Western Europe to pass such a measure. All primary education was made free of charge, irrespective of parental income. There was also a provision for free medical supervision at schools, at the expense of local authorities, and a curriculum for four grades of two years each was established. For many years, primary schools offered the only education for many children and thus tried to provide as much knowledge and as many skills as possible. However, as access to secondary education became more democratic, primary education ceased to be the final educational opportunity. Paralleling this evolution was a change in the aims of primary education toward basic schooling for all children aged 2.5 years to 12 years.

Primary education for children aged 6 to 12 years consists of three stages of two years each, for a total of six years. Five-year-olds can attend primary school under certain conditions stated in the Compulsory Education Act. A student may spend a maximum of seven years in primary school (eight years in exceptional cases), but it is not uncommon for a child to repeat a grade. For instance, in Flanders (1985–86) 88.65 percent of pupils had progressed normally through primary education, 0.83 percent were ahead of their year, 9.9 percent were one year behind, 0.59 percent were two years behind, and 0.03 percent were more than two years behind; 38.79 percent of immigrant children are behind, one year or more. For the most part, these are children of immigrant workers with insufficient knowledge of the Dutch language. Although foreign students account for only 6 percent of the total school population, they are concentrated in a few areas: Limburg (15 percent) and Antwerp (9 percent). Some schools in these provinces have enrollments that are 95 percent foreign.

Teachers for preschool and primary education are trained in teacher-training colleges, which offer a three-year postsecondary non-university program. Although preschool and primary teachers are now trained in separate schools, there is a movement toward greater coordination of these two programs. Primary schools can also hire remedial teachers to work with children who have minor learning problems. Most remedial teachers have attended the usual teacher-training preparation, followed by short courses or in-service courses. In larger schools, there are also special teachers for moral philosophy or religious instruction and for physical education. A school with more than 400 pupils has a head teacher with no teaching duties, who is responsible for administrative and educational management. Many schools involve parents in extracurricular activities.

The syllabi for primary education are organized cooperatively by the bodies responsible for primary education (national, provincial, and municipal governments and private organizations like the Catholic church). These syllabi contain a summary of objectives and delineate the content of courses for each subject and year. Since the 1970's, separate syllabi have been published for each subject. These syllabi are usually reviewed within the educational community and adopted and implemented under the guidance of the school inspectorate. In practice, however, the guidelines for syllabi do not function well. In the organization of their courses, teachers tend to be guided more by existing teaching methods and handbooks and are encouraged to revise the syllabi to suit their local environment. Primary education is charged with the goals of guiding the general upbringing of children, in accordance with their developmental stages; imparting reading, writing, and arithmetic skills; and providing initial education in a variety of subjects so that children can discover their own potential. Attention is increasingly being placed on social and creative expression and on cognitive skills.

Primary education is organized into five-day school weeks, with Wednesday afternoon free. In general, there are four 50-minute lessons in the morning and two in the afternoon, for a weekly total of 28 lessons. Students must attend a minimum of 26 lessons per week. After time for the compulsory subjects on the syllabus has been allocated, the organizing bodies can distribute remaining teaching time among optional subjects. Schools located in a bilingual area such as Brussels must devote more time to instruction in the second language, thus reducing the time available for optional subjects.

The inspectorate has an important task in primary education. A distinction should be made between the State Inspectorate and an inspectorate corps directly linked to nongovernmental, subsidized education. In state education, the State Inspectorate has responsibility for guidance, for pedagogical and didactical implementation of general policy, and for syllabi. In subsidized education, the inspectorates are not paid by the state and have no direct link with the formation of educational policy; however, they issue directives concerning pedagogical and didactic methods. The inspectors for each system provide inspection and advice for the schools within their educational network.

Recently, the method of allocating teaching staff to primary schools has changed. Until 1984, the number of teachers was allocated on the basis of official class-size standards. Since September 1984, teachers have been assigned on the basis of the total number of pupils in the school. Thus each school can determine the distribution of full-time and part-time staff plus special instruction teachers. Although this offers schools opportunities for greater flexibility and innovation, implementation coincided with economizing measures that limited their ability to take advantage of the new system.

Innovation in Primary Education

Two major innovative projects have originated in and been supported by official educational policy: the Renewed Primary Education initiative in Flanders and Cycle 5–8 in Wallonia. The Renewed Primary School (RPS) project in Flanders started in September 1973 with nine schools and expanded rapidly to 275 schools by 1985. (The total number of primary schools in the Dutch-speaking part of Belgium is about 2,500.) The RPS is a large-scale innovative project characterized by its multidimensionality, by a large number of participating schools, and by a complex support structure. Its main goals are (1) enhanced integration and interdependence between preschool and primary education as well as continuity between primary school grades; (2) more individualized instruction in primary schools, particularly in reading and arithmetic; (3) enhanced contact and cooperation between classroom teachers and remedial teachers so that pupils with special problems receive more effective help; (4) increased emphasis on socio-emotional and creative development of pupils though a more child-directed approach; and (5) more effective use of community resources, both in terms of students going into the community to learn and of people in the community serving as resources in the schools. The main philosophical theme of RPS is greater interdependence among educational resources to support a more individualized, humanized, and effective response to pupils.

Parallel to the development of the RPS in Flanders, the Cycle 5–8 project was established in Wallonia in 1977. The number of schools with a Cycle 5–8 course has risen gradually to some 120 schools in the French-speaking network. The main objectives of Cycle 5–8 are to (1) harmonize the transfer from preschool to primary school; (2) reduce the number of failures in primary shcool; (3) achieve global upbringing and training (cognitive, social, emotional, psychomotor, and aesthetic); (4) promote individualized instruction; (5) assist and support autonomy, responsibility, and cooperation; and (6) develop a true local educational community (including parent participation). In Cycle 5–8, structural renewal is emphasized. The observation that the transfer from preschool to primary school, with its emphasis on subject material, causes problems for many children led to a decision to liberalize the subject matter / age-group class structure. A three-year course has been created at the pivotal point between preschool and primary school: the third year of preschool and the first two years of primary school. Three teachers for each of these classes form a team with joint responsibility for the entire group of five- to eight-year-olds. Teaching takes the form of a flexible system of mixed-age groups of pupils and methods that replace conventional teaching.

Secondary Education

Laurent Grimmonprez

THE SUBJECT OF SECONDARY EDUCATION has been discussed on a regular basis at the national level since 1964. Critical issues have been the perceptions of ministers of education of the functions and objectives of secondary education and the participation of the various responsible authorities in the definition of new key objectives and the gradual introduction of reform. It is impossible to overstate the volume of pedagogical work produced in the interim. A revised educational system has meant new timetables and syllabi, training of teachers and counselors, and efforts of individual teachers to analyze implementation measures. The resulting legislation provides a legal framework for secondary education while leaving pedagogical freedom in each of the organizing networks untouched.

The reform of secondary education is still not complete. There are two systems of secondary education in Belgium today: Type I—renewed education, which was introduced in Wallonia in 1969 and in Flanders in 1970; and Type II—traditional education. All state schools use the renewed education system, but the traditional system is still found in many schools run by provincial, municipal, and private authorities, especially in schools in the Dutch-speaking part of the country preparing students for higher education. In 1975, legislation established the equality of Type I and Type II education and the means for transferring from one program to another. All secondary schools, regardless of type or organizing power, follow guidelines established by law and monitored by the Ministries of Education through inspectors and certification of diplomas. These guidelines specify the length of study, conditions of admission, and program requirements. Type I and Type II programs lead to the same academic and professional degrees. The requirements for these degrees are legally specified and monitored by homologation commissions to ensure that the degrees issued by all secondary schools are comparable.

A number of concepts and trends have influenced secondary education in recent years. First, although the various forms of education should be accessible to all young people without distinction, sociocultural background nevertheless remains a determining factor in program selection. Second, the democratization of education has improved the overall cultural level of Belgian society. Third, since specialization inevitably accompanies technical evolution, a major objective of secondary education is to provide a common culture and language to allow mutual comprehension in spite of specialization. Fourth, scientific and technical progress requires a foundation flexible enough to enable retraining and redirection of careers. Fifth, secondary education must train for a specific vocation, for a profession that will require constant retraining, or for further studies. Sixth, although general objectives are the same for all students, differences must be recognized. Pupils beginning their secondary education differ considerably because of sociocultural heritage, the quality of primary education, and the individual student's absorption of that education. Students enter secondary education when they are still in an early stage of development. Secondary reforms have attempted to avoid early streaming of students, to offer remedial and reorientation classes for late-bloomers, and to maintain high standards for talented students. Elements of secondary reforms include (1) observation of pupils throughout their careers to avoid premature and irreversible choices and to select the training that best corresponds to the character and aptitude of individual pupils; (2) continuous assessment rather than final examinations to evaluate student performance; and (3) education at a reasonable cost to the government while maintaining freedom of choice. The third objective has been met by developing secondary education centers and using regional planning to distribute school and program options.

Type I (Renewed) Secondary Education

Type I secondary education has two main channels: *transition*, which prepares students for higher education, and *qualification*, which prepares them for employment after secondary school. Secondary education is further divided into general, technical, artistic, and vocational. General education is always transitional. In modern schools, general and technical education programs are organized into transition and qualification channels beginning in the third year of secondary school. Vocational education, which begins in the second year of secondary school, is always in the qualification channel. Type I secondary education is divided into three phases of two years each.

The first phase, *observation*, begins with a common first-year curriculum. A remedial year is also offered for students with deficiencies. At the end of the first year, students choose to enter either a vocational track or a second year of a common curriculum supplemented with general, technical, and artistic courses designed to provide the opportunity to assess the abilities of individual students. Students are encouraged to explore a variety of study options to awaken dormant abilities and to assess their own progress and potential. They are also helped to build a well-rounded personality: creative imagination, artistic talent, manual dexterity, physical harmony, and good health. A "tailor-made" education attempts to conserve and develop individuality. The first phase of Type I secondary education is usually offered in middle schools specializing in this type of education.

In the second phase, *orientation*, students select a program based on their specialization. Teachers work with students and parents to assess progress in the chosen program and in individual classes and to make adjustments where necessary. Constant self-assessment helps students take responsibility for their work, set goals, and evaluate progress toward their attainment. Educational options become increasingly prescribed as pupils are directed into transition and qualification channels. The timetables for transition programs prescribe 24–25 hours of a 32-hour week in basic education courses. In qualification programs, 7 to 11 hours are devoted to basic education courses. At the end of the fourth year of qualification programs, students can terminate their formal education with a *certificate of qualification* in a particular specialization, enter a reorientation program to move into a different program, or pursue further education in their specialization.

In the final phase, *determination*, two years must be completed in the same study option. Students pursue their study option in more depth while continuing basic courses. Those who successfully complete a transition program receive a *certificate of higher secondary education* giving access to higher education. Students who successfully complete a qualification program receive a *certificate of qualification* in a specialized field.

Type II (Traditional) Secondary Education

Traditional secondary education is now almost nonexistent in the French-speaking part of the country, but is still found in half of the Dutch-speaking, independent schools. It is organized into two cycles of three years each, lower and upper secondary education. General, technical, and vocational programs are introduced in the first year; art education begins in the fourth year following three years of general education. The traditions of general secondary education go back to the 16th and 17th centuries and the influence of the Renaissance and the Enlightenment. General education now includes classical and modern humanities. The classical section has a common first year of Latin. From the second year, a Latin-Greek section focuses on classical literature and antiquity, and the Latin-mathematics section emphasizes antiquity and mathematics. From the fourth year, the Latin-sciences section offers the options of biology, chemistry, and physics. Modern humanities includes general education and family studies at the lower level, and at the upper level Sciences A, emphasizing mathematics, and Sciences B, emphasizing the natural sciences; economics, including modern languages; and social sciences, preparing for teacher-training programs. As in Type I education, technical and art programs can prepare either for higher education or for a profession. Vocational training leads to a professional qualification. Unlike Type I education, students follow the same study option for six years, and opportunities for redirection are limited.

Technical education in the traditional system is a more recent phenomenon. Technical education was organized only in 1933, a time of economic crisis, by the Technical Teaching Code. Even slower was the implementation of a state subsidy system, eventually introduced in 1947. There has since been a gradual structuring, entirely within schools, of training for work. Thus some programs in the technical track offer professional training and sufficient general education preparation to prepare for middle-level positions and redirection of professional orientation, whereas vocational programs offer more narrow training in a trade or craft. However, both types of education have evolved in close consultation with the commercial and industrial world.

In both Type I and Type II education, technical education is at a critical juncture. Very early in a school career, students can select a technical program. However, the changing nature of industry and technology calls into question the training now offered by technical and vocational programs. Modern technology requires technicians with broader, stronger, and more flexible training who are sufficiently prepared in a particular area to begin working immediately. As a result, schools face demands from industry for specially trained employees that may compromise time spent on the humanist and general education components of technical training. Somewhat paradoxically, the education of a modern work force depends on several factors. If technical secondary education cannot adequately prepare students for industrial positions, industry itself must play a direct role in training. Schools are now beginning to call upon the manufacturing and economic world to help train young people by drawing them into real-life situations beyond the traditional notions of "training courses" and "factory visits" currently organized by technical schools. However, industry has not been sufficiently willing to invest in secondary education to finance advanced technologies and to replace outdated school equipment. At the same time, industry has called for schools to give more advanced training to keep up with technological innovation, but is recommending that schools train general technicians. Keenly aware of the risk that technical education will become outdated, industry has placed renewed emphasis on mastery of basics, such as mathematics and languages, to promote employees' versatility. A second line of attack has been the retraining of teachers to close the severe gap that has developed between the training levels of teachers and those demanded by industry.

Universities and Higher Education

Roger Van Geen

BELGIUM HAS A LONG HISTORY of university education. The Catholic University of Louvain, founded over five centuries ago, has long been a center of culture, learning, and science, and educated Erasmus and many other illustrious scholars. Today, Belgian university students follow broad and varied curricula, with a strong emphasis on science. The quality of this training partly explains the large "brain drain" of engineers, researchers, jurists, and economists to other European countries and the United States.

In the middle of the 19th century, Belgium had four full universities: the Catholic University of Louvain; two nonsectarian state universities, one in Ghent and the other in Liège; and the Free University of Brussels, a secular private institution. In addition, there were two specialized institutes of higher education: one for agriculture (Gembloux) and the other for veterinary medicine (Cureghem). The organization of Belgian universities has changed considerably in the second half of the 20th century, through expansion and the introduction of community control.

New Institutions, New Financing System

Belgian governments passed a number of laws after World War II to expand access to higher education. These measures established the equivalency of secondary education diplomas allowing access to university education, very low registration fees, a liberal system of loans and study grants, and legal protection of university diplomas. The most important measures were taken between 1965 and 1971, through the creation of new university institutions and the introduction of a new financing system for all universities.

The higher education system was expanded by creating two-year programs offered regionally and by promoting some institutions of higher education to the rank of universities. In addition, new universities and university institutions were created. This expansion has been financed by a system that is unique in the Western world, but one that has been judged too costly in the current economic crisis. All universities and university establishments are financed by the Belgian state on an equal footing, whether private or public and regardless of the organizing authority. Subsidies are calculated according to the size and composition (arts, laboratory sciences, medicine) of the student body. A government auditor checks that legislation is correctly implemented and that financial management is sound.

Linguistic and Cultural Balance

In the 19th century, Belgian universities were French-speaking institutions and taught only French culture. This was essentially due to the overwhelming proportion of French speakers in the administration, armed forces, education, and church before World War I.

The revival of Flemish nationalism and the search for a Flemish identity crystallized around the call for a Dutch-speaking university. In 1932, the University of Ghent, till then a French-speaking university in the heart of the Flemish provinces, became the first Belgian university where all classes were taught in Dutch. The example was rapidly followed by the Universities of Louvain (Leuven) and Brussels, which soon conducted most courses in both languages. In 1968, following the great sociological upheaval leading to the reform of state structures, each of these two universities split into two separate institutions and campuses. The French-speaking part of the Catholic University of Louvain moved to new campuses in Wallonia (baptized Louvain-la-Neuve) and in Brussels. The Dutch-speaking section changed its name to the Katholieke Universiteit Leuven, reflecting the monolingualism of communities within the restructured Belgium. The splitting of the Free University of Brussels resulted in the French-speaking Université Libre de Bruxelles on the original campus and a new campus for the Vrije Universiteit Brussel. In addition, two new state universities were formed: the Université de l'Etat in Mons in Wallonia and the Universiteit Antwerpen in Flanders. This decentralization movement resulted in a considerable upsurge in the number of students, which doubled within a few years, before stabilizing at around 100,000 per year.

Structure of University and Higher Education

Belgian universities are organized into a number of faculties. Each faculty corresponds to a school or a department. Each full university has at least the four traditional faculties (philosophy and arts, science, medicine and pharmacy, applied sciences) and a variable number of faculties, schools, and institutes in other fields (economics, political science, psychology, education, physical education, etc.). Medical doctors and engineers are therefore educated in universities and not in separate colleges, as is the case in many European countries. Consequently their training is more interdisciplinary, which is a very positive factor in light of current evolution of science and technology. The considerable development of medical technology and physics in Belgium is a result of this organization.

Belgian university education is organized into cycles. Students must successfully complete one cycle before moving on to the next. The first cycle is known as the *candidature* and lasts for two or three years. Generally speaking, students are age 18 to 21. On successful completion of this course, they are awarded a diploma. Candidature classes offer basic preparation for a particular field of study with an intensive mathematics program in most sections. The second cycle lasts for two or three years, and successful students are awarded a *degree*. In this cycle, teaching is more specialized, and students write a thesis. Successful students are awarded a degree or the title of engineer or doctor of medicine, giving them access to the relevant profession.

The third cycle includes doctoral study and original research leading to a dissertation. It is obtained only by high-level graduates, often carrying out scientific research. All these degrees are strictly protected by law. Various additional training cycles (special degrees and postgraduate courses) are offered in a wide range of fields in the sciences, technology, and the arts. Universities are free to decide how they organize this type of teaching.

University Enrollments

Six universities have the traditional faculties of applied science, law, medicine, philosophy and letters, and science as well as the newer faculties of education, political, social, and economic sciences, and psychology: Université de l'Etat à Liège, Université Libre de Bruxelles, Université Catholique de Louvain, Rijksuniversiteit te Gent, Vrije Universiteit Brussel, and Katholieke Universiteit te Leuven. The Université de l'Etat à

Mons has faculties of economic and social sciences, psycho-pedagogical sciences, science, and medicine (first cycle). The Engineering School at Mons is a separate institution. The Universiteit Antwerpen is an amalgamation of three institutions. Ten other institutions of higher education have more limited offerings. Approximately 80 percent of the students attend one of the six full universities. Fifty-four percent are in Dutch-speaking institutions, and 46 percent are in French-speaking institutions.

Higher Non-University Education

Much of the expansion of higher education took place in the non-university sector, where many small institutions were established to offer specialized programs. Legislation in 1970 classified higher education into the categories of university education, higher agricultural education, higher artistic education, higher economic education, higher paramedical education, higher teacher-training education, and higher technical education. The primary task of universities is the preservation, dissemination, and promotion of science and scholarship; the focus of other institutions of higher education is the dissemination of scientific knowledge and its application to professional development. The two types of education are considered to have their own values and purposes that determine their structure and teaching methods.

Higher councils for each language sector and area of study advise on problems related to their fields, either on their own initiative or at the request of the Ministries of Education. This organizational structure promotes interaction among institutions offering programs within a study area, creates bridges for students to move from one type of program to another, and helps organize studies regionally.

Another major development in the 1970's was the restructuring of non-university higher education programs. All non-university programs of study are either short courses (one cycle of two to three years; four years in some art fields) or long courses (two cycles for a total of four to five years). Short courses are not considered to be on the same level as university programs because entrance requirements vary. Some short courses may be offered by only one school or just a few. Others have long, well-established traditions, legally prescribed standards, and demanding curricula because they prepare for specific occupations such as nursing, social work, physical therapy, and primary and lower secondary school teaching.

Long courses are university-level programs with a more applied focus in addition to coursework in the theoretical basis of a profession. The admissions requirements are the same as for universities. Administrative and teaching positions at schools offering long programs require university degrees. Legislation created long programs leading to the title of industrial engineer and architect and defined the schools that could offer these programs. Long programs are also offered in economics.

Another aspect of the 1970 legislation was to halt public support for any additional institutions. Since then, small schools have been closed, and institutions have merged to form more viable centers that share resources and are regionally and financially justifiable.

The Number of Students

The vast expansion in the number of university students can be illustrated by the following figures: 45,000 (1966), 62,000 (1971), 100,000 (1984). The average annual growth rate was about 5 percent until the number of students stabilized at around 100,000 per year because of demographic contraction. Around 44 percent of students are studying social sciences, 37 percent natural sciences and engineering, 17 percent medicine, and 2 percent other subjects.

Problems and Outlook

Belgian university education confronts a number of new challenges on the threshold of the 21st century. These arise from general European integration, economic, technological, and cultural competition with the United States and East Asia, scientific and technological change, and the development of new forms of education, (open university, continuing education).

The National Council for Scientific Policy has made a number of recommendations to the government on ways higher education policy should change in regard to the objectives of universities, teaching methods, and financing. The main proposals were (1) rejection of numerical quotas and continuation of attempts to democratize education; (2) emphasis on varied training; (3) an increase in the links among the various forms of higher education; (4) introduction of modern educational technologies; and (5) creation of education for adults.

Research on Education

Gilbert de Landsheere

BELGIUM HAS A LONG history of experimental, historical, normative, and philosophical research on educational structures, programs, methods, techniques, and assessment of results. This research has had a direct impact on educational policy in modern Belgium. In 1899, Médard Schuyten created an experimental pedagogy laboratory in Antwerp for international research on experimental psychology. Between 1919 and 1927, four Belgian universities set up pedagogical institutes, which have since become faculties of education. The new universities created after 1960 have followed a similar program. Belgium's many researchers in this area give it an opportunity to play a leading role in Western Europe. Experimental educational research has essentially been concentrated in the universities; no other structure for educational research exists.

Two main figures dominated the interwar period, O. Decroly and R. Buysse. O. Decroly, the pioneer of new education, was behind the extraordinary mushrooming of kindergartens in Belgium, which are now attended by more than 95 percent of children in the qualifying age group. His ideas had considerable impact on the "Study Plan of Belgian Primary Education" (1936), the first widescale modern curriculum to be introduced in Europe. R. Buysse, professor at the Catholic University of Louvain, confirmed his position as the unrivaled leader of experimental education with the publication of his masterpiece, *Experimentation in Pedagogy* (1935). In 1960, this author developed the experimental educational laboratory at the University of Liège, on the basis of his experience in the United States. His *Introduction to Research into Education* (1964) has become an international reference work. Similar departments at other Belgian universities are currently experiencing rapid growth and expansion.

Despite its high quality and international reputation, educational research is currently experiencing difficulties in structure and financing. On average less than 1–2 percent of the national education budget is devoted to research. The lack of researchers is severe. General strategy, planning, and coordination would seem to be wanting.

Belgium owes its generally favorable reputation for its research on education to work carried out by individual scientists or small teams, who are not always in a position to influence their own country's educational system. The main activities of these researchers, who belong to large university departments or to regional institutions are summarized below.

Research Methodology

The Belgian A. Quetelet played a considerable role in the development of modern statistics and demography. Belgians have also contributed to the application of statistics to education, particularly in such fields as program assessment, educational administration, the assessment of teacher-training programs, and the development of accurate indexes for examinations.

Curriculum Research

Belgians have played a leading role in the introduction of set theory in the teaching of mathematics, the modernizing of language instruction, and the introduction of modular systems. Belgium also contributed significantly to the editing of school manuals, particularly their readability.

Education Technology

A great deal of research is being done on the application of new information technologies to education, particularly computer-assisted teaching. The French word *informatique* (information technology) first appeared (1970) in Belgium in a pedagogical research paper. Ten years earlier, the Belgian magazine *Education* published the first article in French on computer-assisted education. Though working in a country that did not produce computers, Belgian researchers produced educational software early on. Hardware was not, however, totally absent, as demonstrated by the prototype DOCEO, created in 1965, an audiovisual terminal that could interface with a cassette recorder or a slide projector and was designed with the needs of teachers in mind. In the 1960's, the work of Jones and Martegani established computer-assisted teaching in the Catholic University of Louvain. Some researchers who have been working in the area of computer-assisted teaching for 25 years now anticipated the arrival of high-performance multimedia microcomputers and explored the methodological and technical problems posed by the production of educational software that satisfies rigorous teaching criteria.

Preschool Education

In the past three decades, research on establishments for children age 0 to 6 has accelerated sharply. Belgian researchers have examined why the demand for daycare centers for children under 30 months suddenly soared, both quantitatively and qualitatively. The quantitative rise was found to be related to smaller family size (only the father, mother, and children) and to the higher employment rate for women from all classes. The qualitative rise was due to a desire for a rich educational environment in addition to the traditional need to look after children and keep an eye on their health.

Nursery schools came under the spotlight again in the 1960's when the fight for equality of civic rights was accompanied by a call for equality of educational opportunities. In 1969, thanks to massive support from the Bernard Van Leer Foundation, teams from the Universities of Brussels, Ghent, Liège and Mons were able to begin wide-ranging research on sociocultural handicaps. This highly successful research was the forerunner of many subsequent studies. Queen Fabiola has encouraged research on young children, children at risk, and handicapped children.

Education of Adults and Vocational Training

Belgium has a long history of experience in these two fields. Highly original research has been conducted on the fight against unemployment. Many Belgian researchers have also distinguished themselves in the field of the history of education. The magazine *Paedagogica Historica* is published in Ghent. Comparative education is another choice subject. The Belgian J. Lauwerijs for a long time held the prestigious chair of comparative education at the University of London. This research sector is continuing to expand. In recent years, important studies have been conducted on teaching policy and rejuvenation, as demonstrated by the foundation by this author of the Center for Educational Policy and Innovation in Leuven.

International Activities

Many Belgian researchers play an important role in leading international associations, including the European Network for Research in Education and Training (REREF), the International Association of French-language Experimental Pedagogy (AIPELF), the American Education Research Association (AERA), the European Association for Research on Learning and Instruction (EARLO), the International Association for the Evaluation of School Achievement (IEA), the International Association on Teacher Thinking (ISATT), the International Council on Teacher Education (ICET), the International Standing Conference for the History of Education, and International Cooperation for School Development Research (ICSDR), to name but a few.

Adult Education

Gaston Deurinck

THE OVERALL TREND OF RISING educational levels and the increasing rate of social and economic change have led to a growing concern for adult education, with three main goals: to remedy and/or complement an insufficient level of school education through basic adult education, to maintain and/or to reorient professional knowledge and skills through continuing professional education, and to enable adults to better understand their personal and societal situation through general adult education or "sociocultural work." Each of these goals has an impact on the other; a better knowledge and understanding of the changing social environment, for example, improves ability and motivation in further vocational training. Basic adult education is offered for adults who did not complete their primary or secondary education and allows them to make up for their deficiencies, whether they are working at a job or not. Continuing professional education responds to an ever increasing need to update one's knowledge base and the training acquired during younger years. Finally, the third goal concerns the need to impart a better understanding and a wider participation in the sociocultural life of the country, not to mention measuring the understanding and involvement of citizens in political life at all levels.

The highly decentralized way of life in Belgium greatly influences the nature and structure of adult education. Those activities are largely autonomous and decentralized, whether they are organized by public bodies or by private associations, such as business firms, trade unions, workers movements, or cultural associations.

Education for Social Promotion

Basic adult education offers those who, for one reason or another, did not complete their high school or even their elementary education an opportunity to complete their basic education and acquire further skills related to professional qualifications. The law of July 1963 makes it possible for everyone to pursue education while working and to attain wider professional and social opportunities. This type of education is dispensed in the evening or on weekends. It is under the authority of the Department of National Education. Initially conceived as a means of achieving job advancement for workers, it now constitutes one of the channels of the further education movement. The students in social-promotion education are of different ages, levels of training, social backgrounds, and trades.

Most of the programs include general academic, technical, and practical trade courses. They are given in various vocational fields and offer a wide range of possibilities for advancement in those fields. Courses in many languages occupy an important place in the system. State correspondence courses prepare students for the state examinations for lower and higher secondary education certificates and for civil service recruitment and promotion tests. Further education courses for teachers are also available. All these courses are free.

In 1973 an important step was taken to expand opportunities for workers and employees to acquire further skills and/or a wider basic education. The law of April 1973 established that every worker and employee in private business has a right to an educational leave of absence, at full salary, for up to 90 hours per year. This important legislation was improved and enlarged by the law of 1985 described in the section on vocational training. In 1986 about 230,000 students were engaged in the different courses organized within the social-promotion framework. Fees for those courses are negligible.

Another part of basic adult education is directed at socially or culturally deprived sections of the population: poorly educated youth, older women, the unemployed, immigrants. As in most countries of Europe, it has become apparent that approximately 5 percent of the population is functionally illiterate; their ability to read and write has waned over the years for various reasons. Therefore, literacy courses for adults have been developed in several cities and towns. Furthermore, several experiments have been set up to raise the educational level of poorly educated youth, as the bridge between "schoolbench and workbench." In 1986, it was estimated that about 60,000 youths between 16 and 25 years of age were engaged in such programs.

Vocational Training and Continuing Professional Education

This area of adult education is essentially concerned with the updating of vocational skills and with providing continuing education for those engaged in a profession and/or changing professions.

Vocational Training

Although "education for social promotion" provides more and more opportunities for the updating of skills, specific measures were thought to be necessary to cope with the ever increasing rate of obsolescence in all areas of professional activity. These efforts are related to the problems of unemployment and changes in the economic structure of the nation.

The law of January 22, 1985, enlarged the mission of the National Employment Service. One of its statutory obligations is to help increase the number of qualified workers, whether they are seeking employment or are already employed. People seeking employment but lacking appropriate qualifications are given the opportunity to acquire new knowledge and skills and thus become more eligible for employment. Those with specific qualifications are offered the opportunity of specializing and improving their qualifications in more than one trade, of gaining skills in new technologies, or of developing their basic skills. The service also assists employers with labor problems and with personnel training. The service is capable of offering more than 120 courses, in almost all trades.

In the present economic situation, with a high rate of unemployment and waning employment prospects in many traditional occupations, the existence of a large group of persons with practically no general or technical training is a pressing problem. In 1986, 44,768 unemployed persons were involved in vocational training and continuing professional courses free of charge.

Training courses are also available for the self-employed or those in the free trades. The object of this training is to enable the trainee to acquire the general and vocational knowledge necessary to exercise an independent profession or a trade. The programs are supervised by the Higher Council of the Middle Classes and are delivered in modern and well-equipped centers for free-trade training. There are about 35 centers in the country, with an estimated 4,250 courses and 65,000 students.

Vocational courses in agriculture are organized by recognized bodies subsidized by the community if they satisfy the legal specifications for course instructors, programs, schedules, facilities, and the like. Students must be at least 18 years of age and be working in agriculture or a related sector. Approximately 475 courses are organized each year for 6,500 students.

The important law of March 9, 1985, expanded the law of July 1963 described earlier. The right of every worker and employee to obtain an educational leave with full salary was extended to the whole active population in the private and the public sectors. The appropriate public department reimburses the student's employer for 50 percent of the salary, and a levy of 0.03 percent of the total salary is taken from all companies to fund the program. The number of hours allowed per year was raised to 240 for vocational training and to 180 for general training. In private companies, management submits the overall training scheme to the workers' council. In 1986, 14,800 employees benefited from this scheme, which is free of charge.

Continuing Education in the Professions

The realization of further education needs for persons in the professions has been provoked by the growing complexity and diversity of technology and changes in the socioeconomic environment. Considerable human and financial efforts have been made to establish collaborative structures between industry and other vocational training and educational networks. Highly diversified channels are used to cope with these needs. Besides the role played by the educational systems as such, courses are organized by professional associations, trade associations, in-company programs, consulting firms, and private schools.

In the domain of *management*, a 1955 conference of industry and university leaders led to the establishment of the Industry-University Foundation. The board of this foundation includes representatives of the main universities and of the business community. Its establishment reflects the decision of industry to develop management education in universities, instead of setting up business schools dependent on trade associations or chambers of commerce, as was the case at that time in almost all other European countries. Until 1981, the foundation's primary aim was to stimulate and coordinate initiatives in management education at Belgian universities. It did so by financially supporting the creation of centers and by encouraging doctoral studies in management sciences so as to provide the training centers and universities with highly qualified teachers and researchers. In 1981, an agreement that deepened the industry-university relationship was signed by Belgian business organizations and universities. Since then, the foundation has been concerned with the relationships between industry and the universities for both continuous and basic training. Moreover, it expanded its activities to all subjects related to the development of business: engineering, economics, and human and social sciences.

Universities concentrate their efforts in two areas. First, programs modeled after the master of business administration programs in the United States have been developed and strengthened at all universities. Enrollment has almost doubled since 1981, with an increasing number of adult students with business experience. Second, a large number of short programs are organized in the different universities to meet increasing demands from businesses of every kind and in all major functional areas. In 1986, about a hundred different programs were offered, with an average enrollment of 4,000 students.

However, the universities have not been able to meet the increasing demand for retraining of junior, mid-level, and senior managers. Major companies, especially in the fields of banking and insurance, have thus developed their own facilities and organized "corporate classroom" activities. Trade associations and consulting firms are also meeting a substantial part of the demand, as are technical and professional schools. The cost is born either by the company or by the individual.

In 1982 a similar organization, the Administration-University Institute, was established to cope with the problems of management training in the public administration sector (state, provinces, cities, towns, and related public authorities). Although these programs were very successful with local authorities, they were less successful with the central administration due to a lack of political support and hence of adequate financial and human resources within the universities.

In the field of *engineering*, programs have been developed over the years by the engineering associations. However, since the 1981 agreement enlarging the objectives of the Industry-University Foundation, major steps were taken to expand the involvement of university-based engineering schools in adult continuing education. Under the aegis of the foundation, a consortium of the seven university-based engineering schools was established, with the aim of developing a seven-week training program spread over the academic year. The following programs are now offered: computer-integrated management, telecommunications, computer-controlled measurement systems, new and composite materials, and biotechnology. Furthermore, some engineering schools offer short courses in an increasing number of fields.

In the area of *medicine*, continuing education for physicians in all specialties, but mainly for general practitioners, is regularly offered by the medical schools of all universities. It consists of special lectures by the faculty, reading assignments, special courses, participation in scientific colloquia, and the like. Some of those activities are organized and coordinated on an interuniversity basis. In addition, physicians may participate in local groups that organize periodic meetings with the help of the medical schools. This last development was initiated in 1972, within the framework of a law inviting general practitioners to follow a program of 200 hours of lectures over a period of three years. Upon completion of the program, practitioners are allowed to raise their fees by 10 percent, an amount reimbursed to the patients by the Social Security Administration. Almost 95 percent of all general practitioners participate in this program.

In the *teaching* sector, the need for further education for teachers at all levels is increasingly recognized, but no overall scheme has been implemented by the Ministries of Education. Two main lines of approach are being developed. Either the school as an institution takes responsibility for organizing activities aimed at improving the knowledge and basic skills of its own teachers, mainly through "learning by doing" and stimulated by counseling, attendance at workshops and special meetings, class visits, and the like. Or outside institutions develop training activities especially designed to meet the needs of the profession at different levels.

Teachers are thus invited to participate in courses and seminars organized by the university where they received their basic education, by a number of private institutions, by the social-promotion education system, and by the further pedagogical centers of the Ministries of Education. These pedagogical centers are called upon mostly when new courses are introduced or when there is an important need to improve teaching methods.

Another field of further education is concerned with the improvement of skills in interpersonal relations between teachers, students, and parents and with the overall management of the schools. In 1987, the Ministries of Education budgeted about 2 billion BF to develop these activities. This represents less than 1 percent of the total educational budget of the state.

Sociocultural Education

Belgium, especially the Flemish part of the country, has a long tradition of general adult education, which was called "popular education" or "people's development" in the 19th century and is now called "sociocultural education" or "adult education." The oldest organizations—all voluntary—date to the middle of the 19th century. They reflect the varied ethical, social, and ideological categories of the population, and they all have mixed goals of recreation, social help, defense of their interests, and general and political education.

Public Library Service

A law of October 17, 1921, concerning public libraries was the first major cultural law voted by the Belgian parliament. This law constitutes the foundation of all public efforts to develop education for the people.

The 1921 law was undoubtedly of great merit. It provided a complement to primary education, which had just been made compulsory, and at the same time it provided a useful orientation for the leisure time of workers, who had just obtained an eight-hour workday. In the space of a few years, the very heterogeneous "popular" libraries were transformed into a genuine public service; the taste for reading increased considerably, particularly among the working-class population. In 1921, there were 1,500 public libraries; by 1985, this figure had nearly doubled.

Further Education Organizations

The spectrum of organizations was significantly broadened after World War II, especially during the 1960's and 1970's. Thus, new groups (women, migrant workers, unemployed) were targeted by new types of institutions (educational or neighborhood centers, training centers, cultural houses, etc.). Both the Flemish- and the French-speaking communities developed their own policies from 1965 onwards, but a real policy started only after the installment of "cultural councils" in 1971–72, and the strengthening of Ministries of Culture in both language regions of the country.

Sociocultural Work in Flanders

Voluntary socio-cultural organizations date back to the middle of the 19th century, when the Willemsfond (foundation) was created, followed by the Davidsfond. The latter was a Catholic reaction to the humanistic orientation of the Willemsfond. Also, "people's universities" had the goal of diffusing new scientific knowledge, and "adult Sunday schools" provided basic education for young adults. During the first half of the 20th century, networks of socialist, Christian, and liberal organizations were set up for laborers, farmers, and the middle classes.

Since 1960, a second type of adult education has emerged: the so-called *educational centers* or *folk high schools*. They are aimed at special target groups, offering short courses (2–5 days) on several topics, such as personal growth, group work, societal problems, special skills. There are now about 46 such centers, spread all over the country, mostly in regional towns and big cities.

Since the 1920's, a whole network of organizations devoted to *popular art and drama* has been set up. The oldest are in the areas of popular theater (over 300 local groups), popular music, nature exploration, photography, film, and folk dance. They have a lesser educational impact and stress the development of special skills linked to leisure and recreation.

Finally, within the official spectrum of sociocultural organizations, there is a vast group of organizations that do not have members or regular participants but offer special services to different groups or are temporarily set up to solve specific problems. A special decree has been adopted to provide those organizations with funding and personnel. They either work in areas such as film education, tourism, and audiovisual aids or address special problems, such as unemployment, migration, peace, and disarmament.

Sociocultural Work in the French-Speaking Community

The *Centers of Expression and Creativity* have three main objectives: to promote the values and cultural aims of the community to which they belong (at the local or regional level) rather than the dominant cultural practices and models (those of the privileged section of the public); to promote a wide range of communication abilities, considered as the necessary background for specific projects; and to attempt, as individuals or as a group, to create gradually the conditions for an awareness of and response to the many questions posed by present-day sociocultural life. Since November 1976, the public authorities have recognized and subsidized the Centers of Expression and Creativity, which provide diversified activities, suited both to personal creative projects and to collective activities. These centers are open to all persons and all ages, are autonomous, and have an adequate infrastructure as far as projects and activities are concerned.

Community media facilities include TV programs and new technological elements in telecommunications, microcomputers, local radio broadcasting, videobuses, media centers, super-8 films and video events, and the like. Eleven community TV programs now broadcast, and some 360 local radio stations are recognized and partially subsidized.

Finally, *training for immigrants* has been conceived in response to the needs of this population (integration and the search for identity). The following projects may qualify for subsidies: basic training, languages, publications, and initial assistance.

In conclusion, the *open university* provides opportunities for those who are not eligible to enter the university system to follow special programs organized under the responsibility of a university. Several experiments with this type of education have been carried out by the universities or by further education organizations in liaison with them. The objective of all such experiments has been to offer working adults the chance to follow a university curriculum and obtain a university diploma. The most advanced experiment has been carried out at the Catholic University of Louvain with the establishment of an Open Faculty for Political, Economic, and Social Sciences (FOPES). Most students are young leaders either of the Christian Trade Unions (CSC) or the Christian Workers Movements (MOC).

PART VII

Science

André L. Jaumotte, Coordinator

Introduction

André L. Jaumotte

LOUIS PASTEUR, WHO DID NOT like the common distinction between pure science and applied science, said: "Two sciences do not exist: there is science and there are the applications of science, and the two are related as the fruit is related to the tree." This section deals not with science or the applications of science but with what it takes to grow the tree of science and to reap an abundant and healthy crop. Nevertheless, let me introduce two branches of the tree of science in Belgium that illustrate the Belgian contributions to science: molecular biology and thermodynamics far from equilibrium.

Molecular Biology

A number of discoveries have been made in Belgium in molecular and cellular biology. They are rooted in the techniques of *cell fractionation* developed by a Belgian, Albert Claude, then at the Rockefeller Institute for Medical Research (now Rockefeller University) in New York. These techniques make it possible to break cells open without damaging their structural components and then to separate the components by differential centrifugation. Following separation, isolated fragments can be submitted to a wide range of analyses to determine their enzymatic content and the functional properties of the various intracellular components. At the Catholic University of Louvain (UCL), Christian de Duve considerably improved Claude's techniques and discovered two new subcellular particles. For this discovery, de Duve was awarded the 1974 Nobel Prize for Physiology and Medicine jointly with Claude and George Palade, Claude's main collaborator. The same year, the International Institute of Cellular and Molecular Pathology was created as part of the new School of Medicine in Brussels, a school administered by the UCL.

Among other examples of molecular biology in Belgium in the 1980's is the Molecular Biology Department of the Free University of Brussels (ULB), which has made some fundamental advances since the crucial discovery by Jean Brachet (ULB) of the role of ribonucleic acid (RNA) in protein synthesis. The Catholic University of Leuven (KUL) has an institute oriented toward microbiology and immunology, set up by the late Professor De Somer. It has earned a firm reputation in the areas of interferon, lymphocytes, and cytokines. Finally, Marc Van Montagu and Jeff Schell at the University of Ghent (RUG) have gained international respect for their work on plant molecular genetics and agrobacteria.

Thermodynamics Far from Equilibrium

The study of this branch of thermodynamics can be traced to the work of Théophile De Donder, the founder of the Brussels school of thermodynamics, in the 1920's. De Donder started from the "noncompensated heat" of Clausius, applied it to irreversible processes, and expressed it in terms of the Gibbs chemical potentials. He was thus able to relate the rate of production of entropy to the rate of chemical reactions thanks to a new thermodynamic state function, the *affinity*. In 1945, Ilya Prigogine, a student of De Donder's, formulated one of the first theorems pertaining to situations near equilibrium, the theorem of minimum entropy production. A little later, Prigogine and his coworkers extended thermodynamics to systems far from equilibrium. In so doing, they discovered "dissipative structures," for which Prigogine was awarded the 1977 Nobel Prize for Chemistry. Far from equilibrium, where processes are highly nonlinear, a system can acquire coherent, structured activity in space and in time (auto-organization). Thus the system moves spontaneously from disorder to order. In addition, Prigogine made an essential contribution to elucidating the relationships between the second principle of thermodynamics and molecular dynamics following Boltzmann. The Brussels school of thermodynamics is now internationally recognized as a source of new ideas.

This part deals with the policies and organizations responsible for science and the applications of science in Belgium. The organization of contemporary scientific research in Belgium has a number of characteristics. Fundamental research is concentrated exclusively in universities and in government-funded scientific establishments. Belgium does not have large-scale national laboratories such as those of the CNRS in France or the Max Planck Institutes in West Germany. Military research is practically nonexistent.

Belgian scientific policy is organized in a highly original manner that avoids the typical split between centralized and individual research. Each ministry with an interest in and responsibility for a certain type of research receives a research budget. The Ministry of Science has a separate budget and a double task: to push national programs considered high priorities by the government and to coordinate research at the national level. Thus subsidies go to three different types of activities: priority programs, fundamental research, and applied research. Belgium devotes 1.4 percent of its GNP to research and development (R&D). About 40 percent of this sum is funded directly by the government, half of it to support fundamental science. As much as 10 percent of government-funded research is carried out in the framework of European or international projects.

Supporting fundamental science is the mission of the National Foundation for Scientific Research (Fonds National de la Recherche Scientifique; FNRS or NFWO), a state-run body, which appoints researchers and supports research programs. Selection is through peer review by scientific committees.

Industrial R&D is financed about equally by the private and the public sector. The responsible public agency is the Institute for the Encouragement of Scientific Research in Industry and Agriculture (IRSIA or IWONL). The work is carried out in joint research centers and in a few large industrial laboratories. Universities participate through research contracts. Almost two-thirds of R&D expenditure is focused on two sectors: chemistry, including pharmaceuticals, and electrical engineering, including electronics. The criteria most often used to determine the viability of a program are economic, commercial, and social relevance.

These are the basic characteristics of scientific policy in Belgium. As can be seen, universities play a central role in almost all of science and a considerable part in the applications of science. Therefore, the university-industry interface is of particular importance to technology transfer. The role played by universities is to generate new knowledge and transfer it to the scientific and industrial community. Contract research, with a businesslike approach, is now widespread in the Belgian academic community. The organizational details vary from one institution to another, but three features are frequently seen: a group responsible for promoting or optimizing university research outside the university environment, a science or industrial research park, and a business center. More recently, the group responsible for research promotion and has taken on a new role: starting up new ventures.

Research parks with a university connection date to 1968. Their development was initially slow, but they are now well established. University groups are closely involved in the negotiation of projects proposed by companies. They have a spontaneous and informal relationship with companies operating in the science park. Business centers are also a relatively new invention. Their objectives are to help potential company founders set up a business with maximum chances of success and to help existing companies to develop new industrial or service activities. In this way, universities are fully involved in the process of optimizing research through links with companies. The methods used have created a new climate between the various partners and generated greater enthusiasm in the university-industry dialogue. Academics have learned to work with industry. Biotechnology is undoubtedly the field in which university and industry are the most closely associated.

The last chapter in this section deals with the growing globalization of R&D. Today, both fundamental and applied research need increased financial support over longer periods. Budgets greatly exceed the financial resources of smaller countries. Therefore, considerable efforts are made in Belgium to participate in European and international research programs. At the same time, those areas of R&D are selected where tradition, past results, and qualified scientists can guarantee successful participation in international scientific and technological agreements.

The Organization of Scientific Policy

Roger Van Geen

BELGIAN SCIENTIFIC RESEARCH WAS given its first important boost in 1928 with the creation of the National Foundation for Belgian Scientific Research (FNRS/NFWO), following a famous speech made in 1927 by King Albert I on the importance of the scientific potential of a nation. Another quantum leap was taken in 1947 with the establishment of the Institute for the Encouragement of Scientific Research in Industry and Agriculture (IRSIA/IWONL), which laid the foundations for much more substantial industrial research.

The main features of Belgian scientific research were thus in place before the 1950's, which were characterized by major programs in the space and nuclear sectors. Belgian scientific research is concentrated in the major universities or their peripheral institutions, with the exception of specialized research in the laboratories of a few large firms in the chemical, metallurgical, and electromechanical sectors. One of the chief missions of FNRS and IRSIA is to allocate research grants to universities. The FNRS, for its part, selects programs to support through scientific committees, operating on the principle of peer review. The method used by IRSIA for industrial research support includes assessment of the economic, commercial, and social relevance of the program proposed. The 1960's were marked by considerable expansion of the means and instruments at the disposal of scientific research. This expansion paralleled the introduction in Belgium of the "scientific policy" concept.

Belgian politicians suddenly became aware of the impact of science and technology policy on economic growth and social and cultural development. The general public became entranced by the conquest of space, the splitting of the atom, and the electronic revolution. As a result, a series of measures changed the face of Belgian scientific research. The most important of these were the appointment of a minister for science, the creation of the Scientific Policy Planning Services, and the creation of the National Council for Scientific Policy. As a consequence, a specific decision-making structure and budgetary procedure were set up.

At the same time, university subsidies expanded considerably. The Nuclear Energy Center in Mol underwent large-scale development and became the first (and to date only) extra-university national research center. Four government scientific establishments were established or considerably expanded; namely, the Geomagnetism Study Center, the Space Aeronomy Institute, the Royal Observatory, and the Royal Meterological Institute.

Decision-making Structure and Budgetary Procedure

Industrialized countries have, as a rule, chosen one of two types of science policy. The first is centralized and places all power over science either in the hands of a single minister, a single government department, or a single scientific council. This rather monolithic approach is efficient, improves rationalization, coordinates efforts, and benefits from a certain simplicity. France and the Federal Republic of Germany are good examples of such a structure.

The second approach is the thematic one of entrusting the organization of scientific research within a particular field (medical research, industrial and technological research, public works, fundamental research) to the relevant ministry. This has the advantage of improving the integration of research objectives into the overall policy of the ministry, allowing, for example, improved coordination between hospital policy and medical research, greater coherence between applied research and industrial policy, and so on. Other positive points include a range of better-adapted decision-making centers and a more flexible structure.

Belgium wanted to avoid this dichotomy. It developed in the field of science, as in many other areas, a hybrid and original solution whose structural complexity is often beyond the grasp of the foreign observer. However, in the final analysis it is supple, efficient, and even rather pleasant. The foreign press is often rather ironic about "Belgian solutions," but to understand their dialectic nature, it is important to bear in mind that Belgium is at the crossroads of highly diverse cultures and has been traumatized on several occasions by foreign occupation.

Consequently it has a unique talent for merging Napoleonic centralism, Florentine subtlety, and Germanic rigidity. Under Belgian scientific policy, each minister with an interest in and responsibility for a particular scientific area has a research budget. For example, the medical research budget is drawn from the budget of the Ministry of Health. A Ministry of Science also exists, with its own budget and the twofold task of *motivating and supporting* national programs considered high-priority projects by the national government (e.g., energy research, artificial intelligence) and of *coordinating* research at the national level.

Scientific policy is defined by two coordination and decision-making bodies, the Ministerial Committee for Science Policy, consisting of the relevant ministers, and a committee of qualified civil servants. The Belgian scientific budget is, to a certain extent, calculated with the help of a matrix, whose columns consist of the priorities and choices of each minister and the rows of the programs and fields. Between 1980 and 1985, the amount budgeted came to around 60 billion Belgian francs annually.

The formation of the Scientific Policy Planning Services gave birth to a third method of granting research subsidies, which came to rival those practiced in the cases of fundamental and industrial research. It can be termed the "impetus program method." It consists essentially of finding the most suitable research team for carrying out a particular program, whose objectives have been defined in socioeconomic or cultural terms. Identification of the most suitable team is highly difficult, demanding in-depth acquaintance with the scientific potential of the nation and requiring respect for the delicate philosophical, political, and linguistic balances characterizing Belgium.

The National Scientific Policy Council is the cornerstone of Belgium's scientific infrastructure and stands at the head of all the other scientific policy bodies set up by the government. It has 34 members, chosen for their individual qualities and contributions to the development of a scientific policy to serve national interests. They can be divided into four groups: twelve representatives of research (university chancellors, managers of research centers, foundation leaders), eight researchers from various different scientific disciplines, eight representatives from industry (heads of industrial R&D departments, leaders of federations of employers, managers of large industrial laboratories), and six representatives of the social partners (trade union officials).

The council has the power only to issue *opinions*, but its recommendations carry a certain weight with politicians and academics. The council avoids majority decisions in favor of consensus. In this respect it is a successful example of consultation. The council, and ad hoc committees that assist it in its work, also fulfills an important role as a meeting point between the social partners, university officials, and industry. The council also issues "recommendations" addressed to the government. Its "trend opinions" are regular reports on the state of research, funding, and prospects. A recent report, "Scientific and Budgetary Priorities of Scientific Policy," had considerable repercussions. It contained specific recommendations on, for example, a new university strategy, technological research policy, stimulating research in the social sciences, assessment of innovation policy, and microelectronics research policy and its social consequences. Other recommendations dealt with telecommunications research (an expanding sector), research in the textiles sector (a sector experiencing restructuring), and supercomputer resources. These proved to be very useful documents for political decision-makers.

On a number of occasions, the good quality of Belgian scientific research and the excellent training of researchers have come to the fore. Belgian scientific policy has nevertheless encountered three major problems. These must be dealt with successfully at all costs, particularly with more advanced European integration on the horizon. They are financing, fragmentation, and technological upheaval.

Financing

The scientific effort of a country can be measured by comparing R&D expenditures to a parameter representing growth, for example, R&D as a percentage of GNP, or as a percentage of government spending, the number of researchers per 1,000 inhabitants, and so on. International comparisons of the Belgian effort, for example, within bodies such as the OECD or the EEC, clearly demonstrate that Belgian scientific research suffers from a *lack* of financial and human resources. Table VII.1, extracted from a trend report by the National Scientific Policy Council, shows total scientific research expenditure as a percentage of GNP in

TABLE VII.1
R&D Expenditure as a Percentage of GNP, 1983:
An International Comparison of Industrialized Countries

Country	Total (% GNP)	Private funding (% GNP)	Public funding (% GNP), University	Non-university
France	2.15%	1.22%	0.34%	0.59%
West Germany	2.54	1.80	0.40	0.34
United Kingdom	2.28	1.39	0.31	0.58
Netherlands	2.03	1.09	0.51	0.43
Sweden	2.46	1.66	0.66	0.14
Switzerland	2.28	1.69	0.40	0.19
Belgium	1.40	1.06	0.24	0.10
United States	2.72	1.94	0.36	0.42
Japan	2.56	1.63	0.59	0.34

TABLE VII.2
*Breakdown of Belgian Scientific Research Funding as a Percentage of Total,
by Standardized Objective, 1984–1987.*

Objective	1984	1985	1986	1987
Exploration and exploitation of the earth	2.8%	3.1%	2.5%	2.4%
Infrastructure and amenities	0.6	0.6	0.6	0.6
Pollution and the environment	2.5	2.5	2.4	2.3
Health protection and promotion	2.0	1.9	2.1	2.2
Production and use of energy	12.2	11.3	10.1	9.6
Agricultural productivity and technology	7.2	7.1	7.1	7.1
Industrial productivity and technology	17.9	17.8	16.2	14.8
Life in society	0.4	0.6	0.7	0.6
Exploration and exploitation of space	6.2	6.6	7.2	9.6
Fundamental university research	23.4	22.1	22.8	22.2
Nontargeted research	21.1	21.8	20.5	21.1
Other research	2.4	3.1	6.3	6.5
Defense	1.4	1.5	1.5	1.0
TOTAL	100.0%	100.0%	100.0%	100.0%

TABLE VII.3
*Number of R&D Researchers as a Percentage of the Working Population, 1983:
International Comparison of Industrialized Countries*

Country	Total	Business	University	Non-university
France	3.9%	1.6%	1.4%	0.9%
West Germany	4.8	3.0	1.1	0.7
United Kingdom	3.9	2.9	(1)	(0.8)
Netherlands	3.7	1.5	1.2	0.8
Sweden	3.9	2.2	0.9	0.4
Switzerland	3.4	2.0	1.6	(0.4)
Belgium	3.9	2.0	1.6	0.3
United States	˙6.4	4.7	0.9	0.8
Japan	7.4	3.9	3.0	0.6

NOTE: Estimated values shown in parentheses. Row may not add to totals shown because of overlap in the categories.

1983, broken down into private and public sector contributions. Funding from the public sector is then divided into research expenditure (via government funding) in universities and extra-university research centers. There was no substantial change, except for a slight contraction, in the period 1984–87. Table VII.2 shows the evolution between 1984 and 1987 of the distribution of this funding, using standard categories employed in international comparisons. Table VII.3 shows the number of R&D researchers as a percentage of the working population, for 1983.

These statistics highlight two characteristics that have already been mentioned; namely, the overwhelming role played by universities in Belgian research and the absence of military research. However, the main conclusion to be drawn is that Belgian scientific research suffers from a lack of funding, compared with the European average and compared not only with large but also with small industrialized countries of a similar size, such as the Netherlands, Switzerland, or Sweden, which have been much faster to realize the importance of intangible assets on the threshold of the 21st century.

The National Scientific Policy Council has prepared numerous reports on this alarming situation and proposed a ten-year expansion plan in order to bring R&D expenditure up to the European average of 2 percent. The plan was set in motion, but its implementation has encountered a range of difficulties arising from Belgium's vast budget deficit.

Fragmentation of Research in Belgium

In a 1987 report entitled "Scientific Research at the Service of the Country," the King Baudouin Foundation expressed its support for the conclusions of the National Scientific Policy Committee with regard to certain failings in Belgian research organizations. The report made the following comments:

A new factor has arisen in recent years. The European scientific community in general, and the Belgian one in particular, appears to have overlooked the magnitude, importance, and consequences of this new factor, some of which are already evident. Thus, American and also European firms now have research budgets that amount to hundreds of millions of dollars. Some of them have a research budget which exceeds the entire research budget of Belgium (56.8 billion francs for 1985), including grants to all Belgian universities. . . .

What is the solution for a small country like Belgium where even "big business" is dwarfed by the American giants? Both industry and university are incapable of innovating in isolation, except in isolated cases. An open university-industry system should therefore be created and organized in such a manner as to unite all the forces striving for innovation, which increasingly requires a coming together of various different disciplines. . . .

Some Belgian universities had already put this idea to industry but had failed to first adapt their internal organization, which is a prerequisite for the success of such joint efforts. University research was fragmented among a plethora of departments that are much too small, often consisting of just one person, and divided among a maze of institutions.

Belgian researchers must be given due praise for managing to remain competitive in such conditions, but this competitiveness is draining away and is often too marginal. Universities, through internal restructuring, must reduce the number of their services so that those which remain are of a viable size and dispose of sufficient means. The corresponding services in various universities must form into associations for the purposes of research programs. The idea of a network between Belgian universities must be introduced.

The concept of an interuniversity network is being embodied in the form of a first project: "excellence centers," also termed "interuniversity technological poles of attraction." A second project, the creation of an interactive wide-band optical fiber network between universities, their libraries, computing centers, and audiovisual teaching units, is currently at the study stage.

Coming to Grips with the Technological Revolution

Toward the middle of the 20th century, the adoption of a scientific approach to the "information content" concept caused an epistemological upheaval as vital as that triggered by Newton with the concepts of dynamics and energy. It sparked off whirlwind development of new technologies revolving around computer technology, biotechnology, new materials, and lasers. Comprehension and successful manipulation of these developments require a considerable effort both in fundamental research and advanced technological research. Current technological development is situated at the frontiers of knowledge in physics, chemistry, biology, and mathematics.

This effort must satisfy a certain number of conditions. For example, it must be sufficiently critical, there must be industry-university cooperation, a multidisciplinary approach, and a multinational openness. These criteria can be seen as challenges that must be met.

The impact of the technological revolution is very broad, to the point where it is difficult to quantify its effect. It has changed production relationships, provoked reforms in company structure, overturned education, created the communications society, and churned up ethical questions on social organization, the environment, and information. The future of Europe depends on its ability to come to grips with the social implications of the new technology. Research into the social sciences has been given a new role and a historical dimension.

The National Scientific Policy Council has devoted an important "government recommendation" to the definition of the cornerstones of such research. The scientific and technological revolution has also created problems concerning research structure. The creation of new institutes such as the Microelectronics Research Institute (IMEC), the reconversion of the Mol nuclear center, and the creation of "excellence centers" and "poles of attraction" has been entrusted to the leadership of the university community.

These structural transformations come at a time when the Belgian government is giving more power to the regions (Flanders, Wallonia, and

Brussels) over economic and social affairs. The commanding role played by scientific research in these fields will inevitably lead to a redistribution of power in this area between the central government and the regions. The net result of these changes must be improved and more dynamic scientific potential. To conclude this analysis of the structure, characteristics, and financing of Belgian scientific policy, Belgian research would seem to have the necessary assets to gain a favorable place on the world scientific stage, provided that it adapts rapidly to new factors as they appear in this lively aspect of human activity.

Fundamental Research

Paul Levaux

A nation protects itself from decadence and is sure of remaining strong when it resolutely marches with progress in all fields and applies the best capacities of its citizens to the task of increasing the general well-being. . . . Modern science gives technology new and almost infinite possibilities. Research laboratories are responsible for laying the foundations of tomorrow's industry, and yet one cannot help but be worried by the lack of material means at the disposal of scientists today for the continuation of their studies and work. . . . Considerable and sustained effort and a range of initiatives are essential if we want—and want we must—to maintain our position and our reputation. In this day and age, those who choose not to advance will inadvertently retreat.   —King Albert I, 1927

THE KING'S WORDS STRUCK a chord in national opinion and led to the creation in 1928 of the National Foundation for Scientific Research (FNRS), which was given the task of training researchers and subsidizing their research. The king's appeal for recognition of the fact that research holds the key to national development is now some sixty years old. This axiom is the basis of all hope for progress. In Belgium, fundamental research is carried out chiefly in universities and government scientific establishments. Unlike large neighboring countries such as France and Germany, Belgium generally does not have fundamental research laboratories outside of these institutions.

Fundamental Research Within Universities

Universities are clearly an ideal place for scientific reflection. In all the European research universities, research and teaching both coexist and overlap. Belgium has six universities with a full range of schools: the University of Ghent (RUG), the University at Liège (UEL), the Catholic University of Louvain (UCL; French-speaking), the Catholic University of Leuven (KUL; Dutch-speaking), the Free University of Brussels (ULB; French-speaking), and the Free University of Brussels (VUB; Dutch-speaking). The campuses and the administration of UCL and KUL and of ULB and VUB are separate.

Eleven other institutions of higher education offer teaching at a similar level: the Antwerp University Institution (UIA) and the Antwerp State University Center (RUCA), the State University of Mons (UEM), Mons Polytechnic (FAPOM), the State Faculty of Agronomic Science at Gembloux (FAGEM), the University Faculties of Our Lady of Peace at Namur (FUNDP), the Antwerp St. Ignatius University Faculties (UFSIA), the Catholic University Faculty at Mons (FUCAM), the St. Louis University Faculties at Brussels (FUSEL), the St. Aloysius University Faculties at Brussels (UFSAL), the Limburg University Center at Diepenbeek (LUC), and the Luxembourg University Foundation at Arlon (FUL). Some institutions are interconnected, such as those in Antwerp, and constitute one entity. "Faculty" or "faculties" is frequently used to designate such institutions.

Each university-integrated medical faculty has its own university hospital. In Belgium, both clinical and fundamental medical research depend on the academic and scientific community. In a small yet politically complex country such as Belgium, universities offer the most efficient structure for fundamental research. Staff can assume the dual function of teaching and research and are thus a kind of hybrid between teacher and researcher. Universities are also in a position to encourage the development of promising areas or to reabsorb failing projects without experiencing the major difficulties that plague permanent centers.

Universities encourage the creation of highly active groups operating in a stimulating environment. Such groups can act as an intellectual attraction and stir up a "forum of ideas." Although the system encourages work in groups, it also permits individual expression. However, it can occasionally lead to fragmentation.

The FNRS and its associated funds try to coordinate work in the different universities and to encourage cooperation between them. The FNRS and its associated funds are active in all fields of fundamental research. The FNRS supports individual research projects, whereas the associated funds aid team research programs. The FNRS grants funding to individual researchers, whether working alone, within a laboratory, or within a group.

The associated funds differ from the FNRS in that they support research programs proposed by teams of researchers. Such projects require considerable financial and material resources. The financial support provided enables the promoter to hire the necessary scientific and technical staff, acquire the necessary equipment, and cover operating costs. Each of the associated funds covers a specific research sector. The varying nature of the funds reflects the specific needs they are intended to meet.

The FNRS has the tasks of maintaining the quality of Belgium's scientific potential and of developing its scope, while taking into account the evolution of the country's political structure—the division of decision-making powers at the community, regional, and national levels, its philosophical plurality, and its linguistic specificity. The FNRS must avoid dispersion of its means and encourage interuniversity cooperation and a pooling of efforts.

With this in mind, the FNRS and its associated funds are managed by the scientific community, using the quality of the research as the only assessment criterion. The purely scientific and interuniversity nature of the fund is underscored by the chairmanship of the FNRS Board of Governors: the six chancellors of the major universities chair the board in turn.

Applications are submitted to scientific committees in which the linguistic parity of members is a ground rule. There is one such committee for each discipline, made up of renowned scientists. The committees meet on an individual basis. In all, 300 scientists are members of the 30 scientific committees. External experts can also be invited to attend meetings. The opinions rendered by the committees are based on the scientific interest of the program in question and the originality of the research. They also take into account the implementation possibilities of the project and whether similar research is being conducted by other researchers or other teams.

Fundamental research may also receive financing from other sources. The most important of these are described in the following paragraphs.

Activities of the Ministry of Science Policy

The Ministry of Science Policy funds research sectors considered high-priority areas by the government. These could be in the field of fundamental research, development, or prototype production. Among these initiatives, the Coordinated Research Activities focus especially on fundamental research and aim to spur high-level university teams in particularly important research fields. Teams and programs are suggested by university establishments and are negotiated between the latter and the government. Agreements always contain a clause stipulating that any technology at the disposal of the universities must be transferred to Belgian industry. Joint research activities must aim to attain one or several of the following objectives: the development, within the university establishment, of fundamental research "excellence centers" in areas considered a priority by the establishment in question; the development of interuniversity "excellence centers"; and the development, within the university establishment in question, of "excellence centers" carrying out fundamental and applied research in an integrated manner and aiming for the economic and social optimization of research results.

Other activities developed by the Budget, Science, and Planning Ministry include *interuniversity "poles of attraction"* (pôles d'attraction interuniversitaires), whose goal is to supply the necessary human and material resources to the best fundamental research teams in front-line technologies and to create links between these teams and other universities working in similar fields; the *impetus program for fundamental research in the life sciences*; and the *impetus program in artificial intelligence*, which will train around a hundred researchers in artificial intelligence over a period of five years, reinforce teams active in the field, and start up research in this sector.

As a supplement to joint research activities, the Budget, Science and Planning Ministry also supports national programs whose end objective is applied research and development. Support for such programs is concentrated in priority areas considered to be of general interest. These are defined by the Cabinet and managed by the Scientific Policy Planning Services (SPPS) under the watchful eye of interdepartmental coordination committees. Such programs are implemented by universities, collective research centers, companies, or public research bodies. When the programs are implemented, the fundamental research stage is given marginal financial support.

One such national program deals with aeronautics and related technology. It is divided into three sections: technology directly related to aeronautics, space communications technology, and related technologies, particularly in the field of electronics and telecommunications. A second national program covers "optimization of the life sciences," with the objective of coordinating university collections of microorganisms. A third program studies the earth's land and marine resources by satellite to promote the use of data collected by space remote sensing.

Any work carried out by the Science Ministry and the state secretary for science can be supplemented by individual projects sponsored by each ministerial department in the framework of its own activities and drawing on its own budget. Such ministry initiatives, which may be in the field of fundamental research, can be entrusted to university laboratories or teams. In addition to the fundamental research activities carried out within universities and university centers, 22 state-run scientific institutions also have fundamental research programs. Most notable among these institutions are the Albert I Royal Library, the Royal Meteorological Institute, the Royal Institute of Natural Sciences, the General Archives of the Kingdom, the Royal Observatory, the Space Aeronomy Institute, the Royal Museums of Art and History, the Royal Institute of Artistic Heritage, the Royal Museums of Fine Arts, the National Botanical Gardens, the National Institute of Veterinary Research, the Forest and Hydrobiological Research Station, the National Criminology Institute, the Institute of Hygiene and Epidemiology, and the Royal Museum of the Armed Forces and Military History.

All of these establishments have a special status and are active in a wide range of research fields. They preserve and maximize cultural and scientific heritage. Fundamental research has now become an accepted part of the notion of public service. Some establishments, such as the General Archives of the Kingdom, the Albert I Royal Library, the Royal Museums of Fine Arts, and the Royal Observatory have already celebrated their hundredth anniversary. Others, such as the Royal Institute of Artistic Heritage and the Space Aeronomy Institute, are the product of recent scientific developments. However, all fulfill an essential social need and contribute to defining national identity.

These scientific institutions carry out fundamental and applied research that reflects the nature of their collections and observation data, culminating in the national and international publication of results for use both by specialists and by the general public. They are therefore simultaneously involved in creating, collecting, and disseminating scientific information.

State-run scientific establishments have a special relationship with universities. They place their collections at the disposal of scholars and students for study and for the writing of theses, inform them about their facilities, teach them to use their equipment, and thus pass on essential information. This relationship is reinforced by cooperation at the research level, the implementation of joint programs, often under the aegis of scientific foundations, and by instruction on university premises by the staff of these scientific establishments. It would be extremely difficult to assess the sums spent by such establishments on fundamental research activities. The austerity policy that swept through Belgium in the 1980's forced such establishments to concentrate to a larger extent on public-service activities.

Although in the 1930's no clear distinction was made between fundamental and applied research, a Science-Industry Bureau was set up a little later within the FNRS. This bureau was given the task of carrying out research in collaboration with industry. Just after World War II, the Institute for Encouragement of Scientific Research in Industry and Agriculture (IRSIA) was set up in order to augment these activities. The IRSIA is a state-approved body that stimulates, promotes, and encourages scientific and technical research with the promise of industrial or agricultural progress. It operates by way of subsidies.

The IRSIA also provides grants to people preparing a thesis, as well as research grants and study grants to young university graduates or young researchers whose ambition is to work in the applied research sector. Some work bordering on fundamental research but implemented in the exact sciences and applied research fields thus benefits from IRSIA aid. In 1987, the IRSIA spent a total of 318.9 million BF on grants.

The Past 25 Years

Since fundamental research is chiefly carried out in universities, it is subject to any changes in their form and structure. Moreover, the government has created a number of institutes in response to a desire for greater democracy within higher education. Consequently Belgian scientific potential has been fragmented. The structure of the Belgian state is thus reflected in the structure of the universities, which are individual entities striving to respond to a particular characteristic, whether regional, linguistic, or religious. In the 1987 report "Scientific Research at the Service of the Country," submitted to the King Baudouin Foundation, this is described as "fragmented plurality," which is a Belgian characteristic and is accentuated by community or regional divisions.

The circumstances governing the operation of Belgian universities thus inevitably create a number of problems. For example, mobility of scientists between universities is extremely difficult. Staff recruitment of both academics and scientists tends, for the reasons mentioned above, to take place within the university in question. Moreover, the level of available funding restricts the possibility of hiring more foreign specialists. A corollary of these various barriers is an aging of the research staff within a particular institution.

Structural problems have been confounded in recent years by national budgetary difficulties. Austerity measures have been imposed on universities and consequently on their capacity to subsidize research work from their general budget, which must cover both teaching and research. The quantity of new equipment and the number of new staff have been severely cut. Universities have preferred to reserve the lion's share of their funds for teaching. They have attempted to compensate for their lack of research funding by accepting contract work from firms in the biological, electronics, and computer technology sectors.

Since the 1970's, Belgian research laboratories have therefore been subject to the economic restrictions enforced by the government in an attempt to cope with the economic crisis. This crunch on research activities has been accompanied by a governmental tendency to emphasize applied research in the hope that this will produce rapid technological innovation and therefore boost the country's industrial fabric and economy. Universities now have a much wider operations base, ranging from fundamental research to R&D and research optimization. They either develop their own initiatives, paid for out of their own budget, or seek research contracts.

Belgian Fundamental Research and International Cooperation

Fundamental research cannot be hemmed in within national boundaries. International development within the framework of projects open to all is essential. The need for international cooperation has now become a truism. It forms a component of every national policy and eases exchange of both research workers and ideas across national boundaries. For a small country such as Belgium, participation in international R&D activities is essential. The Budget, Science, and Planning Ministry is thus keen to maximize participation in international programs and willingly provides the additional funding necessary. Researchers in the field of fundamental research cannot go very far without international cooperation. Such relationships grow up spontaneously but must be officially nurtured.

Belgian fundamental research is integrated into European and international research. Belgium participates in the work of umbrella groups for European national foundations, such as the European Science Foundation (ESF) or the Council of Europe, in exchange programs taking the form of scientific grants provided by NATO, research grants from the European Molecular Biology Organization (EMBO), and the European Community Action Program for Student Mobility (ERASMUS) for the stimulation of European cooperation and scientific and technical exchange. In addition, teams of Belgian researchers have participated in the work of the European Laboratory for Particle Physics in Geneva since its creation as the Center for Nuclear Research (CERN).

Industrial Research

Jean Van Keymeulen

THOSE COMPANIES THAT HAVE best integrated R&D into their management structure are also those that are the most prosperous. R&D is the next link in the innovation chain following fundamental research. A distinction must be drawn between fundamental industrial research and applied research. The EEC defines *basic or fundamental industrial research* as a theoretical or experimental activity with the objective of attaining new knowledge or improving understanding of the laws of science with a view to their application to an industrial sector or to the activities of a given company. *Applied research* covers investigation and experiments that draw on the results of fundamental industrial research. It is carried out in order to obtain new knowledge that facilitates the attainment of specific practical objectives, such as the creation of new processes, products, or services.

Applied research often culminates in the production of the first prototype: this is what is known as the *development* stage. Development is taken to mean activities that, on the basis of the applied research, aim to develop new or considerably improved products, processes, or services. Development normally comprises pilot and demonstration plants, as well as the required finishing touches. It results in a set of information allowing passage to the production stage.

The two pillars of R&D are industrial and joint research centers. These are the two places in which industrial R&D is conducted and research capabilities concentrated. However, joint centers focus almost exclusively on research and neglect development. (University-industry cooperation is discussed in more detail in the following chapter.)

Research in Industry

Industrial research (R&D) in companies and in cooperative research centers represents around 70 percent of all research in Belgium. A report issued by the Scientific Policy Planning Services (SPPS) in 1983 shows that total expenditures amounted to U.S. $900 million, or an average annual increase of around 10 percent over the two previous years. In Belgium, R&D expenditures amount to 1.4 percent of GNP. In all, 19,227 people work in industrial R&D. This is equivalent to around 60 percent of all researchers in Belgium, with an average annual growth rate of 4 percent; these researchers consist uniquely of high-level staff and have come to represent a growing proportion of overall employment in business.

A breakdown by industrial sector of R&D expenditures illustrates areas receiving special attention, although it cannot be deduced from this that Belgium specializes in these areas. Four sectors in fact account for three-quarters of R&D expenditures: chemistry (36 percent, including photography and pharmaceuticals), electro-technology and electronics (26 percent), metalworking (9.5 percent, including mechanics), and metallurgy (5 percent, ferrous and nonferrous). Among the leading investors in R&D in chemistry (including nonindustrial chemistry) are Solvay & Cie (Brussels), Agfa-Gevaert (Mortsel), Janssen Pharmaceutica (Beerse), UCB (Brussels), and Smith-Kline (Genval). The leaders in electro-technology and electronics are Bell Telephone Manufacturing Company (Antwerp) and ACEC (Charleroi).

Joint Research Centers

The second pillar of R&D consists in cooperative centers set up and financed by an entire industrial sector. There are currently thirteen technical and scientific centers of this type in Belgium with ties to the main industrial sectors. In 1985, these joint centers employed more than 1,000 people, 40 percent of whom had a university degree. They therefore have considerable research resources capable of bolstering industrial activity.

The centers vary considerably, depending on the size of the sector they represent, the number of sponsors, the technological level, and so on. However, certain common features contribute to their vitality and specialization. The main task of the joint centers is to help firms that are not in a position to pursue technological innovation on their own and to introduce them to new technological trends. A permanent dialogue between centers and their sponsors is a prerequisite, allowing identification of requirements and, after the research phase, transfer of results in a digestible form.

The collective approach is particularly well adapted to the acquisition of know-how of a particular technological or production process. This research-derived know-how can be expressed in practical handbooks designed to improve the quality and the yield of a particular process, through analysis or appropriate checks and optimal working conditions. These aspects can be studied in the joint sectors and adapted to the industry's requirements to the benefit of the entire sector, at minimum cost. Another merit of such centers is the availability of specialists and equipment for companies planning to develop their own goods and systems. Firms can turn to the centers for direct and rapid assistance.

To sum up, the joint approach is particularly useful in the difficult economic situation confronting Belgium and in light of rapid technological change in all fields. In certain instances, it offers the only viable solution. This is why there has been a flurry of new joint research centers. Research projects in joint centers represent between 25 percent and 30 percent of grants made by the Institute for Encouragement of Scientific Research in Industry and Agriculture (IRSIA). The institute is also trying to encourage joint centers to participate in semi-joint research projects. All of the joint centers are briefly described below.

The *Metallurgical Research Center* (CRM) in Liège focuses on the coking process, compounding, blast furnaces, steelworks, ladle metallurgy, continuous casting, rolling, heat treatments, steel working, measuring and inspection techniques and methods, surface problems, physical metallurgy, special products and procedures, and made-up or continuous electroplating.

The *Scientific and Technical Research Center for the Metalworking Industry* (CRIF), headquartered in Brussels, is devoted mainly to the computerization of production workshops (Heverlee); automation and industrial computer technology (Brussels), with a focus on robotics and artificial intelligence; advanced composite materials from plastic resins and fibers and injection molding of thermoplastics (Liège); foundry and boiler construction, casting, injection molding, materials, and computing programs (Ghent); and bridge and framework research dealing with computing problems and the use of metal and mixed concrete-steel structures (Liège).

The *Scientific and Technical Center of "Centexbel" Industry* in Ghent and Verviers conducts research on the spinning, dying, and finishing of wool, cotton, and linen fibers, as well as on the visual inspection of goods in the hosiery and weaving sectors. The *Belgian Ceramics Industry Research Center* in Mons studies new ceramics for (thermo)mechanical applications. The *Road Research Center* (CCR) in Sterrebeek researches limited stress designs and optimal material choice for road construction and surfaces; bridges and other civil engineering works; recycling in road construction; and the adequacy, safety, comfort, and energy savings of structures. The *Scientific and Technical Center of Brewing, Malting, and Related Industries* (CBM) in Asse is devoted to materials and malting technology, quality, brewing technology, protection of acquired quality, and industrial profitability.

The *National Center of Scientific and Technical Research of the Cement Industry* (CRIC) in Brussels studies the character of cement-based materials and their ingredients, the resurfacing of roads with a thin cement-bound surface layer, and the durability of concretes. The *Building Industry Scientific and Technical Center* (CSTC) in Limelette researches materials and structures, and the external appearance of buildings, with an emphasis on energy and comfort. The *Diamond Industry Scientific and Technical Research Center* (CRSTID) in Antwerp focuses on computer-assisted evaluation of uncut diamonds, optimal diamond mounting in finished models, and colorimetric characterization of cut diamonds.

The *Wood Industry Technical Center* (CTIB) in Brussels studies nondestructive inspection techniques, the hygrothermal behavior of roofing, and the classification of local lightwoods. The *Covering, Paint, and Ink Research Institute* (CORI) in Limelette researches mechanisms for the use of paints, the early detection of damage caused by the aging of organic coverings, and the film-forming nature of paints in water dispersion. *Laborelec* in Linkebeek analyzes the management of electricity-generation plants and integrated management of transportation and distribution networks. Finally, the *Belgian Welding Institute* (IBS) in Ghent focuses on traditional and special materials for welding and welded joints from the points of view of economics and safety.

Government Financing of Industrial R&D

The Belgian government grants subsidies to the R&D phase of industrial innovation. These subsidies are used to cover research project risks. Repayable advances may also be made for the construction of prototypes. Finally, special tax provisions may be set up.

Since 1944 the IRSIA has promoted industry-oriented research by way of grants from the budget of the Ministry for Economic Affairs. It is responsible for increasing the quality and capability of industrial research directed toward the technical and economic consolidation of enterprises. To fulfill this task, it collects a wealth of information and uses this information to define its priorities and select its projects.

Subsidies are granted to research projects only if they have a clear program that has been positively assessed by the institute's scientific experts. The funding basis is generally 50/50. In addition to this type of funding, the IRSIA has developed certain activities designed to meet specific needs. First, *exploratory research* can receive an 80 percent subsidy for a period of up to two years. This research must be carried out in university laboratories or in joint centers and must analyze concepts emanating from academic research in order to transfer them to industry. Second, *common core* programs revolve around common research trends identified from the information collected. Programs in new fields such as biotechnology, robotics, and so on are built around existing experience in universities. They are implemented in university laboratories and jointly funded by interested companies and by the IRSIA. Any results obtained are the property of those companies that contributed to the project. From the starting point of common-core programs, satellite projects are generated for specific problems; companies are responsible for optimizing results. Third, for smaller firms or ones with less R&D experience, the IRSIA has organized an improved system for the transfer of information on technological or scientific assessments. This led to the screening of technological changes applicable to the day-to-day running of small and medium-sized companies, the diagnosis of technical shortfalls in firms' manufacturing processes, and a search for external experts and specialists.

This practice led to *technological guidance*. Under this system, information can be transferred and technology made available for specific cases where short-term support can be technically effective. The IRSIA technological guidance concept depends on the initiative and experience of a qualified adviser, the greatest possible degree of personal contact with business, and a research core (joint center) that provides direct contact with modern technology in the relevant field, along with the equipment necessary for testing and measuring.

A guidance network offering a broad spectrum of experience and services has been set up in order to gain the full benefit of this operation. As of 1989, 25 different services were operational and several others were in the pipeline. These services operate in different industrial or technological sectors or subsectors, including casting, digital control, CAD/CAM, transformation of plastics, automation of procedures, the building industry, the textile industry, paints and varnishes, and preservation of fruit and vegetables.

The IRSIA invests $2 million per annum in technological guidance. In operating the technological guidance service, it became clear that short-term research lasting between two weeks and two months was required in each case. Some services set up a small team of researchers so that this consulting work would not interfere with their regular work. These teams can intervene on short notice. Their work is financed 50–80 percent by the IRSIA for small and medium-sized firms. Four such teams are now in place.

Prototype Aid

Money for the financing of prototypes comes from the budget of the Ministry for Economic Affairs at the national level and from the budgets of the relevant ministries at the regional level: Flanders, Wallonia, and Brussels. It is used to finance experimental development work. More often than not, the aid takes the form of repayable advances, designed to prompt firms to make the leap from research results to prototype, new production procedures, or new products. Advances are interest-free but must be repaid in the event of success. These advances are a one-time payment, for the final phase of the innovation process, and are granted to individual companies for a single project.

Stimulus Activities of the Ministry of Science

The Ministry of Science also contributes directly and indirectly to industrial research. It implements multiyear programs that coordinate research in priority economic and social fields of national or European interest. The programs run the whole gamut of activities, from fundamental research, experimental developments, computerized models, and technical and economic studies to demonstration plants. The aim is to achieve an all-around and continuous process of innovation in fields where fragmentation must be avoided at all costs. These programs accelerate progress in priority fields. They are terminated once the objective defined at the outset has been attained. They are replaced by new programs, often concentrating on industry-oriented research.

Tax Provisions for Research Funding

The government has also introduced specific tax provisions to encourage enterprises to carry out research, through a tax-free allowance on profits for each additional staff member taken on for scientific research.

In this way investments in research are granted more favorable tax treatment than ordinary investments.

Belgian industrial research and governmental support are directed to the establishment of teams of excellence in large R&D programs integrated within the European Community. The results of the first years of operation can be considered satisfactory and promising for the coming years until 1992, the year of the unification of the European market.

University-Industry Interactions

Roger Van Overstraeten

DURING THE PAST TWO DECADES, the exploitation of Belgian coal mines became uneconomical, which leaves Belgium without any domestic energy resources. In that respect Belgium differs from most other European countries. Belgium is an exporting country without natural resources. It imports goods, which after transformation and upgrading are exported again. Because of saturation of markets, automation, and rationalization of production in traditional industrial sectors, a large number of jobs were lost in the 1970's. The new jobs created in the expanding sectors of high technology and services could not compensate for these important losses.

In order for Belgium to maintain its standard of living, it has to continue to export more and better products. Belgium has no choice: it has to keep up with technological progress and to use its scientific potential for developing new products and for improving existing ones. In order to compete and because of high wages, it also needs the most rational manufacturing methods.

High technology, however, requires enormous R&D efforts. It often is said that in high technology there is no place for a small country like Belgium, unlike the United States, with its large domestic market and its large expenditures on R&D because of space and military projects. A small country should try to benefit from R&D efforts in the large countries and to apply the results in new applications, often for smaller, or "niche," markets.

Industry

The number of larger Belgian companies with important R&D efforts is limited. Although some of these companies are now part of an international group, they continue with research and product development in Belgium. This is well illustrated in the chemical sector (e.g., Agfa-Gevaert), the pharmaceutical sector (Janssen Pharmaceutica), the materials sector (Glaverbel), and the telecommunications sector (Bell Telephone Manufacturing Company and ATEA). These companies often come up with remarkable new products. Next to the large companies, there is an important number of small and medium-size enterprises. Their own research is limited; their product development depends on research results from university laboratories or on licensing. Also in this category, the number of foreign companies (many American but also Japanese) is large and increasing. They often do the product development or adaptation necessary for the European market. These companies also rely substantially on university laboratories. During the past decade, the number of new high-technology spin-offs from university research laboratories also increased.

This short survey of Belgian industry makes it apparent that because of the small size of companies there is a need for strong, independent R&D laboratories. These should also support the smaller companies in training. The role of university R&D laboratories in research and education is large. Belgium has no national R&D center, except for a nuclear research center. Research in other fields is concentrated in university laboratories or in laboratories linked to the universities.

Since the R&D effort in high technology is very large, no single company and no single country can do it independently. Collaboration between different companies and between industrial companies and university laboratories is necessary on an international scale. To be successful, synergy is needed between university and industry. Only an integration of fundamental research, applied research, product development, and marketing can result in a competitive position for Belgian industry.

University Laboratories

Every university in Belgium has laboratories carrying out basic research. Pure, or fundamental, research remains the first objective of these laboratories. Many inventions leading to industrial applications result from this research. For the past three decades, however, research oriented toward applications, applied research, and sometimes the early phases of product development has received much more attention in university laboratories. This research often parallels more fundamental research, which it helps finance. Many university laboratories are involved now in such research, which is only a few years ahead of industrial needs. The universities possess an important research infrastructure and are willing to make it available to industry without transforming it into an industrial research center. Experience shows that dependence on industry can be limited so that the professors still feel comfortable in this situation.

Interaction between industry and university is not limited to the engineering faculty. It extends to departments of physics, chemistry, mathematics, pharmacology, agriculture, medicine, and even to the social sciences, including law, economics, and of course business. Introduction of new technologies indeed requires participation by everyone. Success in high technology is not only determined by the product. Modern management techniques and new organizational structures are equally important. The manager assumes a key position, and this explains the existence of business schools at all Belgian universities.

University-Industry Interactions on a European Scale

At the beginning of the 1970's, it became evident that the interaction between university and industry could grow only through new facilities and new structures. The university often has too large an administration and does not have the flexibility to deal with industry. Many professors were afraid of becoming corrupted by contract research; most industrial companies were not used to interacting with university laboratories and could not imagine that useful results could come out of university R&D; they preferred making donations to a university rather than making an R&D contract.

Through the late Theo Lefèvre, national R&D programs, including concerted actions, were launched. Industrial spin-offs were stressed. A large number of research programs with collaboration between industry and university were initiated. A major role is played by the Scientific Policy Planning Services (SPPS) of the Ministry of Science and by the Institute for Encouragement of Scientific Research in Industry and Agriculture (IWONL/IRSIA). In the past decade an increasing role was also played by the R&D programs of the Commission of the European Communities. In these programs (such as nonnuclear energy, the European Strategic Program on Research in Information Technologies or ESPRIT, or RACE for research in the telecommunications field), university and industry are involved in joint R&D. The research usually is precompetitive and transnational. These EC R&D programs are now rationalizing efforts on a European scale and stimulating industrial-university interaction.

Most European countries also support the EUREKA initiative. Under this framework, multinational R&D projects that involve industrial companies and academic institutions are carried out. The projects are closer to industrial production than, for example, the ESPRIT projects, which are precompetitive. They therefore easily result in new industrial companies.

Interface Structure and Spin-Off Companies

Every Belgian university now interfaces with industry. The objectives are to valorize the R&D potential of the university, to prospect for projects, and to understand industrial needs. Contract research with industry is always handled through this interface structure. The structure is very flexible. Depending on the funding of the research, either the university or the industry can own the patents on the results. In some cases, the university laboratory receives a royalty on the products based on the research. Additional funding of the project is sometimes obtained from IWONL/IRSIA, from the Ministry of Science, or from the Commission of the European Communities. The interface usually plays an important role in generating spin-off companies from university laboratories in which an idea resulting from university research is exploited in a new company. There already are dozens of examples of spin-off companies. Sometimes they are started by scientists leaving the academic laboratory. In other cases technology or the know-how for a product is transferred to an existing company.

Industrial R&D Parks

Successful examples of R&D parks around large universities like Stanford and MIT in the United States have been well known for many years. They stimulated the creation of similar parks all over Europe. Near every university in Belgium is a research park, allowing the implantation, under favorable conditions, of industrial companies that carry out R&D. The management of these industrial sites usually is done by regional development companies in collaboration with the university. These parks are important for many reasons. First, they stimulate interaction with the university laboratories. Second, employees of small and medium-sized enterprises can be trained at the university. Being close to the university, these companies can benefit from lectures and seminars. Third, these companies can use the university infrastructure (large computers, measurement and analytical equipment). In this respect, it is also worth mentioning that most of these parks have industrial nurseries.

Industrial Nurseries

The objective of these nurseries is to facilitate the start of a new company by reducing the initial risks, by removing a number of initial barriers, and by assisting the new companies in their early development. Several start-up companies with growth potential are located together in an appropriate building. A number of common services (telephone, telefax, office, meeting rooms, shipping) are organized and headed by an experienced manager. This manager also helps beginners with advice. These nurseries are expected to play an important role in the formation of many high-technology companies.

In general, the interaction between universities and industry, started in the early 1970's, is expanding rapidly. This interaction is supported by regional and national governments and by the Commission of the European Communities. It leads to a rational use of R&D potential and results in new and better products and in spin-off companies. The infrastructure created by the industrial parks and by the nurseries helps in consolidating the interaction.

Research Centers on University Campuses

A number of research centers are also located on university campuses. An example is the laboratories of the Scientific and Technical Research Center for the Metalworking Industry (CRIF/WTMC) of the federation of the metal-manufacturing industry. These scientific and technical centers do research in the fields of manufacturing processes (casting, welding, machining, shaping), manufacturing equipment, measurement methods, and automation. The centers can be seen as units at the universities; they often refrain from buying buildings and even sometimes research equipment; they have received considerable support from the universities, which put their facilities at the disposal of WTCM/CRIF. Such centers are located at the Universities of Brussels, Liège, Ghent, and Leuven. Other examples are the International Institute of Cellular and Molecular Pathology of Nobel Prize winner Professor Christian de Duve at the Catholic University of Louvain, and the Plant Genetic Systems (PGS) at the State University of Ghent.

The case described in more detail here is the nonprofit Interuniversity Microelectronics Center (IMEC), set up in 1984 by the regional government of Flanders as part of a comprehensive program to promote education, research, and industrial activities in microelectronics. Because integrated circuits are used in almost every product and production process, microelectronics is of strategic importance to every industrialized country. Technological evolution is based on the reduction of dimensions to the submicron level, on the use of new structures and materials, and on the use of novel design methodologies.

R&D in this area is demanding both of capital equipment and of personnel and therefore requires exceptional means. IMEC's objectives are to carry out advanced research in the field of microelectronics and to organize training of chip designers and processing engineers for industry. The initial investment was $80 million and the annual budget is $30 million, of which 40 percent comes from contract research. IMEC has a staff of more than 300. Although located on the campus of the Catholic University of Leuven, it has links with other Belgian Dutch-speaking universities. At IMEC, students can carry out research leading to an M.S. or a Ph.D. degree. Complementary research is funded at associated universities, and as of 1989 more than ten research contracts with university laboratories had been signed in the fields of physics, chemistry, mathematics, and electronics. Design software for integrated circuits is made available by IMEC on a computer network linking sixteen institutions of higher education (three universities and thirteen polytechnic schools) to IMEC. Through this activity, more than 300 design engineers are trained every year.

This INVOMEC division of IMEC also offers training courses for engineers already in industry. An activity similar to that of INVOMEC in the south of Belgium is organized as the ARAMIS system, linking the Universities of Louvain, Brussels, Liège, and Mons.

Research at IMEC is done in collaboration with more than 80 companies from all over Europe and from the United States. It has excellent relations with national and regional government institutions in the fields of research and industrial development. Guest scientists from universities and from industry are encouraged to research problems of common interest. IMEC improves the position of Europe in the field of microelectronics. It creates the scientific environment needed by high-technology companies in microelectronics to start and to grow. Through technology transfer and through the creation of start-up companies, it enhances industrial potential. A recent example of collaboration is the development of a new photo-resist system known as DESIRE. It was developed by UCB, a Belgian chemical company, in collaboration with IMEC. The system is very important for submicron chips. Industrial production has been initiated at UCB.

Every university in Belgium has laboratories carrying out basic research. In recent years applied research has received more attention. Interaction between universities and industry can now be found in disciplines ranging from the social sciences to natural science, engineering, and medicine. This university-industry interaction is organized through an interface structure at the university. It has resulted in an increasing number of spin-off companies. Industrial R&D parks and industrial nurseries not only help companies get started but also help increase interaction. University-industrial interaction now exists on a European scale. Collaborative programs partly funded by the Commission of the European Communities help integrate R&D efforts in Europe. Next to the university laboratories, a number of large research centers were set up to concentrate the effort in certain fields. These centers interact well with the universities and with industry. Through collaboration between industry and university on a European scale and through integration of these efforts, Belgium is preparing its future in a unified Europe.

Belgian Participation in European and International Research

Alain Stenmans

PARTICIPATION IN INTERNATIONAL RESEARCH is a necessity for Belgium from scientific, economic, and social points of view. For continuing growth, Belgium must modernize production and services while encouraging the incorporation of scientific and technological progress in the lifestyles of the people. This can happen in several ways, first and foremost at the level of individuals—Belgian scientists cooperating with foreign colleagues within formal international agreements. Such relations also occur at the level of institutions. Until the late 1970's, government aid in this area represented around 5 percent of the national scientific budget. This percentage doubled in the following years, largely as a result of European R&D activities.

Belgian scientific teams in both academia and industry also interact with the world scientific community by means of such programs at the level of institutions. Without mentioning all the Belgian institutions that participate in European or international research programs, or all of Belgium's distinguished scientists, this chapter will provide an introduction to international scientific activities in Belgium.

Participation in European Research

European research assumes a multitude of different forms, with extensive Belgian participation. Some programs carry out only fundamental research, whereas others concentrate on applied research; still others range through the entire spectrum from basic research to technological innovation.

European Laboratory for Particle Physics (CERN)

Besides being a world-renowned laboratory, the Geneva-based CERN is a forum for consultation between European states on nuclear research of a purely scientific nature. It also cooperates with nonmember states, in all corners of the world. Professor Léon Van Hove, a Belgian, was director of CERN for many years. Belgium was a founding member of CERN. A number of Belgian laboratories, for example, in Brussels, Mons, and Louvain, participate in experiments carried out at CERN. Many Belgian researchers also visit CERN in connection with their own personal work.

European Community

Belgium, one of the six founding members of the European Economic Community, has participated in EEC research since the birth of the EEC when it focused on coal and steel, agriculture, and nuclear energy. Gradually much wider objectives were selected for the economic development of the community and the social well-being of its inhabitants. Since 1984, EEC R&D has been brought under the umbrella of a multi-year program institutionalized in the 1987 Single European Act. The objective remains the same; namely, to provide the Community with an adequate scientific and technological base from which to develop and maintain its position in the world.

Cooperative research has not superseded national research in the EEC member-states. On the contrary, the EEC uses national programs as a starting point, placing particular emphasis on those in areas of special interest to the Community. In budget terms, EEC-funded research represents around 2 percent of the total of national research expenditures.

The 1984–87 framework program received a total allocation of 3.75 billion ECUs. The 1987–91 program will be granted 6.5 billion ECUs. These sums represent, respectively, $3.3 and $5.72 billion at the January 1986 exchange rate. A small part of this program will be implemented exclusively in the Community's laboratories, situated at Ispra (Italy), Geel (Belgium), Peten (Netherlands), and Karlsruhe (West Germany). The bulk of the program will be carried out, in a coordinated manner, both in these laboratories and in the laboratories of the EEC member-states, with EEC funding supplemented by national funding.

It is now possible to assess the 1984–87 program, as well as the contribution of Belgian scientists. In the area of *agriculture*, the laboratories at the State Faculty of Agronomic Sciences at Gembloux (FAGEM) and the Catholic University of Louvain (UCL) were the main Belgian contributors. Moreover, a number of small and medium-sized firms took part in the BRITE program to modernize traditional industry. Research teams from the ESAT laboratory of the Catholic University of Leuven (KUL) and Bell Telephone participated in research in computer technology and microelectronics. Research teams from the Flemish interuniversity institute IMEC along with the Philips laboratory participated in the ESPRIT program. Laboratories at UCL, the Free University of Brussels (ULB), and the State University of Ghent (RUG) participated in the biotechnology program. IMEC research teams and Bell Telephone, ACEC, GTE ATEA, Adequate Processes, and Mietec participated in preparatory research for the RACE program on telecommunications in the year 2000.

In the *raw materials* area, teams at FAGEM, KUL, UCL, ULB, and the Mons Polytechnic Faculty (FPM) participated in research on primary and secondary raw materials. In the energy area, the Nuclear Energy Research Center (CEN/SCK) at Mol and the company Belgonucléaire took part in research on nuclear energy (reactor safety, fissile materials, fast breeder reactors, etc.). The Mol center, along with the laboratory of the Royal Military School, participated in research on thermonuclear fusion, in close collaboration with the JET study center at Culham (U.K.) and the Jülich Nuclear Energy Center (West Germany). The Mol center and the IMEC laboratory, along with the Building Industry Scientific and Research Center and laboratories at KUL, ULB, UCL, and the State University of Liège (UEL), participated in the program on renewable energy. Belgian scientific research teams are also represented in some thirty activities conducted between the member-states of the European Community or between other European countries in the framework of the COST treaty for European cooperation in the field of scientific and technical research.

European Space Agency

Belgium contributes around 5 percent of the budget of the European Space Agency (ESA). This is the biggest contribution from the agency's smaller member-countries. Belgian participation has been particularly active, in both the scientific and the technological programs of the agency. In the framework of the *scientific programs*, the ESA has launched fourteen satellites, five of which are still in use. These are the ISEE (launched in 1977) and GEOS 2 (1978) for the study of the relationship between the sun and the Earth; IUE (1978) for the observation of stars and galaxies in ultra-violet light; EXOSAT (1985) for the study of X-rays; and GIOTTO (1985) for close-range observation (500 km from the core) in March 1986 of Halley's Comet. A number of other missions are planned for the near future.

Space transport has entered a promising, high-growth commercial-exploitation phase, thanks to considerable developments in the area of scientific, telecommunications, weather, direct television, and Earth observation satellites. Since 1973, the ESA has been working on the ARIANE family of launchers. Evolution in the weight and size of satellites has forced continual improvement in launchers. The agency has kept apace with this evolution, moving from a 970-kg satellite in geostationary orbit (ARIANE 1) to a 4,000-kg satellite (ARIANE 4). ARIANE 5 is currently in the pipeline and will be launching satellites weighing between 5,200 kg and 8,000 kg in 1994. A number of Belgian companies have participated in this program. Since 1978, ESA has been developing *communications satellites*, and several Belgian teams have participated in this program.

Paralleling its development of the ARIANE launcher, ESA has participated in NASA's post-Apollo program and has developed a manned space laboratory (SPACELAB) transported by the U.S. space shuttle. The first SPACELAB flight in 1983 was a manned flight. Of the 77 experiments conducted on board, 51 have been European. They include experiments carried out on behalf of Belgian teams.

ESA is currently involved in research to accumulate knowledge necessary for the survival in space of humans, animals, and plants. With this aim in mind, it is preparing a program of experiments in zero gravity, to be known as the *microgravity program*. Again, several Belgian teams are participating in the design and construction of equipment for this program.

In the future, ESA aims to acquire a *manned space transport* capacity and to create a *permanent space station*. With this aim in mind, it has accepted the U.S. proposal to participate in the creation of an international station. On the European front, such an entity will probably consist of a new-generation ARIANE (launcher, the space plane HERMES, and various elements of the space station, baptized COLUMBUS). Belgium is already participating in the preparatory stage.

The EUREKA Program

EUREKA was created in 1985 by the ministers of seventeen states and representatives of the Commission of the European Communities. EUREKA's objective is to increase the productivity and competitiveness of European industries and national economies in the area of high technology. The infrastructure set up to attain this objective aims to encourage and facilitate industrial, technological, and scientific cooperation on projects concentrating on the development of products, systems, and services that use advanced technologies and have potentially a world market.

EUREKA projects are concentrated on products, procedures, and services in the fields of information and telecommunications, robotics, materials, production software, biotechnology, marine technologies, lasers, environmental protection technologies, and transport technologies. Projects must involve companies or research centers in at least two of the member-countries and be proposed by these same companies or centers.

Of the 108 EUREKA projects approved by 1989, Belgium is participating in 15, and 4 are being implemented in the laboratories of one Belgian company. The 15 projects involving Belgian laboratories are in the fields of microelectronics, computerization technology, flexible automation, materials, lasers, turbines, the environment, biotechnology, and transport. These 15 projects have a total budget of around 300 million ECUs, of which Belgium is contributing 13.3 million. These sums amount, respectively, to $264 million and $11.7 million at the January 1986 exchange rate.

European Science Foundation

The European Science Foundation is a nongovernmental international umbrella organization for research academies and councils in eighteen European countries. It is headquartered in Strasbourg (France) and covers all scientific disciplines. Most of its work is entrusted to permanent or ad hoc scientific committees. Belgian scientists sit on a number of the committees (human sciences, social sciences, comparative law, toxicology, human reproduction, mental illness, technological assessment, atmospheric chemistry, geology, oceanology, polymer science, taxonomy, and space sciences.

Oceanology

The North Sea and the Scheldt estuary are jointly managed and conserved through close cooperation with all bordering countries. Belgium has ratified the relevant international conventions (notably the Oslo and Paris conventions) and is subject to EEC directives that require continual monitoring and inspection programs.

The Mathematical Model Unit for Management of the North Sea and Scheldt Estuary is responsible for optimal management of the different uses of these waters (fisheries, sand and gravel quarries, tourism, controlled waste disposal, port infrastructure, navigation channels). It works closely with similar organizations in other North Sea coastal states. It also has scientific ties with other countries facing similar problems in the Nordic seas, notably Norway.

Research carried out by various teams from Belgian universities and scientific establishments also results in frequent contacts with teams in neighboring countries on specific scientific themes of joint interest, such as monitoring of the marine environment, fishing grounds, pollution cycles, marine ecosystems, physical and biological oceanography, geology, and marine sedimentology.

The oceanographic ship BELGICA, equipped with up-to-date laboratories and built in Belgium, is an important piece of equipment in public-interest research and expeditions. The University of Liège operates the STARESO station at Calvi (France) for submarine and oceanographic research in the Mediterranean. The station is a joint Franco-Belgian venture and is open to researchers of all nationalities who want to take advantage of its facilities for their own observations and experiments. In 1986, the station welcomed 300 researchers, students, and technicians who come to carry out impact studies and do research in animal and plant biology, biogeochemical cycles, physical oceanography, ecohydrodynamics, applied ecology, fishing engineering, and archeology.

Participation in International Research

This section deals with programs involving developing countries, fluid mechanics, civil aviation, energy, and the Antarctic.

In the framework of bilateral cooperation agreements with some twenty countries and through its participation in the activities of around thirty multilateral-cooperation organizations, Belgium helps to train scientists and technicians in developing countries. Activities are centered chiefly around agronomy and foodstuffs, along with the development of natural resources and health. Cooperation links exist with many developing countries, especially with those in sub-Saharan Africa. The Tropical Medicine Institute of Antwerp, several laboratories of RUG, UCL, the Botanical Gardens, and the Royal Museum of Central Africa are particularly active in this field. The Royal Academy of Overseas Sciences has close ties with numerous countries, including developing countries.

The von Karman Institute, set up after World War II to study fluid dynamics, is headquartered at Rhode-St. Genèse near Brussels. The institute was the brainchild of numerous European members of NATO and of the United States and Canada. It trains postgraduates, and Belgian universities are closely involved in its activities. Several Belgian companies contract out research to the institute.

Several Belgian companies were responsible for developing the leading wing edges of the AIRBUS A310 and A320. The FN company is participating with SNECMA (France) and General Electric (U.S.) in the development of engines for the airplanes of several manufacturers.

The firm BARCO, in a joint venture with foreign companies, is developing color visualization systems especially designed to meet aeronautical needs. Other developments involving Belgian companies include high-precision, long-duration digital and analogue servocontrols, fiber filters for the filtering of hydraulic fluids, new types of cables for airplane control surfaces or accessory drive commands, carbon fibers, nondestructive testing apparatus for aeronautic parts, electronic equipment for ground infrastructure, an advanced navigation system, and optoelectronics.

Belgium is a party to around half the research agreements concluded, since the 1973 energy crisis, by the founder-members of the International Energy Agency (IAE). Teams of scientists from Belgian universities or state-run scientific establishments have participated in this research, using as a foundation for their work the 1975–87 national program on energy models, rational energy use, and renewable energy.

Belgium has organized coordinated national research activities in Antarctica, within the framework of the Treaty on the Antarctic, of which Belgium is a consultative party. Research involving teams at ULB, RUG, KUL, UCL, and the Free University of Brussels (VUB) has been determined by national and international priorities and currently includes the fields of planktonic ecology, marine geochemistry, marine geophysics, glaciology, and climatology. All this research is being conducted in collaboration with partner-countries, several of which have hosted Belgian teams on their ships.

A significant amount of Belgian government research funds is earmarked for international cooperation. Within this, European cooperation, sparked by World War II, is becoming increasingly important. The majority of West European countries are in fact striving to compensate for their political fragmentation by pooling efforts on all levels, including science and technology, in order to stimulate lasting growth and harmonious development. Cooperation is essential for Belgium, a small country with a long history of industrialization and a tradition of exporting.

It is not surprising, then, that Belgian participation in European and international research has two main characteristics. The first of these is concentration on advanced fundamental research at the cutting edge (particle physics, astrophysics, plasma physics, molecular biology, oceanology, fluid dynamics, climatology). Second, great importance is also attached to advanced technology research in certain high-potential fields, such as biotechnology, information technology and communications, energy, electronics, optics, lasers, flexible automation, materials, mechanics, and the environment. Although factors unrelated to science and technology are also important to the future of a society, the nature of Belgian scientific activities and their firm anchoring in the international arena are such that Belgium can look ahead with optimism.

PART VIII

Culture

Herman Liebaers and Philippe Roberts-Jones,
Coordinators

Introduction

Herman Liebaers and Philippe Roberts-Jones

THIS LAST PART OF THE BOOK covers cultural life in Belgium. It is by no means exhaustive, and often it refers to subjects covered in the other parts. As elsewhere in the book, the authors have been asked to stress factual information and description. No good contributor can, however, refrain from a quick look beyond the facts, from interpretation, however short, of the identity to which the sum of the facts invites. This is inevitable in cultural matters.

Belgians are proud of the openness of their country. In the nineteenth century the numerous political refugees included Victor Hugo and Karl Marx. They both made historical statements from the Grand Place in Brussels, the most beautiful stage setting in the world. Four centuries of Spanish, Austrian, French, and Dutch rule, with varying degrees of acceptance by the occupied population, molded Belgium into a core representative of Europe's patchwork civilization in a constant process of exchange, of give and take. In the 16th century, the painter Juan de Flandres was a characteristic example; in the 17th century, the complex relation between Rubens and Velasquez revealed another side of this exchange; during the glittering 18th century, the Austrian Low Countries were a wholehearted partner in the *siècles des lumières*; the 19th century ended with a glorious contribution to *art nouveau*. The artistic contribution of this part of Europe is generally ranked with that of Italy. It is never compared with the French one. For centuries European artistic civilization was dominated by two poles: the Italian south and the Flemish north.

To a certain extent, this is true today. In France, Belgian French-language authors are sometimes rightly considered Flemish writers. For many literary Dutch people, Belgian Dutch-language authors write a kind of Dutch translation from the French. Linguistically these evaluations may not be completely wrong, but sociologically they show a lack of geopolitical understanding. These ambiguities and many others make daily life in Belgium's multilingual society highly interesting.

The Literary Scene

Georges Sion and Jean Weisgerber

BELGIUM CAN BE SEEN AS A bilingual country only if one ignores its very small German-speaking minority. This linguistic simplification is often used in Belgium, for the divide between the two larger communities is a convenient political excuse for all sorts of ills. It is, however, a simplification that rings true in the field of literature, for the third national language has not been a magnet for writers. Nevertheless, the proximity of German and the undercurrent of English do play a role. They highlight the marginal nature of Belgian authors in relation to the linguistic and literary entities of which they form a part, particularly with regard to such focal points as Paris or the Dutch *Randstad*. These focal points are situated some distance from Belgium and, what is more important, outside its political boundaries in nations that evolved quite separately. History and geography, which forge a people's destiny, also influence its language. In particular, they lie behind a central and almost existential concern for writers, namely, the choice of idiom. In Belgium, language is not always a given. It frequently has to be attained at the price of strenuous efforts or, at the very least, chosen over dialect or common usage. For many Belgians, a standard language has to be learned. But although Belgian literature sometimes bears the stamp of outside linguistic influence, it can also, as in Canada, Austria, or Switzerland, provide the means for the nation to assert its identity.

This tension that runs through the field of literature can be a source of difficulty or inspiration. It can be found in other cultural fields as well and frequently gives rise to a compromise between pure speculation, an essential ingredient of culture, and overwhelming sensitivity on the one hand and down-to-earth pragmatism on the other hand. It can produce a mixture of bourgeois moderation and Bruegelian earthiness of introverted regionalism and cosmopolitanism.

The ambivalent nature of Belgian writers is reflected in their openness to foreign influences or, rather, their readiness to react to foreign contact. Again, two contradictory trends determine their attitude, one centripetal and the other centrifugal. Sometimes this is expressed by an anarchic individualism, by a refusal to fall into step with Paris or Amsterdam; sometimes it takes the other extreme, in the form of a self-denigration complex, a determined disgust for anything identifiably local. This second trend appears to have reinforced the internationalization of culture since 1945. As a consequence, direct imitations are rare. Belgian literature, rather like Belgian industry, is a processing concern. Rather than aping André Breton, Paul Nougé and his friends were able to adapt surrealism to their needs; at the same time, Emile Claus was inspired by Ezra Pound and James Joyce but never copied them.

It is therefore not surprising that the two literary currents in Belgium have developed along similar lines. In both cases, the beginning of the "modern" era dates back to 1880–90, when the country was experiencing colonial and economic expansion. This period also coincided with democratization and a desire to play an active European role. Rather like James Ensor, Henry Van de Velde (Ysaïe), Emile Verhaeren, and Maurice Maeterlinck were thus able to enjoy an international public, previously attained only by Charles De Coster and Guido Gezelle. International renown would also have been at the fingertips of Stijn Streuvels and Karel Van de Woestijne if their language had not been too little known. This eclectic period, of disconcerting richness and complexity, ended around 1916–17 with the appearance of the avant-garde, incarnated by Paul Van Ostaijen and by *Résurrection*, Clément Pansaers's magazine. Ten years later, orderliness was restored, and the novel moved to the forefront of the literary stage, with Franz Hellens, Charles Plisnier, Robert Vivier, Georges Simenon, Willem Elsschot, Maurice Roelants, Gerard Walschap, and Maurice Gilliams, among others.

The clear parallels that can be drawn between the French- and Dutch-speaking cultures in Belgium should not overshadow their divergencies and individual characteristics. The French-speaking part of the country, for example, has a deep interest in theater, which is less a source of inspiration for the Flemish. Expressionism took a stronger hold in the north of the country, surrealism in the south. This literary dualism is an enriching cultural factor that opens the prepared mind to comparisons and may even contain the embryo of universal brotherhood, which is still a dream for some, despite all the setbacks.

French-Language Literature

Georges Sion

THE TWO MAINSTREAM CULTURES of Belgium have remained quite distinct from each other. Each is connected first and foremost to the central core formed by the language of expression. This independence can conceal the pitfalls of autonomy, but at the same time it gives access to the richness and possibilities of the French language around the world. French is an indigenous and age-old language in Belgium. The most ancient poem in Old French, the *Cantilène de Sainte Eulalie* was written in what is now Belgium. French-language literature in Belgium can cite such ancestors as Commynes (whom it shares with France) and the Prince de Ligne, who in the 18th century wielded one of the most brilliant pens in Europe. It was, however, in the second half of the 19th century that French-language literature in Belgium found lasting expression.

First, in 1867, Charles De Coster (1827–79) published *La légende et les aventures héroïques, joyeuses et glorieuses d'Ulenspiegel et de Lamme Goedzak au pays de Flandre et d'ailleurs*, commonly known as *Tyl Ulenspiegel*, he gave Belgium its first masterpiece. A few years later, Camille Lemonnier (1844–1913) provided Belgium with a different literary foundation: that of naturalism tinged with a kind of lyrical drive. In 1881 he published *Un Mâle* and in 1882, *Happe-Chair*. His work, sometimes considered shocking, was abundant and varied and had a forcefulness that made him worthy of the fame he quickly attained.

Two literary reviews continued the good work. *La Jeune Belgique*, created in 1881 by seventeen-year-old Max Waller and Albert Giraud, proved to be a magnet for young writers. "Let us be ourselves" was their motto. They were inspired by a search for personal development. The adventure lasted only sixteen years. In 1886, Albert Mockel (1866–1945) created *La Wallonie* and thereby invented the name for the Walloon provinces. His publication became a haven for symbolism. Albert Mockel was also a poet in his own right. *Chantefable un peu naïve* or *La Flamme immortelle* contributed a certain fluidity and musicality to poetry.

A Generation of Leading Lights

One generation played a key role in Belgian French-language literature. It includes such names as Emile Verhaeren, Maurice Maeterlinck, Charles Van Lerberghe, Georges Rodenbach, and Max Elskamp. As French-speaking Flemings, they contributed a special spark to French creative arts and revitalized and rejuvenated them.

Emile Verhaeren (1855–1916) was, it is said, swept up in the breezes of the Scheldt, where he was born, and in the colors of Flemish painting. He rapidly acquired a style, rhythm, and drive. He was marked by social evolution, as seen in *Campagnes hallucinées* and *Villes tentaculaires*. The love that filled his life was also a source of inspiration, reflected in beautiful poems of love and happiness such as *Heures claires* and *Heures du soir*.

Georges Rodenbach (1855–98) was born in Tournai, but he joined his contemporary Verhaeren in Ghent. His work was closer to dreams than to reality. Rodenbach joined the ranks of the famous in 1892 with *Bruges-la-morte*, which gave Bruges a strange and lasting image of languor.

Charles Van Lerberghe's (1861–1907) writings were suffused with radiant gentleness, even if he liked sometimes to move beyond this image, as in his plays *Les Flaireurs* and *Pan*. However, Van Lerberghe's true vocation was poetry, as revealed by *Entrevisions* (1898) and even more so with *La Chanson d'Eve*. This awakening of the world and to the world created a magic that was one of the riches of French poetry at the turn of the century.

Maurice Maeterlinck (1862–1949) also came from Ghent. He graduated in the law but began writing poetry very early on. Some of his poems resemble magical nursery rhymes overflowing with regret ("Et s'il revenait un jour . . ."). Others bear troubled witness to the ambiguity of life, such as *Les Serres chaudes*, an innovative work of modern poetry. At the same time, the 25-year-old Maeterlinck was one of the forces behind a new style of theater. He was the author of the intimate *La Princesse Maleine*, discovered by Octave Mirbeau. It was followed by *L'Intruse* and *Les Aveugles*, then *Pelléas et Mélisande*, which Debussy transformed into a major new opera. This active man, who lived life to the full, was also a gifted translator (Ruysbroeck, Emerson, Novalis), an observer of nature (*La Vie des Abeilles*), and a moralist. His reflections on this last theme resulted in *Le Trésor des Humbles* and *Le Sablier*. In 1911, he received the

Nobel Prize for Literature, while he still had a large part of his life before him.

In Wallonia, Hubert Krains (1862–1934) gave his native region, the Hesbaye, a classic in 1904 with *Le Pain noir*, followed by *Au coeur des blés* in 1934. Another great poet was to make a magnificent contribution to this upsurge in poetic activity: Max Elskamp (1862–1931). Elskamp was born in Antwerp and lived his own secret existence. He was very different from the grandiose Verhaeren or the subtle Maeterlinck. Even to express strong passion, he seemed to design, as it were, a work of Chinese calligraphy. *Enluminures* and *La Chanson de la rue Saint-Paul* are admirable works.

This generation was without a shadow of a doubt rich in poetic talent, for it also produced Iwan Gilkin from Brussels, whose obsessions almost seemed to mirror those of Baudelaire. Georges Eekhoud (1856–1927) found his vocation chiefly in writing novels that expressed his literary power and boldness. One of these, *La Nouvelle Carthage*, was a portrayal of his native town of Antwerp. Eugène Demolder (1862–1919), born in Brussels, wrote *La Route d'Emeraude*, a title that became a classic.

The Interwar Period

The period between 1920 and 1940 saw the birth of Fernand Crommelynck's (1886–1970) masterpieces for French-speaking theater. During this time, even if he was only to become famous at the later date, Michel de Ghelderode (1898–1962) wrote almost all the works that epitomize his theatrical genius. Poetry and literature also set off on a flight of fancy, sometimes anchored in national or regional sources of inspiration. This was the case, for example, of Jean Tousseul (1890–1944) and his famous novel, *Le village gris*, and more markedly his five-novel cycle, *Jean Clarambaux*.

Franz Hellens (1884–1975) preserved of his birth in Ghent contacts with mystery and the play of light. His first work was entitled *Les Clartés latentes*. His long, active, and diverse life gave him ample contact with the world. Nevertheless, he remained indelibly attached to his roots, as clearly expressed in the title of the book *Réalités fantastiques*. Hellens tirelessly exploited the ambiguous universe that he inhabited. Sometimes he moved closer to concrete realism, as in *Moreldieu*. On other occasions he let fantasy take over, as in *Mélusine*.

André Baillon (1875–1932), on the other hand, was much more attached to his life as a source of inspiration for his work. He spent the best part of his youth on love affairs and adventures and emerged wounded.

He began at 45 with *Histoire d'une Marie*. He had a great deal of talent but his life was dramatic. *En sabots* also spoke of his youth, but *Un homme si simple*, *Chalet I*, and *Délires* border on the verge of madness and death.

Marie Gevers (1884–1975) was the first woman to take her place among the ranks of the best literary talents. Again, the work was marked by the writer's origins. Gevers was born in Missembourg, in a big and attractive house encircled by trees, not far from Antwerp and the Scheldt. She died at the age of 91 in the same house. She was surrounded by the area of Campine, which at that time was still rural and teeming with tradition and timeless personalities. Books such as *L'herbier légendaire* or *Plaisir des météores* are both rich and enchanting. Novels were, however, her true forte, and in 1932 *La Comtesse des Digues* was published in Paris with a preface by Charles Vildrac. It was followed by *Madame Orpha*, *La Ligne de vie*, and *Paix sur les champs*. Gevers offers a picture of a life that was not easy to live, and transmits the message of the duty and happiness of living. She reached the height of her work with a book of memories: *Vie et mort d'un étang* is a work of art.

Charles Plisnier (1896–1952) gave new inspiration to Belgian literature. He was born near Mons and after a few years at the bar, he made France his home. As a poet, he emerged from surrealism, which gave him the gift of freedom and launched him into a quest that for a long time was devoid of certitude. *Prière aux mains coupées* or *Sacre* are admirable internal songs bordering on cry and incantation. *Ave Genitrix* is, toward the end, the song of a soul that has come to terms with itself. Plisnier's novelistic talents were first demonstrated in a collection of short stories, *Figures détruites*. He then launched himself into a full-length novel with *Mariages* in 1936. Plisnier became a living dilemma: there was much talk of awarding him the Prix Goncourt, but he was a Belgian citizen and there was no precedent for such a move. The Goncourt Academy did not dare take the plunge. The following year, Plisnier published a remarkable collection of short stories, *Faux-Passeports*. He was finally awarded the Prix Goncourt, the first foreigner to receive it. *Faux-Passeports* was the fruit of the writer's bitter experiences. He had marched with the Communists in the years 1920–30 and was then excluded because of his independence. A short story such as *Iégor*, in this collection, was the first to take a line adopted much later by Kravchenko or Koestler. Plisnier then launched himself into his biggest ventures. The *Meurtres* series consisted of five novels, the *Mères* series of three.

Two women were to move to the forefront of Belgian literature. Madeleine Ley (1901–81) wrote novels flooded with fragility and a powerful perception of intimate wounds, such as *Olivia* and *Le Grand Feu*.

Madeleine Bourdouxhe (b. 1906) successfully and exactly perceived the essence of the female universe in *La femme de Gilles*.

Just as Charles Plisnier was about to win the Prix Goncourt, another writer was to take Paris by storm with an almost incredible creativity and fertility. Georges Simenon was born in Liège in 1903. He did a little journalism before launching himself into culinary literature under a number of pen names. He then left for Paris, began to mix in society, created a personality, continually changed genre and tone, spent the war in America, and then set up home in Switzerland. By the age of 60, he had built up a fabulous universe of detective stories with fantastic settings and personalities. Maigret tops the list. The superintendent of police, complete with pipe, appeared for the first time in *Piotr-le-Letton* in 1929. His author was perhaps unaware at that point that he had created a personality who was to live for the entire century and become known the world over. However, he also wrote novels without Maigret, without plots to be unraveled, without twists and turns: *Le Testament Donadieu*, *Trois Chambres à Manhattan*, and a hundred others. This demonstrates the scope of his talent, which is deceptively simple and incredibly rich. Paradoxically, Simenon attempted self-analysis in *Pédigree*, *Je me souviens*, and finally in *Mémoires*, but it was through his novels that he appeared the most forcefully.

Stanislas-André Steeman (1907–1970) wrote highly sophisticated detective novels, but his personal touch was quite different. He was fascinated by the perfect plot. Some of his books rapidly became well known: *Six hommes morts*, *Le mannequin assassiné*, and *L'assassin habite au 21*.

Another writer for those with strong nerves who was active at the same time but became internationally famous later was Jean Ray (1887–1964). Ray had an adventure-filled life: he was a sailor, a con man, and a smuggler and relates these episodes in *Contes de Whisky* and *Les aventures d'Harry Dickson*. He then metamorphosized into a writer capable of creating the tension of anxiety or the fantastic in *Malpertuis*, *Le Livre des Fantômes*, and *La Cité de l'indicible Peur*.

Although during these years the novel was a major art form, poetry also underwent a remarkable development. Highly contradictory concepts of poetry existed side by side. Clément Pansaers (1885–1922), with *Bar Nicanor* and a number of collections, was the perfect incarnation of the subversions of his age. Paul Nougé (1895–1967) was a biochemist, but he was also a Communist activist in the 1920's and followed literary developments with a keen interest. He brought together in Brussels those driven by surrealism: Camille Goemans (1900–1960) and Marcel Lecomte (1900–1966).

Achille Chavée (1906–69) founded in La Louvière the group Rupture, whose name was the expression of its members' quest for total freedom; it was followed by the Groupe surréaliste du Hainaut. He was extraordinarily creative and expressed himself in explosively innocent aphorisms. As he himself put it, he was never one "to walk in single line."

A great poet from Antwerp close to surrealism was Paul Neuhuys (1897–1986). His work was spread over a long life but never lost any of its originality or independence. Jean de Boschère (1878–1953), on the other hand, wrote about solitude and pain. He published a collection of poems entitled *Job le Pauvre* and ten years later a novel, *Satan l'Obscur*.

Another poet seeking spiritual adventure was Ernst Moerman (1897–1944). He lived his life intensely and translated his internal hate into poetry, drawing harsh drafts of freedom, as in *Vie imaginaire de Jésus-Christ* and *Fantômas*. Géo Libbrecht (1891–1976) passed from the war to the vast spaces of Brazil. On returning to Europe, he wrote poetry expressing his experiences and memories. It was published under the collective title *Livres cachés*, a vast expedition into the secrets of life and the world.

However, poetry was not limited to expressions of revolution. Classic poets, sticking closely to traditional forms, spoke in new tones reflecting their individualism. Jean Dominique (1875–1952) contributed, for example, her sensitive impressionism. Thomas Braun (1876–1961) expressed his love for his native Ardennes in *Fumée d'Ardenne* and his serious reflections in *Le Livre des Bénédictions*. Pierre Nothomb (1887–1966) reflected Braun's songlike style in much of his work and, like Braun, originated in the Ardennes. He was much more a man of action, a public speaker, a prime mover, and a historian. From *Risquons-tout* to *Prince d'Olzheim*, he related and retold history, but his poetry for more than half a century was a reflection of the eras of man, of passions lived or conquered, from *Notre-Dame du matin* to *Le Roi David*. Georges Marlow (1872–1947) published relatively little but with *Hélène* in 1926 he fine-tuned his art as a poet of love and regret. Melot du Dy (1891–1956) was a poet of great finesse, and his apparently whimsical work hid deep emotion. He published *Hommeries* in 1924 and *Amours* in 1929.

Although his life was relatively short, Eric de Haulleville (1900–1941) left a profound mark on Belgian literature. He was among the most talented writers of the interwar period. *Le voyage aux îles Galapagos* was published in 1934. If Odilon-Jean Périer's life had not been so short (1901–28), he might also have risen very high. His poetry perfectly reflected his gift: innate grace, renewed inventiveness. His work ranged from *La Vertu par le chant* and *Notre mère la ville* to *Promeneur* and *La Maison de verre*. Auguste Marin (1911–40) devoted himself to the memory of Périer. He displayed the same grace, the same musical fluidity, in *Le front aux vitres*.

It would be unjust to forget the contribution of essayists to Belgian French-language literature. Henri Pirenne (1862–1935), with his *Histoire de la Belgique* and numerous other works, played an important historical role. Two women were leading lights in the study of Hellenism. Marie Delcourt (1896–1979) published *Vie d'Euripide*, *Eschyle*, and *Périclès*, and her humanistic knowledge encompassed absolutely everything about Erasmus. Claire Préaux wrote admirable introductions to Greek culture. Emilie Noulet (1872–1978) was another exceptional woman. Her *Paul Valéry*, her *Oeuvre poétique de Stéphane Mallarmé*, gave ample proof of her critical talents in poetry. Camille Poupeye (1874–1963) had a curious destiny. He spent his youth sailing round the world and studying art, before settling down in later life when his thirst for adventure was quenched by the discovery of new theater of the 1920's, from Shaw to Pirandello, in *Les Dramaturges exotiques* and by the unveiling of *Les Théâtres d'Asie*.

Many Belgians left for Paris and put down roots there. The greatest of them was undoubtedly Henri Michaux (1899–1986), who remains one of the major poetic voices of the 20th century. Françoise Mallet-Joris, born in 1930, has since spread her wings in *Le rempart des béguines* and *La chambre rouge*. Her work has been varied and very rich and promises to astound further in the future.

The organizations or groups active in the interwar period deserve mention. Some of them are still around today. In 1920, a dynamic and well-informed minister, Jules Destrée (1863–1936), created the Royal Academy of French Language and Literature. It was to complement the role of the Royal Academy of Science, Literature, and the Fine Arts, which dates to 1772. This academy resembles the French Academy. It is interesting, however, to look at what makes it different. In addition to its 30 Belgian members, it has ten foreign members, thereby creating a French-speaking community. It is also open to women, which in 1920 was revolutionary. Consequently, Anna de Noailles, Colette, Jean Cocteau, Jean Cassou, Edmée de La Rochefoucauld, Marguerite Yourcenar (twelve years before Paris), Robert de Traz, and Mircea Eliade have been elected members.

Other groups sprung up, some centered around a review, some around research, such as *Sept Arts*, *Libre Académie Picard*, and especially the *Jour-*

nal des Poètes, which is still active today. *Le bon usage* by Maurice Grevisse, which was to become the best reference book for the French language around the world, should not be forgotten in this list.

The Postwar Period

Two of the greatest French-language poets of the first half of the century were Belgian. Marcel Thiry (1897–1977) was one of the adventurers of the poetic mind. After being thrown into the war during his youth, which led him to the Russian front and across a Siberia shaken by the 1917 Revolution, he became an indefatigable seeker after poetry. *Toi qui pâlis au nom de Vancouver*, the magical title of his first collection, was reused as the title for a fifty-year collection in 1975. His novelistic tendencies matched his poetic talent.

Norge (b. 1898) also had an active professional life before devoting himself to poetry. Although he was a prodigious inventor of language, he also stood in awesome contemplation of the internal world, notably with *Joie aux âmes*. He then sharpened his talent with a verve that was both incisive and cordial, as seen in collections such as *La Langue verte*, *Les oignons*, *Le vin profond*, and *Les cerveaux brûlés*.

Albert Ayguesparse (b. 1900) also has a number of different means of expression. He is above all an analyst of the modern world, as seen in essays such as *Machinisme et culture*, but he also tends toward poetry with sharp sensitivity or a poignant sense of friendship. *Le vin noir de Cahors* and *Pour saluer le jour qui naît* are major leaps in a consciousness that alternates between anxiety and fraternity. His talent as a novelist took shape at a later date, chiseled by a divided society, occasionally harsh with its weaker members, where men seek their destiny.

Adrien Jans (1905–73) was able to take enough time off from journalism to write an important work, impregnated with humanism and rich culture. As a poet he touches the soul to the quick in *La tunique de Dieu* and *Chant des âmes*.

Suzanne Lilar (b. 1901) brought an extraordinary richness of style and thought to literature. She passed the bar, dabbled in politics, and made a debut in theater before becoming one of the most important essayists of our time. Between 1945 and 1950, it was on stage that she expressed her vision of a world where nature tries to unite its contradictory forces. Passion was the theme of two novels, one of which, *La confession anonyme*, speaks of the racking of the flesh and became the film *Benvenuta*. Lilar was then at her peak, which began with *Le journal de l'analogiste*, a masterpiece of creative intelligence; then came *Le Couple* and *Le Malentendu du deuxième sexe*. Finally, Lilar displayed the full capacity of her talent, memory, intelligence, and emotion in *Une enfance gantoise*.

When Carlo Bronne (1901–87) published *Les fruits de cendre* in 1929, everyone heralded him as a future poet. But although his diverse talent was evident, it was also clear that history was to become the favorite topic of a man who lived the past as a continuing life and who miraculously harmonized concise information and the art of the storyteller. *Léopold I*ᵉʳ *et son temps*, *L'Amalgame*, *Albert I*ᵉʳ, *le roi sans terre*, and *Elisabeth de Belgique* are major successful works.

Robert Goffin (1898–1984) enjoyed life to the full. He was a pioneer of jazz; the poem *Jazz-Band* dates to 1922. He was a friend of Louis Armstrong and Cocteau and an impassioned exegete of *Rimbaud vivant* or *Mallarmé vivant*. To use one of his titles, he was a firebrand (*Le Voleur de feu*).

Constant Burniaux (1892–1975) was more or less his contemporary, but the two were very different. Burniaux was a very timid and vulnerable person. His novels were built around his experience as a teacher: *La Bêtise*, *Crânes tondus*, and later *Temps inquiets*.

The generation born with this century is also rich in creative personalities. For example, Georges Linze (b. 1900) publishes novels and essays, yet poetry forms the bulk of his work: *Poème de la paix incroyable* and *Poème science du coeur et du monde*. At the outset, Herman Closson (1901–82) seemed to have created a highly original novel form in *Le cavalier seul*. He then switched to essays with *Le Scribe accroupi*. A friend of the surrealists, of Odilon-Jean Périer and Henri Michaux, he was soon to find his true voice in the theater. Albert Dasnoy (b. 1901) was first and foremost a great painter and became a remarkable writer. At the age of 60, he published his major work, *Le Prestige du passé*, a confrontation between the past and its continuation. Ten years later, the painter and the essayist found fresh expression in a superb collection of short stories, *La longueur du temps*.

Paul-Aloïse De Bock (1898–1986) also made a late entrance in literature. He unveiled his first book in 1953: *Terres basses*. His life as a barrister and his involvement in important political cases provided the inspiration for his major literary work, *Les chemins de Rome*, a novel of the antifascist struggle. Constant Malva (1903–69), a miner, the son of a miner, and a populist by nature, incarnated proletarian literature with *Ma nuit au jour le jour*. Roger Avermaete provided a sharp contrast to Malva. Born in Antwerp ten years before Malva, he wrote chiefly in French but also in Dutch and devoted his work to history and the history of art, which brought him membership in the Académie des Beaux-Arts in Paris. He has dozens of books to his merit, including *La conjuration des chats* and *Rubens et son temps*.

Before ending this survey, I should mention the much-appreciated contributions of several active women to French literature in Belgium, such as Marie-Thérèse Bodart (1909–81), who wrote a passionate and disconcerting novel, *Les roseaux noirs*; Louis Dubrau (b. 1904), who took a piercing and merciless look at human passion in *La part du silence* and *A la poursuite de Sandra*; Marianne Pierson-Piérard (1907–81), who was a very sensitive writer combining intuition, attention, and awareness in *Le Tour de soi-même* and *Oslo au mois d'août*; and Sophie Deroisin (b. 1909), who wrote the novel *Les Publicains* and an astonishing study of girl's education, *Petites filles d'autrefois*.

A last group of writers was active during the first half of this century: Alexis Curvers (b. 1906), who wrote a skeptical novel, *Bourg-le-Rond*, and *Tempo di Roma*; Marcel Lobet (b. 1907), who contributed remarkable essays like *Chercheurs de Dieu* and later a powerful novel, *Nathanaël*; and Stanislas d'Otremont (1893–1969), who demonstrated his classical mind and style in his well-known novel, *Thomas Quercy*.

Poetry embarked on a fresh burst of activity, demonstrating that the French-speaking written arts are a permanent feature of Belgian life. Robert Guiette (1895–1976) wrote in a very strict and corseted way about man's essential reasons for existing. His last collection was entitled *L'ombre intérieure*.

Two poets who considered themselves the friends of beings and things must be mentioned here. Robert Vivier, born in 1894, was a leading professor at the University of Liège and at the Sorbonne. He published the fruit of his reflections in *L'originalité de Baudelaire* and in *Et la poésie fut langage*. For sixty years, his poetry has evolved from an encounter with a miracle to day-to-day reality. Armand Bernier also expressed his enchantment with the world and the reality of life. His major work is undoubtedly *Le Monde transparent*, a world which he tasted with pleasure for many years.

Maurice Carême (1899–1978) went through a similar evolution, but his main driving force was poetry for as wide an audience as possible. From *Mère* to *La Lanterne magique*, from *La Maison blanche* to *Heure de grâce*, Carême was inflamed by human tenderness and a song of happiness. Around the same time, Edmond Vandercammen (1901–80) sought to put the discoveries of modernity to the service of everything suggestive of love of the earth and of men as in *Faucher plus près du ciel* or *L'amour responsable*.

Another man emerged, who, outside his personal work, played the role

of discoverer and prime mover. Roger Bodart (1910–73) wrot
deal on poets, covering Charles Plisnier, Maurice Maeterlinck, Ma
Thiry, and Géo Libbrecht in the collection "Poets of Today." But Bodart
was first and foremost a poet. After his early *Les mains tendues*, his art was
to slide imperceptibly toward essential questions, as in *Le nègre de Chicago*
and even more in *La Route du sel*.

Charles Bertin (born in 1919) inherited from his uncle, Charles Plisnier, the gift and also the passion for the creative beauty of language.
He revealed his true colors in the beautiful poems *Psaumes sans grâce* and
Chant noir. Almost at the same time, he made a major entrance into the
theater. But Bertin was attracted by all forms of expression that can serve
a literary passion. *Journal d'un crime* is a lovely novel, and *Le jardin du
désert* a major meditative work. Close to him but totally devoted to poetry
was Jean Tordeur (b. 1920). His *Prière de l'attente* written as a young man
and *Conservateur des charges* in later life reflect the path taken by an anxious soul in poems of rare beauty and intensity. A kindred soul was Jean
Mogin (1921–85), who wrote a cascade of poems, including *La Vigne
amère*, *La Belle Alliance*, and the marvelous *Maison*, written when he was
very close to death.

Some women have contributed exquisite poetry: Lucienne Desnoues
with *Le Jardin délivré*, Andrée Sodenkamp in *Sainte terre*, Anne-Marie
Kegels in *Porter l'orage*, Jeanine Moulin in *Rue Chair-et-pain*, Renée Brock
in *L'amande amère*, and Liliane Wouters with *L'Aloès*.

This still leaves some of the great personalities of Belgian poetry.
Pierre della Faille (b. 1906) has a violent, solitary personality. One of
his books is called *Mise à feu*, another *Le grand Alleluia*. Arthur Haulot
(b. 1913) was well acquainted with social struggle and concentration
camps in the last world war before becoming a commissioner general
for tourism. He established the Biennales Internationales de Poésie. He
paints a picture in his poems of the world of love and humanist faith in
Départ, *Magie*, and *Le Temps intérieur*. Also born in 1913, Fernand Ver-
hesen writes rather bold poetry, as in *Franchir la nuit or Les clartés mitoy-
ennes*. He is well known as a translator of Spanish and Latin American
poems.

Philippe Jones (or Philippe Roberts-Jones) is a man of many talents.
Born in 1924, a university professor, chief curator of the Royal Museums of Fine Arts of Brussels, and now permanent secretary of the Royal
Academy of Science, Literature and, the Fine Arts, he has written a number of top-ranking essays for which he was elected to the Institut de
France: *Du Réalisme au Surréalisme, De Daumier à Lautrec, L'Art majeur*, and
a number of others. At the same time, Philippe Robert-Jones, the poet,

built up an ample and secret body of work in which rigor is the essential language, such as *Graver au vif* and *Racine ouverte*. His compelling poetry is both intense and highly compact.

Henry Bauchau (b. 1913) is the rare writer who allows his talent to mature before revealing it. His first collection of poems was entitled *Géologie*; another is *La Chine intérieure*. Two admirable novels, *La déchirure* and *Le régiment noir*, unfurled the same universe. Francis Walder (b. 1906), with novels such as *Saint-Germain ou la Négociation* (winner of the Prix Goncourt), demonstrates his mastery in resurrecting the past and his hold on classic language.

Thomas Owen (b. 1910) is distinguished by his ample talent and striking personality. A well-known art critic under the name of Stéphane Rey, he rapidly came to the fore with his novels *Les chemins étranges*, *Cérémonial nocturne*, and *Les maisons suspectes*, where fear and mystery slide imperceptibly into everyday life.

Paul Willems (b. 1912) comes from a completely different world and created theatrical work marked by a tinge of poetic transformation and a few novels of unusual tone: *Tout est réel ici* and *La Chronique du cygne*.

Georges Thinès (b. 1923) is an intellectual and a scholar of international status. He received the Prix Victor Rossel for his novel *Le Tramway des officiers*. He publishes poems, puts on plays, writes comment on Kafka, and continues to write remarkable, occasionally mysterious novels, such as *Vacances de Rocroi* and *Désert d'alun*. His contemporary Maud Frère (1923–69) produced a number of highly penetrating novels such as *L'herbe à moi* and *Les temps d'une carte postale*. Gaston Compère (b. 1924) moves between playwriting and poetry with the very beautiful *Profération de la parole perdue* and novels like *L'Office des Ténèbres*. Jacques-Gérard Linze (b. 1925) wrote *La Conquête de Prague* in the refined style of the New Novel and continued his objective exploration of the world in *Le fruit de cendre*.

In a country that is termed materialist and is overflowing with poets, this same generation has also been creatively fertile. Gérard Prévot (1921–75) had a nature that was less inclined to seek out or to renew than to shake up. A novelist in *La Race des grands cadavres*, a fantastic storyteller in *Démon de février*, a playwright in *La nouvelle Eurydice*, he was above all a poet. Similarly, it is difficult to pinpoint the real Hubert Juin (1926–87). He was born in Gaume, which he used as a source of inspiration for his first novels: *Célébration du grand-père* and *Le repas chez Marguerite*. He then left for Paris and did some extraordinary work as a critic. His *Victor Hugo* is one of the major biographies of our time. His path could have crossed that of André Schmitz, born in 1929 in a nearby region. Schmitz, however, after a few years in Africa, came back to his native land as a full-blown poet. *A voix double et jointe*, published in 1965, was an eloquent expression of his profound meditation, as were *Soleils rauques* and *Oiseaux, éclairs et autres instants* in a much harsher manner. Claire Lejeune (b. 1926) is on the contrary a permanent mixture of poetic activity and philosophical work. From *La geste* to *L'atelier*, research is for her a kind of instinctive law.

Literary criticism and first-class essays have always been a source of vitality. Gaston Colle incarnated a happy humanism, for example, in *Les sourires de Béatrice*. Hubert Colleye (1883–1972) dedicated his long life and constant attention to classical culture—literature and fine arts—both in *Hauts-lieux de chrétienté* and in journalism. Charles de Trooz (1905–58) was a master. A man of vast culture, he was gifted with the art of communication. He enriched Belgian intellectual life. *Le Magister et ses maîtres* is a superb essay.

Literary research made Gustave Charlier (1885–1959) one of the best versed connoisseurs of the 20th century and turned Joseph Hanse (b. 1902) into a specialist on Charles de Coster and Maeterlinck, before he became one of the best linguists of the entire French-speaking world. Chairman of the International Council of French Language in Paris, Joseph Hanse has published a *Dictionary of the Difficulties of Modern French*, which is used as a reference work throughout the world.

Let us not forget literary historians. Roland Mortier (b. 1920) is one of the masters of the 18th century and of the Enlightenment, but information and reflection are perfectly combined in a book such as *L'originalité*. During the same years and up to the present time, André Vandegans (b. 1921), with *La jeunesse littéraire d'André Malraux*, is an exemplar of high-level research.

The Present and the Future

A glance at the present gives ample proof of creative vitality that will guarantee the future of French-language literature in Belgium. The novel is an area where very different temperaments have come to the fore. Marcel Moreau (b. 1933) rapidly pressed his violent nature, overflowing with refusal and intensity, onto the literary stage. Novels such as *La terre infestée d'hommes* and *Moreaumachie* and essays such as *Discours contre les entraves* are an expression of rupture and of vast intellectual talents. Conrad Detrez's (1937–85) novels constituted a revolt against everything that left a mark on his youth: religious education, small-town conformity, sexual morality. *L'herbe à brûler* and *Le dragueur de Dieu* are examples of this.

François Weyergans (b. 1940) is a free spirit, full of humor and originality, which allow him to make use of all current techniques without becoming a slave to any of them. Pierre Mertens (b. 1939) is undoubtedly already one of the jewels of Belgian literature and one of its brightest hopes. His first passion was for the way in which the memory records things, as seen in *L'Inde ou l'Amérique* and *La fête des anciens*. He then became engrossed in contemporary social themes: social integration, the fight for freedom, and human rights. From this he has produced vast and demanding works, such as *Les bons offices* and *Terre d'asile*. His last novel, *Les éblouissements*, is a major work (it won the Médicis Prize in 1987).

Françoise Collin (b. 1928) has always been attracted to modernity, as seen in such novels as *Rose qui peut* and even in more technical and analytical works. Marie Denis does not go so far, but her work is in a similar direction. *L'odeur du père* was the first important milestone in her work. Another woman, born in Liège on the threshold of the last war, Véra Feyder, initially chose to give herself up to poetry. Her poems express the anxiety of living. She then switched to novels in *La Derelitta*.

Jacques Crickillon (b. 1940) also has a polymorphous nature. His first collection, *La Défendue*, was the first sign of his vast exploration of an internal universe where anxiety naturally becomes effervescence. This same passion is seen in short stories and novels such as *Supra-Coronada* and *Le tueur birman*.

Bosquet de Thoran (b. 1935) displayed his talents in the novel *Le songe de Constantin* before moving on to essay writing. His last book, *Traité du reflet*, is a highly subtle work of aesthetic reflection. More sociological essay work is evidently not a new phenomenon, as seen in the example of Léo Moulin (b. 1906), a major intellectual, who proved himself an exceptional specialist in the *Monde vivant des religieux* and in *L'Aventure européenne*. Pol Vandromme (b. 1927) is above all an analyst of a certain category of writer, such as Marcel Aymé, Jacques Chardonne, and others.

The surprisingly rich and varied flow of poets has continued. André Miguel (b. 1920) loves exploring verb use and is enchanted by the mystery of poetry and creation in *Corps du jour* and *L'oeil dans la bouche*. André Gascht (b. 1921) has created a poetic universe that is both tender and mysterious, ranging from *Cette âpre douceur* to *Royaume de Danemark*. For his part, Louis Daubier (b. 1924) is a watchful, attentive poet with a kind of secret smile in *La nuit veille, Qui tait la vaste parole?* Jacques

Izoard (b. 1936) uses very tightly knit language bordering on mystery in *Un chemin de sel pur*. Christian Hubin (b. 1941) expresses the adventure of living, the expectation of an unknown light in *Eclaireur* and in *Coma des sourdes veillées*. His contemporary Werner Lambersy (b. 1941) seeks rather a brief upsurge, rupture, or suddenness as in *Maîtres et maisons de thé* and *Paysage avec homme nu dans la neige*, which were written with a glimpse of Japanese poetry.

A total contrast is provided by William Cliff (b. 1946). His poetry relates life with surprising exactitude and nonchalance. *Marcher au charbon* is almost a rhyming novel. Jean-Pierre Verheggen (b. 1942) also uses parody and puns as vehicles of violent questioning, as in *Le degré zorro de l'écriture*. Eugène Savitzkaya (b. 1955) relates in what resembles a dreamlike narrative his expectations, his anxiety, and his vision of beings and things. Here again, mention must be made of those who have left for Paris: Dominique Rolin, Alain Bosquet, and many, many more. All are truly enriching Belgian French-language literature.

Dutch-Language Literature

Jean Weisgerber

"FLEMISH" IS AN AMBIGUOUS WORD because it refers at the same time to a region (Flanders), the people who live there, and the language they speak (also called Dutch). Even as a geographical term, its meaning is complex since it can refer to a medieval county, two provinces of the Belgian state, and more loosely the northern half of Belgium, that is, the territory bounded on the south by the French-speaking area. It is in this —its broadest sense—that the phrase "Flemish literature" is used here, to the exclusion, however, of all the works written in French by people who live in the same area. If Belgium's language problem is something of a Chinese puzzle, it is because it reflects the coexistence of Dutch and French in some Flemish towns.

The emergence of modern literature in Flanders dates to the last decade of the 19th century. It was undoubtedly facilitated by the example of both *La Jeune Belgique* (1881) and *De Nieuwe Gids* (The movement of the '80's, 1885) in Holland. When August Vermeylen, Prosper van Langendonck, Emmanuel de Bom, and Cyriel Buysse founded the journal *Van Nu en Straks* (Today and tomorrow, 1893–1901), Romanticism and Realism had almost written themselves out; the time was ripe for change. But progressive though they were, the innovators were reformers rather than iconoclasts. They did not discard the past *en bloc*, nor did their cosmopolitanism repudiate the national inheritance indiscriminately. On the contrary, they carefully retained what they considered to be sound and useful—some of them revered Guido Gezelle (1830–99), for instance—and got rid only of outdated ideas and techniques. Since they were fully aware of the crisis Europe was experiencing at the close of the century (Symbolism versus Naturalism, Irrationalism versus Collectivism, etc.), they usually adopted a middle-of-the-road policy while drawing the line at making essential concessions. That is why "synthesis" became the distinctive catchword of the movement. The literary code of the periodical and its major contributors (Karel van de Woestijne, Stijn Streuvels, Herman Teirlinck, and Fernand Toussaint, in addition to the founding fathers) is therefore characterized by eclecticism. Naturalism, Aestheticism, Symbolism, and Impressionism are combined, and as a result they lose some of their original stridency. Somehow, Zola is deprived of his scientism, Des Esseintes of his egocentricity, Mallarmé of his abstruseness. By adjusting foreign sources, mainly French, to local conditions, *Van Nu en Straks* also assigned a new function to literature. The Flemish writer's duty no longer consisted in teaching the masses or in pleading the nationalist cause, for the increasing democratization of the state and the progress of the Flemish movement made these tasks less pressing; it was now enough for the individual artist to cultivate beauty, thus improving the taste of the general public and raising the people up to his level. This, however, proved to be wishful thinking, and by and large individualism prevailed.

From a literary point of view, poets such as van de Woestijne (1878–1929) and Van Langendonck (1862–1920) and novelists such as Streuvels (1871–1969) and Teirlinck (1879–1967), as well as Vermeylen (1872–1945), the most active critic of the group, achieved success second only to that of Gezelle. The main feature they shared is overrefinement of language (such refinement characterized neighboring countries at the time). Their indulgence in words, in sound effects and visual images, led them to overemphasize description at the expense of the plot, so that their novels sometimes verge on painting; similarly, their poems are very much like music. This pervasive influence of Impressionism and Symbolism was of historical importance in that it paved the way for subsequent developments. Indeed, though focusing on external reality, the Impressionist merely renders the effect it produces on the senses; things as they really are are beyond our reach, and objectivity is out of the question. It goes without saying that the Symbolists further enhanced this subjective stance, which was eventually to culminate in Expressionism.

A second modernist wave attracted notice in 1916 during the German occupation with Felix Timmermans (1886–1947), whose *Pallieter* is a lyrical novel in praise of life, and with Paul van Ostaijen (1896–1928) and his arresting collection of poems, *Music Hall*. For obvious reasons, the Flemish avant-garde soon identified with the humanitarian wing of German Expressionism. It gratified the young poets' hankering for peace, fraternity, God, and the good life; through political action, they thought the pure in heart would be able to establish a reign of justice and goodwill in Flanders—the millennium. Reacting against individualism, materialism, reason, science, and technology, which they held responsible for war, they extolled collective and idealistic values. Because they believed that intuition could disclose the spiritual essence of things, they regarded sensory data as mere signs of the Idea. Needless to say, this Idea was often nothing else than a projection of the self. Last but not least, instead of depicting the outside world by means of everyday words according to realistic recipes, Expressionism wanted to recreate the universe and language as well. The supremacy of the creative spirit over matter resulted in a political commitment that, ineffectual though it was, made literature once again subservient to the didactic and propagandist tendencies that *Van Nu en Straks* had opposed. Yet the Expressionists did so in a much more sophisticated way than their Romantic ancestors had done for their art, for example, the humanitarian poems and plays by van Ostaijen, Wies Moens, Gaston Burssens, Marnix Gijsen, Victor J. Brunclair (b. 1899), Achilles Mussche, and Anton van de Velde or the magazine *Ruimte* (Space, 1920–21)—it was certainly no popular art.

On the other hand, starting from the same principles, van Ostaijen soon evolved a new poetry theory. His own brand of Expressionism, which he called "organic," aimed at revealing the unknown—the subconscious, the unconscious, and even the metaphysical roots of existence—by the handling of words: poetry thus became a game in which knowledge was at stake. Van Ostaijen was familiar with all aspects of contemporary avant-garde. Not only did he resort to the chaotic typography and layout of Futurism and Dada but, by demanding (while suiting the action to the word) that the poem should grow out of an initial theme through a series of associations (not unlike musical variations), he was also a pioneer. If he is reminiscent of Stramm, he is also akin to Surrealism even though he emphasizes the controlling role of the conscious mind. His finest poems look deceptively simple: they are written in free verse and in a conversational tone that recall the rhythm and style of ordinary speech, but they show such economy of line and they are so rich in meaning that they are extremely elusive. As self-contained verbal objects, they do not explicitly convey any definite "message." More often than not, they offer disillusioned and haunting comments on the world we live in.

True to avant-garde extremism, Expressionism stressed, and so widened, the gap between Collectivism and Aestheticism, two attitudes that *Van Nu en Straks* had tried to reconcile. It lasted only ten years, but its influence extended well into the 1930's, making itself felt, as it happened, in a field it had previously neglected. The novel had been too strongly dominated by Realism to undergo any change, but as time went by, it, too, felt increasingly attracted to the Expressionist doctrine—its worship of the life force, its interest in intellectual or social problems and in formal experiments. In the long run, Expressionism fostered the growth of a new kind of fiction in which characters and ideas were substituted for descriptions and meticulous renderings of sense data. Consequently, the psychological novel and the problem novel became the most significant genres in the prewar decade.

In many respects, novelists such as Willem Elsschot (1882–1960), Maurice Roelants (1895–1966), Gerard Walschap (1898–1989), Raymond Brulez (1895–1972), and Maurice Gilliams (1900–1982) carried on the *Van Nu en Straks* tradition, whose "synthesis" resisted the attacks of Expressionism more successfully than was expected. The younger generation even reached a more satisfactory compromise between social and aesthetic values than Vermeylen and van de Woestijne. History has shown that the humanitarian poets were building castles in the air; the Great Depression and Hitler made van Ostaijen's verbal games utterly irrelevant. The 1930's mistrusted the political wild-goose chase of humanitarianism and refused to separate art from life as van Ostaijen had done. Fascinated by "personalism," they regarded the individual as a member of the community, involved in a network of social and cultural relations. The new synthesis subjected form to the study of humanity, language to the delineation of "personality," for which narration was the ideal medium. Fiction became conscious of its specific character and its own resources. Some of the novels then published in Flanders—Elsschot's *Lijmen* (1924), Gilliams's *Elias* (1936), or Walschap's *Houtekiet* (1939)—are in no way inferior to those written by Huxley or Steinbeck. At the same time, poetry (Richard Minne, Raymond Herreman, Karel Jonckheere) turned back to intimate themes, confession, and introspection.

Such was, roughly speaking, the literary scene when World War II broke out. Things did not change very much at once, for it was not until 1949 that radical alterations would come to the fore. On the surface, budding novelists like Hubert Lampo, Piet van Aken, and Louis Paul Boon were still paying homage to Roelants and Walschap. But some of the magazines that had represented the literary establishment before the war closed down, and in most cases collective action was replaced by individual attempts. Unlike France and Holland, Belgium did not witness a blossoming of Resistance poetry: Belgian writers, whether Flemish or Walloon, chose rather to oppose Nazism in a roundabout way. Brunclair and Kamiel Van Baelen may have died in a German concentration camp, but the voice of freedom and democracy usually made itself heard under the guise of fiction and essays. The defensive response to dictatorship and its catchwords was no less effective for all that, as appears from Boon's first novel, *De voorstad groeit* (The suburb grows, 1943)—a leftist novel that curiously eluded the vigilance of censorship—Van Baelen's Christian idealism, Teirlinck's glorification of the life force, Johan Daisne's (1912–78) magic realism, and Herreman's epicurean *Vergeet niet te leven* (Don't forget to live, 1943). Although few literary works gave immediate expression to the experience of war, occupation, and liberation, these events left a permanent mark on the collective memory, a kind of obsession that has been growing for 40 years, inspiring a series of superb novels from Boon's *Mijn kleine Oorlog* (My little war, 1946) to Ivo Michiels's *Het Boek Alfa* (The book alpha, 1963) to Hugo Claus's *De verwondering* (Astonishment, 1962) and *Het verdriet van België* (The sorrow of Belgium, 1983).

While poetry was stagnating, the novel retained its own momentum. The 1940's considerably enlarged the idea of personality. In addition to psychology, ethics, and social problems, novelists took an interest in the human condition—Sartre and Camus were widely read after the war—in the world of fantasy, metaphysics, and comedy. Above all, Walschap's approach to the novel as a dynamic relation of facts and his mistrust of folklore proved most influential. On the other hand, the genre progressively turned away from realistic observation and representation to modernist experiments with form. Like Gilliams, who patterned *Elias* on the classical sonata, Daisne, Van Baelen, and Boon started dislocating the machinery of the traditional narrative, forsaking the imitation of reality in favor of invention.

Marnix Gijsen (pen name of Jan Goris; 1899–1984), who had made his debut as an Expressionist poet thirty years earlier, published his first and by far his best novel in 1948: *Het boek van Joachim van Babylon* (The book of Joachim of Babylon) is at the same time an autobiographical *Bildundsroman*, a psychological portrait, and a fictionalized essay in which the moralist gives vent to bitter and skeptical comments on human existence. Raymond Brulez likewise made capital of his own past in *Mijn Woningen* (The houses where I lived, 1950–54) and gently satirized Belgian follies in his Voltairian *contes*. While Van Baelen was writing parables that recalled the Expressionist decade as much as they foreshadowed the 1950's and Piet Van Aken (b. 1920) was launching out into a vast panorama of social life in *Het Begeren* (Desire, 1952) and *Klinkaart* (Brickyard, 1954) comparable to Faulkner's and Caldwell's sagas, Johan Daisne, for one, elaborated a new literary program.

"Magic realism" was not actually a new trend, at least not in Germany and Italy, but Daisne was the first European writer to systematize it. A sentimental idealist and Platonist, he expressed his hostility to Nazism by plunging headlong into the realm of ideas. Art, he argued, is a transposition of life; it comes into being in the indefinite borderland between reality and dream where the fantastic background of reality—its essence, or the "other side" of things—becomes visible. Substantially, magic realism consists in combining these two poles, thus producing the magic spark that illuminates the hidden truth. It is, as the title of Daisne's first novel suggests, "a stairway of stone and clouds" (*De trap van steen en wolken*, 1942), which allows the initiate to glimpse the Beautiful and the Good. From a technical point of view, this spiritualism resorts to a montage reminiscent of the cinema by juxtaposing or telescoping contrasting episodes. In *De man die zijn haar kort liet knippen* (The man who had his hair cut short, 1947; filmed by André Delvaux), the author illustrates his theories in a haunting monologue of surpassing beauty.

Hubert Lampo (b. 1920), author of *Terugkeer naar Atlantis* (Back to Atlantis, 1953) and *De komst van Joachim Stiller* (The coming of Joachim Stiller, 1960) was converted to magic realism as early as 1945, but he did not work along the same lines as Daisne. He soon discovered Jung and associated Daisne's program with the collective unconscious and the archetypes to be found in myth, folklore, and dreams, so that his ideas are not unlike those of some Latin American novelists such as Carpentier, Asturias, and García Márquez.

In addition to Daisne, another exceptional talent came to the front during the occupation. At heart, Louis Paul Boon (1912–79) is a fervent socialist; yet his sense of anxiety, loneliness, and alienation brings him closer to Existentialism than to Marxism. If the whole world is going topsy-turvy, he contends, we have only ourselves to blame; the evil is due much more to human perversity than to social and economic factors. So before reforming the world, we need to reform ourselves. As usual, preaching a change of heart proved to be crying in the wilderness. Boon was doomed to record the downfall of all his hopes. But he did so with a passion, a rage, and a fury of impatience to pursue an improbable salvation that belied his pessimism in *De voorstad groeit* (The suburb grows, 1943), *Vergeten Straat* (Forgotten street, 1946), and *De Kapellekensbaan* (Chapel road, 1953). Insofar as he emphasized the human condition rather than social issues, he was led to discard forms that were perhaps appropriate to the novel of ideas but inadequate to describe the complexity of life and, above all, the innermost recesses of the self. In *Chapel Road*, for instance, the threads of several stories, as well as the narrator's comments on them, are skillfully intertwined. Disillusioned idealism is also the keynote of a number of fascinating works in which violent and crude episodes are combined with black humor and poetic delicacy: *Menuet* (Minuet, 1955), *Zomer te Ter-Muren* (Summer in Ter-Muren, 1956), and *De paradijsvogel* (The bird of paradise, 1958).

Boon's career exemplifies literary developments in Flanders after 1950. Existentialism came into fashion; it was soon rivaled by French Surrealism and by the influence of such writers as Eliot, Pound, and Faulkner, and van Ostaijen's poetics made a comeback. The most significant fact, however, was a new avant-garde movement. It was launched by the magazine *Tijd en Mens* (Time and man, 1949–55) led by Jan Walravens, Boon, and Hugo Claus, and it was known by the name "Experimentalism." In essence, it rejects observation, realism, and representational art and prescribes invention in the fullest sense of the word. In principle, the artist breaks away from all the rules of perspective, logic, grammar, genre, and ethics, to handle materials—colors, lines, words—without restraint. In that way, as Paul Klee maintains, art eventually discloses things that are beyond the range of ordinary experience; following the example of van Ostaijen, art becomes once again an instrument of knowledge.

Poetry took the fullest advantage of these ideas, for it was literally rejuvenated by them; Karel Jonckheere, for instance, found his second breath in the 1950's whereas Gaston Burssens, one of van Ostaijen's supporters, was widely read by the new generation. But Experimentalism also consolidated the position of the modernist novel, which Gilliams, Daisne, and Boon had been trying to renew ever since the late 1930's. Suffice it to say that Herman Teirlinck, who had successively contributed to *Van Nu en Straks*, written Expressionist plays, and published "vitalist fiction" such as *Het gevecht met de engel* (The fight with the angel, 1952), turned to modernism in his last and finest novel, *Zelfportret of Het galgemaal* (The man in the mirror, 1955).

Tijd en Mens was an international magazine; it was interested in society and painting as well as in literature, and, on the whole, it took a middle course between aestheticism and Sartre's commitment. It was all for freedom and solidarity, and against dogma, party politics, and "bourgeois" rationalism. Besides Walravens, the most important critic and theorist of the team, a number of young poets caught the public eye: R. C. van de Kerckhove, A. Bontridder, M. Wauters, Ben Cami, and, of course, Hugo Claus (b. 1929).

Claus's first novel, *De Metsiers* (The duck hunt, 1950), which made him famous at twenty, reminds one of Faulkner's *As I Lay Dying*, at least as far as narrative technique is concerned, and early poems such as *Tancredo infrasonic* (1952) and *Een huis dat tussen nacht en morgen staat* (A house between night and morning, 1953) testify to his knowledge of van Ostaijen, Pound, and the principles of both Surrealism and Experimentalism. Claus gave eloquent expression to some feelings prevalent at the time—the consciousness of one's own decay as the years go by, of living in order to die, of being left to one's own devices in an absurd world, and of being sent to one's doom by an anonymous and incomprehensible decree. By way of compensation, he contrasted the weariness of everyday life with the ecstasy of love, and anxiety and experience with nostalgia for the lost paradise of innocence. To him we are mere animals and— as in Blake—the child is irremediably tainted when initiated into adult life. Claus, however, soon extended the scope of his themes. Perceiving that fatalism and instinct had influenced him, he started edging away from Experimentalism. He had recourse to myth, history, and cultural values in *De Oostakkerse gedichten* (Oostakker poems, 1955) and *Het teken van de hamster* (The sign of the hamster, 1963) to call attention to the destructive powers that lie in wait for us. At bottom, indeed, he is deeply committed as is apparent from his keen interest in politics and in the stage. In his great novels, from *De verwondering* (1962) to *Het verdriet van België* (1983), he applied the poetics of quotation devised by Eliot and Pound to full-length narratives blending references to Dante, Sir James Frazer, and medieval theology in the former to alchemy, freemasonry, Plato, and Dante in the latter. Brimming with subtle hints and esoteric allusions, these books epitomize a kind of modern mannerism, although they could be termed postmodernist as well. Since they can be interpreted in terms of several frames of reference, the reader is urged to assume a more active attitude toward literature and to round off, as it were, the story told by the narrator. Unquestionably, Claus is now one of the most significant figures in world literature.

Ivo Michiels (b. 1923) employs different methods, sometimes inspired by the French *nouveau roman*. As stated above, the war provides the backdrop for his work, but he combines this theme with the sense of guilt and uncertainty so typical of the postwar decade. After some existentialist attempts such as *Het afscheid* (Parting, 1957), he resolutely rejected psychology and plot to rely mostly on the resources of language. Owing to the perfect agreement of contents and style, the ideas expressed determine the structure of the sentence in *Het boek Alfa* (1963), an enthralling novel devoted to the problems of doubt, choice, and freedom, which is the first part of a cycle that includes *Orchis militaris* (1968), *Exit* (1971), *Samuel, o Samuel* (1973), and *Dixi(t)* (1979).

A similar social commitment characterizes two further novelists of outstanding merit. If Ward Ruyslinck (b. 1929) sides with the underdog, with the innumerable victims of injustice, he carefully eludes the pitfalls of false pathos; besides being a philanthropist and a humanitarian, he is a satirist endowed with a keen sense of humor, as exemplified by *Het dal van Hinnom* (Gehenna, 1961) and *De heksenkring* (The magic circle, 1972). Jef Geeraerts (b. 1930), who was a territorial agent in Africa, deals with both colonial and sexual themes—the woes of blacks and whites, the alienation of repatriated Belgians—in a way reminiscent of Henry Miller and sometimes of Hemingway, as in *Ik ben maar een neger* (I am but a negro, 1961) and *Gangreen* (Gangrene, 1968–77).

Other prose writers should also be mentioned, notably André Demedts, Libera B. Carlier, Hugo Raes, Paul de Wispelaere, C. C. Krijgelmans, Daniël Robberechts, Gust Gils, Paul Koeck, Fernand Auwers, Clem Schouwenaars, Walter van den Broeck, and Claude van de Berge. Most of them are loath to follow the beaten track.

It is in fiction and poetry that contemporary Flemish literature is at its best. In comparison, except for some good plays by Claus (*Een bruid in de morgen*, A bride in the morning, 1955; *Suiker*, Sugar, 1958; *Vrijdag*, Friday, 1970) and Tone Brulin, the theater does not come up to international standards. Poetry, on the contrary, benefited not only from the example of the Experimentalists but also from the fresh impetus of magazines like *Gard-Sivik* (National guard, 1955–64) and *Impuls* (Impulse, 1968; under Jan de Roek, Marcel Obiak, Roger de Neef), of the mannerism of the so-called Pink Poets (Nic van Bruggen, Henri-Floris Jespers, Patrich Conrad, Michel Bartosik), and of the new realism represented by Herman de Coninck. Some, however, such as Annie Reniers and Eddy van Vliet prefer to go it alone.

Gard-Sivik reacted against the commitment of *Tijd en Mens*, opposed existentialist anxiety, and stressed the formal aspects of poetry. Its tendency was individualistic and literary rather than social. Nevertheless, Hughes Pernath (1931–76) and Paul Snoek (1933–81), its major representatives, expressed ideas that somehow recall those of their predecessors, although Snoek was much more willing than Claus to look on the bright side of things. Pernath, one of Belgium's finest poets, carried terseness to the point of emulating silence and spoke in images of uncommon evocative power. Snoek's originality lies elsewhere. While yearning for happiness, goodness, and freedom, his aggressiveness betrays his vulnerability. In his first poems, melancholy sometimes casts a gloom over his playful imagination; later he wrote some magnificent hymns in praise of the elements (*Hercules*, 1960), and in *Richelieu* (1961) and *Nostradamus* (1963) he posed as a solitary champion of peace and truth.

Looking back on the past century, it is beyond question that Flemish writers listened attentively to Vermeylen's call for "more brains" and originality. Flanders is in perfect harmony with the main trends of world literature, though it always strikes a note of its own.

Architecture, Painting, and Sculpture

Francine-Claire Legrand

SINCE THE MIDDLE AGES, Belgium has brought forth and nurtured painters, sculptors, cathedral builders, and craftspersons of great talent and originality. Museums all over the world testify to Belgium's rich heritage, with paintings, tapestries, and sculptures of every period. It is hardly surprising therefore to find exuberant artistic activity everywhere in Belgium. In painting, this activity finds its inspiration in the earthier Flemish school or the more surrealistic school of Wallonia. Contemporary Belgian artists are well represented in private and public collections worldwide as well as in the numerous art galleries.

Architecture

The old Belgian towns are dotted with elegant cathedral and church spires made of stone lace. In one fluid evolution, the Romanesque style gave way first to the Gothic and then to the Renaissance style. In the old part of Bruges, one can gaze in every direction without encountering a single jarring note, and yet every stage of Gothic architecture is represented, from the most austere to the most ornate. Architecture in Ghent is somewhat less homogeneous and more representative of the 19th century. But here again Romanesque houses lead to the Gothic Cathedral of Saint Baaf before which are "The Kneeling Adolescents" of George Minne, the contemporary symbolist sculptor. The Grand Place in Brussels successfully mingles the Gothic style of the Town Hall and the King's House with the luxurious Baroque style of the guild halls. Antwerp has its cathedral, Liége its episcopal palace as well as modern buildings, and every town in Belgium boasts glorious reminders of the great periods in its history.

At the end of the 19th century, an architectural revolution took place that could have turned Brussels into the most beautiful Art Nouveau town of Europe. Industrialization, financial concentration in the hands of banks, and colonial conquests, tempered by the rise of socialism through the formation of the Belgian Workers Party in 1885, prompted a number of rather bold initiatives. The Neo-classical style was shelved. In liberal upper-middle-class circles, very open to contemporary art, literature, and music, a few innovative architects overturned conventional practices and changed the facades of the new family mansions. They threw out the system of three linked rooms per floor, strangled by a dingy corridor. They opened bay windows and broke the monotony of identical floors by introducing corbeled loggias or winter gardens supported by metallic framework. Harmonious curves flourished in stairways, set off by sinuous ironwork banisters. The basic concept was the creation of a fluid, spacious interior, and to this end walls were removed wherever possible and replaced by double glass doors, interior arcades, and floral skylights. Houses attained a transparency that enhanced a more relaxed family and social life.

However, the greatest changes were seen in the decor, which enjoyed much greater freedom. Iron, glass, often tinted to produce stained-glass windows, and mirrors were used to add form to the bare structure. A proliferation of arabesque and scroll-shaped ornamentation was used to reinforce the impression of lightness. Nature's example was often copied, and its spontaneous pattern was reflected in curves and countercurves. Green plants and a variety of electrical and natural light sources were used to divide up the volume of the house into human-sized living spaces. Very few examples of this architectural exuberance remain. Most did not escape the demolition ball; they were too recent to be registered and classified. The Solvay Mansion, on avenue Louise in Brussels, is one survivor. Victor Horta (1861–1947) designed every last detail of this house, right down to the house number, the door handles, and the light shades. The present owners, in love with their surroundings, have added pieces of Horta furniture, recovered from various sources. The interior is an organic whole, perfectly comfortable and easy to live in. The architect's own house on the rue Américaine was saved from demolition and has been refurnished and transformed into a museum.

Paul Hankar (1859–1902) was a contemporary of Horta's and a great admirer of his. For many years, Hankar's talents were underestimated; however, it was he, rather than Horta, who first introduced arabesque Art Nouveau into ironwork. Typical features of Hankar are virtuoso railings, banisters, and window frames as well as ornate ceilings and paneling. The facade of the house built for the painter Ciamberlani is one remaining vestige of Hankar's work, decorated with sgraffito figures; another is a house in rue Antoine Bréart, that combines arabesque with smoothly balanced horizontals and verticals.

The Art Nouveau style, smothered by the overgenerous ornamentation of poor imitations, gradually went out of fashion. The Palais des Beaux Arts, built by Horta in 1922–1928, marked a return to the straight line. The outside, tucked away on a slope, is not very spectacular, but the interior is spacious and functional. The ceiling of the large concert hall makes use of harmonious curves, and its impeccable accoustics should teach contemporary architects who make exaggerated use of adjustable pendentives.

Henry Van de Velde (1863–1957), a follower of Art Nouveau in its early phases, designed Art Nouveau furniture, useful objects, wallpaper, and dresses. However, he rejected the need for pointless ornamentation and soon adopted an asymmetric and functional style. Belgians thought his work controversial, and he left to pursue a career in Germany and the Netherlands; he later returned to reform the teaching of architecture in Belgium.

Meanwhile, people's attention had turned to the Palais Stoclet, on the avenue de Tervueren in Brussels, built of white marble set off with gold. It was the creation of the Viennese architect Josef Hoffmann during the period when vertical symmetry and clean-cut geometry were in fashion. It was a major model for architects and decorators in the years 1925–30 who were followers of the style known as Art Deco.

The years after World War I were not a period of great inspiration among Belgian architects. However, after 1930, they began to copy the English garden-city style. Making maximum use of green spaces, these "garden cities" either consisted of identical family homes, as at Floreal in Boitsfort, or used natural "accidents" to diversify and personalize housing developments by using pathways to insert space, as seen in the Krieken Put district in Uccle or in Auderghem. Schools, churches, and shops made these districts autonomous. The most recent examples include collective amenities, such as day-care centers and local meeting places.

Many opulent but not very original detached houses have been scattered around the countryside on the outskirts of towns, creating flourishing suburbs, somewhat along the lines of those seen in the United States. However, they differ in that gardens are strictly fenced off, discouraging neighborly contacts. In certain regions, the style of typical Flemish farmhouses, whitewashed and with blue or green shutters, has been used in middle-class dwellings.

At the same time, high-rise council-built housing sprang up here and there, devoid of any town planning or relationship with the environment. A fad for high-rises then afflicted towns. Curtain walls in glass and aluminium served as a pretext for the construction of towers in an anarchic manner that disrupted the urban landscape, even if occasionally the structure was lightened by the use of pillars and new materials such as polyester.

In the center of Brussels, the Bruxelles-Lambert Bank brought in American architects and contractors to produce a building that has often been badly imitated, consisting of prefabricated parts in reinforced concrete stuck together by stainless steel knee-and-socket joints. More recently, some banks and insurance companies have decided to adopt the air of a modern cathedral, with raised archways, as seen in recent buildings in New York. Some companies have moved out of the center in order to have more breathing space. Glaverbel, built in the form of a ring, is distinguished by a crust of blue stone attached to consoles in reinforced concrete. The Royale Belge Insurance Company, situated in a wooded site with mirror-like stretches of water, was built of tinted glass and a type of steel resistant to atmospheric corrosion.

Around 1970, events were to fire the imagination of a new generation of architects. When the Catholic University of Louvain split into two separate entities, one Dutch-speaking and one French-speaking, it was decided to create a small-scale town, rather than a campus, in the Walloon part of Brabant. Louvain-la-Neuve, as this town was baptized, is capable of housing 20,000 students in a center with 50,000 inhabitants, integrated into a site of hills and woodlands. A multilevel platform covers a utilities infrastructure, used for car garages and services. Around the administrative and commercial center, four different districts perch on the hillside. The university faculties are scattered among them and surrounded by different types of housing, at various levels, linked by a maze of pedestrian malls and small, sunny squares. Traffic is relegated to the outskirts of the town and beneath the platform, which thus forms a kind of pedestal. Brick buildings, intermingled with archways and adorned with terraces, give each district its own distinct character, while preserving the architectural homogeneity of the town.

In Woluwé Saint-Lambert, near Brussels, a new university district with a faculty of medicine, housing, restaurants, churches, cultural meeting places, day-care center, kindergarten, post office, and metro station also provided an opportunity for the full flight of architectural fancy. The architect Lucien Kroll concentrated much imagination on the medical center (known as Mémé), all of whose facades are different and which uses six kinds of window frames and three types of materials in four shades. The result is a kind of architectural jugglery.

Brussels is also distinguished by its metro stations, which are often decorated with original works of art. Each station has its own character, for the decoration of each was entrusted to a different contemporary artist of some renown. A representative cross-section of Belgian contemporary art can be appreciated by traveling around the metro.

Finally, in the Liège area in the hilly wooded region of Sart-Tilmant, the university provided the impetus for a series of defiantly modern buildings, which are occasionally highly original. The Physical Education Institute, whose roof is in undulating cement, and above all the hospital center, completed in 1986, are the work of Vandenhove. The hospital's reception hall has a most extraordinary glass roof. It is surrounded by huge concrete floors supported by a sea of pillars; access is provided by elevators and stairways whose sharp diagonals span the entire height of the five towers. Metal service conduits are angled in such a way as to enhance the feeling of height. The fluid impression of space so dear to Horta is raised to monumental level by the interplay of immense square modules. Everything appears big in this building, but not overwhelming. Panels of metallic screen prints by various contemporary artists, including the American Sol Lewitt, give an impression of intimacy and individualize each floor.

Following the destruction of Art Nouveau treasures, architects generally turned their attention to the renovation of buildings and of old districts. In the Grand Béguinage district in Louvain, the past has been brought back to life. The Hors-le-Château district in Liège was renovated and at the same time modernized by Vandenhove. He restored a number of small houses dating back to the 18th and 19th centuries around a quiet square to the state where they can again be used as dwellings. He closed off the square with small new houses. The Neo-classical Royal Monnaie Opera has been completely transformed by elevation of the building, which is accentuated by a band painted the same blue as the doors. Famous foreign artists, including the American Sam Francis, helped with alterations to the interior.

The nature of the site and the architect's imagination prompted Roger Bastin to build the Museum of Modern Art (1984) with a shell-shaped basement wrapped around a well of light that allows daylight viewing of a large part of the collection. The entrance is in the Place Royale, through one of the Louis XVI mansions built according to the plans of Barré and Guimard. The floors of this palace are used for temporary exhibitions. Through the rear windows, one catches sight of the elegant rococo curve of the Palace of Charles de Lorraine, the old court of Brussels. The balustrade, which is the centerpiece of the curved facade, is made less austere by Laurent Delvaux sculptures. A large modern glass roof links the Place Royale mansions to the rear facade, which is a skillful example of the Louis XVI style. The centuries are therefore linked together through the Royal Museum of Fine Arts, so that visitors are gently guided from the preciosity of the early masters to the somewhat bold flights of fancy of modern art.

Painting

Names such as Jan van Eyck, Rogier Van Der Weyden, Hans Memling, Pieter Bruegel, Peter Paul Rubens, and Anthony Van Dyck conjure up some of the wealth of the Belgian artistic tradition. Wide-ranging inspiration, the quest for perfection, and an enthusiasm for great work have been the hallmarks of Belgian art. They fired the genius of James Ensor (1860–1949), who resolutely heralded the age of modern painting. His creativeness subsided at the end of the 19th century, but it was so powerful that many foreign and Belgian artists consider him a guiding light. At the beginning of the 20th century, German painters such as Heckel, Grosz, and Nolde rendered homage to him, and in Belgium all the followers of the imagist movement, from Paul Delvaux to Pierre Alechinsky to Roel D'Haese to Vic Gentils to Landuyt, drew inspiration from him. James Ensor in fact broke down the constraints of traditional painting and opened the art to absolute freedom. He created the freedom to transform, invent, and lose oneself in a frenzy. He opened the way to use of shocking or pearly colors, to free use of brush strokes incorporating all the twists of fantasy, curving or cutting, expressing fury or tenderness. Ensor used light not only to express the image as perceived by the eye but also to reflect the meanderings of subjective thought from torture to triumph.

Ensor and Turner were both masters of light. Ensor was the greatest inventor of hybrid forms since Bosch and Bruegel and succeeded in breathing into them the organic tangibility of insects or reptiles and the force of the wind. Alfred Barr shed some light on his genius when speaking of the *Tribulations de Saint Antoine* (1887; Museum of Modern Art, New York): "Indeed, at this moment in his career Ensor was possibly the boldest living painter. Gauguin was still painting semi-impressionist pictures, and it was only in the following year, 1888, under the burning sun of Arles, that Van Gogh was able to free himself from impressionism."

Ensor is known as the "mask painter" because of his use of masks to attack human vices in the oppressive confines of society. He was also fond of using skeletons, the blood brothers of masks, to mock society and denounce its absurdity. The questioning of his own identity through self-portraits was another modern feature. After Rembrandt, the English painter Francis Bacon is his only rival in this regard. His identification with a misunderstood Christ, however, was not exceptional, for Gauguin did the same during the same period. However, Ensor lived this identification much more intensely, expressing the pangs of persecution that deforms faces and bodies in such works as *L'Homme des douleurs* and *Satan et les légions infernales tourmentant le Crucifié*. The culmination of this clandestine agony came in the vast parade of masks in the *Entry of Christ into Brussels* (1888). Ensor was inspired by the ceremonial "entry of the princes" into the Belgian provinces in the 16th and 17th centuries. The mob, wearing hilarious, gesticulating masks, has forgotten the message of Christ, who is following along behind them, and it transforms what should have been a joyous occasion into a funeral farce denouncing the vanity of glory. The painting, whose size (258 × 431 cm) is disproportionate with respect to works of the same period, is a manifesto because of the boldness of its composition, the aggressive use of colors, the integration of foreign materials, and finally the virulence of its message.

At the end of the 19th century, Symbolism came to cloak Belgium and other European countries in its shroud of mystery and singular narcissism. Poetry and painting became intertwined and were awash with the same questions about the meaning of life, the eternal presence of death, and the weight of fatality. Ensor had certain Symbolist facets and periods, but his ravaging passion broke the silence so dear to the Symbolists, with their literary depression and dandyism. Fernand Khnopff (1858–1921), who had a personality diametrically opposed to that of Ensor, was the perfect incarnation of this movement. His refined aristocratic air, bathed in literary reminiscences, was an enigma that captivated contemporary historians. *L'Art ou les caresses*, a strange tête-à-tête between a cheetah with a human head and a hermaphrodite adolescent, is one of his most famous paintings. His *I Lock My Door upon Myself* (Munich), an affected and complicated image of solitude that would have caused people to laugh 30 years earlier, was perceived as a captivating combination of coded messages.

Léon Spilliaert (1881–1946), although much more simple, was also haunted by the secret of beings and objects in his Symbolist period. Whereas Khnopff accumulated accessories, Spilliaert systematically eliminated them. However, his anxiety came through clearly because of the simplicity of his themes, which included solitary characters and night landscapes. A kind of timeless irreality transfigures the spectacle of everyday life. In his landscapes, his sense of geometry brought him to the edges of abstract art. He was touched by the invisible to a much greater extent than his Symbolist predecessors. However, caught between Symbolism and Expressionism and combining the characteristics of the two, he expanded the latter through the monumental and deformed nature of certain of his subjects. Moreover, his strange and cruel sense of humor rendered his vision of the human race very incisive.

Nothing could be further from the abstruseness and preciosity of the Symbolists than the earthy and healthy art of the Expressionist generation, which began just before World War I but took off in the 1920's. Constant Permeke (1886–1952) was the Belgian cornerstone of this movement. His influence is still felt by contemporary painters. In the village of Laethem-Saint-Martin on the banks of the Leye (Lys), where his predecessors, the sculptor George Minne and the painter Gustave Van de Woestijne democratized Symbolism, Permeke worked in close symbiosis with nature and its simplest inhabitants. The trio that made up the second Laethem group, namely Permeke, Gustave De Smet, and Frits Van den Berghe, were known as the "clog painters" because of their way of life and their choice of subjects. However, Permeke was the only one to raise peasant farmers and fishermen to heroic dimensions. Massive, weighed down by enormous hands and feet, monstrously deformed, his imposing characters were built to stand up to the elements. The affinity of *Le Mangeur de patates* and *Les Fiancés* with the earth almost seems to have given birth to them; Permeke's desire to paint only the essential and thus transmit a vast charge of emotion is seen in *The Separation*, which was inspired by the death of his wife. The passage of the seasons over the flat countryside, tearing open the thick sky that sticks to the fields, and the menacing sea give a spatial dimension that can only be imitated but never equaled. Permeke's earthy sculpted nudes have the vitality of a tree. His painted nudes have a sensuality unequaled in modern painting, even though they defy normal standards of beauty. His house in the Flemish countryside of Jabbeke, an object of much pride to him and now to all Belgians, has become a museum.

Frits Van den Berghe (1883–1939), the intellectual of the trio, was affected by the emphasis on the imagination in Surrealism derived from Bruegel and Ensor. His anamorphoses of flowers, masks, tree-people, fitted easily into contemporary international trends and are occasionally reminiscent of the work of Max Ernst.

The subjects of Gustave De Smet (1877–1943) derive closely from

Flemish folklore. His stylized characters resemble fashion models in their tautness and the emptiness of their gaze. De Smet surpassed his two colleagues in the exceptional subtlety of his palette, which included broken browns, undefinable violets, and pinks and yellows in duo. This quality gave his paintings highly individual tones. Melancholy characterized all his subjects, from the solitary women under their implacable clock to his pipesmokers and drinkers. The fatigue of those broken by physical work is drenched in melancholy; melancholy descends upon the evening landscape and strikes without purpose dull-witted brains.

In Brabant, Jean Brusselmans (1884–1953) was a solitary Expressionist. He was more constructive than destructive. His subjects, objects, and still lifes were borrowed from a suburban environment. He combined a sense of austerity and a static nature, cementing rainbows and waves in his landscapes in an attempt to show that the universe has a coherent and stable structure capable of endowing it with eternity. He was open to all research and was the only one of his generation to lend his support to the Young Belgian Painting movement.

At the same time other, more intellectual trends were vying for attention. The near contemporaries of the Expressionists, a few abstract painters, focused their inspiration on two magazines, one in French, *Sept Arts*, and the other in Dutch, *Het Overzicht*, directed by Michel Seuphor, who was to become a well-known art critic in France. Weakened by the barrage of attention on the Expressionists, this group of artists rarely caught the limelight. Georges Van Tongerloo (b. 1886), sculptor and painter, connected to the de Stijl group of Dutch abstract painters, exiled himself to France. The premonitory quest and the mysterious spirituality of these painters, who were able to create an impression of infinite space by the undulation of a few lines, have been revealed only in recent exhibitions, including one in Washington, D.C. Victor Servranckx (1897–1965), in his best paintings, was inspired by the aesthetic nature of machines, which he transformed into abstract and contrasting forms, shot through with tension. Several painters belonging to this group became discouraged and stopped painting.

In contrast, Surrealism gave birth to a real Belgian star: René Magritte (1898–1967). Magritte did not attempt to produce an attractive picture or a perfect drawing. His objective was not to please and even less to decorate. He was more an intellectual anarchist who wanted to overturn visual habits and sow a fertile disorder in thought processes. He combined precise images of real objects without any logical or natural link between them. He puts caterpillars in the feathers of doves. A floor distorts a woman's body by running over it. He attacks the human face by introducing gaping holes through which a wall of small bells (female symbols) can be seen. He breaks a window and leaves parts of the landscape stuck to the debris. He pigeonholes objects and sticks strange names on them to show the arbitrariness of language. He set fire to a trombone. Under a female head of hair, he replaced the expected face by breasts, a navel, and hairy sex organs, then gave it the title *Le Viol*. Some of his paintings are premonitory. For example, in *L'Homme du large*, a man in a diving-suit, whose face has been replaced by a cutout piece of wood, which is even more enigmatic than a mask, places his hand on the catch of a nonexistent window. Behind him, the sea, perceived as a maternal assailant, is about to swamp the world to later deliver it afresh. Even if it is difficult to follow Magritte's line of thought, his images are fascinating and seem to reveal new truths; after viewing his paintings, the world around us becomes bizzare. His revolutionary nature softened into charm with the years. His painting of a bird against clear clouds on a stormy sky above a night sea is an invitation to evasion and has become the emblem of Belgium's national airline, Sabena. A tender magic impregnates *L'Empire des lumières*, which shows a night street under a day sky cut across by small clouds. The surreal nature of this sight does not become evident at first glance. The blue sky and transparent clouds were images adopted by Magritte after the war and would seem to contain the promise of an unpredictable and serene "elsewhere."

French Surrealist poets adopted the Belgian Paul Delvaux (b. 1897). And yet his method differed from that of Magritte through his senseless fantasizing of intellectual calculations, touched with a degree of subversion or a desire for mystification. Their common point was the revealing shiver that ran through both of them when they viewed the paintings of Chirico. Delvaux's paintings are filled with naked women with empty eyes and heavy breasts who wander aimlessly around ancient ruins. Neither the bodies or thoughts of these women seem to have any sensual power. Male subjects pass them by without seeing them or hold out their arms to them without waiting for them. Some memories of childhood—trains, stations, little girls with long hair—bear witness to the naïveté that drives the painter as if awake in his sleep. Superficial analysis attached the glow of scandal to some of his paintings. In fact, critics should have been struck by their blinding innocence. In *Pygmalion*, which turns the legend on its head, a naked woman embraces a man of stone who, naturally enough, fails to respond. This painting is perhaps a key and an involuntary confession. The problem treated in all of Delvaux's work is the absence of communication between beings on both a sexual and a moral level. In this respect, Paul Delvaux distanced himself from the Surrealists, who were concerned with blazing a trail, and came much closer to the cloistered outlook of the Symbolist Fernand Khnopff. Paul Delvaux had a split personality. On the one hand, he was a likable, simple, and tolerant man; on the other hand, he was a living wall, a sleepwalker lost in a maze of visions.

Although the process of undermining reality epitomized by Magritte and Delvaux survived well beyond World War II, it was not a success among the following generation. The group of painters who reached maturity after 1945 were concerned more with form and craft, with direct expression through drawing and color. The best of the 1945 generation formed part of the Association of Young Belgian Painting, led by the art patron René Lust and by the critic Robert L. Delevoy, future head of the Cambre School of Visual Arts. The latter had already presented them in his Apollo gallery. Ensor was their honorary chairman and Brusselmans offered moral support. The war shut out light for so many years that the beginnings of this movement revealed painters who were still very introspective, producing interiors, portraits of persons close to them, and self-portraits crystallizing their intimist inspiration. This movement continued a trend during the occupation under the aegis of Paul Haesaerts and was known as Animism. A significant number of original personalities were to emerge from the Young Belgian Painting group, including Gaston Bertrand, Louis Van Lint, Anne Bonnet, Marc Mendelson, Lismonde, Jo Delahaut, and Antoine Mortier. No unity of style or doctrine bound them together. The main painters of the Young Belgian Painting movement evolved naturally toward a nonfigurative language. Their desire for freedom prompted them to give up the need for motif, to disconnect colors and forms, and to draw graphism into their caprices and emotions.

In the work of Louis Van Lint (b. 1909), rejection of motif is coupled with a sensual attachment to nature and to tangibility. Practical experimentation, using colored cellophane cutouts placed at random on a rotating disk and projected on a screen, provided his source of inspiration. He passed from the strange *Homme en chemise* (1947) to *Ciel, terre et mer* (1948). Nature, perceived as a green and spatial being, has never left his repertoire. The tendrils of a vine and the swirling of a bird have guided his brush. Transported by a gentle sense of jubilation, colors are both rich and transparent, both delicate and sumptuous.

For his part, Gaston Bertrand (b. 1911) is fascinated by architecture. He has proceeded by identifying the essential part of what he wants to express in synthesis, the inside and outside, relationships of volume with an interiorized space. He is the most traveled of all the Belgian painters.

Periods spent abroad diversified his themes to include the Medici Chapel in Florence, several Spanish towns, the Roman abbey of Montmajour, the vaults of the Paris metro, and the rays of sunshine in the sinuous streets of Provençal villages. They are evoked in smooth paintings, using unexpected colors and elliptic styles of drawing that surprise before they gently seduce. Whereas Van Lint has preserved the wash of brushwork, Bertrand has cultivated a much more airy and effacing technique. He has never abandoned the human figure; his gap-filled portraits, flooded with space, always have a questioning presence. He is as much a soul quantifier as a prier into secret spaces.

The only abstract painter among the Young Belgian painters is an intellectual from Liège. Trained as an art historian, Jo Delahaut (b. 1911) absorbed different ancient cultures to the point where he sent down new roots in them. For a long time, he was preoccupied by rhythmic research and early on discovered a very pertinent principle—repetition or pattern—that seems to find its inspiration in music. His work is characterized by combinations of primary colors, within geometric shapes somehow attached to an open space. He has never been distracted by references to nature. He has always associated increasingly simple and relatively sparse forms. The sense of fluidity is preserved by his use of colors. With age, Delahaut has become both more economical and more monumental, as demonstrated by the 120-meter-long ceramic mural in the Montgomery metro station in Brussels. Since this work, he has moved closer to minimal art, but his movement in this direction has not been deliberate or faddish. Rather, it is the consequence of meditation, which is why his work gives an impression of substance even when portraying emptiness.

Antoine Mortier (b. 1908) and Jan Cox are the two Belgian painters who come closest to action painting; in that movement they play a key role but also display richness and sensuality in their work. Mortier loves the savagery of blacks broken by flashes of color. Before becoming acquainted with the American Franz Kline, he made use of the same voluntary trajectories to cause an explosion within the picture. His painting is stormy, austere, and vehement. He is sometimes classified among abstract painters, but his true source of inspiration is the human body.

Jan Cox was a follower of the Cobra movement, which explains the phantoms in his early paintings. The Cobra movement survived only for a short period, but its spirit is still alive. It was founded in 1949 by the Belgian poet Christian Dotremont and consisted of a core of Danish, Dutch, and Belgian artists. Its objective was to react both against geometric abstract art and against Surrealist imagery by searching for roots in folklore, children's drawings, and the early masters. Cox broke away from the Cobra movement to develop a highly individual sense of the fantastic, notably in his portraits. His long stay in the United States—he taught in Boston—brought him into contact with action painting. Drawing on this and also on a lyrical mythology fired by references to Homer, he introduced within the "action" and through rivers of color semi-human, semi-animal islands. His last paintings were scenes of combat, passing from a crescendo of violence to gentleness, from panting to quiet breathing. As the years went by, his work gained the renown it merited.

Pierre Alechinsky (1927–56) reignited the flame of Cobra. In his paintings, the flame became much more lively, exploding, caressing, and curling up within a twirling style of drawing. His work is reminiscent of Ensor's humor and Ensor's masks, monsters, and the worrying closeness of death. Alechinsky discovered Far Eastern calligraphy during a visit to Japan in his youth. He retained the mastery of the hand and gesture that imperceptibly structures the dynamics of the imagination. India ink remained one of his favorite media both for sketching a drawing and for creating an impression of shadow and light. However, Alechinsky generally painted using acrylics and successfully conferred on acrylics the body and softness of oil paints. He is a virtuoso and also an unrepentant creator and storyteller. Narration is left to his "offhand remarks" at the bottom of the canvas, as a kind of predella cut into episodes, whereas the center is reserved for some action with unforeseeable consequences.

Before becoming Belgian, Bram Bogart, who was born Dutch, had a studio in Paris next to those of the Cobra group of artists. However, they did not get on. Bogart developed as an abstract painter, using both the dripping technique and thick layers of paste. Little by little, thanks to a secret process, the paste rises, producing projections, crests, valleys, nests, and caves that create light and shadow. Occasionally a strange thrust pushes through the various layers of relief and forces them to stand up, as frothy as solidified foam. Large brush strokes scrape the areas of color and organize them. Bogart produced a simple and healthy art, of reassuring vitality.

Marcel Broodthaers juggled with stenciled words, transformed objects, and turned his monogram into a talisman. Mussels, eggshells, pots of jam plastered with images of starlets, are among the accessories of this tightrope-walker/alchemist. The Philosopher's Stone is evoked in a spirit of derision that spares no taboo. He refers a great deal to Magritte, but in a rather provocative tone. Broodthaers's style has been termed neo-Dada.

Surrealism tinted with Symbolist reminiscences has inspired Camille

De Taeye. His paintings could be stood end to end like a Buñel film. He uses cinematic language, in violent short sequences, enigmatic jump cuts, and shock images. He stirs up the kingdom of nature, cuts it up into samples, and assembles the fragments with cruel imagination, producing unpredictable intensity. His work is reminiscent of the collages of Max Ernst. But his extraordinary technical perfection, drawing on classicism and brushing close to trompe l'oeil, is placed at the service of these frenzied visions and forces them into the mold of impeccable pictorial cohesion.

At the other extreme, Marthe Wéry followed in the footsteps of Barnett Newman, Elsworth Kelly, and all the other "color-field" painters. There is no longer any national art. Overinformation has become the evil of our century. Sifting out, choosing, and weaving one's own cocoon of solitude for metamorphosis into the full-blooded artist is all that remains for the most talented. The color-field work of Marthe Wéry has been built on the cutting edge of a highly individual sensitivity. The rediscovery of yellow through red, of red through blue, so that a vibration drawn out by the impression of space is created within a united plane is the culmination of a long and patient maturation. Many contemporary artists are anxious to create a certain atmosphere within an exhibition hall and not merely have a painting hanging on the wall. However, few of them succeed in prolonging this atmosphere beyond the exhibition hall. Marthe Wéry is one of the elite few.

The Young Belgian Painting movement culminated in the creation of an annual prize for which there are hundreds of Belgian entrants representing all styles. The prize competition, restricted to those under 40, creates a joyful fair of modern art that bears witness to enormous faith in the future of art in contemporary society. Many well-known artists have received this prize. Recent promising artists include Jean de la Fontaine, an action painter; Dario Caterina, a representational painter along the lines of Otto Dix; and Damien De Lepeleire, who paints ghostlike dogs woven out of free brushstrokes that seem to fade away in the mist. Prizewinners are immediately taken up by art galleries in highly popular exhibitions that guarantee the indestructible vitality of Belgian painting.

Sculpture

At the end of the 19th century, Belgian sculpture was dominated by two powerful personalities from two different generations but who worked almost at the same time at opposite ends of the spectrum. Constantin Meunier (1831–1905) was deeply affected by the industrial revolution and by the rise of the working class. He drew on a particular region, such as the Borinage or the Pays Noir, and on a specific trade, such as mining or metalworking, to produce heroic poses in an attempt at universal synthesis. In painting, he influenced Charles De Groux into producing austere and sad paintings, depicting poverty in anecdotes on which religion weighed with the full force of convention. Eugène Laermans discovered the pictorial power of a walking crowd using a stylization already slightly distorted toward Expressionism. His painting, which went beyond Impressionism and Symbolism, stood out through an excess of solidity. Meunier the sculptor concentrated on fixing movements and preserving them for eternity. Wax prototypes were shown at the XX (the Twenty) in 1885, the year in which the Belgian Workers Party was formed. However, bronze quickly replaced this, both for monumental works and for statuettes. Meunier immortalized the *Hammersmith* and the *Puddler* in robust figures. France in 1896 and Germany in 1897 welcomed this innovative style.

George Minne (1866–1941) was the only one capable of expressing the existential anxiety of Symbolism in bronze or marble. He transposed the human body into a spiritual form beyond flesh and blood. He continually made use of an ascetic adolescent figure, struggling under a burden known as a "relic" or, more exactly, destiny or fatalism. In one work, five such adolescents surround a well, leaning toward the waters of their internal dream like Narcissuses tearful at being themselves.

The vitality of Belgian art was given a boost by the sculptor and painter Rik Wouters (1882–1916). The naked body of the *Dancer* is brusquely set free and explodes into an unprecedented and unequaled Dionysian series of gestures. Isadora Duncan was the inspiration behind this triumphant work. Her dynamism is a challenge to the fleshy limbs of the model, who was Nelle, the painter's wife. Advocates of sexual freedom could take her as a mascot. Other sculptures by Wouters have the quality of a fugitive in an interplay with light. Wouters the sculptor hit by instinct on the equivalent of pictorial Impressionism, and yet his multifaceted works demonstrate his constructional carefulness. In painting, he tirelessly and intensively sought to strike a difficult balance between mass and light, the permanent and the ephemeral. His *Flutist* playing in a Cezanne landscape and the *Lady in Blue* posing in front of a mirror and dispersing reflections and roses mark the two extremes of this quest.

Later artists can be divided into five groups: Expressionists, classicists, abstractionists, assemblers, and inventors. The work of the oldest among them dates back to the years after World War I, the younger ones are still active today.

Among the abstract painters, Victor Servranckx, who was mentioned above, sculpted a number of pieces in the 1920's. These sculptures are very bare, and their round, hollow, or protruding forms have no significance other than their primary one.

Georges Van Tongerloo, the ascetic painter and inventive sculptor, as well as a resolute constructivist, was distinguished by the harshness of his geometric forms and by his architecture-based work. His airport models (circa 1928) were of a rather pioneering nature, although they have now been surpassed from a technical point of view. He is little known in Belgium, where he is often confused with the de Stijl Dutch artists. But it should not be forgotten that he was one of the first to use, around 1950, free-form plexiglass and plastic to give a new impression of space.

Willy Anthoons, who was associated with the Young Belgian Painting movement, took up the gauntlet. He carves wood with especial sensitivity, producing monoliths streaked with fine parallel cuts, which could symbolize either water or the forest. He also wanted to capture the essence of human relationships through purified forms along the lines of Constantin Brancusi. He ventured into mobile cutouts of metal sheets suspended in the air.

At the 1958 Brussels World's Fair, Jacques Moeschal revealed his true colors as an architect and engineer and a creator of forms slicing through the air with the concrete arrow in the Civil Engineering Pavilion. The apparent carefreeness of this arrow is actually based on exact calculations. Moeschal is only interested in working on a monumental scale. Two concrete road signs, one at the French border and the other toward the coast, were planned to stretch upward toward the sky. Unfortunately, work at a later date changed these sites. On the other hand, the Negev Desert boasts one of these vast signals. A gigantic ex-voto offering dominating the Mexico Olympic Stadium celebrates the faith in the stars of pre-Colombian civilizations. Through economy of means and a sense of grandeur, Moeschal could consider himself the heir of the builders of the pyramids or of the Teotihuacan temples and also as a forerunner of the art of the future. The decoration of the most important and most complex Brussels metro station, the Midi Station, and its integration with engineering work were entrusted to him.

Hilde Van Summere and Jan Dries work in marble. Van Summere carves almost translucent disks, open to light through a slit. Dries's encased stones have a Japanese air about them and are perfectly at home placed on the ground. They are "contemplation stones." Jean-Paul Laenen concentrated his abstract work on color, adding a spatial quality to the elegance derived from Art Nouveau. He was also responsible for urbanization plans, a monument to Maeterlinck based on the geometry of the beehive, and, more recently, through a return to representation for portraits of a dynamism evocative of the Italian futurist Boccioni. Raoul Ubac (b. 1910), painter and sculptor, worked chiefly in slate, which he cut in smooth or grooved facets. He was not very interested in the third dimension. His work draws on the subtleties of light play and often deals with the spiritualized expression of the human torso.

Two other women are worthy of mention alongside Hilde Van Summere. Monique Guébels tirelessly works large stones, respectful of their mass. The grain and nuance of the stone are very important to her. She harmoniously integrates curves and countercurves into a compact volume, destined to be left in the open air. Tapta first of all built sculptures using wool woven into large living and warm masses. Recently she has begun using neoprene, a semirigid material, which she cuts into large forms with pure curves, a welcoming sight for walkers. Her sculptures offer viewers the pleasure of being able to walk right inside them. André Willequet is also situated on the edges of representation. He has mastered wood and stone and shapes them with elegance and reserve.

The classicists, namely George Grard (b. 1901), Charles Leplae (1903–61), Nat Neujean, and Christian Leroy, are fascinated by the human body. They attempt to portray it as well balanced and serene, reflecting the harmony between human beings and the universe, which is part of their philosophy. Grard revels in carnal and fleshy female forms, with an aura of intimacy that underscores their sensuality. His type of woman is close to that of the Frenchman Maillol. Leplae, on the other hand, takes after another Frenchman, namely Despiau, and some of his busts have the same purity. He is more refined and more curious. Leplae is a humanist captured by the beauty of Chinese poetry. In his group works, he attempts to suggest psychological and emotional links between the various figures across the charged space separating them. His *Luco*, a slender adolescent, shivers with a melancholy reminiscent of George Minne. Moreover, Leplae is interested in mingling techniques. With the help of the ceramist Pierre Caille, he encrusts in the ground enameled designs, producing an exotic effect. Both are accomplished artists who are aware of the fact that the eye must be able to look without jarring on all aspects of the whole. Very elaborate links are made between projections and hollows as if the whole were machine-turned, thereby preserving its overall unity and homogeneity. Nat Neujean is known essentially for various studies for a monument to deported Jews. However, he is also an artist who can communicate the subtlety of a sign by a gesture. The bulk of his oeuvre consists of official portraits and commissions.

Expressionism had a much weaker impact on sculpture than on paint-ing. Oscar Jespers (1887–1970), remarkably adept with volume, did not seem to suffer from a tormented soul. His work was varied and evolved right up until his death. Even during the so-called Expressionist phase, his figures maintained a certain stability and placidity empty of strong emotion. It is perhaps more difficult to express strong feelings in bronze than in clay. Jespers retained from Cubism the simplification and geo-metric nature of forms. Even when he became part of *Sélection*, which brought Expressionists together, he did not renounce the principles of frugality and lack of ornamentation. He attempted to express through massive forms a feeling of weightiness and architectonic monumentality. After 1937, he returned to rounded curves, full and smooth volumes, expressing a carnal serenity and generous corporal well-being. He also attempted direct carving, in stone or wood, modeled clay, and hammered out copper. One of his most impressive works is *The Prisoner* in granite, crouching down and compact, seemingly resisting the pressure of destiny through his unshakable robustness.

Joseph Cantré (1890–1957) is not only a sculptor but also a remarkable woodcarver. Linked with Frits Van den Berghe and Gustave De Smet, of whom he carved a double portrait, he devised a precise, pure, and clean style, bringing out the edges of volumes in a geometrical manner remi-niscent of Zadkine, although less lyrical. A sense of propriety linked with a frugality of forms gave his work a rather austere poetic appearance. He also won many commissions for monumental and decorative works, particularly in the Netherlands.

Constant Permeke, as a sculptor, dominated his contemporaries through his Baroque style and the irresistibly vital nature of his human sculptures, which express the crude and violent genius of Permeke the painter. Despite his lack of experience as a sculptor, an art he took up only in 1935, he allowed himself to be guided by his instinct toward distortions as emotionally authentic as Picasso's. He was little concerned with the attractiveness of materials. The poorer and the coarser the bet-ter. Plaster and occasionally cement were a sufficient medium for his message.

Dodeigne had certain similarities, but he was a stonecutter. From blocks of stone he revealed crude and almost incomplete forms, savagely alive rather like primitive humans.

José Vermeersch's recent, rapid rise to the position of one of Europe's most prominent sculptors has resulted from a long and very gradual artistic development. Trained as a painter during the war and immedi-ate postwar years, he became an industrial ceramist in the 1950's and returned to painting only in 1962. At the same time he began to experiment with large-scale ceramic sculptures. The distinctive style and subject matter that appeared full-fledged in his sculptures toward the end of that decade had had their gestation in his earlier paintings, a fact that may seem surprising in view of the strongly sculptural quality of his three-dimensional work. In their extreme nakedness—hairless, smooth, or slightly dimpled—these clay bodies have a memorable physical presence. There is nothing "primitive" in the style of these figures. They represent, on the contrary, a sophisticated lateness—calculated deviations from norms perfectly well understood. To come upon work of such individuality is a surprise and pleasure. It was the privilege of the Stanford University Museum to introduce the art of this Belgian sculptor to an American audience. The exhibition was tragically cut short by the earthquake of October 1989. (This paragraph was written by Lorenz Eitner, chair of the Department of Art and director of the Stanford Museum.)

Roel D'Haese, a full-blooded Expressionist, is, however, somewhat in a league of his own. He is particularly noted for his technical mastery of wax and his lively imagination, which has its roots in Flemish folklore. His work draws on the heterogeneous creatures of Hieronymus Bosch and Pieter Bruegel. His most direct ancestor is Ensor. In much the same manner, he uses masks, a false celebration drowning out the real cause for joy, to demonstrate his cynicism and pride. He denounces hypocrisy and vanity and welcomes the obsessive fear of death. Technically speaking, D'Haese does not represent any fresh evolution. However, his Baroque assemblages of elements where the formless is juxtaposed with the refined have a certain power of bewitchment and an organic truth rivaling that of nature. His brother Reinhoud, a close friend of Alechinsky's, did not step out of the Cobra movement. He cuts up and welds sheets of copper and brass, creating gnomes and hybrid monsters that are an expression more of anti-authoritarianism than of terror.

Vic Gentils is another master of assemblages. He began with reliefs in old frames. By burning them and giving them a sheen, he created stelae that were both baroque in their decoration and austere in their construction. They were like altars in some strange sacrificial religion. He then pulled pianos to pieces and used the ivory and black keys and the small pieces of green or red felt, encrusting them in dark wood a bit like a Nordic mosaicist. Expressionism then gained the upper hand, and grotesque figures and assemblages using existing forms dominated his work. Occasionally the color used underscored the fact that an ironic attack was being made on the human race. Often references to reality were hidden behind the clowning. The sense of derision that swept through contemporary artists was fueled by Flemish colorfulness. In the Middelheim Museum, close to Antwerp, identifiable and varied chess pieces are shown on a chessboard. At the Akademische Ziekenhuis in Antwerp a hommage to Camille Huysmans, the great Belgian statesman, can be viewed. Huysmans's large stature and noble face are perfectly recognizable in the assemblage of pre-existing wood pieces. Second-rate politicians and sycophants press around him in a parody of democracy.

Paul Van Hoeydonck also used assemblages. A small sculpture of his was placed on the moon by American astronauts. His dreams of space discovery were put to use in a variety of manners, from somber plexiglass reliefs in the 1950's, to white mannequins bought from antique dealers in a poetic 1920's style or draped in neo-Grecian hangings, to groups of metallic Martians, terrifying in their ugliness and aggressiveness, conjuring up evil spirits from another planet.

Léonardo da Vinci has inspired Belgian inventor-artists. It is not difficult to take the step from tinkering about to invention. Pol Bury was always fascinated by movement. When he was an abstract painter, he produced "mobile plans" that could be displaced around an axis. He then housed his sculptures in clever mechanisms. Bouquets of antennas proliferated on a flat background, imperceptibly shivering and crackling. Metal balls, driven by magnetization, shiver, brush against one another, slide, and slowly bump into one another. The slowness of the movement and its unpredictability test the patience of impatient people, but they cast a spell on the attentive eye. Bury was able to produce monumental works by using assistants, machines, and industrial processes. The most beautiful of his works are fountains. Parts of tubes and bunches of hollow spheres gradually move around an axis and pour out streams of water. Metal reflections and the iridescent nature of the water combine very attractively. They are 20th-century creations, and yet this subtle interplay is reminiscent of the Mannerist curiosity cabinets and surprising machines designed for the amusement of princes many centuries ago. However, a touch of derisive irony, inherited from Surrealism, lies just behind these inventions.

The flying machines of Panamarenko have a rather poetic appeal. Enormous insects, giant dragonflies, fragile, refined, and poised for flight, seem somehow out of place between the walls of a museum. And yet they are doomed to remain on the ground. They are made of wood, Japanese vellum, nylon, rubber, and wire with metal carcasses. They are spiritually on the edges of our high-tech age, and this is the source of their charm. They seem to be perfectly designed to fly, but they cannot. This powerlessness, opposed to the harm often caused by high technology, gives the machines a nice touch of madness. The only way the machines could fly is in a dream, to reach a different world and a different sky. Panamarenko's ink drawings are meticulous, exact, and perfectly outlined. They are covered in captions, surrounded by engineering calculations, and as enigmatic as magic. Occasionally lightly colored in, they also float in an imaginary world, where magic formulas exist to combine gold and mercury, sulfur and silver. There was therefore something of the alchemist in this inventor of the impossible.

Imagination and a taste for the unusual therefore fertilize art in modern Belgium. Fantasy, irony, and a predilection for investigation are planted on the seedbed of know-how, practical knowledge, experience, and a desire for work well done. There are many experimenters among Belgian contemporary artists, but very few continue in their chosen path. Belgium has seen stars of international art turn their backs on themselves, with geometric becoming Baroque, action painters at the same time practicing trompe l'oeil. Art that sets out to shock crushes any desire for dialogue between the creator and the audience. Violence forms an integral part of the artistic act, as if all modern wars, all the ills of our world, had become inseparable from plastic expression. It is as if the international language of art had deliberately decided to be blasphemous.

Fashions pass so quickly that when their waves sweep across Belgium, which is a small but divided and highly individualistic country, it is much too late to move with the tide. Art that aims to shock is seldom seen in Belgium. In the secrecy of their studios, intimate dialogues are occasionally struck up between the artist and nature in its full range and complexity, in its mysterious continuity reflected in the return of the seasons, birth, development, and death. This intimacy provides fertile ground for the explosion of artistic jubilation. Belgium is and remains a forum for the silent appreciation of the arts of yesteryear and today.

Theater, Dance, and Cinema

Jacques De Decker

AN EFFERVESCENT THEATRICAL LIFE, a cinema industry that has failed to move beyond the craft industry stage but still produces a few major works, and dance centered around one of the brightest figures of our day and age—this is a brief summary of what the words "theater," "film," and "dance" signify in Belgium. In each of these fields, Belgium bears out the saying "small is beautiful" and illustrates clearly that it is the European country with the most highly concentrated and the most varied cultural activities.

Theater

Theater provides the best example of this creative concentration, as can be seen by comparing Belgium with France. The Belgian French-speaking community covers an area equal to two or three French departments. However, in France, all roads lead to Paris, and the regions are lucky if they have one drama center and a handful of modest and temporary performances. In Belgium, on the other hand, the French-speaking community has a national theater whose activities stretch out of Brussels into the regions and the international environment, along with some half-dozen renowned and prestigious theaters. Twenty or so smaller troupes have a reputation that occasionally reaches beyond national boundaries, and a large number of groups, essentially made up of young people, are preparing their members to enter the major companies.

The distribution of theater is somewhat different in Flanders, but there is the same abundance. The difference lies in the fact that there is no single focal point for theatrical life, like Brussels for French-speaking theater. In Flanders, there are in fact three centers. The first of these is again Brussels, which the Flemish consider their capital despite the fact they are in a minority there. The other two are Antwerp and Ghent. Moreover, no town in Flanders lacks a theater of some importance. The most popular one is the Mechel Miniatuur Theater in Mechelen. Some of the most daring shows are put on in Bruges. All of Flanders is therefore drawn into a very dynamic theater network.

The state, too, makes a contribution to theatrical activity. However, the total amount of aid to theaters throughout the country is under 1 billion BF, a rather meager sum for such a flourishing sector. The two communities have distinct theater policies, for this matter is in the hands of community executives and not in those of the national government.

The National Theater of Belgium, the main French-speaking troupe, was founded in 1945 by Jacques Huisman and directed for 40 years by him. This grand old man of Belgian theater was succeeded in 1985 by the Belgian actor Jean-Claude Drouot, who owes his popularity to his leading role in the French television series *Thierry la Fronde*. Huisman had a power of animation without comparison. He strove to provide Belgium with a major international repertoire, always in an attempt to improve the country's general cultural level. He put on plays by Brecht, Arthur Miller, and Dario Fo in the most distant corners of Wallonia. Very open to foreign productions, whether it be Vilar or the Royal Shakespeare Company, and to foreign producers such as Frank Dunlop and Angelo Corti, he did much to introduce the Belgian public to world theater.

Claude Etienne, director of the oldest permanent troupe, Le Rideau de Bruxelles, is another dominant personality in the history of Belgian theater. Etienne is also a great explorer of international theater. His two theaters in Brussels have staged plays by Samuel Beckett, Christopher Hampton, Tom Stoppard, and Botho Strauss. But he is first and foremost the person who has most encouraged Belgian playwriting. Paul Willems, Jean Sigrid, and Liliane Wouters, Belgium's major French-speaking playwrights after the illustrious Maeterlinck, Crommelynck, and Ghelderode, were encouraged by Claude Etienne. An excellent teacher, he has also trained a string of actors who are among the most sought after in the Belgian theater.

In Flanders, the person who has most influenced theatrical activity is not a director (Flemish theater has never found anyone of such permanence as Huisman or Etienne), but rather a playwright: Hugo Claus. Claus makes a success of everything he touches, and the range of his artistic talents has often been compared to that of Cocteau. He is a poet, painter, filmmaker, and novelist. Claus is also an all-around theatrical genius, despite the fact that he has never been an actor. However, he has written some 30 plays, ranging in styles as far apart as realistic drama to psychological comedy; he has also rewritten the great classics (Shakespeare, Ben Jonson, Fernando de Rojas) and modernized ancient tragedy. Deeply cosmopolitan, Claus lived for a long time in Paris, Italy, and the Netherlands before moving recently to Provence. He has forced Flemish theater to cast its gaze on the international arena. In Ghent, his favorite town, he has worked with the municipal group, the Nationaal Toneel Gent, and greatly enriched its repertoire. The best Flemish producers owe part of their style and professionalism to Claus, whether it be Franz Marijnen, who has also taken his career to the Netherlands and Germany, Jean-Pierre De Decker, or Walter Tillemans, for whom Claus wrote a *Hamlet*.

However, to speak only of these leading personalities is to neglect part of Belgian theatrical activity. The theater is equally active on both sides of the linguistic boundary. Flanders, for example, is well known for the postmodern productions of Jan Decorte and his troupe Het Trojaanse Paard, which puts on classics in a style reminiscent of Bob Wilson. The actors of the Flemish troupe Epigonen are invited to all international experimental festivals, for their caustic and hilarious portrayal of everyday life. The sarcastic vision of theatrical tradition held by Jan Fabre is also internationally known. In addition, a large number of French-speaking companies have contributed to the revival of the theater, for example, Albert-André Lheureux and his Esprit Frappeur, who are enamored of theatrical poetry, and the entire critical theatrical movement, influenced by Peter Stein and Patrice Chéreau and represented by Marc Liebens, Philippe van Kessel, or the triumvirate that heads the Varia theater: Philippe Sireuil, Marcel Delval, and Michel Dezoteux. Also contributing to this revival has been the *théâtre du corps* (body theater), represented by Plan K or Banlieue, who travel to the four corners of the world with shows that give special meaning to the term "body language." Such experiments create a pathway between theater and dance, particularly since the companies just mentioned attempt to release theater from the need for verbal language in search of other means of expression.

Dance

To mention the word "dance" in Belgium is to praise the stupendous efforts over 27 years of Maurice Béjart's Ballet du XXème Siècle in Brussels. Thanks to Béjart, who has been to dance what Chaplin was to cinema and Picasso to painting, Brussels was the international capital of choreography for almost three decades.

Maurice Huisman, who headed the Brussels Opera La Monnaie, spotted the young French dancer who, at the time, had organized a few ballets. Huisman gave him a free hand. By 1959, Béjart was producing an unstoppable flood of creations, which cannot be summarized in a few lines. However, some of the high points can be mentioned, such as Boléro, the Neuvième, and the Triomphes, which rapidly became famous worldwide. Béjart's ballet won the heart of audiences all over the world. It was overwhelmingly popular in Japan and enthusiastically greeted in the Soviet Union, despite the long-standing and jealously guarded Soviet ballet tradition. The Béjart phenomenon has been the most remarkable event to mark Belgian cultural life since 1950. This explains the wrench provoked by Béjart's departure in June 1987. Belgians were stripped of one of their symbols. However, Gérard Mortier, the present director of the opera, has hired the talented young American Mark Morris to replace Béjart. Mortier may well be the best opera director in Europe, and he seems to accomplish miracles on a small budget.

Nevertheless, Béjart left his mark on Belgium. He influenced young creators, such as the producer Bernard De Coster, who was his assistant. He molded his disciples to his way of thinking, and they will continue with his tradition, whether it be Micha Van Hoecke, who directs the Tournai Ensemble, or Jorge Lefèvre, choreographer of the Ballet of Wallonia. By founding the Mudra school in Brussels, Béjart not only trained choreographers who went back to revive dance in their respective countries, such as the Frenchwoman Maggy Marin, but also encouraged a strong dance tradition in Belgium, both in Flanders and in the French-speaking part of the country (if it makes sense to speak of linguistic divisions in regard to something as universal as dance).

Even though some of the advocates of new dance techniques are opposed to Béjart's aesthetics, they still inherit his tradition, albeit in a negative sense. Anna-Teresa De Keersmaeker, for example, whose international reputation is untouchable, is closer to Pina Bausch than to Béjart and has reacted against his humanism and philosophical ambitions. In some respects, she is philosophically his bastard child, along with other new dance figures in Belgium, including Patricia Kuypers, Michèle Anne De Mey, Jan Lauwers, Marc Vanrunxt, and Pierre Doulers. Although each has an individual approach, they share a quest for unstressed simplicity, a return to everyday gestures exalted by the simple step of having extracted them from their context.

Cinema

In many countries, no clear dividing line can be drawn between theater and cinema; Visconti, Bergman, and Wajda are stars both of the big screen and of the theater. In Belgium, unfortunately, there are no links between the two. Although the most famous Belgian filmmaker, André Delvaux, one day found himself a producer, it was for an opera and not a theater production. Gérard Mortier, the brilliant successor of Maurice Huisman as head of the Monnaie theater, entrusted *Pelléas et Mélisande* to Delvaux. There are no other examples of someone involved in theater involved in the movies in Belgium. This is all the more astounding in that the two colleges of higher education for the performing arts, at least in the French-speaking region (Insas in Brussels and Iad in Louvain-la-Neuve) train both for the theater and the cinema.

As with dance, the linguistic distinction is not felt very strongly. First, some filmmakers use both languages, and second, English has become the lingua franca of cinema, particularly among Flemish filmmakers. This mirrors a similar trend in the Netherlands (*The Assault*, for which the Dutch producer Fons Rademaekers won an Oscar for best foreign film, was made in English). A number of young filmmakers such as Marc Didden (*Brussels By Night, Istambul*) and Dominique Deruddere (*Crazy Love*) also film directly in English. This was also done by Marion Hansel when she adapted the novel by the South-African J. M. Coetzee in her film *Dust*, which won a Silver Bear at the 1985 Venice Film Festival.

Belgian cinema is threatened by the dominating presence of international companies, the proximity of France, the biggest European producer, and the division of its market into two cultural entities. In Italy, Germany, Great Britain, and Switzerland, cinema would all but have died out were it not for television coproductions, but Belgian television channels are not very active in this field. It is almost surprising that with a low level of public funding (only one-quarter of that granted to theater), films are nevertheless made in Belgium, and great talents brought into play.

This is the case, for example, with André Delvaux, for he has filmed both in French and in Dutch and taken his inspiration from national literature both of Flemish origin (Johan Daisne, Yvo Michiels) and of Belgian French-speaking origin (Suzanne Lilar, Marguerite Yourcenar, whose mother was Belgian). Marion Hansel, following his example, has also sought inspiration among writers. Chantal Akerman's highly individual filmmaking (particularly in the full-length films *Jeanne Dielman* and *Les rendez-vous d'Anna*) is, however, characterized by a very specific treatment of time. The centering makes an Akerman film immediately recognizable.

In Flanders, there was for a number of years a strong trend toward production of films anchored in the Flemish literary tradition. For example, Roland Verhavert adapted Timmermans and Teirlinck, and Hugo Claus made a film entitled *The Lion of Flanders*, the great Flemish national epic. This was before awareness grew that cinema did not exist only to illustrate great literary works. Cinema in Flanders is now tending toward lighter subjects, such as detective stories, adventure, comedy, and eroticism, probably with the hope of creating a cinema industry worthy of the name. However, the general crisis in the cinema industry will not facilitate this development, which has often been announced but has never actually materialized.

In the French-speaking part of the country, filmmakers are examining the possibility of forming a coalition with countries also experiencing difficulties in gaining international recognition for their work. Jean-Jacques Andrien coproduced the latest full-length film by the Indian filmmaker Mrinal Sen, and *Noces en Galilée* by the Palestinian Michel Khleifi, which caused a sensation at Cannes in 1987, was produced with a considerable amount of Belgian funding. This prompted Benoît Lamy to make *La Vie est belle* with a Zaïrean colleague and a majority of black actors. It remains to be seen whether these original and ingenious solutions will bring Belgian cinema out of the backwoods.

It goes without saying that in a country where great painters and comic strips have such a rich history behind them, cartoon films also have their place. Animated cinema and cartoon films have their respective masters in Belgium. Raoul Servais from Ghent has won innumerable prizes and has gathered a considerable following. The Brussels humorist Picha, whose three full-length films (*Tarzoon, The Missing Link, The Big Bang*) have been shown all over the world, carries on the merciless tradition of Rops, Ensor, and, more recently, Franquin.

This rather negative picture of the difficulties facing the Belgian cinema industry should not overshadow the fact that in certain marginal but dynamic cinema circles, Belgium has climbed to the top of the ladder. Jean-Pierre Berckmans is considered a leading international light of musical clips, and a number of firms in Brussels and Antwerp excel in the production of advertising segments. However, it would be a pity if Belgian producers were able to develop their talents only in these secondary sectors, even if they are economically the most profitable ones. The film rights to Tintin, Belgium's most popular national hero, have been bought by Stephen Spielberg. The Hanna-Barbera studios turned the Smurfs, originally christened the Schtroumpfs, into the heroes of the large and small screen. This is to say, Belgians are not lacking in imagination, simply in the means to exploit it.

Music in Flanders

Bernard Huys

AFTER THE INDEPENDENT KINGDOM of Belgium was founded in 1830, musical life had to be completely reorganized. Existing music schools were upgraded to Royal Conservatories (Brussels in 1832, Ghent in 1835), and a network of municipal schools of music was gradually built up. Concert performances took on a new lease on life, too. Conservatory concerts played a bigger role in Brussels, and performances of French operas in Antwerp and Ghent were highly successful.

One of the key figures in the Brussels music world was François-Joseph Fétis (1784–1871), who was appointed director of the Brussels Conservatory in 1833. His cosmopolitan views found a keen supporter in François-Auguste Gevaert (1828–1908), who succeeded him in 1871. Not only were both men composers, they also shared a passion for musicology. As founder and leader of the Société des Concerts du Conservatoire, Gevaert introduced French music to the Brussels public and brought them the leading trends in European music. As an opera composer, he tended to follow French models in such works as *Hugues de Zomerghem, Quentin Durward,* and *Le Capitaine Henriot.* Early composers of opera, like Albert Grisar (1808–69) of Antwerp and Armand Limnander de Nieuwenhove (1814–92) of Ghent, also followed Parisian models and considered such men as Meyerbeer their great idols.

A Flemish national consciousness soon arose in Flanders in reaction to this movement. One of the earliest exponents of this movement was Karel Miry (1823–89), who not only composed numerous operas to Dutch libretti by Van Peene but also wrote a number of songs, including "De Vlaamse Leeuw" (1847), unanimously accepted as the anthem of the Flemish movement. The movement was partly nurtured by a thorough study of Flemish folk songs and their publication by J. F. Willems, F. A. Snellaert, and F. Van Duyse, among others.

However, the greatest exponent of the nationalist movement was Peter Benoit (1834–1901). A pupil of Fétis's in Brussels, he won the first Rome Prize in 1857. During his stay in Germany (1858), he came into contact with German culture, particularly the music of Wagner. In 1860, he went to live in Paris, where in 1862 he became manager of the Bouffes Parisiennes. It was during his stay in the French capital that major parts of his *Quadrilogie religieuse* (*Salut de Noël, High Mass, Te Deum, Requiem*) were composed. Apart from this, Benoit composed a number of motets in this early period, although his religious work from the same period is little known. Many compositions for piano, influenced by the great Romantics such as Chopin, also date from this time. From 1864 on, Benoit was in close contact with the Flemish poet Emmanuel Hiel (1834–99), whose influence led him to secular oratorios and cantatas such as *Lucifer* (1865), *De Schelde* (1868), *De Oorlog* (1873), *De Rijn* (1889), *Rubenscantate* (1877), *De Wereld* (1878), and *Conscience herdacht* (1889). Benoit's romantic nationalism shines through in all of these ambitious works. It was his belief that racial and ethnic origin determine human existence, spirit, and creation, and that this applied to music too. Therefore, every people must have its own music. His innovations in musical education were also based on the use of the vernacular and folk song as a musical source, and they contributed to the flemishization of the Antwerp school of music and its upgrading to the Royal Flemish Conservatory of Music in 1898.

Benoit's ideas crop up again among the enthusiastic throng of young composers who were fervent supporters of the Flemish movement. Jan-Baptist Van den Eeden (1842–1917) from Ghent composed operas, such as *Rhena* (1912), and oratorios characterized by natural spontaneity and a tendency to the dramatic. Hendrik Waelput (1845–85), another citizen of Ghent, wrote two operas (*La ferme du diable*, 1865, and *Stella*, 1881), praiseworthy choral works, and intimate songs to words by Eugeen Van Oye and Karel Versnaeyen; he was also one of the few composers to achieve success in the orchestral field, with his five symphonies and other pieces. Willem De Mol (1846–74), a composer and organist from Brussels, was a convinced supporter of nationalism in music. By the time of his early death, he had already written a major symphony, *De Oorlog* (1873), and impassioned songs like "Ik ken een lied," to words by G. T. Anthuenis. Karel Mestdagh (1850–1924) of Bruges studied under Waelput, Benoit, and others, completing his education in Leipzig. His best-known works are his marvelous songs in the style of Schumann, such as "De Schelde." Jan Blockx (1851–1912) of Antwerp was a pupil of Benoit, and succeeded him as director of the Antwerp Conservatory (1901–12). He was the most gifted opera composer in the Flemish school. An instinctive feel for dramatic action and refined lyrical melody are the characteristics of his lyrical works, such as *Herbergprinses* (1896), *Tijl Uilenspiegel* (1900), and *De Bruid der Zee* (1901). His *Vlaamse Dansen*, composed for orchestra in 1884, show that he, too, was imbued with the spirit of Flemish folk song.

Edward Keurvels (1853–1916), another of Benoit's pupils, founded the Royal Flemish Opera in Antwerp in 1893, together with Henry Fontaine. His dramatic opera *Parisina* (1890) did not enjoy a long run, but his musically refined songs are of lasting value. He was also important as the founder of the Peter Benoit Fund (1902), devoted to the publication and distribution of Benoit's music. Emiel Wambach (1854–1924) was another Benoit pupil and supporter of Flemish national music. In 1913, he succeeded Jan Blockx as director of the Antwerp Conservatory. His best-known works are the drama *Quinten Matsys* (1910); his four oratorios, including *Yolande* (1884) and *Blancefloer* (1889); and many songs and choral pieces. Leo Van Gheluwe (1837–1914), a cantata composer from Oudenaarde, and Gustave Huberti (1843–1910) belong to Benoit's following. It was to Hiel that Huberti owed his love of Flemish music, to which such works as *Een laatste zonnestraal* (1873), *Verlichting* (1883), *Bloemardinne* (1884–86), and *Kinderlust en-leed* (1890) bear witness, as do many songs for orchestra or piano. Emile Mathieu (1844–1932), director at Leuven and from 1898 at Ghent, belongs to the same generation.

Another outstanding personality alongside Benoit was Edgar Tinel (1854–1912), the first director of the Interdiocesan School for Devotional Music at Mechelen and director of the Brussels Conservatory from 1909. Less attracted to Flemish nationalism, he devoted more attention to the classical Romanticism of Mendelssohn, Schumann, and Brahms and to Bach's contrapuntal music. In Flanders, he laid the foundations of the Romantic oratorio with *Franciscus* (1888) and *Godoleva* (1897), and his religious music also includes the spiritual opera *Katharina* (1909), a Te Deum, a mass, psalms, and motets. Nor are his piano works or songs, some of them to words by G. Gezelle, without merit.

After Benoit, a new generation was heralded, led by the trio of Paul Gilson, August De Boeck, and Lodewijk Mortelmans, the last true exponents of musical Romanticism in Flanders. Already less attracted to musical mass demonstrations than to orchestral music, they took the decisive step toward the 20th century.

The central figure is Paul Gilson (1865–1942), a refined artist, great composer, and eminent teacher. Outstanding among his lyrical works are his fairytale opera *Prinses Zonneschijn* (1903), and *Zeevolk* (1904). The cantata *Francesca da Rimini* (1892) also shows a wealth of inspiration. His foremost orchestral pieces include *La Mer* (1892) and *Symphonic variations* (1903), in which his extensive technical knowledge of instrumentation finds expression, as do the great models who inspired him: Wagner, Richard Strauss, and the Russian school. As a teacher too, Gilson was an authoritative figure. He held himself aloof from academe, was open to innovation and evolution, and never tore apart the work of his pupils, preferring to encourage them. This broad vision is well reflected in his unsurpassed *Traité d'harmonie* (1919–23, 3 vols.).

August De Boeck (1865–1937) was a pupil of A. Mailly, H. F. Kufferath, and P. Gilson, who revealed to him the orchestral coloring of the Five Russians. We can find this rich palette of colors in such works as his *Rhapsodie dahoméenne* (1903) and in his symphony. De Boeck was first and foremost a simple lyricist with natural inspiration, as witness his refined songs and his greater lyrical works, such as *Winternachtsdroom* (1903), *Rijndwergen* (1905), *Reinaert de Vos* (1909), and *La Route d'émeraude* (1920).

With Lodewijk Mortelmans (1868–1952), another of Benoit's pupils, and later director of the Antwerp Conservatory (1924–33), the tradition of Brahms, the late Romantic German symphonists, and Bruckner was maintained in works such as *Homerische symfonie* (1898), *In Memoriam* (1917), and his symphonic poems. His opera *Kinderen der Zee* (1920) is well known, as are his many songs to words by Guido Gezelle, so finely crafted that Gilson justifiably crowned him the Prince of Flemish Song.

The trio of Gilson, De Boeck, and Mortelmans had its contemporaries who accomplished praiseworthy work in their chosen fields, without venturing boldly down new paths: the Leuven pianist and composer Arthur De Greef (1862–1940); the Mechelen carillonneur Jef Denijn (1862–1941), founder of the Mechelen bell-ringing school; Remi Ghesquiere (1866–1964) and Oscar Van Durne (1867–1925), both organists and composers of devotional music; Jaak Opsomer (1873–1952); and Alfons Moortgat (1881–1962). Ghent, too, produced some outstanding talents: Paul Lebrun (1863–1920), writer of the symphonic poem *Sur la montagne* (1911) and of a symphony (1911); Oscar Roels (1864–1938); Pieter Franz Uyttenhove (1874–1923), author of the opera *Marieken van Nijmegen* and of inspired songs; Lieven Duvosel (1877–1956), who had a preference for national themes and an Impressionist play of colors in such works as his orchestral piece *Leie-cyclus* (1902–23); Emiel Hullebroeck (1878–1965), composer of songs in a folk style; Georges D'Hoedt (1885–1936), composer of *Korte kronieken uit het Burgerleven*; and Jules Toussaint De Sutter (1889–1959), director of the Ghent Conservatory (1936–54) and composer of symphonies, symphonic poems (such as *Bij de dood van een kind*, 1922), the oratorio *Vlaanderen*, and the opera *Maya*.

A few Flemish composers continued to be open to foreign influence. Flor Alpaerts (1876–1954), an Antwerp man and director of the zoo concerts there, moved from Wagnerianism to French Impressionism, finally to find his own form of expression with *Pallieter* (1921) and the *James Ensor Suite* (1929). The prolific Arthur Meulemans (1884–1966), a pupil of Tinel, composed fifteen symphonies, among them *Dennensymfonie* (no. 3), *Zeesymfonie* (no. 6), *Zwaneven* (no. 7), and *Rembrandtsymfonie* (no. 13), other orchestral works, such as *Pliniusfontein* (1913) and *Stadspark* (1928), chamber music, songs, chorales, and masses (*Sanguis Christi*, 1938). All these works are steeped in the sounds and atmosphere of the late Impressionist era.

Robert Herberigs (1886–1974), also from Ghent, a composer, writer, and talented artist, was inspired primarily by the Impressionism of Ravel. He composed magnificent symphonic poems (*Cyrano de Bergerac*, *Zang van Hiawatha*, *Antonius en Cleopatra*, *Vrolijke Vrouwtjes van Windsor*), refined song cycles to words by Charles Van Lerberghe and Guido Gezelle, a number of masses and other devotional music, and the oratorio *Het Lam Gods* (1949).

Karel Candael (1883–1948) of Antwerp was originally influenced by Wagner. Later, under the influence of the Russian school and Stravinsky, his art expressed itself in an opulent and richly colored orchestral palette, before striving for sobriety and internalization. Important works are the ballet *De Zeven Hoofdzonden* (1925–27), the *Danssymfonie*, and the oratorio *Marialeven* (1941–43).

The Mechelen bandmaster Jules Van Huffel (1883–1953), composer of inspired psalms, motets, and Te Deums, belongs to the same era, as do Gilson's pupils from Antwerp, Jef Van Hoof (1886–1959), late Romantic composer of operas (*Meivuur*, 1916; *Jonker Lichthaart*, 1928), five symphonies, chorales, and poetic songs; and Lodewijk De Vocht (1887–1977), choirmaster and composer of Romantic works (including three symphonies, symphonic poems, and songs).

A group of seven composers was brought together by Paul Gilson under the title Les Synthétistes. The Flemish members of the group were, in addition to Gilson himself, Theo Dejoncker (1894–1964), Marcel Poot (b. 1901), and Maurits Schoemaker (1890–1964). There was no group aesthetic, but Gilson's pupils were open to all the achievements of contemporary music. They also publicized their efforts jointly through the medium of the periodical *La Revue musicale belge*, founded by Gilson.

Three of their contemporaries in Antwerp can be placed in this context: August L. Baeyens (1895–1966), Karel Albert (1901–87), and Willem Pelemans (b. 1901), who were drawn primarily to Expressionism. Marius De Jong (1891–1984) was influenced by Mortelmans. This very prolific composer started out with a neo-classical concept, but subsequently preferred as inspiration chromaticism and color (*Hiawatha's lied, Imitatio Christi*), as well as old Flemish folk songs (*Vlaamse rapsodie, Proverbia Breugheliana*).

Flor Peeters (1903–86), a celebrated organist and composer of devotional music and of numerous pieces for the organ, evolved from his symphonic style to a more linear way of writing. The influence of Alban Berg can be traced in Jef Van Durme (1907–65), who studied in Vienna under the Austrian master. Among his works are seven symphonies and the symphonic poems *Hamlet* and *Beatrice*. Louis De Meester (b. 1904) is an independent figure in Flemish music. This composer of chamber music and orchestral works also wrote electronic music after 1958.

A number of composers born between 1910 and 1920 had a deep admiration for Stravinsky, Bartok, and Schönberg: Renier Van der Velden (b. 1910), a largely self-taught eclecticist with a strong personality, prefers ballet music (*Dulle Griet, Arlequinade, Maskers*), stage music (*De Leeuw van Vlaanderen, Marieken van Nieumeghen*) and songs, some of them to words by K. Van de Woestijne. Jean Louel (b. 1914) wrote almost exclusively instrumental music without a systematic impact. He distanced himself gradually from Ravel and Bartok to reach his own resolutely modern tone language with strong dissonants, polytonality, and the use of clusters. David Van de Woestijne (1915–79) originally composed concert works in a neo-classicist style. His tone language gradually became more expressionistic, culminating in a search for greater sobriety. Victor Legley (b. 1915) is a pupil of Jean Absil, but he also followed the examples of Max Reger and Paul Hindemith. He is one of the few to have achieved international acceptance, with such works as *De Stalen Kathedraal* (1958); he wrote six symphonies, chamber music, and a number of song cycles, all in an ordered, classical structure. Jan Decadt (b. 1914) was another of Absil's pupils. His style was influenced by Honegger, as well as Bartok and Hindemith. He also liked to seek his inspiration in contemporary visual artists such as Constant Permeke (*Permekesuite*) and Octave Landuyt (*Muzikale monografie over een groot schilder*), whom he evokes with plastic orchestrations and expressionistic eloquence.

Other contemporaries are Karel De Brabander (1913–84), a pupil of E. Verheyden and F. Alpaerts, and a composer of orchestral music, including five symphonies, chamber music, chorales, and songs; Ernest Van der Eyken (b. 1913); and August Verbesselt (b. 1919). Verbesselt studied under R. Van der Velden, K. Candael, and Matyas Seiber (twelve-tone music). He has adopted the latest techniques, such as atonality, bitonality, and seriality, but uses them for the purposes of expression (as in *Universum*, 1974). In the meantime, studio work and the broadcasting organizations have also exercised their influence on Flemish musicians, who are gradually integrating new sources of sound into their work. It was to further this process that Louis De Meester founded the Instituut voor Psychoakoestiek en Elektronische Muziek (IPEM) in Ghent in 1962. A number of eminent composers have been members of this institution, among them Karel Goyvaerts (b. 1923), Lucien Goethals (b. 1931), and later Claude Coppens (b. 1936).

Another galaxy of composers born in Flanders between 1920 and 1940 has gone on to enrich the musical spectrum with his or her own aesthetic conception: Peter Cabus (b. 1923), Peter Welffens (b. 1924), Herman Roeselstraete (1925–85), Nini Bulterijs (b. 1929), Frits Celis (b. 1929), Frederik Devreese (b. 1929), Willem Kersters (b. 1929), Raymond Baervoets (b. 1930), Jacqueline Fontyn (b. 1930), André Laporte (b. 1931), Elias Gistelinck (b. 1935), and Vic Nees (b. 1936).

Among those born after 1940, most of them trained in Brussels by Vic Legley, are Marcel De Jonghe (b. 1943), Rafaël D'Haene (b. 1943), Mark Verhaegen (b. 1943), Wilfried Westerlinck (b. 1945), Jean Gyselynck (b. 1946), Gilbert Huybens (b. 1949), Frank Gyselynck (b. 1950), and Floris Jonckheere (b. 1951).

Music in Wallonia and Brussels

Robert Wangermée

THE REGIONS THAT MAKE UP Belgium experienced a musical golden age that began at the end of the 14th century and stretched into the 16th century. During this period, Belgian music served as a model all over Europe. The elaborate style in the main creative centers on both sides of the linguistic border, namely Ghent, Bruges, Antwerp, Brussels, Liège, Tournai, and Mons, was based on a relatively severe polyphony that found expression in motets, masses, songs, and madrigals. This style had its roots in French music, but was international in spirit. The best composers were famous outside Belgium: Guillaume Dufay at the Savoy court and with the pope in Rome, Josquin des Prés in Milan, and Rolandus Lassus in Munich. At the same time, vast numbers of musicians practiced their art in the princely churches and chapels of Europe. Thus they trained local musicians in their style of singing and composing, until the day when counterpoint became unpopular and was overtaken by a style developed in reaction to it. From the Baroque era on, musicians from the southern Netherlands and then from Belgium ceased playing the leading role in international music. Great artists naturally still gained great renown, as seen in the prodigious success of Grétry from Liège and in the comic operas of the late 18th century. But, with variations depending on the period and genre, the majority of composers attached themselves either to French or Italian styles, to the Mannheim or the Vienna school or, more recently, to the Wagner, Debussy, Stravinsky, or twelve-tone styles. They demonstrated an eclecticism corresponding to a tradition of openness to the main musical styles. This did not, however, prevent the best of these composers from developing their own personal style and gaining recognition.

The dominant figure among musicians from Wallonia in the 19th century was without doubt César Franck (1822–90). He was born in Liège at a time when Belgium still had to win its independence, but spent most of his life in Paris. He was a young prodigy of the piano, before moving on to an unstartling career as an organist at the Sainte-Clothide Basilica (1858) and a conservatory professor. However, despite the lowliness of these posts, he was seen by a number of fervent followers as a renovator of French music. His main works are the religious oratorio *Les Béatitudes*, *Trois chorales pour orgue*, long compositions for the piano (*Prélude, aria et finale* and *Prélude, chorale et fugue*), the brilliant *Variations symphoniques* for the piano and orchestra, chamber music (*Quintet with piano, Quartet for strings*, and the *Sonata for violin and piano*), along with the *Symphony in D Minor*, one of the monuments of 19th-century orchestral literature. Their tortured chromaticism, subtle counterpoint, and magnified classical form made Franck one of the great creators of his time. His work considerably influenced French music.

Among all the composers who emulated Franck, Guillaume Lekeu (1870–94), born in Verviers, wrote a number of beautiful pieces, including in particular the *Fantaisie symphonique sur deux airs populaires angevins*, the uncompleted *Quartet with piano* and the *Sonata for violin and piano*.

Franck's prestige in Wallonia was extraordinarily intense and lasting. Many musicians followed his style for a very long time, preserving up to the interwar period his complex harmonies, severity, and seriousness. One of the most original was Joseph Jongen from Liège (1873–1953), pianist, organist, conductor, and prolific composer. Some of his compositions were inspired by Walloon folklore, but more often than not Jongen continued to use large forms (for example, his *Concerto for cello* and *Symphonie concertante avec orchestre*) but along the same harmonic lines as Franck, occasionally with a hint of Debussy. However, with a lighter orchestration his winding and vague melodies always display a very personal touch.

Most other post-Franckists, who for a long time represented an official and rather academic art form in Belgium, were born in Liège. They include Armand Marsick (1877–1959), François Rasse (1873–1955), Jean Rogister (1879–1964), René Barbier from Namur (1890–1981), Léopold Samuel from Brussels (1883–1975), and Raymond Moulaert (1875–1962), who was rather more progressive. Désiré Paque, who based his work on Franck's harmonies, produced atonal compositions that owe nothing to Schönberg.

The strongest influence on the following generation was Paul Gilson (1865–1942), a Flemish composer of considerable experience. In the 1920's and 1930's, he trained dozens of Flemish and Walloon musicians. He imposed no aesthetic guidelines on them, but gave them strong foundations in the art of being a musician. He also produced excellent text-books on harmony and orchestration. Some of his pupils formed a group in 1925 that displayed its eclectic nature through its name: the Synthe-sists. The group was not concerned with promoting any bold musical approach; rather, it integrated certain modern features into music that was essentially traditional. Next to Marcel Poot (b. 1901), who is Flem-ish, the most interesting of the Synthesists were Francis de Bourguignon (1890–1961); Gaston Brenta (1902–69), who was anxious to use all the resources offered by a large orchestra; and René Bernier (1905–85), inti-mist musician, who felt that the Latin civilization was an aesthetic ideal of clarity. Bernier chiefly wrote melodies, choruses, and chamber music.

The relentless organizing talents of Paul Collaer were responsible for giving Brussels a taste of the most innovative music of the 20th century, namely that of Stravinsky, Schönberg, and Bartok or the provocative work of Erik Satie, the works of the Six, and many others. The Pro Arte Concerts, which he organized between 1921 and 1932 with the famous Quartet of the same name, played an important educational role, intro-ducing the public and musicians to works as then unknown in the most daring tone used until then. After Collaer, this role was essentially taken over by the radio, which, like the majority of public service bodies in Europe, expended much effort on supporting contemporary art. Bel-gian radio organized, for example, Experimental Music Days at the 1958 World's Fair, followed later by festivals for the "recognition of modern music" and the "biennale of Belgian music."

In the generation that reached maturity before 1940, Jean Absil (1893–1974), Albert Huybrechts (1899–1938), and Raymond Che-vreuille (1901–76) were undoubtedly those who best assimilated these new styles in order to integrate them into a coherent personal style.

The most striking feature of Jean Absil's work is his quest for poly-phonic composition inspired by the great masters. Three or four lines that seem to be separate from the rest but are in fact closely interdepen-dent can be found in all his works, whether it be choruses, chamber music, or orchestral music. This tight counterpoint, which brings into play complex rhythms, is a modern style without, however, reaching true polytonality. Absil wrote in all genres; his most remarkable works are the *Concerto no. 1 for piano*, which was chosen as an obligatory piece for the final round in the Ysaye Competition in 1938 and won Absil an interna-tional reputation, and his cantata *Les Chants du mort*, in which Absil wrote an admirable piece of music revolving around folklore on the basis of popular Roman funeral songs.

Albert Huybrechts hesitated between the neo-classicism of a musician well acquainted with Ravel and Stravinsky (for example, in his string quartets and the *Sérénade en trois movements* for orchestra) and an Expressionism reminiscent of Alban Berg (*Divertissement pour cuivres et batterie, Chant d'angoisse*). In both styles, however, Huybrechts produced high-quality music.

The style adopted by Raymond Chevreuille, originally guided by an atonality and Expressionism close to Alban Berg, rapidly became more supple. He often made use of the twelve sounds on the chromatic scale, but based his work on chords of traditional tonalities. In his *Symphonie des Souvenirs* or his cantata *Evasions* (based on the nursery rhymes of Maurice Carême), Chevreuille alternated tenderness, dream, and mystery with moments of great dramatic intensity. He composed many pieces in traditional forms (eight symphonies, sixteen concertos, nine quartets) and always demonstrated his great inventiveness in expressing musical colors.

André Souris (1899–1970) was one of the most remarkable and endearing musicians ever. He belonged to the Surrealist Brussels group Correspondance, which differed from the group led by Breton in Paris precisely through its special interest in music. This spiritual commitment led him to question all artistic activities and to think up a musical style consisting of juxtaposed and contrasted clichés, rather like the paintings of René Magritte. His style had certain affinities with that of the Neoclassical Stravinsky, who also had a talent for transforming the hackneyed formulas of past styles. His work *Quelques airs de Clarisse Juranville* for soprano and a few instruments is particularly characteristic of this style; *Le marchand d'images*, which is a long suite for voices and orchestra, incorporates Walloon folk songs in a poetic and refined atmosphere. André Souris also wrote some very functional film scores. He was a remarkable musicologist (his publications of lute music are notable), a lucid and fiery musical philosopher, and a production organizer who, after 1945, brought Schönberg and Webern to the attention of a new generation of composers.

The compositions of his friend Pierre Froidebist (1914–62), organist and musicologist, were influenced by Stravinsky (*Cinq Comptines*), Webern (*Amer Coeur*), and Pierre Boulez (*Stèle pour Sei Shonagon*). He was very active in Liège musical circles and had a number of followers. The best known among them was Henri Pousseur (b. 1929), who rapidly moved beyond Webern-style dodecaphony (*Trois chants sacrés*) to join Stockhausen, Boulez, and Berio in the discovery of new forms of music. By 1957, he was involved in electronic music by itself or combined with other instruments, and he was one of the discoverers of open forms. With the French writer Michel Butor, he wrote a great dramatic piece, *Votre Faust,* whose action can be guided by the audience. At the same time, he has attempted to put forward a method integrating in the serial system all the great styles of the past. In different works, he quotes and parodies (in the aesthetic sense of the term) Monteverdi, Wagner, Schönberg (*Le procès du jeune chien*), Webern, popular songs, and jazz (*Les îles déchaînées*). Henri Pousseur is today director of the Liège Conservatory and of the Musical Research Center of Wallonia. He also guided the first steps of the Paris Institute of Musical Pedagogy. Pousseur has written numerous studies rationalizing his commitment to new styles of music and also placing musical creation in a utopian framework, where music will one day harmonize human relations.

Philippe Boesmans (b. 1936) has had no time for theorizing. His music is based on the tangible, on immediate musical data that can be used to invent a dazzling and multifaceted world that exploits the virtuosity of musicians and caresses the ear (*Upon la-mi*, which won him the Italia Prize; Prize; *Elément-Extensions* for solo piano and instrumental ensemble; *Concerto for violin*). Boesmans has also composed an opera based on a libretto by Pierre Mertens, successfully produced at the Monnaie Theater.

Pierre Bartholomée (b. 1937) is first and foremost a composer. He created and directed the Musique nouvelle ensemble, specialized in the performance and creation of 20th-century works, before taking over as head of the Symphonic Orchestra of Liège and the French-speaking Community. However, his acquaintance with Henri Pousseur prompted him to turn to composition, and he has written highly refined works in a style that is still evolving and tending to become simpler (*Le Tombeau de Marin Marais, Harmonique*).

In what is inevitably an arbitrary selection among a great number of quality composers, Louis Robert (1948–79), who left this world much too soon, must be mentioned. He wrote a number of original pieces (*Miroir des eaux*) for the ensemble Musique nouvelle. Also worthy of mention is Jacqueline Fontyn (b. 1930), who conceals a great deal of daring behind her discretion.

Musical creation in recent years has not only consisted of a search for radicalism. Various musicians have adopted a resolutely modern approach that nevertheless coincides more with symphonic composition or chamber music. Among the most brilliant of these is Frédérik van Rossum (b. 1931), who is not concerned with any particular system but who in all his compositions has given proof of great creative inventiveness (*Der blaue Reiter, Concerto for violin and orchestra*).

Finally, among the followers of Jean Absil, mention should be made of Camille Schmit (1908–76); Marcel Quinet (1915–87), who was also a great teacher; Jean-Marie Simonis (b. 1931); and Jacques Leduc (b. 1932). Despite their very different temperaments, they all strive to express themselves with constant attention to craftsmanship and in a classical form.

The Gastronomical Ecumenism of Belgians

Léo Moulin

AMONG THEIR OTHER QUALITIES, Belgians like eating and are fussy about their food. They have since time immemorial practiced the joys of good living, as attested by Flemish painting and infinitely appreciated by modern tourists. The city of Brussels has around 120 streets, lanes, and cul-de-sacs, often very picturesque, which spill over with the pleasures of eating and drinking. It outstrips all the world's other cities on this point.

Flemish Benedictine monks "invented" beer. Charles de l'Escluse, known as Clusius, who was Flemish, helped publicize the potato throughout Europe. One of the most important cookery treatises of the 17th century was written by Lancelot de Casteau (1604) from Picardy, who for more than fifty years worked for the prince-bishops of Liège. A number of relics of past cooking traditions have been preserved, such as the use of sweet and sour, beer, or *escavèche*. They are greatly appreciated by connoisseurs, as are the range of cakes and sweets. Each town, large or small, has its speciality.

It is impossible to list all the Belgian specialities. Names such as "waterzooi," eels "au vert," and "craquelin" cannot give an idea of the unforgettable richness and variety of Belgian gastronomy. There is only one way to really appreciate them, namely, with knife and fork in hand.

Belgium is unique in that it is open to foreign cooking. But it is not a country lacking in haute cuisine; it has just as many Michelin stars per capita as France. However, as a crossroads between France, Germany, and Great Britain and stimulated by two different turbulent communities, both of which enjoy the pleasures of eating, Belgium benefits from the intermingling of Germanic and Latin culture and is by nature ecumenical.

Belgium can boast of more than 300 different types of beer (some people would even claim 800!), which are among the best in the world.

This does not, however, prevent it from enjoying British, German, Dutch, Danish, Luxembourgeois, Czech, French, and Zaïrean beers.

In Belgium it is possible to find 85 different types of native cheeses, each with its own flavor and texture. Proportionally, this is more than France and more than the Netherlands and Switzerland put together. Even the most humble local grocery sells cheese from ten or twelve different countries, ranging from Yugoslav feta to Bulgarian brinza and Hungarian lifaner.

The same variety is seen in Belgian hams and cooked pork meats, which are excellent and compare very favorably with similar products from neighboring countries. But Belgians, who will try anything new, are also acquainted with Italian San Danieli, German Bierwurst, Bayonne ham, Spanish chorizo, Grison meat, and Polish sausage, producing a symphony of odors and flavors.

Belgium is fortunate not to have any vineyards. As a consequence, a Belgian cellar will boast wine from Chile, the United States, and even Great Britain, Brazil, Greece, and Australia. Belgian restaurants have the most handsomely filled cellars in the world. It is not rare for a restaurant to have between 500 and 600 different wines, much to the delight of both Belgians and tourists.

Naturally, there is an exception to prove the rule. Belgians will tolerate only Belgian pralines, which are reputed to be the best in the world. Over 400 different types now exist.

These are the most noteworthy aspects of the art of culinary appreciation in Belgium. When Belgians display their *joie de vivre*, their eagerness to show others the richness of Belgian cuisine, the surprises reserved by their wine cellars, and a welcome both informal and expansive, it is not difficult to understand why it can be said that life in Belgium is good.

Sociologists may well wonder at this rich gastronomical tradition in Belgium. The historical and geographical reasons for this have already been briefly mentioned. As a disciple of Max Weber, I personally believe in the decisive importance of religion in molding the feeling of a nation. By this I am referring to religion not as an institution or way of education, but rather as a sociocultural foundation underlying the life of every citizen, whether a believer or not.

Max Weber established historical and social connections between the Protestant ethic and capitalism. I believe that this theory can be extended to democracy, scientific research, and culture where the Protestant ethic has emulated the Catholic ethic with a great deal of success (as I said above, I am talking in the sense of a sociocultural foundation, a kind of historical cradle). But the same does not hold true in the field of gastronomy. It is universally recognized that the countries with great culinary traditions are sociologically Catholic nations. I have no intention of making a value judgment here. An English professor at the University of Exeter, Stephen Mennel, wrote in a work of high scientific value, *The Manners of Food* (Oxford, 1985), of the "beheading" of English cuisine. He bases this on historical arguments that seem to me irrefutable. Even though I feel that he underrates the role of Puritanism in this phenomenon, I go along with his views. Moreover, from the point of view of everyday reality, it can be stated that the cuisine of Protestant nations does not export well. The nationals of sociologically Protestant countries throw themselves on the highly varied and refined dishes offered in Catholic countries, whereas people from Catholic countries, after a stay in a Protestant country, have no wish to continue with the habits that they picked up while abroad. This does not mean that culinary tradition in these countries is no good. I have tasted a number of very simple, family dishes that are full of flavor. However, they cannot be held up as monuments to haute cuisine. The clue to these differences may be, as I said one day to a Belgian bishop, the practice of confession. Again, to use Weber's ideas, confession leaves room for a certain degree of sensuality. Sensuality is clearly an important ingredient of good cooking. A bad or a sullen conscience is an uneasy bedfellow to good cooking.

Belgium is sociologically a "Catholic" country, as demonstrated by Flemish painting from Bruegel to Teniers. They clearly depict Belgians' joy in eating, drinking, and singing. Belgium is a mystical and carnal country.

Professor Mennel cited the industrial revolution as one of the main causes of the "beheading" of English cuisine. Belgium was the first country on the continent to make a success of industrial takeoff, although conditions were dreadful, comparable to those in Britain at the time. However, this did not result in the "beheading" of its cuisine and joie de vivre. From this it can be concluded that the cataclysm of the industrial revolution fell on different sociocultural soil in Belgium than it did in England. This is why Belgium has preserved one of the most sumptuous gastronomical palettes of the world. This is why it has, proportionally speaking, as many Michelin stars as France. Life is good in Belgium.

Conclusion

Herman Liebaers and Philippe Roberts-Jones

BELGIUM HAS THE GREAT ADVANTAGE of being a multilingual society. It has always been one. Although the linguistic border is fifteen centuries old, it cannot be seen in the land, except through the decisions of modern bureaucracy, which reflect political measures taken far away from the linguistic border. On both sides people speak a different dialect, a Germanic and a Romance one, but the people are basically identical.

There has been a tendency in Belgium to equate language with culture, which we feel to be a basic mistake. The French-speaking Belgians are not French, the Dutch-speaking are not Dutch, the German-speaking —a tiny minority of 60,000—are not Germans. It would be much closer to reality to state that the French-speaking ones are the northernmost outpost of Latin civilization, the Dutch-speaking ones the southernmost settlement of Germanic civilization. This border between both linguistic groups has created as many apparent links as invisible meeting points; they have forced Belgium to become a cultural entity of its own. Over the centuries this process was almost certainly the product of the linguistic border, but it might as well have been the other way around. The linguistic border is a link between those two basic European civilizations.

In many ways the Belgian linguistic border may be assimilated with the horizontal east-west dividing line, separating northern from southern Europe. This line is 400 years old, whereas the political wall between Western and Eastern Europe dates back only 40 years. It is common knowledge that northern Europe leans toward federal institutional systems, and southern Europe favors centralized state organizations. Opinions are divided, inside and outside Belgium, as to the religious background of this major difference. Is the democratic trend more natural in northern Europe than in the south? American students learn that democracy is confined to Protestant Europe. If this assumption is true, it must be admitted that Belgium is the obvious exception. Although the country is basically Catholic, Amnesty International recognizes Belgium as one of the most democratic countries in the world.

Every nationalism goes down in history as a distortion of the culture it is supposed to represent. All over the world cultures can grow only by respecting other cultures, be they neighboring or distant. When this respect is lost, barbarian nationalism takes over, and it is the end of cultural growth, which is a blow to humanity in general. In a small country this danger is less threatening. Small countries have so many advantages that they make genuine contributions to general well-being, either culturally or materially.

In these paragraphs we have viewed Belgium with a retrospective eye. If we shift from a diachronic to a synchronic point of view, it seems obvious that we move from questions of artistic heritage to current curatorial problems. Many a Belgian art museum has quite recently been renovated, and physically they match their inherited collections. The museums are still understaffed and have no acquisition budgets worth mentioning. The conclusion is obvious: museums, libraries, and other cultural institutions have reached an acceptable degree of development. The national ones among them suffer from the constitutional reform that began in 1970. The Palace of Fine Arts in Brussels has been for over half a century one of the leading cultural centers in Western Europe. Its position has recently been taken over by the National Opera in Brussels. Brussels is also the home of the biennial arts festival Europalia, as befits the title of our capital as the heart of Europe. The Queen Elisabeth musical competition in Brussels has a worldwide reputation.

Cultural ambassadors owe it to the glory of Flemish art to expand the international acceptance of the present-day artist. After all, the historical distance between the painters Hieronymus Bosch and James Ensor is much larger than the aesthetic one. This part ends with a few paragraphs on culinary art, which in all its aspects is a tangible expression of culture. All human activity is embedded in its cultural background. This last part of the book could have been the first one and the preceding sentence the opening one.

Index

STARESO, 453
State, 86–97; and church, 42, 45–
46, 69; reform, 199–200, 217–18.
See also Federalism; Government;
Politics
State Council, 180, 193–98 passim,
219–20
State Faculty of Agronomic Sciences
at Gembloux (FAGEM), 449–50
State Inspectorate, 387–88
Statistics, in education research, 401
Steel industry, 14, 240–41
Steeman, Stanislaus-André, 467
Stein, Peter, 510
Stengers, Jean, 6–9, 86–97
Stenmans, Alain, 448–55
Stillbirths, 363
Stockbreeding, 234, 236
Stock market, 258
Streuvels, Stijn, 462, 479
Strikes, 1960's, 84
"Study Plan of Belgian Primary Edu-
cation" (1936), 400
Subcontracting, SME and, 250, 323
Suffrage: age minimum, 212; for
European Parliament elections (uni-
versal), 128; universal manhood,
50–51, 70, 71, 75, 76, 93, 103, 202,
203; women's, 51, 76, 202
Sugarbeet production, 236
Suicide, 359–61
Supermarkets, 265
Surrealism: Cobra movement and,
498; in literature, 462, 466, 467–
68, 480, 484–85; in music, 524; in
painting, 494, 495–97, 499–500; in
sculpture, 506
SWIFT (Society for Worldwide Inter-
bank Financial Telecommunica-
tions), 254–55
Switzerland, 143, 145, 171, 282
Symbolism, 479, 493–94, 497, 499–
500, 501
Synthesis, in literature, 478–79, 481
Synthesists, 518, 523

De tael is gansch het volk, 94, 95
Taxes, 294, 297, 298; on Congolese

exports, 157; constitution and, 194;
and research funding, 439–40; of
SME, 248
Teachers: continuing education for,
409; primary, 386–87, 388; training, 384, 386–87, 409
Technical education, 264, 393–94
Technical-medical council, 370
Technology: bio-, 418, 450; communications, 268, 318, 322, 430, 451;
education, 401–2; energy, 272;
financial, 256, 317–18; information,
318, 401; labor-saving service, 266;
research and, 425–26, 430, 435–
46 passim, 451–52; seminars in,
264; trade in, 268, 269, 271, 311;
transfer, 417; transport, 268, 451
Teenagers: pregnancies, 363. *See
also* Youth
Teirlinck, Herman, 479, 482, 484, 512
Telecommunications. *See* Communica-
tions
Television, 512
Temperatures, 10, 12, 233
Textile industry, 20–21, 50, 59, 81,
238, 243–44, 436–37
Theater, 508–10; popular, 411;
writers, 462, 464, 465, 469, 470,
486, 509–10
Théâtre du corps (body theater), 510
Thermodynamics far from equilib-
rium, 416
Theunis, M., 144
Thinès, Georges, 474
Third World, 164–65, 453, 473. *See
also* Africa
Thiry, Marcel, 470
Threshold fees, health insurance, 339
Tienen, 22
Tijd en Mens, 484, 486
Tillemans, Walter, 510
Time: school, 387; working, 308–9
Timmermans, Felix, 479, 512
Tindemans, Leo, 115, 117, 128, 132–
33, 141
Tindemans Report (1976), 115, 125,
128, 149–50
Tinel, Edgar, 516

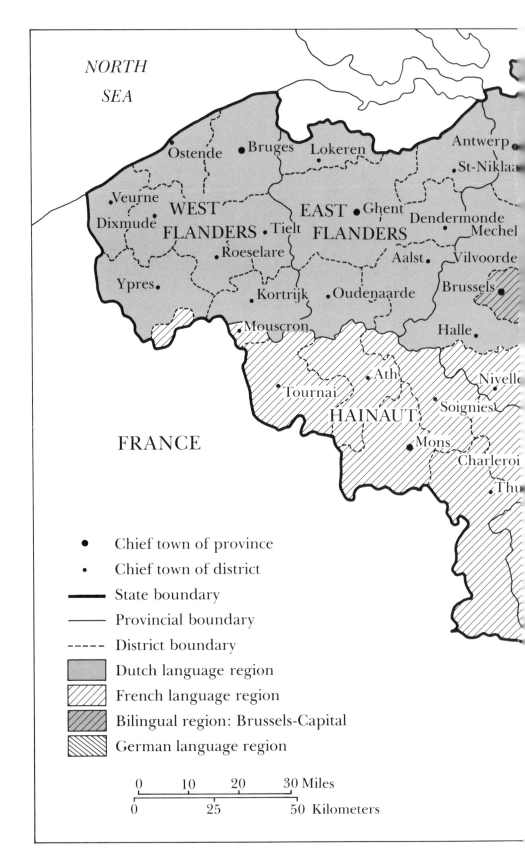

NORTH SEA

Ostende • Bruges   Lokeren   Antwerp
                              • St-Niklaa

Veurne   EAST • Ghent
Dixmude   WEST   FLANDERS   Dendermonde
          FLANDERS • Tielt   • Mechel
          • Roeselare   Aalst • Vilvoorde

Ypres •   Brussels •
          • Kortrijk • Oudenaarde
                                    Halle •
          • Mouscron

                    • Ath   Nivell
          • Tournai   Soignies
                    HAINAUT

FRANCE   • Mons
                                Charleroi
                                  • Thu

● Chief town of province

• Chief town of district

━━━ State boundary

─── Provincial boundary

----- District boundary

Dutch language region

French language region

Bilingual region: Brussels-Capital

German language region

0   10   20   30 Miles
0   25   50 Kilometers